SEVENTH EDITION

Dance A While

Handbook for Folk, Square, Contra, and Social Dance

Jane A. Harris
Formerly of Washington State University

Anne M. Pittman
Formerly of Arizona State University

Marlys S. Waller
Formerly of the University of Washington

Macmillan College Publishing Company
New York

Maxwell Macmillan Canada
Toronto

Maxwell Macmillan International
New York   Oxford   Singapore   Sydney

Cover art: Mechele Herres, Quilter
Editor: Ann Castel Davis
Production Editor: Christine M. Harrington
Art Coordinator: Peter A. Robison
Text Designer: William R. Harrington
Cover Designer: Cathleen Norz
Production Buyer: Pamela D. Bennett

This book was set in Garamond by Carlisle Communications, Ltd. and was printed and bound by Von Hoffmann Press, Inc. The cover was printed by Von Hoffman Press, Inc.

Macmillan College Publishing Company
866 Third Avenue
New York, New York 10022

Macmillan College Publishing Company is part of the
Maxwell Communication Group of Companies.

Maxwell Macmillan Canada, Inc.
1200 Eglinton Avenue East, Suite 200
Don Mills, Ontario M3C 3N1

Library of Congress Cataloging-in-Publication Data
Harris, Jane A.
    Dance a while : handbook of folk, square, contra, and social dance /
    Jane A. Harris, Anne M. Pittman, Marlys S. Waller. — 7th ed.
      p.   cm.
    Includes bibliographical references and index.
    ISBN 0-02-350581-8
      1. Dancing.   I. Pittman, Anne.   II. Waller, Marlys S.
    III. Title.
    GV1751.H322   1994
    793.3—dc20   93-26173
                                                        CIP

Printing: 1 2 3 4 5 6 7 8 9   Year: 4 5 6 7

To Jane Farwell

folklore
village
farm

Foreword

Dance A While is a classic! This book, conceived and first published in 1950 by three young teachers, has become the authoritative, informative, practical, and comprehensive book on the teaching of folk dance in the United States.

The authors, who started writing early in their teaching years, grew every year with more ideas and insights into what was needed by the teaching profession. They never lost their vision to provide an immensely practical and resourceful book while being carefully authentic. This seventh edition is a compendium of the knowledge they have accumulated jointly. It is a book that should be included in every professional and personal library. It is a book that is timeless regarding its content. It is a reliable resource for all those interested in folk dance.

While I was serving as Executive Director of the National Dance Association, I realized the need of NDA to include a good folk dance book on its list of publications. I am happy to say that the NDA agreed and enthusiastically endorsed *Dance A While* for its widely circulated publications list.

Congratulations to the authors on this the seventh edition and another masterpiece. Congratulations to you who have just read this book for the first time and to all of you who have been faithful supporters. You have chosen well. I am proud to lend my name to this edition.

Margie R. Hanson, Ph.D. (Retired)
American Alliance for Health, Physical Education, Recreation and Dance Consultant for Children 1965–1991
Executive Director of the National Dance Association 1971–1989

Preface

It seems like only yesterday that three young, enthusiastic, and energetic physical education instructors on the Women's Physical Training staff at the University of Texas at Austin put together materials used in their folk, square, and social dance classes to fulfill the many requests from their students. Yesterday was 1950; the three young instructors were Jane Harris (Ericson), Anne M. Pittman, and Marlys Swenson (Waller).

Since 1950 *Dance A While* has been available through six editions to students, teachers, and community leaders as a popular source of dance materials and instructional aids. This seventh edition is the culmination of more than forty years of experience in teaching, research, and development of methods and materials that include the best of contemporary materials along with time-honored traditional forms. The time span has made it possible to introduce a new generation of dancers to a number of dance forms so widely enjoyed by their parents and grandparents.

The seventh edition continues to place emphasis on new approaches to teaching and learning by providing a thorough delineation of teaching methods, enrichment activities, locomotor skills, and basic steps necessary to skill enhancement and teaching expertise. Graphic illustrations continue to provide visual cues to movements and dance positions as well as to convey an "around the world" approach to the materials.

The History chapter has been expanded to give insights into dance as a part of the culture of selected countries in the Pacific Rim. The intent is to balance our knowledge and references of traditions from Western civilization with the tremendous dance heritage that emanates from the Eastern part of the world. A brief perspective of the rich heritage of dance from our South American neighbors is included to further remind us of the global nature and importance of dance as it has existed for centuries.

The American Dance Heritage chapter combines a wide variety of American country dances. This includes Round, Play Party, Contra, and Old Time Square Dance. The order of dances begins with a collection of dances brought to America by the early settlers. With the exception of the Loomis Lancers, they are still danced today. Sandy Gallemore presents a major unit on Clog Dance. There are samples of contemporary dances to popular tunes, line dances, and mixers. With the current national "Cajun craze" several Cajun dances have also been included.

The Square Dance chapter includes the rebirth of some older traditional dance materials that have surfaced among dancers of the present generation. Western cowboy–type dances, currently referred to as dances of the fifties, along with the nationally standardized scheme of basics makes this chapter easily span the generation gap.

The Contra chapter combines an interesting balance of traditional dances, sometimes referred to as "chestnuts," and contemporary dances. The contributions of many contemporary callers keep pace with the current contra trends.

The International Folk Dance chapter reflects the considerable expertise of some of the nation's outstanding dance teachers. Expansion in terms of choice in numbers and variety, along with balance in nationality, basic steps, and formations has been achieved by the new contributions of these leaders: Andor Czómpo, Hungarian dances, and motifs; Nelda G. Drury, Mexican dance; George A. Fogg, English Country dances; Karin Gottier, German dances; and Marilyn Wathen, French dances.

Of all the dance forms included in *Dance A While,* Social Dance is growing the most. There is the increasing popularity of Country Western, which includes line dances. There is a resurgence of Swing dance to any rhythm—rock, big band, salsa, country, cajun. And there is continued fascination with the Latin dances, especially Tango and Salsa.

The choice of dance material is still predicted upon the availability of recorded music. Every effort has been made to update music sources to make dance materials in this edition viable. Cassettes and a limited number of compact discs have become the leading sources of music for dancers as well as listeners. *Dance A While* becomes an exceptionally "user friendly" dance source on several dimensions for those who make use of the extensive resources found in the appendixes, bibliography, glossary, and indexes.

The seventh edition of *Dance A While* is dedicated to the late Jane Farwell. Jane was "folk dance!" Many generations derived joy and fun from her holistic approach in recreation, especially dancing, being immersed in and sharing all aspects of the folk setting. Jane's contagious enthusiasm, vision, and trendsetting ideas brought people together from all over the world. It was she who began the idea of weaving together folklore and customs with dance by establishing the first folk dance camp at the Oglebay Institute in Wheeling, West Virginia, in 1941. In her folk songbook *My Heart Sings,* Jane referred to this folk dance camp as "a wondrous tradition that has no ending." She developed a magic formula for planning, pacing, and leading events that appeared to "just happen." She founded Folklore Village on her farm in Dodgeville, Wisconsin, to further expand folk opportunities and to perpetuate her philosophy of enriching lives through understanding one's roots and other cultures. Jane was always "on call" as a leader, a contributor, a resource, and, best of all, a person who made learning easy and fun for all who gathered.

The seventh edition of *Dance A While* is a compilation of all the people, all the places, and all the joys we have been privileged to share along the way with those who love to dance. It has been our means of sharing this activity with a wider audience in the hope that the circle of those who dance will become even larger as the years roll by.

Acknowledgments

The seventh edition is very special since it is, indeed, the result of more than forty years of wisdom shared with us by many outstanding teachers, leaders, and dancers. First, we would like to acknowledge those who have had special impact on this edition and those who have been loyal contributors over the many years.

Dr. Sandra L. Gallemore contributed a complete unit on Clogging for the American Heritage chapter. Andor Czómpo, Hungarian dance specialist, presents historical notes, warmup exercises (motifs), and three exciting dances. George A. Fogg has furnished an interesting collection of English Country dances, including an early American dance in the English style, directions by Charles C. Hendrickson. Nelda G. Drury, Mexican dance specialist, developed historical notes, selected Mexican dances, and has provided a lifetime of companionship and advice. Karin P. Gottier's enthusiasm and knowledge of German dances gives us a new Krüz König more in keeping with the way it should be. Marilyn Wathen's contribution, gleaned from her many visits to France, expands our readers' choices in dances from that country. Ted Sannella has been especially helpful in critiquing the former Contra chapter and with Penn Fix recommended new material. The following have generously contributed one or more original Contra dances to this edition: Don Armstrong, Fred Breunig, Bob Dalsemer, Penn Fix, Gene Hubert, Roger C. Knox, Lannie McQuaide, Glen Nickerson, Al Olson, Tony Parkes, Ted Sannella, and Steve Zakon.

With every production there are the ground troops that lend immediate assistance with facts, ideas, and opinions. Kathy Anderson, Mary Lea Bailey, Luther Black, Dorthalea Horne, Alice Nugent, Judy Robare, and Mary Sarver have been very helpful. Then there are the relatives who are on constant call: daughter Kristina Waller Golden, Michael Golden, and husband Lynn Waller. Merci!

Special kudos to the "nuts and bolt gang" of record dealers who so carefully and generously checked available records and cassettes, namely Jack Geddes, Ed Kremer, Bob Ruff, and Kenneth Spear. John Filcich gave his guidance in assigning "most likely" ethnic group names to dances formerly labeled Yugoslavian.

Thanks also go to the reviewers for this seventh edition: Kenneth R. Aldrich, California State University at Fresno; Rayma K. Beal, University of Kentucky; Elizabeth A. Hanley, Pennsylvania State University; and Martha Kellstrom, Kansas State University.

In the last but not least category, we are ever grateful to those who have contributed to previous editions, material and ideas that continue to be the backbone of today's dance. Those still active and involved include: Glenn Bannerman, Vyts Beliajus, Sunni Bloland, Dick Crum, Henry "Buzz" Glass, Michael and the late Mary Ann Herman, Dvora Lapson, Jack Murtha, Bob Ruff, Country Dance Society of America, Folk Dance Federation of California, Mountain Folk Festival, Berea College, and the Lloyd Shaw Foundation.

Dance A While has been made even more special and valuable in the last several editions with the inclusion of the "History of Contra" by the late Ralph Page, and the Swedish materials contributed by the late Gordon Tracie. The late John Carlson's illustrations have made *Dance A While* as appealing to the eye as it is toe tapping to the feet.

Many thanks to our production staff, consisting of Suzanne Spunar of Lopez Island, Washington, and Judy Schilling of Tempe, Arizona.

The contributions of our colleague Jane Harris Ericson to the previous editions are many. Thanks, Jane, for the continual encouragement on the seventh edition.

AMP
MSW

Contents

Chapter Four
American Heritage Dance   57

Chapter Five
Square Dance   133

Chapter Eight
Social Dance   373

CHAPTER 1
History

The Beginning

Dance and the dancer have belonged to every age and culture since the beginning of time and thus have reflected the human condition and experience in each succeeding age. In the earliest human experience, dance was a functional means of survival. For primitive societies, dance was a psychological and physiological imperative.

Among primitive peoples everywhere, religion was a highly developed notion of a world of unseen powers. Worship was an expression, in one form or another, of the dependence of humans on powers outside themselves. Fear and a universal dependence on nature for sustenance are the two most conspicuous elements in primitive religion. Humans depended on natural phenomena—on the rain to grow plants, on the regular succession of seasons, and on the reproduction of animals. Primitive people feared sickness, death, hunger, drought, storms, and the spirits of the dead, both human and animal. The power to communicate with and manipulate the unseen powers that controlled their lives was engendered by the magic

of rituals and ceremonies designed to please and appease these forces. It is from these ancient mimetic ceremonies and rituals that the oldest of the arts has emerged—the dance.

Primitive people were one with their environment and, as such, were keen observers of the animal life around them. They reproduced with great fidelity the movements of birds and animals in the art of the period. These dancelike movements were unquestionably models for the mimetic movement used in primitive rituals. The observation of the structured movements of bird and animal groups and individuals gave rise to some of the earliest and oldest dance forms still in use today, namely, Circles, Chains, and Processionals.

Forms

The *Closed Circle* is perhaps the most ancient of these forms and is believed to have derived from observation and imitation of the sun's rotation. In the early uses of the Closed Circle, dancers entered into the circle equally without regard for differences in sex or social position. Magic was engendered by simple left-and-right movements around a central object that was the focus of the circle. Breaking the circle allowed the evil spirits out and the good spirits in, or vice versa, depending on the culture of the performers.

A second stage, in which the complexity of the circle increases, reflects the effect of cultural change. A dance for alternating sexes or for only one sex indicates occupational differentiation. Movement directions, forward and backward and weaving in and out, also increase the complexity of the circle. The elaboration of the Closed Circle into the Double Circle with men on the inner circle, women on the outer circle, either facing center or each other, represents forms used for executing occupational dances and fertility rites.

The *Chain* is derived from the Closed Circle. It first occurred, perhaps, when the Closed Circle was broken. Moving, or traveling the chain from one place to another, allows the magic or good luck engendered by the circle to be distributed over a larger area. Chain dances were generally "asexual"; that is, they could be danced by either sex or by a combination of sexes usually placed alternately in line. The Lira vase, modeled and decorated 22 centuries ago by Indo-Europeans, depicts a group of four women linked with three men in a chain who are moving sideways in unison. The *Carole,* a song-dance of the early Middle Ages, was danced in a chain formation. The *Farandole,* a form of Carole, was also danced in a hand-linked line or chain.

1

The *Processional* consisted of a single or double file of dancers. The latter form was more common and consisted of couples, men in one file and women in the other. The Processional, March, or Promenade was once a complete dance; however, it was more commonly used to begin a program of dancing. The Processional form is said to have originated from two important tribal customs, namely, to clean the community after a hard winter and to ensure its continued fertility. In England, whole communities dance the Processional, moving through the town and in and out of houses, cleaning all before them with a May branch or a green broom. It is from the Processional of couples that first the early Processional Court Dance, then the English Longways set and their continental versions, and finally the Couple Dances developed.

Throughout the ages, forms such as these have functioned to describe something about the society and culture of which they were a part. In the early stages of human development, the forms were as simple as humans imitating animals. As society became more complex, dance forms also became more complex. The effects of cultural changes on dance forms are particularly reflected in sexual, occupational, and social-class distinctions. These prehistoric dance forms—the Circle, Chain, and Processional—still exist in present contemporary dance sequences.

Music

Music, the twin sister of dance, has, through the ages, been intimately related to all phases of life—birth, death, love, work, play, war, peace, and religion—and to a myriad of occurrences that arouse human emotions—be they joyous, comedic, or tragic. Because of this intimate relationship with all facets of the human experience, music has had a universal appeal.

Primitive music was spontaneous and improvised, and it was characterized by its nonaesthetic nature and lack of notation. In primitive cultures, music had a magico-functional purpose that served to carry out and perpetuate tribal traditions. The endless singsong of primitive tribal chanters is reflected in early Christian chanting as well as in the droning rhymes of a child jumping rope.

The order in which the elements of music were developed is not known. It is tempting to surmise, however, that primitive humans were not wholly insensitive to the wealth of rhythm in their natural world. The rhythm of seasons, wind, water, and people's own physiological processes were con-

stant cues. There is evidence that primitive people were keenly aware of the two sets of percussion instruments, hands and feet, provided by nature. It is equally tempting to surmise that they vented their feelings of joy and sorrow in bodily motions accompanied by rhythmic noises. These crude rhythmic patterns and raw snatches of melody enacted in pantomime or expressed in grunts and shouts were the antecedents of dance and song.

The origins of instrumental music can be projected on more solid grounds because practically all types of instruments existing today can be traced from primitive and ancient times. Three classes of instruments have evolved: percussion, wind, and string. *Percussion instruments,* predominantly the drum, were used to accompany ritual dances and to communicate. In addition to the drum, rattles, seashells, twigs, bond scrapers, and gourds are examples of percussion instruments employed in primitive cultures.

Wind instruments in the form of flutes, trumpets, and reeds date back to the Stone Age. The flute and the trumpet are associated with magico-religious functions. The trumpet is also known to have been used as a signaling instrument in much the same way as it is used today.

In primitive cultures, the *string instruments* were the least developed. The predominant vocal and rhythmic character of primitive music did not require the use of melody or pitch. Primitive cave paintings, dated 30,000 to 15,000 B.C., reveal a human disguised in an animal skin and apparently playing a bow. This gives rise to the possibility that the hunting bow could very well have been the progenitor of string instruments. Whether rhythm preceded melody, vocal music preceded instrumental music, or, in fact, it all happened simultaneously, music was born.

Cultural Significance

Human history attests to the significance of dance as a serious and sacred activity. It was not a mere exuberant display of motor-rhythmic energy separated from the other institutions of a society. It was, indeed, the basis of the survival of the social system in that it contributed significantly to the society's functional and instrumental needs.

Religion

Among pre-Christian civilizations, dance was a functional part of religion. In Egypt, dance was an essential part of every religious celebration. Worship was predominantly a ritualized concern for death and rebirth. Egyptian art has left lasting tributes to the importance of dance in wall paintings, reliefs, and literary hieroglyphs. The Egyptians were the first to describe dance movement on paper, and so they are the inventors of the art of choreography.

The Bible, particularly the Old Testament, gives abundant evidence of the importance and place of dance in ancient Hebrew religion. Dance was primarily an act of gratitude for victory or an accompaniment for a hymn of praise. Dances were generally joyous in nature and circular in form. Gratitude, joy, and praise are all found in David's dance in leading the procession of the ark and the canticle of the Israelites after the destruction of the Egyptians led by Miriam and "all the women" (II Sam. VI) and David danced before the Lord with all his might (Exod. 15:20).

Education

Dance pervaded the life of ancient Greece, primarily in the form of worship and education. It also penetrated everyday life and achieved perfection as an art form in Greek drama. The Muse of Dance, Terpsichore, was one of the seven Muses. Ancient Greek philosophy defined the soul as the harmony of the body; thus the aim of the Greeks was to develop equally all poses of the mind and the body. Dance, a chief branch of education, was the medium through which total integration of mind, body, and spirit could be achieved.

Dance as it is functionally significant to education has been recognized at various stages throughout human history. The Greeks considered dance a necessary part of education for all people. Plato proposed that all children, boys and girls, be instructed in dance from an early age. He wrote, "To sing well and to dance well is to be well educated" (Lawler 1964; p. 124). The Pyrrhic was the great Greek dance of war. It was accompanied by the flute and danced by armed warriors, who simulated warlike deeds with all the proper maneuvers for attack and defense. Sparta required every child over the age of five to learn the Pyrrhic and to practice it in a public place.

In New England, contrary to popular belief, settlers recommended that the young be taught to dance in order to learn poise, discipline, and good manners. John Locke, the great commonsense philosopher, wrote of dancing, "Nothing appears to me to give the children so much becoming confidence and behavior . . . as dancing" (Damon 1957; p. 3). Elsewhere in the New World, North American Indian war dances and primitive hunting dances were occasions to teach and practice the skills necessary for war and hunting.

Health

The preservation of health and the power to cure ailments through dance rituals are found in every culture. Among primitive people, the *Death Dance* was a united rhythmic effort to remove the ghost, dust the spirits from the house, quiet the emotions, and dispel the fears of those who remained. The 15th century version of the Death Dance was strange in that it happened only in the minds of medical writers and artists. Paintings and woodcuts of the period depict the universality of death, the equality of death, and the vanity of rank and riches. All people, regardless of caste, eventually succumb to the Death Dance. Death also appeared among the living in the form of a skeleton as a warning of impending death.

Captain Cook, of English naval fame, required his crew to dance the *Hornpipe* to ensure immunity from disease. In mid-14th century Italy, the violent, nervous exercise of dancing was believed to relieve the harmful effects or the unreasonable fear of the bite of the tarantula spider.

Devil dances to drive out the ghost of a dead person are thought to be the bases for many funeral dances found throughout history. The Hopi Indians of Arizona use an ancient sand-painting ceremonial for curing purposes. During the four holy days following na ih es, the San Carlos Apache girl's puberty ceremony, the girl's power is believed to be strong enough to cure the sick (Basso 1966; p. 160). So great is the residual power of the dance in this ceremony that it has even been known to cure retarded body conditions such as bowed legs (Goodwin 1969; p. 443).

Fertility

Dance in the form of fertility rites has been universally used by humans to propagate the species and to secure food. Initiation, courtship, marriage, and birth are themes represented by the dance in these rites. In the initiation rite, youth is danced into adulthood. Fertility of the fields and of humans is abduced by the power generated by encircling a maypole, a tree, or a sword. The three themes symbolized by the dance are (1) passage from one phase to another, as from youth to adulthood or from single to married status; (2) transfer of power (e.g., to carry or decorate with green or to encircle another person); and (3) purification, exemplified by leaping through or running around fire. "Sowing and copulating, germinating and bearing, harvesting and delivering are under one law" (Sachs 1937; p. 67).

Dance and the dancer have belonged to every age and culture since the beginning of time. It is evident that dance and the dancer have played a significant role in the evolution of mankind. In all ages, the human body, as an instrument moving in space and time, has made dance unique among the arts. It is this uniqueness that makes dance older than art and thus explains the antiquity and universality of dance.

Pacific Rim Perspective

The Pacific Rim is a vast area extending from the southern tip of the western edge of South America north along the western coast of South and North America; west across the Bering Sea to the eastern edge of the former Soviet Union; south along the eastern edges of the three regional groupings referred to as East Asia (China, Japan, North and South Korea), South Asia (India, Pakistan, Afghanistan, Nepal, and Sri Lanka), and Southeast Asia (Myanmar [Burma], Laos, Thailand, Philippines, Indonesia, Malaysia, New Guinea and hundreds of islands in the South Pacific); to Australia and New Zealand. Historically the area represents the western edge of the 15th and 16th century European expansion and influence and the eastern edge of the Asian expansion and influence. The cultural impact of these two forces is dramatically portrayed in the history of the Philippines, which was dominated by the Spanish; Indonesia, which was greatly influenced by India; and Australia and New Zealand, which are part of the British Commonwealth.

Historically the Western study of the arts, including dance, has been dominated by the arts of European or Western civilization. Until early in the 20th century, little was known of dance as it existed in the eastern part of the European continent, although for centuries it was an important element in the cultures of this portion of the world. In more recent times Western interest, particularly American, has led to increased study and research as well as extensive exposure to Western audiences by performing groups from many of the East, South, and Southeast Asian countries. This heightened interest in dance as part of the culture of many Asian countries has led to the inclusion in this chapter of brief background sketches of dance in a select group of countries in Asia and the island nations of the South Pacific.

India

Dance in India is reputedly the most primitive and at the same time the most sophisticated of the arts.

Historical references record that classical dance existed and flourished for centuries before the birth of Christ and, in fact, all India's theater arts were highly developed. The Hindu god Siva is supposed to have created the world by setting its rhythm in motion by dance. Mythology abounds with descriptions of gods and goddesses dancing to produce blessings or to ward off evil.

Classical dance was intrinsically bound to religion. Temple festivals were inseparable from dance and served as the place for the performance. Temple sculpture depicted gods and goddesses dancing and provided a visual legacy of movement for succeeding generations to study. Temple dancers or "devadasis," servants of the deity, helped develop and preserve dance tradition. It has been said that classical dance might never have survived had it not been for these temple dancers and their teachers.

Classical dance in India is in essence dance-drama. The dancer is a storyteller and through dance movements acts out the cast of characters. The elements found in these dance-dramas are song, pantomime, expression, movement, speech, and scenery. The performance may convey ideas, moral values, moods, emotions, and philosophy. The elements vary with the style and historical time of the dance. Aside from their function as entertainment, dance-dramas played an important role in educating the unlettered masses. It was through theatrical spectacles that the ordinary people learned the benefits of virtue, dangers of vices, legends of heroes, and stories of the gods. The theater, often called the bible of the poor, with its color, sound, action, drama, and splendor, gave the people an opportunity to participate in festivals fit for kings and to enter the world of gods and heroes.

Physical training played an important role in all forms of classical dance. Years of arduous training was necessary to acquire the intricate control, skills, and postures required by the dance. Each body part and individual muscle, large and small, was trained to perform separately. Extensive and intensive work was required to control the muscles of the eyeball, eyelids, and eyebrows. In addition, control of the nose, cheek, lips, chin, and neck muscles along with the ability to produce coloration of the face, perspiration, and tears were all to be acquired for dramatic effect. Lastly, the multi-meaning or vocabulary of the hundreds of hand and finger gestures so typical of Indian dance were to be mastered.

The four classical dance styles in India are *Bharata Natya, Kathakali, Kathak,* and *Manipuri.* All four styles are composed of three common elements: pure dance, mime, and a combination of the two. Pure dance is simply dancing to a rhythmical accompaniment without regard for the theme. Pantomime or mime consisted of expressive gestures that communicated the meanings in the story.

All four styles have a common beginning in the system codified by the poet-sage Bharata in the 3rd century B.C. Although each style was conditioned by the environment in which it developed, all share similar techniques, aesthetic principles, and historical and mythological backgrounds. On the other hand, each style differs in language, technique, music, costume, and physical training requirements.

In Bharata Natya the basic geometrical motif is one of three triangles. The movements are angular, measured, and symmetrical. A rectangle forms the basic posture of the Kathakali style. All movements on the floor or in the air are governed by this geometric form. Kathakali movements are violent and expansive. Kathak emphasizes a straight line and preserving gravity. The movements are light, vague, and vacillating. Manipuri dances are based on the figure eight and circular movements in which the body and limbs move in flowing curves.

Bharata Natya

The Bharata Natya style of dance is the oldest and most classical in India. Bharata, a combined sage and patron saint of dance, wrote in Sanskrit a treatise on dance and drama in approximately the 3rd century B.C. He codified the knowledge and formulated the theories for the practice and study of dance and drama as revealed to him by the gods. This canonical work is referred to as the Fifth Veda (Holy Book) because of Bharata's sacred relation to art and the Hindu religious concept of dance. The traditions he codified indicated an advanced stage of development in the arts in his time. The Bharata Natya is the most brilliant and classical dance in India and thus is the master form and parent for all dance.

Bharata Natya is the dance style of south India, more specifically, the Tamil Nad region, which encompasses a major portion of southeast India. There it has been preserved and practiced. Originally it contained masculine and feminine roles as taught by the god Siva (male) and goddess Paravata (female). The movements of the dance thus displayed the vigor of the active male and the soft passiveness of the female. Today Bharata Natya is a solo dance that developed independently and is distinct from other dance forms. This solo type is thought to be a direct descendant of the dances of the devadasis.

The basic posture of the Bharata Natya is a triangle, in fact, three triangles. The first is formed by the turned-out feet, as in the first position of ballet, and flexed knees. The line across the knees forms the base with the apex at the heels. The second has the apex at the waist sharing the base line at the knees. The third is formed by the shoulder line sharing the apex at the waist. The knees must remain flexed throughout the dance

except during short song sequences whose meanings are danced out by hand gestures and facial expressions. Characteristic movements are terse lines in space and abrupt head and shoulder movements. Outstretched arms and crisp hand movements extend the torso. Leg extensions move from a well-balanced opposite-side base. Leaps are frequent and concise. Vertical elevations are limited. Bharata Natya is characterized by energy, speed, force, exuberance, clarity, and above all physical precision.

Kathakali

Kathakali is the dance-drama of Malabar in southwest India. Malabar is a tropical coastline of some three hundred miles lying between coastal hills and the ocean where the Arabian, Indian, and Bengal seas meet. Its excellent harbors attracted the Greeks, Phoenicians, Arabs, and Chinese a millennium before the Christian era; it was the oldest part of India to have contact with the outside world. This mixed ethnic background is reflected in the dance form.

The dance-drama Kathakali is held outdoors and is an all-night performance ending at dawn. It is usually held during periods of the full moon. The performers, all men, also take women's roles. Dancers appear, not as human beings, but as gods, demons, and spirits from another world. Their actions create certain moods characteristic of a view of life in the abstract.

Kathakali is the culmination of many different theatrical forms existing over time in south India. The dance style is overwhelmingly dramatic. To achieve this dramatic quality a highly developed, complex, and symbolic system of makeup has evolved. Colors are associated with certain moods and sentiments. In facial makeup, green is the color for virtuous characters. A black moustache drawn on the upper lip indicates an angry mood. The color symbolism is carried out in the colorful costumes and headgear, which represent gods and spirits of the world of myth and legend, not of the real world.

Kathakali technique follows other classical styles in that it utilizes pure dance, expressive dance, and mime. However, unlike other styles, Kathakali uses both skeletal and large muscle groups of the body. The geometric pattern is a square or rectangle. The basic posture is feet apart, knees turned out. The dancer moves his feet to all corners of the rectangle. The rectangle is used in hand and arm movements as well. Jumps, spirals, and leaps along with some elevation is characteristic. Facial expressions are of major importance. The most exacting part of Kathakali training is learning to control the eyes, eyelids, eyebrows, and lip movements.

The pantomime aspect of the dance sequence is the test of a great Kathakali dancer. This is the creative portion of the dance in which the dancer can embellish a simple line in a poem into a solo improvisation of great dramatic effect. In mime the hand movements are particularly important in setting the dramatic mood. Some twenty-four hand gestures communicate more than five hundred words and word signs.

Kathakali style is energetic, active, violent, athletic, and acrobatic. It is predominantly masculine in feeling. The conditioning of the body requires that dancers begin at an early age and spend up to ten years in training. Massages and oil baths make the body soft and flexible so that each muscle, joint, and nerve can operate independently when called on. Acrobatics and fencing are used to produce fantastic leg extensions, leaps, jumps, and splits. Eye training is extensive and arduous. The eyes are trained to open to twice their normal size, tremble rapidly, move slowly in tracking an object, and show the whites only. Kathakali training makes the body perform in ways that otherwise seem impossible.

Kathak

Kathak is the dance style of northern India, a section ruled by the Muslims during the 12th to the 18th centuries. During this period, the otherwise religious and temple-oriented Kathak degenerated into a secular form known as Nautch. The vulgarity of Nautch relegated the dance to brothels and Muslim courts where it was performed to please the overlords, not the gods, and for remuneration rather than spiritual reward. Under Muslim influence and material encouragement large numbers of artists pursued their talents in this environment. Since the revival of classical dance in India, Kathak has resumed its rightful place among other forms.

Kathak is characterized by a wide-eyed stare and a whirl and sudden halt. The dancer's feet are percussion instruments that produce rhythmic pulses to vibrate the ankle bells. The dancer can tap out long, involved meters with or against the drum syncopation. Dancers have been reputed to be able to control all bells but one in a percussion action. Kathak movement is neither violent nor overly dainty and the mood is soft and sweet. It can be danced, therefore, by male or female. The latter, however, constitute the majority. Aside from these elements, the dance style is much like other classical forms.

Manipuri

Manipuri dance is at home in the province of Manipur in northeast India along the Myanmar (Bur-

ma) border. This small part of India is a beautiful, fertile, self-sufficient valley inhabited by mixed ethnic groups predominantly of the Vaishnavite Hindu persuasion. The area has been isolated both geographically and for political reasons for many years. Until very recently visitors came only by permission from the government.

According to mythology, Manipur was created so the gods would have a place to dance. Therefore, Manipur is a land of amateur dancers! It is a matriarchal society in which men are idle while women take care of the home and business affairs. It is compulsory for women to dance and optional for men.

Manipur is most celebrated for producing polo and Ras Lila. Polo is known and played worldwide. *Ras Lila,* a dance of ecstasy in heaven, was created by the god Siva and his wife Parvati. Legend further claims that the imitation Ras Lila for which Manipur was founded was Lai Haraoba.

Lai Haraoba, an imitation Ras Lila, is the oldest dance form in Manipur and therefore the basis for all their dance. It is performed for one month, usually April or May, by each village as a religious obligation. It is at once dance, fertility ritual, religious in context, and village entertainment. In reality it is a small-scale version of the creation of the world.

The dance is accompanied by drums and a small string instrument played with an archerylike bow to which bells are attached to add percussion. Dance training is unnecessary in Manipur. The natural grace of its people and their outdoor life give them enough exercise and training to perform the dance. The people literally dance as soon as they walk!

Religion is the focus of the dance and the body movements are considered the highest dedication of the human body to the gods. The Manipuri consider movements in sports as well as dance a means of worship. Gods are worshipped in boat racing, polo, hockey, and mountain climbing. The holy book even suggests offering a stick and a ball to the gods in cases of epidemics. To the Manipuri dance is physical culture made more ornamental for the glory of the gods.

Ras Lila is one of India's most outstanding contributions to the arts. Ras Lila is a love dance or love play as conceived by Joy Singh, a Manipur king who saw and heard it in a dream. In contrast to polo, Ras Lila has never been performed outside of Manipur. It is performed after midnight and staged according to season, usually in a mountain area or a remote temple. Ras Lila is in truth a full-scale opera-drama combining dance, choral singing, and religious cantatas. It is a spectacle of color, glittering jewels, flashing mirrors and mica on flamboyant costumes. It is considered a national treasure and is without a doubt a moving and exciting dance-drama with universal appeal.

Classical dance in India has been revived from oblivion and extinction more than once since its codification by Bharata in the 3rd century B.C. Passed along mainly by rote and practice, the details of the dance-drama grew dim or were lost over succeeding generations. In the mid-eighteenth century Vadivela and Ponniah Pillay, brothers of Tanjori, both masters of the dance, music, and Sanskrit, revised and standardized Bharata Natya. Their expertise uniquely suited them to interpret the literature and theatrical background of the dance; thus they were able to crystallize the repertoire and regulate the dance items into a more classical program.

Subjugated by Muslims, the British, and later influenced by Christianity, dance in India did well to survive at all. However, with independence came a rebirth of interest in all the arts, including dance. Anna Pavlova's Indian tour in 1929 is credited with stimulating renewed interest in classical dance. Her performance, based on Indian themes and music, along with her inquiries and obvious interest in Indian dance, helped awaken national interest. More importantly, perhaps, was the part she played in enhancing the stature of women artists.

Classical dance in India today is the product of some half a century of activity stimulated partly by American interest and wholly by the dedication of many Indian artists. Interest and support of dance by people of a higher caste, particularly women, coupled with travel and performance abroad have been the major forces moving dance from provincial to national stature. Classical dance is India's most significant and unique gift to the world of dance.

China

China is a vast country encompassing a civilization dating back more than four thousand years. Discoveries of late Stone Age sites on the Loess Plateau along the Yellow and Wei Rivers indicate that the Chinese civilization did, indeed, develop independently of South Asian and Western cultures.

The first Chinese state has been traced by scholars to the Shang dynasty (ca. 1766–1122 B.C.). Priests, scholars, officials, and artisans of the Shang dynasty developed agriculture, formalized religion, set up government and legal systems, produced writing and literature, began the tradition of dynasties, and developed handicrafts and metallurgy. All of these accomplishments clearly distinguished China from other cultural systems of the same period. A common means of communication in the written literature has always been a unifying factor between past and present in Chinese culture.

The dynasty system, which began with the Shang and ended with the Qing (A.D. 1644–1911), is one of China's most interesting and unique cultural developments. The cyclic rise and fall of dynasties over the centuries makes it important to understand and cast the study and research of events and the cultural progress of Chinese history against the chronology of this system.

China and India were the two major cultural forces in Asia. As India's influence waned, China, an equally powerful force, began to dominate. China is a gigantic multinational country made up of the Han, the Chinese people, who represent approximately 90 percent of the population, and more than fifty national minorities. It is this mix and the influence they had on one another that created the common cultural tradition of the Chinese people. The bulk of dance before and after liberation has come from the minorities. Unlike the Indians, the Chinese produced little or no dance. China's forte in the arts was the theater, better known as the opera. India cultivated dance and music to the detriment of drama; China developed drama and music to the exclusion of dance.

Despite the domination of the opera there was dance. Thanks to the mountainous bulk of literature the Chinese have produced in written history dating from the most ancient times and to archaeological finds of more recent times dance has been quite thoroughly researched and studied. Of particular importance have been archaeological digs, cave paintings, and murals. These, combined with accounts in poetry and essays from the Han dynasty (206 B.C.–A.D. 220) and the Tang dynasty (A.D. 618–907), indicate that dance and songs were indeed a part of the life of the primitive people who were the forebears of the Chinese people. A Neolithic bowl, one of the oldest finds, depicts a line or circle of dancers holding hands with movement indicated by the angle of the braided hair hanging from their heads. Legends tell of dances developed to serve as fitness exercises and martial dance with weapons to train soldiers. Votive dances related in ancient legends tell of clan or tribal leaders who ordered songs and dances composed to offer as homage to a good harvest, for the pleasure of a god, or to heaven, earth, and the ancestors.

The dynastic system in Chinese history began as a slave society, a period lasting some 1600 years. As was true in most of the world's emerging human societies, people had no means for understanding natural phenomena and thus resorted to shamans to communicate with the gods. During this period shamans practiced their sorcery by singing and dancing. Rain dances, for agricultural reasons, were especially in demand. Dances of exorcism were also used to drive away the demons of pestilence or devils. Dancers wore masks and performed frenziedly to clear out the evil. These dances enjoyed an unbroken tradition of several thousand years.

Dancing slaves represented the gradual entry of dance into the realm of performing art. Rulers of the time considered dance as entertainment and kept troupes of dancing girls in their courts. Legend tells that groups of slave dancers were killed and buried with their owner so they could continue serving their master after death.

The powerful slave state of the Western Zhou (11th century B.C.) appointed a director of music whose task it was to work out a system of ritual music and dance. He collected songs and dances of various clans under previous dynasties and taught them to the members of the court for ritual ceremonial purposes. This system included the dances for votive ritual, a martial type of dance, dances costumed with animal tails or plumage relating to hunting, and music and dance of national minorities such as "Music of Border Tribes." Succeeding generations of feudal rulers praised this system of court ritual as "Music of Early Kings" or as "sublime music."

A slave revolt brought an end to the Western Zhou reign and thus ended the cruel regime and along with it organized court dance and music. China entered a period of turmoil and change, and folk song and dance was left to the vicissitudes and vagaries of the general population. During this period, known as the Spring, Autumn, and Warring States period, groups of poor people roamed the countryside offering their services as actors or dancing girls. Many excellent artists were produced during this period. Performers continued to lead harsh lives during the feudal period but despite this these early professional performers preserved and developed dance in ancient China.

China experienced its first multi-national unified state during the Han dynasty. Unification led to stability, economic progress, and frequent contacts between nationalities within and outside the borders. Under these circumstances literature, art, and dance flourished. A board of music was established to collect and improve folk song and dance. Variety shows became the vogue for performing and entertaining. These shows included acrobatics, martial arts, comic acts, recitals of music, song, and dance as well as other folk arts. The widespread popularity of the variety shows drew audiences from hundreds of miles around.

Archaeological finds have provided a lifelike look at the variety show popular in the Han period. One such group of Han clay figurines on a tray shows the arrangement of musicians, acrobats, and dancing girls. A brick relief shows the *Tray Drum Dance*, an ingenious combination of dance and acrobatics which is a distinctive style in Chinese classical dance. Other artifacts show the *Fish Dance, Dragon Dance,* and *Peacock Dance.* The sleeve movements of a dancer's costume, an ancient tradition in Chinese dance, are also found in figurines and in murals. Stone reliefs and other objects depicting dance have been corroborated by contemporary folk dances such as the *Red Silk Dance* and the *Long Silk Dance* created after Liberation.

During the more than four hundred years of the Han dynasty artists created many dances. Dancers underwent strict training during this time and were successful in raising dance to a new artistic level. However, the low social status of the dancer was such that only the figurines and stone engravings buried with the feudal nobles remain to tell the story of their work.

The development of cities, institution of the guild system, and increased foreign trade led to a prosperous economy during the northern and southern Song dynasties. The arts flourished and expanded with special venues being set aside in the cities to stage shows for increasingly large, eager audiences. These venues were known as Wazi and Goulan. They were places to display all kinds of skills such as poetic dramas, acrobatics, story telling, comic acts, musical acts, wrestling, and dances.

Although the song and dance pieces given at the Wazi were well received, the most popular were the poetic dramas. Dance performances increasingly included sections depicting stories and it was in the telling of these stories that the populace found an avenue for expression suited to their needs. This was in essence the beginning of the traditional Chinese opera. Traditional opera continued to grow from the Song dynasty to the Qing dynasty and proved to be the most popular form of art, becoming China's world-renowned art form.

Under the short-lived Sui dynasty the rulers celebrated the end of the latest period of war and set about unifying China once again. They amassed the traditional songs and dances of the Han dynasty, minority nationalities, and materials from abroad into "Seven Books of Music," later increased to "Nine Books of Music." The books were for the populace as well as for court use. They also continued the variety shows of the Han dynasty. The lavish spending and self-indulgence of the Sui dynasty spelled its doom in some thirty short years.

The golden age of the arts followed under the Tang dynasty (A.D. 618). The Tang court set up offices for music and dance and employed noted artists to train professional performers in a systematic manner. These trained professionals were then dispersed all over the country, which helped ancient and traditional dance to attain a new standard of performance and skill.

The "Nine Books of Music" from the Sui dynasty was enlarged to "Ten Books of Music" by incorporating materials from the minority nationalities, the Yan, Qingshang, Xiliang, Indian, Korean, Kucine, Bokhara, Shula, Samarkand, and Qoco. Of the ten books only Yan and Qingshang music were Han music; the other eight were of other nationalities. The "Ten Books" enjoyed great popularity in the Central Plains.

The "Samarkand Music," commonly called *Dervish Dance,* was the dance of the minority from the northwest boundaries of China. The dance featured whirling movements variously described as "gyrating frenzy like flurrying snow." Most of the Dervish Dances were performed by women and were very popular during the Tang period.

Zuobu Arts and *Libre Arts* were two new categories of dance formed in the Tang period. Zuobu Arts were refined movements performed inside by a small number of dancers. Libre Arts were ostentatious displays of dance performed outside by a large number of dancers. Both were based on the artistic tradition of the Central Plains but largely made up of materials of the national minorities and neighboring countries. The "Taiping Music" in the Libre Arts was also known as the *Lion Dance of the Five Directions.* The Lion Dance appears over several centuries in several cultures in the Asian area and has a particularly interesting history as it relates to China. Although not native to China, lions were often brought as gifts to the Han dynasty court from Afghanistan and Persia. They were viewed as symbols of power and strength. The dance, in its many forms, grew out of the imitation of the lion's appearance and actions and was danced to express what the lion symbolized.

Small-scale dances used at less important or ordinary banquets were classified as *Jian Dances* and *Ruan Dances.* The former were robust dances requiring agility; the latter were more sedate and beautiful in their movements. The *Sabre, Mulberry Branch,* and *Dervish* represent the Jian group while the *Green Waist Dance* was the most famous of the Ruan dances.

"Grand Compositions" and "Folk Song and Dance Drama" were two other forms active in the Tang period. The "Grand Compositions" included song, dance, and poetry while the "Folk Song and Dance Drama" combined singing, dancing, and acting to portray set characters and a plot. Most of the latter consisted of one character and a simple plot; therefore they could not be termed full-fledged song and dance dramas but could be said to be the precursor of China's later world-renowned traditional opera.

Music and dance were the main performing arts during the Tang dynasty. Although based on traditional dance, the choreography was bold and innovative, and embraced many national folk dances as well as those introduced from abroad. It is said that whenever the Chinese adapted anything from abroad it was as if they had taken it as a prisoner to do with as they pleased. Tang arts absorbed everything, and given fairly stable political and economic conditions, a golden era in the development of dance in China's feudal society was created.

National minority dances played an important role in the overall mosaic of Chinese folk dance. Their work, life, love, and customs were bound up in their dance, which was largely passed along by oral tradition. Hand-written historical documents carried few records of their dances. The most influential were the Mongol, Tibetan, Uygar, Miao, Korean, Yao, and Dai minorities. The following are some examples of the style and type of minority dance that was popular in central China.

The *Daola* of the Mongols displayed the strong, vigorous, and rapid whirling action characteristic of the northern border neighbor. The *Guozhuang Dance* from Tibet reflected the hunting life of its people by imitating tigers, eagles, and peacocks. The *Xie* or *Xianzi Da,* the graceful sleeve dance, and the *Duixie* or *Tap Dance,* which beat out rhythm with the feet, were well-received dances from Tibet. The *Long Drum Dance* of the Yao was popular through the Song, Yuan, Ming and Qing dynasties. It is also a present-day favorite of new China. The beautiful *Mynah Dance,* which imitates the movements of the mynah bird, and the *Reed Pipe Dance* of the Miao people are both currently being performed by professional dancers. Other national minority dances known during the feudal periods and which have been drawn upon and used in present-day performances are the Yi people's *Axi Moon Dance,* the Dai *Peacock Dance,* the Li *Money Bell and Double Sword Dance,* the Zhuang *Carrying and Pole Dance,* and the Gaosham *Pestle Dance.*

The Ming and Qing dynasties were the final stages of China's feudal system. Popular thought and action at this time bore the seeds of capitalism and a thriving city life spurred a boon in the arts. Traditional opera, singing, and story telling flourished while dance performances alone were rare. Popular opposition to feudalism found in the opera a means for communicating resistance to the cruel constraints of everyday life, something that dance alone could not do. Dance merged with opera and thus rarely existed as an independent performing art although a wealth of dance was preserved in the opera. Dance continued in the general populace in the form of small song and dance shows put on by amateur performers of working people during slack seasons. These small touring groups of seven or eight actors developed shows from original song and dance pieces such as *Local Flower Drum, Tea Picking Lantern* and other well-known pieces. The resulting shows were widely popular and provided an outlet for the people to pour out their joys and sorrows and make public note of their resistance to feudal rule.

Although dance performances alone were uncommon in the Ming and Qing dynasties, dances at local festivals were widespread. The traditional Lantern Festival held on the 15th day in the first month of the lunar calendar was a particularly joyous occasion for song and dance. Homes and streets were festooned with lanterns, fireworks were set off, drums and gongs sounded, and the *Lion Dance* and the *Monk with the Big Head Dance* were traditional attractions. Chinese literature in the form of books, poems, accounts, and recollections attest to the continued popularity of dance among the populace at festival times.

In the intervening years after the dynasty system became history and the Republic exited to Taiwan, some efforts were made to collect and arrange folk dance materials but the major effort was left to be done after liberation. Almost immediately the Chinese government seized on folk dance as a means of fostering national spirit and to present the people as happy and cheerful members of the new Chinese society.

In 1951, two years after liberation, a large celebration of song and dance called "Great Unity of the People" was held in Tiananmen Square. It was an opportunity for national minorities to demonstrate their dances as well as a national review of the achievements of professional dancers from the folk art tradition of old China. In 1952 the performance toured all areas of China to demonstrate unity and exuberance for the new society.

Under a policy adopted by the Chinese Communist Party and the central People's Government national minority art and literature was to be developed. This policy led to extensive research, study, and rearranging of many of the traditional dances throughout China. Specifically, folk dance disciplines were set up in dance schools, dance teachers collected and arranged dance materials, studies of dance in classical Chinese opera was undertaken aided by older performers in the opera, and in the mid-fifties Chinese dance leaders created a national dance with a distinct style based on the study of national, traditional, and foreign dance forms. The result was "The Precious Lotus Lamp," the first large-scale dance-drama. A second large-scale dance-drama, "The East Is Red," which was especially supported by Premier Zhou Enlai, required some three thousand dancers. This epic covered the various stages of the Chinese revolution.

Suddenly the "Gang of Four" headed by Jiang Qing came to power and brought to a virtual halt all the work in dance and other arts. During the ten years of their influence artists, dancers, singers, and musicians were cruelly treated; they were executed, imprisoned, or sent to the country to do manual labor. In 1976 this foursome was ousted and national art was liberated for the second time. Since the mid-seventies, the national art movement has regained its momentum and is once again teaching, practicing, researching, and staging mammoth and spectacular performances for audiences in China and abroad.

China is presently awash in dance. Dances are created in villages, cities, communes, schools, factories, as well as professional dance schools. It is seen in parks, courtyards, plazas, indoors, and outdoors. A festival held in Beijing in 1972 was reported to have had over two thousand amateur groups performing. Performers, even eight- and eleven-year-olds, are polished, technically adroit, and project theater-quality proficiency.

Dance in China is an expression by and of the people. It is about them and exists for them. The frames of reference are contemporary situations, historical events, revolutionary themes showing workers, peasants, and soldiers as heroes and heroines, and stories of the crimes of the old society. Movement styles come from minority nationality forms, work techniques of the field and factory, old dances of the Tang and other dynasties, and even a touch of Wu Shu, a traditional style of physical culture. Regardless of the style or content, the dance is always presented in a joyous, happy, and exuberant mode.

Content and style is best reflected in dance titles such as *The Spinners and Weavers Dance, Dance of the Steel Workers, Think of the Consumer When Growing Vegetables, On the Way to Battle,* and *The Bayonet Fight.* Titles of dances for children reflect history, vocational preparation, and acquiring attitudes: *The Long March, The Nurses, Friendship Dance,* and *Washing Clothes.*

The new China is clearly allowing for the fullest expression of people's ideas and feelings through dance. And just as the ancient "Book of Odes" suggests, "If words do not suffice, then sigh; if sighing fails, then sing; if singing is not enough, then let your arms and legs dance it."*

Japan

The three professional classic dance forms in Japan are *Bugaku, Noh,* and *Kabuki.* All three are performed by men, confirming Japanese society as indeed a man's world. Each represents an aspect of three different historical socioeconomic groups found in the cultural life of Japan. Bugaku was developed from dances brought from Asia for the imperial courts during the Heian period (794–1185). Noh was developed under the patronage of samurai rulers and aristocracy during the Muromachi

---

*Wand Kefen, *The History of Chinese Dance.* Beijing: Foreign Language Press, 1985, p. 1.

period (1338–1573). Kabuki was a popular form among merchants and townspeople of Osaka and Edo (Tokyo) during the Todugawa period (1600–1867).

Folk dances in general occur as part of the three major religious festivals, Kaura, Ta Asobi, and Obaon. Kagura is the music (god music) and dance of Shinto, the indigenous pantheistic religion of Japan. It includes a wide variety of activities such as dances and ceremonies of the imperial shrines, dances of the Miko or shrine maidens, and numerous regional dance-dramas, martial arts, and animal dances. Ta Asobi or "rice paddy play" refers to a variety of agricultural rites dealing with the cultivation of rice from mid-winter to the fall harvest festivals. Bon dances are performed throughout Japan, generally on the grounds of Buddhist temples. Bon festivals are celebrations of the return of the souls of dead ancestors, who visit the earth once each year in mid-August. Noh performances are also given as a part of some festivals.

Bugaku

Bugaku dance style emphasizes pure dance forms over the dramatic elements. Although dramatic elements exist in some dances, they become mostly topical and little or nothing of the story is communicated. Bugaku emphasizes symmetry of the basic movement patterns in solo dances and the frequent use of paired dancers. The dance setting is usually outdoors or in a simulated outdoor setting in a courtyard, shrine, temple, or the imperial household. The fixed repertoire is composed of some sixty pieces handed down from ancient times. The works are divided into two categories according to basic style and assumed place of origin. The *Left Dance* (Samai) includes dances from China, India, and Indochina along with those from Japan in similar style. The movements are slow, gentle, and elegant. Dancers are costumed in robes of reddish color. The *Right Dance* (Umai) includes dances from Korea and compositions based on Korean dances. The movement is humorous and spirited. Dancers wear robes of a greenish color. In the Left Dance the dancers enter the stage from the left of a large drum located at the rear of the stage or stage right. The Right Dancer enters the stage from the right of the drum or stage left.

Bugaku dances are divided into four types based on content. They are ceremonial (hiramai), military (bumai), running (hashirimai), and children (dodu) dances. Ceremonial dances are performed by two to four unmasked dancers wearing court or ceremonial robes. Military dances are performed in pairs. Dancers wear elaborate warrior robes and simulate battle action with swords and lances. Run-ning dances are performed by solo masked dancers displaying a strong character. Children dances are composed for and performed by children.

Noh

Noh is held to be the greatest dance-drama tradition in human history. After appreciating the visual beauty and traditional conventions of Noh, those who make the effort will experience a powerful expression of the universal nature of man's spirit. The training and aesthetics of Noh were formulated by the writings of the famous performer, playwright, and philosopher Zeami in the mid-12th and early 13th centuries. His writings are still read by students, performers, and connoisseurs of the art and his plays still form the core of Noh repertory.

A combination of the elegant world of the imperial court, Zen in the form of Buddhist meditation, and the code of ethics and conduct of the samurai were the main influences on the content of Noh dance-dramas. These three influences are seen in Noh plays in which samurai, nobles of the court, and Buddhist priests appear as characters.

Noh plays draw on the etiquette of Shintoism, including the carrying of the fan, the use of flute and drum, and on Kagura for ceremony. From Bugaku it drew its structure, namely the use of an introduction, development, and conclusion. Variety came from Sarugaku in the form of magic tricks, humorous skits, and acrobatics. Field music elements came from rice cultivation festivals. Dances performed by Buddhist priests (Ennem) at New Year festivals and popular songs and dances of the period are all part of the background and content of Noh theater.

Set movement patterns, meaning a form either in time or space, are the bases for construction of Noh dances. The movement patterns are composed of position and progression. The basic position requires the torso to be inclined and held in place with no rotation. The back is held in a straight line, knees slightly bent, and arms curved down and forward of the body, elbows slightly lifted to create a line for the large sleeves of the costume. The dancer imagines lines of force coming out of the center of the body to project his energy. This effort can be characterized as a level of high tension without being rigid. Concentration produces the effect of freedom coming from self-control.

Walking is the most characteristic movement. It is the progression that integrates the dance. In addition, it is the element by which the overall skill of the dancer is determined. The walk gives the impression that the dancer is gliding in space without effort. Stamping is also used and the resulting pattern of sound is augmented by placing clay pots under the stage to give resonance to this part of the performance.

The mechanics of turning and locomotion to various parts of the stage are highly codified in Noh. These movements are important to convey traveling to shrines, battlefields, or places in nature. Locale or the place depicted in Noh text is expressed primarily in movement, seldom with the aid of stage properties. Movements such as the activity of looking are depicted by a forward move, raising and pointing the fan, then backing away to add perspective. Some pantomime depicts praying, holding a shield, or riding a horse.

Noh dancing is not verbose in that most movements are minimal and subtle. The goal is to express the highest ideals with the simplest means. Noh has been continued by generations of people who have a great sensitivity to all arts and a special talent for dance-dramas.

Kabuki

Kabuki is one of Japan's most traditional and popular theater arts. Its beginnings date back to the latter part of the 16th century, a time when there was a rigid distinction between the warrior class and the commoners. Kabuki was cultivated by merchants who has become economically powerful but who remained socially inferior. The art of Kabuki was a means for expressing their resentment against the feudal system of the times. Kabuki themes were thus those of fundamental conflicts between humanity and the feudal system. It was the thematic content of Kabuki that endeared it to the public in its early development and even today.

In the beginning the players were women but when they began to attract undue attention from their male audience, public officials banned their appearance in the theater. Male actors became the sole performers. During the two hundred and fifty years that the ban on women dancers was enforced, men actors perfected the art of female impersonation or "onnagata." Onnagata became such an integral part of Kabuki that, if deprived of this element, the traditional quality of Kabuki could be lost forever.

Kabuki has incorporated parts of all preceding theater forms in its extensive and continuous evolution since the 16th century. It drew stage technique and repertoire from Noh. It adopted a comic element from Kyogen plays, which were interludes in Noh performances. It also drew from the puppet theater, which was developing at the same time. And finally, in the 19th century it added literary realism.

Dance-drama constituted a segment of some three hundred plays in the Kabuki repertoire. Actors danced to both vocal and instrumental music. Many of these dramas told complete stories; others were primarily pure dance. Historical dramas presenting accounts of warriors and nobles and domestic dramas depicting plebeian life constituted the remaining repertoire.

The aesthetic principle underlying Kabuki is formalized beauty. To prepare for their roles, actors study the style modeled by their predecessors. Over the years these model styles become highly formalized and symbolic even if they are intended to present realism. Thus in acting, gestures became more like dancing than acting, posture and poses placed more emphasis on statuesque beauty, vocal delivery became elocution accompanied by music and sets. Kabuki costumes and makeup are recognized as the most lavish and extravagant in the world. Audiences enjoy this spectacle of dazzling and superb color even if unconvinced by the plot of the story. Visual beauty sustains the popularity of Kabuki even today.

The modern Kabuki theaters are built largely in Western style but have retained some significant features of the traditional theater. Two of these are the flower-walk ramp and the revolving stage. The flower-walk ramp (Hanamichi) is a passageway connecting the left side of the stage with the back of the hall. The ramp passes over the seats at head level with the audience. Actors enter and exit along the passageway as well as at the right and left exits on the stage. The passageway is part of the stage and often actors give important scenes of the play on the flower-walk. The revolving stage was invented in Japan some three hundred years ago and is a major contribution to theater around the world.

Kabuki's greatness is primarily due to its actors, many of whom come from families of Kabuki actors that date back to the feudal era. To acquire all the skills needed, an actor must begin in childhood. The family system not only allows for early development but has made it possible to preserve the art of Kabuki.

The Kabuki actor of today no longer specializes in a particular role but has become more versatile. This is true except in the role of onnagata or female impersonation. In this role, specialization is still the rule. Formerly actors were popular among the masses but considered to have low social status. Today actors are held in high esteem and many have been elected to the Academy of Art of Japan. Kabuki enjoys wide popularity in Japan today, although its content does not depict contemporary themes. The principle reason for its sustained popularity lies in the fact that it has become a crystallized art form and thus seems destined to retain the affection and pride of the nation.

Bali

The word Bali conjures up romantic associations such as South Sea islands, tropical beaches, coconut trees, and a world of magic and enchantment. The island of Bali is a ninety- by fifty-mile speck off the east coast of Java. Bali is a country of spectacularly gifted people of mixed race, endowed with a great sense of humor and united by an ancient oral tradition to their revered ancestors.

The wave of Hindu culture and religion that flowed through Java found its terminal point in Bali. Today, Bali is the only Hindu country in the world outside of India. The Balinese are the recipients of India's highly developed music, dance, and aesthetic philosophy.

Communal village-centered life is the norm in Balinese culture. Yet over the centuries villages have bound together to form a highly sophisticated and interdependent wet-rice agricultural system. The need for cooperation is emphasized in ancient Balinese teachings from manuscripts dating back to the 8th century. Religion and spirituality are integral parts of life and making offerings in the form of food and flowers is considered a continual act of devotion. Dance is considered as one very special form of communal offering and it plays a vital part in all ceremonies.

Each village has three temples, the Ancestor Temple, the Community Temple, and the Temple of Death. Within the most sacred inner temple courtyard the Wali or most sacred Balinese dances are performed. Both the temple and the dances are thought to be of indigenous origin; however, some Hindu-Japanese elements may be seen in the dances. Temple form and layout date back to the Neolithic culture of ancestor worshippers who migrated to Bali from Southeast Asia between 2500 and 1000 B.C.

The Balinese observe an elaborate schedule of festivals according to the Hindu-Balinese religious calendar or Odalan. The Wali or group of dances performed in connection with religious rituals involves going into a trance in which the dancers are possessed by divine or sometimes demonic spirits. These dances also require a strong element of village and audience participation. They are performed in the sacred inner temple courtyard before the shrine of the gods. Prominent in the Wali or most sacred category are *Berutuk, Sang Hyang Dedari, Rejang,* and *Baris Gedes.*

Berutuk

The Berutuk rite is performed by young bachelors wearing sacred masks, dressed in large aprons made from dried banana leaves and carrying a long fiber whip. The whips are used to ward off the audience, who cheer and tease the dancing monsters, hoping to get a piece of the sacred banana leaf costume. The dance-drama lasts all day. It is a performance that combines aspects of a game, a ceremony, and a ritual drama.

Sang Hyang

Sang Hyang Dedari is an ancient dance in a group known as Sang Hyang. Dances in this group all involve putting one or more dancers in a trance by means of incense, prayers, and chanting to receive the gods. Once possessed the dancers interact with the audience by dancing, mimicking animals, and sometimes speaking as oracles. Possession differs among the many varieties of Sang Hyang. There is an element of ritual purification and exorcism in most Sang Hyang dances. Sang Hyang Dedari is one of the best known of these possession rituals. It means "Honored Goddess Nymph" and is performed by selected preadolescent girls from the village. Sang Hyang Dedari is not on the calendar of festivals and is performed as needed in cases of epidemic or disaster. Once the dancers are possessed by the deities they speak to the villages, giving the cure or remedy for whatever sickness or disaster has occurred.

In other trance dances an animal spirit enters the body of the dancer. In *Sang Hyang Jaran,* a horse spirit invests the body of a male dancer who, once possessed, runs barefooted through hot embers astride a straw hobby-horse. In *Sang Hyang Celing* a pig-spirit has the dancer symbolically eat the filth or impurities responsible for the disaster.

Rejang

Rejang is an important category of Balinese religious dance in which the performance is given for the gods rather than by the gods, as in Sang Hyang and Berutuk. The gods descend into doll-like wooden effigies called pratima. They are brightly decorated with flowers and placed in a portable shrine for the festival. Rejang is an ancient formal and elegantly dignified processional group dance performed by forty to sixty women of all ages in the village temple. It is performed in the daytime and dancers are dressed in formal traditional Balinese costumes topped off with fresh flowers. Dancers form four rows in front of the shrines where the pratima are placed and in turn the dancer at the head of each row dances forward toward the shrine. Once they reach the shrine the lead dancers move off to each side and the next dancer in line moves forward, repeating the action. Once all have danced up to the shrine with the pratima in it the dance is over.

Baris

The Baris dance dates from the 16th century in Indonesia and is the most important ritual dance in Bali. Baris is essentially a warrior's drill dance that ancient Balinese soldiers used to protect their kingdom. Baris is derived from the word *bebarison* which means line or file formation. Even today there are many of these martial dances, each distinguished by the weapon being carried by the soldier. Weapons commonly used are spears, lances, shields, daggers, or even, in some villages, rifles.

In Baris the dancer-soldier wears a triangular-shaped headdress or helmet and performs stylized military movements, attacking and defending in turn. The movements are done in unison. The dance is performed by men in groups of four to sixty, accompanied by the traditional Balinese musical orchestra gamelan gong. Aside from the ritualistic formation the show of physical maturity in handling weapons adds a patriotic element.

Baris is based on the pokok stance, which has to do with the contact of the dancer's feet on and with the earth and the special alignment of the legs and torso. The Pokok stance is the basic posture of all Balinese dance. It pays homage to Balinese origin and roots and that is why the foot contact with the earth is important, since it symbolizes the flow from and the connection with the earth as the foundation. Pokok is the point of departure for all dance steps. It is the connection with ancestral origins and provides the spiritual nature to the dance. Baris, therefore, demonstrated the sacred postures of the warrior of Eastern traditions and the martial origins of the dance. It is the preparation for and introduction to the dances of Topeng, the masked theater of Bali. Balinese actors are trained in the pokok stance as a foundation from which all dance movement springs.

The 19th century saw the emergence of professional dance groups that traveled from village to village performing for hire at Odalan and other festivals. It was, therefore, no major step for these dance companies to begin performing at hotels for the tourist trade in the early 1920s.

The 1930s saw tourism increase to a steady flow and an increased demand for dance performances. Repetitive performances in village settings and structured performances at hotels led to adapting traditional forms and creating dances in response to the tourist market. A revue-style presentation featuring short versions of several dances became common.

By the 1980s tourism reached the million mark. Balinese dance companies were in demand not only at home but also abroad. Revenue from dance performances coupled with mass production of handicrafts became important to the economic life of the villages. Although contemporary forces have been rapid and extensive, the age-old tradition of unity and cooperation has served to integrate all that is foreign in philosophy, culture, religion, and politics into distinct Balinese forms.

Maori

Polynesia is a collection of large and small islands in the south Pacific Ocean. It is best envisioned by imagining a triangle formed by Hawaii on the north, Easter Island on the east, New Zealand on the south, and the Society Islands in the center. Settlement of the area is theorized to have been from a gradual west to east population flow out of Southeast Asia. Traditions and archaeological evidence seem to support this theory. The area has been the home of Polynesians for more than four thousand years. The Society Islands appear to have been the dispersing point for population movement to all parts of the area. In their sturdy longboats a hardy and courageous people took their common language, religion, myths, traditions, and cultural materials wherever they traveled. Wherever they settled, these elements united them and identified their kinship over the vast triangle. These are the ancestors of the Maori people of New Zealand.

New Zealand was settled, it is believed, in the mid-14th century as a result of a series of migrations. The last and largest was the Fleet. It is from the leaders and chiefly families of the Fleet of seven canoes that the Maori proudly trace their descent. The canoes were seventy or more feet in length and carried food, water, seed, and livestock. They landed at various points on the north island of New Zealand. Tradition among the Maori tells the story of each canoe, its landing place and settlement. And until modern historical findings indicate otherwise, these traditional accounts of the settlement of the Maori in New Zealand will stand.

Much of the pre-European picture of the Maori can be attributed to Captain James Cook and his keeping of a daily account of his observations of the Maori. He was known for his care for his own men as well as his humane dealings with the Maori. From these and other early accounts a picture of the lifestyles and activities of the Maori have come.

The European explorers' first encounter with a group of foot stomping, finger quivering, eye rolling, and tongue protruding dancers accompanied by a roaring chorus of rhythmic chants caused many captains and their crews to weigh anchor and sail away. To those who weathered the encounter, it appeared to be a war dance. To the Maori it was *Laka*, the vigorous posture dance that symbolized the vitality of Maori manhood. More careful reading of early accounts of the dance interpret it as a formalized pattern of challenge to a stranger to determine if his intentions were friendly or hostile.

Since it was more often used to welcome guests this theory is well supported.

Poi, not described until the 19th century, is a woman's dance unique to New Zealand and is considered to be the most graceful in all Polynesia. It consists of twirling a small ball made of dry leaves on a cord. Several variations exist including twirling the ball on a short cord with the right hand while beating it with the left hand and touching the head, shoulders, and hips between beats. The dance is performed sitting or standing, often accompanied by foot movements. It is a dance of precision, harmony, and beauty and is accompanied by a lilting song.

Maoritanga is a modern movement to revive and preserve Maori culture and foster cultural pride. To many Maori, the most real and tangible expressions of their culture are their songs, games, and dances.

Philippines

The Philippine archipelago lies some 500 miles off the southeast coast of Asia and is an integral part of the cultural emanating from southeast India and China. Early inhabitants of the more than 7000 islands came from south China and the Malay Peninsula. Some parts were occupied by the Indo-Malayan empire of Sri-Vishaya in the 3rd century A.D. and later the Japanese empire of Madjapahit. In the 15th century Arabians and Indians moved into Mindanao bringing the Islamic and Hindu religions to this southernmost part of the country. The remote mountainous regions of the northern islands became the home of the earliest inhabitants, the pygmy tribes. These influences serve as a basis for a very diverse cultural beginning.

The colonial period began with the discovery of the islands by Ferdinand Magellan of Spain in 1521. The Spaniards brought Christianity to the islands, which was a strong and lasting influence for some 400 years. Today, except for the Muslim south and pagan north, the Philippines is the only Christian country in the Asian sphere.

In 1898 the United States took control and the American influence lasted for some fifty years. The Philippines became an independent country in 1946. Filipinos refer to their cultural heritage as "400 years in a convent and 50 years in Hollywood." Nevertheless, the Philippines are a rich mixture of Asian, European, American, and native cultures.

Although subdued by the missionary zeal of Christians and Muslims, culturally dance and drama are derived from four elements: Spanish, residual Filipino, Igorat (Aboriginal), and Muslim. In most provinces local folk dance is Spanish in name as well as movement, for example, *Polkabal, Mananguete,*

Surtido, and *Los Bailes de Ayers.* In the large city ballrooms Filipinos execute rumbas, tangos, sambos, and paso dobles in a characteristically graceful Filipino style.

Among some of the remaining most conservative and aristocratic families, formal balls are still opened with the stately quadrille *Regadon d'Honor.* For the Regadon d'Honor ladies wear ternow or mestiza dresses with the renowned butterfly sleeves made of pineapple cloth, silk, satin, or brocade. The men wear black pants, shoes, socks, and the barong tagalog shirt made of fine linen or pineapple cloth with hand embroidery or ruffles and frills down the front. The *Maria Clara,* a minuetlike dance full of bows and curtsies, is also a popular replica of the past. The Maria Clara, popular toward the end of the Spanish rule, is often performed for formal occasions and as a part of historical stage dramas. For the Maria Clara the characteristic costume consists of a light blue dress with starched white long frilly sleeves, wide collars, and fans for the ladies and a velvet jacket and tight-fitting trousers for the men.

Two of the most well-known dances representing the residual or Filipino-derived dances are the *Binusan Candle Dance* and the world-renowned *Tinikling.* The Binusan dance consists of a series of virtuoso feats including a rollover on the floor while balancing lighted candles in a glass tumbler on the head. Historically, this feat appears in many dances from various provinces. The *Pandaggo su Illaw* or dance of the lights is a couple dance from Mindoro in which lighted oil lamps are balanced on the head and back of both hands. Tinikling is undoubtedly the most widely known dance associated with the Philippines. Its popularity makes it almost a national pastime. An early version or sighting described the dance as having four long bamboo poles and danced in 4/4 time by four dancers. The version most widely used, however, uses two bamboo poles struck together in 3/4 time. The latter version appears in *Philippine National Dances* by Francisca Reyes Tolentino, published in 1946.

Dances performed among the Igorat (aboriginal inhabitants or tribes of the northern Luzon) are authentically primitive. Dances occur during feasts, weddings, when conferring tribal title, at rice planting and harvest festivals, when headhunting, and at moon or star worshipping ceremonies.

During American times headhunting was discouraged, except briefly during the Japanese occupation. Now a nut from a fern tree or a carved wooden head serves the purpose. Headhunting dances are performed when a tribe member dies from an accident or lightning strike or as a cure for illness. If all other remedies fail, dance is certain to cure the sick and ailing.

Tribal dances are performed by both men and women. They generally move clockwise in a circle accompanied by songs and gongs. Shouting, clapping, and stamping make these tribal dances more energetic and vigorous than those found in the lowlands. Costumes and dances vary among mountain tribes but all are colorful. Elaborate headdresses of native flowers, beads, turbans, and crowns made of bamboo adorned with rooster feathers are common. Necklaces of dog or pig teeth, colored beads, or metalwork highlight the costumes.

Dances among the Christian Filipinos center around fiestas held to honor patron saints. The Black Nazarene festival in Manila, a nine-day celebration, begins the year-round calendar of festivals. St. John's Day and St. Augustine's Day include colorful processions of people often led by dancers. In the province of Bulucan the *Obando Dance* is performed during celebration of the feast of Saint Clare. The dance is a fertility dance performed by childless married women who believe the dance prayer will give them children.

Harvest festivals are a time for singing, dancing, and eating. Courtship and wedding dances are the highlights of these most beloved Philippine festivities. Formal occasions such as inaugural balls for state and provincial officials or to entertain official guests are traditions carried on in cities and provinces. So it seems that Christians do, indeed, dance.

Perhaps the most important dancing in the Philippines, artistically and visually, is found among the Muslims or Moro (Mohammedans) in the southern part of the Sulu archipelago, Mindanao, and Palowan. Dance among the Mohammedans is a curious phenomenon since traditionally their religion does not tolerate dance. The mix of cultures including Hindus, who foster dance, and perhaps the remoteness of the southern islands from the mainstream of Islam produces less antipathy and intolerance of dance. Regardless of the reasons, the Muslim area of south Philippines has more dance variety and quality than all other areas of the country. The dances are in fact vestigial remains of dances of India and Indonesia with flowing movements of the arms, facial expressions, and extreme flexibility and use of the fingers. Ankle bells and fan manipulation complete the inheritance from southeast Asia.

The legacy of folk dance of the Philippines is found in the survival of the manuscript of the book *Philippine National Dances* by Francisca Reyes Tolentino, published in 1946 by Silver Burdett Company of New York. The manuscript was received in New York in 1941 but was not published until after the liberation of the Philippines from the Japanese in 1945. After the war contact was reestablished with Mrs. Tolentino, who reported that all her resource materials, books and records, pictures, costumes, and musical instruments were burned or destroyed during the war.

The book contains fifty-four dances with brief historical notes, costume descriptions, and pictures along with full piano scores for each dance. The piano scores are themselves of unique historical value. Mrs. Tolentino, who was physical education director of women students at the University of Philippines, was encouraged and supported in her original research of dances of less-developed regions of the country by the farsightedness of Dr. Jerge Bocobo, then president of the university. The first materials gathered between 1924 and 1926 were used for her master's thesis, which was later published in book form as *Philippine Folk Dances and Games*. Interest in Philippine dances was stimulated by the University of Philippines and the Bureau of Education as a valuable part of the curriculum of physical education classes in public schools. The result was a revival of interest and soon dance exhibitions and competitions were an integral part of school programs. The effect was an awakening of national pride.

As a result of this impetus, additional research was officially carried on by Lt. Antonio Buenaventura, Ramon P. Tolentino, Jr., and Mrs. Tolentino under the auspices of the University of Philippines President's Committee on Folk Songs and Dances. Costumes, music, and musical instruments were collected as well as songs and dances. This research produced the manuscript that was published in 1946 as *Philippine National Dances*.

Many of the native dances show unmistakable Spanish influence; others reflect French, English, and Malayan influences to a degree. Performances over a long period of time, however, have given them the unmistakable stamp of Filipino interpretation, execution, and expression.

Hawaii

Before European contact, music in Hawaii was a completely integrated system based on the use of poetry, rhythm, melody, and movement, which served the gamut of social needs from prayer to entertainment. Without a written history or literature to refer to, Hawaiians used musical poetry to call on the gods, honor their chiefs, lament the dead, tell of the creation, and perpetuate their history down through the generations. Poetry, therefore, was functional to their religious and social organization. Dance was an extension of poetry in the form of stylized visual accompaniment.

Traditional Hawaiian dance, unlike Asian and Indonesian forms, contained no theatrical or dramatic characterizations. Dance movement interpreted specific words of a poem or described a characteristic or thing mentioned in the poem. There was no dialogue or pantomime in indigenous poetry meant to be accompanied by dance. Poetry was divided into two main types: all poetry not intended to be used with dance (*oli*) and poetry meant to be accompanied by dance (*mele hula*). The former (oli) was done as a solo while the latter (mele hula) was performed by a group.

Performers were trained in hula schools (lalau) by a teacher (kumu lula), a priest (kahuna) under a strict religious system imposed by the patron goddess (Laka) of hula. Hulas were performed, therefore, only by dancers who had graduated from a hula school. Although there were a great many taboos and religious rites connected with the training, many were anxious to learn since training was an entree into the life of the courts of the chiefs. Schools were subsidized by the chiefs for reasons of prestige and entertainment. The primary functions of the hula dance at court was to honor the gods and sing praises of the chief and his ancestors.

The traditional hula was performed standing or seated. The seated version was more strenuous since the dancer raised and lowered as well as circled the torso from a kneeling position in which the dancer sat between the legs. In addition, the dancer often played an instrument. The standing hula was, as they are today, movements done while standing.

Mele hulas or name chants were composed to honor a person. They became the property of that person and were passed down through generations. They told the story of the honoree in terms of his or her high birth, genealogy, or something for which the person was noted. The general structure of a performance consisted of music, usually percussion; reciting the poem, which was a two-line couplet; and movement or dance. Movement described specific words of the poem such as hands forming a flower or arms indicating the flight of a bird. If the dancer played an instrument, the body movements were used to convey the meanings.

Hulas are generally classified according to their instrumental accompaniment. The hula pohu (drum) is an important type danced to honor chiefs of high distinction. The *hula pa ipu* is danced accompanied by a gourd instrument struck by the hand or on the ground. The *hula uli uli* is a seated dance accompanied by a feathered rattling gourd. There are many hulas and instrumental combinations, including the unique *hula pa'uimauna* in which the chest and thighs are struck to generate two different sounds.

The modern-day hula is the result of Hawaiian contact with Western civilization. Captain Cook's visit in 1778 set in motion the change from a Neolithic society to one that integrated the cultural traits and values of Western civilization. Music and dance were most affected by the arrival of Christian missionaries in 1820. For a period of time after the influx of missionaries, Western values were represented on the one hand by sailors and on the other by missionaries. The contrast was at once bewildering if not at times humorous. The influence of the missionaries won; the dancers were clothed and the dance movements damned as lustful and evil. The dances, missionaries declared, not only violated Protestant values but took the Hawaiians from their work in the fields. The result was that the hula went underground.

In 1874 Kalakaua came to the throne and called hula teachers to his court to revive the dance and court dance troupes. The success of his effort culminated in an invitation for a Hawaiian dance group to perform at the 1893 World Columbian Exposition in Chicago, Illinois. This was the first time the dance of Hawaii, the hula, was treated with the respect due an art form.

The revival of the hula was not without loss of the old and emergence of the new. The costumes became the "ti leaf" hula skirt and the long white frilly dress with fitted sleeves. The dance lost its religious restrictions and became open to everyone, not just trained professionals. Kalakaua's court marked the end of the traditional hula and the beginning of accultured dance and music.

For over half of the 19th century Hawaiian music and dance was persecuted but was saved by the tenacity of a few conservative families. Traditional dance and music thus made its way into the 20th century to be publicly recognized by a statewide program to study and teach the ancient hula. In 1970, some two hundred years after Western contact, only five individuals were known to be hula experts. Statewide conferences have since been held to revive and preserve the knowledge held by the remaining experts and to reinstate this ancient art form.

American Perspective

Dance heritage in the United States is a matter of perspective. Historically, we Americans have alluded to "our heritage" as being from Europe. This perspective is true if, in fact, we view our heritage as consisting of all the facets of culture brought by explorers and settlers from Europe.

Is there another perspective? What about our heritage from the Western hemisphere, from North,

Central, and South America? Was the New World only a vast undeveloped land mass waiting to be discovered by Europeans? A second perspective, one that views our heritage from the Americas, is long overdue.

The sounds of Native American drums echoed through the Americas long before the arrival of the first Europeans. Over untold centuries, immigrants traveled across the Bering Straits into North America, Mexico, Central America, and South America. These early arrivals, whom we refer to as Indians or Amerinds, were loosely organized into tribes that varied enormously in appearance, language, and culture. Even a cursory recounting of their progress and achievements is enough to warrant a second perspective, a view that includes our heritage from the Americas.

Just what were the accomplishments of these aboriginal Americans? It has been estimated that three-fifths of the modern world's agricultural wealth is derived from plants first domesticated by American Indians. They cultivated corn to its environmental limit long before the first Europeans arrived. In addition, they grew potatoes, sweet potatoes, manioc, varieties of beans, squash, pumpkins, peanuts, tomatoes, chocolate, rubber, long-staple cotton, and tobacco. Their domestication of these plants was the basis for their civilizations and a heritage we enjoy daily in modern American life.

In the 15th century, the most developed cultures, with histories that reach far into the mythical past, were the Aztecs in the Valley of Mexico, the Maya in the Yucatan Peninsula, and the great agrarian culture, the Inca Empire of the South American Andes. The height of their civilizations is evidenced by the cities they built with richly carved stone; their knowledge of mathematics and astronomy applied to the development of a calendar that required no leap year and predicted the eclipses of the sun; their construction of strong governments; and their recognition of the need for a division of labor. Although these were essentially Stone Age civilizations, astronomy, mathematics, writing, fine arts, and the ability to work gold, silver, copper, and various alloys with artistry flourished in them.

In the arts, there existed a rich culture of music, song, and dance used in sacred ceremonies and secular festivals. Aztec musical instruments included drums, hunting horns, whistles, flutes, pipes, and bells made of precious metals and gems. Early Spanish missionaries wrote of the Mayan "House of Song," in which professors of music, song, and dance trained the young to perform so that they could participate in the constant rituals and celebrations. From *Historia de las Indias* by Diego Duran, Giselle Freund quoted an early Spanish missionary:

> There were songs and dances of great solemnity, with a rhythm measured and austere; others, for less serious occasions, were lighter and sang of love and happiness. Most elaborate of all were those that accompanied the floral offerings of the gods. The richness of the dance costumes imitating fruits and flowers, birds, and animals; the grace of the dancers representing the gods and their worshippers; and the strange and stirring music; all made Duran declare that this was "the most beautiful and solemn dance this nation possessed," and he never expected to witness again anything more wondrous. (Bauer and Peyser 1967; p. 50)

The Aztec, Inca, and Mayan empires were the centers from which flowed the cultural stimuli to the more primitive regions in the Americas. Cultural artifacts, such as rattles, flutes, whistles, bull roarers, Apache fiddles, and the most revered of all instruments—the drum—offer evidence of this stimulus and the cultural link in music, song, and dance throughout the Americas. We must begin today to appreciate the scale, the complexity, the host of accomplishments, and the long cultural evolution that mark the cultures of the Americas. This, then, is our American perspective, a dance heritage yet to be claimed.

CHAPTER 2
Effective Group Instruction

The nature and purpose of the dance curriculum are results of a continuous and judicious mixture of factors relating to the learner, the learning process, the dance content, and the demands of the culture. The two ingredients that combine to produce effective group instruction are the teacher's ability to analyze and cope with variables operative in groups, and the teacher's thorough knowledge of dance materials and resources. Facilities and equipment are the keys to accomplishing the purposes and objectives of a dance program.

Facilities

A well-ventilated room with good acoustics, adequate lighting and heating, and sufficient floor space are essential. An area too small may limit the freedom of movement and the type of dance. An area too large may generate acoustical problems that can distort the music and verbal instructions, and destroy the spirit of the occasion. Also, dancers may feel uncomfortable with too much space; it is better to be slightly crowded.

Floor

The condition of the floor is of vital concern. The different dance forms require varying degrees of slickness. There is considerable difference between a floor constructed specifically for dance use and one constructed for another use. The basic essential for all forms is cleanliness.

Acoustics

Permanent acoustical treatment is very expensive and is seldom found in the variety of buildings used by dance groups. Poor acoustics is a handicap to a dance group. The following practical suggestions have proven useful in improving the sound in halls and gymnasiums adapted to use for dance.

1. Drapes of any material (burlap, flannel, rugs, blankets) suspended from the ceiling can improve sound.
2. Acoustics in an ordinary gymnasium can be improved by hanging mats around the walls.
3. Ceilings can be lowered with crêpe-paper streamers or similar decorations.
4. Human bodies absorb sound. The sound system adjusted to an empty room is not always adequate when the room is filled with dancers. This fact should be kept in mind when the sound system is set up for a large crowd.

Equipment

Sound Systems*

Regardless of the size of the group, equipment for quality sound reproduction is essential to instruction and participation in all forms of dance. Technology has made it possible to select from a wide variety of sound systems of high quality. Manufacturers offer a wide range of models, each equipped with as few or as many features as the consumer wishes to purchase. Common features include amplifier mixer, equalizer; variable speed turntables; separate tone and volume controls; multiple speaker and microphone outlets; tape decks for recording and playing; standing, portable, and remote microphones; and monitor speaker attachments. Custom-made sound systems can be assembled to meet special needs.

---

*Refer to *Contra Dance Calling, A Basic Text,* by Tony Parkes, pp. 97–112. Sound equipment, up-to-date and inclusive information.

Dance music and dance calling need adequate coverage in all three noise ranges—high range for melody instruments like the fiddle, low range for rhythm instruments like the guitar and bass, and midrange for the human voice.

Some **considerations for selecting a system** are (1) the size of the largest crowd it will serve; (2) the degree of portability, sturdy handles for carrying (sometimes handles are poorly attached to cases), and time required for setup; (3) the number of mikes (a band requires 6–8); (4) the stage monitor (a small speaker that allows musicians to hear themselves); (5) the complexity of the system (fewer controls are desirable); and (6) the cost, ownership, and storage.

Speakers are the most important part of the sound system. They should be placed in front of and away from the microphone to avoid possible feedback. Tripod speaker stands are handy. The usual practice is to place the speakers on each side of the stage (teaching area), at least *3 feet above the heads of the dancers,* and pointed down toward the heads of the dancers.

Microphones are the second most important feature of a sound system. To some extent, a better microphone will compensate for deficiencies in the sound system. If using one a great deal, consider buying your own microphone before investing in a complete sound system. Know the different mechanisms and pickup patterns. A foam windscreen allows the user to get closer to the mike. Small telescoping boom or gooseneck stand attachments are useful. Wireless mikes are effective when you are out on the floor teaching. There are three types: lapel, handheld, and headworn. Most teachers prefer the headworn style. If a teacher is "yelling instructions" it's time for a wireless mike. The tone and volume control for the microphone should be separate from the rest of the system. Generally men's voices require an increase of treble in the tone and women's voices require an increase of bass.

Turntable and CD Player

A turntable needs to be located for easy access for teaching and on a stand that will not be jarred by dancing feet. On gymnasium floors, needle bounce is common. The player may be located in a console. Seventy-eights are not being produced, but some distributors have some in stock and many schools/clubs have them. Therefore, a machine that has three speeds, 33, 45, and 78 rpm, is desirable. Dance music is also produced on compact discs, which requires use of a CD player. The quality of the music is extremely important in generating enthusiasm and style in dancers.

The essential features needed in a turntable are manual arm control, variable speed, volume and tone control, and microphone. The *variable speed* really facilitates teaching. The quality of the sound is directly related to the quality of the cartridge and needle. The magnetic cartridge gives a truer tone quality than the crystal type. The diamond needle will last longer than the sapphire needle.

Care of Turntable and Records

Keeping the needle clean and changing it as needed are important. Taking care of the records will increase their longevity as well as improve their music. Store records in a vertical position in a case, dividers between each record. A thin foam cushion on the bottom protects rims, and a tight cover keeps the dirt and dust out. The 45-rpm discs should be stored flat, in jackets.

Tape Deck

A variable speed capacity is important. Recording the music on 2 or 3-minute tapes is beneficial (one dance per side). Putting six dances on one tape is neither efficient nor conducive to good instruction. The "stop-go" to find the counter takes time. The convenience of practice tapes encourages students to spend additional time practicing, especially if the teacher superimposes cues over the music.

Camcorder/VCR

The camcorder is a readily portable piece of equipment, and it records action and sound. A VCR and monitor are necessary for playback. As well as providing the novelty of watching one's self, this instrument is especially helpful in developing style and working with performing groups.

Music

Recordings

Recordings on discs and tapes are the primary sources of musical accompaniment for dance. The recording industry for dance is in a state of flux. Fewer companies are producing music for folk dancing. The most useful and practical recording type (record/tape) is not settled, but the cassette is gaining. So the availability of recordings to match one's equipment can be difficult to find. The problem of the **ethics** of copying music from someone and passing it along is increasing. It is driving dedicated companies out of business. Recorded music of superior quality and variety is available, making it possible to have colorful and authentic music for instruction and participation. The wide variety of domestic and foreign recordings available makes it necessary for the teacher or the leader to be discriminating in choosing musical accompaniment. The following suggestions may assist in making appropriate choices:

1. The music should include an introductory passage so that the dancers can begin in unison.
2. A steady tempo is desirable unless a change is appropriate to a particular dance.
3. The music should be authentic; that is, if a dance is traditionally done to a special tune and the recording is available, it should be used.
4. The phrasing should be clear and definite.
5. Albums are not always preferable to single records, because multiple recordings often include titles that are not usable.
6. The nonbreakable recording is preferable.

The following suggestions are appropriate to the selection of recordings for dance areas included in *Dance A While*.

Folk Dance

There are often several recordings available for the same Folk Dance. The record that corresponds in sequence to the direction for the dance should be selected. It is generally advisable to use the record recommended by the dance reference. Since no list of suggested records can be kept completely up to date, it is advisable to request the record shop or company to make a substitution when requested records are no longer available.

Square Dance

The problems of selection in the Square Dance area center around finding records that are suitable to the caller's voice and have the desired tempo and rhythm. Callers should make selections only after listening and practicing to a variety of records. There are several advantages to records with calls: They can be used as models for learning to call, as supplements to live calling for calls not in the musical key or vocal range of the teacher, and as opportunities for a group to dance to a wide variety of callers.

Contra Dance

Only a few of the Contra Dances require special music; for instance, Rory O'More uses the tune by the same name. Therefore it is the teacher's choice to select appropriate music for the specific flow of figures (storyline) in a given dance. Some dances suggest a Jig, others a Reel, others a March. Finding a recording that arouses the dancers and the caller is the next step. Eventually the teacher will rely on

certain tunes for specific dances, because they "fit like a glove."

Social Dance

The criteria for selecting Social Dance records include finding recordings that have a definite beat and a regular tempo and that are appropriate for listening. Longplay albums are advisable and economical for those who specialize or teach several classes in one type of dance, such as Latin or Jazz. Albums featuring a variety of dances on one record are recommended for those who teach few or occasional classes. The specialist needs greater variety in music. The radio is a continuous source of current and standard music. Jotting down the title and name of the recording artist aids in securing records from local shops and in keeping a current collection for teaching.

Teaching with Recordings

Some of the techniques for teaching with recordings are the following:

1. Before using a recording in class, know the music and be familiar with the phrasing as well as the way the dance sequence fits the music. It is an advantage to be able to hum or whistle the tune.
2. All recordings to be used in an instructional period should be preselected and arranged in order of use.
3. Isolating a musical phrase on recordings is difficult. Knowing the music is the key. Experience and practice will develop the technique for setting and picking up the needle arm on a phonograph to isolate desired musical phrases.
4. Play the music for the group to hear before presenting each part of the dance.
5. Verbal cues should be in time with the music.
6. Give the starting signal at the appropriate time according to the introduction on the record. Tell the group when the record has no introduction.
7. An adjustable speed control allows practice at a variety of tempos. If there is no speed control on a machine, a part of the dance should be practiced without music and then the tempo should be speeded up gradually with verbal cues until the dance can be done at the tempo of the recording.

Live Music

There is a resurgence of live music for dancing. A live band or orchestra accents the color, flavor, and festive atmosphere of the occasion. The opportunity for recreational musicians to play enhances country dances. Many ethnic groups, such as Scandinavian and Slavic groups, have developed musicians' groups playing native instruments for their dances. Even in Social Dance, Big-Band Sound, Country Western, and Salsa, musicians are available.

The best musicians, colorful as they may be, should blend with the group. The dancers are the focal point of the dance and, although musicians should enter into the spirit of the occasion, they should not become a distraction.

The instruments commonly used for Square Dance and Contra Dance are the fiddle, the piano, the banjo, the bass violin, and the guitar. The fiddle is sufficient for small groups if the fiddler is good. A combination of three to five instruments is most desirable.

The instruments used for International Folk Dance vary. Accordions, horns, and reed instruments, as well as foreign musical instruments native to a particular country, are used with more common combinations of instruments.

For Social Dance, a three- to seven-piece band is usually adequate, depending on the talent of the group. Keyboards are also available. An audition is usually advisable when an unknown band is being considered. Small bands or combos can sometimes be assembled from talent in the community or the school. In all cases, the band should be notified about the specific type of music planned. The type of music varies with the age and interest of the group to be entertained.

Dance musicians need an understanding of the dance itself and should realize that the character of the dance is influenced by the manner in which they play the tune. The tempo must be steady. As they play, the musicians need to watch the dancers, sometimes adjusting the tempo or emphasizing a phrase. Phrasing is extremely important for all dances.

Teaching with Live Music

Some dance teachers are very fortunate to have a fiddler, an accordion player, or a trio to work with, particularly for workshops. Very few institutions still have an accompanist. The primary advantage, beside the stimulation of live music, is the time saved by not having to attend to and adjust mechanical devices during the presentation of a lesson. Flexibility in applying music to the dance-teaching sequence is perhaps even more of an advantage than saving time. The accompanist can introduce music with the movement very early and make the rhythm clear and definite. The beginner is able to hear the beats of the music better. The introduction of accompaniment in the early stages trains dancers from the beginning to let the music help cue them in pattern and step changes, so counting is avoided.

As the teacher and the accompanist work together, the accompanist will sense when to start playing while the group is practicing.

The working relationship between teacher and accompanist is important. They should begin by establishing certain vocal and hand signals. Most important, the teacher should stand at all times in view of the accompanist so that signals can be clearly seen or easily heard. Common vocal communications between the teacher and accompanist are "ready and" and "ready begin." Common hand signals are lowering the hand palm down to indicate a slow tempo, raising the hand palm up to indicate a faster tempo, nodding the head or raising the hand above dancers' heads to signal a stop at the end of the music, and waving the hand back and forth above the dancers' heads or saying "stop" to stop the music immediately.

The teacher can do a great deal to make the accompanist an integral part of the group. When the accompanist becomes a real part of the group, and not just a tool, everyone benefits because the involvement stimulates greater interest. The music should complement the activity; it should not dominate it.

Great care should be exercised in the selection of an accompanist. An accompanist should:

1. Have thorough musical training.
2. Play in a steady rhythm, accenting certain parts to help the dancers while they are learning a new dance.
3. Know the music well enough to be able to give attention to the group and the teacher during performance.
4. Rehearse all new music prior to the class.
5. Adjust the tempo to the dancers' ability or change the rhythm to accompany the teacher's analysis.
6. Know dance and be sensitive to ways in which cooperation between teacher, dancer, and accompanist can be enhanced.
7. Be able to develop and vary the music to make it interesting for the dancers because most folk music is noted simply.

Planning Instruction

Purpose

An individual's initial interest and desire to participate in dance are signaled when he or she joins a group. The purpose in joining can be learning how to dance, learning to dance better, or learning more about dance. Once an individual's initial interest has been demonstrated, it is the unique responsibility of the teacher to maintain and develop that interest, both as a benefit to the individual and, if possible, as a contribution to the general skill with which particular dance forms are executed. In general, experience has demonstrated that dancers share a common desire to perform dance skills well enough to enable them to join community dance groups in order to enjoy the resulting social relationships and to have a good time. The purpose and subsequent objectives of those who join groups for more technical than social reasons may be to acquire and/or increase their repertoire of dances, to develop a technical understanding of dance fundamentals and techniques, and to increase and perfect their performance skills. Either purpose is a viable reason for participating in a dance program, and both are important factors to be considered when learning experiences are being planned.

Objectives

Educational objectives are a concern of the professional teacher and have a variety of functions. They serve as a guide for selecting content and learning experiences. They provide criteria for what to teach and how to teach it. They set the scope and limits for what is to be taught and learned and are the basis for the evaluations that appraise student achievement.

Objectives function at several levels. They generalize the relationship between the needs of society and those of educational philosophy. They describe the outcomes intended by a particular curriculum. And, most important, they describe the particular behavior to be learned in a unit or a lesson, or upon the completion of a grade level. Objectives are implicit or explicit statements about what a teacher wants to teach. Well-stated objectives clearly identify what a student is to learn and/or is capable of performing as a result of instruction.

Performance Objectives

By design, performance objectives, formally behavioral objectives, place the emphasis on what a student will be able to do at the completion of an instructional unit and are therefore particularly suited to the instructional unit in dance. The terminology employed in the performance objective is critical to the successful learning experience. Statements should describe as specifically as possible exactly what the student is to be able to do. The more specific the teacher can be, the greater the chances are of success in getting the student to do it. The performance objective should clearly describe the observable behavior that the teacher expects the student to exhibit and should include both the conditions under which the student will

perform and the criteria to be achieved in order to be successful. The following statements illustrate how performance objectives are stated:

1. "The student will be able to dance the Two-Step," does not indicate which behaviors are to be observed, the conditions under which the demonstration occurs, or which criteria the teacher would use in judging or rating the performance.

2. "The student will be able to dance the Two-Step in time with the music," means the teacher can observe whether or not the student executes the Two-Step in time with the music. However, there is still no description of the conditions and/or any indication of the criteria for judging.

3. An example of what might be a good performance objective is: "The student will be able to dance the Two-Step with a partner around the gymnasium floor for the length of one 45-rpm record and demonstrate the ability to dance forward, backward, and sideways, and to turn clockwise as well as counterclockwise, in time with the music." In this example, the conditions are "dance with a partner around the gymnasium floor for the length of one 45-rpm record." The criterion for judging is indicated in "ability to dance forward, backward, and sideways, and to turn clockwise as well as counterclockwise, in time with the music."

Assessing Group Variables

Assessing skills, knowledge, attitudes, and characteristics is an important first step in formulating objectives and selecting learning experiences. Some common group variations and suggested adaptations follow.

Range of Skill and Motor Ability

Skill is seldom distributed evenly in a group. Although it may be clustered at one end or the other of a continuum, it will still represent a range. In an advanced group, the range is as apparent, although not as formidable, as in a beginning group. Materials should be selected to accommodate all skill levels and, at the same time, to provide for sequential progression toward a minimum standard of accomplishment for all. Dances involving locomotor skills can keep the level of participation and incentive high until the skill range of a group is narrowed to a manageable range.

Range of Experience and Association

Experience implies formal learning, such as a class or a club membership. Informal experiences like imitating dance movements without formal instruction and/or participation in rhythmic activities—such as marching in a band or a drill team, twirling a baton, or reacting to television or radio music—represent a type of association that constitutes a viable background for dance. Selection of familiar or currently popular dances may help maintain the interest and enhance the progress of individuals with either or both types of experience.

Range of Intellectual Capacity

This is an ever-present problem in interpersonal communication. In dance, however, verbal instructions can be greatly enhanced by active demonstration and practice accompanied by verbal cues. Material that lends itself to demonstration should be selected when a lack of intellectual capacity or verbal sophistication is apparent.

Range of Purpose

Individuals may join a group for the conscious purpose of learning to Square Dance or the unconscious purpose of finding fellowship. Awareness of the two purposes for membership in a group should occur to the teacher who may be pressing for perfection in dance skill rather than planning for adequate skill and general sociability.

Group Structure

Groups seldom appear in even numbers or in alphabetical order. Having equal numbers of men and women in a group is seldom the rule. Dances for threes, mixers, and nonpartner circle dances help solve these ever-present imbalances. Group size is also a problem. Groups may be too large or too small. Size presents problems in how much, how little, and how rapidly materials can be covered and learned.

Content Selection

After diagnosing group needs and formulating objectives, the teacher must search dance literature for specific dance materials with which to build content. The search for dance content is more efficient and need serving when the teacher selects materials in terms of dance structure.

Dance structure refers to the component parts or basic elements that make up a dance. For most dance forms, these elements are basic step, position, formation, nationality, degree of difficulty, and musical meter. In Square Dance, these elements are patter, singing, basics, and figure type.

Refer to the classified dance indexes listing the structural parts of each dance in each section.

Total Dance Program

School Curriculum

In the formal school situation, the total dance program consists of a planned progressive sequence distributed throughout the entire school curriculum from first grade through graduation. The total dance program may be planned for six to eight grades in elementary school, three in junior high, and three to four in high school, depending on the numerical breakdown of the individual school system.

The year's program, at any school level, is further subdivided into units of instruction and daily lesson plans. Each subdivision is organized systematically, with specific objectives, content, learning experiences, and appraisals in the form of evaluations. Each part of the total program should combine with the others to form one sequentially related dance program.

Materials selected for a specific unit should be related to the overall plan. The overall program should be flexible enough to allow for adaptation of materials in smaller units to meet specific or unique needs of a particular group within the total system. Evaluation of the individual units in terms of stated objectives should provide information necessary for revision of the sequential program in relation to the changing needs of students.

Extracurricular Opportunities

The total dance program should not be an isolated experience to be participated in, in lockstep fashion, throughout the school curriculum. Ideally, the instructional phase of the total school program should be augmented by many extracurricular opportunities. Clubs, exhibition groups, festivals, and celebrations of special events and holidays are all opportunities for enriching formal learning sessions. In addition, dance may be integrated with other subject areas, for example, language courses or dramatic presentations such as operettas and musicals.

Dance Unit

A *dance unit* is a period of time during which a planned sequence of learning experiences concentrates on a specific form of dance. The dance unit is a segment of the total dance program. Units should be planned and linked together to offer progressive experience in each dance area included in the total program. The dance unit is not an isolated learning experience but rather one of many stepping stones that provide sequential learning experiences in each dance area included in the total dance program. The following factors should be considered in planning a dance unit: (1) general purposes or objectives of the unit; (2) age, sex, skill, and dance experience of the participants; (3) facilities and equipment; (4) time allotment (class periods per week, continuous or divided, number of weeks per unit); (5) relationship of unit to school curriculum; (6) leadership experience and background; (7) relationship to community recreational program; and (8) enrichment activities.

Dance Lesson

The *dance lesson plan* is a written outline of specific procedures and materials to be presented in a given period of time. Written lesson plans assure progression, unity, and completeness in teaching each class period. Lesson plans are functional tools that provide effective guides for learning experiences. They should not be considered inflexible. Lesson plans should be adapted to meet any unforeseen changes that can occur within the group or the class situation.

The extent of detail to be included in a lesson plan varies, depending on the experience of the teacher. The beginning teacher understandably will need more detail than the experienced teacher. The following paragraphs list the component parts of a lesson plan. The use of component parts varies, depending on the location in the sequence of the unit and the purpose of the lesson. The first lesson, for example, would have no need for review of old materials, although other lessons could be devoted entirely to review.

General Objectives

General objectives are statements in broad terms that indicate the instructional goals to be accomplished by the unit. The statement, "The student will be able to perform six traditional dance steps," is an example of a general objective broadly stated for a unit. Each lesson would, in whole or in part, be a step toward accomplishing this as well as other general objectives of the unit.

Performance Objectives

Performance objectives state in behavioral terms exactly what a student should be able to do at the end of the instructional period or a learning experience. The behavior should be observable, and the conditions under which the skill is executed and the criteria used for judging the completed skill should be understood by the student. Performance objectives serve two func-

tions: They become terminal objectives for the instructional activity, and they are congruent with items used in evaluation.

Terminal objectives are the results of analyzing and rewriting general unit objectives as performance objectives. Test items are and should be wholly a function of the performance objectives on which they are based. If a performance objective asked the student to execute a Two-Step with a partner, moving forward, backward, sideways, and turning clockwise and counterclockwise for the length of one 45-rpm record, and the test item asked the student to write an analysis of the Two-Step and give a Two-Step sequence, then the test item would be wholly incongruent with the stated objective.

Procedure and Organization

Procedure and organization is the portion of the lesson plan that outlines the order of materials to be presented. There are essentially five sections dealing with class management and teaching procedures. Class organization, progression, and methods are outlined as needed and integrated under any or all main sections. The review section, for example, may require one type of class organization, but the new material section requires another. The same is true for methods used in review as opposed to methods used in presenting new materials. A brief demonstration without detailed analysis may suffice in review, although a step-by-step analysis and walk through may be needed for presentation of new materials. Progression may occur in cumulative fashion from the beginning to the end of the lesson plan or in any one part of the lesson. Progressive or teaching sequences occur in any one part of the lesson or in the whole lesson and move from simple to complex or from part to whole.

Lesson Plan

The following five sections of the lesson plan do not necessarily need to be used in the order presented here. The innovative teacher will want to vary the daily class lesson procedure to provide variety and an air of expectation.

1. **Roll call and announcements.** This is the business management section of the lesson and should be accomplished without taking undue time away from instructional activities. Procedures used in this section of the lesson plan should not detract from the friendly and informal nature of the dance activities. This section should be planned so cleverly that it is hardly noticeable as a "daily business task." Some suggestions for making it a more integrated part of

the learning experience include: employ the bulletin board for class announcements; arrange name tags on the bulletin board for roll-checking purposes; use the section as a rest period in the middle of the class after a vigorous review or a concentrated presentation of new materials; hold it at the end of the instructional period, thus leaving students in a less boisterous mood for the more formal classroom atmosphere of other school subjects.

2. **Review.** Review is a formal or informal runthrough of previously learned materials. The review may be conducted as a formal part of the lesson by the teacher or it may be an informal student-participation session. The review section serves two purposes: to refresh the students' memory of previously learned dances and to help students who have been absent. Making equipment available for students to carry on self-directed activities before the formal lesson can make this section a barometer of student interest in the class. Formal review does not necessarily have to be a part of every lesson. It is wise, however, to devote one or several whole lessons to review. Holding the review section at the beginning of the class period is more a tradition than a requirement. It can be an attractive and pleasant mixer session when placed from the middle to the end of class. Dance favorites or well-known dances can be an enjoyable conclusion for any daily class period, especially before holidays.

3. **New materials.** This section of the lesson is for the introduction of materials not covered in previous lessons in the unit. New materials may be in the form of a fundamental step (such as the Mazurka or the Magic Step), a new Square Dance figure, an early American dance, or an international Folk Dance. New materials may also appear in the form of an adaptation of a dance, such as a conversion of a routine into a mixer. This section may not appear in every lesson plan because it may take more than one lesson to complete the presentation of certain materials. The new material may be presented in any part of a class period. Beginning the lesson with new material is a means of varying class procedure as well as providing a longer segment of the class time for presentation and practice. Ending with new material is possible, if the material is short, lively, and especially designed as a fun ending to the class period.

4. **Activity.** This is the section of the lesson plan in which the new material is done in its entirety and repeated for fun and enjoyment. Completing the instructional section of the lesson as efficiently as possible allows for a greater portion of the lesson time to be spent on dancing and enjoying what has been taught. Getting to the activity—dancing—makes the class period seem more successful to both teacher and student, and this should be a major objective for every lesson.

5. **Evaluation.** Evaluation is an ongoing process and should be a part of the daily lesson. Clearly stated performance objectives predict the desired student behavior and, when the test items correspond directly to the desired student behavior as stated in the objectives, simple daily tests can be devised to assess the progress of the students as well as the effectiveness of the instructional process. Clearly stated performance objectives for each lesson make self-ratings by students, subjective ratings in pairs, and small-group ratings by the teacher effective within the class period. The bulletin board, when used as an instructional aid, can be of value and save time. If, for example, "to be able to write an analysis of the mechanics of the Two-Step" is a performance objective of a lesson, the teacher can post footprint diagrams and an analysis several days prior to the specific lesson. On the day of the lesson, responses to one or two questions may be written on index cards. Then the cards can be collected in class or deposited in a container on the bulletin board at a later time. Results can be posted before the next class period.

Orientation to the Dance Class

Setting the Stage

Dance is ideally and culturally best conducted in a coeducational setting. There is a need to set the stage for sociability. Enthusiastic participation and promotion by both men and women faculty members is helpful. Group participation in planning the coed dance unit enhances understanding and creates greater enthusiasm. A coed steering committee can serve to generate interest and assist in promoting the idea of coed dance classes.

Etiquette

Simple good manners and courtesy are part of helping everyone in a group have a good time. It is the teacher's responsibility to create the kind of atmosphere that contributes to easy social adjustment and relationships among members of the dance group. Assisting members in becoming acquainted with each other and learning to mix are the most important social responsibilities, and they all add to the fun and pleasure of the occasion. Etiquette is everybody's responsibility.

The teacher's language (his or her choice of words and phrases) can remind group members of simple courtesies. Gentle admonitions are helpful;

for example, "thank your partner for the dance and invite another lady to be your new partner," "get together with the couple nearest you, introduce your lady and exchange partners," "escort your lady off the floor and introduce her to someone who is sitting out," and "there are a few extra ladies (men), and so between dances will the ladies (men) who are dancing take turns trading out so that everyone will get a change to dance." These simple pleasant directions set the tone for interpersonal relationships necessary in the dance group.

The following are a number of techniques for bringing about social intermixing to provide opportunities that gradually develop into pleasant habits.

Social Aids

The use of an attractive name tag helps people to get acquainted and feel at ease. Square and Folk Dance clubs use them with tremendous success. They are equally welcomed by students in a class.

Still another successful idea has been the appointment of a host and hostess for each session. They have the responsibility of seeing that everyone has a chance to dance, that name tags are out and ready, that visitors are included in the activities, and that guests are met and made to feel welcome. In a large group, members can take turns playing host-hostess so that everyone has an equal opportunity to participate in the dancing.

Fun with Cutting In

In almost every mixer, there is a break during which an extra person can step in and steal a partner, which automatically puts someone out. This can be good fun if everyone gets into the spirit of it. If the leader shows the group how and encourages stealing partners during the mixers, the problem of extras in a group is reduced.

Cutting in is a fun technique also used in Square Dancing. However, it should be stressed that the skill of cutting in lies in the ability to cut the other person out and yourself in without breaking the continuity or rhythm of the figure.

Cutting in in Social Dance can also be made into a fun situation; for example, use one or two couples, give the girls a peach, the boys a lemon, and they cut in by passing the peach or lemon to another boy or girl.

Uneven Numbers

Uneven numbers are a rather common occurrence and therefore a problem in all dance situations, except in clubs that restrict membership to couples. Leaders need to be particularly alert and unusually resourceful in handling this situation. An extensive repertoire of nonpartner dances, dances for threes, and simple partner-exchange mixers are necessary for instructional and recreational success in any group.

Holding Hands

Sometimes boys and girls are reluctant to hold hands. Starting with catchy, novelty, nonpartner dances gets them moving. Grand Marches, Virginia Reels, and partner dances with little contact like Tennessee Wig Walk or line dances like Cotten-Eye Joe are nonthreatening. One thing naturally flows to another like a Big Circle Mixer and suddenly they are ready to swing.

Students with Special Needs

The terminology and practices for this group of students continue to evolve and become better. For "students who are handicapped," formerly special education students, the emphasis is on "student" rather than "handicapped." Another term is "special needs children." In the school setting these students are "mainstreamed." The terms "integration of children" and "inclusive schools" are also used.

In mainstreaming handicapped students, the choice of dances is again important so that all participants feel successful and have fun. Start with dances that have very few changes.

First Class Meeting

The first class meeting should be carefully planned to create a general feeling of success in learning as well as in social interaction and good fellowship. Significant factors to be considered in planning the first class meeting include the following:

1. Consider carefully how to have students start dancing. The strategy needs a well-thought-out plan. Some teachers prefer a short talk defining the general rules of behavior to make students feel more secure. Others select a simple dance, usually a nonpartner dance, and "up" music that relates to the students' age. The teacher needs a clear mental picture of how to move students from the side to the center and dancing. While all dances should be "winners," if the first three catch students' interest, the session should move smoothly.
2. Early instruction in social etiquette is helpful. Help students learn how to introduce partners to others, how to ask for a dance, and how to thank partners for a dance.
3. Provide name tags to help students get acquainted.

4. **Organize devices for getting and changing partners.** Automatic partner-getting devices used early in the dance unit build morale since partner formation is by direction rather than choice. When students become better acquainted, they may be allowed to choose partners at appropriate times.
5. **During the first lesson avoid asking boys to choose partners, lining students up in rows to secure partners, or allowing them to sit down with boys on one side of the room and girls on the other.**
6. **Use quick, easy sequences for forming sets of three, four, six, and eight.** Dances may be arranged in the order of numbers involved, thus making it easy to change from one formation to another.
7. **Mixers are a must, especially during the first few lessons.** Include a generous number of nonpartner dances in the course content. They reduce the class time it takes to choose partners or arrange formations, thus increasing class time for instruction and participation.
8. **Use appropriate material for the age level.** Contemporary music should be used for novelty mixers and other routines where the recorded music for a dance has an out-of-date sound.
9. **The class should be activity oriented.** Long waits or lectures about what is going to happen dampen interest. Keep activity high by talking less.
10. **End the lesson with an exciting hint about something special in the next lesson.**

6. Frequent partner changes should be used.
7. Plans should allow time and include opportunities for the group to be social.
8. Put new steps to use in the normal dance setting as soon as possible. Example: a Ballroom Dance step taught in a line or a circle formation should be danced in Ballroom fashion as soon as possible.
9. Include new and review material in each lesson after the first lesson.
10. Arrange the lesson content to provide for periods of activity and rest, contrast in style and steps, and variety in formation. Examples: circles, lines, sets, and so on.
11. To stimulate interest, presentation of material should include cultural information about the dance. This adds meaning to the dance and enhances understanding of style.
12. Discuss the unique features of a dance to help dancers distinguish one dance from another.
13. Allow ample time for practice, questions, requests, and suggestions, so that you can give individual assistance.
14. Encourage original work. Social dancers are particularly anxious to be free from set routines. Similarly, dancers in other forms enjoy creating their own routines for the Schottische, the Polka, and the Waltz.
15. Visual aids supplement teaching. Pictures, diagrams, maps, cartoons, articles, movies, and special demonstrations stimulate interest. Costume dolls and other bits of folklore add to the cultural understanding of the dance. Learning is enhanced when dance titles are posted so that dancers can check their spelling and pronunciation.

Class Procedure

Strategies for Selecting Material and Presentation

The suggestions that follow constitute rather specific guidelines for class procedures relevant to selecting materials, achieving variety within a class period, and using enrichment materials to make the class period a warm, friendly, and informative experience.

1. Materials should correspond to the skill level of the group.
2. Beginning activities should include the entire group. Nonpartner Circle Dances are recommended.
3. The first dances should be simple and short.
4. Plan materials in progressive sequences so that each succeeding part relates and depends on the preceding part.
5. Plan activities that make use of uneven numbers of men and women. Examples: dances for three, nonpartner Circle Dances.

Teaching a Specific Dance

Teacher Preparation

The teacher's preparation to teach a specific dance should include:

1. Knowledge of the basic steps.
2. An understanding of the sequence of the step patterns and their relation to the music.
3. A knowledge of the music (introduction, sequence, and tempo).
4. The ability to demonstrate the steps accurately, with or without music.
5. An organization of all materials that makes the best possible use of class time.

Presentation of the Dance

The analysis of each dance to be taught varies. However, many of the steps in the analysis are similar for all types of dance.

1. Give the name of the dance. Write it on the board. If it is unusual and uncommon, have the class pronounce the name.
2. Give the nationality of the dance and any background that will add interest and make the dance more meaningful. Such information need not be given all at once but can be interspersed here and there between steps.
3. Play a short part of the record, enough to give the class an idea of the character, the quality, and the speed of the music.
4. Arrange the group in the desired formation. It may be practical to do this first.
5. Teach the difficult steps or figures separately. Refer to the suggestions for teaching basic steps on pages 45–46.
   a. Teach basic step patterns, such as the Waltz or the Polka, independently of the dance. They should be mastered before being used in a dance.
   b. If the dance has steps that can be learned better in a line or a circle formation, isolate these and teach them before starting to teach the dance.
   c. If a specific step and pattern are involved, teach the isolated step first, then the figure. Talk the step through while demonstrating it and then direct the entire class in the pattern at the same time.
6. For dances with short sequences, demonstrate the entire dance and cue the class as they do it. For dances with long sequences, analyze the part, try it without music first, and then with music. This process continues for the entire dance.
7. Give a starting signal. "Ready—and" is a helpful signal in getting everyone to start together. There is usually a pause between "ready" and "and." Accent the word *and*. The first step of the dance comes on the next accented beat after the word *and*.
8. Demonstrate with a partner as each part is explained to the group. It is not necessary to have a special partner. For many dances, the teacher can select an alert member of the class. As the teacher explains the step and demonstrates and leads the action, the partner should be able to follow easily. For a more difficult pattern, the teacher should practice with the student a few minutes before class begins. Do not use the same student all the time.
9. Correct errors in the whole group first. Give individual help as it is needed later.
10. Start the music slowly and gradually speed it up to normal tempo. When working with a record player without a speed-control mechanism, gradually speed up the dance by verbal cues until it is the same tempo as the record. For additional ideas refer to "Teaching with Record-

ings," p. 21, or "Teaching with Live Music," p. 22.
11. Use the blackboard to help explain and clarify rhythm patterns. Have the group clap difficult tempos and rhythms.
12. Teach first the repeated part of a dance. For example, teach the chorus and then the first verse. If the dance is long, it is not necessary to teach all the verses on the same day.
13. Give lead reminders to help the man guide his partner into the figure or the pattern of steps.
14. Demonstrate and practice the style along with the step pattern. For example, the manner in which the foot is placed on the floor, the resultant body action, and the position of the arms is a total relationship that should be learned at one time. If it requires unusual coordination, style can be taught separately. For specific styling comments, refer to the directions given in Chapter 3, Dance Fundamentals.
15. Cue the dance steps on the microphone until the dancers have had sufficient practice to remember the routine. Cueing by the use of descriptive words in time to the music is very helpful. For example: step, point, step, point, slide, slide, slide. If the cue is to remind dancers of the next sequence (Black Hawk Waltz, "crossover") it should be given just before the new phrase. Otherwise the cue would be given on the beat of the step. The timing of the cue depends on its purpose.
16. Videotapes for instructional purposes are appearing on the market. Also, an instructor is sometimes able to make a video of a performing group. When a class is ready to perfect its style, a short video presentation gives the students a visual image for which to strive.
17. Change plans if a dance is too difficult or a poor choice for the group. Select another dance.
18. Be confident in correcting your own errors in teaching. All teachers make errors now and then. It is wise to correct them immediately. This can be done with a sense of humor or a light touch.
19. Be generous with praise and encouragement to the group.
20. Show personal enthusiasm and enjoyment for the dance. A teacher's enthusiasm and genuine interest in teaching does much to help others enjoy it.

Review

1. Review verbally, having the class tell the sequence of the dance. Then try the dance with the music while cueing the important changes.
2. Pick out the spots that need review and practice them. Point out the details of style and leading. Repeat the dance.

3. Announce the dance several days later, play the record, and see how far the dancers can progress without a cue.

4. Avoid letting the class form the habit of depending on a cue to prompt them. Cueing is only a teaching device.

5. Make records or practice tapes available for those who wish to practice. Have the music playing when students come into class to encourage them to practice and to establish an appropriate atmosphere.

Evaluation

In the school situation where a final grade is required for each student in a dance class, some consideration must be given to a fair means of evaluating the students. While some teachers feel that it destroys the recreational value of a class to conduct tests, most students are anxious to be graded if they feel that they have had a reasonable opportunity to show what they know.

Occasional tests serve to stimulate better learning, to show progression and accomplishment, and to serve as a booster to those who are slow or disinterested. From the teacher's point of view, they focus attention on the students who need special help or encouragement and on the material that needs review. Students are very interested in how grades are computed. They want to know the relationship (percentage of points) of written tests, practical tests, attendance, and improvement to the final grade. Students deserve a clear statement that coincides with the department's philosophy. There are two kinds of tests: the practical or skill test and the written test.

Practical Test

A *practical test* assesses the student's ability to perform a dance skill. For example, a test on the Waltz, the Schottische, or the Polka; a test on the fundamentals of Square or Contra Dance; or a test on the basic steps in Social Dance. The following are types of practical tests that have been used for dance with reasonable efficiency and success.

1. *Subjective rating.* A subjective rating is determined from scores on a prepared check sheet. Five students at a time can be checked as they perform a skill individually or with partners. The sheet is given to the student so that he or she may benefit from comments; afterward, he or she signs it and turns it in.

2. *Systematic use of an achievement chart.* Each student can be checked off on an achievement chart as a few at a time are observed during the last ten minutes of a series of class periods.

3. *Accumulative grade system through use of name tags or numbers.* The teacher circulates and writes down a grade for each of the students as they dance. This should be done several times so that an average grade can be taken. If the students wear name tags throughout the course, the teacher can jot down grades at frequent intervals and thereby keep a progress chart on each student. Improvement may be quite evident with this system of checking.

4. *Colored tags used for grading.* The teacher circulates and gives each student a colored tag that represents the teacher's opinion of the student's ability (blue—excellent, red—good, yellow—fair, green—poor, and white—no opinion). At the end of the period, each student writes his or her name on the tag and turns it in. This method is effective in grading Ballroom Dance and can be used for each type of dance, including the Rumba, the Tango, and the Waltz.

5. *Student check list.* Students check each other on a prepared check list. For example: good rhythm, poor lead, inconsistent step, and so on. They can check five persons with whom they dance. The student should sign the check list. The teacher can then draw up a summary of the opinions. This is very helpful in grading and also in knowing which students need extra help.

Written Test

The knowledge test gives every student a chance to show what he or she has learned, even though he or she may perform the skill poorly. More than one written test should be given, so that the student has a better understanding of how the questions will be phrased. For many, this is a different vocabulary. The student-teacher should respond to more information than a service student. Two kinds of written tests have proved most satisfactory for grading.

1. *The short quiz* is a five-minute test in which the student is asked to identify a fundamental step, a rhythm pattern, a specific style, a position, or a lead. It should require only a few words and should have a specific positive answer. These can be corrected in class.

2. *The objective test* is usually given as a final test. It should be given far enough in advance to get the papers corrected, returned, and discussed in class, with time allowed for questions and corrections. The objective test in dance should be set up to include material on etiquette, fundamental steps, rhythm, position, style, and history. There should

be several types of questions, including true or false, multiple choice, and identification. Directions should be clear so that students will not need to ask questions on procedures. The method of scoring should be indicated on the test paper.

A Model for Test Construction is presented in Appendix A, pp. 475–483. Sample questions illustrate how test questions are phrased in a variety of ways to gain the same knowledge. Some types are more difficult than others. The model is helpful to students in teacher training and service classes, as well as to teachers.

Grading the Class

Grading the class should be handled efficiently in order to avoid long periods of inactivity and subsequent loss of interest. All cards, tags, pencils, numbers, and other materials should be ready to use before class begins. A group that is prepared for the testing period in advance is usually cooperative and helpful. With proper motivation, the dancers should feel that they can have as much fun as usual even though they are aware of being graded.

Grading should not take up an entire period. Each class period should include some dancing just for fun, free from grading. This will restore the spirit and relieve the tension that is sometimes present during the grading time. Grading should be scheduled throughout the semester and not left until the end. All final grading should be finished before the last week so that the last two periods can be devoted to perfecting the dances and enjoying the activity as pure recreation.

Enrichment Activities

Class Projects

Whether the class is oriented to teacher preparation or a regular "service" class, the opportunity for projects is rewarding. It recognizes the enthusiasm of those who want to do more and offers an opportunity for the student who may not perform well but excels in other skills related to the subject.

1. Make arrangements for a guest teacher to come and prepare written instructions.
2. Prepare a research paper related to a specific aspect of the dance or its country.
3. Prepare an audiovisual presentation (video, movie, or slides) of a specific dance or dance event.
4. Teach one dance in class.
5. Plan and execute a One-Night Stand event.

Bulletin Boards

The class bulletin board is a place to share ideas and interests. It is a vital link between the teacher, the students, and the enrichment materials. It is an important teaching aid. The bulletin board can be used effectively in three ways: instructionally, promotionally, and creatively. A bulletin board theme can be developed around any of the following dance-related topics: basic skills, national background, region or geographic location, age groups, instruction, recreation, promotion, manners and customs, proper dress or costume, international politics, ethnic groups, seasons, holidays, states, female names, and many more. For example: take state names and symbols or slogans (state: Alabama; slogan: heart of Dixie; dance title: "Are You from Dixie"). Students could put up one bulletin board with all materials relating to this theme or make it a continuous project by putting up materials during the lesson before the lesson in which the dance is taught.

A teacher who maintains an informative and attractive bulletin board and brings interesting bits of information, pictures, clippings, and articles to the class is the teacher who turns the ordinary into the extraordinary and opens a whole new world of meaning and understanding.

Culminating Activities

Interest and enthusiasm generated by a series of lessons or a season of dancing often culminate in the desire for a special event that appropriately celebrates the achievements in skills and fellowship attained by the group. The following suggestions assist in planning such an event.

1. Several beginning classes could be combined for a late afternoon or evening dance party.
2. A guest caller or teacher could be invited to make the last class session a special occasion.
3. The group could attend a festival or a jamboree together.
4. School groups could culminate their work by giving a demonstration for a school assembly, a parent-teacher association, or a service club group.
5. An exhibition team could be invited to put on a performance for the group. The exhibition group could teach and dance at least one simple dance with the group.
6. A list of community dance opportunities could be posted on the bulletin board. The list could include classes, clubs, summer camps, workshops, clinics, festivals, and leadership-training sessions.

Community Resources

Ethnic groups, foreign students attending local high schools or colleges, Square and Folk Dance clubs, museums, libraries, and art galleries are found in almost every community and can be involved in the school dance program in many ways.

Foreign students often can show regional or national costumes and musical instruments typical of their homelands and slides or movies of their homelands. Their presence in a community offers an obvious opportunity for cultural exchange.

Ethnic groups often carry on many of their former customs and can be invited to share and compare their culture in appropriate ways with the dance class. Many ethnic groups in America have forgotten specific dances but, because they retain their native language to a greater extent than other customs, they can share songs and music if not dances.

Teacher Resources

The teacher must bridge the gap between the daily task of teaching dance skills and the vast amount of dance-related information if the instructional experience is to be more than a social and psychomotor experience. Keeping current is a constant task in the teaching profession, and, if the dance teacher is to keep current, reviewing periodic literature in dance and dance-related periodicals is a necessity as well as an efficient means of keeping abreast of the field. Current magazines carry information about other literature, including books, films, records, and costumes, and so make it possible for the teacher to be more selective about the materials to be reviewed in depth.

A teacher who participates in the dance groups and the related activities in a community enriches and improves his or her instructional skill in an enjoyable and pleasant manner. Encouraging students to attend concerts, foreign films, festivals, art shows, exhibitions, plays, and selected television performances is important, but it is equally important that the teacher also participate in these cultural opportunities.

Traveling abroad has been a tradition with American school teachers, and it is a valuable professional as well as personal experience. Traveling at home is equally important. In fact, getting to know your state and region is important. Language, customs, dress, dances, songs, humor, and stories are different for every section of the United States. These regional differences are a rich part of our heritage and are the fabric of our culture. Visiting, talking, dancing, sightseeing, and sharing individual differences around a campfire, along a mountain trail, and across a tennis net are what learning and teaching are all about.

Organizing Special Activities

Family Dances

Those who have had their children later yearn for a dance activity that involves the whole family. A sensitive leader and cooperative parents can make family dances work. Everyone looks forward to the occasion. *Coming on time* is important as the easiest dances come first. But the committee (leader) needs to have some activities ready to go—blowing up balloons, moving chairs, mixing lemonade, drawing with color markers on butcher paper attached to the wall with a theme, i.e., "spring green." Parents need to participate too, even in some table games. Two activities are enough until enough are present to "circle up" and dance. These are called "ice-breakers." Start with simple dances to peppy music, circle left and right, and play party games like Skip to My Lou, Herr Schmidt, Ach Ja. Obviously the adults need to split up and dance with the children. Grand Marches are excellent. The families need to agree on a length of time for the very elementary dances. The program depends on the ages, ability, and flexibility of the group. *A good program does not just happen.* It takes thought and planning, reaching out to the dancers' level of ability and accommodating odd numbers. Singing, playing games, eating, and creating skits are other activities to have besides dance.

There needs to be a clear understanding of purpose and a group effort for success. Those with children may leave after the first hour; some may want to have another activity available after the first hour for the restless, so that the rest of the family can dance a while longer. Some of the children will prance on the side of the stage, perfectly happy, as the group moves on to more complicated dances. Family dances are very rewarding.

One-Night Stand

A class barn dance, church dance mixer, wedding, or special celebration is the occasion for a one-night dance party—thus the term **One-Night Stand.** An experienced leader is often brought in from outside the group to conduct party games and run the program. There are many unknown factors that make planning difficult: The number of participants is often indefinite; the range of ability may vary; and the balance of sexes, more often than not, may be uneven. The one thing the group has in common is a desire to have a good time. An effective leader should be guided by these principles:

1. People enjoy group participation if they are allowed to join in willingly and are not forced to take part.
2. Plan a simple flexible program that can be quickly adjusted to the moods and the caprices of the situation.
3. Nonpartner dances, novelty activities, and mixers that are learned quickly are effective in these unpredictable groups.
4. Dances for threes or odd numbers are especially suitable when there are more of one sex than the other.
5. A high level of performance is not necessary. The group needs only to do the dances well enough to feel comfortable and have fun.
6. Careful planning includes getting the group active as soon as possible and moving from one activity to the next in **well-planned transitions.**
7. A dance or a mixer that has been particularly satisfying may be worth repeating. The group may even request a repeat. The leader can work request dances into the program when they are appropriate for the majority of the dancers.
8. A sensitive leader knows when to stop. Any **single dance or mixer should not last more than five minutes.** An hour of organized mixers and dances is generally sufficient. Square or Ballroom Dancing can be used to vary or extend the time. Other forms of social recreation—such as games, skits, stunts, and refreshments—can supplement the party.
9. Ballroom Dance is an all-time favorite dance activity for single sessions. An evening of Ballroom Dancing requires a minimum of planning, and leadership for program direction is not necessary. The primary objective is to create an evening of easy, pleasant activity during which old and new friends can meet and dance. A few mixers are appropriate and useful. Mixers should be of an informal partner-exchange type, carried out when couples are arranged informally around the floor. This is preferable to the circle-patterned step mixers associated with Square and Round Dance. The inclusion of a currently popular novelty dance provides a change of pace and adds to the fun of the evening. The planning committee should be cautioned to resist the temptation to turn this type of session into a grand mixer.

The Special Party

The program for a special party for members of a regular dance group should include familiar dance favorites. It is not an appropriate time to teach new dances or techniques. The general fun and enthusiasm can be enhanced with skits, novelty mixers, and exhibition numbers by special guest performers. Added festivity can be achieved by planning the program, decorations, and refreshments around a theme.

The Theme Party

An example of a plan for a theme party is one based on a circus motif.

Occasion: Last club meeting.
Theme: Circus.
Promotion: Appropriate posters based on circus slogans: "Under the Big Top," "Greatest Show on Earth."
Costumes and decorations: Provide construction paper, wallpaper, and crêpe paper along with string, cellophane tape, and scissors, so that guests can construct clown hats to wear during the evening. Each guest can also make one item to hang on the wall for decoration.
Name tags: The guests' first names plus the name of a traditional circus animal organize the group into animal families for a special dance number, such as an animal Square Dance with each square made up of one type of animal. Examples: Gus Elephant, Diane Tiger, Willie Monkey, Jean Lion.
Master of ceremonies: The caller or the dance leader, depending on the type of dance group, leads the circus parade from outside in or around the dance floor. Followers mimic animal walks appropriate to their last names. Music should be a rousing circus-type march.
Program: Rename dances to fit the theme. For example: High-Wire Two-Step, Elephant Stomp, Trapeze Square, Tightrope Mambo, Tattoo Tango.
Last dance of the evening: All dancers gather in Square Dance sets or circles according to family name on name tag and, after the last dance, sit down on the floor in family groups.
Refreshments: A parade of animals, some juggling cookies or donuts and others carrying water pails of punch to fake dousing the guests, parade into the room led by the famous two-person horse. The horse is two dancers under a blanket or sheet, one as the head and the other as the rear end. A horse head can be made by simply drawing a likeness on a flat piece of posterboard. After the parade antics are over, the guests are served from the pails and the cookie platters brought in by the animals.

Physically Disabled Persons

Dance is a socially acceptable and rewarding activity for physically disabled persons. Therapeutic professionals use dance as one activity in the rehabilitation of certain disabilities. Three objectives of the rehabilitation program are to eliminate the physical disability; to reduce the physical disability; and to retrain the person to work within his or her physical disability. Below are two sources for teaching dance to the physically disabled.*

Senior Dances

A variety of Senior Dances are scheduled to meet different needs and interests. In general the seniors thoroughly enjoy dances that they did in the 1940s, during World War II and immediately afterwards. Ballroom dancing, especially the jitterbug and Latin dances, brings them to the floor along with the slow Fox Trots. They dance a smooth jitterbug. They like a few mixers and pattern dances—not too many sequences to remember. Seniors enjoy the comfort of the familiar, limited new challenges, and

---

*Hill, Kathleen. *Dance for Physically Disabled Persons. A Manual for Teaching Ballroom, Square, and Folk Dances to Users of Wheelchairs and Crutches.* Washington, D.C.: American Alliance for Health, Physical Education and Recreation, 1976.

Mason, Kathleen Criddle, editor. *Dance Therapy: Focus on Dance VII.* Washington, D.C.: American Alliance for Health, Physical Education, and Recreation, 1974.

the opportunity to repeat every week the dances they know. If the seniors live in rural areas or in an ethnic community, they would like other dances too. For instance, the Scandinavians smile and dance when the Schottische, Scandinavian Polka, or Hambo are played. If the seniors were especially active in square dance circles in the 1940s and 1950s, that's what they will seek out.

A leader needs to *listen* and be receptive to the seniors as they recall favorite dances. Find the music and include them. The chances are good that others know the dance or that the person would be willing to teach it. Seniors prefer to come to events scheduled in the daytime. They are reluctant to drive or take public transportation in the dark.

Senior or community centers will draw a regular following, even once a week. Sometimes a group of retired musicians form a band and delight in playing for the gang regularly. Sometimes the local musician's union will sponsor a monthly dance for seniors with live music.

Ethnic museums or lodges sponsor senior dances.

Retirement homes may sponsor two types: a regular dance or a very modified program for seniors with limited ability to move. Dances are modified considerably to meet their ability. Some enjoy sitting in a chair (wheelchair) and moving their arms to different dance rhythms. The leader has to be creative and use ingenuity to appeal to the residents. Even the adapted movement will bring joy as they remember other days.

CHAPTER 3
Dance Fundamentals

Rhythm and Meter

Rhythm

Rhythm is the regular pattern of movement and/or sound. It is a relationship between time and force factors. It is felt, seen, or heard.

Beat

Beat is the basic unit that measures time. The duration of time becomes established by the beat, or the pulse, as it is repeated. It is referred to as the **underlying beat.**

Accent

Accent is the stress placed on a beat to make it stronger or louder than the others. The primary accent is on the first beat of the music. There may be a secondary accent.

When the accent is placed on the unnatural beat (the off beat), the rhythm is syncopated.

Measure

A *measure* is one group of beats made by the regular occurrence of the heavy accent. It represents the underlying beat enclosed between two adjacent bars on a musical staff.

Meter

Meter is the metric division of a measure into parts of equal time value and regular accents. Meter can be recognized by listening for the accent on the first beat.

Time Signature

Time signature is a symbol (e.g., 2/4) that establishes the duration of time. The upper number indicates the number of beats per measure, and the lower number indicates the note value that receives one beat.

2/4 — Two beats to the measure–accent on first beat–quarter note gets the beat.

3/4 — Three beats to the measure–accent on first beat–quarter note gets the beat.

4/4 — Four beats to the measure–accent on first beat–quarter note gets the beat.

¢ — **Cut time** plays the accented beats of the measure. Speed is often faster. Two beats to each measure. Same as fast 4/4 or 2/2 time.

6/8 — Six beats to the measure–accent on first beat–eighth note gets the beat.

Note Values

whole note

half note

quarter note

eighth note

sixteenth note

dotted quarter or dotted eighth notes
A *dotted note* increases the value by one half. Therefore the dotted note equals one and a half value of the original symbol. A dotted quarter note, then, is equal to a quarter plus an eighth; a dotted eighth is equal to an eighth plus a sixteenth.

triplet
A group of three notes played in the usual time of two similar notes. It would be counted *one-and-a* for one quarter note.

Line Values

Whereas the musical notation establishes the *relative value of beats,* these same relative values can be represented by lines:

one whole note	————————————
two half notes	———————— ————————
four quarter notes	——— ——— ——— ———
eight eighth notes	— — — — — — — —
sixteen sixteenth notes	– – – – – – – – – – – – – – – –

Phrase

A musical sentence, or *phrase,* can be felt by listening for a complete thought. This can be a group of measures, generally four or eight measures. A group of phrases can express a group of complete thoughts that are related just as a group of sentences expresses a group of complete thoughts in a paragraph. Groups of phrases are generally 16 or 32 measures long.

Tempo

Tempo is the rate of speed at which music is played. Tempo influences the mood or the quality of music and movement. Sometimes at the beginning of the music or the dance, the tempo is established by a metronome reading. For example, metronome 128 means the equal recurrence of beats at the rate of 128 per minute.

Rhythm Pattern

The *rhythm pattern* is the grouping of beats that repeat for the pattern of a dance step, just as for the melody of a song. The rhythm pattern must correspond to the underlying beat. Example: meter or underlying beat 4/4.

4/4   rhythm pattern
       underlying beat

Even Rhythm

When the beats in the rhythm pattern are all the same value (note or line value)—all long (slow) or all short (quick)—the rhythm is **even.** Examples: walk, run, hop, jump, leap, Waltz, Schottische.

4/4   rhythm pattern
       rhythm cue*
       underlying beat
       counts

Uneven Rhythm

When the beats in the rhythm pattern are not all the same value, but are any combination of slow and quick beats, the rhythm is **uneven.** Examples: Two-Step, Foxtrot.

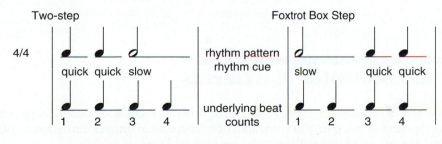

Two-step   Foxtrot Box Step

4/4   rhythm pattern
       rhythm cue
       underlying beat
       counts

———————
*S = Slow; Q = Quick.

A *dotted beat* borrows half the value of itself again. Examples: skip, slide, gallop.

When the note comes before the bar, it is called a *pick-up beat*.

Broken Rhythm

Broken rhythm is a combination of slow and quick beats when the rhythm pattern takes more than one measure. A repetition begins in the middle of the measure. Example: Magic Step in the Foxtrot.

Analysis of a Basic Rhythm

A teacher should thoroughly understand the complete analysis of each basic dance step to be taught. The following example shows the eight related parts of an analysis. Each basic dance step has been analyzed in this manner (including the basic steps of Social Dance in Chapter 8).

Two-Step

2/4	/ step	close	step	name meter 2/4 accent step pattern
	quick	quick	slow	rhythm pattern rhythm cue underlying beat
	1	and	2	counts
		uneven rhythm		type of rhythm

Fundamental Locomotor Movements

Movement through space is called *locomotion*. The following eight locomotor steps are simple ways to transfer weight in moving from one place to another. Locomotor movement forms the floor pattern of circles, squares, and longways in our Folk, Square, and Social Dances.

Walk

1. Even rhythm.
2. Steps are from one foot to the other, the weight being transferred from heel to toe.

Run

1. A fast, even rhythm.
2. A run can be compared to a fast walk except that in the run the weight is carried forward on the ball of the foot.

Hop

1. Even rhythm.
2. A transfer of weight by a springing action of the foot from one foot (push off and land on ball of foot) to the same foot.

Jump

1. Even rhythm.
2. Spring from one or both feet and land on both feet.
3. Feet push off floor with strong foot and knee extension, the heel coming off first and then the toe.
4. On landing, the ball of the foot touches the floor first and then the heel comes down and the knees bend to absorb the shock of landing.

Leap

1. Even rhythm.
2. A transfer of weight from one foot to the other foot, pushing off with a spring and landing on the ball of the foot, letting the heel come down, and bending the knee to absorb the shock.

1. Uneven rhythm   (6/8 ♪ ♩ or 2/4 ♩♩♩) .
2. 1–2 ratio; short–long.
3. A hop and a step on the same foot. Alternate feet.
4. Actually starts with a step.

Slide

1. Uneven rhythm   (6/8 ♩ ♪ or 2/4 ♩♩♩) .
2. 2–1 ratio; long–short, long–short.
3. Movement sideward can go right or left.
4. A step on the right foot, on the slow beat, close the left foot to right, shifting the weight quickly onto the left foot on the quick beat.
5. One foot maintains lead.

Gallop

1. Uneven rhythm   (6/8 ♩ ♪ or 2/4 ♩♩♩) .
2. 2–1 ratio; long–short, long–short.
3. Movement forward, knee action, heel leading.
4. A step followed by a run.
5. One foot maintains lead.

2/4	step	run	step	run	step	run	step	run
	R	L	R	L	R	L	R	L
	1	and	ah	2	and	ah	1	and	ah	2	and	ah

uneven rhythm

Exercises for Fundamental Locomotor Movements

1. Practice each movement while clapping or playing rhythm instruments.
2. Vary the energy, space, direction, and style.
3. Put three different movements together and repeat the combination four times. For instance: run, run, leap, run, run, jump. Repeat four times. Write the rhythm pattern in counts and lines.
4. Compose a two-part dance (A, B) for 16 counts. Clap the rhythm or use rhythm instruments.

Basic Dance Steps

Shuffle, Dance Walk, or Glide

1. An easy, light step, from one foot to the other, in even rhythm.
2. Different from a walk in that the weight is over the ball of the foot.
3. The feet remain lightly in contact with the floor.

Two-Step

1. 2/4 or 4/4 meter.
2. Uneven rhythm.
3. Step forward on left foot, close right to left, take weight on right, step left again. Repeat, beginning with right.
4. The rhythm is quick, quick, slow.

2/4	step	close	step
	L	R	L
	Q	Q	S
	1	and	2

uneven rhythm

Polka

1. 2/4 meter.
2. A bright, lively dance step in uneven rhythm.
3. Similar to a Two-Step with the addition of a hop so that it becomes hop, step, close, step. The hop comes on the pick-up beat.

2/4	hop	step	close	step	hop	step	close	step	hop
	L	R	L	R	R	L	R	L	L
	ah	Q	Q	S	ah	Q	Q	S	ah
	ah	1	and	2	ah	1	and	2	ah

uneven rhythm

Schottische

1. 4/4 meter.
2. Smooth, even rhythm.
3. Three running steps and a hop or a step, close, step, hop.

4. The Schottische dance form is four measures (step, step, step hop; step, step, step hop; step hop, step hop; step hop, step hop).
5. Common and popular variations are to hold, turn, or swing the free leg on the fourth count instead of hopping.

Waltz

1. 3/4 meter—accent first beat.
2. A smooth, graceful dance step in even rhythm.
3. Consists of three steps; step forward on the left, step to the side with the right, close left to right, take weight on left.

	3/4	fwd	side	close	fwd	side	close
		L	R	L	R	L	R
		S	S	S	S	S	S
		1	2	3	1	2	3

even rhythm

4. The **Box Waltz** is the basic pattern for the Box Waltz turn. Step left forward, step right sideward, passing close to the left foot, close left to right, taking weight left; step right backward, step left sideward, passing close to the right foot, close right to left, take weight right. *Cue:* Forward side close, back side close.

	3/4	fwd	side	close	back	side	close
		L	R	L	R	L	R
		S	S	S	S	S	S
		1	2	3	1	2	3

even rhythm

5. The **Running Waltz** used so often in European Folk Dances is a tiny three-beat running step with an accent on the first beat, three beats to each measure.
6. **Canter Waltz** rhythm is an uneven rhythm in Waltz time with the action taking place on beats one and three. The rhythm is slow, quick; slow, quick or long, short. (Refer to Canter rhythm, p. 509.)

uneven rhythm

Mazurka

1. 3/4 meter.
2. Strong, vigorous, even three-beat rhythm—accent second beat.
3. Step left, bring right up to left with a cut-step displacing left, hop right while bending left knee so that left foot approaches the right ankle. Repeat, left foot leading.

3/4	step L	cút R	hop R	step L	cút R	hop R
	S	S	S	S	S	S
	1	2	3	1	2	3

even rhythm

Basic Dance Turns

Using the fundamental dance steps, partners may turn clockwise or counterclockwise. Basically, if the man is leading with the left, the turn is counterclockwise; if he is leading with the right, the turn is clockwise. But in Folk Dance, the majority of the partner turns are clockwise. A successful turn actually starts with the preceding step, the man's back to center and his body moving into the turn. The man steps left backward in the line of direction, which allows his right foot to lead on the second step.

Schottische Turn Clockwise

The Schottische rhythm is even 4/4 meter. The pattern is step, step, step hop; step, step, step hop; step hop, step hop, step hop, step hop. The last two measures of four are used for the partner turn. The starting position is generally a closed position or a shoulder-waist position. By turning gradually, the couple can make only one turn clockwise on the four step hops, or, by turning a half-turn clockwise on each step hop, they can make two full turns. They progress forward in the line of direction on each step hop.

Two-Step Turn Clockwise

The Two-Step rhythm is uneven 2/4 or 4/4 meter with a quick-quick-slow pattern. There is a half-turn on each measure (2/4 meter). The starting position is closed, with the man's back to center of the circle. *The turn is on the second count.*

Left-Foot Sequence (Man)

Count 1	Step left sideward.
Count and	Close right to left, taking weight on right.
Count 2	Step left around partner, toeing in and pivoting clockwise on the ball of the foot a half-turn around.

Right-Foot Sequence (Lady)

Count 1	Step right sideward.
Count and	Close left to right, taking weight on left.
Count 2	Step right forward between partner's feet and pivoting clockwise on the ball of the foot a half-turn around.

Note

The man starts with the left sequence, the lady starts with the right sequence. After a half-turn, the lady then starts with the left sequence and the man with the right sequence. They continue to alternate. By this process of *dovetailing with the feet,* man and lady can turn easily without stepping on each other's feet. Couple progresses in the line of direction as they turn.

Style

The steps should be small and close to partner. The body leans back and aids in the turn. The turn is on the ball of the foot. Each partner must give the impetus for the turn by pivoting on his or her own foot.

Lead

Closed position, the man should have a firm right hand on the small of the lady's back so that she can lean back against it. His right arm guides her as he turns.

Cues

1. Left-Foot sequence: side close around.
   Right-Foot sequence: side close between.
2. Practicing together in closed position.
   Side close turn, side close turn.

Polka Turn Clockwise

The **clockwise turn** is used almost always for a Polka partner turn in Folk Dance. The Polka rhythm is uneven 2/4 meter. The pattern is hop, step, close, step. With the addition of a quick hop (pick-up beat) before each Two-Step, all the directions described for the Two-Step turn can be applied to the Polka turn. The starting position is generally a closed position or a shoulder-waist position.

Waltz Turn

The Waltz rhythm is even 3/4 meter. Three patterns are presented: the Box Waltz, traditional step-side-close, and Running Waltz pattern.

Box Waltz Turn—Clockwise, Counterclockwise

The Box Waltz turn is used in social dancing and in some American Folk Dances and can go either to the left in a counterclockwise turn or to the right in a clockwise turn, depending on which foot leads the turn. (These turns are described under the Waltz box turn, pp. 435–436.)

Clockwise Turn

The clockwise turn is the turn most often used for Folk Dances. Two patterns are presented, the first based on the traditional step-side-close pattern and the second on the running Waltz pattern. It is in 3/4 meter.

Step-Side-Close Pattern (Traditional)

Left-Foot Sequence (Man).   Step left around partner, pivoting on the ball of the foot a half-turn clockwise (count 1). Step right sideward in line of direction (count 2). Close left to right, take weight left (count 3).

Right-Foot Sequence (Lady).   Step right forward between partner's feet, pivoting on the ball of the foot a half-turn clockwise (count 1). Step left sideward in the line of direction (count 2). Close right to left, take weight right (count 3).

Note

The man starts with the left sequence, the lady with the right sequence. After a half-turn, the lady starts with the left sequence and the man with the right sequence. They continue to alternate. By this process of dovetailing the feet, dancers can turn easily without stepping on each other's feet.

Style

The steps are small and close to partner. The pivot halfway around is on the ball of the foot on the first count. Each partner is responsible for supplying the impetus for the ball of the foot turn.

Lead

The man has a firm right hand at the lady's back. She leans back and is guided into the turn by his firm right hand and arm.

Cues

1. Left-foot sequence: around side close.
   Right-foot sequence: between side close.
2. Practice together in closed position.
   Turn side close, turn side close.

Step-Step-Close Pattern

Left-Foot Sequence (Man).   Step left in the line of direction (toeing in, heel leads), pivoting on the ball of the foot and starting a half-turn clockwise (count 1). Take two small steps, right, left, close to first step, completing half-turn (counts 2 and 3).

Right-Foot Sequence (Lady).   Step right in line of direction (toeing out) *between partner's feet,* pivoting on the ball of the foot, starting a half-turn clockwise (count 1). Take two small steps, left, right, close to first step, completing half-turn (counts 2 and 3).

Note

1. When the man steps backward left, the right foot leads the clockwise turn.
2. The man starts with the left sequence, the lady with the right sequence. After a half-turn, the lady starts with the left sequence and the man with the right sequence. They continue to alternate. When doing left-foot sequence, step backward in line of direction; when doing the right-foot sequence, step forward (but not as long a step as the first step in the other sequence). The dancers are turning on each count, but steps on counts 2 and 3 are almost in place. *Both feet are together on count 3.*

Lead

The man has a firm right hand at the lady's back. She leans back and is guided into the turn by his firm right hand and arm.

Cues

Left-Foot sequence: Back turn turn.
Right-Foot sequence: Forward turn turn.

Reverse Direction of Turn

If turning counterclockwise, the left foot leads. If turning clockwise, the right foot leads. To change leads from left to right or right to left, one measure (3 beats) is needed for transition. A balance step backward or one Waltz step forward facilitates the transition. Or turning counterclockwise, after a left Waltz step, immediately reverse direction with a right Waltz step, turning clockwise (a more difficult maneuver). Eventually the lead comes back to a left one, and another transition occurs.

Suggestions for Teaching Basic Dance Steps

The level of ability of the student and the degree of difficulty of the basic step will influence the manner in which a step is presented. The factors involved are interdependent and may be used in various combinations when the steps are being taught. The sequence of the factors and the starting point for teaching vary. Sometimes it is necessary to go back in the teaching process to an easier form. Several approaches may be necessary for everyone to learn the step.

Analysis of Rhythm of Basic Step

Explain and discuss accent, time signature, even or uneven rhythm, and foot pattern in relation to rhythm.

1. Listen to music.
2. Clap rhythm with students.
3. Write out on blackboard.
4. Demonstrate action.

Method of Presentation

1. Walk through with analysis and demonstration.
2. Practice.
3. Apply basic step in simple sequence.
4. Use basic step in simple dance.

Interdependent Factors Influencing Procedure

1. Position of teacher in relation to group. Ideally the teacher should be a part of the group, standing in the circle, two steps inside the circle, or facing the line. Avoid standing in the middle because the back is to part of the group. The dancers cannot hear, and the teacher is unaware of whether they understand. In large groups, the teacher is on a platform, slightly above the group so that he or she may be seen and heard. Otherwise, a mike is necessary. With a wireless mike, there is more flexibility of position.
2. Demonstrations. If facing lines, mirror demonstrate, rather than turn back on group. If demonstrating in the circle, give demonstration several times, moving to different locations, especially directly across the circle. Dancers tend to mirror what they see in a circle and forget to translate demonstration to the same foot and direction.
3. Formation of group for teaching.
   a. Line.
   b. Single circle.
   c. Double circle.
4. Position of people.
   a. Alone.
   b. With partner.
      1) Varsouvienne, couple, promenade, open, or conversation position.
      2) Closed or shoulder-waist position.
5. Accompaniment—with or without music.
6. Cue—with or without verbal cue.
7. Direction of movement.
   a. In place.
   b. Forward and backward.
   c. Sideward or diagonal.
   d. Turning.

Procedure for Teaching Basic Dance Steps and Turns

Schottische and Clockwise Turn

Directions are for man; lady's part is reverse.

1. **Single circle,** facing line of direction.
   a. Beginning left, take two Schottische steps, moving forward in the line of direction. Rock forward on first step hop, rock backward on the second step hop, rock forward on the third step hop, and backward on the fourth step hop. Repeat.
   b. Beginning left, take two Schottische steps moving forward in the line of direction. Turn clockwise by rocking forward and backward twice to make one complete turn. Repeat. Discourage any body sway that may accompany the rock as soon as the pattern of turning is learned.

2. **Double circle,** take open position, facing the line of direction. Beginning left, take two Schottische steps, moving forward in the line of direction. Take closed or shoulder-waist position. Turn clockwise by rocking forward and backward twice to make one complete turn. Repeat. Emphasize the importance of turning to face partner on the last Schottische step so that the turn starts on the first step hop. Encourage more advanced dancers to make two turns.

3. Use a simple dance to practice Schottische step. For example: Schottische, p. 96, Road to the Isles, p. 274.

Progressive Two-Step

1. The forward Two-Step can be taught simply by moving forward on the cue **step, close, step,** alternately left, then right.
2. Take couple position. Take the Two-Step face to face and back to back, progressing in the line of direction.

Two-Step Turn Clockwise

1. **Double circle formation,** man with his back to the center of the circle. Take closed position. Begin on man's left, lady's right.
   a. Moving toward the line of direction, take four slides, pivoting around clockwise on the last slide so that the man faces the center of the circle. Take four slides to the man's right still in the line of direction, pivoting on the last slide clockwise so that the man is back in original position. Repeat. Emphasize that the last slide is the pivot clockwise and that the man must lead the lady with his right arm as he goes around so that they can turn together.
   b. Moving to the man's left (line of direction), take two slides and pivot clockwise halfway around on the last slide. Then, reaching in the line of direction, take two slides to the man's right and pivot clockwise to original position. Repeat.
2. Use a simple dance to practice Two-Step turn. For example: Boston Two-Step, p. 103.

Polka

1. Step by step rhythm approach.
   a. **Single circle,** all facing line of direction.
      1) Analyze the Polka very slowly and have class walk through the steps together in even rhythm (hop, step close step).
      2) Gradually adapt the rhythm until there is a quick hop and a slower step close step.
      3) Gradually accelerate the tempo to normal Polka time. Add the accompaniment.
   b. **Double circle,** take promenade, Varsouvienne, or couple position, facing line of direction. Polka forward with partner.

   c. Use a simple dance to practice Polka step. For example: Klumpa-kojis, p. 320.
2. Two-Step approach
   a. **Single circle,** facing the line of direction. Beginning left, Two-Step with music, moving forward in the line of direction. Gradually accelerate the tempo to a fast Two-Step and take smaller steps. Without stopping, change the music to Polka rhythm and precede each Two-Step with a hop. If musician is available, this rhythm change can be made with music. Otherwise, cue without music until step is learned and then use Polka recording.
   b. **Double circle,** take promenade, Varsouvienne, or couple position, facing the line of direction. Polka forward with partner.
   c. Use a simple dance to practice Polka step. For example: Jessie Polka, p. 115.
3. **Slide approach**
   a. **Single circle,** all facing center, hands joined.
      1) Take eight slides to the left and eight slides to the right. Take four slides to the left and four slides to the right. Take two slides to the left and two slides to the right. Repeat the last group of two slides over and over. *Emphasize that in order to change direction each time, a hop is added.* This last series of slides with the hop is a Polka step.

2) Repeat this last series of slides, moving forward toward the center of the circle and then moving backward away from the center.
b. **Double circle,** take promenade, Varsouvienne, or couple position, facing the line of direction. Polka forward with partner.
c. Use simple dance to practice Polka step. For example: Jessie Polka, p. 115; Heel and Toe Polka, p. 104.

Polka Turn Clockwise

1. Learn the basic Polka step forward.
2. Repeat the process, describing how to learn the Two-Step turn clockwise, p. 47.
   a. When a change of direction is made on the fourth slide or on the second slide, *add a hop.*
   b. When a change of direction is made on a pivot, *add a hop,* as the pivot is made.
   c. *Cue:* Slide and step hop, slide and step hop.
   d. Then put the hop first and *cue:* Hop, slide and step, hop, slide and step.
3. Practice individually and then with a partner. Dovetail feet as in two-step turn.
4. Use a simple dance to practice Polka turn. For example: Doudlebska Polka, p. 307.

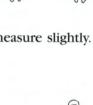

Running Waltz

Single circle, hands joined. Move one step with each beat of music. Accent first step of measure slightly.

Box Waltz and Turn

1. Learn box pattern individually.
2. Take closed dance position with partner. The man steps forward on the left and the lady backward on the right.
3. Practice turning left and right. *Cue*: Turn side close, back side close.
4. Use a dance with a box waltz to provide practice. For example: Black Hawk Waltz, p. 107.

Waltz Turn Clockwise

1. Learn step pattern, turning clockwise individually. Sometimes to establish a complete half-turn, it is helpful to travel the length of the hall and indicate one wall to be faced on the first measure and the other wall to be faced on the second measure. The dancers try harder to complete one turn and always face the correct direction.
2. Partners take closed position and practice turn together.
3. Use a simple dance with a clockwise turn. For example: Swedish Waltz, p. 251.

Pivot Turn

The continuous pivot turn, used in Folk Dance and Social Dance, is a series of steps turning clockwise as many beats as desired and to different rhythms.

1. Slow, slow, slow, slow.
2. Quick, quick, quick, quick.
3. Slow, slow, quick, quick.
4. Slow, slow, quick, quick, quick, quick.

The man should be careful that he has room to turn, as the pivot turn progresses forward in the line of direction if done properly, and he should not turn so many steps as to make his partner dizzy. The principle involved in the footwork is the dovetailing of the feet, which means that the right foot always steps between partner's feet and the left foot always steps around the outside of partner's feet.

Analysis of Pivot Turn

Take closed or shoulder-waist position. Preparation to start clockwise turn is the **preceding beat** of the pivot turn.

Rhythm Cues	Steps
Slow	**Preliminary step.** Man steps right between partner's feet, and leads into the turn by bringing his left shoulder toward his partner, increasing the body tension, shoulders become parallel and remain in that position for entire pivot.
Slow	Step left, toeing in across the line of direction and rolling clockwise, three-quarters of the way around the ball of the left foot.
Slow	Step right, between partner's feet forward in the line of direction, completing one turn.

Last two steps repeat alternately.

Lady

The lady receives the lead as the man increases body tension. She does the same. She places her right foot forward in between his feet on the line of direction, left foot across the line of direction, right foot between, left across, and so forth.

Style

The hips and legs are closer together than most steps. They both must lean away, pressing outward like "the water trying to stay in the bucket." The concept of stepping each time in relation to the line of direction is what makes it possible to progress while turning as a true pivot turn should do.

Note

1. In Scandinavian pivots, some have found it helpful to step on the right heel, transferring the weight to the sole of the foot; step left on the sole of foot, in effect pivoting on the right heel, left sole.
2. For further analysis, see Pivot Turn, Social Dance, p. 431.

Twirl

Whenever the lady is turned under her arm one or more turns (twirls), it is important for the man to hold his left hand over the apex of her head; joined hands should be loose to allow turn.

Dance Positions

1. Back Cross

2. Butterfly

3. Challenge

4. Closed

5. Conversation

6. Escort

7. Inside Hands Joined. Side by Side. Couple

8. Left Parallel. Side Car

9. Open

10. Pigeon Wing

Detailed description for each position is given in the Glossary.

Dance Positions (con't)

11. Promenade, Skaters

12. Reverse Open

13. Reverse Varsouvienne

14. Right Parallel. Swing, Banjo

15. Semiopen

16. Shoulder-Waist

17. Swing Out. Flirtation

18. Two Hands Joined. Facing

19. Varsouvienne Jody

20. Wrap

Dance Formations

The dance formations are representative of the dances in this book. There are many other variations.

1. NO PARTNERS

Single circle

Broken circle

Line, side by side

File, one behind
each other

Key:

☐   Man

○   Lady

→   Direction facing

△   Caller and/or music

Head couple is nearest to the
caller and/or music.

2. COUPLES IN A CIRCLE

Single circle, facing center

Single circle, man facing
the line of direction, lady
facing the reverse line of
direction

Double circle, couples
facing the line of direction

Double circle, partners facing,
man's back to center

3. THREE PEOPLE

Set of three in a line,
side by side

Set of three, facing
set of three

Single circle,
facing center

4. TWO COUPLES

Set of two couples,
partners facing

Sicilian circle, sets of two
couples, couples facing

5. COUPLES IN A FILE DOUBLE FILE

Longway or contra set,
couples facing head

6. COUPLES IN A LINE

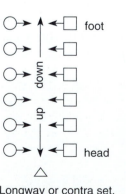

Longway or contra set,
partners facing

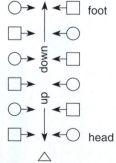

Couples 1, 3, 5 cross over
Contra Set

7. FOUR COUPLES

couple 3   foot

couple 4   couple 2   side

couple 1   head

Set of four couples

Music in Relation to Dance

One problem that plagues the dance teacher more than any other is how to teach a student to hear and move to the beat of the music. A person who cannot hear the beat and constantly fumbles with all the relationships in movement that depend on being on the beat has a psychological handicap. Perhaps there are some basic understandings that can be learned and explored.

Listen to the Beat

The underlying beat is usually carried by the string bass, the piano, and the drums. In Latin rhythms, the beat is carried by the bongo drum, the clavs (sticks), or the wood block.

The Beginner

The beginner should try to pick out a steady beat that is most dominant and synchronize his or her step with this downbeat. Quite often, people who think they have no sense of rhythm can clap a consistent pattern of beats but do not know what to listen for. If an individual can clap accurately to the basic beat and can depend on this beat to be consistent throughout a piece of music, he or she usually has the major problem solved. Regular practice moving with the beat brings confidence for dancing.

When an individual cannot clap to a regular beat and cannot hear a beat, the only way for him or her to learn is to:

1. Visually follow the clapping of the teacher or someone else in class.
2. Try to relate this with listening for the basic beat of a very obvious piece of Square Dance or march music. Mark time in place with feet and then try to walk to this beat alone.
3. Gradually progress to other music that has a less obvious beat.
4. Walk with a good partner and try to feel the relationship of the movement to the beat until the individual can move with the beat.

The melody or the vocal can be very distracting to the individual who has difficulty with rhythm, and he or she tends to speed up or slow down. The more a dancer is concentrating on a dance step pattern, style, or lead, the easier it is to forget about listening to the music. A teacher can help in this case by calling attention to listening for the music. Thorough understanding and practice of the difficult step without music also permits greater freedom to listen to the music.

The Dancer

When one has accomplished the hurdle of being able to dance to the beat of the music, the next step is to learn to listen to the rhythmic changes in the music.

1. The dancer should be able to recognize the beginning and the end of a phrase and anticipate this in his or her movement or call.
2. He or she should be able to recognize and adjust the movement to changes of tempo.
3. He or she should be able to identify the parts of a dance by the melodic changes in the music and therefore be able to make smooth transitions in movement or position.
4. He or she should be able to note the quality of the various parts of the music and be better able to interpret the appropriate style.
5. He or she should learn from experience with different types of rhythm to correctly identify one basic rhythm from another.
6. And finally, with experience, he or she should be able to interpret the music and in combining dance steps feel the relationship of the step to the music.

How to Recognize Music for Dance

Certain facts must be learned in order to recognize music for specific dances.

1. Each dance rhythm is in a definite meter. For example, the dancer learns to recognize Waltz music if he or she knows to listen to 3/4 meter with an accent on the first beat.
2. Each dance has a pattern of movement, the quality or feeling of which should identify with the quality of the music. For example, the dancer needs to know the Rumba has a smooth, rolling Latin quality; the Samba has a faster, bouncy, rocking quality; and the Mambo has an offbeat, heavy, sultry quality. By trying to recognize this quality in the music, the dancer can usually identify the appropriate music.
3. Some types of dances have particular instruments that carry the base or the melody. For example, the Latin American dances have the bongo drums, the sticks, the wood blocks, and the maracas, one or two of which carry the basic beat and another the rhythm pattern.
4. In Folk Dance, the music, the pattern of steps, and the style often relate to the meaning or the origin of the dance, and this association helps the dancer to remember and identify the music.

Rhythm Training and Appreciation

There are different approaches for understanding rhythm. The Orff-Schulwerk process is one that is meeting success. It is a sequential approach to music education that uses all the elements of music (rhythm, melody, form, timbre, and harmony) in the development of conceptual understandings. Movement is one aspect. Teachers should explore a variety of approaches to this subject.

The teacher can contribute to rhythm training and appreciation through dance by following these guidelines:

1. Be thoroughly familiar with the music used for any specific dance, in order to
   a. Give verbal cues in the correct rhythm.
   b. Give the starting cue at the appropriate time.
   c. Cue the group with regard to the length of the musical introduction before the dance begins.
2. Direct the group to clap out difficult rhythms.
3. Point out rhythmic changes in the music and allow time for listening to the transitions from one part to another.
4. Point out and allow the class to listen to particular instruments or qualities in the music that help them remember the dance.
5. Provide frequent opportunities for student identification of music rather than announcing the dance.
6. Plan the program to include interesting cultural contrasts in music and dance.
7. Use words and meanings to folk songs that accompany dance.
8. Add significant authentic sounds to the recorded music, such as:
   a. Appropriate shouts or claps.
   b. Appropriate percussion instruments, such as tambourine or drum.
   c. Appropriate words or yodeling.
9. Explain meanings of music or dance and add highlights of folklore or background information.
10. Allow sufficient practice and review of dances so that the group can know dances well.

Dance Style

The Beautiful Dancer

A beautiful dancer is one of the most satisfying sights to watch. It is really not the intricate steps or figures that are noticed, but rather the rhythmical way the dancer seems to glide around the floor. There is an alertness, a vitality, a strength, and a beauty that transmits the feeling of complete control over the entire body.

The dancer receives more pleasure by continuously striving for the special style that makes each dance—Square, Tango, Country Western, Scottish Reel—different. It is as important to execute the style and mannerisms inherent in the dance of any country as it is to be able to dance the steps and pattern sequences. If twirls, whoops, and yells are added to every dance, the dances lose their individuality and become uninteresting. Without care, a fast clogging routine blurs into the intricate Slavic Kolos.

Ear and Ankle Alignment

The subtle thought of maintaining ear and ankle alignment in an easy, natural way gives a person the poise and confidence so rightfully desired by all. The dancer who practices this secret of body balance will not tire as easily. Dancers who adopt the "ear to ankle lineup" as a slogan, whether dancing a favorite Folk Dance, in a Square Dance set, or on the ballroom floor, will have more assurance of what to do and how to do it, will wear their dress (costume) with greater charm and distinction, and will have a great deal more fun. The body carriage adds style to the dance pattern performed and gives the dancer that "finished look."

Good Posture—Key to Body Balance and Control

1. Keep yourself upright—do not lean forward or backward. Do not stick out in the rear.
2. Keep your weight up—not dragging over your feet. This cultivates that "light on your feet" feeling.
3. Keep yourself a moving weight—alert all the way through your body—not planted on every spot you take.
4. Transfer weight smoothly and evenly from foot to foot without unnecessary motion of the hips from side to side or of the body up and down.
5. Move on a narrow base with the feet and legs close together.
6. Practice walking backward—the lady must learn to keep her balance when taking long, gliding steps backward.
7. Keep your eyes off the floor and the feet.
8. Bend the ankles, the knees, and the hips when executing a dip—not the back and head. The trunk is held erect.
9. Be at ease but in complete control of all parts of the body.
10. Relax, listen to the music, and *enjoy* dancing!

Achieving Appropriate Style

One needs to make a conscious effort to develop style. Observation of dancers who have good style is a starting point; careful analysis and application must follow.

1. The expression on the dancer's face should reflect enthusiasm and a friendly, relaxed attitude. Dance with joy and pride.

2. Proper body mechanics are influenced by optimum posture. Age, body type, and personality influence the style, but still the goal is the same: smoothness, graceful carriage, and appropriate action for the dance. The position (contact) of the arms and hands for the different positions influence the style. *Resistance,* or "weight," is essential in partner dances. The tendency to stare at one's partner is uncomfortable for both, but occasional eye contact and focus toward partner or over partner's shoulder is important. Refer to dance walk, leading and following, and closed position in Chapter 8, Social Dance, for specific details as they are fundamental to style.

3. The blending of one step or figure to the next is important. The body position adjusts in preparation for a different step, figure, or direction. Smaller footsteps frequently solve some basic problems.

4. A study of different nationalities, their culture, and their way of life, all give the dancer a broader understanding of the movement itself. Consider the influence of the costumes on the dance movement. For instance, tight jeans and large silver buckles have an influence on Country Western dance style.

5. Consider the movement of a particular ethnic group and look carefully at their method of walking and their body movement. Is the upper body flexible or rigid above the waist? Basic body movements tend to reflect basic feelings and attitudes. Do they move quickly or slowly? Are they "happy go lucky," temperamental, quiet, or reserved?

Teaching Style

Some already have an innate sense of how to achieve style or have had a fair amount of dance training. Here the focus is making the dance style unique.

The average dancer has difficulty developing style and may feel that style is a nebulous thing or that the dance is for "fun" and is an end in itself.

1. The teacher must consciously incorporate the element of good style in his or her teaching, whether its's for a one-night stand, a class, or a performance.

2. The teacher, by virtue of his or her own posture, style of movement, and exemplification of different styles, sets an example—a visual one—that stimulates the dancer in an indirect way. A teacher should take every opportunity to attend workshops given by ethnic dance teachers to learn style firsthand. A live experience surpasses every written description.

3. The careful selection of music for each dance is important. A recording with native instruments, quality live music, and arrangements that are versatile and interesting all add flavor to the dance and encourage the dancer to aspire to better dancing.

4. In an atmosphere of gym shorts and tennis shoes, the teacher is challenged to promote appropriate style. All teachers know how much they may request students to bring shoes that will slide more easily and clothing that would be worn for informal dancing.

5. Special clothing frequently enhances the dance. Full skirts are very much a part of Mexican dances and Square Dances. The opanci—a soft, leather, moccasin-type shoe worn in Slavic dancing—allows for the rolling forward and backward action of the feet. This is a specific type of footwear that allows the feet to respond closely to the Slavic style. The movement pattern of the dance frequently relates to the costumes of the period and nationality.

6. The teacher should experience greater success in developing style among dancers when only a few specific suggestions are made for each dance presented.

7. The teacher should point out the exact position of hands in relation to the waist and clothing; the action of hands and arms as in the manipulation of a skirt; any unusual body position, as in arching the upper torso in a draw step; the position and interaction of the individual in relation to partner and group; the details of footwork in terms of length of step, foot mechanics, and quality of step; the amount of energy expended in a movement; and the facial expression, including the focus of the eyes and the direction of the head.

8. The teacher should invite dance studio professionals, club dancers, foreign students, or community ethnic groups to dance with the students on special occasions or show films or videotapes of special styles. A visual experience with the real flavor of a dance often encourages dancers.

9. The use of mirrors and/or videotapes gives dancers an opportunity to see themselves and study specific movements.

10. Sometimes, if the teacher actually *moves* the dancers' arms or heads in the desired pattern, a kinesthetic sense of the movement is established, which is more meaningful than a verbal or a visual explanation.

11. The discipline that results from polishing a specific dance for an audience has a carry-over value for individual dancers as, subconsciously, they tend to apply better body control, precision, focus, and projection in their future dancing. Their attitudes and emotional responses are also different. To perform for others stimulates dancers to accept the demands of repetitive practice and achieve at a higher level. Even costuming excites and brings pleasure to the dancer.

CHAPTER 4
American Heritage Dance

the square formation, to the New World. There are records of Morris and Court dances too.

Country dancing in the United States was the primary recreation for all classes. The majority of the settlers in the North were lower and middle class. In the South some had more money and also had the assistance of the slaves to work the land, which meant they had more time for amusements. During the colonial period the upper class eventually began to dance the dances of the European courts.

Dances from the European Courts to the American Ballrooms

Historians refer to the period of 1600–1700 as the Age of Enlightenment. Everything was ordered: the architecture, the nomenclature of flora and fauna by Linnaeus, the box hedges and the formal gardens, and even the dances of the courts. France was usually thought of as the base of the Enlightenment, and French was the established language of international diplomacy, culture, and polite society. In matters of dress, literature, art, architecture, and home furnishings, London set cultural models and standards that were accepted by all the colonies. The wealthy colonists sent their children "home" to England to be educated. With this cultural flow, it was natural for the latest Court dances to be very much a part of American society balls. Through mimicry, the bonded servants and slaves transplanted the court dances into their culture.

The sophisticated, polished group dances with set figures, such as the Minuet and Cotillon (sometimes referred to as the German dance), were the most popular dances at the balls before the Waltz. It was common to use the European music in the American ballroom. The *Minuet* is based on triple meter, and it appeared in many formations: two men and a lady, Longway sets (Ford 1943; p. 96), Quadrille sets (Ford 1941; p. 35), and later as a couple dance (Ford 1943; p. 112). Every action was studied. The stately, stylized posturing, promenading, deep bows, and curtseys of the Minuet are an excellent example of a dance being influenced by the dress of the day; the elaborate headdresses, the heavy panniered skirts, and the powdered wigs of

American Heritage Dances are the dances that the people—"the plain folk," "society," "young folk," "old folk," and "breadwinners"—enjoyed in the past for their own pleasure. Yesterday's Social Dances are today's Folk Dances.

Our dances come from several sources: the Country Dance tradition of England and Scotland, as evidenced by the Contra Dances; the Square and Circle Dances of New England; the Kentucky Running Sets of Appalachia; the Play Party Games; the dances of the French court; the Spanish-Mexican dances in the southwest and early California; and the syncopated rhythms of the blacks.

The dance scene in western Europe in the 1600s and 1700s was the foundation of our Social Dance tradition. English country dances were the rage in England and France. The French called them *contree-danse.** The settlers brought these dances, the progressive longways for "as many as will" and

---

Contree-danse was shortened through usage to *Contre*. *Contre* dances were square and longways. In those days a "contre dance" (country dance) could be either formation. In 1918 Elizabeth Burchenal's *American Country Dances* book reflects "twenty-eight Contra Dances," quadrille, longways, and Sicilian Circle formation. Almost all the dances were from New England and reflected the notion that the terms "country dance" and "contra dance" were synonymous. At some point "contra dance" applied only to progressive longway dances.

the women and the lace cuffs falling below the wrist and the brocade knee britches of the men reflected the style and the pattern of the Minuet. The Oxford Minuet is one of the variations of the Minuet still danced today. The *Gavotte,* closely related to the Minuet, preceded such familiar American round dances as the Badgers Gavotte and Glowworm Gavotte.

The Waltz, the Polka, and the Varsouvienne arrived on the Social Dance scene and sent couples whirling around the dance floor. The dancing master established his trade and traveled from town to town to teach the finer points of dance. Americans began to publish books such as *The Art of Dancing,* written by Edward Ferrero and published by Dick Fitzgerald in 1859.

The Unique Contributions of Afro-Americans

In the history of European dance, the Spanish-Moorish dances express African characteristics, as do the musical rhythms of tambourines, castanets, and stringed instruments. Some Catholic fiesta dances from the Middle Ages have links with Africa. Indirectly the African influence was brought to the New World by the Europeans.

As a direct influence, consider the eight million Africans who were imported as slaves during the 17th and 18th centuries. Afro-Americans in the South brought with them the most primitive instrument of all—the human body. Bare feet stomped, hands clapped, and voices sang songs, albeit aboard a slave ship, on the auction block, or on their white master's plantation. Dancing, whether by command or choice, furnished a meaningful link with the past and a temporary escape from the present.

Dancing depended on the whims of the white owners. Some encouraged dancing and even provided the fiddle, thus recognizing dance as a means of entertainment for both the Afro-Americans and their owners. A good fiddler was prized by his owner not only for his ability to play for plantation balls, but also for the higher price he brought at auction. It was common for Afro-American musicians to furnish music for dancing at the Big House, and many times they also called out the dance figures.

Whereas Europeans traditionally accent the first beat of a measure, Afro-Americans accent the second beat, the upbeat. Soon beats were skipped and the accent was placed on unexpected counts. This different accent is now labeled syncopation. As the result of an uprising in 1739, the slaves were forbidden to use drums, so they transferred their rhythm to their feet, shook tambourines (perhaps

acquired from the Spanish Creoles of the South), clacked bones (like castanets), and changed the African bonja (gourd with strings) to the banjo.

Afro-American dancing was generally of two kinds: dance movements that pantomimed animals and highly acrobatic movements that required endurance and skill. The *Pigeon Wing, Buzzard Lope,* and *Turkey Trot* mimed animal movement, and, as in the case of the Buzzard Lope, acted out the story of a buzzard seeking and finding food. The *Buck* and the *Jig* dances were of the individual acrobatic type and were the objects of dance contests sponsored by the white owners. The *Cake Walk,* although used in contests, was mostly a festival dance common at harvest or crop-over times. Many of the dances were done with a container of water placed on the head—a continuation of the African custom of carrying burdens in this manner.

The house servants were the link between the Big House and the field hands in matters of manners and fashions. It was through them that the field hands learned the fashionable Quadrilles, Cotillon, Reels, and Big Circles of the day. In the latter days of slavery, white influence was very apparent in black dance.

Afro-Americans enjoyed dancing on special occasions such as Christmas, corn shucking, quilting bees, weddings, and funerals, but most of all on Saturday nights. Saturday night was a celebration of the end of the work week and was looked forward to and sung about in the fields all week in anticipation. Dancing included Set Dances (Squares), Quadrilles, Jigs, cutting the Pigeon Wings, Cake Walks, and Virginia Reels.

From the days before the American Civil War came such folk dances as Juba, Ole Aunt Kate, Jimmie Rose, Brother Eprum, Got Corn, and Gone On. Juba was quite famous in Georgia and the Carolinas. It was considered a simplified version of the African *Giouba.* The *Shout* and *Ring Shout* were sacred dances that remained on the plantations and in the Protestant churches. Shuffling, clapping, and singing in a ring that circled around and around was a way of retaining some vestige of their African heritage.

New dances continue to appear from the Afro-American culture's never-ending creativity. Afro-Americans have made a major contribution to American music and dance.

The Spanish-Mexican Influence

The explorers and colonizers from Spain came across the Caribbean to Mexico and Central and South America and eventually to the American Southwest and California. Although they tried to colonize New Mexico during the 1500s, the Spanish rule and culture were not established there until 1692. The New Mexican colonial dances, Spanish in origin, also reflect the influence of the native Pueblo Indians of the area. Although both the Spanish and English claimed California, the first settlement, in San Diego in 1769, was Spanish and the Franciscan fathers soon began to establish some 21 missions along the coast.

Two types of Spanish dance were brought to America: the classical dance by the Spanish artists who set up schools in the East and the dances of the people brought along by the colonists, which were later influenced by the native Mexicans. The second type is seen mostly in the Southwest and California. The early isolation of the territories resulted in the dances becoming well established, thus retaining their European characteristics. The music and dance forms were the social dances of the settlers during this era. El Jarabe, El Fandango, La Bamba, and the Minuet were some of the oldest dances. Song games such as El Burro and El Caballo, and the Fandangos, Bailes, and Fiestas were all a part of this early tradition.

Dances of the People

It is important to remember that the social dances traveled from the court to the middle-class drawing-room to the dance hall just as the dances of the common people moved upward to elite society. This phenomenon occurred in the 1600s just as it does today, the dances taking on the flavor of local traditions and the manners of a given lifestyle.

Square Dances

The American Square Dance is truly a product of American culture, although it originated with the Quadrilles of the French court and the Country Dances of England and Scotland. The prompter became the caller who cued the dancers and established the rhythm of the dance with a running pattern of rhymes along with figure commands. Refer to Chapter 5, Square Dance, History, for further elaboration.

Play Party Games

Play Party Games, sometimes referred to as Folk Games, are actually dances. They were developed mostly by the early settlers in Tennessee, Kentucky, West Virginia, and Ohio, and traveled westward with the pioneers. The dancers made their own music by singing the verses and the people on the sidelines joined in the song, clapping their hands and stamping their feet to add to the jollity of the occasion.

American Play Party Games were definitely courtship dances that were eagerly endorsed by the young people. Although many religious groups opposed dancing and thought the fiddle was an instrument of the devil, Play Party Games (as opposed to the Hoedowns*) were approved by the elders, because even they remembered playing the same games when they were courting. The simplicity, the social interchange, and the opportunity for young people to "kick up their heels" all contributed to the spread of Play Party Games, particularly in rural America where people had to rely on their own resourcefulness for their amusements.

The songs and figures of many Play Party Games came originally from Scotland, England, Ireland, and Germany, where they were among the customs and the traditions that the early settlers brought with them from the Old Country.** Similar types of dances, such as Old Dan Tucker, Paw Paw Patch, Bingo, Yankee Doodle, and Shoo Fly, are as American as apple pie. They were passed from one generation to the next by word of mouth, and, of course, many versions of a song or a dance appeared for the same tune. Today, many of these same Play Party Games are kept alive as children's dances in elementary schools or by fun-loving recreational leaders who incorporate them into one-night stands and parties for young people, suggesting some of the charm and dramatics that accompany the dance. With this spirit, modern dancers enjoy them just as much as the pioneers did.

Round and Novelty Dances

The American dancing public quickly adopted the Waltz, the Polka, the Schottische, and the Varsouvienne as their favorites. From these couple dances, the popular round dance movement was born. Newly arranged dances done to popular tunes based on basic steps appeared regularly. After World War II, this practice mushroomed. A similar situation occurred in the 1600s: when John Playford's *English Dancing Master* first appeared, it contained 104 dances; 17 editions later, 918 dances were included. With the mass of newly composed American Round Dances, the prompter has again appeared on the scene to cue the dancers through the

---

*Although *Hoedown* is a dance step (see Kentucky Running Set, p. 76), the term eventually was used to refer to rural dancing with instrumental music, usually fiddlers.
**For example: "Ach Ja," Germany; "Ja Saa," Norway; "A Hunting We Will Go," England; "Pop Goes the Weasel," England.

sequence. The old favorites persist and are referred to as old-time dances or pattern dances. The newly composed ones are here today, gone tomorrow.

Nonpartner dances like Ten Pretty Girls have mushroomed since World War II, and even more so in the '80s and '90s. Today the trend for set patterns to peppy tunes like Twelve Street Rag, or dances like Amos Moses, the Hustle, and Achy Breaky all become a part of the scene.

Contra Dances

The English Longway Dances, Irish Cross-Road Dances, and Scottish Reels are the backbone of American Contra dancing. Contra dancing was best known in New England. It is currently enjoying a surge of popularity all over the United States and the world. The late Ralph Page, dean of American Contra Dancing, wrote eloquently about its history in Chapter 6, Contra Dance.

Appalachian Clog Dances

The popularity of the *Appalachian Clog Dance* has continued to grow throughout the United States since the mid-1960s. Clogging is believed to have originated in the Appalachian Mountains. There are three styles of clogging: freestyle clogging (which evolved from buck dancing), square dance clogging, and precision clogging. Refer to History of Clogging on page 82.

Cajun Dance

Cajun dance is an excellent example of a dance tradition whose roots go back to France. In 1604 the French colony of Acadie was established in Nova Scotia. Eventually the colonists were deported and a large number migrated to Louisiana. Cajun music and dance is a live tradition that has evolved from contact with the French, Spanish, English, black Creoles, East Texans, even rock and roll. Only a few dances remain, but they are very popular. Refer to Cajun Dance, page 112.

Music

The tunes for dance came from the Old World, dance patterns blending with the new environment, variants and new dances arising with westward expansion, and transmission from generation to generation. The Ballroom Dances used the European melodies. Eventually, new tunes were created for dance.

The violin (fiddle) has long been the traditional instrument for dance accompaniment. In New England the transverse or German flute was also used along with the violin in the late 18th century. The banjo, the guitar, the bass, and the harmonica are frequently parts of the musical group. Different sections of the country favored special instruments, usually developed from the settlers' own creativity, for they were long accustomed to "makin' out" with whatever they had and using substitutes. The mountain folk of Appalachia made a cornstock fiddle for their children; a long-necked gourd became a "banjer"; the mouth harp, a small whistle imitating a recorder; and the dulcimer. But the fiddle was their favorite. In the absence of musicians, the hand clapping and feet stomping of spectators and/or the patter rhymes of the caller established a rhythm and excitement for square dancers. Play Party Games illustrate a group of courting dances that move to the joyous singing of the dancers. Military brass bands were popular in America in the mid-1800s for fancy balls, but for the parlor or drawing-room a piano or a violin alone was preferred. A combination of two violins, flute, clarinet, cornet, and bass was used, however, in larger rooms.

One way or another, if the people wanted to dance, they made their own music even when a musician was not present. Although live music is always vibrant and stimulating, the record player and tape recorder make it possible for more people to dance to good authentic recordings. True music for recreational Folk Dancing is growing.

Dress

The clothing that a particular class of people wore during a particular era is the cue to what they wore for dancing. The lower classes and the working classes have traditionally worn garments that fit more loosely and allow greater freedom of movement. The construction and the material of shoes determined the action of the feet (for example, the boots of a cowboy). Fancy ball gowns represent just one class of American society. Wigs and panniers were worn in colonial times, hoops in antebellum and Civil War times, and bustles in the 1870s and 1880s. The garments definitely restricted the movement of the dancers. Probably one of the greatest changes in style for women occurred when Irene Castle wore clothing of lightweight material and full skirts, thus setting a casual style.

Almost anything goes as long as the dancer is comfortable. Whether the lady wears a dress, slacks,

Levi's, or shorts, she is more concerned about dancing for fun and is likely to wear what her peers do. But, without a doubt, the graceful movement of a full skirt enhances many a dance.

A Social Occasion

Dancing is a social occasion. It is a time to visit, to greet, to meet new people, to court, and to celebrate. Whenever people gathered together for barn raisings or quilting parties, the dancing began when the work was accomplished. Different parts of the country had their traditions, but, from the beginning, pushing back the furniture in the kitchen (New England) or dancing on the porch (Appalachia) was a common practice. Eventually, the school house, the Grange, the barn and, in the warmer climates of California and the Southwest, the courtyards, allowed for more couples on the floor. To be sure, the upper level of society had their ballrooms and others had their dancehalls and saloons. But, for a large segment of America, dancing was a family affair. The stories of bundling children down at Square Dances on the frontier are common. With the advent of night clubs, children were no longer part of the adult dance scene. Granges, community clubs, some churches, and some ethnic groups sponsor dances where children are welcome.

Although the dancing masters helped to establish the etiquette of the period for the upper class, the plain folk were also concerned with courtesy in dance. It is interesting to note the presence of the "address, honor, and salute" in the dances of the court (Minuet, Lancers, Quadrilles) and the absence of them in the Kentucky Running Set and Play Party Games. "Honor your partner" is part of the Square Dance tradition; yet it is absent in the Big Circle, Contra, and Sicilian Circle.

The social dances of a particular era reflect the social customs of that era. At Contra Dances in the 1990s the practice of changing partners after each Contra leads to a scramble for the next partner of choice, leaving the last partner in the middle of the floor; either person may ask another for the next dance. From the disco period, two or more people of the same sex might dance together or even one dance alone. Country Western dancers follow the older tradition of always escorting their partner back to the side.

The social dances are a vital part of the school recreational program. More churches today incorporate dancing activities into their recreational programs. And dance clubs and dancehalls specialize in different kinds of social dance.

Revival of Folk Traditions

Prior to the First World War, folk traditions began to be revived. Folk dance was introduced in public schools and was encouraged by the efforts of Henry Ford and the activities of the WPA during the Depression. After the World War II another surge of interest came, particularly in square dancing. Ballroom dancing has returned, especially Swing. In the '90s Contra and Country Western are extremely popular.

Country dancing is a term that has returned to common usage. The cornerstone to the revival of old-time country dancing is live music. Contras and Squares dominate the program with a few Round Dances, ranging from a Waltz to a lively Polka, or Mixers sprinkled in. Because dancing is definitely a social occasion, dancers change partners after every Contra or after two Squares. The dancers enjoy variety but do not care to remember sequences from one week to the next. The caller gives a quick walk-thru and away they go.

More opportunities for the family to dance together are created. Dance programs and family camps consider the range of abilities. Adults who have had their children later like having the family dance together. More dances are scheduled for seniors. They enjoy the dances of the '40s and also pattern dances.

The Melting Pot versus Ethnic Identity

The colonists, the immigrants, the explorers, the slaves—each brought their culture and their dance with them, blending their ways with the New World as they established roots. Many were anxious to lose their old-world identity and their old languages and traditions and take on the new ways quickly. Yet others clung together, still holding fast to their traditions and continuing to pass these down to their children even while they learned the American way of life. The Greek and Yugoslavian communities illustrate this point well, particularly at their weddings and baptisms.

The concept of the melting pot dominated American thinking until around 1940. Then interest in ethnic identity, particularly among the minorities, began to grow. Native Americans, Hispanics, and Afro-Americans have received in recent years considerable federal assistance to reinforce their ethnic heritages. As a result, other ethnic groups have found a rekindled interest in keeping their traditions alive and meaningful, including music, dance, dress, and art.

All Americans have benefited from this movement. Each group has greater pride and all Americans have gained a greater understanding and appreciation for the contributions that each group has made to society.

Conclusion

The heritage of the dances of the American people was presented to illustrate the cultural patterns, beginning in 1620 and continuing to the present. The dances that have been included in this chapter are viable in that they trace a dance tradition, are still danced today in the communities (in schools, recreational groups, and dancehalls), and represent various dance formations and basic dance steps. At different times in history, each type has enjoyed great popularity in a particular area and with a special segment of society.

This chapter also includes contemporary folk dances, recently composed. Some follow a pattern from long ago; many are composed to popular tunes; some are line dances, which not only accommodates situations where there is an unequal number of men and women, but allows for individuals "to do their own thing"; and many are mixer-type dances, which allows for changing partners. In the past many of these dances would be considered "ice breakers." Most of these dances are *pattern dances,* set sequences (the exceptions would be the waltz, polka, schottische, and two-steps) and therefore are placed in the folk dance section as opposed to the Social Dance chapter.

The diversity of American traditional folk dance continues to flourish as a means of understanding our heterogenous heritage. And it allows for countless opportunities of social exchange and recreation. Yes, American dance is alive and doing well!

Teaching Suggestions

Various Approaches

1. **American heritage dances:** The American Heritage Dances include examples of the following: Quadrille, Lancer, Square Dance, Contra, Running Set, Play Party Games, Round Dances, and Mixers. A sampling of these types reinforces the history of our dance.
2. **Basic steps and formations:** Select dances that include walk, Schottische, Two-Step, Polka, Waltz, Mazurka, as well as nonpartner, couples, Square, set of three, Longway, and Circle with sets of two couples.
3. **Old-time dances, novelty dances, mixers.**
4. **Exhibition dances:** Prepare for a program and/or incorporate customs, dances, and costumes with a theme illustrating an American tradition, such as a kitchen junket, fiesta, quilting bee, or barn raising.
5. **Party time or special fun dance:** Plan a class period or a special event to dance the favorites of the group with a theme, a few traditions, maybe a game, a song, or a skit. Encourage dancers to dress specially for the event, and plan refreshments to relate to the era or the theme.
6. **Local community identity:** Relate choice of material to local community, particularly local ethnic groups, and invite local citizens to share their talents with the group.
7. **Related curriculum:** Wherever possible, relate American dances to other subjects in the school curriculum or to local events.

❧ Grand March

Let the dance begin! The *Grand March* has long been a part of American dance tradition. At ceremonial occasions and balls, the instrumental groups would play a short concert prior to the dancing. Then the floor managers of the ball would signal for the dance to begin: The instrumentalists would play a march and the couples would begin a grand promenade around the room for the Grand March. Today, for special occasions, dance festivals, and one-night stand dance parties, the Grand March is part of the program. It may not be first but perhaps after the intermission. Dancers look forward to that moment of everyone dancing together, winding in and out from one pattern to the next.

The Grand March may be used as an end in itself, since it is impressive and stimulates group feeling, or it may be used as a means for organizing a group quickly for another activity. A Grand March is most effective when many people participate. Since guests do not always arrive punctually, this fact should always be considered in scheduling a Grand March.

Music: Any lively March, Two-Step, or Square Dance tune.

Position: Escort.

Formation: Double circle, couples facing the line of direction, or two single files, men in one and ladies in the other.

■ Directions for the Grand March

Leadership

The leader stands at either the front or the rear of the room. A change in pattern is indicated as the group nears the leader. It is helpful if the first two or three couples are familiar with the various figures to be used in the Grand March. Experienced couples will follow the leader's cues more easily and set the pattern for the others to follow. An assistant standing at the opposite end from the leader facilitates the flow.

Beginning

A Grand March may be started either in couples or from two single files of individuals. The latter is particularly suited for groups not already acquainted.

1. **Two single files:** Men line up on one side of the room and ladies on the other. Both files face either the front or the rear of the room as indicated by the leader. **Note:** The leader must be careful to indicate the proper direction for the two files to face so that the ladies will be on the right side of the men when couples are formed. Each line marches toward the end of the room, turns, and marches toward the opposite line. The files meet, forming couples in escort position, ladies to the right of the men, and march down the center of the room.
2. **Couples in a double circle:** Couples in escort position form a double circle and march counterclockwise. One couple is selected as the leader and that couple, followed by the others, moves down the center of the room.

Figures

These figures may be used in any order as long as they flow from one to the other.

1. **Single files**
   A. **Inner and outer circle.** When each couple reaches the front of the room, partners separate, men left and ladies right, and travel down the side of the room until they meet at the opposite end. Then the lines pass each other. The ladies travel on the inside, men on the outside, and down the side of the room until they meet again at the front of the room. They pass again, the men traveling on the inside, ladies on the outside, and down the sides of the room.

Grand March (continued)

B. **The Cross (X).** When each file reaches the rear corner, the leader of each file makes an abrupt turn and travels diagonally toward the front corner on the opposite side. Both files cross in the center of the room, lady crossing in front of partner. The files travel down the side of the room toward the rear corners. The diagonal cross is repeated, the man crossing in front of his partner.

C. **Virginia Reel.** Couples move down the center in double file. When each couple reaches the front of the room, partners separate, men left, ladies right, and travel down the sides of the room to form two files about 10 to 15 feet apart. Both lines face each other. The head lady and the foot man meet in the middle and dance away. Then the head man and foot lady meet in the middle in like manner and dance away. This process is repeated until all have partners and are dancing.

2. **Couples**

A. **Four, eight, or sixteen abreast.** When the couples marching down the center arrive at the front of the room, the lead couple turns to the right, marches to the side of the room, and back toward the rear of the room. The second couple turns left, the third right, and so on, and march to the side and back to the rear of the room. When they meet at the rear of the room, the two approaching couples march down the center of the room together, thus forming a group of four abreast. At the front of the room each group of four marches alternately to the right and left, down the sides and at the rear of the room they form a line eight abreast. The same procedure is followed to form lines of 16 or more abreast. After the group has formed lines of 16 abreast they may be instructed to mark time in place.

B. **"Ring up" for squares.** If groups of eight are desired for the next activity, for example, a Square Dance, the couples mark time when they are eight abreast. Each line of eight then "rings up," or makes a circle.

C. **Over and under.** When the couples are four abreast, the two couples separate at the front of the room, one turning right, the other left. When the couples meet at the rear of the room, the first couple of the double file on the right side of the room makes an arch. The first couple of the other double file goes under the arch and quickly makes an arch for the second couple they meet. All couples in both double files are alternately making an arch or traveling under an arch.

D. **Snake out.** When the couples are 8 or 16 abreast, the person on the right end of the front line leads that line in single file to the right of the column of dancers and in between lines two and three. As the person on the left end of the first line passes the person on the right end of the second line, they join hands and line two then follows line one. The leader then leads the line between lines three and four and again as the last person in the moving line passes the right end of the third line, they join hands and line three joins with lines one and two. The moving line weaves in and out of the remaining lines and each time the person on the end of the moving line passes the right end of the next line they join hands and continue weaving in and out. After all lines have been "snaked out," the leader may lead the line in serpentine fashion around the room and eventually circles the room clockwise in a single circle, all facing the center.

E. **Danish march.** When the couples are in a double circle or double file, partners face and stand about 4 feet apart. The first couple joins hands holding arms out shoulder height and slides the length of the formation used. The second couple follows, and so on. When couples reach the end, they join the group. This may be repeated with partners standing back to back as they slide.

F. **Grand right and left.** When couples are in a single circle, partners face and start a grand right and left. This may continue until partners meet or until the leader signals for new partners to be taken for a promenade or other figure.

G. **Paul Jones.** When couples are in a single circle, any of the figures for a Paul Jones may be used. See p. 72.

Ending

There is no set ending for a Grand March. However, the ending should be definite so that there is a feeling of completion and satisfaction. It may end with people in groups for the next activity or in a circle with everyone joining in a song or dancers may swing into a Waltz, a Polka, or some other planned activity.

✣ The Loomis Lancers

The *Lancer Quadrilles* are also a part of the fabric of American dance and a part of the evolution of Square Dance as it is done today.

A variant of the Cotillon developed on the Continent and in England and became known as the Quadrille. Originally there were six figures in a Quadrille, but later it became established as five figures and even later shortened to three. One of the Quadrilles, known as "Quadrille a la Cour," became known as "Les Lanciers" in England. Lancer Quadrilles were written in America as early as 1825 (Czarnowski 1950; p. 141) and were extremely popular.

A Lancer has five parts, each danced to specific rhythms: part I, 6/8; II, 2/4; III, 6/8; IV, 6/8; V, 4/4. The figures were prompted by the caller and dance movement reflected the courtly mannerisms of the day. With live musicians, shifting rhythms and specific tunes for each of the figures was readily accomplished. With the trend toward using records, the lack of proper recordings for Lancers, as well as the length of the dance routine, undoubtedly contributed to their fading from the dance scene. The dances of the people that came with the westward expansion were more informal.

The *Loomis Lancers* was one of the most popular Lancers in New England around the turn of the century. It was named after Loomis, a dancing master who presented new Lancers regularly. The traditional music for the Loomis Lancers was "Abonnement," composed by Edward Beyer.

The dance, as presented here, was workshopped by the Lloyd Shaw Dance Fellowship in 1963 and is included with the permission of the Lloyd Shaw Foundation.* The last two figures have been combined in the Loomis Lancers.

Record: Lloyd Shaw, American Dance Treasurers 1001/1002.

Formation: Set of four couples in Quadrille (Square Dance) formation, couples numbered 1, 2, 3, 4 counterclockwise around the set.

Basics: Dance walk (all begin left foot), right-hand star, promenade, do-sa-do, ladies chain, grand square, left allemande, right allemande.

Style: "The dancing of a lancer is an exercise in courtesy."

1. **Address, honor, salute (your corner, your partner):** These are all "bows." Variations are in the timing, depending on the exact number of counts of music allowed. "Address" usually takes 8 counts; "salute" may be momentary. These bows may be done holding hands in a circle or with no hand holds.
   A. **Bow** (man's part); **slight bow:** facing lady, man bends from waist, both feet together, offering right hand, palm up. Left hand placed, palm up, at about the back left hip pocket, fingers extended; **deep bow:** facing lady, man steps back on left foot, bending left knee slightly, and extends right leg forward, pointing toe down; he offers his right hand, palm up.
   B. **Curtsey** (lady's part); **slight bow:** facing man, lady steps back on her right foot, bending right knee slightly, and extends left leg with toe pointed to floor. She places fingers of her left hand lightly in man's upturned palm. Her right arm is gracefully extended to side about waist high, palm down and fingers softly straight. Keep head erect and smile; **deep bow:** facing man, lady crosses her right foot behind left, keeping torso erect, lowers her body deeply or sits on her foot. Her left foot is extended in a point toward gentleman to match his. Or lady may cross right foot behind left and, bending both knees, lower self to semikneeling position, sitting on right heel. Free arm extended as above.
2. **Minuet position:** Man extends right arm forward about waist high or to accommodate lady, bending elbow slightly and with palm down, fingers straight. Lady places her left hand, palm down, lightly upon his, keeping her forearm close to his, with her right arm at side as in curtsey. Arms are horizontal, partners side by side. Hand hold may be reversed as in some parts of grand square; lady's right and man's left are joined.
3. **Pigeon-wing hand hold:** Man and lady, facing each other, place their forearms, held vertically, close together, the palms held together, open and upright, elbows almost touching.

The Loomis Lancers (continued)

---

*Excerpts on styling from the Loomis Lancers brochure (*The Loomis Lancers, An American Dance Treasure*. Editor: Dorothy Shaw, reprinted with the permission of the Lloyd Shaw Foundation. Style suggestions were researched by Dena M. Fresh, Mary and Fred Collette, Carlotta Hageman, and Calvin J. Campbell.

4. **Hands in general:** Never let the hands be stiff. Ladies, let the fingers hang softly, not like semaphores. Let the wrists lead and the fingers follow. Men, let the hand lie lightly on the hip pocket. And let the hands be as long as possible.

■ Directions for the Dance

Measures

Introduction (2–4 count chords): **Honor your partner. Honor your corner.**

Meter 6/8

Figure I

1–4   Pattern: **First four forward and back** (8 counts). Head couples (1 and 3), in Minuet position, take three steps forward and on fourth count man makes slight bow, ladies a little curtsey to opposite, while pointing free foot lightly forward; couples back up to place taking four steps, closing feet together on fourth count.

5–8   **First four half-promenade the inside and take the side lady to a line of three** (8 counts). As each couple backs into the opposite position, the man takes his original right-hand lady's right hand in his left (number 1 man takes number 2 lady, and so on) into a line of three. Men pass left shoulders on count 3, turn on counts 4 and 5, take corner lady and back into line of three on counts 6, 7, and 8. Action is smooth and Minuet position maintained. Inactive men now stand alone.

9–12   **Lines of three forward and back** (8 counts).

13–16   **All turn partners by the right** (8 counts). All dancers take pigeon-wing hand hold with partner, walk around and back into position.

17–20   **All chassez by corners and return** (8 counts). Sliding, men pass behind ladies to left; ladies in front of men to right (4 counts) and back to place passing the same way (4 counts).

21–24   **All turn corners with a left-hand turn** (8 counts). Use pigeon-wing hand hold.

Dance Figure I four times, head couple leading out first and third times; side couples, second and fourth times.

Meter 2/4

Figure II

1–2   Introduction (4 counts): no action.

1–4   Pattern: **All eight forward and back** (8 counts). All hands joined, moving forward, swinging hands forward and upward (4 counts) and back out, lowering hands (4 counts).

5–8   **Turn the ladies to the center and back to place** (8 counts). Couples take Minuet position. All ladies walk three steps around and into center, so they describe a half-circle, to end facing own partner, ladies back to back. Men take a quick bow, ladies a brief curtsey on fourth count. Ladies return to place, backing up (4 counts).

9–12   **Turn the gentlemen to the center and back to place** (8 counts). In same manner, men move into center (back to back), bow, and return.

13–16   **All four ladies take the gentlemen in a right-hand star** (8 counts). Maintaining Minuet hand hold, ladies move into center to form right-hand star and start to turn star clockwise. Take time to form star and spread star out as far as possible.

17–20   **And star promenade around to place** (8 counts). Continue star promenade to complete one full revolution and step back into home position.

21-24   **All turn corners by the left** (8 counts). Use pigeon-wing hand hold.

Repeat above routine as follows:

All eight forward and back (8 counts).
Turn the gentlemen to the center and back to place (8 counts).
Turn the ladies to the center and back to place (8 counts).
All four gentlemen take the ladies in a left-hand star (8 counts).
And star promenade back to place (8 counts).
And turn partners by the right (8 counts).

Repeat entire routine (96 counts) once, ending in Quadrille formation.

Meter 6/8

Figure III

1-4   Introduction (8 counts): no action.

1-4   Introduction: **Do-sa-do corners by the right shoulder** (8 counts).

5-8   **Do-sa-do partners by the left shoulder** (8 counts).

1-4   Pattern: **All hands joined, go forward, salute, and back** (8 counts). All hands joined, move forward three steps, pointing right foot with a bow (curtsey) on the held note on fourth count. Take three steps backward, closing right foot to left on fourth count.

5-8   **All circle to the right, salute, and circle back** (8 counts). All hands joined, walk three steps in line of direction, point right foot forward in line, making a bow on the held note on fourth count. Ladies look back over their shoulder at their partner as man bows. Walk four steps clockwise, back to place.

9-16   **Four ladies chain across and chain back** (16 counts). All four ladies form a right-hand star and cross to opposite man, to a position on the right of opposite man, and turn right face into place beside him. No courtesy turn, only a momentary hand hold in Minuet position with a brief bow on eighth count. Ladies form a right-hand star again and continue action, returning to place.

17-20   **All hands joined, go forward, salute, and back** (8 counts).

21-24   **All circle to the right, salute, and circle back** (8 counts).

25-32   **Four men chain across and chain back** (16 counts). All four men star right across set, turn left face into place beside opposite lady. Repeat action, returning to place.

Repeat entire routine of pattern, measures 1-32.

Meter 4/4

Figure IV

1-2   Introduction (8 counts): no action.

1-4   Pattern: **First four leading grand square** (16 counts). When couples are side by side, take Minuet position, moving forward or backing away.

5-8   **Reverse** (16 counts).

9-10   **First couple faces out, other couples form column** (8 counts). During first four counts, first couple turns in place in a small semi-circle to face out (head of hall). During second four counts, side couples fall into a column behind first couple, second couple ahead of fourth, third remaining in place.

The Loomis Lancers (continued)

11-12　**All chassez, and turn to face** (8 counts). Ladies moving left in front of partners, men right, take three slides and step touch (4 counts) and slide back to place (4 counts), turning at end to face partners in Contra formation (ladies on prompter's left) and instantly wheel into position with two head men (1 and 2) facing two foot ladies (3 and 4) diagonally across set and two head ladies (1 and 2) facing two foot men (3 and 4).

13-16　**Arch and under across the set, and return** (16 counts). Men holding inside hands **high** make an arch and ladies take promenade position (traditionally left joined hands on top for Lancers). Head men and foot ladies cross the set diagonally, ladies passing under arch (4 counts). On fourth count each two turn toward each other (ladies **do not let go of hand position,** men change to hold new inside hands). Head two ladies and two foot men repeat above action (4 counts). Head two men and two foot ladies return to place (4 counts). Head two ladies and two foot men return to place (4 counts). Men must hold arch high enough so ladies may pass under without bending.

17-18　**Lines of four go forward and back** (8 counts). Four ladies and four men join hands in their line, move forward toward each other four steps, with a slight bow (curtsey) on fourth count; take four steps backward.

19-20　**All turn partners to place** (8 counts). All four couples make a two-hand turn back to original positions in set. Each man must end up with his lady on his right. Second and fourth couples need to practice to move home smoothly without interfering with each other. Use all eight counts to complete the maneuver.

21-22　**Left allemande corners** (8 counts). Pigeon-wing hand hold.

23-24　**Right allemande partners** (8 counts). Pigeon-wing hand hold.

Repeat entire routine four times as follows:

First time: As described.
Second time: Side couples start grand square moving to center, head couples separating and reverse. Measures 9-10, second couple faces out, first couple falls behind second couple, third couple behind first, and fourth couple remains in place.
Third time: Grand square and reverse as described. Measures 9-10, third couple faces out, fourth couple falls behind third couple, second couple behind fourth, and first couple remains in place.
Fourth time: Repeat grand square and reverse as second time. Fourth couple faces out, third couple falls in behind fourth, first behind third, and second remains in place.

Ending

Partners bow, and men escort partners off the floor.

🎶 Virginia Reel

The *Virginia Reel,* known as Sir Roger de Coverley in England, was first published about 1685. This was one of many dances the colonists brought to America, and the name eventually changed to Virginia Reel. It was danced in the ballrooms as well as on the village greens, by all. The Virginia Reel is a Contra Dance that children today learn in school and fondly remember as part of their American heritage of dance. Adults enjoy the dance at one-night stands and family gatherings.

Virginia Reel is a traditional Contra. It is a longways dance and there is progression (the head couple moves to the foot at the end of the dance). The directions presented are for one of the common ways that recreational groups dance the Virginia Reel today because everyone is dancing most of the time.

Records: "Irish Washerwoman" or any good Hoedown. DC 162303; EZ 706, 728; FD LP 3; Grenn 16016; High/Scope RM3; Mac 7345; MAV Album 3; MH 74; WT 10023.

Cassettes: DC 162303, 487; MH C74; High/Scope RM3.

Music: Irish Jig tune such as "Irish Washerwoman."

Meter: 6/8

Formation: Contra Dance formation. Four to eight couples, partners facing.

◼ Directions for the Dance

A1   **Forward and bow** (8 counts). Lines walk forward, curtsey and bow to partners and walk backward to place.

       Forward and right hand 'round (8 counts). Lines walk forward, partners join right hands, turn clockwise once around, and move backward to place.

A2   **Forward and left hand 'round** (8 counts). Lines walk forward, partners join left hands, turn counterclockwise once around, and move backward to place.

       Forward and two hands 'round (8 counts). Lines walk forward, partners join two hands, turn clockwise once around, and move backward to place.

B1   **Forward and do-si-do** (8 counts). Lines walk forward, partners do-si-do, and move backward to place.

       Head couple sashays down the center and back (8 counts).

B2   **Head couple, right arm to partner and reels** (sequences of 8 counts). To reel, partners hook right elbows in middle of set and turn clockwise once and a half, separate; head man turns next lady counterclockwise in line, with left elbows hooked once around as head lady turns next man in line with left elbows hooked once around; head couple meets in middle of set, partners hook right elbows, turn clockwise once around. Head couple moves down set turning alternately next person in line with left elbow and then each other with right elbow, until they reach foot of set.

       Head couple sashays back. Partners turn each other a half-turn (now on original side), join two hands, slide to head of set.

       Head couple casts off, forms an arch. Partners separate and walk down outside of set, man left, lady right, to foot of set. Each person in line follows the head person, single-file. Head couple join two hands to form an arch at foot of set.

       Pass thru and form your sets. Partners join inside hands as they go thru arch and promenade to head of set. Head couple is now at foot; original second couple is now head couple.

Continue to repeat dance until couples are back to original positions. Wait for the beginning of a new phrase to repeat the dance.

Note

Although most figures are based on 8 counts, the number of couples in a set influences the length of the music for one complete round of the dance.

Grand Square Quadrille

The Quadrilles originated in the French court ballet, became established in the British Isles, and were very popular among the colonists in America. Quadrilles are still danced today, particularly in New England. The Quadrille originally had six parts (Czarnowski 1950; p. 141), but later was shortened to five parts. A different piece of music is played for each figure, with a pause between figures for the dancers to catch their breath and an introduction of music before each figure. Eventually the Quadrille was reduced to three parts. The numbering of couples differs from Square Dances in that the head couples are 1 and 2, side couples, 3 and 4. Quadrilles are traditionally **prompted;** that is, the caller gives the name of the figure.

Grand Square Quadrille is still danced today, particularly in New England. This version is based on a call by Bob Osgood of Sets In Order American Square Dance Society. Although the call **grand square** is known today by square dancers as one of the basics and is used as a break in Square Dance, the figure as such was part of many of the Lancers, namely the fourth figure (Czarnowski 1950; p. 145).

Records: Any march music may be used. Suggested records: Folkraft 102; EZ 717, 730; LS E-34; E 34.

Formation: Set of four couples in Square Dance formation. Couples are numbered as in square dancing today.

■ Directions for the Dance

Meter 4/4

Measures

1–2	Introduction (8 counts): no action.
1–4	**Grand Square** (16 counts). See Square Dance section, grand square, p. 152 for directions.
5–8	**Reverse grand square** (16 counts).
	Figure I
9–12	**Head couples right and left thru and back** (16 counts).
13–16	**Side couples right and left thru and back** (16 counts).
9–12	**Head couples to the right, right and left thru and back** (16 counts).
13–16	**Side couples to the right, right and left thru and back** (16 counts).

Chorus

1-4   **Grand square** (16 counts).

5-8   **Reverse grand square** (16 counts).

Figure II

9-12   **Head ladies chain over and back** (16 counts).

13-16   **Side ladies chain over and back** (16 counts).

9-12   **Head ladies to the right, chain over and back** (16 counts).

13-16   **Side ladies to the right, chain over and back** (16 counts).

Chorus

1-4   **Grand square** (16 counts).

5-8   **Reverse grand square** (16 counts).

Figure III

9-12   **Head couples half-promenade and right and left home** (16 counts).

13-16   **Side couples half-promenade and right and left home** (16 counts).

9-12   **Head couples half-promenade right and right and left home** (16 counts). Couples 1 and 2 (couples 3 and 4) half-promenade with each other and right and left home.

13-16   **Side couples half-promenade right and right and left home** (16 counts). Couples 2 and 3 (couples 4 and 1) half-promenade with each other and right and left home.

Chorus

1-4   **Grand square** (16 counts).

5-8   **Reverse grand square** (16 counts).

Notes

1. The caller prompts by giving the directions for the next maneuver on the last two to four counts of the preceding eight-count phrase.
2. Dancers dance to the music, using the exact number of beats to execute each maneuver, with action flowing from one pattern to the next.

✍ Paul Jones Your Lady

During the 19th century, the group dances with set figures, like the Quadrille, the Lancers, and the *Paul Jones,* allowed for the interchange of partners. Paul Jones, formerly danced in the ballroom and frequently used as the first dance at a party, is still danced today as a lively mixer. In some parts of the West, the same dance is called *Circle Two-Step* or *Brownee.*

Music: Any lively two-step.

Position: Promenade.

Formation: Double circle, couples facing line of direction.

Steps: Shuffle, Two-Step.

■ Directions for the Mixer

The leader calls out each figure and signals clearly. Each figure is danced briefly as it is merely a method of changing partners.

I. Paul Jones Your Lady or Promenade
Couples promenade around room in one large circle.

II. Figures
A. **Single circle.** Couples form a single circle, hands joined. Slide left, right, and/or shuffle to center and back. Each man takes his corner lady for a new partner.

B. **The basket.** Ladies form an inner circle, hands joined and slide left. Men form an outer circle, hands joined, and slide right. Both circles stop. Men raise joined hands. Ladies move backward through arches made by men and stand beside a man. Men lower arms. Everyone slides left, then right. Each man takes lady on right for a new partner.

C. **Across the circle.** Couples form a single circle, hands joined. Slide left, right, and shuffle to center, back, and center. Each man takes lady across the circle as a new partner.

D. **Grand right and left.** Couples form a single circle, hands joined. Slide left, right, and shuffle to center and back. Face partner and grand right and left around the circle. Each man takes lady facing him or lady whose hand he holds when leader signals for new partners.

E. **Gentlemen kneel.** Couples form single circle and face partners. Men kneel, ladies move in reverse line of direction, weaving in and out between kneeling men. Each man takes lady facing him when leader signals for new partners.

F. **Count off.** Double circle, couples facing counterclockwise. Ladies stand still and men move forward, counting off as many ladies as indicated by leader. Men may stand still while ladies move forward and count off in like manner.

III. Two-Step
Couples in closed position, Two-Step about the room. Upon signal "Paul Jones Your Lady," they again fall into a double circle and promenade counterclockwise around room until the signal for a new figure action is given.

🌿 Ninepin Reel

Ninepin Reel is danced traditionally in America and England and was formerly known in Scotland. There are variations of figures but all have the common figure of five men circling in the center of the square and suddenly a break occurs; all choose a new partner; obviously, one is not able to claim a partner, and thus there's a new "ninepin." Some American versions have a caller who calls various Square Dance figures and when the call "ninepin" occurs, each man changes partners and once again there is a new "ninepin."

Elizabeth Burchenal in *American Country Dance* (1918; pp. 61–62) has recorded two Quadrille dances from New England with an extra man in the center: John Brown and Old Dan Tucker. There are dances for nine in Scotland, England, America, Germany, Sweden, and Finland with different names and many variations, from simple musical game types to very complicated figures.

This particular version was presented to Skandia Folkdance Society about 1952 by a Canadian couple attending summer school in Seattle, Washington. The pattern is similar to the English dance, Cumberland Square Eight.

Records: Any reel music. E2 5008.

Formation: Set of four couples in Square Dance formation. Extra man or lady stands in middle of set and is referred to as "ninepin." In this case, directions assume "ninepin" is a man. If more than one set, arrange sets in file and line formation.

Steps: Slide, buzz step, Polka, shuffle.

■ Directions for the Dance

Meter 2/4 • Directions are the same for both lady and man, except when specially noted.

Measures

Figure I. Slides

1–4   In closed position, head couples take eight slides (man beginning left, lady right) across set, exchanging places. Couples pass to the **right** of the "ninepin." If more than one set, couples may travel through other sets in a straight line, always passing to the right of "ninepin." Couples **do not** turn at end of eight slides.

5–8   Head couples take eight slides (man beginning right, lady left) to return home, passing to **left** of "ninepin" (ladies' backs to "ninepin").

9–16   Side couples repeat action of measures 1–8.

Figure II. Circle left and right

17–24   Head couples join hands in circle ("ninepin" in middle) and circle left, taking eight slides or four Polka steps; circle right, taking eight slides or four Polka steps.

25–32   Side couples repeat action of Figure II, measures 17–24.

Figure III. Swing

1–16   "Ninepin" swings (waist swing, buzz step) lady of couple 1 (8-count swing). While "ninepin" swings, displaced partner moves to center of set and waits for each displaced partner to join him. At completion of swing, lady returns home; "ninepin" travels around set to each couple (2, 3, 4), swinging each lady and each displaced partner moves to center; ladies remain in home position.

Figure IV. Circle

16–23   At conclusion of last swing, "ninepin" travels to center to join the four men. All men join hands, circle left and right, taking Polka steps or slides. **At any point, "ninepin," as he takes lady of his choice, calls "break."** Other men hurry to take new partner. Everyone swings to completion of musical phrase. Obviously, there is a new "ninepin." Couples take home position of lady to swing and to repeat dance.

Ninepin Reel (continued)

Figure V. Swing

24–32   All couples swing (see note 3).

Notes

1. Ninepin Reel is obviously a rollicking, fun-loving mixer that absorbs extra people. Remember the "ninepin" can be a man or a lady and each set can differ.
2. Everyone enjoys sliding (galloping) through more than one set, sometimes the length of the hall. Dance etiquette implies that one couple does not pass a preceding couple while galloping.
3. In Figures IV and V, if the "ninepin" is a real "swinger," he might call "break" after a couple measures of circling; whereupon there is a longer swing. On the other hand, the "ninepin" may prefer to complete the circling figure and call "break" at measure 24. The element of suspense created by the "ninepin" deliberately waiting until the last minute to indicate his choice of partner adds to the spirit of the dance.
4. Extra dancers on the sideline have been known to cut in when the "ninepin" calls "break," by casually waiting behind a couple. Someone from the original set must retreat to the sidelines or cut in on someone else at the earliest opportunity.

🌀 Portland Fancy 🌾

Portland Fancy is a traditional Contra.

Records: "Portland Fancy," Folkraft 1131, 1243; EZ 4004, 5003; Fretless FR203; or similar Jig.

Cassette: New England Chestnuts ACL 203/4.

Music: "Portland Fancy," Ford, Henry, *Good Morning,* 4th edition, p. 52; "Portland Fancy" and "Blackberry Quadrille," Page, Ralph, *An Elegant Collection of Contras and Squares,* pp. 78, 79.

Formation: Sets of four couples, Contra formation, two couples facing two couples. Sets may be in a circle.

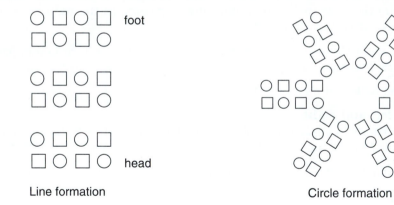

Line formation   Circle formation

■ Directions for the Dance

A1   **Circle left eight hands around** (16 counts).

A2   **Right and left thru, right and left back** (16 counts). Opposite couples, right and left.

B1   **Ladies chain over and back** (16 counts).

B2   **Forward and back** (8 counts). Join hands in line, take four steps forward and four steps back.

      Forward again and pass thru and face a new foursome (8 counts).

Variation

Pass thru two groups and face a new foursome.

Lovely Lane Chain*

Lovely Lane Chain was composed by Bob Dalsemer for the wedding of Bruce and Susan Edwards, April 30, 1983 at the Lovely Lane United Methodist Church in Baltimore, home of weekly contra dancing for nearly twenty years. Lovely Lane Church, founded in 1784, was the first Methodist congregation in the United States; the current church was built in 1884 for the 100th anniversary of the congregation.

Lovely Lane Chain was inspired by a 19th century country dance called variously La Tempête, The Tempest, and Tom Pate that has survived in several folk forms.

Lovely Lane Chain is a Progressive Dance with minor sets of four couples.

Record: "Beaumont Rag," McLain Family Band, The McLain Family Band, Country Dance Album CLR 16L.

Cassette: "Beaumont Rag," McLain Family Band, The McLain Family Band, Country Dance Album CLR 16C.

Music: "Peacock Rag," Brody, David, *The Fiddler's Fakebook*, p. 215.

Formation: Double contra with minor sets, four couples, two couples facing two couples. Sets are in a line and shown by the diagram.

Line formation

■ Directions for the Dance

A1 **Opposite ladies chain, over and back, roll away with a half sashay** (16 counts). At the end of the ladies' chain, the lady turns counterclockwise once, crossing to her partner's left side. Man gives her a slight pull with his left hand.

A2 **Go forward and back** (8 counts). All join hands in the lines, go forward and back.

All do-si-do the opposite (8 counts).

B1 **Ends balance and swing the opposite, while middle four right-hand star and left-hand star back. All face your partner** (16 counts). End facing original partner.

B2 **Grand right and left around your group of eight, pass four** (10–12 counts). Right hand to partner, men travel clockwise, and ladies counterclockwise. Four changes. The grand right and left is *contrary to usual direction.*

Swing your partner (4–6 counts). Each couple will be diagonally across the set from their original position during the swing. At the end of the swing, each couple turns their backs on the original set and faces a new line. Lady will be on man's right.

Starting position

Ending position

Note

On the repeat, the ends become the middles; the middles become ends. With each repeat, each couple alternates position in line.

---

*Lovely Lane Chain included by permission of Bob Dalsemer, Brasstown, NC.

🌿 Kentucky Running Set

Cecil J. Sharp, authority on Country Dances of England, in search of traditional songs and ballads, traveled in southern Appalachia and heard about the *Running Set*. Although the natives refer to this particular dance as a Square Dance, the expression is used "to run a set." Perhaps from this Sharp established the term **Running Set,** a term commonly used within a variety of combinations to refer to the Square Dances of southern Appalachia.

As the result of his experiences at Pine Mountain Settlement School and on other occasions in Kentucky in 1917, Cecil J. Sharp, along with Maud Karpeles, wrote *The Country Dance Book Part V.* This classic book records his conclusions that the Running Set contains figures of early English country dancing that precede the dances described by John Playford in the *English Dancing Master,* written in 1650. Sharp suggests that possibly these dances came from the northern counties of England and the Scottish Lowlands, areas from which the early Appalachian settlers came during the 18th century. The geography of southern Appalachia and the lack of mobility until recently kept their tradition of song and dance and their dialect, too, alive and relatively untouched. These dances have been handed down orally.

The Kentucky Running Set has always generated a great deal of historical interest because it is part of the ancestry of American Square Dance as performed today. Although there are many variants of the Running Set, this material is presented as an American Heritage Dance of the 1920s, based on Cecil J. Sharp's accounts. The step, the promenade, the swing position, and the concept of one couple visiting at a time differ from that of the Big Circle Square Dance. The Running Set is still danced today in many sections of the South, but its purest forms (Hipps and Chappell, 1970) are found in the mountains of Georgia, Kentucky, North Carolina, Tennessee, and Virginia.

Music: Fiddle or fiddle and banjo reinforced with "patting" are typical instruments for accompaniment. A common practice was for the fiddler and the banjo player each to have assistants (referred to as "beaters," according to Thomas and Leeder, 1939), who sat at right angles to their instruments and beat with two flexible sticks the strings between the bridge and the players' left hands. If there were no musicians, they danced to the rhythm of the "patting" by those standing or sitting on the sidelines. The rhythm is established by stamping the right foot on the accented beat and clapping hands together on the secondary beat. Jig tunes are typical. Many different tunes are played, one after another, as musicians desire, during the dancing of one set. The tempo of the music controls the pace of the step, but the step tends to be faster with "patting" alone. Suggested tunes are "Cripple Creek," "Sally Goodin'," and "Old Joe Clark."

Records: Many tunes available. "Boil Them Cabbages Down," MacGregor 1100; Country Dance Album CLR 16L.

Cassette: Country Dance Album CLR 16C.

Formation: Even number of couples stand in a single circle, lady is on right side of partner. Four couples are preferred.*

Steps and Style: A swift, short, slightly springy running step, very smooth like an English Country Dance running step. The step is close to the floor; the ball of the foot pushes off the floor, with more elevation than a walk. The dancers appear to glide while running; the body moves freely, leaning slightly in the direction of movement and arms hang loosely at sides, swinging naturally, when not involved with specific figures. No skipping. During the promenade, a dancer may interject his or her personal style by kicking up the heels, doing a hoedown step (heel and toe, shuffle, or clog dance step), or even dragging the feet. Sharp (1918; p. 21) wrote that the dancers appeared to be "detached," "impersonal," and "moving in a dream." Today dancers reflect their joy.

The Caller: One of the group, not necessarily a dancer in the set, calls the figures to cue the dancers. The caller uses a variety of figures, one pattern leading to the next.

---

*Although Running Sets today are danced with many more couples, during the early 1900s the size of the porch or the room in the house with furniture pushed against the wall had to be considered, and usually there was barely enough room for four couples to dance.

■ Directions for the Dance

The basic structure includes an introduction; a chorus (usually a grand promenade) preceding each figure; and an indefinite number of figures, with the closing figure returning dancers to their places.

Introduction

The following is a suggested introduction:
All join hands and circle left
Grand promenade
Everybody swing
First and third go forward to back
First and third go forward
And cross over and change places. (Opposites pass right shoulders.)
Repeat to return home.
Repeat action for side couples.

Chorus

Usually a **grand promenade** precedes each figure. Grand promenade: partners turn clockwise with a two-hand swing (four steps); they separate and each turns his or her corner with a two-hand swing (four steps), comes back to partner, takes promenade position, and promenades counterclockwise once around the set to home position.

Figures

Each couple, starting with couple 1, leads out to the right, dances the figure with couple 2, and then progresses around the circle; then couple 2 leads out and progresses around the circle. Each couple eventually leads, visits each couple, and repeats the same figure. Suggested figures are: Shoot the Owl, p. 81. Bird in the Cage, Lady 'Round the Lady, see p. 80.

Ending

The last figure usually involves the action of all the dancers and brings the dancers back to their places.

Notes

1. At the time Cecil Sharp recorded his observations, the length of one set lasted about two hours; today, one set might last about fifteen minutes, the guidelines being the endurance, agility, and interest of the dancers.
2. Today's dancers prefer to have more couples active; for instance, couples 1 and 3 lead out, or all couples dance the figures (odd couples facing even couples) and the specific figure is changed frequently.
3. The do-si-do (Texas-Southwest style) in a circle of four is a common figure, either as a separate figure or as a conclusion of a figure, before traveling on to the next.

❧ Big Circle Square Dance ❧

Very much alive today in the southern Appalachian region and a variant of the Running Set is *Big Circle Square Dance,* a dance that is known by many names, such as the Mountain Square Dance, Appalachian Big Circle, and Great Circle.

It is interesting to note that the concept of the Big Circle with sets of two couples (active and inactive couples, or odds and evens) is known throughout the United States. New England does a version referred to as the Circle, Sicilian Circle, or Cirassian Circle, which has traveled to the four corners of our country. In 1945, when the authors were teaching at the University of Texas, the Big Circle was a common dance, both as a traditional form in the community and as a teaching method for Square Dance.

The Big Circle Square Dance has much in common with the Kentucky Running Set. At this time, there is an effort to differentiate between the two. Glenn Bannerman, professor of recreation and outdoor education, Presbyterian School of Christian Education, Richmond, Virginia, has researched and assisted in keeping the western North Carolina style alive. The ideas presented follow this style.

The Big Circle Square Dance is a social occasion. The dancers come to see their friends, and during the Big Circle, friends greet one another and quiet exchanges of news may go on during the dance. It differs from the Kentucky Running Set as follows: A walking step is danced even on the swing and is referred to as "smooth dancing," or single- and double-clog steps, by the spirited dancers; the Varsouvienne position is used for the promenade; and there are more people involved, maybe as many as 50 in a circle, all couples dancing and the figures changing frequently.

Records: Many tunes available. Appalachian Clog Dancing & Big Circle Mountain Square Dancing AR53C; Big Circle Mountain Dance Music LP 36L; Big Circle Mountain Square Dancing AR 52L; "Boil Them Cabbages Down," MacGregor 1100; Country Dance Album CLR 16L; Dances from Appalachia II BER 2L; Mountain Dance Music Comes Alive AR 82L; Old-Time Music Dance Party FF 415L; "Old Joe Clark," Folkraft 1071.

Cassettes: Appalachian Clog Dancing & Big Circle Mountain Square Dancing AR53C; Country Dance Album CLR 16C; Dances from Appalachia I BER 1C; Mountain Dance Music Comes Alive AR 82C; Old-Time Music Dance Party FF 415C.

Formation: Couples, lady on partner's right, in large single circle. Even-numbered couples. Prior to dancing, determine head couple and number couples 1, 2, 1, 2, and so forth, so that at the call "odd couple out to the even couple," couple 1 moves into the circle (backs to center) to face couple 2 (face center). Couple 1 always progresses on the inside in the line of direction (counterclockwise) to the next couple; couple 2 progresses on the outside in the reverse line of direction (clockwise).

Steps and Style: A walking step, even on the swing, swing position. When moving in one large circle or in small circles, joined hands are held at shoulder height. Promenade in Varsouvienne position.

The Caller: Preferably the caller (lead man or lady of head couple) calls from the floor while dancing. If the group is large, then he or she stands by the musicians and uses a microphone.

◾ Directions for the Dance

The caller uses a variety of figures, one pattern leading to the next. The basic structure includes: an introduction (with the whole group in a large circle), a series of figures (with the group in small circles), and a closing (with the group in a large circle again).

Introduction

Large-circle figures are called involving the whole group in a large circle. Any of the following large-circle figures may be called: circle left and right, promenade, swing partner, swing corner, promenade single file, grand big left, queen's highway, king's highway, shoo fly swing, and Georgia rang tang.

■ GEORGIA RANG TANG

Circle left

The other way back

With the Georgia rang tang. The leader releases his left hand with his corner and travels through the arch made by his partner and her corner; then he continues to weave in and out through the arches made by each succeeding two dancers, his partner and other dancers following in and out. Do not let go of hands. The circle continues to move right until everyone has completed the figure. The leader may go on with endless rhyme such as:

Make your feet go whickety whack.

Hurry, hurry, hurry.

■ KING'S HIGHWAY

Promenade.

Gents turn back on the king's highway. The head man steps behind his partner, turns right, and travels in the reverse line of direction around the circle, followed in succession by the men behind; the ladies continue to travel forward.

Promenade. When each man meets his partner, he crosses to the inside of the circle, **behind** his partner, and they promenade in the line of direction.

■ QUEEN'S HIGHWAY

Promenade.

Ladies turn back on the queen's highway. The head lady turns right and travels in the reverse line of direction around the circle, followed in succession by the ladies behind; the men continue to travel forward.

Promenade. When each lady meets her partner, they promenade.

■ SHOO FLY SWING

Shoo fly swing around the ring. The man of the head couple faces his partner (man's back to center of circle).

Right to your own. He swings his partner by the right hand.

Left on the side. She swings the man of the next couple (to the lady's right) by the left hand. Now back to own partner with the right, left to the next man (second couple to right), and so on around the circle. Her partner follows on the inside of the circle. After the first couple has passed three couples, the next couple starts the same pattern. Each couple continues until they are back home.

Figures

Odd couples out to the even couples. They join hands, circle four to the left until a small circle figure is called. Any of the following small-circle figures may be called: circle left and right, right- and left-hand star, ladies chain, right and left thru, butterfly twirl, bird in the cage, take a little peek, lady 'round the lady, dive for the oyster, and shoot the owl. At the call "odds on to the next," the active couple moves forward on the inside to the next couple and circles four.

■ THE BASKET

Circle four hands around.

Ladies join your hands.

The men the same. Ladies join two hands across, men join two hands above the ladies.

Ladies bow the gents know how. The men raise their arms over the heads of the ladies (ladies bow under) and lower them behind ladies' backs.

The gents bow, the ladies know how. The ladies raise their arms over the heads of the men and lower them behind men's backs.

Circle left. With right foot forward, scoot to the left with a modified buzz step.

Break and swing your corner. And now your own. And on to the next.

Big Circle Square Dance (continued)

■ BIRD IN THE CAGE

Circle four hands around.
Cage the bird with three hands 'round. Active lady steps in center. Inactive couple and active man join hands and circle around active lady.
Bird flies out, crow hops in. Active man steps in center as active lady joins circle with inactive couple.
Ring up three and you're gone again.
Crow hops out and make a ring.
Swing your partner and on to the next.

■ BOX THE GNAT AND BOX THE FLEA

Circle four.
With your opposite box the gnat.
Now box the flea. Same person.
Do-si-do. Same person.
Now swing that gal high and low.
And circle four.
Repeat call with own partner.
And lead onto the next.

■ BUTTERFLY TWIRL

Ladies twirl. Ladies turn in place.
Gents twirl. Men turn in place.
Everybody twirl a butterfly twirl. Everybody turns in place.
Now swing your corner girl.
And swing your own.

■ DIVE FOR THE OYSTER

Circle four.
Dive for the oyster. Without releasing hands, active couple moves forward through an arch made by the inactive man and back to face the inactive couple; the active man stands in place.
Now circle four once around and on to the next.

■ LADY 'ROUND THE LADY

Lady 'round the lady and the gent solo. The active lady leads, her partner following, and goes between the inactive couple; the lady goes behind the inactive lady, around her and in front while her partner goes behind the inactive man, around him and back to face the couple.
Lady 'round the gent and the gent don't go. The active lady goes between the inactive couple, travels behind and around the inactive man and back to face the inactive couple; the active man stands in place.
Now circle four once around and on to the next.

■ MOUNTAINEER LOOP

Circle four.
Mountaineer Loop. The even couple raise their arms for the odd couple to pass thru. The odd couple releases man's right, lady's left, as they go thru the arch; man turns left, lady right and travel back home, the even couple turning under their arch. Odd couple rejoins hands.
And circle left.

■ POP THEM THRU

Circle four.
Back with a left-hand star.
Then gents reach back and
Pop them through to a right-hand star. Men reach across their chests with right hands (under left arm) for their opposites' right hand. All release star as men turn their opposite under their right arms and all form right-hand star.
Gents reach back and
Pop them back. Men repeat above action using left hand to form left-hand star.
Swing your opposite on the same old track. Men turn to swing the lady following them in the star.
Swing your partner
And onto the next.

■ SHOOT THE OWL

Three hands 'round if you know how. Active man circles three with inactive couple.
When you get right, shoot the owl.
Two hands up, the gents shoot under. Circle three once and a half. Inactive couple "shoots" active man under arch to partner.
Grab your partner and swing like thunder. Active couple swings.
Circle four and on to the next.

■ TAKE A LITTLE PEEK

Around that couple and take a little peek. Active couple separates, lady peeks right, man peeks left around behind inactive couple.
Back to the center and swing your sweet. Active couple swings.
Around that couple and peek once more. Couple repeats "peeking" action.
Back to the center and circle four.
Lead to the next.

Ending

Large-circle figures are called involving the whole group in a large circle.

Notes

1. When determining the active and inactive couples, always count around the circle counter-clockwise. Also, do not let the couple to the left of the head couple start counting clockwise; it adds to the confusion, especially if there is an uneven number of couples present.
2. During the small circle figures, at the call "odds on to the next," the active couple moves forward to the next couple. They join hands and circle four to the left until a new figure is called.
3. If dancers become mixed up, call "find your partner, and everybody swing."
4. There is no end of figures that may be used, once the format of the Big Circle Square Dance is learned. The figures presented are just a few.

⚘ Clogging*

■ HISTORY

Clogging is a dance of sound. An American folk dance form enjoyed by people of all ages and all ability levels, clogging is primarily a combination of the rhythms, motions, and steps of the English, Scottish, and Irish immigrants who settled in the Appalachian area of the South during the 1700s and 1800s. Clogging is sometimes called Appalachian Mountain Style Dancing because the Appalachian area between southern Pennsylvania and northern Georgia is the primary area where this dance form has been preserved.

Historically, the style that generally today is simply called "clogging" included such terms/styles as clog dance, foot stomping, dancing, hoedowning, jigging, surefooting, flatfooting, little chugging, buck and wing, shuffling, heel and toe, buck dancing, and old English stepdancing.

Buck Dancing

The style of clogging called buck dancing originated in the Appalachian mountain area. Although the origin of buck dancing is not clear, generally it was considered a solo dance form. Some cloggers today view buck dancing as solo clogging; others view it as a unique form of dance separate from traditional clogging.

In buck dancing, the feet remain very close to the floor. With the exception of the legs, little body movement is used. The accompaniment is simple (perhaps only a fiddle). The steps used in buck dancing were learned from the slaves brought to this country from Africa. Added to these steps were some of the ceremonial dance steps of the Cherokee Indians.

Step Dancing

Step dancing, a predecessor of clogging and a popular dance form in Canada, came to Ontario via early Irish settlers. The movements in step dancing are performed on the balls of the feet with the heels rarely touching the floor, a style distinctly different from the flat-footed action of buck dancing. Like traditional buck dancing, however, the movements originally were restricted to the legs and feet. Today, clogging taps are used on the shoes and the steps use more total body movement.

The Term Clogging

In 1939 the Soco Gap Dancers from western North Carolina performed for King George VI and Queen Elizabeth of England when they visited the White House. The queen commented that the dance looked like the English clogging. Thereafter, the term clogging began to be used for all styles of clogging.

Three Styles

Three main types or styles of clogging popular today are freestyle clogging (which evolved from buck dancing), square dance clogging, and precision clogging. Freestyle clogging is a solo dance. It includes a wide variety of step variations and combinations that use lively foot stomping, leg swinging, and considerable body action.

From early times, in addition to the freestyle solo clogging, dancers clogged in a square dance formation using traditional square dance movements. Originally, people danced using simple fast walking steps, adding clogging steps only occasionally. Clogging during the entire square dance did not become common until the 1930s. The steps performed in square dance clogging generally are freestyle in nature, with individual cloggers using steps of their own choosing. Such freestyle clogging is also performed in Big Circle Mountain dance.

Precision clogging, which began in the late 1950s, uses the same types of steps as freestyle clogging, but the dancers perform prescribed routines. James Kesterson's Blue Ridge Mountain Dancers in western North Carolina were possibly the first dancers to perform using this style. Of these three styles, precision clogging is the most spectator-oriented. Clogging routines in which individual dancers, partners, and groups perform a set sequence of dance steps have become popular with education and recreation groups, as well as with exhibition groups.

---

*Clogging was written by Dr. Sandra L. (Sandy) Gallemore, Georgia Southern University, Statesboro, GA 30460-8076.

Clogging Competitions

Clogging competitions exist for advanced dancers who wish to exhibit their skill. The first recorded clogging team competition occurred in 1938 in Asheville, North Carolina, at Bascom Lamar Lunsford's annual Mountain Dance and Folk Festival, the oldest folk festival in the country. The winners of the competition, Sam Queen's Soco Gap Dancers, performed a combination of freestyle clogging and mountain-style square dance figures. Queen was well known for his own dance ability, as well as for his leadership of dance teams in the western North Carolina area.

In the 1940s, interest in clogging increased and, as a result, wearing special costumes and shoes became customary. Clogging began to attract spectators as a popular form of entertainment, making the activity more performance-oriented than had been the case in earlier years.

Clogging in Early Physical Education Programs

During the 1920s and 1930s, clogging, frequently called clog dance, was taught in public school and university physical education departments. These dances (frequently referred to as character dances) often had a dramatic quality not evident in today's clogging. These early clog dances appear to be related more closely to tap dance than what today is called clogging.

National Organization

Originated in 1976, the National Clogging and Hoedown Council (NCHC)* was formed to help preserve traditional clogging by collecting information about clogging styles and steps, as well as assembling historical material on clogging. In addition, to assist with communication among cloggers about more current dance routines, as well as the historical materials, NCHC has established a written vocabulary of basic terminology.

■ COSTUMES AND SHOES

Although recreational cloggers wear any comfortable clothing, exhibition cloggers traditionally wear costumes very similar to those used in square dance. The major difference between exhibition square dance attire and exhibition clogging attire is the length of the women's skirts; cloggers usually wear shorter skirts than do square dancers.

Shoes

The clogging shoes of today, quite different from the practical and comfortable dancing shoes of earlier times, hold a special fascination for both dancers and spectators. Clogging shoes are low-heeled shoes. Clogging (or "jingle" or "staccato") taps are attached to the heels and toes of the soles. This type of tap creates a louder tapping sound than regular taps because the clogging tap has a loose two-part construction that allows metal to flap against metal and produce a jingle or rattle sound. Popular styles include square dance or tap dance shoes and lace-up shoes. It is critical that the shoe stays securely on the foot.

Taps on the shoes are not essential for participating in clogging. Many individuals clog successfully in shoes with a smooth sole (leather preferred). The main advantage of taps on the shoes when learning to clog is the feedback the learner receives from the sound produced.

■ MUSIC

Traditional clogging music, sometimes termed "old-time" folk music, used primarily fiddle and/or banjo and on occasion another instrument, such as a guitar. It was the music of the 19th century and earlier.

Fiddle/banjo bluegrass or hoedown music is the accepted traditional form of clogging music today. Clogging instructors find the same hoedown musical selections with a definite repetitive beat and little melody that the square dance caller uses for patter calls appropriate for clogging.

Clogging (continued)

---

*National Clogging and Hoedown Council (NCHC), 507 Angie Way, Lilburn, GA 30247.

The use of more current country and pop music is gaining in popularity for modern cloggers. Cloggers of today dance to almost any kind of music with a strong 2/4 time signature and an appropriate tempo for the skill level of the participants.

■ STYLE

Clogging style and steps, as they have been since early times, frequently are regional in nature.

Traditional clogging style calls for a torso that is almost motionless, even though the footwork consists of quick-moving intricate steps. Characteristic of the footwork is the use of the flat-foot action. When performing various steps and step patterns, both legs are straight (but not stiff) or both are slightly bent. The arms are relaxed and used only for balance, although in some modern exhibition clogging arm movement or claps may be included in the choreography.

Leg Action

When the heel is sounded against the floor, the legs are flexed. They straighten on count "and" of the music. The result is the customary up-and-down body movement identified with clogging. This up-and-down movement is combined with the forward-and-backward sliding motion of the feet to achieve the characteristic body action associated with skillful cloggers.

Most step patterns in clogging are designed so that when one foot has taken the weight the opposite foot is lifted from the floor (the lift may be very low to the ground or moderately high, depending on the steps involved). Although the legs bend and straighten to produce the appropriate style, looseness in the legs is needed for smoothness in the up-and-down bounce and also for the dancer to be ready to perform the following step.

■ BASIC CLOGGING STEPS

Eight basic steps or movements adopted by the National Clogging and Hoedown Council in 1978 are the basis for a wide variety of steps and combinations of steps used in clogging. Generally, the steps are performed in place. These basic movements are divided into two categories: heel movements and toe movements.

Heel Movements

The heel movements (step, slide, heel) take place on the downbeat (accent) of the music. Both legs are slightly bent. Heel movements are accented as the weight is transferred to the entire sole of the foot.

2/4	/		/		/		/	
	heel movt L		heel movt R		heel movt L		heel movt R	
Q	Q	Q	Q	Q	Q	Q	Q	Q
&	1	&	2	&	1	&	2	&

Toe Movements

The toe movements (rock, drag, toe, double-toe, brush) occur on the upbeat (count "and") of the music. Both legs are straight (but not stiff).

2/4	/		/		/		/	
toe movt R	toe movt L		toe movt R		toe movt L		toe movt R	
Q	Q	Q	Q	Q	Q	Q	Q	Q
&	1	&	2	&	1	&	2	&

The basic clogging steps are presented in the order taught. The usual abbreviation for the movement found on clogging cue sheets is included, i.e., Step (S), Rock (R).

Step (S)

1. 2/4 meter.
2. A flat-footed **heel** movement on the downbeat (accent); a weight-bearing movement.
3. Both knees are slightly bent on STEP left, on the following upbeat (count "and") both knees straighten; repeat beginning right.
4. Both feet remain close to the floor, alternating left and right.

2/4		/		/			/		/	
		Step		Step			Step		Step	
		L		R			L		R	
Q		Q	Q	Q	Q		Q	Q	Q	Q
&		1	&	2	&		1	&	2	&

Rock (R)

1. 2/4 meter.
2. A **toe** movement on the upbeat (count "and").
3. A weight-bearing movement in which the weight is taken on the ball of the foot, which usually is placed directly under or slightly behind the center of gravity.
4. Both knees are straight (not stiff) on the ROCK; on the following downbeat (accent) of the music, both knees bend slightly while performing the next movement.
5. Both feet remain close to the floor.

2/4		/		/			/		/	
Rock		Step	Rock	Step	Rock		Step	Rock	Step	Rock
L		R	L	R	L		L	R	L	R
Q		Q	Q	Q	Q		Q	Q	Q	Q
&		1	&	2	&		1	&	2	&

even rhythm

Drag (DR)

1. 2/4 meter.
2. A **toe** movement on the upbeat (count "and").
3. A weight-bearing movement, which may be performed on one foot or on both feet simultaneously.
4. Similar to a chug step, the DRAG is a movement that scoots **backward** a few inches as the weight is shifted to the balls of the feet. Heels skim the floor during the movement.
5. Both knees are straight (not stiff) on the DRAG; on the following downbeat (accent), both knees bend slightly while performing the next movement.
6. In the analysis below, one may start on the **and** with a DRAG or on the **accent** with a STEP.

2/4		/		/			/		/	
Drag		Step	Drag	Step	Drag		Step	Drag	Step	Drag
L		R	R	L	L		R	R	L	L
Q		Q	Q	Q	Q		Q	Q	Q	Q
&		1	&	2	&		1	&	2	&

even rhythm

Clogging (continued)

Slide (SL)

1. 2/4 meter.
2. A **heel** movement on the downbeat (accent).
3. A weight-bearing movement, which may be performed on one foot or on both feet simultaneously.
4. Feet scoot **forward** a few inches as weight is shifted from balls of feet to heels. Heels skim along the floor.
5. Both knees are slightly bent on the SLIDE; on the following upbeat (count "and"), both knees straighten while performing the next movement.
6. The combination DRAG SLIDE performed on one foot is much more difficult than performing the combination on both feet simultaneously. In the analysis below, during the first measure the left foot remains in contact with the ground while the right foot/leg is off the ground; the style of both knees bent on the SLIDE and both straight on the DRAG refers to performing this movement on one-leg combination as well as on both simultaneously.

2/4		/		/			/		/	
Drag		Slide	Drag	Slide	Drag		Slide	Drag	Slide	Drag
L		L	L	L	L		both	both	both	both
Q		Q	Q	Q	Q		Q	Q	Q	Q
&		1	&	2	&		1	&	2	&

even rhythm

Toe (T), Heel (H), Touch (TCH)

1. 2/4 meter.
2. The TOE step is a weight-bearing **toe** movement on the upbeat (count "and"). It must be followed by a HEEL step.
3. The HEEL step is a weight-bearing **heel** movement on the downbeat (accent).
4. A variation of the TOE is the TOUCH, which involves no change of weight. The ball of the foot touches the floor on the upbeat (count "and") and lifts on the downbeat (accent) as another movement is performed.
5. The weight is shifted to the ball of the foot for the TOE step; this leg is very slightly bent and the opposite leg is straight.
6. The weight then shifts to the entire sole of the foot for the HEEL step as the heel slaps the floor; legs bend slightly.

2/4		/		/			/		/	
Toe		Heel	Toe	Heel	Toe		Heel	Toe	Heel	Toe
L		L	R	R	L		L	R	R	L
Q		Q	Q	Q	Q		Q	Q	Q	Q
&		1	&	2	&		1	&	2	&

even rhythm

2/4		/		/			/		/	
Touch		Heel	Touch	Heel	Touch		Slide	Touch	Slide	Touch
L		R	L	R	L		R	L	R	L
Q		Q	Q	Q	Q		Q	Q	Q	Q
&		1	&	2	&		1	&	2	&

even rhythm

Double-Toe (DT)

1. 2/4 meter.
2. A **toe** movement on the upbeat (count "and").
3. No weight change occurs in the DOUBLE-TOE. The foot performing the movement makes two clicking sounds with the ball of that foot. A small brushing movement of the ball of the foot forward and a small brushing movement backward occur during the "and-ah" count.
4. The DOUBLE-TOE action generally occurs slightly in front of the center of gravity.
5. The knee of the supporting leg is straight; the knee of the leg performing the movement straightens on the small brushing movement of the ball of the foot forward and relaxes on the small brushing action backward. On the following downbeat (accent), both knees bend slightly while performing the next movement.

2/4			/				/		
Brush Fwd	Brush Bkwd	Step	Brush Fwd	Brush Bkwd	Step	Brush Fwd	Brush Bkwd
L	L	L	R	R	R	L	L
Q	Q	S	Q	Q	S	Q	Q
& – ah		1	& – ah		2	& – ah	

uneven rhythm

Brush (BR)

1. 2/4 meter.
2. A **toe** movement on the upbeat (count "and").
3. No weight change in the BRUSH. The leg performing the movement swings forward as the ball of the foot brushes the floor. Generally the brush and following action is within a few inches of the floor.
4. Brushes also may cross in front of the body or swing out to the side. Less frequently they are performed brushing backward.
5. Both legs are straight; on the following downbeat (accent), both knees bend slightly while performing the next movement.

2/4	/				/			
Brush	Slide	Toe	Heel	Brush	Slide	Toe	Heel	Brush
L	R	L	L	R	L	R	R	L
Q	Q	Q	Q	Q	Q	Q	Q	Q
&	1	&	2	&	1	&	2	&

even rhythm

■ TEACHING CLOGGING

Progression

The following order for teaching the basic steps is suggested: Drag and Slide, Step, Rock, Toe and Heel, Double-Toe, Touch, Brush.

The instructor should develop sequences in phrasing with the music for practicing and learning to combine step patterns. For most musical selections routines should use the same step or step pattern for four or eight measures.

The instructor may wish to use only selected parts of dance routines choreographed by others. The dance routines included in this text are written so that dancers can eliminate any 16-measure part that is not appropriate to the students at a given point in the instruction.

Evaluation

Students may be evaluated for the purpose of assigning a grade on clogging performance and clogging knowledge. Appropriate competencies for performance evaluation include the following:

1. Students will demonstrate each of the basic steps in clogging.

Clogging (continued)

2. Students will demonstrate a variety of step combinations.
3. Students will demonstrate appropriate clogging style.
4. Students will combine steps in a manner that compliments the phrasing of the music.
5. Students will perform dance routines accurately and skillfully.

Appropriate competencies for knowledge evaluation include the following:

1. Students will exhibit knowledge about the proper techniques of performing the basic steps.
2. Students will exhibit knowledge about clogging style.
3. Students will exhibit knowledge about the relationship of music to the steps and the step combinations used in routines.
4. Students will exhibit knowledge about the history and background of clogging.

◢ Clogging 101

Clogging 101 was composed by Sandra L. "Sandy" Gallemore, Statesboro, Georgia.

Music: Any 2/4 music; bluegrass or hoedown suggested.

Formation: Scattered, all facing music.

Steps: Double-toe, step, rock, toe, heel, touch, brush, drag, slide.

■ Directions for the Dance

Meter 2/4

Measures

Part I

1–4 Beginning right, double-toe step (right), rock step (left, right); double-toe step (left), rock step (right, left); double-toe step (right), rock step (left, right); double-toe step (left), rock step (right, left).

5–8 Beginning right, double-toe step (right), double-toe step (left); double-toe step (right), rock step (left, right); repeat sequence beginning left foot.

9–16 Repeat action of part I, measures 1–8.

Part II

1–4 Beginning right, double-toe step (right), toe heel (left, left); toe heel (right, right), toe heel (left, left); double-toe step (right), touch heel (left, right); touch heel (left, right), touch heel (left, right).

5–8 Beginning left, repeat sequence part II, measures 1–4.

9–12 Beginning right, double-toe step (right), brush slide (left, right); double-toe step (left), brush slide (right, left); double-toe step (right), drag slide (right, right); drag slide (right, right), drag slide (right, right). The drag-slide combination may be performed on both feet or on the designated foot.

13–16 Repeat action of part II, measures 9–12, beginning on left foot.

🐚 Fancy Step Out 🐚

Fancy Step Out was composed by Sandra L. "Sandy" Gallemore, Statesboro, Georgia.

Music: Any 2/4 music; bluegrass or hoedown suggested.

Formation: Scattered, all facing music.

Steps: Double-toe, step, rock, toe, heel, brush, slide.

■ Directions for the Dance

Meter 2/4

Measures

Part I

1–4   Beginning right, double-toe step (right), touch (out to side) heel (left, right); touch (cross in front) heel (left, right), touch (out to side) heel (left, right); repeat sequence beginning left.

5–8   Repeat action of part I, measures 1–4.

9–12   Beginning right, double-toe step (right), toe heel (left, left); toe heel (right, right), rock step (left, right); repeat sequence beginning left.

13–16   Repeat action of part I, measures 9–12.

Part II

1–4   Beginning right, double-toe step (right), double-toe step (left); double-toe step (right), double-toe step (left); double-toe step (right), rock step (left, right); double-toe step (left), rock step (right, left).

5–8   Repeat action of part II, measures 1–4.

9–12   Beginning right, double-toe step (right), double-toe step (left); double-toe step (right), double-toe step (left); double-toe step (right), brush slide (left, right); double-toe step (left), brush slide (right, left).

13–16   Repeat action of part II, measures 9–12.

Part III

1–4   Beginning right, double-toe step (right), rock step (left, right); rock step (left, right), rock step (left, right); repeat sequence beginning left.

5–8   Beginning right, double-toe step (right), double-toe step (left); double-toe step (right), double-toe step (left); double-toe step (right), rock step (left, right); double-toe step (left), rock step (right, left).

9–16   Repeat action of part III, measures 1–8.

Part IV

1–4   Beginning right, double-toe step (right), double-toe step (left); double-toe step (right), rock step (left, right); repeat sequence beginning left.

5–8   Beginning right, double-toe step (right), brush slide (left, right); double-toe step (left), brush slide (right, left); double-toe step (right), brush slide (left, right); double-toe step (left), brush slide (right, left).

9–16   Repeat action of part IV, measures 1–8.

🎵 Southern Special

Southern Special was composed by Sandra L. "Sandy" Gallemore, Statesboro, Georgia.

Music: Any 2/4 music; bluegrass or hoedown suggested.

Formation: Scattered, all facing music.

Steps: Double-toe, step, rock, touch, heel, drag, slide.

■ Directions for the Dance

Meter 2/4

Measures

Part I

1–4   Beginning right, double-toe step (right), double-toe step (left); double-toe step (right), double-toe step (left); double-toe step (right), touch (forward) heel (left, right), touch (backward) heel (left, right), touch (forward) heel (left, right).

5–8   Repeat action of part I, measures 1–4, beginning left.

9–12   Beginning right, double-toe step (right), rock step (left, right); touch heel (left, right), touch heel (left, right); repeat sequence beginning left.

13–16 Repeat action of part I, measures 9–12.

Part II

1–4   Beginning right, double-toe step (right), rock step (left, right); double-toe step (left), rock step (right, left); double-toe step (right), double-toe step (left); double-toe step (right), rock step (left, right).

5–8   Repeat action of part II, measures 1–4, beginning left.

9–12   Beginning right, double-toe step (right), drag slide (right, right); drag slide (right, right), drag slide (right, right); repeat sequence beginning left. The drag-slide combination may be performed on both feet or on the designated foot.

13–16 Repeat action of part II, measures 9–12.

Double Toe Tapping

Double Toe Tapping was composed by Sandra L. "Sandy" Gallemore, Statesboro, Georgia.

Music: Any 2/4 music; bluegrass or hoedown suggested.

Formation: Scattered, facing music.

Steps: Double-toe, step, rock, drag, slide, brush.

■ Directions for the Dance

Meter 2/4

Measures

Part A

1-4   Beginning on the right foot: double-toe step, rock step; double-toe step, rock step; double-toe step, double-toe step; double-toe step, rock step.

5-8   Repeat measures 1-4 of Part A beginning on left foot.

9-16   Repeat measures 1-8 of Part A.

Part B

1-4   Beginning on the right foot: double-toe step, rock step; drag slide, drag slide (the drag-slide combination may be done on both feet or on the designated one).

5-8   Repeat measures 1-4 of Part B beginning on left foot.

9-16   Repeat measures 1-8 of Part B.

Part C

1-4   Beginning on the right foot: double-toe step, brush slide; double-toe step, rock step; double-toe step, double-toe step; double-toe step, rock step.

5-8   Repeat measures 1-4 of Part C beginning on left foot.

9-16   Repeat measures 1-8 of Part C.

Part D

1-4   Beginning on right foot: double-toe step, double-toe step; rock step, brush slide; double-toe step, double-toe step; double-toe step, rock step.

5-8   Repeat measures 1-4 of Part D beginning on left foot.

9-16   Repeat measures 1-8 of Part D.

🌿 Tricky Footwork

Tricky Footwork was composed by Sandra L. "Sandy" Gallemore, Statesboro, Georgia.

Music: Any 2/4 music; bluegrass or hoedown suggested.

Formation: Scattered, all facing music.

Steps: Double-toe, step, rock, drag, slide, brush.

■ Directions for the Dance

Meter 2/4

Measures

1–4   Beginning right, double-toe step (right), rock step (left, right); double-toe step (left), rock step (right, left); double-toe step (right), double-toe step (left); double-toe step (right), double-toe step (left).

5–8   Repeat action of measures 1–4.

9–12   Beginning right, double-toe step (right), brush slide (left, right); double-toe step (left), brush slide (right, left); double-toe step (right), drag slide (right, right); drag slide (right, right), drag slide (right, right). The drag-slide combination may be performed on both feet or on the designated foot.

13–16   Repeat action of measures 9–12 beginning left.

Alabama Gal

Alabama Gal, a Play Party Game, was taught by Jane Farwell at the Oglebay Folk Dance Camp, Wheeling, West Virginia, in 1948.

Record: World of Fun M112.

Formation: Longway sets, men on left, ladies on right, partners facing. Large groups should be divided into sets of 16 couples or less.

Singing Call

Alabama Gal

Comin' thru in a hur-ry, Comin' thru in a hur-ry,

Comin' thru in a hur-ry, Al-a-bam-a gal.

Verse 2
You don't know how how
You don't know how how
You don't know how how
Alabama Gal.

Verse 3
I'll show you how how
I'll show you how how
I'll show you how how
Alabama Gal.

Verse 4
Ain't I rock candy
Ain't I rock candy
Ain't I rock candy
Alabama Gal.

■ Directions for the Dance

1. Everyone or just the caller sings the verses.
2. Head couple joins two hands, extending arms shoulder height. Slides down and back between two lines.
3. Head couple reels down the set by starting with a right-hand swing, once and a half. When the active couples reach the foot of the set, they join the lines.
4. As soon as all four verses have been sung, next couple starts to slide down center and back and reel. Therefore, each time the first verse is sung, a new couple starts "comin' thru in a hurry." The fun comes when a new couple begins to slide through the set while the reeling continues!

ᔥᕲ Nobody's Business

Nobody's Business is a fun-loving American Play Party Game. The tune is catchy and it is an excellent mixer.

Record: Folk Dancer MH1107.

Cassette: Play Party Dances for Early Childhood, Can-Ed Media Ltd.

Formation: Single circle, couples facing center, lady to right of partner, hands joined.

Singing Call

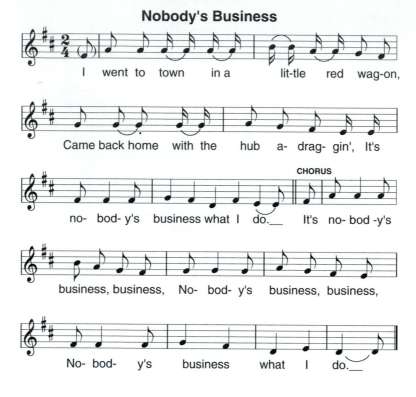

Nobody's Business

I went to town in a lit-tle red wag-on,

Came back home with the hub a-drag-gin', It's

no-bod-y's business what I do.__ It's no-bod-y's

business, business, No-bod-y's business, business,

No-bod-y's business what I do.__

Verse 2
Way down yonder about a mile and a quarter,
Some old man's going to lose his daughter,
It's nobody's business what I do.

Verse 3
Butterbeans has killed my baby
Popcorn has killed the old lady,
It's nobody's business what I do.

Verse 4
I've got a wife and she's a daisy,
She won't work and I'm too lazy,
It's nobody's business what I do.

■ Directions for the Dance

1. Everyone sings the verses with the chorus between each verse.
2. For each verse, all join hands and circle to the left, walking briskly.
3. For the chorus, release hands, partners face, ready for a grand right and left with an elbow swing. Partners hook right elbows and make one complete turn (each turn lasts one line of the chorus). Each meets the next person, men always progressing counterclockwise, ladies clockwise, with a left elbow swing; then the next with a right elbow swing. There are three elbow swings. Complete the last swing, men taking this one for their new partners.
4. For the next verse, all join hands and circle left. Continue alternating the action with each verse and chorus.

Hokey Pokey

Hokey Pokey is a modern Play Party Game popular with young and old, an adaptation of Looby Lou. The music was written by the Sun Valley Trio, Tafft Baker, Larry La Prise, and Charles Macak, natives of Washington, in 1947. Tafft Baker wrote the words and tried them out on his girlfriend Jean. Jean and Tafft married and traveled around the U.S. promoting the song and dance. Acuff-Rose Opryland Music pressed the record in 1950 and the rest is history. The action sequence on several records with calls varies slightly from the one given here. The tune is simple and may be easily done without musical accompaniment. The leader may sing the call for the group or have them sing and perform the action.

Records: Can-Ed DC 74528, LS E38; Capitol 6026, EZ726; MacGregor 6995.

Cassette: DC 13X.

Formation: Single circle, individuals face center; or single circle, couples face center, lady to right of partner.

◼ Directions for the Dance

Call

You put your right foot in. Place foot forward into circle.
You put your right foot out. Place foot back away from circle.
You put your right foot in.
And you shake it all about. Shake foot toward center of circle.
You do the hokey pokey. Place palms together above head and Rumba hips.
And you turn yourself around. Individuals shake arms above head and turn around. If couples, man turns lady on left once and a half with right elbow and progresses one position clockwise.
That's what it's all about. Clap hands four times.

Repeat the above call, substituting the following parts of the body: left foot, right arm, left arm, right elbow, head, right hip, whole self, backside.

Ending

You do the hokey pokey.
You do the hokey pokey. Raise the arms above head and lower arms and head in a bowing motion.
You do the hokey pokey. Kneel on both knees and raise arms above head and lower arms and head in a bowing motion.
That's what it's all about. Slap the floor six times.

✍ Schottische

Music: Any Schottische. Schottische melodies and styles of arrangements relate to the quality of movement: a lively, bouncy one for step-hops; a smooth one for Ballroom variations and Texas Schottische variations.

Position: Open, couple, or conversation.

Steps: Schottische.

■ Directions for the Dance

Meter 4/4 • Directions are for man; lady's part reverse.

Measures

Basic

1 – 2 Open dance position. Beginning left, move forward in line of direction with two Schottische steps.

3 – 4 Closed position or waist position. Turn clockwise with four step-hops. Progress in line of direction.

Variations

I. Lady's Turn

1 – 2 Repeat action of measures 1 – 2 in basic Schottische.

3 – 4 Four step-hops, man moves forward, while the lady turns clockwise under upraised left arm of partner. Lady may make one or two complete turns. Progress in the line of direction.

II. Man's Turn

1 – 4 Directions are the same as for the lady's turn, except man turns clockwise under upraised right arm of lady.

III. Both Turn

1 – 2 Repeat action of measures 1 – 2 in basic Schottische.

Four step-hops, partners turn away from each other, man to his left, lady to her right. Partners may make one or two complete turns.

IV. Diamond

1 – 2 Man and lady take one Schottische step diagonally forward away from each other. Man and lady take one Schottische step diagonally forward toward each other. Progress in the line of direction.

3 – 4 Repeat action of measures 3 – 4 in basic Schottische.

V. Wring the Dish Rag

1 – 2 Repeat action of measures 1 – 2 in basic Schottische.

3 – 4 Partners face, join two hands and with four step-hops turn back to back (turning to man's left, lady's right) and continue roll until face to face. Join hands and swing through between couple, below waist, and quickly overhead. The couple may make one or two turns.

VI. Rock

1 – 2 Repeat action of measures 1 – 2 in basic Schottische.

3 Step forward on left, take weight (counts 1 – 2). Step backward on right, take weight (counts 3 – 4). Rocking effect is produced by swaying body forward and backward.

4 Repeat action of measure 3.

VII. Ballroom Schottische

1 – 2 Repeat action of measures 1 – 2 in basic Schottische. On count 4, the hop is omitted and the free leg swings forward, toe pointed close to floor.

3 – 4	Closed position. Beginning left, pivot turn clockwise four steps, progressing in line of direction.

VIII. Schottische for Four—Horse and Buggy Schottische

Two couples stand one behind the other, both facing the line of direction. Join inside hands with partner. The outside hands joined link the two couples together. The front couple is number one, the back couple is number two.

1 – 2	Repeat action of measures 1 – 2 in basic Schottische.
3 – 4	Four step-hops. No. 1 couple releases partner's hand and turning away from each other, man left, lady right, they move around couple No. 2 on the outside and come in behind them. Joining hands with partner, they therefore become the back couple and No. 2 couple, the front couple. Or No. 1 couple may take step-hops backward through the upraised arms of No. 2 couple. This action will cause No. 2 couple to turn the dish rag in order to become straightened out. After turning No. 2 couple becomes the front couple. These variations, if repeated, will return couples to starting position.
1 – 4	Repeat the entire action of measures 1 – 4 with No. 2 couple turning out or moving backward with step-hops, to return couples to original positions.

Mixer

Double circle, couples facing line of direction. Dance basic Schottische. The lady moves forward to a new partner on the second Schottische step.

Style

Three styles are used in this Schottische: Traditional—the Schottische step is danced as a step, close, step, hop. Barn dance—the Schottische step is danced as a step, step, step, hop or run, run, run, hop. Ballroom dance—step, close, step, lift. The hop is replaced by a slight lift of the body. Point toe of the free foot. The step-hops are replaced by a step-lift, with a rocking action forward and back.

The American style is to swing the free leg forward on the hop and the pattern is very smooth. The European style keeps the leg under the body and the hop has a bouncy action.

❧ Ping-Pong Schottische ❧

Position: Varsouvienne.

■ Directions for the Dance

Meter 4/4 • Directions are same for man and lady.

Measures

1	Beginning right, place heel, then toe by left foot.
2	Take one two-step, moving forward.
3 – 4	Beginning left, repeat action of measures 1 – 2.
5 – 6	Beginning right, take eight count grapevine, traveling sideways to right; stepping to right side (count 1), then left behind right (count 2), step side right (count 3), cross left in front of right (count 4), step side right (count 5), cross left behind right (count 6), step right (count 7), bring left to right but do not take weight (count 8).
7 – 8	Beginning left, repeat action of measures 5 – 6, traveling sideways to left.

🎵 Texas Schottische Variations

The *Texas Schottische* was first seen by the authors as part of an exhibition danced and taught by Herb and Pauline Greggerson. The Texas Schottische was also referred to as the El Paso Schottische, because El Paso was home base for the Greggersons in those days. There are many Texas Schottische variations such as Douglas, Belen, and Scotch. As originally danced, these steps were not done in any special sequence.

Records: FD LP 4; MAV Album 4; Shaw E 23, or any smooth Schottische.

Position: Varsouvienne.

Steps: Variations of grapevine, Schottische and Two-Step.

■ Directions for the Dance

Meter 4/4 • Directions are same for man and lady.

Measures

I. Military Schottische

1	Point left toe in front of right foot (counts 1 – 2). Point left toe sideways to left (counts 3 – 4).
2	Step left foot behind right (count 1). Step right foot to right (count 2). Close left to right (count 3). Hold (count 4).
3 – 4	Beginning right, repeat action of measures 1 – 2.
5 – 6	Beginning left, two walking steps forward followed by one Two-Step.
7 – 8	Beginning right, repeat action of measures 5 – 6.

II. Peter Pan Schottische

1	Step forward left (counts 1 – 2). Step forward right (counts 3 – 4).
2	Step forward left, right, (counts 1 – 2), step left and pivot to own right (count 3), swing or lift right leg (count 4). Couple now faces in the reverse line of direction.
3	Moving backward, step right, lift left (counts 1 – 2). Step left, lift right (counts 3 – 4).
4	Step right, left, right, pivoting to own left (counts 1, 2, 3, 4). Couple now faces line of direction.

III. McGinty Schottische

1 – 2	Step forward, slightly to left, with left foot, close right to left, step left, and swing right across left with a slight kick. Repeat stepping forward, slightly to right, with right foot. (Right, close, right, swing left across right with slight kick.)
3 – 4	Beginning left, take four step swings (kicks), moving forward in line of direction: step left and swing right across in front of left, step right in front of left and swing left across in front of right; repeat action. Body sways with a roll during the step swings.

IV. Blue Bonnet

1	Beginning left, take one Schottische step to left, sideways, stepping left, step right behind left, step left, swing right in front of left as body rises and lowers on left foot.
2	Take one Schottische step to right, sideways, lady rising and lowering on step swing.
3 – 4	Partners release left hands. Man and lady take 12 small steps in a quick quick slow rhythm (four times). Lady, beginning left, takes three small steps (quick, quick, slow), turns right face to face partner, and moves so right arms are almost extended; lady travels around her partner, to man's right, behind him, to his left side, and back to original Varsouvienne position while taking three more series of small steps to the rhythm of quick, quick, slow. On the last quick, quick, slow,

the lady turns clockwise under her right arm as she moves into her original position. As the lady is sweeping around the man, the man guides her raising his right arm and circling his right hand above his head (lariat fashion); and the man takes 12 steps to the rhythm of quick, quick, slow, four times almost in place, moving slightly to assist the movement of his partner. See Note 2.

Notes

1. In El Paso, Texas, McGinty is the name for a "big beer." In Lloyd Shaw's *The Round Dance Book* (1948), under Texas Schottisches, this variation is listed as Drunken Schottische.
2. Although **quick quick slow** is a Two-Step rhythm, the Greggersons did not Two-Step this figure; rather, they used a smooth travel of steps.

Texas Schottische for Three*

During World War II, the Texas Schottische and Put Your Little Foot were the two Round Dances most frequently danced between squares in the Southwest. Following the folk-transmission process, set patterns known as the *California Schottische* and *Oklahoma Mixer* have come from variations of the Texas Schottische. Jane Farwell adapted the Oklahoma Mixer and named it *Texas Schottische for Three,* partly to compensate for the man shortage during the war.

Records: Any smooth Schottische. MAV Album 4; Shaw E23; World of Fun MH 130.

Formation: Line of three, man between two ladies, facing line of direction; man reaching back holds outside hand of each lady, ladies join inside hands behind man.

Steps: Two-Step, walk, heel toe.

■ Directions for the Dance

Meter 4/4 • Directions are same for man and lady.

Measures

1–2 Beginning left, take two Two-Steps, moving diagonally left, then right.

3–4 Beginning left, four walking steps forward.

5–6 Place left heel forward, place left toe close to right instep (counts 1–4). Ladies release inside hands. Man backs up three steps, pulling ladies around in front, as ladies take three steps (left, right, left) in line of direction, turning back to face reverse line of direction. Man faces line of direction, ladies face reverse line of direction. Beginning right, repeat heel, toe. Man gives a slight pull of hands, then releases hands, as all take three steps (right, left, right) forward. Man passes between the two ladies, and joins hands with new partners; ladies turn towards each other, pivoting on third step to face line of direction.

Notes

1. A marvelous mixer for extra men to cut in, and, in Jane Farwell's words, "snatch two women" leaving another man to become one of the "thieves."
2. An excellent dance to teach the Schottische steps.

---

* Texas Schottische for Three included by permission of the late Jane Farwell, Folklore Village Farm, Dodgeville, WI.

🌾 Ten Pretty Girls

Ten Pretty Girls is usually identified as originating in Texas. The Schottische pattern of Ten Pretty Girls and that of the Military Schottische, one of the Texas Schottische variations, are identical. According to Herb Greggerson, well-known Square Dance caller and leader of the famous Blue Bonnet Set of El Paso, Texas, which toured New York City* in 1939, the name of this dance is credited to the popular extravaganza producer Bill Rose, who upon seeing the dancers in El Paso exclaimed, "Give me ten pretty girls and I'll use that dance at the Casa Mañana" (the 1936 Fort Worth extravaganza of the Texas Centennial).

Records: MAV Album 2, FD LP2, EZ 5003, 6004, LS E 36; World of Fun MH 130; DC 162402.

Cassette: DC 162402.

Formation: Lines of three, four, six, or as many as desired; arms around neighbor's waist; facing line of direction.

Steps: Grapevine, walk.

■ Directions for Mixer

Meter 4/4 • Directions are same for man and lady.

Measures

1   Beginning left, tap left to side twice, grapevine to right stepping left behind right, right to side, cross left in front of right (slow, slow, quick, quick, slow).

2   Beginning right, tap right to side twice, grapevine to left stepping right behind left, step left to side, and cross right in front of left (slow, slow, quick, quick, slow).

3   Beginning left, walk forward four steps.

4   Swing left forward, swing left backward, stamp three times in place. Body leans backward and forward with action of leg swing.

Repeat dance beginning right.

---

* Herb Greggerson and the Blue Bonnet Set appeared at the New York World's Fair, Madison Square Garden, and Chesterfield Radio Broadcast Center during their 1939 tour.

✿ Salty Dog Rag

The *Salty Dog Rag* is a novelty dance composed to a popular tune, based on the Schottische rhythm.

Records: DC 73304; High/Scope RM 9; MCA 60090; Nama LP 2.

Position: Promenade.

Steps: Grapevine Schottische, step-hop

■ Directions for the Dance

Meter 4/4 • Directions are same for man and lady.

Measures

1 - 8   Introduction: no action.

      Part I

1 - 2   Beginning right, take two grapevine Schottische steps, moving diagonally forward right (step right, step left behind right, step right hop) diagonally forward left (step left, step right behind left, step left hop).

3 - 4   Moving forward, take four step-hops (or step swings).

5 - 8   Repeat action of measures 1 - 4.

      Part II

1   Dropping right hands, left hands remain joined, lady turns to face partner on her first step. Beginning right, take one grapevine Schottische step sideways to own right (partners move away from each other).

2   Beginning left, each takes a three-step turn, turning left, toward partner. Begin impetus for turn by each pulling joined hands slightly, then drop hands to complete solo turn.

3 - 4   Catch right hands, shoulder height, elbows bent. Beginning right, take four step-hops (or struts), making one complete turn clockwise.

5 - 8   Repeat action of part II, measures 1 - 4. On last step-hop, take promenade position and face line of direction.

      Part III

1 - 2   Beginning right, place heel forward, step right in place; place left heel forward, step left in place; rise on both toes swinging heels out (pigeon-toed); click heels together; stamp right, stamp left.

3 - 4   Take four step-hops forward.

5 - 8   Repeat action of part III, measures 3 - 4.

Note

Many people dance parts I and II alternately, omitting part III.

🌀 Glowworm

Glowworm Gavotte is the complete name of this dance. This version was taught at the Lloyd Shaw Cheyenne Mountain School.

Records: DC 162303 LP; FD LP 3; EZ 5012, 6013; HLP 4028; LS E 46, 106; MAV Album 3; Windsor 4613.

Cassette: DC 162303.

Music: Lincke, Paul, "The Glow Worm," Edward B. Mark Music Corp, RCA Building, Radio City, NY.

Position: Inside hands joined.

Steps: Walk, slide, Two-Step, grapevine, dip.

■ Directions for the Dance

Meter 4/4 • Directions are for man; lady's part reverse.

Measures

Part I

1 - 2   Walk forward three steps, left, right, left. Touch right toe forward (count 4). Beginning right, repeat.

3 - 4   Partners face, join two hands. Take grapevine step left, right, left, and swing right across in front of left (count 4). Beginning right, repeat moving in the reverse line of direction.

5 - 6   Beginning left, man and lady exchange places taking three steps, turn and point, lady turning counterclockwise under man's upraised right arm. Man walks across, passing right shoulders with lady. Beginning right, repeat exchange to end in original position.

7 - 8   Closed position. Four two-steps turning clockwise and progressing in line of direction.

Part II

9   Couple position. Walk forward three steps left, right, left, and touch right toe forward (count 4).

10   Partners face, join two hands. Beginning right, take two slides in reverse line of direction. Step right and dip backward left by shifting weight to left and point right toe forward (count 4), facing reverse line of direction. Body leans toward pointed foot.

11   Beginning right, repeat action of measure 9, continue in reverse line of direction.

12   Beginning left, repeat action of measure 10, taking dip with weight on right and point left toe forward, now facing the line of direction.

13 - 14   Closed position. Beginning left, take six steps (counts 1, 2, 3, 4, 1, 2) or two Two-Steps. Man steps in place, lady turns three times clockwise under man's upraised left arm (2 counts to each turn). Dip back on left (count 3). This is like a Tango Corté. Step forward right (count 4).

15 - 16   Beginning left, four Two-Steps turning clockwise, progressing in line of direction.

Style

This is a very stately dance. Careful footwork and an upright body will give the dance a Minuet-like quality.

Boston Two-Step

The *Boston Two-Step,* of English origin, has become part of the American fabric of dance and is an old-time favorite still danced at the Grange halls and dancehalls, where social dances (Foxtrot, Waltz) prevail. The dance programs feature occasional pattern dances like the Boston Two-Step.

Records: RPT LP106; Shaw E 46.

Position: Partners face, man joins lady's right hand with his left or join two hands.

Steps: Step swing, three-step turn, Two-Step.

■ Directions for the Dance

Meter 2/4 • Directions are for man; lady's part reverse.

Measures

Part I

1	Beginning left, step in place, swing right over left.
2	Step right in place, swing left over right.
3–4	Release hands. Traveling in the line of direction, take one three-step turn (man turning counterclockwise; lady clockwise) and swing right over left.
5–8	Join hands. Beginning right, repeat action of measures 1–4, three-step turn, moving forward in the reverse line of direction.
9–12	Join hands. Beginning left, repeat action of measures 1–4, three-step turn moving forward in the line of direction, **stamp right** (instead of last swing). Place weight on right foot.

Part II

13–16	Closed position. Beginning left, take four Two-Steps, turning clockwise, progressing in the line of direction.

Variation

In Part II, a pivot may be substituted for the last two Two-Steps or for all four Two-Steps.

🎵 Heel and Toe Polka

Music: Any lively polka.

Position: Closed or shoulder-waist.

Steps: Heel and Toe Polka, Polka.

■ Directions for the Dance

Meter 2/4 • Directions are for the man; lady's part reverse.

Measures

I. Heel and Toe Polka

1 – 2   Moving to the left, hop right (count **and**), place left heel close to right instep (count 1), hop right (count **and**), place left toe close to right instep (count 2), take one Polka step to the left (counts 1 **and** 2).

3 – 4   Moving to the right, repeat action of measures 1 – 2, hopping on right.

5 – 8   Repeat action of measures 1 – 4.

II. Polka

9 – 16   Take eight Polka steps, turning clockwise, progressing in the line of direction.

Polka Variations

1. **Crossover Polka:** Varsouvienne position. Man and lady both begin Heel and Toe Polka by hopping right. Without releasing hands, lady crosses over to man's left on the hop step, close, step, man dancing almost in place. Lady crosses back to original position on second Heel and Toe Polka. This action repeats. Second part, couple takes eight Polka steps, moving forward in the line of direction.
2. **Crossover Polka with Three-Step Turn:** During the Crossover Polka, part I, lady makes a three-step turn to cross over and back. Heel toe, heel toe, release right hands and turn under left arm, stepping left, right, left; rejoin right hands. Repeat to right, releasing left hands for turn. Part II, Polka forward.
3. **Slide Polka:** Closed position, man's back to center of circle. Heel toe, heel toe, take four slides, traveling in the line of direction (the last slide is not completed in order to change direction). Repeat traveling in the reverse line of direction. Take eight Polka steps, turning clockwise, progressing in the line of direction.
4. **Falcon Hop:** In 1950, at the after parties of the National Folk Festival, St. Louis, Missouri, it was fun to dance with the Polish-American dancers. To sprightly Polka tunes, especially the Polish ones, in closed or shoulder-waist position, they danced the Falcon Hop. The Falcon Hop is a small Polka step, turning clockwise as they progressed forward, but actually not traveling very far. The dancers appeared to "jiggle" as they hopped.

🎵 Cotton-Eyed Joe

Dorothy Scarborough identifies *Cotton-Eyed Joe* as an authentic slavery tunesong in her book *On the Trail of Negro Folksongs*. One that antebellum blacks played and sang was one that dealt with Cotton-Eyed Joe. Judging by the many verses—all in the same vein—he was a tantalizing, intriguing, and devilish character.

> Hadn't been for Cotton-Eyed Joe
> I'd 'a' been married twenty years ago
> With an old gourd fiddle and a cornstalk bow
> None could play like Cotton-Eyed Joe.

The fiddle tune, written in 2/4 meter, may be found in several references, one being Ira W. Ford's *Traditional Music of America*. Some references present the same tune in 4/4 meter.

According to Uncle Dave Dillingham (Pittman, Swenson, Sanders 1947) of Austin, Texas, who learned the dance in Williamson County in the early 1880s, Cotton-Eyed Joe is nothing but a Heel and Toe "Poker," with fringes added. For the most part, the fringes, or variations, over and above the Heel and Toe Polka were originally clog steps, which required skill as well as extroversion on the part of the dancer.

Uncle Dave, at age 81 (1947), recalled the visits of Professor Whitehead, the visiting dancing master, who dealt with the finer points of ballroom dancing. The dancing master taught the Heel and Toe Polka in every community he visited, along with the Waltz, and so forth. But the short duration of his visit, the scarcity of students, and the ability of dancers no doubt contributed to the fact that the Heel and Toe Polka was not mastered by the majority of the dancers. In addition to these difficulties, the fringes that really make the dance were for the most part made up of clog steps, which not only require skill but also require an extroversion that is not a common trait attributed to the average dancer but is easy for the "Fancy Dan" who was, and still is, an exception on the dance floor. The dance as described is a simple version, commonly danced in Texas.

Records: Belco 257; Express 405; EZ 715, 6003, LP 506; FD LP 5; MAV Album 5; HM 35, 74; LS E 35; World of Fun MH 130.

Cassettes: DC 162105; MH 35, C 74.

Music: Dave, Red River, "Cotton-Eyed Joe," Southern Music Co., San Antonio, TX.

Position: Closed.

Steps: Polka, Two-Step, push step.

Directions for the Couple Dance

Meter 2/4 • Directions are for man; lady's part reverse.

Measures

I.   Heel and Toe Polka

1-2   Hop right, touch left heel out to the left (count *and* 1). Hop right, touch left toe behind right foot (count *and* 2). Polka to left (counts *and* 1, *and* 2), in the line of direction.

3-4   Repeat beginning with hop on left foot and travel in the reverse line of direction.

II.   Individual Turn

5-8   Three Two-Steps turning in a small circle. The man turns counterclockwise, the lady turns clockwise. Finish with three quick stamps in place, facing partner.

Cotton-Eyed Joe (continued)

III. Push Step

9-10   Chug left foot sideward in line of direction (count 1), place the weight momentarily on the right (count *and*), push back onto left foot, chugging left sideward again and flip right heel out to the side (count 2). Push with the right (count *and*), chug left (count 1), push with right (count *and*), chug left (count 2). Weight remains on left.

11-12   Repeat action of measures 9-10, starting with the right foot, and moving to the right.

IV. Two-Step or Polka

13-16   Four Two-Steps in closed dance position, turning clockwise, progressing in the line of direction. These may be Polka steps.

Variations

The dancers perform the variations at random, measures 9-16. After the variation, the Heel and Toe Polka and the individual turn are repeated.

1. **Two-Step Away and Toward Partner:** Moving away from partner, takes four small Two-Steps; step left directly behind right (count 1), step right in place (count **and**), step left in place (count 2); step right directly behind left (count 1), step left in place (count **and**), step right in place (count 2); repeat. Moving towards partner, take four small Two-Steps.

2. **Hooking:** Partners grasp right hands, free left arm curved and raised shoulder height as each dancer hops on left, extending right foot to meet partner's right foot, hooking foot just back of partner's right ankle. Take eight hops, couple turning clockwise in place. Reverse direction, grasping left hands, hooking left ankles, and taking eight hops, beginning left. Couple turns counterclockwise. Partners lean away from each other, slightly offering resistance or counterbalance as they turn; hooked leg is straight.

3. **Jig Steps:** These Jig and Clog steps are listed for historical significance and for the advanced dancer to pursue. They are not analyzed. Partners face each other and do Jig or Clog Dance steps such as shifting sands, seven steps, grapevine twist, pigeon wing, double shuffle, buzzard loop, triple step, and rock the cradle. Uncle Dave Dillingham at 80 would dance these steps, doing a solo, while his partner marked the rhythm, moving ever so lightly in place, perhaps working her skirt "à la Square or Mexican" dance styling.

■ Directions for the Line Dance

Formation: Lines of three, four, six, or as many as desired, arms around neighbor's waist, facing line of direction. Lines move like spokes in a wheel. Or lines of two in Varsouvienne or Promenade position.

Steps: Kick, Two-Step.

Meter 2/4 • Directions are same for man and lady.

Measures

I. Kicker

1   Beginning left, cross left foot and knee in front of right knee; kick left foot forward.

2   Back up, taking one Two-Step.

3-4   Beginning right, repeat action of measures 1-2.

5-8   Repeat action of measures 1-4.

II. Two-Step

9-16   Beginning left, take eight Two-Steps in line of direction.

Improvisation may take place in part II, such as turning, backing up, or walking around.

Black Hawk Waltz

The *Black Hawk Waltz* was taught at the Lloyd Shaw Cheyenne Mountain School, August 1943, 1946, and 1947.

Records: Folkraft 1046; EZ 6008; Lloyd Shaw 104.

Music: *The Folk Dancer,* Vol. 6, No. 11, November 1946, pp. 10–12.

Position: Closed.

Steps: Waltz, balance.

■ Directions for the Dance

Meter 3/4 • Directions are for man; lady's part reverse.

Measures

	I.	**Balance Waltz**
1–4		Balance or rock forward on left, balance backward on right. Repeat balance forward and backward.
5–8		Beginning left, four Waltz steps, turning clockwise, progressing in the line of direction.
9–12		Repeat action of measures 1–4.
13–16		Beginning left, two Waltz steps, followed by six walking steps forward.
	II.	**Cross Step**
17		Man places left (lady right) across in front of right, letting it take weight.
18		Place right across left in the same manner.
19–20		Cross again with left followed by step sideward to right with right, step with left behind right and finally, point right sideways to right (weight remains on left).
21–24		Beginning right, repeat action of measures 17–20, moving to left on the completion.
25–32		Repeat action of measures 17–24.

Note

The first 16 measures of balance and Waltz steps may be done as follows: Balance forward and back, two Waltz steps. Repeat three times.

Style

During the crossing step, the foot is extended and the toe is pointed to the side. This is accompanied by a turn of the body in the new direction.

🌀 Blue Pacific Waltz

The *Blue Pacific Waltz* was composed by Henry "Buzz" Glass of Oakland, California.

Records: LS E 48; Windsor 7609.

Music: *Over the Waves.*

Position: Inside hands joined.

Steps: Waltz, three-step turn.

■ Directions for the Dance

Meter 3/4 • Directions are for man; lady's part reverse.

Measures

I. Three-Step Turn and Swing

1 — Beginning left, step left and swing right across left, turning slightly away from partner.

2–3 — Beginning right, take a three-step turn clockwise (lady counterclockwise) exchanging places with partner (holding count 2, move on counts 1, 3, 1). Swing left across right, turning slightly away from partner (counts 2–3). The rhythm of this figure is known as the Canter. Lead: Man draws lady across in front of him into the turn with his joined hand, releasing just in time to make the turn, and then catches the opposite hand after the turn.

4–5 — Beginning left, repeat action of measures 2–3, swinging right across.

6 — Step right, turning to face partner. Touch left to right, keep weight on right. Take closed position.

7–8 — Two Waltz steps turning clockwise, progressing in line of direction.

9–16 — Repeat action of measures 1–8.

II. Twinkle Step

17 — Semi-open position, facing line of direction. Step left forward, swing right forward.

18 — Step right forward, step left in place facing partner, step right in place facing reverse line of direction (counts 1, 2, 3). This movement is called the twinkle step (Waltz time).

19 — Step left across right in reverse line of direction, step right in place, facing partner. Step left in place to face line of direction in open position.

20 — Step forward right, touch left to right, keep weight on right.

21–28 — Repeat action of measures 17–20 twice.

29 — Step left forward, swing right forward.

30 — Man: Step right across left, close to left toe (count 1). Pirouette on toes turning one-half counterclockwise (counts 2–3). Lady: Three little steps (right, left, right) and follow man's turn counterclockwise, walking around him.

31–32 — Closed position. Two Waltz steps turning counterclockwise. Open into couple position to repeat dance from beginning.

Note

For simplification of measures 30–32, step right forward, touch left to right, keep weight on right and take closed position. Two Waltz steps turning clockwise.

Garden Waltz

The *Garden Waltz* is a German-American Waltz for three dancers from New Braunfels, Texas, with two rhythms, Waltz and Polka.

Record: Bellaire 5031.

Formation: Set of three, man between two ladies, facing line of direction. Man's arms around ladies' waist, ladies' inside arm around man's waist, or hook elbows.

Steps: Hesitation Waltz, Waltz, Polka, or Two-Step.

■ Directions for the Dance

Measures

Meter 3/4 • Directions are same for man and lady.

	I. Waltz Forward
1 – 16	Beginning left, take 16 Hesitation Waltz steps forward. Hesitation Waltz step: Step forward left, knee slightly bent (count 1), bring right to left, rising on balls of both feet (count 2), end weight on left (count 3). Repeat beginning right. Styling: body falls count 1, body lifts counts 2 and 3, similar to body action in a step-swing.

Meter 2/4

	II. Polka Turns
1 – 16	Release hold. Beginning left, man takes 16 Polka or Two-Steps, first hooking right elbows with right-hand lady, turning clockwise with four Polka steps; then hooking left elbows with left-hand lady, turning counterclockwise with four Polka steps. Turn right-hand lady, then left-hand lady again. If quick, turn each four times alternately.

Variation

Meter 3/4

Waltz Turns

1 – 8	Beginning left, take eight Hesitation Waltz steps forward.
9 – 16	Inside hands joined with man, raise arms. As man takes eight Waltz steps forward, two ladies spin under raised arms away from man, right-hand lady counterclockwise, left-hand lady clockwise. Ladies may take eight Waltz steps turning.

Meter 2/4

Polka Turns

1 – 8	Elbow Turns: All dance eight Polka steps as man hooks right elbows with right-hand lady, turn with four Polka steps, then hooks left elbows with left-hand lady, turn with four Polka steps.
9 – 16	Arches: All take eight Polka steps: right-hand lady travels under arch made by man and left-hand lady, then back to place; man turns under his left arm; left-hand lady repeats.

❧ Waltz of the Bells ❧

The *Waltz of the Bells* was composed by "Doc" and Winnie Alumbaugh, Alhambra, California.

Records: Folkraft 4605; Lloyd Shaw 109; Windsor 4605; World of Fun Vol. 2.

Position: Inside hands joined.

Steps: Waltz, three-step turn, rock step.

■ Directions for the Dance

Meter 3/4 • Directions are for man; lady's part reverse.

Measures

| | **I.** | **Swing and Waltz** |

1–2   Beginning left, step forward and swing right forward. Step right backward and swing left slightly across in front of right. Joined hands swing forward and back.

3–4   Repeat action of measures 1–2.

5–6   Beginning left, two Waltz steps. Partners turn away from each other, making one full turn, lady right, man left, and progress in line of direction. End with two hands joined, facing partner.

7–8   Step left, draw right to left. Step left, draw right to left, keeping weight on left. (Holding count 2, move on counts 1, 3, 1, 3.) This is known as canter rhythm.

9–16   Beginning right, repeat action of measures 1–8, progressing in reverse line of direction.

II.   Step Close and Lady Turn

17–18   Partners facing, join two hands, Beginning left, step sideward left, in line of direction. Close right to left. Step sideward left, close right to left (holding count 2, move on counts 1, 3, 1, 3).

19–20   Man takes step left, close right, step left, touch right in place keeping weight on left. Lady takes a three-step turn clockwise under man's upraised left arm (counts 1–3, 1) to face partner, close left to right, keeping weight on right (counts 2–3).

21–24   Repeat action of measures 17–20, moving in reverse line of direction, lady turning under man's right arm. **Note:** In the original dance, man turned lady with the trailing arm, but it is generally not danced this way.

III.   Rock Step and Waltz

25–26   Partners facing, man's right hand holds lady's left. Rock back on left away from partner, then rock forward on right toward partner.

27–28   Repeat action of measures 25–26. Take closed position on the last rock step together.

29–30   Two Waltz steps, turning clockwise, progressing in line of direction.

31–32   Six little steps, man stepping in place and turning lady clockwise under his upraised left arm.

〰️ Varsouvienne ❧

The *Varsouvienne* is also known, especially in Texas, as *Put Your Little Foot.*

Records: Folkraft 1165; Windsor 4615; LS E 45; EZ 715; World of Fun MH 130.

Music: Lloyd Shaw, *Cowboy Dances,* p. 392.

Position: Varsouvienne.

Steps: Mazurka.

■ Directions for the Dance

Meter 3/4 • Directions are same for both lady and man.

Measures

I. Long Phrase

1	Swing left heel across in front of right instep (count 3, pick up beat). Step left, close right to left, weight ends on right (counts 1–2).
2	Repeat action of measure 1.
3–4	Swing left heel across in front of right instep (count 3, pick up beat). Step left, right, left (counts 1, 2, 3) and point right foot to right (counts 1–2).
5–8	Beginning right, repeat action of measures 1–4.

II. Short Phrase

9–10	Repeat action of measures 3–4.
11–16	Beginning right, repeat action of measures 9–10 through three times.

Variations for Measures 3–8 (Part I)

1. **Crossover:** Beginning left, the man moves the lady across in front of him to his left side with three steps. Beginning right, he moves her back to his right side.
2. **Turnback:** During the three steps, make half-turn clockwise and point in opposite direction. Beginning right, turn counterclockwise. **Note:** Forward or backward movements with a pivot on first or third step may be used.

Variation for Measures 9–16 (Part II)

Swing In and Out: Beginning left, repeat action of measures 3–4 as follows: Man: Take steps in place. Lady: Release man's right hand and take three steps toward center of circle to face reverse line of direction, out to the left and slightly in front of man. Beginning right, take three steps turning counterclockwise under man's upraised left arm and finish in original position. Repeat action toward center and back to original position.

Mixer

On measures 15–16 in the swing in and out variation, lady may move in reverse line of direction to a new partner and turn counterclockwise into place beside him in Varsouvienne position.

Note

Since parts I and II of the music vary on different records, the repetition of the action should vary accordingly.

❧ Cajun Dance ❧

Cajun dance, music, and food are very popular. In the 1980's Chef Paul Prudhomme of New Orleans attracted nationwide attention with his Cajun cooking and references to Cajun culture. Cajun culture suddenly bounced all over the United States. It exemplifies a true spirit of *joie de vivre*. The Cajun heritage is keyed to family, music, and the French language.

The word "Cajun" evolved from the word "Acadian" with the loss of an unstressed syllable (*cf.* Injun from Indian). The Acadians originally came from the French provinces of Normandy and Picardy along the English Channel. The first French colony, Acadie,* was established in 1604 in Nova Scotia, Canada. For political reasons the British deported the Acadians in 1755. Some migrated south, finally settling in the flatlands and bayous of Louisiana with other French. This coastal area, actually 22 of the 64 parishes of Louisiana, is referred to as Acadia, Acadiana, or Evangeline country.

From France the Acadians brought their 17th–18th century culture to the New World. Their culture evolved and adapted with that of the French, English, Spanish, and Afro-Americans. The white French-speaking people of Acadia are referred to as Cajuns; the black French-speaking people are Creoles. (These are not the same Creoles that settled New Orleans.)

Families have always gathered together for social occasions, first at homes and later at barns and dancehalls. Music, French ballads, dancing, cards, and of course food were enjoyed. These gatherings were called *fais-dodo* ("go to sleep") because the children were bedded down in another room while the parties lasted till the wee hours. When the halls became night clubs, the children were excluded.

■ MUSIC

Originally the fiddle was the primary instrument and someone sang old French ballads. The interaction of the Acadians and Creoles influenced the music. The singing became less important as two fiddles played, one melody, one rhythmic backup. More French songs were lost in the 1880s when the German immigrants introduced the button accordion. By the 1920s, the accordion had displaced the fiddles. But during the '30s and '40s fiddles returned as the Cajun musicians were influenced by their Texas neighbors' Country Western music. Later Bob Wills's western swing, Nashville Country Western music, and rock and roll all touched Cajun music too. After World War II Cajuns returned home with a sense of pride and a rebirth of Cajun music took place. The folk festivals also encouraged traditional Cajun musicians to come forward. Michael Doucet is to be credited with his leadership in restoring interest in traditional Cajun music, encouraging acoustic playing, and playing outside the lounges.

Today the button accordion is the lead instrument and the accordion player also sings French songs. The fiddle and small triangle make up the band. In larger bands there are guitars, spoons, drums, bass, and sometimes brass. Of course there is electric amplification. Cajun music, sometimes referred to as "Chanky Chank" sounds, is a mix of sounds, styles, and cultural history.

A relatively new offshoot of Cajun music is Zydeco, a combination of Cajun and rhythm and blues with a Caribbean musical pulse. The band includes a piano accordion and a metal washboard (or vest, strapped on the musician, who also wears metal casings on the fingers that produce a myriad of sounds), along with the other instruments. The songs are in English or French. The rhythm is 4/4, a strong 1-2, 1-2 beat.

■ DANCE

The Acadian dance repertoire included the quadrille, lancer, polka, mazurka, play party types referred to as *Danserond,* and contredanse. Many dances were performed without instrumentation during the 40 days before Lent, so they sang, which helped to keep the language alive. Young and old danced, especially those of a "marrying age." The contredanse was more like the Appalachian Big Circle—a country dance. In the late '40s the Cajun round dance scene was very similar to that in Texas. It is almost a step back in time to watch the Cajuns dance the waltz, two-step, one-step. There is jitterbug and Zydeco is the latest dance.

---

*Acadie, which the French called their settlement, was a descriptive word of the Micmac Indians, members of the Olgonquin tribe.

Records: Cajun: *Parlez Nous á Boire* (two-step, swing, blues, waltz), CD 322; *Allons á Lafayette, Bayou Boogie,* Bcausolcil; *Stir Up the Roux,* Brucc Daigrcpont. Zydcco: *Louisiana Blues and Zydeco,* Clifton Chenier, CD 329; *Louisiana Zydeco Music,* Boo Zoo Chavis.

Cajun Waltz

Meter 3/4 • Directions are for man; lady's part reverse.

Forward Waltz: Closed position. The man pulls the lady close, wrapping most of his right forearm around the lady's shoulder blades. Moving in the line of direction, step on each beat (left, right, left). The first step is longer, followed by a shuffle, shuffle. The man travels forward, lady backward, most of the time; minimal turning. Two measures (6 steps) to turn in place counterclockwise; may turn clockwise.

Lady's turn: Couple travels forward. Man releases right hand and steps slightly to left side (count 1) and forward (count 2, 3) as lady turns clockwise under his left arm, 3 steps. As she turns, she places her left bent arm behind her back. As she completes the turn the couple resumes the closed position.

Double turn: Couple travels forward and man releases right hand. Man takes three steps forward as lady turns with three steps clockwise under his left arm, places her left arm behind her back; lady continues to travel backward as the man turns counterclockwise three steps under his left arm; resumes the closed position.

Style: The dance is smooth as if gliding on ice. A fluid movement is achieved by dancing on the balls of the feet and absorbing the movement with bent knees.

Cajun Two-Step

Meter 2/4 or 4/4 • Directions are for man; lady's part reverse.

Closed position. The man pulls the lady close, wrapping most of his right forearm around the lady's shoulder blades. Progressing forward, the couple turns slowly counterclockwise, step-close-step touch. Step to the left side, and slightly forward, close right to left, step left in place, touch right to left instep (4 counts). May turn clockwise.

Style: The dance is smooth. In some areas, dancers rock slightly side to side.

Cajun One-Step

Meter 4/4 • Directions are for man; lady's part reverse.

Closed position. Travel forward stepping side to side on each beat (side touch, side touch). Turning counterclockwise, step side touch near instep, step side touch near instep, step side touch near instep, step side touch near instep.

Transition one-step to two-step or vice versa. The change of pattern is made when the feet are together.

🌿 Cajun Jitterbug 🌿

Cajun Jitterbug is frequently danced to two-step music. The steps are smooth with many variations.

Meter 2/4 • Directions are for man; lady's part reverse.

Two hands joined. The basic step appears to be a "slight limp" with weight on right foot. Step left and lightly drag the right to the left, accent the second and fourth beats as the body drops (knees bend) ever so slightly. Step is smooth, (not a jerk or bounce). Step-close, step-close, (one and two and). The lead may change to right close, right close or during the moves, step alternately left, right on each beat like Four Count Swing, coming back into step close, step close. The arms push-pull like a parllelogram; arms held chest-high push to right side, pull left arm back, shift right side to right side and pivot clockwise using side close, side close or buzz step. Reverse to left side by side without losing a beat. The arms are never straight, sometimes referred to as "noodle arms."

    The man leads the moves. All the figures are smooth, one leading to the next as the dancers cover a circular space. Refer to Swing, pages 386–398, for different figures. Additional figures resemble Bavarian Laendler.

🌿 Amos Moses 🌿

Amos Moses is a novelty dance with no partner.

Meter 4/4 • Directions presented in beats.

Records: High/Scope RM8; RCA 447 0896.

Cassette: High/Scope RM8.

Formation: Scattered, all facing music.

Steps: Grapevine, stamp.

■ Directions for the Dance

Beats

1–4   Beginning right, place right heel forward, step right in place; place left heel forward, step left in place.

5   Grapevine in direction of music: pivoting a quarter turn left, step sideward right.

6   Step left behind right.

7   Step sideward right.

8–9   Turning right one-half turn, step left, right in place.

10   Stamp left foot, taking weight, and at the same time clap hands.

Note

After each sequence all will face one-quarter turn to the right.

Jessie Polka

In Country Western dance, the *Jessie Polka* is also known as the *Cowboy Polka* or the *Eight-Step Shuffle*.

Records: EZ 5004; High/Scope RM8; MacGregor 5001; National 4533.

Cassette: High/Scope RM8.

Music: Any good Polka.

Position: Form groups of two or more in a line, with arms around each other's waists. Groups progress counterclockwise around the room.

Steps: Two-Step or Polka.

■ Directions for the Dance

Meter 2/4

Measures

	I.	**Heel Step**
1		Beginning left, touch heel in front, then step left in place.
2		Touch right toe behind, then touch right toe in place, or swing it forward, keeping weight on left.
3		Touch right heel in front, then step right in place.
4		Touch left heel to the left side, sweep left across in front of right. Keep weight on right.
	II.	**Two-Step or Polka**
5–8		Four Two-Steps forward in the line of direction. Four Polka Steps may be used if preferred.

Variation

This dance may be done in a Conga line, one behind the other, with the leader moving in a serpentine on the four Two-Steps.

Mixer

Couples in line alternate lady and man. The lady may turn out to the right on the last two Two-Steps and come back into the line behind her partner. The lady at the end of the line rushes up to the head of the line.

🌀 Popcorn

Popcorn is a novelty dance with no partner. It is also known as *Alley Cat*.

Meter 4/4 • Directions presented in beats.

Records: "Popcorn," (fast) Eric 4009; High/Scope RM 3, 7; Musicor 1458, 1959; "Alley Cat," DC 687, 73304; (moderate) Atlantic 13113.

Cassette: High/Scope RM 3, 7.

Formation: Scattered, all facing music.

Steps: Touch, kick, jump.

■ Directions for the Dance

Beats

       Introduction: no action.

1–4   Beginning right, touch right toe in front, then touch along side left. Repeat.

5–8   Beginning left, repeat action of beats 1–4.

9–12   Beginning right, touch right toe backward, then touch alongside left. Repeat.

13–16   Beginning left, repeat action of beats 9–12.

17–20   Kick right, knee up in front of left knee and return. Repeat.

21–24   Kick left, knee up in front of right knee and return. Repeat.

25–28   Repeat action of beats 17–24. Action is double time.

29–30   Clap both hands together once.

31–32   Jump and turn a quarter turn to right.

       Repeat dance from beginning making a quarter turn to right at end of each sequence.

Note

Introduction: "Popcorn" 24 beats; "Alley Cat" 1 beat.

🎵 Twelfth Street Rag

Twelfth Street Rag is a novelty dance composed to a popular tune.

Records: DC 74505; High/Scope RM5.

Cassettes: DC 15X; High/Scope RM5.

Formation: Single circle, hands joined; scattered; or lines of four to five, hands joined, facing line of direction.

Steps: Strut, Charleston, grapevine.

■ Directions for the Dance

Meter 4/4

Measures

1   Beginning left, strut four steps forward.

2   Point left toe forward, then to side. Beginning left, take three steps backward.

3–4   Beginning right, repeat action of measures 1–2.

5   Beginning left, take seven quick steps sideward to left. Type of step options could be shuffle, step close, grapevine, and swivel steps.

6   Beginning right, take seven quick steps sideward to right.

7–8   Beginning left, take two Charleston steps in place.

Repeat dance.

Interlude

1   Jump forward on both feet, throwing hands up in air. Jump backwards on both feet, throwing hands back, turn and face the other way.

2   Turn individually to own right, taking three steps (strut right, left, right) and clap own hands on fourth count. Improvise during interlude.

🌿 Steppin' Out

Steppin' Out was composed by Roger and Jean Knapp of Corpus Christi, TX.

Record: Blue Star 1528.

Formation: Scattered, all facing music.

■ Directions for the Dance

Beats

Part A

1-4   Beginning left, step left, brush right forward, brush right backward across in front of left, brush right diagonally forward to the right.

5-8   Grapevine. Step right to right side, step left behind right, step side right, step left behind right.

9-12   Step right, brush left forward, brush left backward across in front of left, brush left diagonally forward to the right.

13-16   Grapevine to the left (left, right, left, right).

17-24   Turn a full turn around to left: step left, brush right forward, step right, brush left forward. Repeat two more step brushes.

25-32   In place, repeat the action of the first 4 beats. Then stamp right, left, right, turn a quarter turn right on last stamp and hold. Couple dance, face partner on stamps.

33-64   Facing a new direction, repeat the action of Part A. On the last three stamps, do not turn. Remain facing the same direction. Couple dance, move to own right, face line of direction on stamps.

Part B

1-8   Walk forward four slow steps and snap fingers between each step (left, snap, right, snap, left, snap, right, snap).

9-16   Step forward left, hold one count. Then with weight on left (left knee slightly bent for balance), with right toe describe a circle, brushing forward, out to the side, around behind, and back to place (two counts). Stamp right, left, right in place.

17-32   Repeat all of Part B again.

Sequence of Dance: A A B A three times.

Note

The first time through the pattern, there is full musical accompaniment. Second time, just the rhythm. Third time, silence until the last part. If the dancers keep a steady rhythm, they will step down on the left foot of Part A to full musical accompaniment.

Plain and Novelty Mixers

Gain or Exchange Partners

1. **Upset the Cherry Basket:** When the music stops, the leader requests that everyone change partners. If couples are asked to change with the couple nearest them, everyone is involved, and no one walks to the side for the lack of a partner.

2. **Snowball, Whistle Dance, Pony Express, or Multiplication Dance:** One to three couples start to dance. When the music stops, each couple separates and goes to the sidelines and gets a new partner. This is repeated until everyone is dancing.

3. **Line Up:** The men line up on one side of the room, facing the wall; the ladies on the other side, facing the wall. When the signal is given, each line backs up until they gain a new partner.

4. **Arches:** All the dancers form a single circle and walk counterclockwise around the circle. Two couples form arches on opposite sides of the circle. When the music stops, the arch is lowered. Those caught in the arch go to the center of the circle, gain a partner, and go back to the circle to form new arches. Eventually, just a few dancers will be walking through the tunnel of arches. When all have partners, the dancing proceeds.

5. **Star by the Right:** Six men form a right-hand star in the center of a single circle formed by the group. The star moves clockwise, and the circle counterclockwise. As the leader gives the signal, six ladies hook onto the star; alternate sexes are called out until all have hooked onto the star. A little spice is added if the last person on each spoke winks or beckons a specific person from the ring to join his or her spoke. When the star is completed the lady dances with the man on her right.

6. **Matching:** Advertising slogans (Ivory Soap—99.9 percent pure, it floats), split proverbs (a rolling stone—gathers no moss), famous couples (Romeo—Juliet), pairs of words that belong together (ham—eggs), playing cards (spades match with hearts for each number, clubs with diamonds), pictures cut in half (cartoons), or songs may be used for this mixer. Half of the slips of paper are given to the men, and the corresponding halves are distributed to the ladies. As the people circulate, they try to find the person with the corresponding half of their slogan, proverb, cartoon, or whatever has been selected to be matched. When everyone has found his or her partner, the dancing proceeds. If songs are used, each person sings his or her song until he or she finds the person singing the same song.

7. **Musical Chairs:** Set up a double row of chairs, back to back, almost the length of the room. Leave space between every group of four chairs so that partners can get together. The group marches around the chairs. When the music stops, each person tries to gain a seat. A man must sit back to back with a lady. These two become partners and proceed to dance while all the others continue to play the game until all have partners. When all are dancing, the next signal is given and partners separate and rush for a chair, thus providing a change of partners. **Musical knees:** Played like musical chairs, except that on a signal, the men get down on one knee and the ladies rush to sit on a knee. Those left out go to the side.

8. **Ice Cube Pass:** Double circle, men on the outside, ladies on inside. Pass an orange around men's circle; an ice cube around the ladies' circle. When the music stops, the man with the orange and lady with the ice cube step to center of circle or its outside and become partners. Repeat over and over, until all have partners. Several oranges and ice cubes may be passed simultaneously.

9. **Mexican Broom Dance.*** As couples are dancing, an extra man with a broom knocks the broom handle on the floor several times. Partners separate, ladies line up on left side of man with the broom and men on right side. The two lines are about five feet apart. All clap their hands while lining up and until they get a new partner. After everyone is in line, the man with the broom goes up and down the line and decides with which lady he wants to dance. When he has made his choice, he drops the broom and grabs his partner, while everyone else takes a partner too, and dancing resumes. Then the extra man picks up the broom and the procedure starts all over again. More fun is added to the mixer if the man in going up and down the line pretends to drop the broom but actually keeps on looking for a better partner.

*Herb Greggerson, author of *Herb's Blue Bonnet Calls*, saw this mixer danced in Mexico and presented it for the first time at a Square Dance institute at the University of Texas, April 1948. Directions were first printed in *Foot 'n' Fiddle*, Editors, Anne Pittman, Marlys Swenson, and Olcutt Sanders, May 1948, p. 4.

Trade Dances

1. **Are You on the Beam?** While everyone is dancing, a spotlight is suddenly focused on a specific area. Those people standing in the rays of the light are requested to give a yell, sing a song, or trade partners.
2. **Hats Off!** Four hats are distributed among four couples. Each couple with a hat places it on one member of another couple. When the music stops, the couples with the hats must change partners.

Tags

1. **Ladies' Tag or Men's Tag:** Certain dances may be designed as ladies' tag or men's tag.
2. **Similarity Tag:** Either a man or a lady may tag, but the person tagging can only tag someone who has a similar color of hair, eyes, shirt, shoes, and so on.
3. **"You Take the Lemon, I'll Take the Peach":** A few lemons or other designated articles are distributed among the men or the ladies. Anyone who holds the article may tag. Additional fun may be had by stopping the music periodically and anyone holding the article pays a forfeit. Later the forfeits are redeemed by performing a humorous stunt.

Elimination Dances

1. **Number Please?** Each couple is given a number. Each time the music stops, a number is called out and the couple or couples having the numbers called sit down. Numbers are called out until only one couple remains.
2. **Lemon Dance:** An object—for example, a lemon—is passed from couple to couple. When the music stops, the couple with the object sits down. Eventually one couple is left.
3. **Dance Contest:** Determine the type of dancing for the contest, for example, Waltz or Jitterbug. It should be conducted in a casual manner with qualified judges. Gradually, the contestants are eliminated until one or two couples remain. Choosing two couples, instead of one, for the winners keeps competition from becoming too keen.
4. **Orange Dance:** Each couple balances an orange or a tennis ball between their foreheads and proceeds to dance. Slow music like a Tango allows the dancers to concentrate on keeping the orange in position and still move to the music. When a couple drops the orange, they go to the sidelines. Eventually one couple is left and the rest have enjoyed the antics of those trying to keep the orange in position. Change the rhythm of the music to match the ability of the dancers.

All-American Promenade

The *All-American Promenade* was composed by "Doc" and Winnie Alumbaugh, Alhambra, California.

Records: CAN-Ed A784; Folkraft 1482; Windsor 4605.

Position: Inside hands joined.

Formation: Double circle, couples facing line of direction.

Steps: Walk, balance.

■ Directions for the Mixer

Meter 4/4 • Directions are for man; lady's part reverse.

Measures

I. Walk Step

1 – 2   Beginning left, walk four steps forward, turn toward partner on fourth step to face reverse line of direction, join inside hands. Back up four steps in line of direction.

3 – 4   Repeat action of measures 1 – 2 in reverse line of direction.

II. Balance, Exchange Places

5   Beginning left, balance away from partner (counts 1 – 2), balance toward partner (counts 3 – 4). Face line of direction during balance.

6   Beginning left, man walks four steps behind lady to opposite side. Beginning right, lady takes one four-step turn counterclockwise in front of man to opposite side. Man assists turn with right hand, releases during turn and catches inside hand at end of turn.

7   Beginning left, balance toward partner (counts 1 – 2), balance away from partner (counts 3 – 4).

8   Beginning left, man walks four steps, crossing behind lady, and moves forward to meet a new partner. Beginning right, lady takes one four-step turn to original side and moves back to meet a new partner.

Variation

Measure 8, beginning left, man takes four steps diagonally forward to inside of circle to meet a new partner. Beginning right, lady takes one four-step turn, moving behind man to outside of circle to meet new partner.

🌿 The Digging Dutchman* 🌿

The Digging Dutchman is an Anglo-American mixer adapted by Jane Farwell from the *Circle Mixer*, a dance called by Dick Witt of Devon, England, and published in the book *Everyday Dances* by Nibs Matthews. The Circle Mixer was inspired by the English folk dance the Lancashire Reel. The tune "The Digging Dutchman" was composed by Douglas Clark, a musician and dancer at Folklore Village. For years, Jane has been trying to grow a forest around Folklore Village. The tree-transplanting machine, called "The Digging Dutchman," was the source of inspiration for both the tune and the dance.

Record: Folklore Village FLV 103.

Music: "The Digging Dutchman," Werner, Robert, *The Folklore Village Saturday Night Book,* p. 25.

Formation: Double circle of couples, Varsouvienne position, facing line of direction.

Steps: Walk, balance, swing.

◼ Directions for the Mixer

Meter 6/8

Measures

A1   1–8   Walk eight steps forward in line of direction. Man moves on to the next lady. Take Varsouvienne position and together walk eight steps forward.

A2   1–4   Face new partner, man's back to center. Do-si-do partner. For a smooth transition from promenade to do-si-do, release left hands, man passes right arm over lady's head and both pull toward each other as they move into the do-si-do.

       5–8   With person diagonally left, join left hands and turn once around.

B1   1–4   Do-si-do partner, passing left shoulder first.

       5–8   With the person diagonally right, join right hands and turn once around.

B2   1–8   Return to partner, balance and swing.

---

*The Digging Dutchman included by permission of the late Jane Farwell, Folklore Village, Dodgeville, WI.

🎵 Glowworm Mixer

Records: Folkraft 1158, 4139; MAV Album 3, EZ 5012, 6013; Windsor 4613.

Cassette: DC 14X.

Position: Inside hands joined.

Formation: Double circle, couples facing line of direction.

Step: Walk.

■ Directions for the Mixer

Meter 4/4 • Directions are for man; lady's part reverse.

Measures

I. Forward

1   Beginning left, walk four steps forward in line of direction.

II. Away

2   Partners face, beginning left, man walks backward into center of circle four steps as lady walks backward away from center of circle four steps.

III. Diagonal Left

3   Both man and lady face diagonally to their own left. Beginning left, walk four steps forward to new partner.

IV. Turn Four

4   Beginning left, hook right arms with new partner and turn around in four steps, ending in couple position. (The lady needs to spin around on the last beat to face line of direction.)

Note

This may be danced to other four-beat music. It needs a newer tune now and then. For example: "Swedish Rhapsody," "Hello Dolly," "Hey Look Me Over," "Up with People," "A Spoonful of Sugar," "Hava Nagila," "Jingle Bells" (at Christmas), and current rock tunes.

🌿 🍃 Levi Jackson Rag*

The *Levi Jackson Rag* is an Anglo-American Mixer for a five-couple set. It is a sprightly dance and ragtime-style tune by the late Pat Shaw, and was commissioned by the Mountain Folk Festival, Adult Section, of Berea College in 1975. The Adult Festival is held annually at Levi Jackson State Park near London, Kentucky.

Pat Shaw had a passionate interest in music and kept his interest in both folk song and dance centered in his life. He contributed significantly in the research, publication, and composition of music and dance, and in the leadership of the folk dance movement.

Records: Country Dance Album CLR 16L; Festival 801; LS E 28; Folklore Village FLV 103; Shaw E 28.

Cassette: Country Dance Album CLR 16C.

Music: "Levi Jackson Rag," Werner, Robert, *The Folklore Village Saturday Night Book,* p. 35.

Formation: Five-couple set, one head couple and four side couples.

Steps: Walk, swing.

■ Directions for the Mixer

Meter 2/4

Measures

1–4   Introduction: no action (8 counts).

A 1–18   Side couples right and left thru and back with opposite side couple. For measures 3–4, head couple, inside hands joined, walk halfway down center of set; for measures 7–8, continue to foot of set.

9–12   Side couples join hands with opposites to circle four left once around, while head couple separates, casts back to home place.

13–16   All partners do-si-do.

B 1–4   All five ladies chain to third man: right-hand star past partner and next man to third man, who turns lady with a courtesy turn. Head man should chain his lady around fairly fast, so that she may get back into the star that follows.

5–8   All five ladies chain on two more places as above where they meet their new partners (their original corners).

9–10   Promenade new partner in line of direction to next place, taking four steps.

11–12   Balance partner right and left.

13–16   All swing new partners in new places.

Repeat whole dance four more times, ending in original position.

*Levi Jackson Rag included by permission of Mountain Folk Festival, Berea College, Berea, KY.

🪶 Jiffy Mixer

Jiffy Mixer was composed by Jerry and Kathy Helt, Cincinnati, Ohio.

Records: Windsor 4684; LS E 35; DC 74506.

Position: Butterfly.

Formation: Double circle, man's back to center of circle.

Steps: Balance, walk, chug, step-close-step, heel and toe.

■ Directions for the Mixer

Meter 2/4 • Directions are for man; lady's part reverse.

Measures

1 – 4	Introduction: Wait 2 measures. Beginning left, balance away from partner (step touch), balance together (step touch).
1 – 4	Beginning left, heel, toe, heel, toe, step side in line of direction, close right to left, step side left, touch right toe to left.
5 – 8	Beginning right, repeat the action of measures 1 – 4, moving in the reverse line of direction.
9 – 12	Release hands. Take four chug steps away from partner (both are backing away from each other), clapping between each chug. Chug (count 1), clap (count 2). The clap is on the upbeat of the music.
13 – 16	Beginning left, take four slow, swaggering steps, diagonally right, each progressing to a new partner. The ladies move forward in the line of direction; men in the reverse line of direction. Take Butterfly position to begin dance over.

Variation

An easier version, no partners, single circle, hands joined, all facing the center. Everyone begins the dance on the left foot, doing the same foot work. After the chug step, rejoin hands and travel in the reverse line of direction four slow steps *or* turn left, making a small circle, solo, four slow steps, to face center. Join hands and repeat dance.

🌀 Mexican Mixer

The *Mexican Mixer* is a popular Texas-Mexican Mixer dating from the French influence in Mexico. According to the noted Mexican dance authority Nelda Drury, San Antonio, Texas, the dance was introduced into Mexico during Maximilian's time and was danced to Viennese music.

Records: "Atotonilco," Musart 1154; MAV Album 7, FD LP7; Folkraft 1516; DOM 8102; High/Scope RM3; or any good Mexican Polka.

Cassette: High/Scope RM3.

Music: "Trompeta Magica," Werner, Robert, *The Folklore Village Saturday Night Book*, p. 24.

Formation: Double circle, couples facing line of direction.

Position: Promenade position.

Steps: Walk, balance, step swing.

■ Directions for the Mixer

Meter 4/4 • Directions are for man, lady's part reverse.

Measures

Walk and Grapevine

1–2   Beginning man's left, walk forward four steps. Face partner, give eye contact, hold right hands; man steps left to side, right behind left, steps left to side, swing right across left or stamp right lightly, no weight.

3–4   Moving forward in the reverse line of direction, repeat action of measures 1–2. Man begins right.

Balance and Turn

5   Single circle, man's back to center, lady faces center, partners' right hands joined, left hand to dancer on the left (corner). Beginning left, balance forward and back.

6   Release left hands. Turn partner with right-hand hold halfway around with four steps. Now men face center, ladies face out.

7   With partners' right hands joined, man joins left hands with dancer on his left. Beginning left, balance forward and back.

8   Release right-hand hold, turn with left-hand hold half around counterclockwise with four steps. End with new partner in promenade position facing line of direction.

Show enthusiasm by occasionally yelling or put tongue against upper teeth and make a continuous sound.

Patty-Cake Polka

Records: Folkraft 1260; Windsor 4624; EZ 3008, 6002; LS 228, E 24.

Cassette: DC 887.

Position: Partners face, two hands joined.

Formation: Double circle, man's back to center.

Steps: Heel and Toe Polka, slide, walk.

■ Directions for the Mixer

Meter 2/4 • Directions are for man; lady's part reverse.

Measures

	I.	**Heel and Toe Polka and Slide**
1-2		Beginning left, place left heel to left, place left toe to right instep. Repeat.
3-4		Take four slides in line of direction.
5-8		Beginning right, repeat the action of measures 1-4, moving in reverse line of direction.
	II.	**Claps**
9		Clap own hands, clap partner's right hand.
10		Clap own hands, clap partner's left hand.
11		Clap own hands, clap partner's hands (both).
12		Clap own hands, slap own knees.
13-14		Hook right elbows and walk around partner and back to place.
15-16		Man moves forward in line of direction to new partner. Lady spins clockwise twice, as she moves in reverse line of direction to new partner.
		Variation
9		Clap partner's right hand three times.
10		Clap partner's left hand three times.
11		Clap partner's hands (both) three times.
12		Slap own knees three times.

🎵 Oh Johnny

Oh Johnny is a popular singing call that may be done as a Square Dance or large Circle Mixer.

Records: Blue Star 1690; EZ 718, 721; Folkraft 1037, 2042; MacGregor 2042.

Formation: Single circle, couples facing center, lady to right of partner, hands joined.

Steps: Shuffle.

■ Directions for the Mixer

Singing Call

Oh, you all join hands and circle the ring. Circle moves clockwise.

Stop where you are and you give her a swing. Gents swing partners.

Now swing that girl behind you. Swing corner girl.

Go back home and

Swing your own if you have time. Swing with partners.

Allemande left with your corner girl. Allemande left with corner.

Do-sa 'round your own. Do-sa-do (sashay) around partner.

Now you all run away with your sweet corner maid. Promenade counterclockwise with corner lady for a new partner.

Singing, oh, Johnny, oh, Johnny, oh! Repeat call to end of recorded music.

Red River Valley

Records: Can-Ed A783; EZ 3003, 6015; Folkraft 1269; Pioneer 3007; Windsor 753; World of Fun Vol. I.

Position: Set of three, man between two ladies, arms linked.

Formation: Two sets of three, facing each other in large circle. Each set alternately faces line of direction and reverse line of direction.

■ Directions for the Mixer

Swinging Call

Verse 1

Now you lead right down to the valley. Walk diagonally forward to right and pass opposite set to meet new set.
Circle to the left, then to the right. All join hands and circle left, then right.
Now you swing with the gal in the valley. Man swings (elbow or waist swing) right-hand lady.
And you swing with your red river gal. Man swings left-hand lady.

Verse 2

Now you lead right on down the valley. Each set links arms. Walk diagonally forward to right and pass opposite set to meet new set.
Circle to the left, then to the right. All join hands and circle left, then right.
Now the girls make a wheel in the valley. Four ladies make right-hand star, walking clockwise once around and return to place.
And the boys do-sa-do so polite. Two men do-sa-do, passing right shoulders.

Verse 3

Now you lead right on down the valley. Each set links arms and passes opposite set as before to meet new set.
Circle to the left, then to the right. All join hands and circle left, then right.
Now you lose your gal in the valley. Two right-hand ladies change places crossing diagonally.
And you lose your red river gal. Two left-hand ladies change places in same manner. Each man now has two new partners for repeat of dance.

✂ Tennessee Wig Walk ✂

Records: "Tennessee Wig Walk," MCA 60051; "Hey Good Looking," Wagon Wheel 824.

Version I

This dance was composed by Harry and Dia Trygg, Tucson, Arizona, in 1954.

Formation: Double circle, couples, right-hand star position, men face line of direction, ladies face reverse line of direction.

Steps: Grapevine, walk.

■ Directions for the Mixer

Meter 4/4 • Directions are for man; lady's part reverse.

Measures

1–2 Introduction: no action.

1–2 Beginning left, point left toe across in front of right, point left toe to left side (slow, slow); exchanging places, grapevine, step left behind right, step right, cross left in front of right, hold (quick, quick, slow, slow). Man now on outside, lady inside, both facing original direction. Change to left hand star.

3–4 Beginning right, repeat action of measures 1–2 with opposite feet, returning to original position.

5–6 Right hand star position. Turning clockwise, make one full turn, stepping left, right, left, brush right; right, left, right, brush left. End facing original direction.

7–8 Release hands. Leave partner and move forward with step, step, step, brush step, step, step, brush. Man progresses in line of direction, lady reverse line of direction, passing first person on first "brush"; meeting next person on second "brush." Join right hands.

Repeat dance from beginning with new partner.

Version II

This dance was composed by Jane A. Harris Ericson, Pullman, Washington.

Formation: Double circle, men on inside, partners facing.

Steps: Walk, draw.

■ Directions for the Mixer

Meter 4/4 • Directions are for man; lady's part reverse.

Measures

1–2 Introduction: no action.

1–2 Beginning left, step left; draw right foot up to left, taking weight on right. Repeat. Step left; clap hands.

3–4 Beginning right, repeat action of measures 1–2, moving right.

5 - 6	Man moving right, lady right, move both feet together, toes first, then heels moving sideward. Repeat three times. Each ends up in front of a new partner (7 quick counts, hold eighth count).
7	Beginning left, take two steps turning (man left, lady right) in place in front of new partner (slow, slow).
8	Slap knees, clap own hands, clap partner's hands (quick, quick, slow).

Repeat dance from beginning, getting a new partner.

🌿 Teton Mountain Stomp 🌿

The *Teton Mountain Stomp* was composed by "Doc" Alumbaugh, Arcadia, California. It was adapted from the old *Buffalo Glide*.

Records: CAN Ed A783; Windsor A 7S3, 4615.

Position: Closed.

Formation: Single circle, men facing in line of direction.

Steps: Walk, pivot, Two-Step.

■ Directions for the Mixer

Meter 4/4 • Directions are for man; lady's part reverse.

Measures

	I.	**Side Step and Stamp**
1 - 2		Beginning left, step toward center, close right to left, step left toward center, and stamp right next to left.
3 - 4		Beginning right, repeat action of measures 1 - 2, moving away from center of circle.
5 - 6		Step left to side, stamp right beside left. Step right to side, stamp left beside right.
	II.	**Walk**
7 - 8		Left reverse open position. Walk four steps in line of direction (lady moves backward).
9 - 10		Right reverse open position. Walk four steps backward in line of direction (lady moves forward).
11 - 12		Man takes half-turn to face line of direction and walks four steps forward to meet the second lady for new partner. Lady walks four steps forward in reverse line of direction to meet second man for new partner.
	III.	**Two-Step, Pivot**
13 - 16		Closed position. Take two Two-Steps, turning clockwise, and four pivot steps. End with man facing line of direction.

CHAPTER 5

Square Dance

History

Antecedents

The antecedents of modern American *Square Dance* are the English Country Dances and the French Contredanse—Cotillon and Quadrille. The English Country Dances—the *Rounds, Longways,* and *Square Eight*—were introduced into France in the late 17th century. The Round and Square Eight forms were transformed by the French into the *Contredanse Francaise* and a later form called the *Cotillon.* The Contredanse and the Cotillon were dances for two and four couples in a square formation.

The word *Cotillon* means "underpetticoat" and comes from a French peasant song to which it was danced. The Cotillon was strictly a square in formation. Writers of the time used the terms *Contredanse* and *Cotillon* interchangeably, making it difficult to clarify the early development of these dance forms. Historians, however, agree that these forms were the antecedent of the Quadrille and thus of our modern Square Dance.

The Quadrille was a five-figure dance done by four couples in a four-sided figure or square. In its early form, the Quadrille consisted of four of the most popular Contredanses of the time. A fifth figure derived from the Cotillon—*Le Final*—was added at a later date to make the traditional five figures of the dance. The five figures were *Le Pantalon, L'Ete, La Poule, La Frenis,* and *Le Final.* French Quadrilles were for two, four, or any number of couples, and each remained vis-à-vis dancing only with each other. In England, it was danced with only four couples. Quadrille music was as exciting as the many and varied dance figures. The French used semiclassical music, light opera tunes, and music composed especially for the Quadrilles by well-known composers of the time.

Couple dances were also gaining in popularity at the same time the Quadrilles were in vogue. The Waltz, Polka, Mazurka, and Redowa were exciting new dances featuring daring dance positions and flying feet! The coexistence of the two resulted in combining Quadrilles with couple-dance steps. Waltz Quadrilles were especially numerous and popular.

The *Lancers* was a very elegant and elaborate form of the Quadrille. It must, therefore, be counted among the antecedents of our modern Square Dance. The Lancers consisted of four couples arranged vis-à-vis, and the five figures were danced with the opposite couple. In reality, the Lancers was a sequence of five Square Dances, each part danced to a different tempo. The fifth figure was usually a rousing military style 4/4 tempo. The well-known "Grand March" is actually the fifth figure of a long-forgotten Lancers. Although a Quadrille, the Lancers was listed and thus distinguished from Quadrilles on the dance program of the day.

Lancer music was usually written by well-known composers of the time and played by live full orchestras. Many American Lancers were danced to Gilbert and Sullivan melodies and some to Stephen Foster songs. Although known and danced in the early 1800s, Lancers did not become popular until the mid- to late 19th century. In America, the French Quadrilles were cast aside in favor of Lancers in all the major urban areas of the time.

These were the dance forms flourishing in western Europe. And like all other parts of the culture brought by immigrants to the New World, they were subjected to the test of a radically different environment and those dances that survived emerged irrevocably altered. Just as the individual identities of colonial Americans were being molded from, for example, Scotch-Irish to New York citizen to loyal American, so were dance forms being molded and shaped into new forms with new identities.

Colonial America inherited a rich dance tradition. It is no wonder that dance was one of the most significant features of colonial life. Indeed, dance was reported to be the chief amusement. Dance was not limited by social class or ethnic group, but was enjoyed by people of all stations. The dance map was becoming clear. Dances of English and French origin were being done throughout the colonies from north to south. Pockets of Scotch-Irish, Germans, Dutch, and others were maintaining the Old World dance traditions wherever they settled. Blacks in the middle and southern colonies brought their own dance traditions. American Indians continued their dance heritage despite colonial intrusion. It seems clear that colonial America enjoyed a healthy and heterogeneous dance repertoire.

New England

The early part of the 19th century saw America becoming a dancing nation. Dancing masters were everywhere for hire; the new minister was welcomed at an Ordination Ball; even teachers and ministers doubled as dancing masters to augment their salaries. Plain folks danced everywhere and on all occasions, in taverns, town halls, and kitchens; at barn raisings, husking bees, and roof raisings.

New Englanders cast aside the five-part Quadrille for a simpler, free-flowing adaptation—the *Singing Quadrille.* These "modern Quadrilles" were set to such dashing American folk tunes as "Darling Nellie Gray," "The Girl I Left Behind Me," and "Hinkey Dinkey Parley Voo." The latter was perhaps a salute to the French Quadrille, its forerunner, and to the predominance of French dancing masters. In any case, the tunes, the dances, and the rhyming caller became widely popular. Singing calls by the hundreds were invented and flourished from New York to Maine. The French-Canadian populace of New England were especially enthusiastic participants, and they are credited with embellishing these modern Quadrilles with the long count swing and buzz step.

Nineteenth-century Singing Quadrilles settled comfortably along beside the New England Contra to become widely known as New England–type dancing. Little did the average New Englander of the time suspect that this new American hybrid would be the basis for 20th-century Square Dance.

The South

The *Running Set* is a dance form of the people of Kentucky and the southern Appalachian Mountains who came to the New World from northern England and the lowlands of Scotland. They found, in the hills and valleys, an isolation that for many years permitted them to practice and thus preserve almost unchanged the customs and traditions of their homelands. It was this isolation that allowed the vigorous folk strain of rounds and chain dances to ferment, and later to flow over the trails of the western frontier.

Cecil J. Sharp, the noted English folklorist, came to the Appalachian Mountains in 1917 in search of early English ballads and songs. While there, he observed the dance form known as the *Running Set.* His scholarly observations and inquiries led him to conclude that it was, indeed, the earliest form of the English Country Dance. The absence of courtesies such as bowing, saluting, and honors indicated to him that the dances were uninfluenced by court manners and thus predated dances found in Playford's first dance book of 1650. He further suggested that the history of the Running Set might date back to 17th-century England and Scotland or even earlier to the May Day Rounds, a pagan quasireligious ceremonial of which the Maypole Dance is the best example.

The Running Set was more in the tradition of the Round Eight than the Square Eight. The dance action moved around the square as opposed to across it. The Running Set was danced in either a big set or circle for as many couples as desired or, as was more typical, in a square or set for four couples. The typical dance action consisted of the first couple leading to the right, dancing a figure, then to couple three repeating the figure, and then couple four repeating it. As the action began with couple four, couple two began the "follow up" action with couple three. The do-si-do, a staple of Western Square Dance, was used to finish off the figures. The "follow up" action allowed for 12 repeats of a figure in a square and as many repeats as there are couples in a "big set or circle." The dance done in either form was long and very vigorous!

The characteristics of the Running Set as danced in Kentucky and the southern Appalachian Mountains make it the most immediate antecedent of the Western brand of Square Dance. The two most enduring characteristics are the use of a caller and the figure action of moving or visiting around the square.

In the Running Set, the caller either called from within the set, prompting the dancers, or from outside the set. If calling from outside the set, the caller would add folksy, rhythmic lines of "patter" to the directions for executing the figure. This was the forerunner of the colorful Western patter calls of the early 20th century. The caller is truly an American innovation whose role particularly in the early days, was to keep the dance alive by passing along calls and figures from generation to generation solely by oral tradition.

The step used was a bouncing run that beat out the rhythm against the dance floor. Dancers appeared erect with loose jigging action of the arms and limber disjointed action of the legs and feet. This style, or clogging action, is the trademark of the Running Set. In early times, the sound of the rhythm of the feet was the music for the dance. Play Party Games, or dancing without fiddle music, was then an offspring of the Running Set. Play Party Games allowed dancing to continue and thus endure times of fanatical religious disapproval. (Refer to Play Party Games, p. 59.)

Texas Square Dance

Texas Square Dance heritage came largely from the South with the settlers who moved to the frontier after the Civil War. Before the war, East Texas settlers developed the area into a replica of Southern plantation life with an economy based on cotton farming and slaves. A festive social life soon developed. Balls and parties attracted guests to around-the-clock dancing from as far as 20 miles away. Settlers brought with them not only their love of dancing, but also their dance traditions—the visiting couple figures, do-si-do, and Square Dance caller.

The Civil War and Indian depredations retarded settlement in west Texas. Once the vast area was opened, social life was patterned around ranching and the demands of ranch life rather than cotton farming. The sparseness of settlements and the distances to be traveled made social gathering rare but highly prized. In west Texas, the two most important ingredients of social life, women and fiddlers, were as scarce as "hen's teeth."

Fiddlers were so rare that many callers began the dance with "Honor the Fiddler!" Although honored at dances, expressions such as "lazy enough to be a good fiddler" and "thick as fiddlers in Hell" attest to their general personality types. Regardless of their shortcomings, pioneer fiddlers enjoyed their art and would often get together for an evening of straight fiddling. When an itinerant fiddler showed up in ranch country, a dance was arranged regardless of the day of the week. The first band to play in the Texas panhandle came from Fort Worth, some 277 miles away, to play for a ball held in 1889. Fiddlers and their music were in short supply in west Texas, but the enthusiasm for dancing to the sounds of the "fisky fiddle" was not.

The sparseness of settlements and the scarcity of women made any kind of social gathering of the two sexes as rare as a "fiddler beyond the Pearly Gates!" Usually there were three times as many men, even counting all the females from the youngest to the oldest. At dances in the early days, wallflowers were nonexistent. Women prided themselves on being able to dance all night without missing a set, and, more often than not, they would easily wear out their shoe soles in one evening.

Cowboys were said to have noticed that "slabsided," or fat, women were often more durable than "scantlings," or skinny, women as dance partners. Social gatherings were so important to the cowboy that he thought nothing of riding a great distance to "squire" a lady to a dance. One cowboy is reputed to have ridden 10 miles to hire a buggy, 15 miles to get the lady, 15 miles to the dance, 15 miles back to the lady's home, 15 miles to return the buggy, and, finally, 10 miles on horseback to reach home—a total of 80 miles. Square Dancing was serious business in Texas, and the conditions of frontier life made it possible for the Square Dance to become firmly embedded in Southwestern culture before the region began to suffer from the inroads of urban civilization.

Texas became the home and stronghold of the colorful patter call and the intricate dance figures that were created by the uninhibited imagination of the callers. Texas Square Dancing was the product of the oral rather than the written tradition. Calls were passed along and repeated as remembered. Unaware of the more traditional spelling of Square Dance terms, cowboy callers called them as they sounded; thus "dos-a-dos" became "do-see-do," "chassez" became "sashay," and "allemande" became variously "al-a-man" or "alamand."

Early Leaders

In the early 20th century, when Square Dancing was at a low ebb in other parts of the United States, folks in west Texas were working hard all day and dancing harder all night. One of the most important pioneers of this period was H. F. Greggerson, Jr., of El Paso, Texas, better known as Herb. Greggerson was a dancer, caller, and writer who used his feet as a mail carrier during the day and, in his leisure moments, as a dancer at a faster tempo at night. He was a strong force in helping El Paso build its reputation as the center of Western cowboy Square Dancing. Before World War II, dancers by the hundreds attended Herb's "barn" to learn and dance to his directions, which were embellished by colorful patter and delivered with a twinkle in his eye.

Greggerson and his wife Pauline traveled and danced throughout west Texas and New Mexico collecting old-time calls and dances. The resulting collections were published in two books, *West Texas Square Dances* and *Herb's Blue Bonnet Calls*, the latter copyrighted in 1937.

In 1939 the Greggersons traveled with their exhibition group, The Blue Bonnet Set, as guests of the Highway 80 Association to the World's Fair in New York. The occasion was a showcase for different dance groups from all parts of the United States. The opportunity for fellowship and exchange between dancers and callers led to a greater appreciation and awareness of the status of Square Dance in America. Exhibitions at the Roosevelt Hotel in New York and at the Edgewater Beach Hotel in Chicago earned them the title of World Champion Square Dancers. The authors of *Dance A While* recognize the work of Herb Greggerson in collecting, teaching, and calling the traditional dances of the Western cowboy as a major contribution to the history of Square Dance in America.

Lloyd Shaw and his wife Dorothy were two giants among the few of their kind in the early development of Square Dancing in the West. In addition to his talent as a teacher and writer, Shaw was more importantly an innovative and creative leader. Early in pursuit of his interest in Square Dancing, he envisioned a future in which all Americans would be Square Dancing. His Cheyenne Mountain Dance Group showed America the joy and spirit of the dance. He further ensured his vision by spending his summers instructing hundreds from all walks of life how to teach Square Dancing.

As principal of the Cheyenne School in Colorado Springs, Colorado, Shaw's first interest in dance came from searching for an adjunct to the school's athletic program. He began teaching European folk dance and, after winning over the football team, the dancers became an official group. The Cheyenne Mountain Dancers' first performing tour found them doing all European dance. Later they added some American dances from the Henry Ford "Good Morning" collection of New England Contras and Quadrilles. It was not until Shaw became interested in the dances that were indigenous to the Colorado Mountains in which he lived that the Cheyenne Mountain Dancers became an all-cowboy dance group.

The Shaws' love of the mountains and the indigenous activities made it a labor of love to research and collect from old-timers the dances of miners, prospectors, and cowboys in the Rocky Mountain West. The dances they found had come along with settlers migrating West and were the offsprings of the Southern mountain Running Set, four-couple squares with patter calls and figures reflecting western ways in their titles. In 1939, Shaw published *Cowboy Dances,* his collection of calls and figures gathered in Colorado and the surrounding mountain area. This was followed in 1948 by the *Round Dance Book.* Important as his writings and teachings were, it was his high-school exhibition team, the Cheyenne Mountain Dancers, performing cowboy dances for the American public in the 1930s and 1940s that aroused a spirited and wide-spread interest in American dance. Getting America interested in American dance was his vision, and it happened!

The Lloyd Shaw Foundation is an incorporated, nonprofit organization founded by former summer-class members to perpetuate his memory, his work, and his special philosophy. The foundation trains teachers and dance leaders; produces records and teaching materials; sponsors recreational dance weeks; publishes books and pamphlets; and collects and disperses dance material of historical interest.

Post–World War II

The rapid growth and expansion of Square Dance after World War II was largely the outgrowth of population movements and technical advances in sound equipment. Population movements were of two kinds: movement to urban areas because of continued industrialization and population displacement associated with service in the armed forces and employment in defense-related industries. The technical improvements in the quality and availability of sound equipment made teaching and calling to groups of all sizes possible and effective. Portable equipment made ownership by schools, families, teachers, and callers a reality, thus multiplying the opportunities for dance experience. In addition, the durability and availability of properly recorded music provided the correct dance tempo and authentic sounds for dancing.

The American penchant for following the latest fad was also a factor. In the 1940s and 1950s, Square Dance hobbyists contributed greatly to the popularity of Square Dance through public performances and exhibitions that introduced nonparticipants to the dance. The precision and style of these exhibitions became a standard for performance for other dancers to emulate, thus raising the skill level of the dance. As an added bonus, the massive effort to serve the social needs of wartime America created a rich opportunity for developing leadership in Square Dance for the future. These are the factors that made it possible for thousands of Americans to be introduced to their own heritage, the American Square Dance.

The postwar years were characterized by mass participation in Square Dance. Classes for over a hundred at a time were common. Communities vied to host the largest and best jamborees, festivals, or Square Dance contests. The major special events, such as inaugurations, patriotic celebrations, and civic anniversaries, featured Square Dance as a main social event. Crowd estimates at these early dance events ranged from 5,000 to 10,000 people. This formerly quiet, predominantly rural form of recreation had suddenly become the mass mania of urban living.

The fast-growing Square Dance population became the target market for a host of goods and services. Among the services were Square Dance publications. The first such publication, *Foot 'n' Fiddle,* a Texas Square Dance magazine, began publication in November 1946. The editors were Anne

Pittman and Marlys Swenson Waller, physical education instructors at the University of Texas, and Olcutt Sanders, head of the American Friends Service committee. The headquarters was in Austin, Texas. The magazine chronicled the early years of the Square Dance movement in the southwest from the mid-1940s to the late 1950s.

A second publication, *Sets In Order,* appeared in November 1948, in response to the growing population of dancers in southern California. The editor, Bob Osgood, combined his enthusiasm for Square Dancing with considerable journalistic skills to launch what became the number-one Square Dance magazine in America. *Sets In Order,* later known as *Square Dancing Magazine,* chronicled the Square Dance movement in the United States and points overseas from 1948 until it ceased publication in December 1985.

Other commercial ventures included merchandising of current dress styles for men and women. Recording companies flourished by providing a wide assortment of recordings and sound equipment. Teaching materials in the form of books, pamphlets, and recorded teaching progressions became available. Former part-time teachers and callers became full-time professionals. Summer calendars began to be filled with institutes, workshops, and vacation-oriented opportunities to dance in exotic places. In 1970, a group known as Legacy was formed to provide a vehicle for communication between manufacturers, producers, publications, and Square Dance associations. Square Dancing had arrived in the marketplace.

As dance skill and experience increased, dance moved from a mass activity into smaller organized units. The dance club became the heart of Square Dancing. Club calendars included classes, interclub exchanges, and travel to major special events. Associations were the outgrowth of club activities. Today there are over 300 Square Dance publications and associations in the United States.

Solid growth in regional organization in various parts of the country made the step to a national-level organization easy and logical. Annual national Square Dance conventions began in 1952, at a time when interest in the movement was on the upswing. Since the first convention, cities from North to South and coast to coast have hosted the national convention. Attendance figures for early conventions were between 15,000 and 20,000. Attendance figures for the 1970s have exploded to between 40,000 and 50,000. It is estimated that at present over 6,000,000 people Square Dance. American Square Dance is in vogue as an international form of recreation in Canada, Japan, Australia, England, Germany, and many other countries. A world Square Dance directory is available for those who wish to become international square dancers.

Square Dance is no longer a quaint cowboy or country hillbilly activity. Media coverage, movies, and television have been instrumental in making Square Dance a familiar activity to an extensive American audience. A commemorative stamp issued by the United States Postal Service in 1970 increased the visibility of Square Dance. The third week in September has been set aside as Square Dance Week and has been officially proclaimed by mayors and governors across the country. The spirit of Square Dancing is found in the simple cooperative effort dancers engender by dancing. Square Dance is truly America's folk dance.

Standardization of Basic Movements

The picture of Square Dance in its formative years was a mosaic of regional dance differences. The two dominant types were the singing calls of the eastern states and the patter calls of the western states. The upsurge of interest in Square Dance led to a natural flow of dances from one section of the country to the other. Western Square Dance became popular in the East while at the same time singing calls became popular in the West. Although the skilled and experienced dancer could travel and dance comfortably in any area, the regional differences in basic steps, promenade positions, dance tempos, type and duration of swings, balance steps, and stylings gave the Square Dance movement a "Tower of Babel" effect. There was no common vocabulary of dance terms understood and used by teachers, callers, or dancers. In effect, there was your way and my way, but no common or right way to perform basics. The increased number and mobility of square dancers within and between regions made this a major problem.

The widespread enjoyment of Square Dancing is largely due to the fact that dancers from coast to coast and overseas execute the same fundamental movements, called basics. The dance movements and steps, and the styling of hands, arms, and positions, are all taught and executed in the same manner. The rationale behind this standardization of basics and learning progressions is to make it possible for dancers to learn calls in any given area and thus be skilled enough to dance to calls anywhere, across the country or overseas.

The guiding force behind the movement to standardize Square Dance movements and teaching procedures has been Bob Osgood of Los Angeles, California, a teacher, caller, and long-time editor of *Sets In Order,* later known as *Square Dancing Magazine,* the official publication of the Sets In Order American Square Dance Society. As early as 1960, a booklet describing 30 basics was available from *Sets In Order.* The work was the result of a cooperative study Osgood made with the help of prominent callers across the country. The success and acceptance of this early work led Osgood to head a larger study in 1969, which resulted in organizational changes to facilitate the work of standardization. The work of standardization, adoptions, and changes was carried on by *Callerlab,* an arm of the International Association of Square Dance Callers. All standardized movements and plateaus, or ability levels, were published in *Square Dancing Magazine* as a joint venture with Callerlab. Over 30 years of study and experimentation have gone into developing the following plateaus and movement basics.

The *Basic Plateau* covers 1–49 basics. It has been estimated that the Basic Plateau or level can be mastered in ten $2\frac{1}{2}$-hour lessons. *Extended Basics* is the next plateau to be achieved. The third plateau is *Mainstream,* which consists of 85 basic movements. The correlation between the number of basics being learned and the frequency of dancing is a factor to be considered at this point. *Plus Movements* take the dancer one step above Mainstream. Dancers may, if time and interest allow, move on to the *Advanced Plateau,* or *Challenge Plateau.* Clubs identify their dance-skill levels in this manner. Match a club's plateau with your plateau and qualify to join in an evening of modern Square Dancing anywhere across America.

Square Your Sets

Modern Square Dance requires that dancers learn a number of basic movements or fundamental techniques. Basics are nondirective one- or two-word commands such as "ladies chain," "wheel around," "pass thru," or "do-sa-do." The Square Dance call is made up of these basics. Contemporary Square Dance movement and style have been standardized by Callerlab, an International Association of Square Dance Callers, and are taught and danced uniformly internationally.

Basics must complement each other and fit in a logical movement sequence so that each call puts the dancers in position to execute the next call. The basic "allemande left" puts dancers in position to do "do-sa-do," "grand right and left," or "weave the ring." The modern Square Dance caller must have command of a large number of basics, and he or she can call them in any order so long as the movement of one complements each subsequent basic called.

Calling

Patter Calls

The two calling styles in modern Square Dance are patter and singing calls. *Patter calling* is competitive calling in that the caller is free to call extemporaneously from an extensive knowledge of basics and their interrelationships. Patter calling allows the caller to call a wide variety of basics, thus challenging the dancers' expertise, concentration, and attentiveness.

Patter calls are made to the beat of the music. The hoedown or instrumental music selected should have a pronounced and compelling rhythmic beat. In addition, the musical key in which the music is played should be comfortable and in the caller's vocal range. Most Square Dance instrumentals or hoedowns are written in 2/4 rhythm and are keyed (A, D, G, C, F) to the average vocal range of most callers.

The timing of the patter call is important. Basics are short word commands that cue action rather than phrases that describe action; therefore commands must be called in rapid and overlapping order to keep the dance action flowing from one movement to the next. During the first call, "Head couples dance forward and back," which requires eight beats to execute, the caller gives the next call, "Forward again and pass thru," thus overlapping the call for the second action over the execution of the first call.

Singing Calls

Singing calls follow a set sequence and are arranged to the melody of a song. The better singing calls use some of the words of the song. The usual sequence is opener, main figure, break, main figure, and ending. In singing calls, the opener, break, and ending are often the same. Dancers tend to memorize dance action in singing calls, so they are not wholly dependent on the live or recorded caller for directions as in patter calls. Singing calls follow popular trends and are continually being choreographed to the latest hit tunes. This is at once both fortunate and unfortunate. It is unfortunate in that popular records become obsolete and therefore unavailable. It is fortunate in that the fad to Square Dance to the latest tunes keeps the singing call readily available and in ample supply.

Keys to Good Calling

The caller is a teacher and a group leader and, in like manner, the teacher is a caller and a group leader. The success of a series of Square Dance lessons depends on creating a pleasant, friendly, and fun-filled atmosphere in a class or club setting. The caller-teacher must be an accomplished dancer in order to demonstrate the movements and dance style effectively; the caller-teacher must be a trained teacher in order to select and present materials in an orderly progression. The keys to good calling are clarity, rhythm, command, judgment, and enthusiasm.

Clarity: Enunciate clearly and emphasize the "action words" and short directive phrases. *"Ladies star left go once around." "Allemande left." "Grand right and left."* Know how to use the sound equipment to achieve clarity. Add treble volume for low voices and bass volume for high voices.

Rhythm: Keep an active, "patting foot" call on the beat of the music. Call the next movement while dancers are executing the last call. Be keenly aware of musical phrases; begin the call on the phrase of the music or on the downbeat.

Command: Project calls out; do not swallow or mumble the calls. Voice is important in establishing a sound of authority and confidence. Call extra directions where beats allow to clarify any momentary directional or action confusion. *"Left, left,* allemande *left!"* Rights and lefts are often confusing in fast-paced dance action. Call within the framework of dancers' knowledge and ability.

Judgment: Adjust dance progressions and practice time to the ability level of the dancers. Be patient with progress! Review often and interestingly by calling the basics in a variety of combinations. Practice with music. Avoid endless walk- and talk-throughs without music. Music gives life and zest even to the mistakes.

Enthusiasm: Approach each lesson in a natural, sincere, and friendly manner. A display of humor increases the fun for teacher and student. Reward progress and encourage the better dancers to dance with and upgrade the skill level of the other dancers. Remember, you were a beginner once.

Styling

Dancing style begins with the dance step. The step should be a gliding shuffle with each step on the beat of the music. The result is a smooth, flowing movement enjoyable to the individual and the dance group. From the first musical note, dancers should begin to respond to the rhythm by taking three small steps and a touch forward then backward. Dancers not involved in the call should maintain this rhythmic action in order to be ready to move into the call.

Styling results from executing basics in the proper number of counts or beats of music. Timing varies, but it is an important part of learning the basics. Ladies chain over and back, including the courtesy turn, takes 16 counts. Ladies move across and courtesy turn in eight counts and repeat to home position in eight counts. Hand clasps, arm holds, wrist holds, swing and turn positions are all part of the style, comfort, and logic of dance movement. Dancing the basics in the proper counts gives style and elegance to the dance action. Teach styling and

timing techniques with each basic. Dancers will enjoy and take pride in making the right moves.

Parts of a Square Dance

There are four parts of a Square Dance: *opener, main figure, break,* and *ending.* The caller chooses breaks to contrast and complement the main figure. Breaks are used after the first and before the second call of the main figure when there is no partner change. For main figures requiring partner changes, the break may be used after each call of the main figure. Example: opener, main figure, break, main figure, break, and ending. Breaks may involve eight or four dancers and should be short and not cause partner changes. The following are some criteria to be considered in selecting breaks: Breaks should (a) contrast and complement main figure, (b) shorten or lengthen the call, (c) provide smooth transition at the beginning or end of the main figure, (d) get dancers out of numbered sequence (4, 2, 3, 1) or back into numbered sequence (1, 2, 3, 4), and (5) get dancers in home positions. The opener, break, and ending are often the same in singing calls.

Sample Call

The caller selects the opener, break, and ending to complement and contrast the action of the main figure. A continuity line may need to be added to any calls that do not have a final line instructing the dancers to be in position for the next call. Example: Add "and home you go."

Opener
All join hands and circle to the left.
Now reverse go single file.
Home you go and swing a while.

Main Figure
One and three lead.
1 and 3 lead to the right.
Circle four, head men break and form a line.
Go forward up and back.
Roll away to a half sashay.
Pass thru and U-turn back.
Right and left thru, turn your girl.
Pass thru and bend the line.
Right and left thru, turn your girl.
Pass thru and bend the line.
Do-sa-do across from you.
Cross trail thru.

Break
Allemande left and allemande thar.
Go right and left and form a star.
Men back up but not too far.

(continued)

Shoot that star to the heaven whirl.
Go right and left to another pretty girl.
Men back up and you form that star.
Shoot that star and find your maid.
Take your gal and promenade home.

Repeat figure for 2 and 4.

Ending
Allemande left with your left hand.
Right to your partner and right and left grand.
Meet your own, promenade home.
Now bow to your partner, corners too.
Wave at the gal across the hall.
And that is all.

Use of Records With Calls

In public schools and recreation groups the use of records with calls serves to keep the class dance materials current, provides an opportunity to dance to a professional caller, and serves as a model to upgrade the teacher-caller's live-calling ability. Records with a call on one side and instrumental on the flip side provide an inservice opportunity for the less-experienced teacher-caller to emulate the professional caller's style and calling techniques.

Overuse of records with calls can restrict the class to one type of call and thus distract from the spontaneity and challenge of live calling. Dependency on the call on the record can also contribute to poor preparation by the teacher-caller. Live calling reinforces knowledge of the call pattern and increases the teacher-caller's understanding of how basics interrrelate in modern Square Dancing.

Teaching a dance with the call on the record presumes that the teacher knows and has danced the call and that all basics involved have been taught and used in other dances. A suggested teaching progression follows.

1. Play the record to accustom the class to the sound of the caller's voice and tempo. This also gives the class a preview of the basics involved in the dance.
2. Analyze and walk the class through the opener. Remember, openers are often used as breaks and endings.
3. Call the opener live and up to tempo, no music.
4. Dance opener to recorded call and music.
5. Repeat steps 2–4 for main figure. **Note:** Recording equipment will allow user to stop a record or tape at any point to give oral instructions, then begin again at the same point.

Mixers for Square Dance

Frequent changes of partners and sets are needed to help class members get acquainted and to establish a good rapport within the group. Mixers are of prime importance in dealing with extras and with groups in which the number of men and/or ladies is uneven. Random changes can serve to mix ability groupings and upgrade the overall dance-skill level. Meeting a variety of class members adds to the fun, sociability, and feeling of fellowship.

Mixing can also be an intentional but seemingly unintentional means of breaking up cliques and getting the attention of inattentive class members. Mixers can work as a gentle and even pleasant way to apply discipline, particularly when working with school and recreation groups. In any event, it is always wise to have a "pocket full of miracles" in the form of mixers when teaching dance.

Mixers to meet the demands of a variety of circumstances can be found in Chapter 4 under Plain and Novelty Mixers, and Paul Jones Your Lady. The following are samples of the kind that would accomplish the uses suggested in the foregoing discussion. All mixers should be done to musical accompaniment. Square Dance mixers should be called as illustrated by the following samples.

Big Circle Mixers

1. Couples promenade counterclockwise. Men turn left and roll back to promenade the lady in the trailing couple.
   Promenade go two by two
   Gents roll back and promenade that gal behind you.
2. Couples promenade counterclockwise. Men move forward to the next lady and promenade.
   Promenade this little pal
   Now move up one and take a new gal
   And all promenade
   Promenade a little bit more
   Move up one as you did before
   And all promenade.

Methods for Squaring Up

1. **Grand March:** The Grand March is a traditional way of squaring sets. It serves chiefly as a mixer of couples rather than individuals. It is a particularly good and efficient way of organizing a large crowd into sets. Refer to p. 63 for a detailed description of the procedure.
2. **Paul Jones:** This procedure will enable a group to get partners for forming sets. Ladies form a single circle facing out, circle to the left. Men form a single circle around the ladies, facing in, circle to the left. The larger group usually forms the outside circle. When the music stops, the men take the ladies directly opposite or nearest them for partners. Refer to Paul Jones Your Lady, p. 72, for additional variations.

3. **Circle Two-Step:** Once partners are secured, the leader may call out "circle four," "circle six," "circle ten," or any even number so that partners are not separated. Eventually "circle eight" may be called and sets arranged for dancing. Younger groups may enjoy this procedure: The leader blows a whistle or claps hands to indicate the number of couples he or she wishes to have form a circle.

4. **Grand Promenade:** After partners are secured, the leader may use the following call to organize the group into sets.

> Promenade go two by two
> Now promenade a little bit more
> Pick up two and make it four
> Promenade and don't be late
> Grab a four and make it eight
> Line up now and keep it straight
> Spread that line way out wide
> And circle up eight on all four sides.

5. **Promenade Around the Hall:** This call may be used at the beginning of the dance or at the end of any one call during the dance to arrange couples in different sets for the next call.

> Promenade one and promenade all
> Promenade around the great big hall
> Circle up four with any old two
> Go 'round and 'round like you used to do
> Now break that four and circle up eight
> Hurry up gents now don't be late
> Find your place right in that set
> Stand right there, we ain't through yet.

Variation: The following variation of the preceding call may be used to break up the sets and arrange the dancers in formation for a round dance.

> Break up your sets and promenade all
> Promenade, go around the hall
> Around the great big beautiful hall
> Now stand right there upon the floor
> Stand right there, we'll dance some more.

Methods for Changing Partners or Moving to a New Square

1. **Promenade out of the Square:** During a call, usually where a trim or break is in order, the caller may change a couple or couples from one set to another and finish the call with new couples in every set. The following call indicates how this may be done.

> One and three—promenade
> Right out of that square
> And find yourself a brand new square
> Promenade, go anywhere
> Just find yourself a brand new square
> Look for hands around the floor
> Fill in there—they need two more
> There's a spot—go over there

> They need two more to make a square
> One for the money, two for the show
> All get set—'cause here we go!

Variation: While the promenading couples are relocating, the caller may keep the other couples dancing by calling a ladies chain, right and left thru, or do-sa-do. The following call indicates how this may be done.

> One and three—promenade
> Right out of that square
> And find yourself a brand new square
> Now two and four—while they are gone
> Circle up four and carry on
> Do-sa-do in the middle of the set
> 'Cause one and three ain't ready yet
> Two and four go home to your places
> And take a look at the brand new faces.

2. **New Partner Calls:** The following may be used to secure new partners at the end of a call.

> Honor your partner and thank her too
> Now swing the gal to the left of you
> Swing your corner, that pretty little maid
> Keep this gal and all promenade
> Honor your partner, corners too
> Swing that gal across from you
> Swing that gal but not too hard
> Stand right there with a brand new pard!

3. **Directed Changes:** The leader may direct dancers to change places as follows.

   a. All ladies move one position to the right in the set.

   b. Each gentleman takes his opposite, corner, or right-hand lady for a new partner.

   c. All the ladies or gentlemen move to the adjacent square and take the same positions in the new set.

   d. Ladies (gents) leave the set and move anywhere around the room to a new square. Dancers should be in new square before the next dance call begins.

> Gents (ladies) to the center
> And stand right there
> Ladies (gents) run away to a brand new square
> Sides (heads) to the center
> And hold on there
> Now the heads (sides) promenade right out of that square
> Go anywhere I don't care
> And find yourself a brand new square.

4. **Scoot and Scat:** Scoot is the cue for the men and scat is the cue for the ladies. In general, the leader must explain the action to the group so that they will respond in the desired manner. The ladies or men may be directed to form a star in the center of the set; while the star is rotating, the leader calls "scoot" and the men leave the square and go to another one to form a star.

If ladies are directed into a star figure, on the call "scat," the ladies leave the square and get into another to form a star.

Scoot and Scat may also be called as part of Texas Star. If the men are on the outside spokes of the star, "scoot" is called. The ladies continue to star and the men hook onto the spoke of the ladies' star in another set. When all squares have eight people, the caller continues the Texas Star. New partners promenade to the home position of the lady.

5. **Birdies in the Cage:** The following variation of the regular Bird in the Cage—Seven Hands 'Round (refer to p. 169) may be used as a mixer.

> All four gents swing your right-hand lady
> With a right hand around
> Partner left with a left hand around
> Corner lady with a right hand around
> Now swing your partner with two hands around
> And cage those birds as you come around
> Now four hands up and away we go
> The birds fly away through that open door!

All four ladies are placed in the center of the set back to back. The men join hands and circle left around the ladies (birds). The men hold their hands up high, forming arches through which the ladies (birds) fly on the call, "The birds fly away through that open door." The call may be repeated with the "crows," the men, in the center and the ladies circling around with joined hands raised high. The "crows" fly away on the call, "The crows fly away through that open door." The "birds" or "crows" simply go to any new set and take a new partner for a repeat of the call.

Teaching Approaches

Teachers may choose one of two approaches for teaching the beginning Square Dance basics. The *Big Circle approach* makes use of the single circle, double circle, and Sicilian circle for teaching and practicing basics that can be done without reference to the square formation. The *Set approach* begins with the dancers in the square formation and teaches the basics in reference to positions and movement directions as they evolve from the use of a simple Square Dance call.

The Big Circle approach is immediately attractive in that it allows all class members to be active at once; since the teacher makes the class "odd or even" in numbers, there can be no extras. The single circle is particularly useful for demonstration. Dancers can see the mechanics and style of a basic. Basics appropriate to the single circle are the shuffle (circling left, right, forward and back), do-sa-do, swing, allemande left, honor, twirl, single-file prom-

enade, grand right and left, and forearm turns. The double circle is appropriate and useful in teaching promenade, California Twirl, you turn back, box the gnat, and wheel around. The Sicilian circle is a formation in which two couples face, one faces clockwise, the other counterclockwise. It is useful in teaching ladies chain, right and left thru, pass thru, box star position, do paso, square thru, and star thru.

The Big Circle approach is useful for class warmup and review. Once again it allows all class members to be active, including the teacher, who may fill in if there is an extra dancer. It may also be used as a part of a lesson to present and demonstrate new basics. The Big Circle approach is versatile and should be used throughout a series of lessons whenever appropriate and needed.

The Set approach combines maneuvering in the square with learning the basics as they occur in a given Square Dance. After all, the set is only a "square" in concept. Once dancers respond to a call, the set can become a single circle, double circle, or parallel lines. This is an exciting approach because it plunges the dancers into full Square Dance action. Their objective, "to learn to Square Dance," happens in the first lesson and is not delayed by practice and drill on style and technique. In a short series of lessons, getting to the "nuts and bolts" of the dancing motivates the dancer to listen and learn. Lesson planning, however, is more difficult and important. The teacher must be sure that all parts of the Square Dance (opener, main figure, break, ending) are utilized to teach basics and that each lesson builds progressively on the preceding lesson's content.

Planning Units and Lessons

The basics in this book provide materials for a beginner and intermediate course in Square Dance. Beginning materials are covered in levels 1, 2, and 3. Intermediate materials are covered in levels 4 and 5. There are ample singing and patter calls for each level. The material covers 50 basics and sufficient content for 30–35 lessons.

Public schools and recreation groups may find it advantageous to divide the materials into a series of five to six lesson units progressively linked and scheduled throughout the year. Recreation groups and after-school clubs can easily cover 50 basics in one year.

Three six-lesson units allow for orderly and progressive distribution of basics 1–33, covering beginner levels 1, 2, and 3. Planning in relation to a specific "on the job" situation provides the best estimate of class length and content to be covered. A rule of thumb suggests that instruction should go slowly enough for dancers to learn and enjoy each lesson and fast enough to hold their interest and provide a challenge. The overall objective should be to provide a sound skill basis in an atmosphere of fun and fellowship and challenge enough for dancers to choose Square Dance as a lifetime recreational pursuit.

A daily lesson plan is a systematic checklist of progress toward the overall goal of learning to Square Dance. Mastering a few skills during each lesson makes teaching and learning a pleasant and enjoyable occasion. The framework for conducting any given lesson may include:

1. Warmup and review of basic movements in a circle to include all class members. Or dance a figure using previously learned basics.
2. Presentation of new basics. Isolate each one from any specific dance and include a walk-through and practice call.
3. Call and dance one or more dances containing new basics with combinations of several previously taught basics.
4. Culminate lesson with previously learned dances or allow class to request favorites.

Fifty Basic Movements of Square Dance

The Square Dance basics included in this book are aimed at the beginning and intermediate dancer and teacher-caller. The materials included in the Square Dance chapter will provide students and teachers with a sound foundation for further skill acquisition at more advanced levels.

Level 1A: Beginner Basics 1–8

1. Shuffle
2. Honors
3. Do-sa-do
4. Promenade
5. Twirl
6. Single-File Promenade
7. Waist Swing
8. Allemande Left

Level 1B: Orientation to the Square

a. Forming the Square
b. Maneuvering in the Square
c. Practice Basics 1–8

Level 2: Beginner Basics 9–20

9. Grand Right and Left
10. Split the Ring
11. Pass Thru
12. Separate Go Around One
13. Texas Star Basics
14. Forearm Turns
15. Courtesy Turn
16. Ladies Chain
17. Circle to a Line—Lines of Four
18. Bend the Line
19. Right and Left Thru
20. Weave the Ring

Level 3: Beginner Basics 21–33

21. Four Ladies Chain
22. Do Paso
23. All Around Your Left-Hand Lady—Seesaw
24. California Twirl
25. Drive Thru
26. Ends Turn In
27. Roll Away to a Half-Sashay
28. U-Turn Back
29. Cross Trail Thru
30. Grand Square
31. Box the Gnat
32. Allemande Thar
33. Rip and Snort

Level 4: Intermediate Basics 34–44

34. Buzz Swing
35. Single-File Turn Back
36. Square Thru
37. Star Thru
38. Double Turn Back from Grand Right and Left
39. Three-Quarter Chain
40. Box the Flea
41. Alamo Style
42. Wheel Around
43. Slip the Clutch
44. Double Pass Thru

Level 5: Intermediate Basics 45–50

45. Wheel and Deal
46. Eight Chain Thru
47. Turn Thru
48. Ocean Wave
49. Swing Thru
50. Circulate

Teaching Progression and Analysis for Basic Movements of Square Dance

The 50 basic movements of Square Dance have been arranged from simple to complex in a recommended teaching progression. Basics may be combined and called to practice interrelated movement patterns within the overall progression. The progression is designed to give the teacher-caller full information germane to each basic. The information includes: analysis or description of movement, specific teaching suggestions for each movement, diagrams for visual aid, calls for practicing basics as used in a dance, and recommended singing and/or patter calls using the basics in a dance figure.

Level 1A: Beginner Basics 1–8

The beginning basics 1–8 should be practiced in a single circle to provide opportunity for all class members to participate regardless of class size. The single-circle formation allows for easy demonstration and viewing of class progress from the center of the circle. The teacher-caller may also "dance and call" from this formation or simply call out basics from the center of the circle.

1. Shuffle

An easy, light, walking action in even rhythm, with the ball of the foot kept lightly in contact with the floor. The action should be in time with the music. The body is held upright.

Teaching aids: (a) Practice in a single circle moving left, right, forward, and back. (b) Styling of hand clasp: man's palm up, lady's palm down. (c) Move with small steps, synchronize with partner, and step to the beat of the music.

2. Honors

Partners turn slightly to face each other while shifting the weight to the outside foot and pointing the inside foot toward partner. Often called Bow to Partner.

Teaching aids: (a) One may dip slightly, keeping the back straight and the weight over the outside foot (man's left, lady's right.) (b) The action can take four counts in all: shift weight and dip (count 1), hold (2), and recover facing the set (counts 3 and 4).

3. Do-Sa-Do

Partners face, pass each other right shoulder to right shoulder, move around each other back to back and return to original position facing partner.

Teaching aids: (a) Dancers should learn to keep hands and arms down to the sides and slightly behind. (b) Dancers can turn slightly on a diagonal in passing so as to make it easier to get around without bumping.

Practice call 1 (using first three basics)
All join hands and circle left
Everybody go forward and back
Face your partner, do-sa-do
Bow to your partner.

4. Promenade

Partners take promenade position (see Glossary) and move counterclockwise around the circle.

Teaching aids: (a) The joined right hands are on top. (b) The hands are joined (man's palm up,

lady's palm down) at about waist level. (c) The man may take the initiative to lead slightly as they move forward. (d) A clockwise direction is called a **wrong-way promenade.**

5. Twirl

Partners face, join right hands. Man lifts right hand, turning lady under man's right arm once clockwise. As lady completes turn, man takes her left hand. Couples resume promenade position or as directed by caller.

Teaching aids: (a) Lady must move along line of direction while turning to stay slightly ahead of man who is following lady's turn. (b) A good demonstration helps dancers style the twirl. (c) Twirl is not always called. It is a styling movement done automatically. **Note:** In practice call 2 the twirl may be done twice, once after each call "right to your partner, promenade."

Practice call 2 (using the first five basics)
All join hands and circle to the left
Now circle to the right
Everybody go forward and back
Do-sa-do your partner
Right to partner, promenade
All join hands to forward and back
Do-sa-do your corner
All join hands and circle to the left
Now circle to the right
Face partner, do-sa-do
Right to partner and promenade.

6. Single-File Promenade

Dancers turn to face counterclockwise and shuffle one behind the other single-file around the circle.

Practice call 3
All join hands, circle left
Break, promenade single file
The other way back
Face the center, go forward and back
Honor your partner.

Practice call 4
Bow to partner, promenade
Promenade single file
Home you go and do-sa-do.

Teaching aid: Dancers may go into single-file promenade from a promenade. The lady steps in front of the man, and they move one behind the other counterclockwise around the circle.

7. Waist Swing

Partners take swing position (see Glossary). Dancers shuffle (gliding walk) around each other, turning twice around clockwise in four or eight counts.

Teaching aids: (a) Body erect, lean back from waist and look at each other. (b) Lady rolls off man's right arm to next position called or may twirl to a promenade position. (c) More advanced styling may be added later (i.e., buzz step swing and twirl.)

8. Allemande Left

Corners take a left forearm grasp and turn each other once around and go back home.

Teaching aids: (a) Left elbow is bent, dancers pull away slightly on the turn. (b) Grasp forearm with palm of hand rather than fingers.

Practice call 5 (using basics 1–8)
Honor your partner, swing your partner
All join hands and circle left
All to the center and back
Now swing your partner round and round
Promenade her single file
Join hands and circle left
All to the center and back
Allemande left your corner
Do-sa-do your partner, do-sa-do corner
Swing your partner
Bow to your partner and stand right there.

Practice call 6
Promenade go around the hall
Let's all dance and have a ball
Now hook up two and line up four
You are lined up four don't be late
Hook four more and make it eight
Move that line and keep it straight
Spread all eight way out wide
Join all hands and circle left
Allemande left and don't be slow
Back to your partner and do-sa-do
Do-sa-do your corner girl
Back to your partner and swing and whirl
Now bow to your partner bow down low
That's all there is there ain't no more.

Level 1B: Orientation to the Square

Dancers need to learn how to form a square and to understand and practice the movement possibilities based on its structure.

A. Forming the Square

1. Four couples form a square. Each couple forms one side of the square. All couples face the center of the square, each man with his partner on his right. This is **home position** for each couple.
2. Couples are numbered counterclockwise or to the right around the square. Couple 1 always has their backs to the caller and music; couple 2 is to the right of couple 1; couple 3 is across from couple 1 and to the right of couple 2; couple 4 is across from couple 2 and to the left of couple 1.
3. Couples 1 and 3 are called **head couples** and are numbered 1 and 3 in most of the calls. Couples 2 and 4 are called **side couples** and are numbered 2 and 4. □ = man, ○ = lady.
4. The lady to the left of each man is the **corner lady**. The lady in the couple to the right of each man is the **right-hand lady**. The lady directly across from each man is the **opposite lady**.
5. Couples are called **active couples** when their number is called for an action. **Inactive couples** are those not called for an action, but they may be involved in an action by the active couples. The active couple is also called the **lead-off couple**.

Practice call 7 is designed to provide practice in learning home positions, couple numbers, individual numbers, and interaction with partner and corner. Basics 1–8 are used as they relate to the square formation. For full and complete practice the call sequence should be: opener, main figure for ladies, break, repeat main figure for gents, repeat break (gives extra allemande left practice), and add the ending.

Practice call 7
Opener
Honor your partner, honor your corner
All join hands and circle left
Circle right the other way back
Into the center and give a little yell
Back right out and circle left
And home you go.

Main Figure
Two little sisters form a ring
   (Ladies 1 and 2 join hands in center of square)
Circle left don't be slow
   (Ladies 1 and 2 circle once around)
Home you go and do-sa-do (or swing)
Three little sisters form a ring
   (Ladies 1 2, 3)
Circle left don't be slow
   (Circle once around)
Home you go and do-sa-do (or swing)

(continued)

Now four little sisters form a ring
  (Ladies 1, 2, 3, and 4)
Circle left don't be slow
Home you go and do-sa-do (or swing).

Break
Allemande left that pretty maid
Back to your partner and promenade
Once around the square you go
Home you go there is more.

Repeat figure for gents

Ending
Honor your partner, corner too
Thank you folks, I'm all through.

Note: Teachers may wish to teach basic 14 "forearm turn" and use it as a "single arm swing" rather than using the waist swing at this early stage of learning. This would be a good choice in classes that have more women than men. More important, there is less style and technique in the "forearm turn" used as a "single arm swing," thus allowing the class to go through the first eight basics and get to a whole Square Dance in the very first lesson.

B. Maneuvering in the Square

Maneuvering in the square means learning to move in relation to eight dancers. It is a group action and therefore requires group timing in order to achieve smooth interaction and transitions. The following "traffic" rules will help dancers move as a group more efficiently. The teacher-caller should alert dancers to these techniques of group movement as they present new basics and figures.

Rule 1: Keep the feet moving: From the first beat of music to the last, all feet should keep time with the music. Standard practice is to dance forward and back with three small steps and a touch on fourth count. Throughout the call, this dance action is continuous. Never stop and start to get into a movement.

Rule 2: The caller is always one call ahead of the dancers: While dancers are executing the first call, they should listen for the next call. The caller will overlap the action of the first call with the second call. Dancers should always finish each call before moving into the next. Remember, patter calls can be extemporaneous; dancers must listen!

Rule 3: Keep the square closed in to normal size: Size of the square may be kept compact by the men promenading with left shoulders pulled in toward the center of the square. Distance to

home position is shortened and movement is better timed. Men may practice twirling partner into home position during the last few steps of promenade. (See Twirl in Glossary.)

Rule 4: Inactive couples move in: When a couple or individual dancers move around the outside of the square, dancers should move to center as they pass. Makes a shorter and better-timed dance action around the square.

Rule 5: Promenading around the ring: Men should always promenade ladies (own or new one) to the man's home position. A promenade may be called for less than once around (i.e., one quarter, one half, three quarters). These fractional promenade distances may be danced outside or inside the square. Individual dancers may be called to promenade in any of the foregoing ways.

Rule 6: Dancers are always in home positions at the end of the dance. Although out of sequence or with different partners during the call, dancers should understand that it is the caller's responsibility to end the dance with all in home position.

Rule 7: When everybody is mixed up: The best solution to a mixup in execution of the figure is to go to home position. This will allow the figure to become untangled and dancers may "pick up the call" and continue dancing in good order.

Rule 8: How far to promenade: The rule of thumb is: If the distance is one quarter or more to home position, simply "go home"; if the distance is less than one quarter (you are almost home), you should respond to the call and "go full around to home position."

Rule 9: Lead to the right: Designated couples move as a couple to stand in front of the couple on the right. Example: Couples 1 and 3 move to the right and stand in front of couples 2 and 4, respectively. The same call for 2 and 4 puts them in front of couples 1 and 3, respectively.

Rule 10: Dancers should react to the various positions in the square rather than to the person who is supposed to be there. Example: Allemande left, dancers should go to the corner position that is a known part of the square and simply wait for the dancer to come to the position.

Rule 11: In sequence and out of sequence: Dancers are in sequence when they are in the original order in the square (i.e., as numbered 1 to 4 counterclockwise). Dancers are out of sequence when any two have changed places (i.e., couples 1 and 3 pass thru or all couples pass thru or as individuals change in two ladies chain).

Rule 12: Swing the opposite lady: The call is for men only. Men move simultaneously, allowing the man on the left to pass across in front before reaching opposite lady. Men swing opposite and return home in like manner. Or men may make a brief right-hand star as they move in the center to opposite, swing, and return with a brief right-hand star to home position. The technique is learned by the dancers, not called.

Rule 13: Swing the right-hand lady: A call for men only. Men move to the right across in front of partner to right-hand lady, swing, and face center. Wait for call to move home.

Level 2: Beginner Basics 9–20

9. Grand Right and Left

Partners face and join right hands, move forward, pass partner, extend left hand to the next dancer, right to the next, and so forth, until dancers meet original partner. Men move counterclockwise; ladies move clockwise.

Teaching aids: (a) Dancers release hand grasps quickly as they pass. (b) Dancers meet partner or person with whom they began the figure. Listen for next call; it could be "swing partner," "do-sa-do" or "promenade home." (c) To promenade, man should take lady's right in his right and turn lady clockwise into promenade position.

Practice call 8
Face your partner
Grand right and left
Meet partner, promenade.

Practice call 9
Allemande left with your left hand
Right to partner, keep going
Right and left grand
Meet partner, promenade.

10. Split the Ring

The lead-off couple moves between the man and lady of the opposite couple.

Teaching aids: (a) Couple being "split" moves sideways and apart to let lead-couple through. (b) After moving through, lead-couple must listen for next call. **Example:** "Separate go around the outside ring, home you go and swing."

Practice call 10
First couple go down the center
Split the ring, separate,
Go back home
Everybody do-sa-do.

Repeat for each couple.

Practice call 11
1 and 3 go forward and back
Forward again, face the sides
Split the ring, separate
Go back home, do-sa-do.

Repeat for 2 and 4.

11. Pass Thru

Two couples face. Dancers move forward passing opposite dancer's right shoulder to right shoulder.

Teaching aid: Dancers pass thru and listen for next call.

Practice call 12
1 and 3 pass thru
Separate, come around two
Right back home
2 and 4 go forward and back
Everybody do-sa-do.

Repeat for 2 and 4.

Square dance: Four-Leaf Clover.

12. Separate Go Around One

Men move left, lady right to separate. Dancers then move around the nearest inactive dancer to face partner in center of square. Wait for next call.

Practice call 13
1 and 3 pass thru
Separate, go around one
Come in between the sides
Go into the middle
Pass thru, split the next two
Separate, go around one
Come down the middle
Pass thru face partner
Swing and square set.

Repeat for 2 and 4.

Square dance: Split the Ring, Go Around One.

Practice call 14
1 and 3 pass thru
Separate, go around one
Line up four, go forward and back
Center four join hands
Circle four halfway 'round
Pass thru, split two
Separate, go around one
Line up four, go forward and back
Allemande left.

Repeat for 2 and 4.

13. Texas Star Basics

The following basics are used in the dance figure Texas Star. However, they may be used separately in other combination.

Four Gents Star: Men go to the center, touch hands, fingers up, and move around the center of the ring.

Teaching aids: (a) The men make a right-hand star, turning clockwise, and a left-hand star, turning counterclockwise. (b) When changing from a right-hand star to a left-hand star, the men release with the right hand, make a right face turn, and form the star with the left hand. (c) The four ladies may form the star in the same manner.

Star Promenade: Four couples move in same direction. Men star with left hand moving counterclockwise. Women star with right hand moving clockwise.

Teaching aids: (a) Men put right arm around lady's waist, lady's left arm should rest on man's upper right arm. (b) Ladies need to move toward man to be picked up to begin the star. Remember, men are holding hands in a left-hand star as they start the pickup.

Gents Swing Out Ladies Swing In: Men break the star and back up, turning as a couple counterclockwise. Ladies move into center to form a right-hand star. The "swing out and in" may be a half turn or a turn and a half to put the ladies in the star.

Box Star Position: Dancer (man or lady) places right or left hand on the wrist of the dancer in front. This wrist hold is also called a *packsaddle*.

Square dances: Texas Star and Gents Star Right.

14. Forearm Turns

A means of turning in place with the use of a forearm grasp. This basic may be used instead of or along with the waist swing as a "single arm swing." It is easy to learn and is useful in classes where there are more women than men, or vice versa.

Teaching aid: Dancers should pull away slightly, keeping the elbow bent, the arm firm, and palm against the partner's arm.

Practice call 15
All face your partner
Turn partner right arm round
Men star left in the center
Meet your partner, do-sa-do
All join hands and circle left

Go once around and get back home
Now gents star right, one time around
Pass your partner, allemande left
Come back to partner and swing.

Square dances: Arkansas Traveler and Mañana.

15. Courtesy Turn

Couple face in same direction. Man takes lady's left hand in his left, places right arm around lady's waist. Couple turns as a unit, man backing up as couple turns counterclockwise to face original direction or as caller indicates.

Teaching aids: Lady's right palm should rest lightly on her right hip over man's hand.

16. Ladies Chain

Two couples are facing each other. The two ladies take right hands and pull by and then give a left hand to the opposite man. The man takes her left hand in his left and does a courtesy turn, turning once around to face the other couple. The two ladies have changed partners. Repeat to home position.

Teaching aids: (a) Couples 1 and 3 execute ladies chain across in the square formation. This acts as a demonstration for other couples. Repeat for couples 2 and 4. (b) Men should take Two-Step to the right after releasing lady and reach out with left hand to receive new lady for courtesy turn. (c) Dancers may also practice all at once in a diagonal formation (i.e., couples 1 and 2 chain as couples 3 and 4 chain). (d) Use practice call 16 for all four couples to practice on the diagonal (i.e., couple 1 with 2 and couple 3 with 4). (e) Use practice call 17 in the set or square formation. (f) Use practice calls 18 and 19 to teach and practice four ladies chain or grand chain.

Practice call 16
Bow to your partner
Bow to your opposite
Two ladies chain across
Chain right back
All four go forward and back
Two ladies chain
Now chain 'em back.

Practice call 17
Bow to your partner
Couples 1 and 3 promenade outside
Go all the way around
Couples 2 and 4 ladies chain

2 and 4 chain back
Couples 2 and 4 promenade outside
Go all the way around
1 and 3 ladies chain
1 and 3 chain back
All join hands and circle left
Break and promenade single file
Home you go, everybody swing.

Practice call 18
All join hands and circle left
Go once around
1 and 3 ladies chain across the set
2 and 4 ladies chain across the set
All four ladies chain right back
Bow to your partner.

Practice call 19
Heads promenade, go halfway around
Just halfway and all four ladies
Chain across the middle of the ring
Now side couples promenade
Just halfway 'round and all four ladies
Chain across the ring
All join hands and circle
Just halfway around
Break and swing
Promenade home.

Square dance: Hurry Hurry Hurry.

17. Circle to a Line

Couples 1 and 3 (or 2 and 4) lead to the right, circle two-thirds around; active man drops left hand grasp and pulls the line out straight.

Teaching aids: (a) To get the notion of couple positions in the line, simply have couples 1 and 3 (or 2 and 4) move over and stand beside couples 2 and 4. Men 1 and 3 will be opposite their home position. (b) Practice having 1 and 3 (or 2 and 4) move from home position, circle with 2 and 4 into position as in (a). The inactive ladies should turn counterclockwise under partner's right arm to move comfortably into position at end of line.

18. Bend the Line

From any line of an even number (usually four people), the line breaks in the middle, the centers of the line back up, and the ends of the line move forward until both halves of the line are facing.

Teaching aids: (a) The center two people release hands and back up at the same time that the two end people move forward so that each half of the line pivots to face the other. (b) When two lines of four face each other, bend the line; the result

is that two new lines of four are formed, facing each other in the new direction.

Practice call 20
1 and 3 lead to the right
Circle, break and make a line
Go forward up and back
Bend the line
Go forward up and back
Bend the line
Join hands and circle right
Home you go and do-sa-do.

Repeat for 2 and 4.

Practice call 21
1 and 3 lead to the right
Circle, break and form a line
Go forward up and back
Pass thru and bend the line
Go forward up and back
Pass thru and bend the line
Go forward up and back
Pass thru and bend the line
Go forward up and back
Pass thru and bend the line
Now all join hands and circle eight.

Repeat for 2 and 4.

Square dances: Easy Bend the Line and Bend It Tight.

19. Right and Left Thru

Two couples face each other. Dancers join right hands and pull past opposite, passing right shoulder to right shoulder. Couples have backs to each other. Courtesy turn to face again and repeat to original place.

Teaching aids: (a) Practice in square formation or on the diagonal as suggested for ladies chain. (b) The call is not necessarily followed by a "right and left back" call. Dancers must listen to caller for directions. (c) Use practice call 22 on the diagonal and calls 23 and 24 in the square formation.

Practice call 22
Honor your partner
Honor your opposite
Go right and left thru
Right and left back
Do-sa-do your opposite gal
Go right and left thru turn your pal
Now do-sa-do opposite, don't be slow
Right and left thru and back you go.

Practice call 23
Bow to your partner
1 and 3 go right and left thru across the set

(continued)

Right and left back
2 and 4 go right and left thruRight and left back
1 and 3 ladies chain across
2 and 4 ladies chain
All 4 ladies chain back
Join hands, circle left
Home you go.

Practice call 24
Couples 1 and 3 go right and left thru
Couples 2 and 4 go right and left thru
Couples 1 and 3 go right and left back
2 and 4 go right and left back
Head ladies chain across
Side ladies chain across
All 4 ladies chain back.

Square dances: The Route, Promenade the Outside Ring, Split the Ring Variations, and Old-Fashioned Girl.

20. Weave the Ring

Same as grand right and left except that dancers do not touch hands when passing each other.

Teaching aid: Dancers may turn slightly on a diagonal when passing so as to pass each other closely without bumping.

Practice call 25
All join hands and circle left
Break, reverse, go single file
When you get home, swing your partner
Allemande left and weave the ring
In and out 'til you meet your maid
Take the little girl and promenade.

Square dances: Four-Leaf Clover, substituting weave the ring for grand right and left.

Level 3: Beginner Basics 21-33

21. Four Ladies Chain

All four ladies move to the center, touch right hands, and move clockwise to opposite man. Opposite man and lady courtesy turn, ladies move back into center, touch right hands clockwise to home position, and courtesy turn. Basic also called grand chain.

Teaching aid: The four ladies need to keep track of where they are so they will only pass one man and be turned by the opposite. Use practice calls 18, 19, 23, 24.

Square dances: Bad Bad LeRoy Brown and Tie Me Kangaroo Down.

22. Do Paso

Starting position is a circle of two or more couples. Partners face, take a left forearm grasp, and turn

each other counterclockwise until facing the corner. Turn corner with right forearm grasp until facing partner. Take partner with the left hand, and man turns lady with courtesy turn.

Teaching aid: Practice first in circle of four or more couples, then practice in circle of two couples.

Practice call 26
All join hands, circle left
And around you go
Break into a do paso
Partner by the left, corner by the right
Now turn your own if it takes all night
Join hands, circle.

Repeat all.

23. All Around Your Left-Hand Lady

Often used with seesaw your taw. Corners move one time around each other in a loop pattern, the man starting behind the corner, on around her and back to place, the lady starting in front of him and around him back to place. This completes half of the loop. Seesaw your partner is a similar action that completes the other half of the loop.

Teaching aid: Dancers learn that these are companion figures, but the second loop does not always follow the first loop; it depends on the call.

Practice call 27
Walk all around your left-hand lady
Oh boy, what a daisy
Seesaw your pretty little taw
She's the best you ever saw.

Square dance: Goodbye My Lady Love.

24. California Twirl

The same as the frontier twirl. This basic is used by a couple to reverse the direction they are facing. If they are facing out, they turn to face in, and vice versa. Partners join inside hands (man's right, lady's left). The man walks around the lady clockwise as he turns her counterclockwise under his right arm.

Teaching aids: (a) The lady begins and ends on the man's right side. (b) They must let the hands slip easily around each other so as not to twist the wrist. (c) Both actually turn a half-turn.

Practice call 28
Head couples pass thru
California twirl
Side couples pass thru
California twirl.

Repeat all.

25. Dive Thru

Two couples are facing each other. The couple whose back is to the center of the square makes an arch by joining inside hands. The couple facing them ducks under the arch and moves forward. The arching couple now facing out turns a California twirl.

Teaching aid: The California twirl is done automatically from this position. The caller does not call it.

Practice call 29
Head ladies chain across
But don't chain back
1 and 3 lead to the right
Circle halfway 'round
Now dive thru pass thru
There's your corner
Allemande left.

Repeat for 2 and 4.

26. Ends Turn In

Starting position is when two lines of four are facing out. The two persons in the center of the line form an arch, and the two persons on the ends of the line drop hands, walk forward, and go together under the arch, moving into the center of the square. The arching couple California twirls.

Teaching aid: To practice, direct 1 and 3 men to stand next to corner ladies and 1 and 3 ladies stand next to corner men. The two facing lines move forward, pass thru and join hands, lines are facing out. Repeat practice for 2 and 4.

Square dances: Ends Turn In and Inside Arch Outside Under.

27. Roll Away To a Half-Sashay

Partners are side by side, facing same direction, lady on the man's right. The lady rolls across in front of the man to his left side. As she rolls, she makes one complete turn counterclockwise.

Teaching aids: (a) The man guides the lady across with his right hand and simultaneously steps to his right so that they end up having exchanged places. (b) He will release her left hand and take her right in his left. (c) In star promenade position, the man will have his right arm around the lady's waist and will help her roll across in front of him to the other side. (d) Dancers learn to respond to this basic as half-sashay, roll away, or whirl away (synonymous terms).

Practice call 30
All join hands and circle left
Roll away with a half-sashay
Circle left in the same old way

Ring, ring, ring, I say
Roll away with a half-sashay
All you gents listen to my call
Swing the girl across the hall.

28. You Turn Back

An individual turn or about-face to move in opposite direction.

Practice call 31
1 and 3 pass thru
U-turn back
2 and 4 pass thru
U-turn back.

Repeat all.

Practice call 32
1 and 3 roll away with a half-sashay
Up to the center and back that way
Pass thru and U-turn back
Right and left thru on the same old track.

Repeat for 2 and 4.

Square dances: Roll Away Combo #1 and Gentle on My Mind.

29. Cross Trail Thru

Two couples are facing each other. Each person passes by the opposite right shoulder to right shoulder and then the lady crosses to the left in front of the man. The man crosses to the right behind the lady. They all stop facing out, side by side, lady on left of man, and follow the next call.

Teaching aids: (a) Next call may be "go around two." (b) May be done from line formation; couples end up facing out. When facing out in a line, the two in the middle of the line are corners and will turn to face for allemande left. End dancers will find corners behind them on the end of the opposite line.

Practice call 33
1 and 3 cross trail thru
Separate and go around two
Home you go, pass by your own
Allemande left
Honor your partner at home.

Repeat for 2 and 4.

Practice call 34
1 and 3 promenade the outside ring
Go just halfway round
Same two cross trail thru
Now allemande left with your left hand
Right to partner, shake her by the hand
And there you stand.

Repeat for 2 and 4.

Practice call 35

1 and 3 lead to the right
Circle, break, and make a line
Go forward up and back
Right and left thru
Now ladies chain on the same old track
Turn 'em boys and chain 'em back
Now pass thru and bend the line
Go right and left thru
Now cross trail thru, you're facing out
Allemande left.

Repeat for 2 and 4.

Square dances: Another Trail, Roll Away Combo #2, Arkansas Traveler with Cross Trail, and Split the Ring Variation #2.

30. Grand Square

A no-patter call. Dancers walk individually around a square pattern on the floor. Each side of square is four counts. Dancers move along each side with three steps and turn or hold as indicated.

Teaching aids: (a) All dancers should practice action from the head and side couple position. (b) Caller may cue with word cues as in practice call.

Practice call 36

Honor your partner—the lady fair   ⎫
All get set for grand square   ⎬ A
Walk 2 3 turn   ⎫
Walk 2 3 turn   ⎪
Walk 2 3 turn   ⎪
Walk 2 3 reverse   ⎬ B
Walk 2 3 turn   ⎪
Walk 2 3 turn   ⎪
Walk 2 3 turn   ⎪
Walk 2 3 hold.   ⎭

A. Introduction to music *on* last eight counts of phrase.
B. First 32 counts of music. Start figure with new phrase.

Grand square figure:

Heads
1. Go forward three steps and turn on fourth count to face partner.
2. Take opposite's hand beside you and back up three steps, turning on fourth count to face the person by your side.
3. Drop hands, back away from this person three steps, turning one-quarter on fourth count to face partner.
4. Move forward three steps toward partner and hold the fourth count (do not turn).

Reverse
5. Move backward away from partner three steps, turn one-quarter on fourth count to face the opposite person.
6. Move forward toward opposite three steps, turn one-quarter on the fourth count to face partner.
7. Take opposite's hand beside you and move forward three steps, turning on the fourth count to face opposite.
8. Drop hands, take partner's hands, back up three steps into home place, and hold the fourth count.

Sides
Start with 5, 6, 7, 8, 1, 2, 3, 4.

Square dances: Grand Old Flag using grand square for opener, middle break, and closer, or any previous Square Dance, using grand square as trim.

31. Box the Gnat

Partners face, join right hands and exchange places, as the lady turns counterclockwise under the man's right arm, man walks around lady clockwise. Partners end facing having exchanged places.

Teaching aids: (a) The hands are allowed to slip easily around each other so as not to twist the wrists. (b) Dancers should learn to listen for "box the gnat, pull by," in which they hold on with the right hand after box the gnat and use that hand to pull by that person. (c) Practice this first with partner, then with corner, and then use practice calls 37 and 38.

Practice call 37

1 and 3
Roll away to a half-sashay
Box the gnat across the way
Pull by for a right and left thru.

Repeat for 2 and 4.

Practice call 38

1 and 3 go forward and back
Right to opposite, box the gnat
Pull her thru and U-turn back.

Repeat for 2 and 4.

Practice call 39

1 and 3 cross trail thru
Separate come around 2
Meet your partner, box the gnat
Same lady do-sa-do
Allemande left
Swing your partner.

Repeat for 2 and 4.

Square dances: There's Your Corner and Marianne.

32. Allemande Thar

A star formation for all four couples in square. Dancers allemande left, back to partner with right, pull by to next with left forearm grasp. Men turn this lady a half-turn counterclockwise until men can make a box star (packsaddle) in center. Men travel backward in the star, ladies travel forward. On call "shoot the star," men release box-star position, turn lady on left arms halfway around; ladies are facing clockwise, men counterclockwise. Dancers release arm position, move forward to the next with right hand, pull by, a left forearm grasp to the next, men turn as before into box star backing up. "Shoot the star" again and turn the lady halfway around, move forward to meet original partner and follow the next call.

Teaching aids: (a) The key word to this basic is *thar*. (b) Men should let ladies set movement pace in box star. (c) Allemande thar star is used as a trim and as part of a patter call any time from a left-arm turn.

Practice call 40
Allemande left and allemande thar
It's right and left and form a star
Gents back up in a right-hand star
Now shoot that star to the heavens whirl
Go right and left to a brand new girl
And form that star again
Back 'em up boys but not too far
Shoot that star and find your own
Promenade, go right on home.

Practice call 41
Four men to the center
With a right-hand star
Turn partner left to an allemande thar
Men roll to a promenade
And home you go.

Square dance: Woman in Love.

33. Rip and Snort

Basic use in a circle of eight. The designated couple, without releasing hands, lead across the center and under arch formed by opposite couple, pulling the whole circle under arch. Once under, lead couple drops inside hands. Lady pulls her line round to the right as the man pulls his line left and back to place. The arching couples turn under their own joined hands without releasing hands to face center of circle.

Practice call 42
First couple rip and snort
Down the center, cut 'em short

Lady go right, gent go left
Pull 'em through
Join hands, circle eight.

Level 4: Intermediate Basics 34–44

34. Buzz Swing

A more advanced swinging technique. Dancers are in the same position as they were for the shuffle swing. They turn twice around as before and open up facing the center of the square. The difference in the buzz swing is that the rhythm is uneven. Instead of being an even beat shuffle (♪♪), it is a long-short-long-short (♪.♪) rhythm.

Teaching aids: (a) Each person places the outside of the right foot close to partner's right foot and turns the foot a little each time, pivoting around a center point between the two dancers. The right foot takes the long beat, and the left foot takes the short beat and acts in a pushing motion to propel the turn around. (b) Dancers should lean away from each other and take advantage of the centrifugal force. (c) Momentum must be stopped near the end of the turn so that they can make a controlled stop in place. (d) The buzz swing should be very smooth. Avoid bobbing up and down.

35. Single-File Turn Back

From a single-file promenade, traveling counterclockwise, either man or lady may be designated by the caller to step out of the circle, about face to the right, and go the other way, making another circle traveling clockwise.

Teaching aid: The designated person who steps out and goes in the opposite direction will go all the way around. Since the inside circle is also traveling forward, partners pass each other halfway around and meet the next time to go into the next call.

Practice call 43
Promenade single file
Gents turn back on the outside track
Go once around
Meet partner, right
Go all the way around
Allemande left.

Practice call 44
Promenade single file
Ladies turn back on the outside track
Go once around, do-sa-do partner
Box the gnat, pull by
Allemande left.

36. Square Thru

Two couples are facing each other. Right square thru, starting with the right hand, will be described here. The square thru may be full-square thru (four hands), three-quarters-square thru (three hands), half-square thru (two hands), or square thru five hands, as described below.

Full-Square Thru: Face opposite, take right hand, pull by, turn one-quarter to face partner, give left hand, pull by, turn one-quarter to face opposite, give right hand, pull by, turn one-quarter to face partner, give left hand, pull by, and stop.

Teaching aids: (a) Take four hands, R, L, R, L, hand over hand; the ladies travel counterclockwise around the center of the square; the men travel clockwise. (b) Drop the hand after pulling by. (c) Do *not* turn the last time. (d) Each person ends facing his or her corner.

Three-Quarters-Square Thru: Take three hands, R, L, R.

Teaching aids: (a) Do *not* turn the third time. (b) Each person ends facing out.

Half-Square Thru: Take two hands, R, L.

Teaching aid: Do not turn the *second* time.

Square Thru Five Hands: Take five hands, R, L, R, L, R.

Teaching aids: (a) Do not turn the *fifth* time. (b) Will end facing out.

Note: A left-square thru is executed in the same manner, beginning with the left hand.

Practice call [45] (full-square thru)
1 and 3 square thru
Count four hands, R, L, R, L.
Then split the outside two
Go around one and come back home.

Repeat for 2 and 4.

Practice call [46] (full-square thru)
1 and 3 promenade halfway 'round
Same two square thru
Split the outside two
Come around one to the middle
Cross trail thru
Allemande left.

Repeat for 2 and 4.

Practice call [47] (three-quarters-square thru)
1 and 3 up and back
Square thru three hands 'round

Then separate, go 'round one
Into the middle
Square thru three-quarters 'round
That's what you do
Split the sides, go 'round one
Into the middle, cross trail
To a left allemande.

Repeat for 2 and 4.

Practice call [48] (half-square thru)
1 and 3 half-square thru
Right and left thru with the outside two
Dive thru, pass thru
Allemande left.

Repeat for 2 and 4.

Square dances: Easy Square Thru, Pitt's Patter #3, Half-Square Thru Combo, Half-Square Thru and Then Three-Quarters, Five Hands, Just a Breeze, Half-Square Thru and Box the Gnat Hash, A Fooler A Faker, and Don't Let the Good Life Pass You By.

37. Star Thru

When two couples are facing, each person works with the opposite. The man takes the lady's left hand in his right hand and turns her one-quarter counterclockwise as he walks around her one-quarter clockwise. They end up side by side. This lady is now his new partner on his right.

Teaching aids: (a) The new couple has made a quarter-turn and ends up facing the other couple who were their original partners. (b) The fingers need to slip around each other's easily in order to feel comfortable.

Practice call [49]
1 and 3 go forward and back
Star thru, star thru again
Cross trail back and find the corner
Allemande left.

Repeat for 2 and 4.

Practice call [50]
1 and 3 star thru
Now pass thru, split the ring
Go around one, come down the middle
Star thru, pass thru
Allemande left.

Repeat for 2 and 4.

Square dances: Star Thru—California Twirl, Star Thru Square Thru Combo, New Star Thru, Pitt's Patter #4, Go the Route, and Chime Bells.

38. Double Turn Back From Grand Right and Left

While doing grand right and left, dancers meet partner, take a forearm grasp, and turn each other halfway around to face back the way they came. They grand right and left the wrong way 'round until they meet partner and with a forearm grasp turn one-half again to face the original grand right and left direction. They grand right and left and meet partner the third time and promenade or follow the call.

Teaching aids: (a) The cue is "meet partner and turn right back, go the other way." (b) The turn back may also be done with box the gnat and pull by.

Practice call 51

Allemande left, grand right and left
Corn in the crib, wheat in the stack
Meet your honey and turn right back
Up the river and around the bend
Meet your honey turn back again
Meet your partner and promenade.

39. Three-Quarter Chain

The designated ladies make a right-hand star in the center and pass two positions, or three-quarters of the way around the ring and meet the man in the third position, who will turn her with a courtesy turn.

Teaching aids: (a) If starting from home position, the ladies will travel three-quarters of the way around the ring and be courtesy turned by their original corner. (b) The man may do this same maneuver, called three-quarter star, and the call will indicate some other move when the men get three-quarters of the way around in place of the courtesy turn.

Practice call 52

Four ladies chain three-quarters 'round
Roll away with a half-sashay
Circle left in the same old way
Home you go.

Square dances: Sail Away, Mucho Combo, and Grand Old Flag.

40. Box the Flea

Similar to box the gnat except that both man and lady use the left hand instead of the right. The lady is turned clockwise under the man's right arm; the man walks around her counterclockwise. They end up facing each other but have changed places.

Teaching aids: (a) The hands slip easily. (b) Dancers should listen for a pull by to follow.

Practice call 53

Allemande left your corner
Meet partner, box the gnat
Pull by and with your corner
Box the flea, pull by
Swing your partner.

Square dance: Gnat and Flea Combo #1.

41. Alamo Style

A variation of grand right and left. All eight dancers do an allemande left, hold on to the corner, but shift to a hands-up position and take partner right with a hands-up position, making a complete circle with the men facing in and the ladies facing out (diagram a). Dancers balance a short step forward and a short step back. Release the left hand and turn partner with a right hand halfway around so that the men now face out, the ladies face in. Join hands in the circle (diagram b). Repeat balance forward and back. Release with the right hand and turn with the left hand halfway around. Rejoin hands in the circle. Repeat balance and right-hand turn. Repeat balance and left-hand turn. There is your partner, follow the call.

Teaching aids

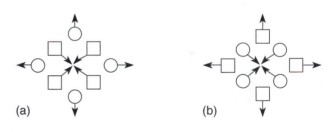

(a)   (b)

Practice call 54

Allemande left, Alamo style
Right to your own, balance a while
Turn with the right half about
Balance in and balance out
Turn with the left and balance Joe
Balance again and don't be slow
Turn with the right on the same old track
Balance forward, balance back
Turn with the left—one more time
Find your own, you're doing fine
Swing.

42. Wheel Around

From a promenade, a couple will turn half-way around counterclockwise to face the couple behind them.

(continued)

Teaching aids: (a) Keeping the promenade position, the man will back up and the lady will move forward so that the move is a pivot in place. (b) The man who was on the inside for the promenade is now on the outside. (c) The dancers should learn to listen for the cue "promenade but don't slow down." (d) The caller may call "all four couples wheel around," in which case they will all be promenading the wrong way around with the lady on the inside. (e) The caller may call "1 and 3 wheel around," in which case 1 turns to face couple 4 and 3 turns to face couple 2. All should adjust slightly so that couples 1 and 2 are in line facing couples 3 and 4. If the caller calls "2 and 4 wheel around," then couples 2 and 3 are in line facing couples 4 and 1. (f) The next call might be "pass thru go on to the next," and couples will pass thru the couple they are facing and proceed as a couple around the circle of couples in the direction they are facing, to meet the couple coming toward them.

Practice call 58

Ladies to the center, back to the bar
Gents center, right-hand star
All the way 'round
Turn partner left, corner right
Partner left to an allemande thar
Slip the clutch to an allemande left.

Square dance: Pitt's Patter #2.

44. Double Pass Thru

A simple pass thru done by four couples instead of two.

Teaching aids

(a) Starting position facing in:

(b) Finish position after both couples passed thru facing out:

Practice call 55

Promenade but don't slow down
First and third wheel around
Go right and left thru
Cross trail to an
Allemande left.

Repeat for 2 and 4.

Practice call 56

Promenade but don't slow down
First and third wheel around
Go right and left thru
Pass thru to a brand new two
Right and left thru
Cross trail, there's your corner
Allemande left.

Repeat for 2 and 4.

Practice call 57

All promenade don't slow down
Couples 1 and 3 wheel around
Star thru, dive thru
Pass thru right and left thru with the outside two
Then dive thru and pass thru
Right and left thru with outside two
Then star thru and cross trail
Find your corner, allemande left.

Repeat for 2 and 4.

Square dances: Duck and Wheel Around, Pitt's Patter #5, I Had Someone Else, and Truly Fair.

43. Slip the Clutch

Start from the allemande thar star. Man will release partner on his left arm, move forward one place to the corner for an allemande left, and follow the call.

Practice call 59

2 and 4 right and left thru, same ladies chain
Now 1 and 3 promenade outside halfway 'round
2 and 4 star thru, double pass thru, first couple left
Next couple go right, right and left thru, turn this girl
Cross trail thru to an allemande left.

Repeat starting with 1 and 3.

Square dance: Four in the Middle.

Level 5: Intermediate Basics 45–50

45. Wheel and Deal

From a line of four, the right couple in line pivots counterclockwise halfway around the person nearest the center. The left couple moves forward two steps and then pivots clockwise halfway around the person nearest the center and comes in behind the right-hand couple. Starting formation: two lines of four facing out.

Teaching aid: When the couples have completed the figure, they are lined up in double file, left-hand couple behind the right-hand couple. Both are facing the same direction.

Practice call 60

Side ladies chain
1 and 3 lead to the right
Circle to a line

Pass thru
Wheel and deal
Center four star thru
Cross trail
Left allemande.

Repeat for 2 and 4.

Practice call 61 (combine with double pass thru)
1 and 3 lead to the right and form a line
Forward up and back you reel
Pass thru wheel and deal
Double pass thru
First couple left, second couple right
Meet the next two
Go right and left thru
Cross trail to an allemande left.

Repeat for 2 and 4.

Square dances: Sides Break to a Line, Now Hear This, Hello Dolly, and King of the Road.

46. Eight Chain Thru

For starting position, 1 and 3 take the opposite and face the sides as shown in the diagram. Four couples are lined up across the floor, two are on the outside facing in while two couples on the inside are facing the couples on the outside.

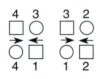

The action is like grand right and left across the set and back, using a right and left thru when facing out.

Teaching aid: Inside couples start with a right and left thru; outside couples give a right hand, pass by to inside, give a left to the inside couple, pass by, and then do a right and left thru to turn around. The process is repeated to get them back to starting position.

Practice call 62
1 and 3 go forward and back
Take your opposite, face the sides
Now everybody eight chain thru
All the way over and back
Meet that couple, right and left thru
Allemande left.

Repeat for 2 and 4.

Square dances: Eight Chain Combo 1 and Combo 2 and A Long Way Over.

47. Turn Thru

Two dancers are facing each other. They take a right forearm grasp and turn each other around clockwise 180 degrees, so as to end up facing the direction they had their backs to when they started.

Teaching aids

(a) Start facing   (b) Turning clockwise   (c)

(d) When dancers are turning, they are actually side by side because of the forearm grasp. (e) After turning halfway around, pull past each other and release grasp.

(e)

Practice call 63
Partners face
Turn thru
Now allemande left the corner
Go back and bow to partner.

Practice call 64
Head couples turn thru
Separate, go around one
Come into the middle
Turn thru, meet your corner
Allemande left.

Repeat for side couples.

Practice call 65
Heads square thru, four hands
Split the outsides, around one
Line up four
Turn thru, bend the line
Turn thru
Allemande left.

Repeat for side couples.

Practice call 66
Head ladies chain
Heads roll away to a half-sashay
Star thru, circle four
Head men break to a line
Turn thru, bend the line
Turn thru, cross trail
Allemande left.

Repeat for side couples.

Practice call 67

Promenade but don't slow down
1 and 3 wheel around
Right and left thru
Turn thru, bend the line
Turn thru, bend the line
Cross trail thru to the corner
Allemande left.

Repeat for 2 and 4.

Square dance: Turn Thru Combo 1.

48. Ocean Wave

A line of dancers, usually four, facing in alternate directions.

Teaching aids: (a) The call usually is "do-sa-do to an ocean wave." Two couples facing each other do-sa-do with opposite all the way around and step forward as if to pass thru and stop when they get four in line. (b) Note diagram. Man and lady of couple 1 face one direction and man and lady of couple 3 face opposite direction. (c) All join hands in line, hands up, elbows down.

(d) All four balance forward (step touch) and backward (step touch). On the backward balance, dancers should reestablish relationships with their own partners by noting which one is facing the same direction as they are. (e) If the next call is right and left thru, they pull by the person who has their right hand and reach for partner with left for courtesy turn. (f) If the next call is box the gnat, it is done with the person who has their right hand in the line. (g) If next call is pass thru, then release hands, and move straight ahead. Same action for starting cross trail thru.

Practice call 68

1 and 3 go forward and back
Now do-sa-do, go all the way 'round
To an ocean wave
Rock it up and back
Do right and left thru
And cross trail
To an allemande left.

Repeat for 2 and 4.

Practice call 69

1 and 3 bow and swing
2 and 4 promenade half the outside ring
Come into the middle and do-sa-do
All the way 'round to an ocean wave
Rock it up and back

Box the gnat across the track
Change girls, box the flea
Join hands and circle left
Allemande left.

Repeat for 2 and 4.

Square dances: Easy Wave.

49. Swing Thru

From an ocean-wave position, the two on each end of the line turn each other with a right arm halfway around. Then the two in the center turn each other with a left arm halfway around. All balance forward and back and follow next call.

Teaching aids: (a) Dancers must have joined hands in the up position, palm to palm. A firm grasp when turning permits the turn to be quick and controlled.

(b) Swing thru may be repeated before adding anything else. (c) The figure ends with lady 3 and man 1 facing the same direction, and man 3 and lady 1 facing the same direction. They would be partners if the next call were right and left thru, pass thru, cross trail, and so on. Box the gnat would be done with person holding the right hand.

Practice call 70

1 and 3 go forward
Swing thru in the middle of the set
Right hand first, then centers left
Go forward and back
   (here note, each has a new partner)
Swing thru one more time
Balance forward, back, you're doing fine
   (here note, each has original partner)
Cross trail, find your corner
Left allemande.

Repeat for 2 and 4.

Practice call 71

1 and 3 half-square thru
Count two hands, then U-turn back
Box the gnat
Swing thru
Swing thru
Pull by to your corner
Left allemande.

Repeat for 2 and 4.

Practice call 72

1 and 3 star thru
Swing thru
Swing thru
Pass thru, allemande left.

Repeat for 2 and 4.

Square dances: Ocean Wave and Swing Thru Combo #1, Happiness Is, and Ocean Wave and Swing Thru Combo #2.

50. Circulate

From two ocean-wave lines, dancers on the outside or the inside of the line may circulate by moving forward to the next end position in a circle.

Teaching aids

(a) If men are circulating, they move clockwise one place.

(b) If ladies are circulating they move counterclockwise one place.

(c) If all circulate, they have moved up two places. (d) After bend the line, the men may be on the inside and the ladies on the outside. The same situation may develop with swing thru.

Practice call 73

1 and 3 go forward to the center
Face the sides
Do-sa-do to an ocean wave
Go forward and back
Men circulate
Girls circulate
Men circulate
Girls circulate
Right and left thru
Dive thru, star thru
Cross trail thru
Allemande left.

Repeat for 2 and 4.

Square dances: Ocean Wave and Circulate and Circulate Sue.

Patter Calls

Notes on the Dance Figures

Only the basic figures are presented in these dances. The caller must select an opener, break, and ending in order to choreograph a full Square Dance call. The basics used in these dances are fully explained for teaching and calling purposes under Teaching Progression and Analysis for Basic Movements of Square Dance, earlier in this chapter. Each basic in the teaching progression is accompanied by an analysis or a description of the movement, teaching aids, diagrams, and suggested dance figures using the basic. Basics are also analyzed in the Glossary.

Each patter call brings the dancers back to a promenade or an allemande left position. If the dance ends with "promenade" or "allemande left," the caller must make up a continuity line to direct the dancer to home positions. When there are exceptions, a note will indicate to the caller where the dancers end up and how to repeat the call in order to bring them to home position. When the call is given for couples 1 and 3, it should be repeated for couples 2 and 4. When the call is given for couple 1, it should be repeated for all couples. The calling sequence for singing calls will be noted at the end of the call when necessary.

■ Promenade the Ring

Basics: Preliminary basics.

Bow to your partner
Heads promenade go halfway 'round the outside ring
Sides up to the middle and back
Sides promenade go halfway 'round
Heads up to the middle and back
All join hands circle left
Go halfway 'round
When you get home face your own
Do-sa-do your partner
Same lady swing and promenade
Promenade single file
Go back home, face your own
Bow to your partner, corner too
Wave at the girl across from you.

■ Gents Star Right

Basics: Star halfway 'round, preliminary basics.

Gents star right, just halfway 'round
Turn your opposite left

(continued)

Now star back home and here we go
Meet your partner do-sa-do
Now gents star left go all the way 'round
Meet your partner right, right arm 'round
To the corner, allemande left
Back to your partner, right and left grand
Hand over hand till you
Find your own, promenade
Come right on home.

■ Bend It Tight

Basics: Split the ring, pass thru, bend the line.

1 and 3 do a pass through
Split the ring and go around two
Hang on tight form two lines
Go forward and back keep in time
Pass thru and bend the line
Pass thru now and bend it tight
Circle up eight and keep it right.

■ Texas Star

Basics: Four gents star, star promenade.

Ladies to the center and back to the bar
Gents to the center and form a star
Right hand crossed
Back with the left and don't get lost
Meet your pretty girl, pass her by
Hook the next gal on the fly
  (Star promenade)
The gent swing out, ladies swing in
Form that Texas Star again
Break that star and everybody swing
Promenade home with the new little thing.
  (Men have new partners)

Repeat 3 times until ladies are back to original
partners.

■ Arkansas Traveler

Basics: Forearm turns.

1 and 3 go forward and back
Forward again
Turn your opposite right arm 'round
Partner left, left arm 'round
Corners right, right arm 'round
Partner left, left arm 'round
Promenade your corner as she comes around.

Note: Gent promenades the corner each time until
he gets his original partner back. Called four times.

■ Easy Bend the Line

Basics: Do-sa-do, bend the line.

1 and 3 promenade three-quarters outside
Go 'round the ring

Line up four with 2 and 4
It's forward up and back
Do-sa-do across the way
Bend the line, that's what I say
Now do-sa-do in the center once more
Then circle eight, go 'round the floor.

Note: Two lines face each other on the diagonal.

■ Split the Ring and Around Just One

Basics: Pass thru, split the ring.

1 and 3 bow and swing
Up to the center and back to the ring
Pass through, separate
Come around just one
Go down the middle, pass thru
Split the ring, separate
Go around one down the middle
Pass thru, separate
Come around one, pass thru
Meet your corner, left allemande
Right to partner, right and left grand.

■ Arkansas Traveler With a Cross Trail Thru

Basics: Forearm turns, cross trail thru.

1 and 3 go forward and back
Sides do cross trail thru, separate
Go around the outside track
Heads go forward
Turn your opposite, right arm around
Partner left, left arm 'round
Corner right, right arm 'round
Partner left, left arm 'round
Promenade your corner as she comes around.

Note: Couples 1 and 3 are doing the Arkansas
Traveler figure, while 2 and 4 cross trail, separate,
and go around the outside. At home, they must
pass by partner to be ready to meet corner with
right arm around.

■ The Route

Basics: Ladies chain, right and left thru.

1 and 3 bow and swing
Lead to the right
Circle, break, and form a line
Forward eight and back you go
Forward again do-sa-do
Go right and left thru across the set
Right and left back, you're not thru yet
Chain those ladies across the hall
Turn and chain them down the line
Chain those ladies across the hall
Chain those ladies down the line

All join hands and circle left
And home you go.

Repeat for 2 and 4.

Note: When ladies chain across hall and down the line, not all couples have the same amount of turn on the courtesy turn, so all need to adjust so that the timing works out right.

▪ Promenade the Outside Ring

Basics: Right and left thru, ladies chain, bend the line, promenade three-quarters, pass thru.

1 and 3 promenade three-quarters 'round the outside ring
While the roosters crow and the birdies sing
Line up four with the sides
Diagonally now go forward and back
Go right and left thru
Right and left back
Two ladies chain, chain back
Forward eight and back in time
Pass thru and bend the line
Now right and left thru, you're doing fine
Forward eight and back once more
Pass thru and bend the line
Go right and left thru to your own land
Allemande left, go right and left grand.

Note: "Line up four with the sides" means to go to the far side of the line nearest home.

▪ Split the Ring Variation 1

Basics: Split the ring, pass thru, ladies chain, right and left thru.

Four ladies chain across the hall
Chain them back and don't you fall
1 and 3 pass thru, go round one
Into the middle, right and left thru
Turn on around right and left back
Pass thru, split the ring
Come 'round one, go down the middle
Pass thru, 'round one into the middle
Right and left thru
Turn on 'round right and left back
Pass thru
Watch out man there's your corner
Left allemande.

▪ Roll Away Combo 2

Basics: Roll away to a half-sashay, right and left thru, bend the line, cross trail thru, U-turn.

1 and 3 lead to the right
Circle, break, form a line
Roll away to a half-sashay
Pass thru, U-turn back

Right and left thru, turn your girl
Pass thru bend the line
Right and left thru
Pass thru bend the line
Do-sa-do
Cross trail thru
Allemande left.

▪ Ends Turn In

Basics: Split the ring, pass thru, California twirl, dive thru, ends turn in.

1 and 3 go forward and back
Pass thru split the ring
Go around two and line up four
Forward eight and back with you
Pass thru, join your hands
Arch in the middle, the ends turn in
Circle four in the middle of the floor
Go one time around, same two
Pass thru, split the ring
Go around one and line up four
Forward eight and back with you
Pass thru, join your hands
Arch in the middle, ends turn in
Circle four in the middle of the floor
Go one time 'round, same two
Pass thru, watch out man
Left to your corner left allemande
Right to partner, right and left grand.

▪ Roll Away Combo 1

Basics: Roll away to a half-sashay, pass thru, split the ring, U-turn back.

1 and 3 roll away to a half-sashay
Pass thru separate come around one
Into the middle, pass thru, split two
Go around 1, down the middle
Pass thru, U-turn back
Allemande left.

▪ Box the Gnat—Pull By

Basics: Roll away to a half-sashay, box the gnat, right and left thru, ladies chain.

Head 2 couples do a half-sashay
Come up to the middle and back that way
Right to opposite and box the gnat
Pull by for a right and left thru
Same two pass thru and separate go 'round one
Meet in the middle for a right and left thru
Same two pass thru and split the outside
Go around one to a line of four
Forward eight and back like that
Right to opposite box the gnat, pull by

(continued)

Right and left thru
Ladies chain across the track
Chain back in the usual way
Roll away to a half-sashay
Join hands circle eight
Allemande left.

■ Split the Ring Variation 2

Basics: Promenade halfway, right and left thru, pass
thru, cross trail.

1 and 3 promenade halfway 'round
Go forward up and back
Pass thru, separate, go 'round one
Into the middle, pass thru
Split the ring, go 'round one
Into the middle, right and left thru
Cross trail thru
Left allemande.

■ Another Trail

Basics: Roll away to a half-sashay, right and left thru,
cross trail thru.

1 and 3 do a half-sashay
Up to the middle and back that way
Pass thru and U-turn back
Go forward and back on the same old track
Pass thru separate come into the middle
Pass thru split the ring, go 'round one
Come into the middle, right and left thru
Now cross trail thru, find your corner
Left allemande.

■ There's Your Corner

Basics: Roll away to a half-sashay, pass thru, box the
gnat, cross trail thru.

1 and 3 roll away to a half-sashay
Up to the middle and back that way
Pass thru, split the ring, go 'round one
Come into the middle, box the gnat
Right and left thru the other way back
Turn on around and pass thru
Split the ring and around just one
Come down the middle, right and left thru
Turn your girl and cross trail back
Separate, come around one into the middle
Box the gnat, pull her by
There's your corner, allemande left.

■ Easy Square Thru

Basics: Right and left thru, dive thru, square thru.

1 and 3 square thru
Right left right left

Right and left thru with the outside two
Dive thru, pass thru
Right and left thru with the outside two
Dive thru, pass thru
Allemande left.

■ Pitt's Patter 3

Basics: Cross trail thru, square thru, box the gnat.

1 and 3 do cross trail thru
Go 'round one, that's what you do
Down the middle, pass thru
Split two, go 'round one
Cross trail in the center once more
Round just one, into the middle
Full square thru to the tune of the fiddle
Face your partner, box the gnat
And swing—she's your own.

■ Half-Square Thru Combo

Basics: Right and left thru, dive thru, box the gnat,
U-turn back, half-square thru.

1 and 3 half-square thru
Right and left thru, outside two
Dive thru, pass thru
Right and left thru with outside two
Dive thru, half-square thru
Separate, go 'round one
Come into the middle, box the gnat
U-turn back
Left allemande.

■ Just a Breeze

Basics: Square thru three-quarters, half-square thru,
bend the line.

1 and 3 lead to the right circle four
Go once around and a quarter more
Now pass thru, on to the next around the ring
Right and left thru, turn on around
Square thru three-quarters, hear me shout
Two lines of four facing out
Now bend the line and pass thru
On to the next right and left thru
Square thru three-quarters 'round
Then bend the line when you come down
Do a half-square thru, look out man
There's your corner, left allemande.

■ Five Hands

Basics: Square thru one-half, three-quarters, five
hands.

1 and 3 square thru, four hands
Right and left thru, outside two

Dive thru, square thru three-quarters 'round
Split the sides, go 'round one
Into the middle, half-square thru
Right and left thru, outside two
Dive thru, square thru five hands
Allemande left.

■ **Half-Square Thru and
Then Three-Quarters**

Basics: Half-square thru, three-quarter square thru.

1 and 3 forward and back
Half-square thru, two hands 'round
Right and left thru with outside two
Turn on around dive thru
Square thru three-quarters, three hands 'round
Then split thru, separate, go 'round one
Right and left thru, go down the middle
Allemande left.

■ **Half-Square Thru and
Box the Gnat Hash**

Basics: Right and left thru, roll away to a half-sashay, box the gnat, half-square thru, box the flea.

Head couples go forward and back
Right and left thru across the track
Right and left back in the usual way
Roll away to a half-sashay
Right to your opposite, box the gnat
Hang on tight for a half-square thru
Right and left thru with the outside two
Same two do half-square thru
You're facing out in lines of four
Forward four and back like that
Bend the line and box the gnat
Change hands, box the flea
Change girls, box the gnat
Change hands, allemande left.

Repeat for side couples.

Note: After twice through, everybody will be home.

■ **Sail Away**

Basics: Three-quarter chain, roll away with a half-sashay, bend the line, cross trail, U-turn back.

Four ladies chain three-quarters 'round
Turn her left then settle down
1 and 3 will swing and sway
2 and 4 roll away with a half-sashay
Heads pass thru go 'round just one
Line up four, let's have some fun
Forward eight and back you sail
Bend the line, then cross trail
U-turn back and join hands circle left

Then roll away to a half-sashay, circle left in the
   same old way
Allemande left.

■ **Star Thru Square Thru Combo**

Basics: Cross trail thru, star thru, square thru.

Heads promenade just halfway 'round
Go down the middle, right and left thru
Then heads lead right—circle break
And make a line
Go forward and back—star thru
Square thru, four hands 'round
Now bend the line, then
Cross trail thru to allemande left.

■ **Star Thru—California Twirl**

Basics: U-turn back, box the gnat, California twirl,
   half-square thru, star thru.

1 and 3 star thru
California twirl
Star thru
Right and left thru
Half square thru
U-turn back
Box the gnat
Change hands
Allemande left.

■ **Pitt's Patter 4**

Basics: Bend the line, dive thru, star thru, box the
   gnat.

1 and 3 lead to the right
Circle, break, and form a line
Forward eight and back you go
Pass thru and bend the line
1 and 3 dive thru
Make a line, bend the line
Pass thru, bend the line
Right and left thru
Pass thru and bend you do
Pass thru to a brand new two
Star thru, right and left thru, box the gnat
Swing your own, circle eight.

■ **Gnat and Flea Combo 1**

Basics: Box the gnat, box the flea.

1 and 3 go forward and back
Right to opposite, box the gnat
Pull 'em thru and separate go 'round just one
Down the center, pass thru
Split the ring to 'round one
Come down the middle, left to opposite

(continued)

Box the flea, pull 'em thru
Separate, go 'round one—come into middle
Swing your own right there at home.

■ New Star Thru

Basics: Star thru, cross trail thru, box the gnat, roll
    away to a half-sashay.

1 and 3 go forward and back
Pass thru U-turn back
Now star thru
Right and left thru the outside two
Now dive thru, star thru
Right and left thru
Same ladies roll away to a half-sashay
New star thru across the way
Right and left thru with the outside two
Turn your girl
Dive thru, star thru
Right and left thru
Now cross trail thru go 'round one
Come into the middle
Box the gnat, pull her by
Allemande left.

■ Go the Route

Basics: Star thru, square thru, dive thru, bend the
    line.

Head two ladies chain to the right
New side ladies chain across
Turn this girl is what you do
Now face the middle, star thru
Right and left thru and turn your Sue
Then pass thru, star thru to lines of four
Forward eight and back with you
Forward again, star thru
Then dive thru, pass thru
Square thru with the outside two
Four hands 'round, you go the route
Two lines of four, facing out
Now bend the line and star thru
Right and left thru and turn your Sue
Then dive thru and pass thru
Square thru with the outside two
Count four hands, you go the route
Two lines of four, you're facing out
Bend the line, go right and left thru
Allemande left.

■ Pitt's Patter 5

Basics: Wheel around, star thru, dive thru, pass
    thru, full-square thru, U-turn back

All eight swing twice around
Promenade don't slow down

1 and 3 wheel around
Star thru, dive thru
Pass thru in center
Dive thru, pass thru in center
Star thru, pass thru
Bend the line
Full-square thru
You're doing fine
U-turn back
Right and left grand.

■ Mucho Combo

Basics: Three-quarter chain, half-sashay, star thru,
    square thru three-quarters.

Four ladies chain
Turn 'em boys and don't get sore
Ladies chain three quarters 'round
Take her by the left, turn her around
1 and 3 do half-sashay
Up to the middle, back that way
Go forward again and star thru, face the sides
Right and left thru the outside two
Then dive thru and pass thru
Star thru the outside two
Right and left thru, turn this girl
Pass thru, on to the next, star thru
Square thru three-quarters
Find the corner, left allemande.

■ Pitt's Patter 2

Basics: Allemande thar, slip the clutch.

1 and 3 bow and swing
Promenade the outside ring
Sides pass thru
Step in behind the old head two (2 behind 3, and 4
    behind 1)
Gents turn back in a right-hand star
Gals progress just as you are
Pass your honey and turn the next
To an allemande thar
Back up boys, not too far
Slip the clutch to an allemande left
Back to your partner, pass her by
Swing the next girl on the fly
Promenade.

■ Sides Break to a Line

Basics: Wheel and deal, double pass thru, cross trail
    thru.

1 and 3 lead right, circle four
Head gents break, line up four
Forward eight and back you reel
Pass thru, wheel and deal

Inside two pass thru, right and left thru outside two
Turn your girl and circle four
Side gents break and line up four
Forward eight and back you reel
Pass thru, wheel and deal
Double pass thru, first couple left, second couple
   right
Pass thru the first two, meet the next
Cross trail thru
To a left allemande.

■ Duck Then Wheel Around

Basics: Roll away with a half-sashay, star thru,
   wheel around, ends turn in, cross trail.

First and third go forward and back
Do a right and left thru across the track
Roll away with a half-sashay
Star thru and hear me say
Split the sides
Go 'round one and make a line of four
Forward eight and back you do
Forward again and pass thru
Join hands centers arch
Ends turn in
Go into the middle
Wheel around in the middle of the square
Do a right and left thru
With the outside pair
Dive thru
Right and left thru in the middle of the set
Pass thru
Split two go around to a line of four
Forward eight and back once more
Pass thru and join hands
Ends turn in—go into the middle
Wheel around in the middle of the square
Do a right and left thru
With the outside pair
Dive thru, pass thru
Split two and around one
Down the middle
Cross trail and find the corner
Left allemande.

■ Four in the Middle

Basics: Ladies chain, roll away to a half-sashay, bend
   the line, California twirl, double pass thru.

Four ladies chain across the way
1 and 3 roll away to a half-sashay
Couple 1 down the middle
Split couple 3, around 1 to a line of 4
Forward 4 to the middle of the ring
Bend the line and face those two
Double pass thru that's what you do

First couple California twirl
Guess who, the corner girl
Left allemande.

■ Now Hear This

Basics: Star thru, double pass thru, wheel and deal,
   square thru three-quarters.

1 and 3 go forward up and back
Cross trail thru, separate go 'round two
Line up four, forward up and back
Star thru, double pass thru
First two left
Next two right
Meet two, pass thru
Wheel and deal
Inside two square thru three-quarters
Left allemande.

■ Eight Chain Combo 1

Basics: Square thru, eight chain thru.

Heads to the center and back you do
Forward again do a full square thru
Count four hands don't get mixed
Right and left thru the outside two
Eight chain thru
All the way over and back you bet
Meet that couple right and left thru
To a left allemande in front of you.

■ Eight Chain Combo 2

Basics: Star thru, eight chain thru, cross trail thru.

2 and 4 go right and left thru
Turn on around
1 and 3 lead right, circle, break to a line
Forward and back
Star thru, right and left thru
Eight chain thru across the land
Don't just stand, count to eight
All the way over and all the way back
Don't be late, then star thru and
Cross trail to an allemande left.

■ A Long Way Over

Basics: Star thru, square thru, eight chain thru,
   wheel around.

Promenade, don't slow down
1 and 3 wheel around
Right and left thru the couple you've found
Star thru, eight chain thru
It's a long way over and then right back
Right and left go along the track
Square thru with the same two

(continued)

Go all the way 'round make two lines
You're facing out, bend those lines
Star thru across from you
Square thru three-quarters, right left right
Allemande left.

■ Turn Thru Combo

Basics: Ladies chain, bend the line, turn thru, ends turn in, square thru, star thru.

Head ladies chain
Heads star thru, pass thru
Split those two, go around one
Lines of four go forward and back
Turn thru, bend the line
Pass thru, bend the line
Turn thru
Centers arch, ends turn in
Square thru, four hands
Separate around one
Into the middle, star thru
All four to your corner
Allemande left.

■ Inside Arch and Outside Under

Basics: Dive thru.

Couple one bow and swing
Lead to the right and circle half
Inside arch and outside under
Cross the hall and go like thunder
Some will arch, some dive under
Hurry up boys, don't you blunder
Lead to the next, circle half
Dive thru, lead to the next
Circle half and here we go
Inside arch and outside low
Dive thru, don't you blunder
Inside arch, outside under
Home you go and everybody swing.

Note: Inside arch and outside under is continuous until the lead couple is in the middle of the set and can lead to couple 3. The side couples are opposite home. The repeat will take everybody home.

■ Easy Wave

Basics: Square thru, ocean wave.

1 and 3 square thru
Count four hands that's what you do
Do-sa-do to an ocean wave
Balance forward up and back
Right and left thru turn your girl
Dive thru, pass thru
Do-sa-do to an ocean wave
Balance forward up and back

Right and left thru, turn your girl
Dive thru, pass thru
Allemande left.

■ Ocean Wave—Swing Thru Combo 2

Basics: Wheel around, ocean wave, swing thru, box the gnat, star thru.

Four men do a right-hand star
Back by the left not too far
Meet your own and
Promenade, but don't slow down
1 and 3 wheel around
Do-sa-do to an ocean wave
Swing thru, balance back
Box the gnat, go right and left thru
Star thru, dive thru
Pass thru, do-sa-do to an ocean wave
Swing thru, balance back
Box the gnat, go right and left thru
Star thru, cross trail thru to an
Allemande left.

■ Ocean Wave—Circulate

Basics: Square thru, ocean wave, circulate.

1 and 3 square thru
Count four hands
Do-sa-do to an ocean wave
Balance forward and back
Men circulate
Go right and left thru
Turn your girl, dive thru
Pass thru
Do-sa-do to an ocean wave
Balance forward and back
Men circulate
Right and left thru
Turn your girl and dive thru
Pass thru to an allemande left

Repeat for 2 and 4, ladies circulate.

■ Ocean Wave—Swing Thru Combo 1

Basics: Box the gnat, star thru, swing thru, box the flea, ocean wave.

Heads star thru, pass thru, do-sa-do
All the way round to an ocean wave
Forward up and back then swing thru, go up and back
Box the gnat, pull by for right and left thru
Now dive thru, pass thru
Do-sa-do the outside two
Make an ocean wave with the same pair
Go forward and back, swing thru
Box the gnat, now listen to me
Pull on by, face partner

Everybody swat the flea
Change hands to right and left grand.

■ Circulate Sue

Basics: Square thru, ocean wave, circulate.

1 and 3 square thru
Four hands 'round in the middle you do
Now do-sa-do to an ocean wave
Go forward up and back
Men circulate
Girls circulate
All circulate
There's your corner, allemande left.

Supplementary Square Dance Patter

■ Openers

Honor your partner, lady by your side
All join hands and circle wide
Break and trail along that line
The lady in the lead, the gent behind
Now you're home and now you swing.

Clap your hands
Now slap your knees [twice]
Bump-si-daisy if you please [partners bump hips together].

Hi diddle, diddle
All eight to the middle
Back right out and swing your own
To the tune of the fiddle.

Honor your partner, lady by your side
All join hands and circle wide
Break and trail along that line
Lady in front and the gent behind
Home you go, you're doing fine.

All jump up and never come down
Swing your partner 'round and 'round
And promenade, boys, promenade.

Bow to your partner, corner too
Swing that pretty little girl with you
Promenade.

■ Endings

Honor your partner, corners all
Honor your opposite across the hall
And that is all.

Promenade—you know where
And I don't care
Take her out and give her air.

All you folks listen to the call
Thank you, ladies—that will be all.

Honor your partner, corner all
Wave at the gal across the hall
Thank you, I guess that's all.

Honor your partner and your corner too
Now wave at the gal across from you
Thank you folks, I'm all through.

Allemande left with your left hand
Bow to your partner and there you stand.

■ Roll Away

1 and 3 roll away to a half-sashay
Box the gnat across the way
Pull her thru with a
Right and left thru.

■ Breaks

Allemande left, say what do you know
Back to your own and do-sa-do.

Wham bam, left allemande.

Allemande left as pretty as you can
Right to your honey
And a right and left grand.

Promenade around the ring
While the roosters crow and the birdies sing.

Here we go in a little red wagon
Rear wheel's broke and the axle's draggin'
Promenade, boys, promenade.

With your big foot up
And your little foot down
Promenade, go 'round and 'round.

Promenade, go 'round and 'round
Like a jaybird hoppin' on the frozen ground.

Allemande left with your left hand
Right to your partner
And a right and left grand
Promenade eight when you come straight.

Ace of diamonds, jack of spades
Meet your honey and all promenade.

Two, four, six, and eight
All promenade when you get straight.

Swing the girl across the hall
Go back home and swing your own.

Alamo style
Allemande left in Alamo style
Right to your honey and balance awhile
Balance in and balance out
Turn with the right hand half about
Balance out and balance in
Turn with the left hand half about
Balance in and balance out
Turn with the right hand half about
Balance out and balance in
Turn with the left hand half again
Swing your partner and promenade.

(continued)

■ Breaks for Fours

Half-square thru
1 and 3 go forward and back
Now half-square thru around the track
Right and left thru with the outside two
Dive thru, pass thru to an allemande left.

Square thru
Heads go forward and back you do
Forward again and full-square thru
Now count four hands is what you do.
Head two couples go square thru
Right, left, right, and pass a few
Partner left and now you're thru.

Star thru
Heads go forward, back with you
Go forward again and pass thru
Around just one is what you do
Into the center and star thru
Cross trail thru, look out, man
There's your corner, left allemande.

■ Breaks for Eights

Wheel and deal
Head two couples swing and sway
Side ladies chain across the way
Heads go right and circle four
Head gents break to a line of four
Forward eight and back you peel
Pass thru, wheel and deal
Inside two square thru three-quarters
Don't stand, left allemande.

1 and 3 right and left thru
Lead to the right, circle to a line
Ladies chain
Pass thru
Wheel and deal
Centers pass thru
Box the gnat
Right and left grand.

Wheel around
1 and 3 wheel around
Square thru three-quarters 'round
Go on to the next
Left square thru all the way 'round
Allemande left.

Promenade and don't slow down
Keep on walking that girl around
Heads back track and pass thru
Sides back track and follow those two
Lead two couples wheel around

Box the gnat with the two you found
Do a right and left thru

The other way back
Turn this girl, and
Cross trail thru.

Promenade, but don't slow down
First and third, wheel around
Right and left thru
Cross trail back to an allemande left.

Promenade, but don't be slow
1 and 3 wheel around
Star thru, square thru
Four hands count 'em too

Go on to the next, cross trail
Allemande left.

Gimmick for bend the line
Fourth couple bow and swing
Couple 1 promenade three-quarters to the right of
    number 4
Forward 4 and back
Couple 2 bow and swing
Up to the middle and split those four
Separate, go around two and line up six
Couple 3 promenade around one
Crowd into the line and make it eight.

Red Hot
Promenade red hot
Turn the right-hand lady, right arm 'round
Partner left, go all the way 'round
To your corner right, right arm 'round
Partner left, go once around
Promenade your corner as she comes 'round.

Do paso
Eight hands up and away we go
Circle left and don't be slow
Break right out with a do paso
Partner left, corner right
Back to your partner
Turn that gal if it takes all night.

Roll away
Ring, ring, ring I say
Roll away with a half-sashay.

Rip and snort
First couple go down the center with a rip and
    snort
Down the center and cut 'em short
Lady go gee and the gent go haw
Circle eight as you come straight

Double back track
Corn in the crib, wheat in the stack
Meet your honey and turn right back
Up the river and around the bend
Meet your honey turn back again
Meet your partner and promenade.

Listen folks to what I say
Meet your gal and go the other way
Whirl the rope and jerk the slack
Meet your partner and turn right back
Promenade, boys, promenade.

Meet your honey and sing a little song
Turn right back you done gone wrong
Meet your honey and sing once more
Turn right back as you did before
Meet your partner and promenade.

Western Cowboy Square Dance

The figure is the dominant characteristic of the *Western Square Dance*. The caller follows the figure but may change and use any opener, break, or ending. If the figure is long, the breaks should be short. If the figure is short, the breaks can be longer and more complicated. Breaks should be chosen to complement the formation the dancers are in at the time it is to be used. When dancers are circling four, use a break-form four.

The dances included in this section are representative of the following figure types: symmetrical, Forward Up Six, Catch All Eight, Sides Divide, Bird in the Cage—Seven Hands 'Round, and Tea Cup Chain; double lead out, Forward Up and Back, and Milagro Square; single visiting, Sally Good'in; accumulative, Cowboy Loop. Chapter 4 lists several "visiting couple" figures—such as Shoot the Owl, Take a Little Peek, and Lady 'Round the Lady—under the title Big Circle Square Dance. These figures may also be done in the square formation. So now "Buckle up your belly bands, loosen up your traces, all to your place with a smile on your face and let's do some old time square dancin'."

■ Bird in the Cage—Seven Hands 'Round
First couple bow, first couple swing
First get out to the right of the ring
Turn the right-hand lady right arm around
Back to your partner, left arm around
Opposite lady, right arm around
Partner left and left arm around
Corner lady right arm around
Swing your partner with two-hand swing
Cage that bird in the middle of the ring
   Lady 1 whirls into center.
Seven hands up and circle left
   All remaining dancers circle around bird.
The bird hops out and the crow hops in with bird
   Gent 1 exchanges places with bird in the center.
Seven hands up we're gone again.

Crow hops out with an allemande left
   All dancers allemande left.
Meet your partner and right and left grand.

Repeat for gents 2, 3, and 4.

■ Catch All Eight
First couple balance and swing
Down the center and split the ring
   Couple 1 goes across set and walks between (splits) couple 3.
Lady go gee, gent go haw
   Lady goes right, gent goes left.
Meet your honey in the hall
   Couple 1 meets in home position.
Catch all eight with the right, go half way around
   All swing partner half turn around clockwise with right forearm grasp.
Back with the left go all the way around
   All swing partner one full turn counterclockwise with left forearm grasp.
Swing your corner with a two-hand swing
   Join both hands with corner, turn once around clockwise.
Meet your partner pass her by
   Pass partner's right shoulder.
Pick up the next girl on the fly and promenade.
   Promenade new partner (right hand lady) to gents' home position.

Repeat for couples 2, 3, and 4.

■ Cowboy Loop
First couple out to the couple on the right
Circle four with all your might
Break and trail that line to the next
   Gent 1 breaks circle by unclasping left hand, leads line of four to couple 3.
Two hands up and four trail thru
   Couple 3 raises joined inside hands, line of four passes under arch.
   Couple 3 walks forward over line to position 1 in set.
Turn right around and come back thru
   Gent 1 pulls line around toward center of set and prepares to go under arch the second time. Couple 3 does California Twirl, walks back to position as line of four passes under arch to center of set.
And tie that knot like the cowboys do
   Gent 1 turns right and pulls the line through arch formed by last couple in line.
Circle up four and away we go
Pick up two and make it six
Circle left till all get fixed
   Gent 1 breaks circle with left hand and picks up couple 3 on left side.
Break and trail that line to the next
   Gent 1 breaks circle with left hand, leads line of six through arch formed by couple 4.

(continued)

Two hands up and six go thru
>Couple 4 raises joined inside hands, line of six passes under arch.
>Couple 4 walks forward over line to position 2 in set.

Turn right around and come back thru
>Gent 1 pulls line of six around toward center of set and prepares to go under arch the second time.
>Couple 4 turns around, walks back to position as line of six passes under arch to center of set.

Tie that knot like the cowboys do
>Gent 1 turns right and pulls the line through arch formed by last couple in line.

Now circle up six and keep it straight
Pick up two and make it eight
>Gent 1 breaks circle with left hand and picks up couple 4 on left side.

Circle eight and here we go.
>(Use any appropriate break.)

Repeat calls for couples 2, 3, and 4.

◼ Forward Up and Back

Couples 1 and 3 go forward and back
Forward again and right and left thru
Right and left back in the same old track
Circle up four in the middle of the floor
>Break for circle of four.

Couples 2 and 4 go forward and back
Forward again and right and left thru
Right and left back on the same old track
Circle up four in the middle of the floor
>Break for circle of four.

Head ladies chain and chain right back
Side ladies chain and chain right back
Now all four ladies chain
Grand chain your ladies.
>Break for eight.

Variation

1 and 3 right and left thru
2 and 4 right and left thru
1 and 3 right and left back
2 and 4 right and left back
Head ladies chain
Side ladies chain
Head ladies chain and chain 'em back
Side ladies chain and chain 'em back
All four ladies chain
Grand chain the ladies.

◼ Forward Up Six

First and third balance and swing
Now whirl your girl to the right of the ring
>Gent 1 twirls lady 1 to gent 2. Lady 1 stands to the left of gent 2 to form a line of three, facing center. Gent 3 whirls lady 3 to gent 4. Lady 3 stands to the left of gent 4 to form a line of three, facing center. Gents 1 and 3 remain in home positions. Join hands in each line.

Forward up six and back you go
>Lines of three go forward and back.

Two gents loop with a do-sa-do
>Gents 1 and 3 execute a do-sa-do.

Now right hand up and left hand under
>Gent 2 twirls the left-hand lady under the arch formed with right-hand lady to gent 3. Right-hand lady is twirled outside and over left-hand lady to gent 1. Gent 4 twirls the ladies in the same manner with his left-hand lady going to gent 1 and his right-hand lady going to gent 3.

Twirl those girls and go like thunder
Form new threes and don't you blunder
>Gent 3 now has lady 4 on the right and lady 1 on the left. Gent 1 has lady 2 on the right and lady 3 on the left. Two new lines of three are formed.

Repeat call three times beginning with "Forward up six and back you go," to return ladies to the right side of original partner. Then use any appropriate trim.

Note: Vary the call "Two gents loop with a do-sa-do" by calling "Two gents loop with a right elbow" or "Two gents loop with a left elbow."

◼ Milagro Square

First four lead to the right
>Couples 1 and 3.

Go around that couple and take a little swing
>Couple 1 separates, lady goes right, gent goes left, and swings *three times* around behind couple 2. Couple 3 does the same around couple 4.

Center couples form a ring and circle once around
>While couples 1 and 3 swing, couples 2 and 4 circle *once* around in center of set.

Pass right through, just you two
>Couples 2 and 4. Do not turn back.

And around that couple and take a little swing
>Couple 2 moves forward, separates and swings behind couple 3. Couple 4 moves forward, separates, and swings behind couple 1.

Center couples form a ring and circle once around
>While couples 2 and 4 swing, couples 1 and 3 circle once around in center of set.

Pass right through, just you two
>Couples 1 and 3. Do not turn back.

And around that couple and take a little swing
>Couple 1 moves forward, separates, and swings behind couple 2. Couple 3 moves forward, separates, and swings behind couple 4.

Center couples form a ring and circle once around
>While couples 1 and 3 swing, couples 2 and 4 circle once around in center of set.

Pass right through just you two
>Couples 2 and 4. Do not turn back.

And around that couple and take a swing
>Couple 2 moves forward, separates, and swings behind couple 3. Couple 4 moves forward, separates, and swings behind couple 1.

Center couples form a ring and circle once around
  While couples 2 and 4 swing, couples 1 and 3 circle once around center of set.
Pass right through, just you two
  Couples 1 and 3. Do not turn back.
Circle with the next and around you go
Break right into a do paso
Take her home and everybody swing.

Repeat calls for couples 2 and 4 or side four.

■ **Sally Good'in**
First gent out and swing Sally Good'in
  Gent 1 swings right-hand lady Sally Good'in with right arm around.
Now your Taw
  Gent 1 swings own partner left arm around.
Swing that girl from Arkansas
  Gent 1 swings opposite lady (Arkansas) with right arm around.
Then swing Sally Good'in
  Gent 1 swings Sally Good'in with left arm around.
And now your Taw
  Gent 1 swings own partner right arm around.
Now don't forget your old Grandma
  Gent 1 swings corner lady (Grandma) with left arm around.
Home you go and everybody swing
  Swing with waist swings.

Repeat call with gents 1 and 2 leading out and doing the figure simultaneously.
Repeat again with gents 1, 2, and 3 leading out and dancing the figure simultaneously.
Repeat, fourth time, "All Four Gents" leading out and dancing the figure simultaneously.

■ **Sides Divide**
First four forward and back
  Couples 1 and 3.
Forward again on the same old track
Swing in the center and swing on the side
  Gent 1 swings lady 3, gent 3 swings lady 1. Simultaneously couples 2 and 4 swing.
Now swing your own and sides divide.
  Couples 1 and 3 swing own partners in center. Side couples separate, ladies go left, gents right. Move one quarter around set, meet opposite and swing.
Circle four in the middle of the floor
  Couples 1 and 3.
Sides divide and swing some more.
  Sides separate. Move one quarter around set, meet partner and swing.
Do paso and don't get sore.
  Couples 1 and 3 in center.
Sides divide and swing some more.
  Sides separate. Move one quarter around set, meet opposite and swing.

Up the river and around the bend
Sides divide and swing again
  Sides separate, meet partners in original home position and swing.
And promenade your corners all
  Gents have new partners.
Hold that gal don't let her fall
Promenade around the hall.
  Promenade new partner home.

Repeat call for couples 2 and 4.
Repeat from beginning until ladies are back in home positions.

■ **Tea Cup Chain**
The patter figure Tea Cup Chain was choreographed by Mrs. Pat Morrison Lewkowicz of Chicago, formerly from Austin, Texas. She worked out the figure of the coffee table using tea cups from her collection as ladies and gents, thus the name "Tea Cup Chain." Later she worked it out with members of the Lone Star Square Dance Club of Austin, Texas.

General Directions: Tea Cup Chain is a symmetrical figure in which all couples begin moving simultaneously. The head and foot gents always send their ladies to the center and receive a new lady from the gent on the left. The side gents always send their ladies to the gent on their right and receive their lady from the center. Head and foot ladies start with the right hand and continue alternating right, left, right, etc. The side ladies start with the left hand to partner and continue alternating left, right, left, etc. Gents alternate similarly, taking whichever hand is extended to them. The ladies progress counterclockwise, moving to the right-hand gent each time. When the gent receives a lady, he turns her in place as in a regular ladies chain, always backing up in place. When he receives a lady's left hand, he turns her counterclockwise. If he receives her right hand, he turns her clockwise and sends her to the center or side as the case may be.

Specific Figure Directions: All couples begin moving simultaneously.

Head and Foot Ladies: The ladies move to the center, grasp right hands and turn three quarters around clockwise in the center; give left hand to side gent. Lady 1 goes to gent 2 and lady 3 goes to gent 4, who turns ladies counterclockwise.

Side Gents: Pass ladies on to the right-hand gent. Gent 2 sends lady 1 to gent 3 and gent 4

(continued)

sends lady 3 to gent 1, who turns ladies around with the right hand clockwise.

Head and Foot Gents: Send ladies to the center. Ladies grasp left hands and turn counterclockwise one and a fourth in the center and give right hand to side gents. Lady 1 goes to gent 4 and lady 3 goes to gent 2.

Side Ladies: Side gents turn their ladies around counterclockwise and send them to the gent on the right. Lady 2 goes to gent 3 and lady 4 goes to gent 1.

Head and Foot Gents: Turn ladies around with the right hand clockwise and send them to the center. Ladies grasp left hands and turn counterclockwise one and one-fourth in the center and extend right hand to side gent. Lady 2 goes to gent 4 and lady 4 goes to gent 2.

Side Gents: Turn ladies clockwise and pass them on to the right-hand gent. Lady 2 goes to gent 1 and lady 4 goes to gent 3.

Head and Foot Gents: Turn ladies clockwise and send them to the center. They grasp right hands and turn three quarters clockwise and go on to original partner who turns them in place.

Notes: (a) Once the figure "Tea Cup Chain" is called, any patter may be used to fill in the execution time. (b) All couples work together so that while two are turning in the center, two ladies are being turned on the side and passed on to the right-hand gent. (c) The figure is usually repeated twice. (d) Select an opening and break to suit the figure.

Singing Calls

■ Hurry, Hurry, Hurry

Records: EZ 733; Grenn 12223; Windsor 4405B.

Cassette: "Smoke on the Water" Square Dance Classics by Bob Dalsemer, TC 123C (with calls), TC 124C (without calls).

Basics: Ladies chain.

Opener
Everybody swing your partner
Swing 'er high and low
Swing that next girl down the line [to the left]
Don't let 'er go
Cross the hall and swing your own
And swing and swing and swing
Promenade that pretty girl around the ring.

Figure
First couple lead to the right
Circle four around
Leave that girl, go on to the next
And circle three around
Take that couple on with you
And circle five hands round
Now leave those four
And join the line of three [on the corner beside partner]
Ladies chain across the hall
But don't return
Chain those ladies down the line
Watch 'em churn
Turn and chain across the hall
Don't you fall
Chain the line and swing your honey home.

Break
Allemande left with your left hand
'Round the ring we go
It's grand old right and left
Walk on your heel and toe
When you meet your honey boys
Try a do-sa-do [or swing 'er high and low]
Promenade that pretty girl right on home
Hurry, hurry, hurry, hurry home.

Sequence: Opener, figure, and break for each couple.

■ Alabama Jubilee

Records: EZ (LP) 506; Folkraft 1136; Windsor 4144, 4444.

Cassette: "Smoke on the Water" Square Dance Classics by Bob Delsemer, TC 123C (with calls), TC 124C (without calls).

Basics: Sashay, promenade, allemande left, grand right and left.

Four little ladies promenade inside of the ring
  Ladies move in single file, counterclockwise, around inside of set.
Back to your partner and give him a swing
Sashay 'round your corner girl
  Either sashay or do-sa-do.
Bow to your partner boys, give her a whirl
Now four little gents promenade inside of the ring
  Gents move single file, counterclockwise, inside of set.
Sashay 'round your partner, give your corner a swing
  Either sashay or do-sa-do.
You promenade just you and me
  Gents promenade corner lady.
To the Alabama Jubilee, yeah man
To the Alabama Jubilee.

Break

Turn the left-hand lady with a left hand 'round
    Turn corner once around. All turns with forearm
    grasp.
A right to your partner go all the way 'round
    Turn partner once and a half.
The right-hand lady with a left hand 'round
    Turn right-hand lady twice around.
Now swing your little honey
    Waist swing.
'Till her feet leave the ground
It's an allemande left, a right and left grand
Meet your little honey, take her by the hand
You promenade, just you and me
To the Alabama Jubilee, yeah man
To the Alabama Jubilee.

Repeat figure and break three times until ladies are
    returned to original partners.

■ Hello Dolly

Caller: Marshall Flippo.

Music: The Texans.

Record: Blue Star #1729, flip side.

Basics: Allemande thar, box the gnat, half-square
    thru, star thru, wheel and deal.

Intro, break, ending

Four ladies chain across that ring, turn 'em all a
    left-hand swing
Then roll away and circle, don't take long
Do an allemande left and allemande thar, right and
    left the four gents star
You're going you're still going you're still going
    strong
Shoot that star full around like that, with the corner
    girl you box the gnat
Pull her by and turn your own and then [prome-
    nade]
Promenade fellas, have a little faith in me fellas
Dolly's never going 'way again.

Figure

The head two couples half-square thru, then do-
    sa-do the outside two
Face the same little girl, star thru [and then]
Pass on thru and wheel and deal, star thru the
    center two
Half-square thru, then do-sa-do that outside two
    again
Star thru and pass thru, and wheel and deal go two
    by two
Centers pass on thru and then swing [promenade]
Promenade fellas, have a little faith in me fellas
Dolly's never going 'way again.

■ Mañana

Record: Windsor 4887.

Basics: Forearm turns, with all ladies.

Opener

Now you honor your chiquita
Give your corner girl a weenk
Allemande left your corner
Grand old right and left I theenk
Now when you meet your enchilada
Do-sa-do her neat
Swing your chili pepper and
Promenade the street.

Figure

Vaqueros star across the set
A left-hand turn that girl
Star back home again real quick
Another left-hand whirl
A right arm 'round your corner
Give your own a left-arm swing
Now promenade that corner girl
And everybody sing
Mañana, Mañana,
Mañana is good enough for me.

Chiquitas star across the set
A left-hand turn that man
Star back home and turn your hombre
With the old left hand
A right arm 'round your corner
Give your own a left-arm swing
Now promenade your corner girl
And everybody sing
Mañana, mañana,
Mañana is good enough for me.

Break

Allemande left your corner
And pass right by your own
Allemande right your right-hand girl
And leave your own alone [pass by]
Now allemande left your corner
And give your own a swing
Promenade to Mexico
And everybody sing
Mañana, mañana,
Mañana is good enough for me.

Sequence: Opener, figure, break, figure, break.

■ King of the Road

Caller: Bob Ruff.

Music: Wagon Masters.

Record: Wagon Wheel WW922 flip side.

(continued)

Basics: Cross trail, star thru, wheel and deal, double pass thru.

Intro, break, ending
Join hands, circle left you know
All the way around 'til you get back home
Left allemande your corner, then come back and do-sa-do
Allemande your corner, then you weave the ring, promenade
Ah, but two hours of pushin' broom buys an eight-by-twelve four-bit room
I'm a man of means by no means, king of the road.

Figure (twice for heads, twice for sides)
Heads forward up and back, a right and left thru
Cross trail, to your corner, then star thru
Pass thru, wheel and deal, double pass thru
First one left, the next one right and do the right and left thru
Star thru, corner swing and whirl, promenade, go around the world
I'm a man of means by no means, king of the road.

Alternate verses for middle break and ending
I smoke old stogies I have found, short, but not too big around
I'm a man of means by no means, king of the road.
Trailer for sale or rent, room to let, fifty cents
I'm a man of means by no means, king of the road.

■ **Just Because**

Caller: Mike Michele.

Record: Western Jubilee No. 500.

Cassette: "Smoke on the Water" Square Dance Classics by Bob Dalsemer, TC123C (with calls), TC124C (without calls).

Basics: Allemande left, allemande right, grand right and left, ladies chain, see-saw, star.

Opener
Honor to your partners and to your corners all
Swing that opposite lady, she's the one across the hall
Now run away back home, swing and whirl your own
Thank your stars the bird ain't flown
Allemande left with the ol' left hand
Partner right and a right and left grand
Hand over hand around that ring
Right and left with the pretty little thing
Now promenade your partners, boys, shout and sing
Because, just because.

Figure
Now the two head ladies chain across, chain right over that ring

Send 'em right on back, take your own and give her a swing
Side two ladies chain across, chain right over that ring
Send 'em right on back, take your own and give her a swing
Allemande left your corner, allemande right your partner
Swing your corner lady around and around
Now promenade that corner, boys, shout and sing
Because, just because.

Break
It's all around your corner, that the gal we call Grandma
See-saw round your partner, she's the prettiest in the hall
All four gents center and star with the ol' right hand
Circle to your corner with a two-time allemande
Turn 'em once, turn 'em twice, back right off and bow real nice
Then a grand ol' right and left around the ring

Note: All four gents step to center, form a right-hand star, walk all around new corner. Gents take corners with left forearm hold breaking their star and walk two complete turns around with corners. At the end of the turns, gents should all be facing counterclockwise around the set, ladies clockwise. Slip hands down from forearm hold to a hand hold, step back arms length and bow, then take partners right hand for the grand right and left.

Now promenade that dear old thing,
Throw your heads right back and sing
Because, just because.
    (On meeting partners across set, promenade home.)

Repeat Figure and break three more times.

■ **Gentle On My Mind**

Caller: Bob Ruff.

Music: Wagon Masters.

Records: Wagon Wheel WW911. EZ Album 5, LP506.

Basics: Weave the ring, ladies chain, pass thru, right and left thru, roll away.

Opener, break, closer
Allemande your corner
Do-sa-do your own
Four men make a left-hand star around
Turn your partner right
Your corner allemande
Partner do-sa-do
Weave the ring now
Meet partner, do-sa-do, promenade.

Figure

Four ladies chain
Turn your girl and then
1 and 3 go right and left thru
Turn your girl
Roll away—circle left
Four girls pass thru
Turn left, go single file
Men pass thru, swing
Promenade.

Sequence: Opener, figure twice for 1 and 3, break, figure twice for 2 and 4, closer.

■ Marianne

Record: Folkraft 1282, flip side.

Basics: Ladies chain, cross trail, box the gnat.

Opener and ending

Four little ladies chain across
You turn 'em with your left hand
You chain those ladies back again
You turn your Marianne
Do-sa-do your corner, do-sa-do your own
Bow to your corner, but swing your own (hurry up now).

Chorus

All day, all night, Marianne (promenade 'em)
Down by the seaside along the sand (sing it)
Even little children like Marianne (swing 'em)
Down by the seaside along the sand (square sets).

Figure

Head two couples pass thru
Around just one you know
Go down the middle and cross trail thru
Around just one you go
Box the gnat at home
Four gents a left-hand star around
Now go back home and do-sa-do
Your corner swing (don't rush me).

Chorus.

Sequence: Opener, figure twice for head couples, figure twice for side couples, ending.

The chorus is not repeated after the ending.
Last line: But swing your Marianne.

■ Old-Fashioned Girl

Caller: Bruce Johnson.

Records: Instrumental: Windsor 7504A. With call: Windsor 4405A; Lloyd Shaw E–31.

Basics: Ladies chain, right and left thru, single-file turn back.

Opener

Honor your old-fashioned girl
Hold her close and swing and whirl
Then promenade that ring
Promenade in single file
Lady in the lead, Indian style
Gents step out, ladies left-hand star
Do-sa-do your honey when she comes around to you
Swing 'er once or twice just like her daddy used to do
Promenade that gal—she's just like the gal
That married dear old dad.

Figure

Head gents swing your maids
Take those girls and promenade
Just halfway 'round that ring
Now right and left thru across the middle
Hurry boys keep time with the fiddle
Chain right, your right-hand ladies chain
All four ladies chain across the hall
Chain 'em right back and don't you let 'em fall
Promenade that pearl
She's just like the girl
That married dear old dad.

Break

Do-sa-do your corner girl
Go back home and swing and whirl
Swing like your daddy said
Allemande left with your left hand
Right to your partner, right and left grand
Hand over hand around the ring you go
Do-sa-do your honey
When she comes around to you
Swing her once or twice
Just like her daddy used to do
And promenade your old-fashioned girl
She's just like the girl
That married dear old dad.

Sequence: Opener, figure twice for 1 and 3 (second time, left-hand ladies chain), break, figure twice for 2 and 4, break.

■ Grand Old Flag

Caller: Dan Dedo.

Record: Pilgrim 1007, flip side.

Reference: *American Square Dance Magazine.*

Basics: Grand square, box the gnat, allemande thar, three-quarters chain.

Opener (sides face—grand square)
You're a grand old flag, a high-flying flag
And forever in peace may you wave
You're the emblem of the land I love

(continued)

The home of the free and the brave
Left allemande the corner girl
Then weave that ol' ring
Go in and out and then you promenade
Should old acquaintance be forgot
Keep your eye on that grand old flag.

Figure
1 and 3 [2 and 4] promenade the outside ring
And then side ladies chain across the floor
Sides do-sa-do, it's back to back you go
Box the gnat, star right around the floor
With that corner allemande, it's do-sa-do your own
Take that corner and promenade
Should old acquaintance be forgot
Keep your eye on that grand old flag.

Middle break and closer
Walk around that girl, seesaw your taw
Join your hands, circle left, go 'round the ring
Do an allemande left, go allemande thar
Go right and left, you've got a star
Shoot that star, four ladies chain three-quarters and then
Roll promenade with your maid
Should old acquaintance be forgot
Keep your eye on that grand old flag.

Sequence: Opener, figure twice, middle break, figure twice, closure. **Note:** Middle break may be substituted for opener or grand square may be used for opener, break, closer.

■ Don't Let the Good Life Pass You By

Caller: Bob Vinyard.

Records: Red Boot 118, Dance Ranch 601; S.D.T. 4001.

Basics: Weave the ring, square thru.

Opener, middle break, closer
Circle left
Did you ever lie and listen to the rain fall?
Did you ever own a homemade apple pie?
Left allemande then turn the partner right
Left allemande then weave the ring
Man was made for loving not for buying
Do-sa-do around then promenade
Look my friend there's happiness in living
Somewhere between broke and being free.

Figure
Heads [sides] square thru four hands around now
Face the sides make a right-hand star
Go once around heads [sides] star by the left
Pick up that corner arm around
Back out, circle round the ring now
Swing the nearest girl promenade
Look my friend there's happiness in living
Just don't let the good life pass you by.

Center break
Did you ever hold a woman while she's sleeping?
Did you ever sit right down and have a cry?

Closer break
Did you ever hold a hand to stop the trembling?
Did you ever watch the sun desert the sky?

Tag
Just don't let the good life pass you by.

Sequence: Opener, figure twice for heads, middle break, figure twice for sides, closer, tag.

■ Happiness Is

Caller: Walt McNeal.

Music: Rhythmaires.

Record: Belco #B–109.

Basics: Roll away to a half-sashay, square thru, swing thru.

Opener, break, and ending
Four ladies chain, go straight across that ring
Turn the girls, roll away, you circle left and then
You roll away again, your own a do-sa-do
Allemande the corner and promenade your own
Happiness is, happiness is, happiness is
Different things to different people
That's what happiness is.

Figure
Now heads [sides] square thru four hands around you go.
Do-sa-do with that corner one you know
You swing thru and then, boys trade again
Swing the corner lady and you promenade that ring
Happiness is, happiness is, happiness is
Different things to different people
That's what happiness is.

Sequence: Opener, figure twice heads, break, figure twice sides, ending.

Note: "Boys trade" means that the two men who just turned each other in the swing thru, turn again halfway around so that each man meets his corner lady on the outside for a swing.

■ Truly Fair

Caller: Marshall Flippo.

Music: The Shannoniers.

Record: Blue Star #1774, flip side.

Figure
1 and 3 lead out to the right and circle half-way around
Dive thru make a right-hand star, and ride the merry-go-round

When you meet that corner lady left allemande and maybe
Promenade your own gal go walking 'round the ring and now
Head 2 you wheel around right and left thru with the two you found
Star thru, then pass thru and swing
Swing that little old girl around and do a left allemande
Do-sa-do go round your own, then weave around that land
Singing truly truly fair, truly truly fair
When you meet you do-sa-do and promenade the square.

Sequence: Twice with head couples, twice with side couples.

Note: Centers swing the one they meet in the center; ends swing girl they passed thru with. Take this girl as a new partner each time through the dance.

■ I Had Someone Else

Caller: Andy Andrus.

Record: Blue Star #1727.

Music: The Texans.

Basics: Wheel around, right and left thru, cross trail, weave the ring, square thru three-quarters, box the gnat.

Opener, middle break, and closer
Allemande left that corner girl
Then swing with your own
Promenade around that ring you roam
Those heads wheel around, right and left thru you go
Cross trail, left allemande and weave the ring you know
You needn't stay, go any day
Promenade with me baby, but listen while I say
I had someone else before I had you
I'll have someone after you're gone.

Figure
Those head two pass thru
Go round one you do
In that middle square thru three-quarters 'round
Allemande left that corner girl, and partner box the gnat
You pull her by and swing that corner 'round
Then join eight hands and circle left, go 'round that ring
Allemande left new corners, come back, swing that Jane
Promenade around that ring, and listen while I sing
I'll have someone after you're gone.

■ Chime Bells

Record: Grenn 25316.

Basics: All around left-hand lady, right and left thru, star thru.

Intro, break, ending
Walk around that corner, then you seesaw your taw
Join hands circle round that hall
Allemande the corner, do-sa-do your own
Four men star by the left around you go
Turn the partner by the right and go left allemande
Come back and promenade around the ring (all the way)
Chime bells are ringing on the mountain so high
Upon a summer's eve.

Figure
Four ladies chain, turn a little girl and then
Heads promenade halfway you go
Down the middle go right and left thru, turn the gal I say
Star thru, pass thru, circle up four halfway
Swing that corner girl and go left allemande
Come back do-sa-do and promenade
Chime bells are ringing, on the mountain so high
Upon a summer's eve.

Alternate ending
Sleep my little lady on a mountain so high
Upon a summer's eve.

■ Woman in Love

Record: Grenn 12128.

Basics: Four ladies chain, allemande thar, do paso.

Figure
Docey round your corner, a left-hand turn your own
All four ladies chain across and don't you roam
Keep this girl and promenade, you see
She's got the ways of a woman in love
Join hands and circle left, go walking 'round and 'round
Allemande left with an allemande thar, go right— left—
Gents walk in, make a back-up star, you see
She's got the ways of a woman in love
Shoot that star, go full around, your corner box the gnat
Pull her by, your partner do pas so-so-so-so-
Corner by the right-hand round, a left-hand turn your own
All four ladies chain across and don't you roam
Keep this girl and promenade you see (full around)
She's got the ways of a woman in love.

Note: Keep promenades shoulder to shoulder. Always, full promenade!

Sequence: Figure, four times through.

Goodbye My Lady Love

Caller: Chip Hendrickson.

Record: Top 25306.

Basics: All around left-hand lady, weave the ring, promenade three-quarters, right and left thru.

Intro, break, and closing
Circle to the left, eight hands around you go
Walk all around the corner girl, seesaw your partner
Men star by the right, you turn it once around the set
Allemande left the corner, and you weave the ring
[Singing] Goodbye my lady love, farewell my turtle dove
When you meet your darling, you do-sa-do
Promenade her back to me, and love her so tenderly
So goodbye my lady love, goodbye.

Figure (twice for heads, twice for sides)
Heads promenade three-quarters, 'round the ring
Side couples right and left thru, turn your girl and pass thru
Circle four halfway, one-quarter more
Right and left thru, turn your girl and cross trail
Go to the corner, allemande left, well go forward two and then
Right and a left, full turn 'round and promenade
[Singing] Goodbye my lady love, so long my turtle dove
Promenade her home, well by and by.

Tag at end: Goodbye my lady love, goodbye!

A Fooler a Faker

Caller: Bob Fisk.

Music: The Blue Star Rhythmaires.

Record: Blue Star #1962, flip side.

Basics: All around your left-hand lady, weave the ring, dive thru, pass thru, square thru.

Intro, break, ending
Walk around that corner girl, seesaw your partner
Join hands and circle 'round that ring
Men star right now go once around that ring, pal
Left allemande, now weave the ring
Weave in and out around that ring and when you meet your maid
Do-sa-do around, hey promenade
You're a fooler, a faker, a little heartbreaker
You're the sliest gal I've ever known.

Figure
1 and 3 you promenade, go halfway around now
Down the middle and square thru you do
Four hands around go hey do a do-sa-do
Once around and then go right and left thru

Dive thru, pass thru and then
Hey swing the corner girl and then promenade her, Joe
You're a fooler, a faker, a little heartbreaker
You're the sliest gal I've ever known.

Tie Me Kangaroo Down

Caller: Andy Andrus.

Music: Blue Star Band

Records: Blue Star #2011, flip side; EZ 5012.

Basics: Four ladies chain, right-hand star, do-sa-do, allemande left.

Opener, middle break, and closer
Four ladies chain across, Jane
Turn 'em left around,
Chain back across, Jane
Promenade her around (all together now)
Tie me kangaroo down sport,
Tie me kangaroo down,
Tie me kangaroo down sport, Tie me kangaroo down.

Figure
Heads go up and back, Jack,
Do-sa-do around,
Make a right-hand star and turn it once,
Once around that old town,
Allemande the corner girl, Earl
Do-sa-do your own,
Swing that corner gal, Al
Promenade her back home (all together now)
Tie me kangaroo down sport,
Tie me kangaroo down,
Tie me kangaroo down sport,
Tie me kangaroo down.

Promenade patter (second change for heads)
Loose me tie when I die, Si
Loose me tie when I die,
Don't you go and cry, Si
Loose me tie when I die.

Promenade patter (second change for sides)
Tan me hide when I'm dead, Fred
Tan me hide when I'm dead,
So they tanned his hide when he died, Clyde
And that's it hanging on the shed.

Sequence: Opener, figure twice for 1 and 3, middle break, figure twice for 2 and 4, closer.

Houston

Caller: Bob Ruff.

Record: Wagon Wheel 924.

Basics: Allemande left, weave the ring, pass thru, star right, swing, do paso.

Opener, middle break

Circle left and around you go
Circle left you do a do paso, your partner left
Turn your corner by the right
Partner courtesy turn, everybody circle left again
Circle left just a little bit more
Left allemande and weave the floor
In and out and when you meet her, you swing
Swing your lady and promenade the ring
Promenade to Houston, Houston, Houston.

Figure

1 and 3 (2 and 4) pass thru, separate go around 2
Home you go and do-sa-do your lady too
2 and 4 pass thru, separate around 2
Home you go and do-sa-do your lady too
All the men star right around the land
With your corner girl you go left allemande
Do-sa-do your partner, your corner swing
Keep this lady and promenade the ring
Promenade to Houston, Houston, Houston.
  Twice for head couples, twice for side couples.

■ If They Could See Me Now

Caller: Bob Ruff.

Record: Wagon Wheel 915.

Basics: Swing, allemande, grand right and left, do-sa-do, promenade, forearm turn, courtesy turn.

Opener, middle break, ending

All four ladies promenade inside, once around that ring
Come on back and swing, your partner you swing
Join hands and circle, go walking hand in hand
Allemande that corner, do the right and left grand
Grand old right and left you go until you meet your
  own
Do-sa-do your lady, promenade her home
Promenade your lady, go struttin' high and low
If my friends could see me now.

Figure

Ladies center back to back, men promenade outside
Once around you go, turn your partner by the left
  (forearm)
(Turn) your corner right (forearm)
Your partner courtesy turn (to face center of set)
Men center back to back, ladies promenade outside
Pass this guy, promenade the next, say "Hi"
Promenade this partner, go struttin' high and low
If my friends could see me now.

Sequence: Opener, figure twice, middle break, figure twice, ending.

■ Robinson Crusoe

Caller: Bob Ruff.

Record: Wagon Wheel 917.

Basics: Four ladies chain, allemande left, do-sa-do, promenade.

Opener, middle break, ending

Four ladies chain, you turn 'em and then
Four ladies chain back again
Join hands and circle, walking hand in hand
Allemande left the corner, right and left grand
On this island of wild men, there must be wild
  women
Do-sa-do your gal and promenade
And what did Robinson Crusoe do, with Friday on a
  Saturday night.

Figure

1 and 3 promenade, go round the outside
All the way around the ring, face the couple on your
  right
  1 face 2, 3 face 4.
Two ladies chain, you turn 'em and then
Two ladies chain right back home again
Allemande left with the corner, your partner do-
  sa-do now
Take your corner lady, promenade
And what did Robinson Crusoe do, with Friday on a
  Saturday night.
  Twice for head couples, twice for side couples.

■ Smoke on the Water

Caller: M. R. "Pancho" Baird.

Records: Western Jubilee No. 598; EZ 526.

Cassette: "Smoke on the Water" Square Dance Classics by Bob Dalsemer, TC 123C (with calls), TC 124C (without calls).

Basics: Allemande left, star, grand right and left, turn back, sashay, pass thru.

I. Opener

Now you allemande left your corner
Then you walk right by your own
Right hand swing ol' Sally Goodin
  (Right-hand lady)
Swing left hand there at home
Those four little ladies to the center
Make a star with your right hand
Then allemande left your corner
Partner right go right and left grand.

Break

There'll be "Smoke on the Water on the land on the
  sea"
Right hand to your partner, turn around and go back
  three
Let's do a left, a right, a left-hand swing
Go all the way around, right hand to your partner
Twirl her home and settle down
  (Don't promenade, should be at home position)

(continued)

II.

Four gents center make a circle
  (Circle left)
You turn it once around, go back home sashay your
  partner (Pass right shoulders go back to back)
Gents star right when you come down
Turn that star out in the center
'Til your corner comes around
Then you allemande left your corner
Grand right eight go round the town

Repeat break: "There'll be Smoke on the water, etc."

Figure

Head gents bow down to your partner
Swing that lady round and round
Pass right through right down the center
Separate go round the town
(Lady goes right gents go left to home position)
Then you walk right by your corner
Sashay round your partners all
(All sashay partners passing right shoulders then
  back to back)
Then you allemande left your corner
Grand right eight go round the hall

Repeat break: "There'll be Smoke on the Water,
  etc."
Repeat II call: "Four gents center, etc."
Repeat figure for "Side gents."
Repeat break: "There'll be Smoke on the Water,
  etc."
Repeat opener: "Now you allemande left, etc."
Repeat break: "There'll be Smoke on the Water, etc."

■ Shindig in the Barn

Caller: Bob Ruff.

Record: Wagon Wheel 921.

Basics: Four ladies chain, allemande left, grand right
  and left, do-sa-do, promenade, right and left thru,
  courtesy turn.

Opener, middle break, ending

All four ladies chain, you chain across the ring
Turn and chain them back again
Join all of your hands and circle to the left
Allemande left your corner, grand right and left
Right and left you go until you meet her
Do-sa-do your gal and promenade
Promenade the ring, lift your heads up and sing
We're going to have a shindig in the barn.

Figure

1 and 3 (2 and 4) lead to the right and circle 4
Heads break and make a line, go up and back
Do the right and left thru, turn the girls and then
Same two right and left thru again
Allemande left with the corner, your partner do-
  sa-do

Take your corner lady, promenade
Promenade the ring, lift your heads up and sing
We're going to have a shindig in the barn.
  Twice for head couples, twice for side couples.

Tag Ending

Allemande left your corner, come back and bow to
  your partner
We're going to have a shindig in the barn.

Write Your Own Singing Calls*

The topic of writing, or rewriting, singing calls is
nothing new to experienced caller-teachers. This
section is presented to give the newer caller-teacher
helpful ideas on how to use existing recordings to
enhance the instructional program and develop a
higher degree of class interest and motivation at the
early learning stages.

In recent years, Square Dance record companies have provided callers and dancers with many
excellent recordings of singing calls. The musical
instruments and their use in the arrangements reflect modern changes in Square Dance music. Dancers have for the most part expressed enthusiasm
and enjoyment with this new sound.

The problem that most caller-teachers have
with the existing recorded singing calls is that they
are too advanced. Few of them are usable for
beginner classes because they require mastery of 40
or more basic movements. Recognizing the need to
bring singing calls within the range of enjoyment
for beginners, we have made an effort here to help
teachers learn how to write their own singing calls.

Structure of a Singing Call

Most singing calls are made up of a standard eight-
line, 64-beat chorus, which is played seven times
through. It is made up of two separate parts, the
break (opener, middle part, and ending) and the
figure, which is done four times, twice for the head
couples and twice for the side couples in the
following sequence:

1. Break (opener)
2. Figure (heads active)
3. Figure (heads active)
4. Break (middle break)
5. Figure (sides active)

---

*This section was written by Bob Ruff and Jack Murtha.
(Bob Ruff is a former teacher in the Los Angeles City
schools, and owner of Wagon Wheels Records; Jack Murtha
is assistant superintendent of Instructional Services of
Sutter County, California.) Through their records,
workshops, and institutes for teachers, they have made a
tremendous contribution to school physical-education
dance programs.

6. Figure (sides active)
7. Break (closer)

Teachers should practice writing eight lines of eight beats each, moving the dancers through the basics desired and getting the dancers back home. Generally, the directions for basic movements take six lines and the last two lines use the original words of the song while dancers are promenading around the ring and back home.

The following movements are simple basics for use in writing breaks. The action should flow together without keeping the dancers standing. The actions must fit together logically.

Allemande left	8 steps
Circle left	8 or 16
Circle right	8 or 16
Do-sa-do	8
Forward and back	8
Grand right and left	8
Ladies promenade inside	8
Left-hand star	8
Men promenade inside	8
Promenade, couples	8 or 16
Promenade, single file	8 or 16
Right-hand star	8
Swing	8

Samples

Join all of your hands and circle to the left	(8)
Circle left go all the way around	(8)
Circle to the right now go the other way	(8)
All the way until you're home again	(8)
Face your partner do-sa-do	(8)
Swing your partner 'round and 'round	(8)
Promenade	(8)
Promenade	(8)
All four ladies promenade inside the ring	(8)
Swing your partner, everybody swing	(8)
All four men promenade inside you go	(8)
Come back to your partner, do-sa-do	(8)
Allemande left the corner	(8)
Swing your partner 'round and 'round	(8)
Promenade go round the town	(8)
Promenade go round the town	(8)

The figures of singing calls usually have two couples active, either head or side couples. It is possible to have only one couple active at a time. Also it is possible to have all four couples or all four men or all four ladies active in a figure. At the end of the 64 beats, dancers should progress to new partners. Either the corner lady or the right-hand lady can become the new partner. All dancers should be back in home position after four times through the figure.

Writing the Singing Call

A melody must be selected that is available on a record. This can be determined by watching in the Square Dance magazines for listings of the available tunes. Usually the record will have a flip side, which means that a caller is calling a dance on one side and the other side is the same tune without a caller. The teacher can use this instrumental side to write and call a simpler singing call. The melody should be one that can be sung easily and a tune that will appeal to the beginning dancer. Next the teacher should make a list of the basics the students know and select which ones to use. Write the break first, as it is simple and is repeated three times in the dance. Then write the figure. It is fun to use words and phrases from the original song, particularly on the last two lines of the eight-measure phrase. Arranging and rearranging the words until they fit the melody and feel comfortable to sing is the tricky part. The beginning caller should keep the actions simple at first. Some find it easier to write if they refer to the original words of the song to get the feel of the words in relation to the rhythm and the melody.

Samples of Singing Calls

■ Four-Leaf Clover (Song)
I'm looking over a four-leaf clover
that I overlooked before.
One is for sunshine, the second for rain,
the third is the roses that bloom in the lane.

Now there's no use explaining, the one remaining,
is somebody I adore.
I'm looking over a four-leaf clover
that I overlooked before.

■ Four-Leaf Clover (Dance)

Records: MacGregor 1096; Lloyd Shaw 503, 504; Dance Ranch 711 LP.

Basics: Promenade, do-sa-do, allemande left, grand right and left.

Opener, break, closer
All four ladies promenade the inside ring
Swing your partner, everybody swing
All four men you promenade, inside you go
Come back to your partner, do-sa-do
Allemande left your corner
Grand right and left to Dover
Meet your partner, promenade
You are looking over a four-leaf clover
That you overlooked before.

Figure (call twice for heads, break, twice for sides)
Heads promenade outside, go one time around
Sides, face your own, do-sa-do

(continued)

Sides circle inside one time you know
Heads face partner, do-sa-do
Then join your hands and circle, go once around the
  ring
You're looking over a four-leaf clover
That you overlooked before.

■ Take Me Home Country Roads (Song)

Almost Heaven, West Virginia
Blue Ridge Mountains
Shenandoah River
Life is old there
Older than the trees
Younger than the mountains
Growing like a breeze
Country roads take me home
To the place I belong
West Virginia, Mountain Mama
Take me home, country roads.

■ Take Me Home Country Roads (Dance)

Record: Bogan 1242.

Basics: Promenade, allemande left, do-sa-do.

Opener, break, closer
Join hands circle around the ring go
All the way around, get back home again
Circle to the right, the other way around
All the way you go back to your hometown
Allemande your corner girl once around
Do-sa-do your partner there and promenade
To West Virginia, Mountain Mama
Take me home country roads.

Figure (call for couples 1, 2, break, and then 3 and
  4)
Number one promenade all the way around
All the way round that ring get back home again
Number two promenade go walking the land
All the way around and when you're home again
Allemande left your corner lady

Do-sa-do your partner, promenade
To West Virginia, Mountain Mama
Take me home country roads.

■ Bad Bad Leroy Brown (Song)

Well the south side of Chicago
Is the baddest side of town
And if you go down there, you better just beware
Of a man named Leroy Brown.

Chorus
He was bad bad Leroy Brown
Baddest man in the whole darn town
He's badder than old King Kong
And meaner than a junkyard dog.

■ Bad Bad Leroy Brown (Dance)

Record: Wagon Wheel 912.

Basics: Four ladies chain, allemande left, weave the
  ring, do-sa-do.

Opener, break, closer
Four ladies chain that ring now
Chain the ladies back home
Join hands circle left and then
Allemande left and weave the ring
In and out around you go
Do-sa-do and promenade
He's badder than old King Kong
And meaner than a junkyard dog.

Figure (twice for heads, break, twice for sides)
Heads circle four once around you go
Back out at home, face your own and do-sa-do
Sides circle four one time you know
Back out at home, face your own and do-sa-do
Circle eight go 'round the ring
All the way home, take the corner promenade
He's badder than old King Kong
And meaner than a junkyard dog.

CHAPTER 6

Contra Dance

History

by Ralph Page

Contra Dances and northern New England are fast becoming inseparable concepts in American dance. Far from being antiquated relics rescued for the tourist trade from a limbo of forgotten Americana, they are today as vigorously alive and as much loved among us as were their ancestors—the English "Longways for as many as will," the Irish "Crossroad" Dances, and the vibrant Scottish Reels—at the time of the settling of Maine, New Hampshire, and Vermont. Over 2000 American Contras have been recorded in dance books published in this country since 1790.

Special Appeal

Literally, *a Contra Dance is a dance of opposition, a dance performed by many couples face to face, line facing line.* Contra Dances came to this country from the British Isles; every one of the 13 colonies knew them; they were danced by people from all walks of life, especially by the country people.

Contras are said to appeal to a special type of dancer, and that could be true. At least one has to be able to count to eight and to dance in time with the music. To live more or less unchanged for 300 years or so, these dances must have something. Why have New Englanders retained their love of Contras when elsewhere in the United States they have fallen from favor? Perhaps it is a combination of English resentment of change, Irish bullheadedness, and Scottish stubbornness, for, in the beginning, at least 90 percent of our early settlers came from these three portions of the British Isles.

In Olde England

Contras, or Longways, were the rage of England in the 17th century. The peasantry and bourgeoisie of the country developed the Contredanse to its highest complexity. For example, the number of corresponding Country Dances of England in 1728 numbered some 900 in all and explored every form of crossover and interweaving, with numbers of participants varying from four to an indefinite number. Sometimes each couple in succession led through the figures, sometimes alternate couples, and sometimes the whole group "for as many as will" performed them simultaneously.

Is it any wonder, then, that during the 16th and 17th centuries the English were known as the "dancing English"? Country Dances were the ordinary, everyday dances of the country folk, performed not merely on festal days, but whenever opportunity offered. The steps and figures, while many in number, were simple and easily learned so that anyone of ordinary intelligence could qualify as a competent dancer. Truly, they were dances of the people.

Royal Flavor

The Tudor royal family was passionately fond of dancing and introduced many court masques that embodied many of the Country Dances of the day and period. In the reign of James I, it was said that it was easier to don fine clothes than to learn the French dances and that therefore, "none but country dances must be used at court."

There is a legend that Queen Elizabeth bestowed the office of lord chancellor on Sir Christopher Hatton, not because he had any surpassing knowledge of the law, but because he wore green bows on his shoes and danced the Pavane to perfection. No wonder her court produced so many fine dancers.

Playford Collection

No doubt it was some royal personage who commissioned John Playford to collect and set down all the

Country Dances of England. This he did, and, since he was a bookseller and a musician of considerable ability, he found no difficulty in publishing a series of books. *The English Dancing Master—Plaine and Easy Rules for the Dancing of Country Dances, with the Tunes to Each Dance.*

The first of these volumes was brought out in 1650 and the last in 1728. Obviously, the books had great popularity and were continued by Playford's successors. While the majority of the dances in the Playford collection were not pure Folk Dances, they certainly had a folk basis. The Country Dance ordinarily consisted of a series of figures arbitrarily chosen to fit a given tune; only in certain instances did a particular combination of figures prove so enjoyable as to achieve universal acceptance. The country people never lost their love of these old dances and they still survive from Cornwall to the border counties.

This, then, was the status of Country Dancing at the time of the first settlements in New England. No one will ever make me believe that the English colonials did not bring with them their love of dancing. Not all of the Puritans were "pickle-faced joy-killers."

So much for England. Let us turn northward and see what was happening in Scotland during this same period.

Our Debt to Scotland

From time immemorial, the Scots have followed all facets of Country and Highland Dancing with delight and enthusiasm. Their fondness for it amounts almost to a passion. All efforts of the Kirk to put down "promiscuous dancing" have been failures. Scots dance naturally and intuitively, which seems logical enough when we remember their great love of music. However, descriptions of the early dances of Scotland are very meager, although we know the names of many from the old ballad "Cokelkie Sow," wherein 20 dances are mentioned.

The reason for this poverty of description is that the Scots, while practicing the musical arts, had not reached the point of penning treatises on any of them; and then came the times of John Knox, when dancing was looked upon as a sin and only spoken of to be inveighed against. We must remember that dancing or sports of all kinds had very much obscured the original significance of religious ceremonies, and the Puritans were but endeavoring to return to the simplicity of ancient times when they sought to curtail somewhat the amusements of the people.

By 1723, however, a weekly dancing assembly was established in Edinburgh and was largely patronized; in 1728, the town council of Glasgow appointed a dancing master with a salary of 20 pounds "to familiarize the inhabitants with the art." By 1768, we read that the "Rev. John Mills includes dancing—and Church music, among the many things necessary for a Gentleman's education."

Dancing at weddings was a common custom among the Scottish people. In the 18th century, dancing took place on the green when weather permitted, and the first reel was danced by the newly married couple; next in line were the bridesmaids and their escorts. The first reel was called "shemit," from the supposed bashfulness of the young couple.

From the wedding to the deathbed is a sad journey, but extremes meet. On the night after a death in Scotland, dancing was kept up until the next morning, just as it was at a wedding. If the dead person was a man, his widow—if he left one—led the first dance; if the deceased was a woman, the widower began the measure.

Scottish Reels

When one thinks of Country Dancing in Scotland, one thinks of the Reel. The Scots dance their Reels for the Reel's sake. The dance is not an excuse for a social gathering or a means of carrying on a flirtation. The Scottish gentleman arrives on the dance floor as he would on the drill square, and he dances until he is tired out. When performed by two couples, the Reel is called a foursome Reel; when danced by three couples, it is called a sixsome Reel, and so on, the difference being in the music with a corresponding difference in steps. It might also be noticed that the Scot did not depend always on the playing of some instrument to accompany the dances, but often Reeled to his or her own music.

How the ballet step known as *Pas de Basque* found its way into the Scottish Reels is a most intriguing and controversial question. The logical answer seems to be that it came from the French dancing masters. But perhaps this is too logical an answer. What was the Reel step before the introduction of the Pas de Basque?

The Longway dance was equally as popular in Scotland as in nearby England and was danced and enjoyed in the Lowlands and Highlands alike. In fact, the Reel and the Longway have never ceased to be danced in the smaller communities.

Irish Influence

The Irish possess a natural flair for both music and dancing, and the Irish Jig has a most wonderful influence over an Irish heart. You can get into all kinds of trouble and arguments over the origin of the word *jig*. Whatever may be its origin, in Ireland it has long stood for a dance popular with young and old in all classes.

Few meetings for any purpose took place in Ireland without a dance being called for. It was not unusual for young men, inspired by their sweethearts, to dance away the night to the music of the pipes (the bagpipe is not used exclusively in Scotland). Every village had its piper, who, on fine evenings after working hours, would gather all the people of the town about him and play for their dancing. Before the gathering broke up, the piper would dig a small hole in the ground before him and, at the end of the next dance, all present were expected to toss coins into this hole to "pay the piper his due." One very old tune of this character was called "Gather Up the Money." Another tune often used was the one now known as "Blackberry Blossom."

Harp Tunes

The harp is really the national instrument of Ireland, and Irish harpers were unsurpassed in skill. Many of the tunes to which we now dance contras were once songs written for the harp.

An Irish wake meant dancing; not in delight because of the passing, but rather in the deceased's honor and as a mark of the esteem in which he or she was held. If no musician was present at the time, then they danced anyway to their own music, which was called "lilting" a tune. Some of these lilts have found their way into the dance music of Ireland.

It is difficult today to realize the extent to which Irish dance and music permeated English life in the 16th and 17th centuries. In *Playford's Dancing Master,* there are many Irish dance tunes given with a key to the dance that was performed to each tune (some 14 in all, in the earlier editions).

It is in the realm of music that the Irish have contributed most to New England Contras. Who does not know and love such tunes as "The White Cockade," "Irish Washerwoman," "The Girl I Left Behind Me," "Turkey in the Straw," and numberless more of similar nature? Some of these very tunes were brought over to New England by immigrants in the first wave of colonization.

Our Early Settlers

The English, Irish, and Scottish nationalities constituted the largest numbers of early settlers in northern New England. All three had an inborn love of dancing and were well versed in Longway-type dances: the English and the Scots with their highly developed techniques and exactness of steps in Reels and Longways; the Irish with their well-developed skill in music; and the Irish and Scottish with their well-known fondness of holding to the old traditions and ways of their ancestors. Is it any wonder that Contra Dances flourished from the first

in Maine, New Hampshire, and Vermont? Is it to be wondered that we still love them? With our preponderance of natives still of the same racial stock, how could it be otherwise?

I know of no New England Contra that is completely Irish in character and figures. The side step-seven and threes—which is the basic step in Irish dancing—is entirely absent from our Contras. Yet the music played for dozens is a direct importation from the "Ould Sod."

Scottish Influence

The Scot, on the other hand, has had a big influence on the steps and figures of many of our line dances. Three favorites come quickly to mind: Money Musk, Petronella, and Hull's Victory. The music that we play for Money Musk was written by a butler in the household of Sir Archibald Grant of Money Musk, in the Lowlands of Scotland. History tells us that the butler's name was Donald or Daniel Dow and apparently he was a musician of no mean ability, for an early collection of Scottish and Irish airs published by Buntings of London contains many tunes attributed to him. The dance was originally known as "Sir Archibald Grant of Moniemusk Reel." As you would suspect, it was too unwieldy a title to have a long life and it was soon shortened to "Money Musk."

Hull's Victory is almost step for step the same dance as one known in Scotland as the "Scottish Reform." The same may be said of Petronella. New England dancers for generations have called it "Pat'nella." Further proof of these statements may be found by reading the *Scottish Country Dance Books.* The English also have an interesting Money Musk. The Scottish dance "Strip the Willow" is an interesting version of Virginia Reel, in turn a descendant of "Sir Roger de Coverly." A still closer relative to "Sir Roger" is the Scottish dance "The Haymakers."

Poussette and allemande were both methods of progression in Scottish Country Dances, neither of which is practiced now in our New England Contras, although once they were common terms with us. Many old manuscripts of the last century contain both terms over and over again. I have copies of several of these dance manuscripts dated from 1795 to 1816, and they are full of combinations of dance terms, half or two-thirds of which are English terms and the rest, Scottish; an interesting bit of data it seems to me. That was just after the Revolutionary War, and, no doubt in many districts of New England, the English were far from being loved, and other terms began to creep into our Contra Dances. Still others began to be omitted entirely and American substitutions replaced them. *Set* is one term in particular quite common in both English and Scottish dances, corresponding to the New England *balance.*

Ralph Page

Ralph Page is fondly remembered as the dean of American Contra Dancing. Ralph was born January 28, 1903, in Munsonville, New Hampshire, and died February 21, 1985, in Keene, New Hampshire.

A lifelong occupation and love of dancing came to Ralph naturally. Irish minstrels and musicians, and even a dancing master, were all part of his Scotch-Irish heritage. An excellent musician, he composed many tunes for dancing. He was recognized as an outstanding Square Dance caller, but it was in the realm of Contra Dancing that he truly left his mark as a teacher, caller, and writer.

In 1943, in the midst of World War II, Ralph began calling Square and Contra Dances on a weekly basis at the YWCA in Boston, Massachusetts. Servicemen and women, as well as many students in the greater Boston region, discovered the fun and spirit of Contra Dance at the Boston Y. For 24 years, Ralph made the weekly trip to Boston from Keene, New Hampshire.

A strong proponent of live music for dancing, he gave continuous encouragement to folk musicians. He recognized the special talent of those fiddlers of French-Canadian descent and of their fiddle tunes. The long swing, attributed to the fun-loving French-Canadians, was central to his calls, but for no more than 16 counts.

Like the dancing masters of yore, he urged decorum on the floor. He believed in smooth dancing, and he felt we should dance our American Folk Dances with pride and a "wee bit of elegance." He set the pace with a twinkle in his eye.

Ralph was a popular teacher at major dance camps and schools across the United States. Internationally he had successful teaching tours in Canada, Japan, and England. With his longtime partner and wife Ada, he founded the New Hampshire Folk Dance Camp. His leadership was ever present in New England and was especially evident with his founding of the New England Folk Festival Association (NEFFA) in 1944 with Mary Gillette and Philip Sharples.

One of three books published in the 1920s and 1930s that started the revival of Square Dance nationally was *The Country Dance Book* by Beth Tolman and Ralph Page.

A long relationship with Michael and Mary Ann Herman produced many good things, including Contra Dance records under the Folk Dancer label, with Ralph calling to lively New England folk music.

Northern Junket, a magazine devoted to New England Folk Dance, particularly Contra, was begun by Ralph in April, 1949, and published and edited by him until his death.

With his dedication to dance and love of history, many hours were spent in research and working with local historical societies. As a result, he assembled a significant collection of dance music, old dance books, and manuscripts. The following books are to his credit: *The Country Dance Book, The Ralph Page Book of Contras, An Elegant Collection of Squares and Contras,* and *Heritage Dances of Early America.* Together, these significantly enrich our understanding of past and present New England dance.

In 1964, the authors of *Dance A While* invited Ralph to write a Contra chapter for the third edition. He wrote a colorful history of Contra Dancing and presented a sample of nine Contra Dances. This same history introduces an expanded chapter intended to keep pace with the current popularity of Contra Dance.

All over North America, the tradition of Contra Dancing is being carried on today by many who had the good fortune to encounter Ralph in his travels or who fell under his spell at the Boston YWCA. Long live Contra Dancing!

French-Canadian Influence

Within the past 100 years, New England has experienced another flood of immigration—the French-Canadians. Especially is this true of New Hampshire; thousands of French-Canadians from Quebec have poured across our borders, first to work in our lumber camps, later to become textile workers. So many are now here that within another two or three generations New Hampshirites of French-Canadian descent will outnumber all others. They are delightful and fun-loving people who dearly love to sing and dance.

They have had little or no influence as far as bringing with them from Canada Contra Dances of their own. However, so adaptable are they in all things that they have taken to our Contras like "young ducks to water," and their contagious laughter and mimicry are now mingled with Irish tunes and English and Scottish figures and everybody loves it immensely.

French-Canadian fiddle tunes are used more and more for our New England dances, both Square and Contras. Some of our finest folk musicians are of French-Canadian derivation, and they are without peer in this field.

Without a doubt, the French-Canadians have had the strongest influence on *our long New England swings*. To them should go the credit—or the blame—for the frequent eight- to sixteen-count swings.

Yankee Musicians

We have never lacked for fiddlers capable of playing the proper tunes for our Contras. This could be because you can find a touch of the Gael in most of our fiddlers. Itinerant fiddlers traveled over the countryside, sure to find a warm feeling of welcome wherever night found them. Word soon spread of their presence in town, and neighbors came from far and near to listen and, oftentimes, to dance a Contra or two with the fiddler standing in an out-of-the-way corner of the room. After playing a few figures, the musician would pass the hat, collecting from each person whatever could be afforded. The total amount collected decided how long the fiddler would continue to play.

For larger parties in the local town hall, for the many balls and assemblies (or any other name you cared to give them), other instruments were added and the traditional orchestra of our mothers' day consisted of first and second violins, cornet, "clarionet"—that's the way they spelled it then—double bass and, if the occasion warranted it, a violincello and a flute. Later an organ was added, and, by the turn of the century, it was in turn replaced by the piano. My earliest recollection of dancing recalls an orchestra of two violins, clarinet, cornet, and piano.

And Yet They Live

For more than half a century, dance manuals did their best to kill Contra Dances. Such dancing masters as Elias Howe, Edward Ferraro, William B. DeGarmo, C. H. Cleveland, Jr., and Thomas Hillgrove proclaimed bitterly against them and considered them unfashionable. Characteristically, northern New Englanders paid no heed to such "high falutin' fiats" and continued dancing Contras with as much verve and zest as ever.

There are those who hold that Puritanism took the merriness out of Merry England, but it didn't take the merriness out of the stock that came from Old England to make New England. Neither did John Knox drive it completely out of the minds and the customs of the Scottish immigrants. Nor could Cromwell drive it out of the lives of the Irish folk coming to America by the thousands. Perhaps all this persecution only made our pioneer ancestors more determined than ever to carry on the customs of their native lands here in New England.

Contra Dancing Moves into the 21st Century

Contra dancing has made a big leap forward in popularity, not only across the U.S.A., but internationally too. Several factors have contributed to the increased enthusiasm. The interest of musicians has kept pace with the expansion of Contra dancing. They enjoy dancing as well as providing live music for dancing, adding "zing" to the dance floor. The availability and talent of bands specializing in Contra music continues to grow. They bring fresh energy to old tunes, introduce appropriate music, and compose new melodies. They have joined rank with callers and teachers with a common cause. The continued mobility of leaders, dancers, and musicians from New England to the West Coast, North, South, and vice versa have all added to the Contra dance scene.

Expressions change. People will say "they are going to a Contra dance." In actuality there may be a few squares and round dances during the evening. People are looking for a dance activity to which they can come independently, meet friends and new people, and not have the pace and rigidity of the Club Square Dance program. It is interesting to note that squares are still popular, but they are the golden oldies of the '50s–'60s that the contra dancers enjoy. More people are using the term "country dancing" again. Country dancing is the umbrella term for contra, square, couple, mixers, and even a few line dances. The contra groups enjoy perfecting their round dance skills like the waltz and add other dances to their repertoire like English country dancing, Swing, Cajun, Salsa, Clogging, and even the Hambo.

Camps, workshops, and visiting callers have multiplied, with a focus on Contra and then one or two added attractions like Cajun, Country Western, caller workshops, and special musicians' clinics. The organization of the weekly dances tends to be minimal. The free spirit of the contra dancer resists a "constitution" and "limited membership."

With all the enthusiasm, the group faces some of the dilemmas that the square and round dance people had with standardization, proliferation of new dances, and burnout. Family dance camps are coming back as a way to sustain those who are having their families later. Interesting research has been stimulated. Many fine books appear yearly. Talented musicians have the opportunity to play. But few callers and musicians can make a living on this alone. The annual Ralph Page Legacy Weekend, the Ralph Page Library collection, and the CDSS library all contribute to the scholarship of researching Contra dance.

Once again the tradition of Contra Dancing is firmly established. People enjoy dancing contras for the same reasons as long ago. The sense of community and fellowship is strong. It's part of our heritage. It's "good fun." Yes, Contra Dancing moves into the 21st century with vigor!

Contra Dance Basics

Contra Set, Longway Set, or Contra Dance Formations

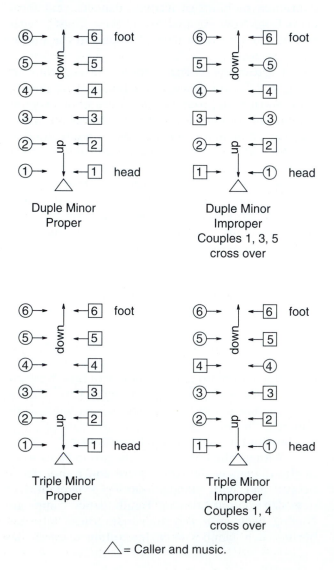

Duple Minor
Proper

Duple Minor
Improper
Couples 1, 3, 5
cross over

Triple Minor
Proper

Triple Minor
Improper
Couples 1, 4
cross over

△ = Caller and music.

Formation of Set

Couples form two parallel lines, partners facing, ladies to the left of the caller, men to the right. Dancers stand four feet apart. This is referred to as a Contra or Longway set, or Contra Dance formation. **Ladies' line** and **men's line** are terms that refer to the original lines, even when couples cross over before the dance begins. The head of the set is nearest the caller; the other end is the foot. Although as **many** dancers may dance in a single Contra set as **space** allows, in a shorter set, the inactives reach the **top** sooner, to become active.

Active and Inactive Couples (1s and 2s)

In most Contras, couples are either **active** or **inactive.** The call is addressed to the active couples, even though all may be dancing, **because** the active couples take the lead or do something different from the inactive couples. The actives are moving down the set one position for each time through the dance, unless it is a double progression, when they move down two positions. The inactives are moving up the set, to become active. Some teachers prefer to use the terms "1 and 2" instead of "active and inactive."

Minor

Most of the dances in this chapter are duple or triple minor, which means that, within the Contra set, smaller units dance together; these are referred to as a **minor set.**

Duple Minor, two couples
Triple Minor, three couples

The first couple in each of these minor sets is active; the others, inactive. The term *inactive* is a misnomer; in the popular Contra Dances, the inactive couple dances almost or as much as the active couple. But the term persists. It is necessary to determine the minor sets to establish which couples are dancing together, as well as which couple is active.

Methods for Numbering Off

From the head of the set:

Duple Minor

1. Every two couples join hands. The couple facing down the set is active; the couple facing up is inactive. The caller may call "hands four from the top."
2. Each couple counts off 1, 2, 1, 2, 1, 2. Ones are active; twos are inactive.

3. Each couple numbers off consecutively (1, 2, 3, 4, 5, and so forth) to the foot. The odd-numbered couples (1, 3, 5) are active; the even-numbered couples are inactive.
4. The caller may announce "first, third, and fifth active."

Triple Minor

Transpose the above methods for three couples, with first couple active and second and third couples inactive in each minor set.

Contra Dance Fundamentals

Proper/Not Cross Over

A Contra Dance that is **Proper/Not cross over** is one in which ladies remain on the original side to start the dance. **Duple proper** means minor sets of two couples each dance together; they begin the dance on the original side, and the first couple in each minor set is active. **Triple proper** means minor sets of three couples each dance together; they begin the dance on the original side, and the first couple in each minor set is active.

Improper/Cross Over

A Contra Dance that is **improper** is one in which the active couples cross over (partners exchange places) before the dance starts (See diagram of Contra Dance formations.) **Duple improper** means minor sets of two couples dance together; the first couple in each minor set is active, and active couples cross over (partners exchange places). **Triple improper** means minor sets of three couples dance together; the first couple in each minor set is active, and active couples cross over (partners exchange places).

Active and Inactive Couples, Neutral

When actives reach the end of the line, they wait once through for duple minor (twice for triple minor) before dancing again, this time as an inactive, moving up the set. A couple waiting out at either end is called "neutral." For **triple minor** when the active couple is in the next to the last place, they dance with an imaginary couple (couple 3). Then they move to the bottom and are neutral. On the next repeat they are the number 3 couple in the new minor set. Thus they only wait once through before dancing again. If dance is improper (cross over), dancers must remember to cross over to original sides before dancing as inactives. When the inactives reach the head of the set, they wait once through for duple minor (twice for triple

minor) before dancing again, this time as actives. If dance is improper (cross over), dancers must remember to cross over before starting to dance as an active.

Above and Below, Up and Down

Above means toward the head of the set. **Below** means toward the foot of the set. Or **above** means the active couple doing something with the couple or couples standing above you up the hall, while **below** means the active couple doing something with the couple or couples standing below you down the hall. **Down the hall** would mean walking toward the foot of the set and **up the hall** would mean walking toward the head of the set.

Progression

Progression is the most important thing in Contra Dancing. **Progression** means movement of couples to a new position during one complete time through the dance, so as to allow the actives to move down the line of dance, forming new minor sets each time, and to allow the inactives to keep moving up, so they will eventually be active. **Single Progression** means each couple moves one position during the dance; actives move down one, inactives move up one. New minor sets are formed. **Double Progression** means each couple moves two positions during the dance; the actives move down two, inactives move up two. Then new minor sets are formed.

Methods of Progression

1. Swing
2. Right and left thru
3. Arch, walk thru
4. Walk to a new place
5. Cast off
6. Allemande once and a half (either hand)
7. Do-si-do once and a half

Cast off means the actives go around one person, finishing one position below, facing partner. The path of the walk around or the turn in the men's line is counterclockwise. In the ladies' line, it is clockwise. Usually the cast off occurs coming up the set as the active couple is between the inactive couple of their minor set or line of four when they approach their original position.

a. Walk Around. Active couple separates, walks around the inactive and finishes below inactive, facing partner. Inactives do not turn.
b. Arm Around. Active couple separates and the inactive couple faces up the set. The active and inactive put their nearest arm around each other's

waist. They may be of the same sex. The inactive person acts as a pivot or backs up, turning as the active moves forward, the two turning side by side. The active ends one position below; all are now facing partners.

c. Unassisted, Two Dancers. Like the "arm around," the two dancers stand side by side, shoulders close together. They turn as a unit, active ends one position below, both facing partner.

d. Hand Cast Off. Active couple separates and joins nearest hand with inactive, joined hands shoulder height, elbows down. Hands may be already joined with inactive from coming up in a line of four. The inactive acting as a pivot, the two turn. Active ends one position below; all are now facing their partners.

e. Two Couple. Active couple leads up the set, followed by inactive. Active couple separates and travels in a small circle to one position below inactive. The inactive couple separates and turns almost in place, backing into the line above the active couple.

f. Separately. Sometimes one person casts off, as in a star figure, and the other person casts off in the next figure.

Sometimes the progression comes in the middle of the dance sequence; not always, but 30 percent of the time. In other words, there may be more figures to dance with the couple you cast off, but you are in position to start the beginning of the dance with the couple below when the right time comes.

Basic Step and Style

A light, rhythmic walking step with the music is used throughout the dance, except for special steps such as swing and balance. There are a few Contras that use the Waltz step (Hills of Habersham) or Polka step (Jenny Lind Polka) as the basic step.

A dancer may start on either foot, except for the swing and the balance, which start on the right. Therefore it is easier to start all figures with the right foot.

The arms hang freely at the side unless they are used to execute a figure. There is a slight motion of the body while standing in place. Sometimes a dancer adds a scuffling step or sways from side to side a bit in response to the music. When in a neutral position waiting to reenter the dance, a couple may swing or dance some fancy steps, solo, but they must be ready to enter on time. Grace in style and timing are most important.

Basic Techniques, Figures, and Styles

Most of the basic techniques and figures of Contra Dancing are the same as those in Square Dancing.

Balance, circle 4 or 6, do-si-do (do-sa-do), forward and back, ladies chain, promenade, right and left thru, sashay, star, and swing are some that are commonly called. Balance, right and left thru, and swing differ from those in Square Dancing.

Balance (4 counts)

The Contra balance step varies in different parts of the country. It may be a step swing; a step-hop swing; or a step touch, rising on the balls of both feet, then lowering heels. Right hands are joined (if more than two people, adjacent hands are joined, shoulder height, elbows bent); all step right first, then left. If style is optional, step touch is recommended.

Right and Left Thru, Right and Left Four

The two terms are used interchangeably. The floor pattern is the same as Square Dancing, but the dancers do not touch hands as they pass right. Dancers travel the same as a courtesy turn, side by side, with no contact of hands; the couple turns as one unit. They may join hands for the courtesy turn. Two men may pass thru with two women, in which case they do not join hands for the courtesy turn (side by side, almost touching) or put their nearest arm around the other's waist. In some areas, dancers may touch right hands as passing thru. The general rule is: If a hand is offered, take it in yours.

Swing

The hand holds vary in different parts of the country, but swing position (right parallel) is most common. Both dancers step into the swing on the right foot. A walk around or buzz step may be used. Knees are slightly bent. Counterbalance is important, with feet close together, upper bodies bowed like a top. The length of time to swing depends on the call—8, 12, or 16 counts.

Contra Corners Turn (16 counts)

Contra corners are diagonally across the set for each person. The *first contra corner* is diagonally right and the *second contra corner* is diagonally left. For the call "turn contra corners," active partners crossing set, take right hands, turn halfway, take left hand of *first contra corner*, turn all the way around, take right hand of partner, turn three-quarters around in middle of set, take left hand of *second contra corner,* turn all the way around and return to center of set and await next call. The actives use their right and left hands alternately; the corners *always* use their left hands. Each turn is 4 counts.

Gypsy (8 counts)

Two dancers face each other and continuing to face each other with eye contact, move clockwise around each other once. "Left gypsy," travel counterclockwise.

Hey for Four (16 counts)

Four dancers in a line, center two facing, weave without touching hands, moving in a figure-eight pattern with an additional loop in the middle.

To begin, two ladies face each other, man behind each lady; they pass right shoulders, traveling toward the end of line (opposite side), pass left shoulders with approaching man. The ladies continue making a loop to left to face center, pass next man left; ladies pass right in center, pass man left, loop to the left to face center, pass next man left and are back in original position. The men make a small loop to left (four steps) while the ladies start; then, following the path of the lady in front of them, pass left shoulders with the other lady, right shoulders with man in center, left with his partner, and loops left to face center. Men return passing lady left, man pass right in center, then lady left, loops left, and is home. The floor pattern is the same path as in a ladies chain. The man follows the same pattern as the lady. Some heys begin with the men starting; some with the inactives or actives starting.

Timing

Proper timing is important in Contra Dancing. The dancers must execute each step on the beat and use the proper number of beats for each figure. The basic figures of Contra Dances are done in the same number of counts that it takes to dance them in Square Dances. Here are a few of the basic Contra figures and the number of counts required to dance them properly.

1. Balance (4 counts)
2. Down the center (down and back) (16 counts)
3. Forward and back (8 counts)
4. Ladies chain (over and back) (16 counts)
5. Right and left four (over and back) (16 counts)

Calls

Sometimes the caller is referred to as the *prompter.* The calls are basically cues that give direction to the dancer, with a minimal amount of rhyming patter. Calls for each dance have been suggested, but the caller is free to use his or her own ingenuity in calling the cues.

The call precedes the action, so timing of the call is important. All Contras require 64 counts. The music is AABB. Therefore all figures must be danced to the proper counts and in the correct sequence. If there is a mixup, the dancers stop, get into correct positions, and pick up the dance at the next figure. Contra Dances are not forgiving like old-time Square Dances, where a call such as "everyone go home and swing" covers for too many errors and brings all the squares together again. If the caller wants all to have a chance to be active, he or she should note the couple at the head of the set before the dance begins in order to get that couple back to place before the dance ends. The caller must learn to space the calls so that the dance will move along continuously and so that the dancers will not have to wait at the end of each figure or have to run to keep up.

After the dancers are very familiar with the pattern, the caller usually stops calling. To reaffirm the sense of community, the caller returns to cueing about the last two times and calls an ending to bring the dance to a close.

Dance Structure

1. A dance usually lasts 6–8 minutes, depending on the length of the sets and whether it is duple or triple minor. (Triple is longer.)
2. The dance begins with the first figure.
3. Live music: The caller needs to agree with the musicians about the music introduction, so that both the caller and the dancers can get off to a good, crisp start. A two- or four-beat introduction or a chord are typical.
4. Records: Sometimes there is a clear introduction, but other times the dance begins with the first beat. The caller must know the records, so he or she can cue dancers properly for the first figure.
5. Ending: When ready to terminate the dance, the caller signals the musicians "two more times," or whatever is needed during the B2 music (away from the microphone) and proceeds to call the dance. A "bow to your partner" may end the dance, yet some dances lend themselves to a different ending in the last phrase, and others may need additional music, possibly 32 beats. New figures introduced must flow together with

the dance. The caller should know in advance an appropriate way to end the dance.

   a. Bow to your partner.

   b. Swing.

   c. Everybody forward and back (8 counts)

      Forward again and swing your partner (8 counts)

      Everybody promenade

      Promenade anywhere/somewhere (16 counts)

   d. All join hands in your lines

      Go forward and back (8 counts)

      Forward again and pass thru

      Turn around and join hands (8 counts)

      Forward and back (8 counts)

      Forward again and pass thru (8 counts)

      And everybody swing (partner) (16 counts)

Music

Contra Dance music is traditionally Irish, Scottish, English, or French-Canadian. Most of the dances are Jigs, Reels, Hornpipes, sometimes a March. The flavor of the music is important to the dance. A Southern or Western hoedown would not be appropriate. The music is written in 2/4, 4/4, and 6/8 meter. The 6/8 rhythm is counted like two beats, each beat being worth a triplet (first beat 1, 2, 3; second beat 4, 5, 6).

The tunes have two parts, A and B, or verse and chorus. Each part has eight measures, repeated twice, AABB. Contras follow the AABB pattern; the figures match the 64 beats precisely. Today, only a few contras are done to a specific tune; e.g., "Hull's Victory," "Money Musk," "Chorus Jig," "Rory O'More," "Petronella," and "Pop Goes the Weasel." Except for these special contras, it is permissible to interchange similar tunes for those suggested.

The interchange of dance to other tunes is permissible if the phrasing is exactly the same. The choice of tune is important. Some tunes "fit" a dance well; some tunes are chosen to match the character of the dance. Irish music is joyous and carefree; Jigs bouncy; Reels energetic and flowing. The music should reflect the spirit and build-up of the dance. The musicians should make the music match the excitement as a dance builds up to its high point. Although a medley of tunes is acceptable, more often the same tune with creative variations is played.

Card File

A card file (3 × 5-inch cards) is an excellent device to record new Contra Dances. Each person develops a unique system for filing. Note that the sample records the date and location that caller-teacher learned the dance; the name of the person that taught the dance (in this case the teacher and originator of the dance are the same person—but both pieces of information are handy); duple or triple/proper or improper; and that key cues are capitalized. In phrase #4, the caller-teacher uses "1s and 2s" as an alternative shorthand for "actives and inactives." On the back, any helpful information for teaching purposes and interesting facts are listed. It is wise to record the dance as taught because, in referring to it later, there is less error. The card may be carried to class and used for a quick refresher or a "crutch."

		Lady of Lake '85
PIERCE'S HALL STROLL		By Fred Breunig
		Duple, improper
A1:1	LADIES DO-SI-DO	
2	GENTS DO-SI-DO left shoulder 1½ & go to PARTNER	
A2:3	Everyone SWING your OWN on sides of set	
4	(long swing) end {1s face down, 2s face up} escort position	
B1:5	"STROLL" promenade along lines, turn as couple	
6	And RETURN look for opposite couple	
B2:7	RIGHT HANDS ACROSS turn 1½ round	
8	GENTS DROP OUT to original side	
	Ladies continue to turn right to LADIES CHAIN HALFWAY	

Community hall, East Putney, Vt., where Fred B. calls dances. Composed for the Sesquientennial, 1982.

Note:

#2	Gents LEFT shoulder do-si-do 1½ to face partner on her side
#6	Must recognize opposite couple at end of promenade Star position—shake hands
#7	Emphasize turning STAR 1½, until Gents get back to their original (improper) sides! Must turn star with *DETERMINATION* or Not on Time
#8	At end of Ladies ½ Chain, gents can direct (lead) ladies into their do-si-do of next lady

Teaching Suggestions

Teachers will have greater success if they know how to dance Contra Dances. In a dance methods class, if dancing is introduced to students not familiar with this type of dance, it is advisable for a master teacher to present several Contras first to the class so that students can become familiar with the form, the unique differentiations, and particularly the concept of active and inactive couples and progression. Then students will enjoy this type of dance and be more successful in interpreting directions and trying Contras as student teachers.

Sicilian Circle or Square Dance

An excellent lead into Contra Dance figures are dances using the Sicilian Circle formation. This is a convenient formation to teach right and left thru and ladies chain. Square Dancing also uses these two figures. If the students know a right and left thru and ladies chain, there is a greater choice of dances.

Ways to Form a Set

Usually the caller says "form your Contra sets!" At a One-Night-Stand, sets may be formed from a Grand March or Square Dance into Longway sets. Every two couples hold hands from the top, reminding the couples facing the "foot" that they are "active" and those facing the "head" that they are "inactive." Cross over if improper dance.

Length of Sets, Extra Couples

Short sets (six to eight couples) are more desirable for teaching, because dancers experience the active and inactive roles more frequently. Extra couples start dancing the second time through the dance. If there is lots of action in the dance for everyone, or double progression, then longer sets are better.

Triple Minor

Start with seven couples in each set. There is less standing around.

Actives, Inactives, Neutral

The call is addressed to the active, but frequently the inactive is involved. Stress the direction that they travel and what happens when a couple reaches the head or foot of the set; namely, they must cross over if improper dance. Refer to Active, Inactive Couples, Neutral, page 189. Coach inactives nearing the head to watch what the actives do so that the transition from inactive to active is smoother. At the foot, the other transition is easier, as the active will bring the inactive along. The inactives need to continually move up toward the head of the set while dancing, otherwise there will be a large gap between the caller and the set. Some dancers will move intuitively; others need a specific cue.

Neutral couples may join in with some figures like a promenade. Discourage neutral couples from swinging. They frequently miss their cue to come back into the dance on the beat. They tend to disrupt the nearby dancers.

Choice of Dances

For the first dance, select a winner, one that has a simple progression (swing neighbor) and peppy tune that gives the dancers an immediate sense of unity, fun, and success. When all of the dancers change direction and figures simultaneously on the beat, they intuitively have a sense of unity. Avoid taxing their memory of figures. Dancing to the *phrases* and the progression are the two important skills to establish. Unless the dancers are familiar with the figure, save "ladies chain" for the second dance and "right and left thru" for the third or fourth dance so that they know a "courtesy turn." When the dancers are quite familiar with the basics and the different progressions (including cast offs), then introduce triple minor dances, Contra corners, and hey for four.

Presentation of Dance

Have one or two walk-thrus as needed. Remember to have dancers return to their original positions. If there is confusion, have everyone watch one minor set demonstrate the figure.

Hey for Four

1. The starting position and ending varies, depending on the preceding and following figures.
2. Walk through a ladies chain. In a hey for four, dancers follow the same path as the ladies in a ladies chain. Repeat without touching hands, lady going around the man to the left, man standing in place (no courtesy turn).
3. Stand in line of four and walk the pattern. Each man follows his partner, but someone passes between him and his partner regularly. Men should not dance the beginning loop until the pattern is established.
4. If necessary, demonstrate.

Triple Minor Dances

1. Teach the dance with only seven couples in each set.
2. Identify the minor sets of three couples. After one time through the dance, identify the new minor sets. Inactives alternate between being #2 and #3 inactives; thus their dance role varies. Return to original positions after walk-thrus.

3. At the head of the set, inactives wait out two turns before becoming active. At the bottom of the set, when only two couples remain, the active continues to dance with an imaginary third couple. Then they become inactive.
4. While waiting at the head or foot or set to dance, the couple may swing or dance solo fancy steps.

Turn Contra Corners

1. Each dancer should identify his or her "Contra corners." Contra corners are diagonally across the set for each person. The "first contra corner" is diagonally right and the "second contra corner" is diagonally left.
2. The corner always gets a left turn.
3. In duple minor contras the inactives will get two consecutive turns, both left, from two different actives.

Be My Valentine*

Be My Valentine is a contemporary Contra, composed by Ted Sannella, February 13, 1984 for a dance on February 14, 1984.

Music: Any lively jig.

Formation: Becket Formation. Couples stand side by side, lady to right of her partner, facing another couple across the set. If there is an uneven number of couples, extra couple stands, at the foot, facing up, till a couple is available to dance with them.

```
5   6    foot
5   6
3   4
3   4
1   2
1   2    head
```

■ Directions for the Dance

A1 Opposite gents allemande left once, right to your own and balance four in line (8 counts) Opposite men allemande left once, give right to partner (ladies face left) forming a line, hands are joined. Balance right and left.

```
①  1  2  ②
```

All swing your partner (8 counts).

A2 Circle left with the opposite two (8 counts).

Same four right hands across, then gents loop left (8 counts). Each pair (two men, two ladies) join right hands, elbows slightly bent, traveling clockwise. Men dropping hands, turn away, traveling in a small circle (loop) preparing to receive opposite lady for a courtesy turn.

B1 Ladies chain, over and back, end with extra one-quarter turn (16 counts). From the right hand across, the ladies continue with a ladies chain, give left to opposite man for courtesy turn and continue ladies chain, ending with an extra quarter turn so that *mens' line faces up and ladies' line faces down.*

B2 Promenade up or down, turn as a couple (8 counts). Moving well in the direction facing, take 6 steps forward. Those approaching end of set, turn to follow behind other line. Counts 7–8, turn as a couple to face the opposite direction.

Promenade back, pass the couple you danced with (8 counts). Now ready to begin dance again (gents allemande left) with a new couple.

🌿 Becket Reel 🌿

Becket Reel is an original dance by the late Herbie Gaudreau of Holbrock, Massachusetts. He named it "Becket Reel" in honor of Camp Becket in the Berkshire mountains of western Massachusetts, where he first called this dance while attending Charlie Baldwin's square dance camp. In some parts of New Hampshire it is known as Bucksaw Contra or Reel. It is similar to Slaunch to Donegal.

Record: Any preferred traditional-type Reel. Grenn 12239.

Cassette: "Woodchopper's Reel," Kitchen Junket ALC 200 A/BC.

Music: "Reilly's Own," Cole, M. M., *One Thousand Fiddle Tunes;* "Reel a Pitou," Page, Ralph, *An Elegant Collection of Squares,* p. 91.

Formation: Becket formation. Couples stand side by side, lady to right of her partner, facing another couple across the set. Or Contra Dance formation, duple improper. Minor sets of two couples, circle halfway to left. If there is an uneven number of couples, extra couple stands in line on caller's right and comes in on right and left on a diagonal, at the foot, facing across.

■ Directions for the Dance

A1 **Allemande left your corner** (8 counts). Individuals at extreme ends of each line cannot do this. They stand in place.

Come back and swing the one you left (8 counts). Partners swing.

A2 **Opposite ladies chain over and back** (16 counts).

B1 **Right and left thru with the left-hand two** (8 counts). From lines, each couple does a right and left with couple in opposite line on left diagonal. Courtesy turn partner to face middle of set.

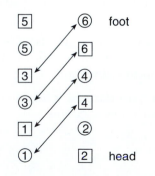

Do the same across from you (8 counts). From lines, each couple does a right and left with couple directly opposite. Courtesy turn partner to face middle of set.

```
 5 <    > ③   foot
 ⑤ <    > 3
 6 <    > ①
 ⑥ <    > 1
 4 <    > ②
 ④ <    > 2   head
```

B2 **Same two couples star by the left. Back by the right** (16 counts). As you come out of right-hand star, movement flows into left allemande at the beginning.

🙠 The Belles of Auburn*

The Belles of Auburn is an original dance by Roger Knox. As the story goes, Roger was calling a dance in Auburn, New York, in 1958. While he was trying to remember another dance, this one surfaced. According to Ted Sannella, he was probably trying to remember Beaux of Oak Hill, a similar dance.

Record: Suggested, "Maple Leaf Jig," "Hold the Mustard Jig," Hold the Mustard HTM IL.

Formation: Contra Dance formation. Couples 1, 3, 5, and so on, active, cross over (duple, improper).

■ Directions for the Dance

A1 **Sashay down with the next below** (8 counts). Actives move to the center, partners stand back to back, join two hands with the one below. All couples slide down the set.

Sashay back to place (8 counts).

A2 **Balance and swing with the same** (16 counts). Same couples, balance and swing. End swing with lady on right side of partner, facing down the set, four in line. Join hands.

B1 **Down the center four in line, turn as a couple** (8 counts). Walk down the set. Counts 5–8, couples turn to face up the set.

Four in line, come back to place (8 counts). Join hands, walk up the set.

B2 **The same two ladies chain, over and back** (16 counts).

Note

Roger Knox writes that he sometimes calls "bend the line" just before "two ladies chain," a more recent term that moves the two couples face to face from a line of four for a ladies chain.

---

*The Belles of Auburn included by permission of Roger Knox, Ithaca, NY.

🌿 British Sorrow

British Sorrow is a traditional Contra.

Record: Lloyd Shaw 169 (flip) (4/4) or preferred march.

Music: Suggested tunes, "Jack's Life" or "The Tower of London Quickstep," Page, Ralph, *The Ralph Page Book of Contras,* p. 7.

Formation: Contra Dance formation. Couples 1, 4, 7, and so on, active, *do not* cross over (triple, proper).

■ Directions for the Dance

A1 **Active couples cast down the outside below two** (8 counts). Active couples turn out (man left, lady right) and walk down outside of set past two couples. Counts 7–8, cut into center of set. Facing up the set, partners join inside hands.

Up the center and cast off (8 counts). Walk up the center, separate, and cast off with inactive couple (couple 2); active's arm around inactive's waist. Active couples have progressed one position down.

A2 **Right-hand star with the couple below** (8 counts). Active couple and the couple below (couple 3) form a right-hand star.

Left-hand star with the couple above (8 counts). Active couples move naturally into left-hand star with the couple above (couple 2).

B1 **Circle six to the right** (16 counts). All three couples join hands and circle right once around, falling back into lines at end of sequence. Actives are between #2 and #3 dancers.

B2 **Right and left thru with the couple above** (8 counts). Active couple and couple above (the couple with whom they cast off) right and left thru.

Right and left back (8 counts).

Notes

1. During the walk-thru, it is important to identify the triple set of couples dancing together. The active couples move down one position each time the dance is repeated. The active couples remain the lead couple in the triple set until they reach the foot. The relative position of the inactives changes too. At the head of the set, inactives wait two times to become active. (See 4th sequence.) At the foot the *active continues to dance* with an imaginary 3rd couple (ghost) until they are at the foot. Otherwise, the last couple will never move up.

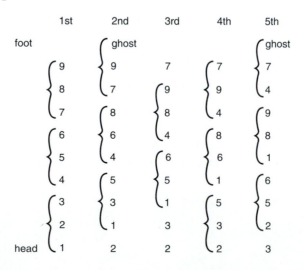

2. The same dance with actives cross over (improper) is known as Ottawa Special.

Broken Sixpence*

Broken Sixpence is an original dance by Don Armstrong.

Record: Lloyd Shaw 155/156 (flip) or lively Contra music.

Formation: Contra Dance formation. Couples 1, 3, 5, and so on, active, cross over (duple, improper).

■ Directions for the Dance

A1 **With the one below you do-si-do** (8 counts). Actives face down the set, inactives face up. Actives do-si-do the one facing.

Now just the men do-si-do (8 counts). Men do-si-do in center of set.

A2 **Now just the ladies do-si-do** (8 counts). Ladies do-si-do in center of set.

Active couples swing (8 counts). Swing in center of set, ending with lady on man's right, facing down the set. Active couple is between the inactive couple (couple below) in a line of four.

B1 **Down the center four in line.**

Turn alone (8 counts). Join hands in line of four. Walk down the set; counts 7–8, release hands, turn individually to face up the set.

Come back home (8 counts). Join hands. Walk up the set.

B2 **Circle four** (8 counts). From line of four, inactive couple joins hands and all four circle left once around.

Star by the left, the other way back (8 counts). From left-hand star, active couple will move naturally into beginning of dance to "do-si-do the one below."

---

*Broken Sixpence included by permission of Don Armstrong, Canon City, CO.

✿ The Brown-Eyed Maid*

The Brown-Eyed Maid is a contemporary Contra. It is an original dance by Glen Nickerson, introduced February, 1980, at the Boeing Employees, Contrails Dance Club, Sweetheart Cotillion. The Waterfall Musical Group had just learned the tune "Mistwold" from Dudley Laufman, who had recently been in the Seattle area. Glen composed a dance specially for the tune, so that the musicians could play "Mistwold," and named the dance for his "brown-eyed maid," his wife Flo.

Record: "Mistwold," Farm and Wilderness, F and W, F74-FW-5 (4/4) or similar tune with a stately feeling.

Formation: Contra Dance formation. Couples 1, 3, 5, and so on, active, *do not* cross over (duple, proper)

■ Directions for the Dance

A1 **Right-hand star below** (8 counts). Active couple right-hand star with the couple below.

Left-hand star the other way (8 counts).

A2 **Four in line down the center** (8 counts). Active couple steps between inactives to make line of four, facing down the set. From left-hand star inactive lady turns clockwise and inactive man cuts star short to form line of four.

Walk down the set.

Counts 5–8, inactives release hands, actives turn as a couple; counts 7–8, inactives turn alone toward center to face up the set. Rejoin hands.

Come back to place and cast off (8 counts). Counts 5–8, active couple release inside hands, cast off (hand cast off) with adjacent dancer to face center. Actives have progressed one position down.

B1 **Ladies chain over and back** (16 counts).

B2 **Left-hand star with same couple** (8 counts).

Actives only half figure eight around the ones above (8 counts). (A) Actives cross to opposite side, lady crossing in front of partner, moving up and around inactive above on the outside and coming into the line one position below. (B) Each active is now on original side, down one position and ready to dance "right-hand star below" with new inactive couple.

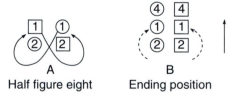

A
Half figure eight

B
Ending position

Inactives should adjust in the half figure eight by moving slightly down the line and in, then back up and out to make room for the actives so that they do not have to travel so far to get around.

*The Brown-Eyed Maid included by permission of Glen Nickerson, Kent, WA.

C. D. S. Reel*

C. D. S. Reel is a contemporary Contra. It is an original dance by Ted Sannella, composed in September, 1984. The Country Dance Society (C. D. S.) is the publisher of Ted's book, *Balance and Swing*.

Record: "Golden Wedding Reel," Hold the Mustard HTM IL.

Music: "Swinging on a Gate," Sannella, Ted, *Balance and Swing*, p. 69.

Formation: Contra Dance formation. Couples 1, 3, 5, and so on, active, cross over (duple, improper).

■ Directions for the Dance

A1 **Swing your neighbor** (8 counts). Each man swings lady on his left. Lady ends on man's right side, facing across.

All go forward and back (8 counts). Join hands in line, move four steps forward, four steps back.

A2 **Big circle, all go left** (8 counts). Head couple joins hands and foot couple joins hands to complete the oval, which moves left.

Big circle, go right back to place (8 counts). Circle moves right. **Note:** Each man locates his partner to form left-hand star, on call.

B1 **Left-hand star three-quarters with the opposite two** (8 counts). Active couple with couple above form left-hand star, turn three-fourths around.

All swing your own (8 counts). Men turn right to swing lady behind. Lady ends on man's right side.

B2 **Gents allemande left, go once and a half** (8 counts). Two men allemande left, once and a half.

Swing your neighbor (8 counts). Men will swing the same person as the beginning; lady ends on man's right side. Active couples have progressed one position.

---

*C. D. S. Reel included by permission of Ted Sannella, Wiscasset, ME.

🌿 The Caller's Wife*

The Caller's Wife is an original dance by Ted Sannella, composed July 29, 1973.

Record: "Poor Auld Woman," Farm and Wilderness, F-72-FW3 or similar Reel.

Music: "Reel du Petit Minou," Sannella, Ted, *Balance and Swing,* p. 83.

Formation: Contra Dance formation. Couples 1, 3, 5, and so on, active, cross over (duple, improper, and double progression).

■ Directions for the Dance

A1   **Allemande left the one below once and a half** (8 counts). Active couples end one position down (first progression).

      Ladies chain (8 counts). Ladies do not return.

A2   **Long lines go forward and back** (8 counts). Join hands in the lines. Walk four steps forward and four steps backward.

      The same two couples circle left three-quarters around and pass thru, up and down the set (8 counts). Active couple joins hands with the couple above, circle left three-quarters. Active couple will end facing down the set. Up and down the set, active couples pass thru the couple facing (second progression).

B1   **Do-si-do the one you meet** (8 counts). From the pass thru, active couple do-si-do the person they are facing, which is the second inactive couple.

      Swing the same (8 counts). Swing the same person, ending with lady on man's right, facing across set.

B2   **Promenade over to the opposite side** (8 counts). Active couple promenades with the ones they swung.

      Right and left thru back to place (8 counts). With same couple, right and left.

---

*The Caller's Wife included by permission of Ted Sannella, Wiscasset, ME.

Chorus Jig

Chorus Jig is a traditional Contra. "Chorus Jig" is a Reel (2/4), not a Jig (6/8).

Record: "Chorus Jig" Cantebury Country Dance Orchestra F & W 3L.

Cassette: "Chorus Jig," New England Chestnuts, Vol. 1 & 2 ALC 203/4C.

Music: "Chorus Jig," Page, Ralph, *An Elegant Collection of Contras and Squares,* p. 39, *Fiddler's Fakebook,* p. 68; *New England Fiddler's Repertoire,* no. 96.

Formation: Contra Dance formation. Couples 1, 3, 5, and so on, active, *do not* cross over (duple, proper).

■ Directions for the Dance

A1   **Actives down the outside and back** (16 counts). Each active walks down the outside of the set, turning on counts 7–8, and return to place.

A2   **Actives down the center and back, cast off** (16 counts). Active couples walk down the center, counts 7–8, turn alone. Return to original position. Cast off, counts 5–8, arm around the inactive person, progressing one position down. Inactive does not turn.

B1   **Turn Contra corners** (16 counts). Active person, identify his "Contra corners" to the right and left of his partner. Active partners crossing set, touch right hands, turn "first Contra corner" with left hand, turn partner with right hand in middle of set, turn "second Contra corner" with left hand, and return to center of set.

B2   **Actives balance and swing** (16 counts). End swing facing up the set, moving to go down the outside below the person you cast off.

Note

Inactive person receives two consecutive turns, both left-hand turn, by two different people.

Dud's Reel

Dud's Reel is an original dance by the late Dudley Briggs of Massachusetts. It was introduced in 1953.

Record: "Indian Reel," English Folk Dance and Song Society RP 500.

Cassette: "Indian Reel," Southerners Plus Two Play Ralph Page, RP 500C.

Music: "Once Upon My Cheek," Cole, M. M., *One Thousand Fiddle Tunes.*

Formation: Contra Dance formation. Couples 1, 3, 5, and so on, active, cross over (duple, improper).

■ Directions for the Dance

A1   **Balance and swing the one below** (16 counts). Actives balance and swing the one below. Leave lady on man's right, all facing center of set. Active couples have now moved down one position; inactives have moved up one position. Active couples continue to dance with couple above until dance repeats.

A2   **Opposite ladies chain** (8 counts). Men chain ladies they have swung.

     And chain right back (8 counts).

B1   **All forward and back twice** (16 counts). Long lines join hands. Take four steps forward, four steps backward. Repeat.

B2   **Circle four with the couple above** (8 counts). Active couples circle four with the couple above.

     Left-hand star back to place (8 counts).

Fiddle Hill Jig

Fiddle Hill Jig is an original dance by the late Ralph Page of Keene, New Hampshire in the late 1950s. Fiddle Hill Jig was named for a road and hill in the town of Winchester, New Hampshire.

Cassette: "Shandon Bells," Kitchen Junket ALC 200 A/BC.

Music: "Fiddle Hill Jig," Page, Ralph, *The Ralph Page Book of Contras,* p. 19; "Maple Leaf Jig" or similar 6/8 tune.

Formation: Contra Dance formation. Couples 1, 3, 5, and so on, active, cross over (duple, improper).

■ Directions for the Dance

A1   **Do-si-do the one below** (8 counts).

     Do-si-do your partner (8 counts).

A2   **Allemande left the one below** (4 counts). First couples swing your partner in the center (8 counts).

     Actives swing your partner (12 counts). Active couples swing your partner in the center.

     End swing with lady on man's right facing down the set.

B1   **Down the center four in line, turn alone** (8 counts). Active couple in the middle joins hands with inactive couple, line of four. Walk down the center, counts 7–8, turn alone.

     The same way home (8 counts). Ends turn in to form a circle.

B2   **Circle four hands once around** (8 counts). Circle left.

     Left-hand star back to place (8 counts). Active couples will be one position down and begin dance with the couple below.

Flirtation Reel*

Flirtation Reel is a contemporary Contra, written by Tony Parkes, 1985.

Music: Any preferred traditional Reel.

Formation: Contra Dance formation. Couples 1, 3, 5, and so on, active, cross over (duple, improper).

■ Directions for the Dance

A1 **With the one below, go down the set four in line, turn alone** (8 counts). Actives move to the center, join hands with adjacent couple below. Walk down the center, counts 7–8, each turn alone to face up the set.

  Return to place and face your neighbor (8 counts).

A2 **Hey for four across the set** (16 counts). Start hey passing neighbor by the right. The inactives will pass left shoulders in the middle.

B1 **Dance a gypsy round your neighbor** (8 counts). Pass right shoulders, traveling clockwise.

  Swing the same (8 counts). End with lady on right side of man, couple facing center. Actives have progressed one position down.

B2 **All go forward and back** (8 counts). Join hands in the long lines, walk forward and back.

  Actives swing in the center (8 counts). At the end of the swing, actives face down, ready to begin the dance again with a new couple.

---

*Flirtation Reel included by permission of Tony Parkes, Arlington, MA.

Hills of Habersham

Hills of Habersham is an original Waltz Contra Dance by the late Mary and Fred Collette of Atlanta, Georgia. The Hills of Habersham refer to the mountains of north Georgia. The action of the dance is suggestive of the Chattahoochee River, winding its way to the Gulf. The tune is the ancient Irish melody, "The Bonny Cuckoo."

Records: Folklore Village, FLV 7802* (3/4); Lloyd Shaw 181 (flip) (3/4).

Music: "Star of Country Down" (3/4) and "Si Bheag, Si Mhor" (3/4), Werner, Robert, *The Folklore Village Saturday Night Book,* p. 53.

Formation: Contra Dance formation. Couples 1, 3, 5, and so on, active, *do not* cross over (duple, proper). In Contra lines, hands joined, held at shoulder height, elbows V-shaped.

Note: Instructions presented in measures, Waltz rhythm. No call. Could prompt.

■ Directions for the Dance

Meter 3/4

Measures

Introduction:* no action.

A 1 – 2   Beginning right, take six steps; all move forward, partners passing right shoulders (drop hands and rejoin) to the opposite side. Now both lines face out from set.

3 – 4   Balance right and left, step swing or step touch.

5 – 6   Release hands. Beginning right, travel six steps clockwise, individually, in a circular pattern, about four feet in diameter, to face center of set. **Rejoin hands in lines.**

7 – 8   Repeat action of measures 3 – 4, balancing right and left.

9 – 16   Repeat action of measures A 1 – 8, returning to original position.

B 1 – 4   Active couples, face up the set. Men turn left, ladies right, and travel down the outside of set (twelve steps) passing two inactive couples. Cut thru the line to meet partner in middle of set and join inside hands.

5 – 6   Moving up the set, take six steps to the inactive couple that was originally below them at beginning. Join hands in a line of four, facing up the set.

7 – 8   All beginning right, balance right and left.

9 – 10   Inactives release actives' hands and continue to face up. Actives wheel around, man backing up, lady moving forward, taking six steps to face up. Line of four rejoin hands.

11 – 12   All beginning right, balance right and left.

13 – 14   Active couples release inside hands. Taking six steps, active person casts off with adjacent inactive person, hands still joined. Active is now below inactive, facing center. Both couples have progressed one position.

15 – 16   Rejoin hands in Contra lines. Balance right and left.

---

*Folklore Village record—Introduction: chord.

Notes

1. Hills of Habersham was originally duple improper (actives crossed over). For beginners, this version (duple, proper) is easier to learn.
2. The balance of the original dance was step right, touch left toe, foot arched to right, body rising slightly on count 2, body lowering on count 3.
3. Dancers momentarily inactive balance right, then left alternately, keeping the Waltz motion constant.

❧ Hull's Victory ❧

Hull's Victory is a traditional Contra. This dance honors the battle between the U.S. ship *Constitution*, commanded by Captain Isaac Hull, and the English ship *Guerriere*, commanded by Captain D'Acres.

Record: Traditionally danced to tune of the same name.

Cassette: "Hull's Victory," New England Chestnuts, Vol. 1 & 2 ALC 203/4 C.

Music: "Hull's Victory," Cole, M. M., *One Thousand Fiddle Tunes,* p. 103; Page, Ralph, *An Elegant Collection of Contras and Squares,* p. 57.

Formation: Contra Dance formation. Couples 1, 3, 5, and so on, *do not* cross over (duple, proper).

■ Directions for the Dance

A1 **Right hand to your partner, left land to your neighbor.**

Balance four in line (8 counts). To form a line of four, active couples walk to center, join right hands, turn halfway and, still holding hands, join left hands with neighbor (inactive) across set. Men face down the set, ladies up. Balance four in line, step forward touch, step back touch.

Allemande left your neighbor twice around (8 counts). Actives drop partner's hand, and allemande left neighbor twice around.

A2 **Allemande right your partner once around** (4 counts). Actives allemande right once around and form a line of four again.

Balance four in line (4 counts).

Actives swing in center (8 counts). End swing with lady on man's right facing down set. Join inside hands.

B1 **Down the center** (8 counts). Active couple walks down the set, counts 5–8, turns as a couple to face up.

And back, cast off (8 counts). Couples walk up the set, and cast off with original neighbor. Two men turn, arm around waist, as a couple; two ladies do same, to face center. Active couples have progressed one position.

B2 **Right and left thru.**

Right and left back (16 counts). Same two couples right and left over and back.

Note

Use pigeon-wing position for balance and allemandes.

🌿 Jefferson's Reel

Jefferson's Reel was composed by the late Dudley Briggs in 1954. It is based on an older dance, Jefferson and Liberty.

Record: "Jefferson Reel," Lloyd Shaw E-18, Grenn 15008.

Music: Suggested tunes: "Golden Stairs," "Durang's Hornpipe," "Lamplighter's Hornpipe."

Formation: Contra Dance formation. Duple proper or duple improper. Presented as duple proper. Couples 1, 3, 5, and so on, active, *do not* cross over.

■ Directions for the Dance

A1 **Circle left with the next below** (8 counts). Active and inactive couple join hands and circle left.

   Circle right, the other way back (8 counts).

A2 **Right-hand star with the same** (8 counts).

   Back with a left-hand star (8 counts).

B1 **Actives down the outside, go single-file** (8 counts). Men turn left, ladies right, and walk down outside of the set. Counts 7–8, turn to face up the set.

   Return up the outside to place (8 counts).

B2 **Down the set four in line** (8 counts). Active couple move to middle of set between inactive couple. Join hands in a line of four and walk down the set.

   Inside couple arch, outside under, return to place (8 counts). Active couple raise inside hands to form an arch; outside people walk under arch, join inside hands, and walk up the set. Active couple release inside hands, turn toward each other to face up the set; join inside hands and walk behind inactive couple to place. Both couples will have progressed: inactive up one position; active down one position.

Notes

1. When the dance repeats, inactive couple with inside hands joined will be ready to join hands with new active couple to circle left. Active couple will release inside hands, turn towards each other to join inactive couple below to circle left.
2. If the group is predominantly one sex, presenting the dance as proper is less confusing.

Joy*

Joy is a contemporary Contra. It is an original dance Lannie McQuaide wrote to express her appreciation to Mary D. and F. Howard Walsh, Lloyd Shaw Foundation members, for their graciousness and generosity, and for the joy they have given to so many people. It was presented on the Littlest Wiseman Pilgrimage in December, 1980.

Record: "Jack's Life," Southerners Plus Two Play Ralph Page, English Folk Dance and Song Society RP 500; or a joyous tune.

Cassette: "Jack's Life," Southerners Plus Two Play Ralph Page, RP 500C.

Music: "Jack's Life," Page, Ralph, *The Ralph Page Book of Contras,* p. 7.

Formation: Contra Dance formation. Couples 1, 3, 5, and so on, active, *do not* cross over (duple, proper).

■ Directions for the Dance

A1   **All go forward and back** (8 counts). Join hands in the lines, walk four steps forward and four steps back.

    Actives cross over, go below one (8 counts). Actives passing right shoulders in the middle, cross to opposite side, moving around inactive person, on the outside and coming into the line one position below.

A2   **Right-hand star above** (8 counts). Active couple with inactive couple above form a right-hand star, opposite people join right hands across.

    Those two ladies chain (8 counts). Ladies only chain across with courtesy turn. While ladies start the chain, men make a small loop left out of the star while waiting to receive lady approaching.

B1   **Hey for four across the set, ladies pass by the right to start** (16 counts).

B2   **Same two ladies chain** (8 counts). Ladies only chain across with a courtesy turn.

    Actives half figure eight thru same couple (8 counts). Actives cross to opposite side, lady crossing in front of partner, moving up and around inactive person above, on the outside and coming into the line one position below. Each active is now on original side.

A   B
Half figure eight   Ending position

---

*Joy included by permission of Lannie McQuaide, Columbus, OH.

✿ Lady of the Lake ✿

Lady of the Lake is a traditional Contra.

Cassette: "Lady of the Lake," New England Chestnuts, Vol. 1 & 2 ALC 203/4C.

Music: "Miller's Reel," Cole, M. M., *One Thousand Fiddle Tunes.*

Formation: Contra Dance formation. Couples 1, 3, 5, and so on, active, cross over (duple, improper).

■ Directions for the Dance

A1 **Balance and swing the one below** (16 counts).

A2 **Actives balance and swing** (16 counts).

B1 **Actives down the center and back, cast off** (16 counts). Active couples, inside hands joined, walk down the center; counts 7–8, turn alone to face up the set. Return to original position. Counts 5–8, cast off, walk around inactive person, progressing one position down. Inactive does not turn.

B2 **Ladies chain with the couple above** (16 counts). Ladies chain over and back.

✿ Lady Walpole's Reel ✿

Lady Walpole's Reel is a traditional Contra. As the story goes, Lady Walpole composed this dance, as it was socially necessary for her to dance with her estranged husband. To note, each lady spends little time dancing with her partner. Frequently danced at weddings.

Record: "Lady Walpole's Reel," Fretless FR 203.

Cassette: "Lady Walpole's Reel," New England Chestnuts, Vol. 1 & 2 ALC 203/4C.

Music: "The Reel of Stumpey," "Massai's Favorite," Page, Ralph, *An Elegant Collection of Contras and Squares,* p. 27.

Formation: Contra Dance formation. Couples 1, 3, 5, and so on, active, cross over (duple, improper).

■ Directions for the Dance

A1 **Balance and swing the one below** (16 counts).

A2 **Actives down the center and back, cast off** (16 counts). Active couple walk down the center. Counts 7–8, turn alone. Return to original position. Arm around cast off, counts 5–8, progressing one position down. Inactive does not turn.

B1 **Ladies chain with the couple above** (16 counts). Ladies chain over and back.

B2 **Promenade across the set** (8 counts).

Right and left home (8 counts). Opposite couples right and left thru.

The Malden Reel

The Malden Reel is an original dance by the late Herbie Gaudreau of Holbrook, Massachusetts.

Record: "Snowflake Breakdown," Fourgone Conclusions, Front Hall FHR 029; or similar Jig or lively Reel.

Music: "Smash the Windows Jig," Cole, M. M., *One Thousand Fiddle Tunes.*

Formation: Contra Dance formation. Couples 1, 3, 5, and so on, cross over (duple, improper).

■ Directions for the Dance

A1   **Do-si-do the one below** (8 counts).

   You swing the same (8 counts). Leave lady on man's right. Active couples have progressed one position down.

A2   **Circle four with the opposite two** (8 counts).

   The other way back with a left-hand star (8 counts).

B1   **All promenade up and down** (8 counts). At end of left-hand star, two couples separate and promenade in opposite directions by couples up and down the hall. Active man and lady he swung promenade **up** the hall, active lady and man she swung promenade **down** the hall. Man takes lady's left hand in his left; his right arm around her waist. Counts 5–8, turn as a couple to face opposite direction.

   The other way back (8 counts). End in long lines, facing across.

B2   **Same two ladies chain over and back** (16 counts).

🌿 Mason and Garden*

Mason and Garden is a contemporary Contra. It is an original dance by Al Olson, created in March, 1979. Many New England Folk Festival Association (NEFFA) dances are held at the First Church, Congregational, located at the corner of Mason and Garden streets, near Harvard Square in Cambridge, Massachusetts.

Music: Any preferred lively Reel.

Formation: Contra Dance formation. Couples 1, 3, 5, and so on, active, cross over (duple, improper).

■ Directions for the Dance

A1 **Balance and swing below** (16 counts). Actives balance and swing the one below. Leave lady on man's right, all facing down the set.

A2 **Down four in line, turn alone** (8 counts). Form line of four. Active couple separated is on the outside of line and inactive couple in the middle. Move down the set. Counts 7–8, turn alone to face up the set.

The same way back, ends turn in (8 counts). Move up the set. Counts 7–8, active couple join hands to form a ring of four.

B1 **Circle right, go once around** (8 counts).

Allemande left below, go once and a half around (8 counts). Actives allemande left the one below, turn once and a half.

B2 **Hey for four across, ladies pass by right to start** (16 counts).

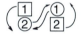

At the conclusion of the hey, the active couple will be ready to dance with the next inactive couple below them.

---

*Mason and Garden included by permission of Al Olson, Chicago, IL.

🎵 Needham Special

Needham Special is a contemporary Contra. It is an original dance by the late Herbie Gaudreau of Holbrook, Massachusetts.

Record: Any preferred Reel or Breakdown.

Cassette: "Mouth of the Tobique," Kitchen Junket ALC 200A/BC.

Music: "Good for the Tongue," Cole, M. M., *One Thousand Fiddle Tunes;* "Le Breakdown de Pontneux," Page, Ralph, *An Elegant Collection of Contras and Squares,* p. 107.

Formation: Contra Dance formation. Couples 1, 3, 5, and so on, active, cross over (duple, improper, and double progression).

■ Directions for the Dance

A1 **Balance and swing the one below** (16 counts). Actives balance and swing the one below. End swing with lady on man's right, facing down the hall.

A2 **Down the center four in line. Turn as couples** (8 counts). Join hands in line of four, walk down the center. On counts 5–8, each couple wheels around to face up the hall. Join hands in line of four.

The other way back (8 counts). Line walks *up* the set, returning to place. Active couples release inside hands and back into long line. Active couple ends one position down (first progression).

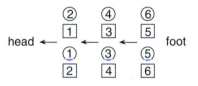

B1 **And the same two ladies chain over and back** (16 counts).

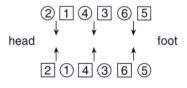

B2 **Everybody pass thru. Turn alone** (8 counts). Pass right shoulders of opposites, turn individually toward new neighbor.

With your new neighbor promenade across (8 counts). Each man takes **new neighbor** and does a half promenade to original side; lady ends on man's right side. Active couple progresses one position down at end of promenade (second progression).

🌿 The Nice Combination* 🌿

The Nice Combination is a contemporary Contra, composed by Gene W. Hubert in September, 1985. The name of the dance comes from the simple, natural sequence of figures and clean phrasing, a "nice combination of figures."

Music: Any lively Contra music.

Formation: Contra Dance formation. Couples 1, 3, 5, and so on, active, cross over (duple, improper).

■ Directions for the Dance

A1   **Balance and swing your neighbor** (16 counts). Each man swings lady on his left. Lady ends on man's right side, both couples facing down the set in a line of four.

⬜1⬜ ② ⬜2⬜ ① ↑

A2   **Go down the center four in line, turn as a couple** (8 counts). Join hands in line of four and move down the set. Turn as a couple, man backing up on a pivot, and lady moving forward to face other direction.

      Return and fold the line (8 counts). Join hands, move up the set, counts 7–8, outside people move toward each other to form a circle.

⬜1⬜ ①↑
② ⬜2⬜↓

B1   **Circle left three-quarters** (8 counts). Extend circles so that it is spacious.

      Swing your partner (8 counts). Everyone swings partner, men on original side.

B2   **Ladies chain across** (8 counts). Do not return. After chain active couples have progressed.

④ ⬜4⬜↑
⬜1⬜ ①
② ⬜2⬜

      Same two couples, left-hand star, go all the way around (8 counts). From the courtesy turn, the two couples flow into a left-hand star. At the end of the star, actives are looking down, inactives looking up, ready for the next call, right hand to neighbor to balance and swing (the beginning of the dance).

Variation

B2   **Forward and back** (8 counts). **Ladies chain across** (8 counts).

This works well for beginners.

---

*The Nice Combination included by permission of Gene W. Hubert, Bethesda, MD.

The Nova Scotian

The Nova Scotian is an original dance by Maurice Henneger of Halifax, Nova Scotia, which was arranged by the late Ralph Page of Keene, New Hampshire.

Records: "Glise a Sherbrooke," Folk Dancer MH 45 10073; "Portland Fancy," Fretless FR 203.

Music: "Speed the Plough," Cole, M. M., *One Thousand Fiddle Tunes.*

Formation: Contra Dance formation. Couples 1, 3, 5, and so on, active, cross over (duple, improper).

■ Directions for the Dance

A1   **Allemande left with the one below** (8 counts). Active couples allemande left with one below.

     Come back to the middle and swing your own (8 counts). Active couples swing in center of set.

A2   **Go down the center three in line** (4 counts). Active couple and #2 lady (active man has a lady on either side of him, partner on his right, corner lady on his left) take four walking steps toward foot of set.

     Right hand over, left hand under, return to place (12 counts). Active man makes an arch with his right hand and his partner's left, left-hand lady walks under this arch as man's partner walks to other side, taking left-hand lady's place in line, and man now turns under his own right arm (4 counts). All are now facing up the set. Line of three return to place with four walking steps.

B1   **The ladies chain and don't return** (8 counts). Ladies chain to opposite side. Do not return.

     Circle four hands once around (8 counts). Circle left.

B2   **Same two couples right and left four** (16 counts). Over and back.

🦢 Pedal Pushers* 🦢

Pedal Pushers is a contemporary Contra, composed by Bob Dalsemer in September, 1989 to honor Jon and Sue Simmons of Greensboro, Maryland, as they departed on a 1500-mile bicycle trip—Seattle to San Diego.

Cassette: "Growling Old Man and the Grumbling Old Woman," Yankee Ingenuity, Kitchen Junket ALC 200A/BC or similar tune.

Music: "Growling Old Man and the Grumbling Old Woman," Brody, David, *The Fiddler's Fakebook,* p. 128.

Formation: Contra Dance formation. Couples 1, 3, 5, and so on, active, cross over (duple, improper).

■ Directions for the Dance

A1 **Two gents allemande left once and a half** (8 counts).

Pick up your partner and half promenade across to gent's original side (4 counts). Men still holding left hands pick up their partner, right arm around her waist and continue turning as in a star promenade till men are on original sides. Men release left hands.

Wheel around as a couple, gents backing up (4 counts).

A2 **Two ladies walk around each other passing by the right shoulder, return to partner** (8 counts). Ladies travel as in a gypsy, always facing each other.

Swing your own (8 counts).

B1 **With opposite two, balance in a ring** (4 counts). Join hands in ring of four, balance forward and back.

Pass thru across, all make a one-quarter turn individually to the right (4 counts).

In your group of four, promenade single file three-quarters around to progressed place. Gents turn back to face neighbor (8 counts). Travel clockwise.

B2 **Balance and swing your neighbor** (16 counts). Finish facing across, with men looking diagonally to the left ready to begin dance again.

Note

B1 "Gents turn back." For experienced dancers, call "Gents turn right" and eliminate the "Balance" in B2. It becomes a smoother dance as dancers move right into a 16-count swing.

---

*Pedal Pushers included by permission of Bob Dalsemer, Brasstown, NC.

🎵 Petronella

Petronella is a traditional Contra. It is an original dance introduced by Nathaniel Gow of Edinburgh, Scotland, in 1820. Gow's version danced a poussette; the American version a right and left thru.

Record: Traditionally danced to tune by same name. Folkraft 1139, F & W 3L.

Cassette: "Petronella," New England Chestnuts, Alcazar ALC 203/4.

Music: "Pat'nella," Page, Ralph, *An Elegant Collection of Contras and Squares,* p. 73.

Formation: Contra Dance formation. Couples 1, 3, 5, and so on, active, *do not* cross over (duple, proper).

■ Directions for the Dance

A1 **Actives balance** (4 counts). Beginning right, active couples balance in center of set.

Turn right a quarter (4 counts). Individually traveling on a right diagonal, turn clockwise three-fourths, taking four steps (right, left, right, left) to face partner. Men will face up the set, ladies down.

Actives balance (4 counts).

Turn right a quarter (4 counts). Repeat three-quarter turn, diagonally right. Dancer will be in partner's original position.

A2 **Actives balance** (4 counts).

Turn right a quarter (4 counts). Men will face down the set, ladies up.

Actives balance (4 counts).

Turn right a quarter (4 counts). Dancers will end in original positions.

B1 **Down the center, turn alone** (8 counts). Active couple walks down the center, each person turns alone, counts 7–8.

Back to place and cast off (8 counts). Active couple returns to original position, separate and walk around the one below and progresses down the set one position.

B2 **Right and left thru** (8 counts). Active couple and couple above right and left thru, two men passing right shoulders with opposite two ladies. No hands used in right and left thru. Two men and two ladies turn as a unit.

And right and left back (8 counts).

Note

For the above dance, the active couples have most of the action. It is best to limit the number of couples in a set.

Variation

A1, A2 In minor sets, join hands. Balance right; drop hands and individually turn clockwise, three-quarters (right, left, right, left) and travel one position to the right (8 counts). Join hands and repeat three times till in original position (24 counts).

🌀 Pierce's Hall Stroll*

Pierce's Hall Stroll is a comtemporary Contra. It is an original dance by Fred Breunig, composed for the Sesquicentennial (1982) of the community hall in East Putney, Vermont, where Fred calls a monthly dance.

Music: A march like "Scotland the Brave."

Formation: Contra Dance formation. Couples 1, 3, 5, and so on, active, cross over (duple, improper).

◼ Directions for the Dance

A1   **Ladies do-si-do** (8 counts).

   Gents do-si-do left shoulder once and a half (8 counts). Men will end on same side as partner.

A2   **All swing partners** (16 counts). After swinging, take escort position. Active couple on men's side face down the set, inactives on ladies' side face up the set.

B1   **"Stroll"** (8 counts). All couples promenade in the direction facing. Those approaching end of the set turn to follow behind other line. Dancers are promenading in a continuous ellipse, counterclockwise. Counts 5 – 8, couples wheel around to face opposite direction.

   And return (8 counts). All couples promenade in the reverse line of direction (clockwise) to original position.

B2   **Right hands across, turn once and a half** (8 counts). Each minor set forms a star with right hands joined as in shaking hands (not a "box star" position).

   Gents drop out to original side. Men will have progressed one position.

   Ladies continue to turn by the right into ladies chain halfway (8 counts). Ladies chain away from partner to opposite. Courtesy turn. Ladies will be on original side and have progressed one position.

Note

All couples are equally active in this dance. This dance illustrates the notion that the term **inactive** is a misnomer.

---

*Pierce's Hall Stroll included by permission of Fred Breunig, Putney, VT.

Pop Goes the Weasel

Pop Goes the Weasel is a traditional Contra.

Records: "Pop Goes the Weasel" or any Jig. DC 162303; EZ 3002/903; Folkraft 1007, 10014, 1329; Lloyd Shaw E-7, E-21; MAV Album 3; Windsor A75-3. Methodist World of Fun 104.

Cassette: DC 162303.

Music: Ford, Henry, *Good Morning,* 4th edition, p. 62.

Formation: Contra Dance formation. Couples 1, 3, 5, and so on, active, *do not* cross over (duple, proper).

■ Directions for the Dance

A1 **Active couples down the outside and back to place** (16 counts). Active couples, man turns left, lady right, walk down outside of set; counts 7–8, turn to face up the set. Return to place.

A2 **Down the center and back to place** (16 counts). Active couple join inside hands, walk down center of set; counts 7–8, release hands, turn individually to face up the set. Return to place and face down the set.

B1 **Circle right with the couple below** (8 counts).

To the left all the way around (8 counts).

B2 **Inactive couples make an arch.**

And pop active couple thru one place. (4 counts).

Everybody swing (12 counts). Active couple moves down the set one position when going thru arch.

Note

Sometimes the tune "Pop Goes the Weasel" seems juvenile. Try another Jig: The action is fun!

🌿 Rory O'More

Rory O'More is a traditional Contra. Samuel Lover, the grandfather of Victor Herbert, wrote the words and music of "Rory O'More."

Records: Traditionally danced to tune by same name.

Cassette: "Rory O'More," New England Chestnuts, ALC 203/4C.

Music: Cole, M. M., *One Thousand Fiddle Tunes*, p. 62.

Formation: Contra Dance formation. Couples 1, 3, 5, and so on, active, *do not* cross over (duple, proper.)

■ Directions for the Dance

A1 **Actives cross over and down the outside. Down below one** (8 counts). Actives pull by with right hands joined, crossing to opposite side; walk down the outside of line, go around one person, and cut into middle of set to meet partner, join inside hands.

Up the center, cross over. Cast off and actives join hands in the center (8 counts). Walk up the center, release hands, cross to own side, lady crossing in front of partner; cast off, walk around the couple originally below the active couple, to face center. Active couples have now progressed one position down. Active couples move to center of the set, partners join right hands, and join left hands with adjacent active couple. Three lines will exist, two on the outside (inactive dancers) and one in the middle (active couples).

A2 **Balance right and left and slide right** (8 counts). Actives balance right and left. Release hands, take three slides and a step to right, past partner. Join left hands with partner and right hands with neighbor.

Balance left and right and slide left (8 counts). Actives balance left and right. Release hands, take three slides and a step to left, past partner.

B1 **Turn Contra corners** (16 counts).

Actives balance and swing in center of set (16 counts). At end of swing, dancers back into position in line.

Sackett's Harbor is a traditional Contra.

Music: Any lively Contra music.

Formation: Contra Dance formation. Couples 1, 4, 7, and so on active, *do not* cross over (triple proper).

■ Directions for the Dance

A1   **Forward and back** (8 counts). Long lines, join hands, walk forward and back.

   Circle left six hands three-quarters around (8 counts). In minor sets of three couples, join hands and circle left three-quarters. Men will end facing up the set, ladies down.

A2   **Active couples go down the center, turn alone and return and cast off** (16 counts). The actives move through the 2 couples below for 6 counts; turn around (7–8) and return. Actives cast off (1s with 2s/4s with 5s) arm around. Actives have now moved down one position.

head ①¬ 1 ④¬ 4 foot   head ② 2 ⑤ 5 foot
      ② 2 ⑤ 5   ① 1 ④ 4
      ③ 3 ⑥ 6   ③ 3 ⑥ 6
      "Down the center"   "Cast off"

B1   **Turn contra corners** (16 counts). Active couples turn contra corners, ending in starting position. *Do not* touch partner after the "second contra corner," but return immediately to starting places.

B2   **Forward six and back** (8 counts). Join hands in each line, walk forward and back.

   Circle right six hands three-quarters around (8 counts). End circle so that men are in men's line, ladies in the ladies' line. Form new triple sets with actives dancing with the next 2 couples below them.

Sackett's Harbor (continued)

Notes

1. During A2 the dancers move down the center; called "down the center," actually they move "across the hall."
2. During the walk thru, it is important to identify the triple set of couples dancing together. The active couples move down one position each time the dance is repeated. The active couple remain the lead couple in the triple set until they reach the foot. The relative position of the inactives changes too. *At the foot the active continues to dance with an imaginary 3rd couple, (a ghost), until they are at the bottom, otherwise the last will never move up! At the head of the set, inactives wait two times to become active. See the fourth sequence.*

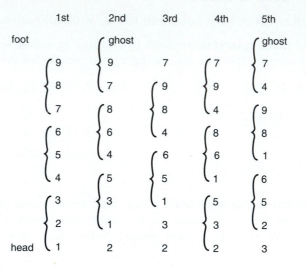

🐟 Salmonchanted Evening*

Salmonchanted Evening is a contemporary Contra, composed by Steve Zakon, March, 1987. Steve wrote the dance in honor of the band Fresh Fish, just before going on a three-week tour with them. Originally the dance was called "Not Tonight, I've Got a Haddock." Within a week it was renamed "Salmonchanted Evening"—a nonsense word, a delightful play on the words "some enchanted evening."

Music: Smooth tunes, well phrased, such as Jigs.

Formation: Contra Dance formation. Couples 1, 3, 5, and so on active, cross over (duple, improper).

■ Directions for the Dance

A1   **Allemande right below once and a half** (8 counts). Actives allemande right your neighbor once and a half. Actives end one position below.

     Men allemande left once and a half (8 counts). Men end on opposite sides, partner on right side.

A2   **All Gypsy partner on the side** (8 counts). Gypsy with partner by the right shoulder.

     All swing your partner (8 counts).

B1   **Chain the ladies over and back** (16 counts).

B2   **Half right and left** (8 counts). Right and left thru. *Do not return.*

     Circle left three-quarters round, pass thru (8 counts). Join hands and circle left three-quarters. Active couples will face down the set, inactive couples will face up the set to pass thru. Each couple will face a new couple to start the dance over.

---

*Salmonchanted Evening included by permission of Steve Zakon, East Sullivan, N. H.

🦢 Scout House Reel*

Scout House Reel is a contemporary Contra. It is an original dance by Ted Sannella, written in 1979. It is named in honor of the Scout House in Concord, Massachusetts, formerly the Concord Girl Scout House, a popular site for Boston-area Square Dances.

Record: Medley Reel including "Flowers of Edinburgh," Lloyd Shaw 308.

Cassette: "Reel de Montreal," Kitchen Junket ALC 200 A/BC.

Music: "Laura Susan Reel," Sannella, Ted, *Balance and Swing*, p. 109.

Formation: Contra Dance formation. Couples 1, 3, 5, and so on, active, cross over (duple, improper).

■ Directions for the Dance

A1 **Go down the center four in line, actives in the middle turn alone** (8 counts). Actives move to the center, join hands with adjacent couple below. Walk down the center, counts 7–8, each turn alone to face up the set.

And return, ends close in (8 counts). Counts 7–8, ends of line turn in, to form a circle.

A2 **Circle left once around** (8 counts). Circle left.

Ladies chain (8 counts). Ladies chain over. Do not chain back.

B1 **Ladies do-si-do once and a half** (8 counts). Ladies end on original side.

Swing the opposite man below (8 counts). Ladies swing opposite man. End with lady on right side of man, couple facing center. Actives have progressed one position down.

B2 **Long lines go forward and back** (8 counts). Join hands in the lines, walk four steps forward and four steps backward.

Active couple swing, face down the set (8 counts). Active couples end facing down the set, ready to join hands with next couple below in a line of four. Start dance from the beginning.

---

*Scout House Reel included by permission of Ted Sannella, Wiscasset, ME.

Settlement Swing*

Settlement Swing is a contemporary Contra. It is an original dance by Penn Fix. Settlement Swing is named after the Old Settlement Road School House in Priest River, Idaho, where monthly dances were held.

Music: A lively Reel.

Formation: Contra Dance formation. Couples 1, 3, 5, and so on, active, cross over (duple, improper).

■ Directions for the Dance

A1   **Do-si-do the one below** (8 counts).

Gents face out and ladies face in, join hands along the lines. After the do-si-do, all turn individually one-quarter to the left to form a long line. All men are facing out, ladies are facing in. Join hands along the lines.

Balance right and left (4 counts).

Turn by the right once all the way around (4 counts). Active persons allemande right the one below (right-hand person).

A2   **Turn by the left once all the way around** (4 counts). Active persons allemande left the one above (left-hand person).

Swing your neighbor (12 counts). Neighbor is the original "one below," the same person you allemande right. End with lady on man's right.

B1   **Ladies chain** (16 counts). Ladies chain over and back.

B2   **Actives balance and swing** (16 counts). End swing facing down the set ready to "do-si-do the one below."

*Settlement Swing included by permission of Penn Fix, Spokane, WA.

Shadrack's Delight*

Shadrack's Delight is a contemporary Contra. It is an original dance by Tony Parkes. The dance was named for Betty and "Shadrack" McDermid.

Records: Well-phrased Jig. "Lamb Skinnet," Folkraft 1501; Lloyd Shaw 193/194 (flip).

Music: Scottish Jig suggested.

Formation: Contra Dance formation. Couples 1, 3, 5, and so on, active, cross over (duple, improper).

■ Directions for the Dance

A1 **Do-si-do the one below, go one and a quarter** (8 counts). End in a line of four across the set, actives face down the set, inactives face up the set.

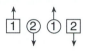

Balance four in line (4 counts). Begin balance on right foot. Look at the person in the direction of the balance.

Turn half by the right (4 counts). Turn neighbor by the right half-way. Actives end facing up the set, inactives facing down the set. Join hands in line of four.

A2 **Balance four in line** (4 counts).

Gents turn half by the left (4 counts).

All swing your own (8 counts). End with lady on right side of man, line of four, facing down the set, hands joined. Active couple will be in the men's line, inactive in the ladies' line.

B1 **Down the set go four in a line, turn as a couple** (8 counts). Turn as a couple, counts 5–8.

Return to place, cast off (8 counts). Cast off counts 5–8; each couple, arm around waist, take four steps, turning out to face center.

Right and left thru across (8 counts). Active men will have progressed one position down.

Same two ladies chain (8 counts). Ladies progress one position down, progression complete.

Note

Sometimes danced without the cast off for a smoother transition in the lady's line.

---

*Shadrack's Delight included by permission of Tony Parkes, Arlington, MA.

Spring Fever*

Spring Fever is a contemporary Contra, composed by Tony Parkes.

Music: Any lively Contra music.

Formation: Contra Dance formation. Couples 1, 3, 5, and so on, active, cross over (duple, improper).

■ Directions for the Dance

A1 **All go forward and back** (8 counts). Long lines join hands, walk forward and back.

    Swing your neighbor (8 counts). Actives swing the one below.

A2 **Men allemande left once and a half** (8 counts). In the center, men allemande left once and a half, ending on the opposite side.

    Swing partner (8 counts). And face across the set.

B1 **Join hands and circle left** (8 counts).

    Left hand star (8 counts).

B2 **Half promenade** (8 counts). With your partner promenade across the set and face the opposite side.

    Ladies chain (8 counts). The active couple will be ready to dance with a new couple after the forward and back.

*Spring Fever included by permission of Tony Parkes, Arlington, MA.

✺ Tamarack Reel*

Tamarack Reel is a contemporary Contra, composed by Penn Fix in 1983. Tamarack is the name of a deciduous conifer in eastern Washington and Idaho. This dance is dedicated to Dean Kenty, who died in a climbing accident. Dean played in a Portland, Oregon, band called Tamarack.

Music: Any preferred traditional Reel.

Formation: Contra Dance Formation. Couples 1, 3, 5, and so on, active, cross over (duple, improper).

■ Directions for the Dance

A1   **Down the center four-in-line, turn alone, and return** (16 counts). Actives move into the center, join hands with couple below. Walk down the center, counts 7–8, each turn alone to face up the set. Join hands in line of four, walk up the set, returning to place. Counts 15–16, ends of line turn in, to form a circle.

A2   **Circle left** (8 counts).

Actives half figure eight above (8 counts). Actives cross to opposite side (lady crossing in front of partner), moving up and around inactive above, on the outside and coming into line one position below. Actives can make a wider arc around the inactives using all 8 counts.

A   B
Half figure eight   Ending position

B1   **Actives turn contra corners** (16 counts).

B2   **Actives balance and swing your partner** (16 counts). Actives finish swing facing down the set, lady on partner's right, ready to dance with the next inactive couple.

---

*Tamarack Reel included by permission of Penn Fix, Spokane, WA.

∾ The Tourist*

The Tourist is a contemporary Contra. It is an original dance by Ted Sannella. This version was arranged by Ralph Page.

Record: "Frenchie's Reel," Fourgone Conclusions, Front Hall FHR 029.

Music: "Lamplighter's Hornpipe," Cole, M. M., *One Thousand Fiddle Tunes.*

Formation: Contra Dance formation. Couples 1, 3, 5, and so on, active, cross over (duple, improper).

■ Directions for the Dance

A1 **Down the outside of the set, turn** (8 counts). Active couples (1, 3, 5, and so on) turn out and walk down outside of set, behind their own respective lines, eight steps. Counts 7 – 8, each turns toward center of set.

Come right back (8 counts).

A2 **Into the center with a do-si-do** (8 counts). Active couples step to middle of set and do-si-do.

Circle four hands once around (8 counts). Opposite couples join hands, circle left once around.

B1 **Balance and swing the one below** (16 counts).

B2 **Opposite ladies chain over and back** (16 counts).

---

*The Tourist included by permission of Ted Sannella, Wicasset, ME.

🌿 With Thanks to the Dean* 🌾

With Thanks to the Dean is a contemporary dance composed by Steve Zakon. This dance salutes the dean of Contra Dancing, Ralph Page. Steve wrote the dance in Ralph's memory to thank him for his efforts to keep Contra Dancing alive and vital for generations to follow.

Music: Smooth flowing tunes, usually Reels.

Formation: Contra Dance formation. Couples 1, 3, 5, and so on, active, cross over (duple, improper, and double progression).

■ Directions for the Dance

A1 **Allemande left below, go once and a half** (8 counts). Actives, allemande left the one below, turn once and a half.

   Ladies chain (8 counts). *Do not* chain back.

A2 **Ladies allemande right** (8 counts). With right hand, ladies turn once around.

   Swing your partner (8 counts). Everyone swings partner. Men are on original side.

B1 **Circle left, move once around along the sides** (8 counts). Join hands and circle left once. All couples slide to the left (along the line), picking up the next couple (first progression). Men take responsibility to slide left with your partner.

   Circle left with the next three-quarters round (8 counts).

circle left   three quarters round

B2 **Do-si-do your new neighbor** (8 counts).

   Allemande right the same once and a half (8 counts). The active couple progresses one position down at the end of the allemande (second progression).

   The left hand is free to start the dance over with "Allemande left."

head   foot

---

*With Thanks to the Dean included by permission of Steve Zakon, East Sullivan, N. H.

CHAPTER 7

International Folk Dance

Introduction

Throughout human history nothing has approached the significance of dance. Indeed, it has been the basis for the survival of social systems in every decade. The story of people and their culture from ritual to art is the history of *Folk Dance*. In the transition from rite to art, it has been the social and pleasurable qualities of Folk Dance that have survived above all the rest. In each dance, however, we still can find a storehouse of traditions that were an intimate part of the culture of the people from whom the dance is derived. Although cultural traces become dim with time, there is more to a folk song than its tune and more to a dance than its movement. In these ongoing traditional expressions are recorded the early and ever-growing and -changing social lives of a people. These folk traditions are living history.

The impact of the modern industrial revolution in both Europe and America threatened to blot out the natural flow of folk expression. The threatened disappearance of folkways, songs, music, costumes, and dances spurred governments, private individuals, and organizations into concerted efforts to preserve these traditions. Organized efforts to revive interest in folk traditions began at different times in different countries, but in each the main thrust was to collect, note, and preserve in national repositories the finest examples of folk song, dance, music, costume, and art, as possible.

Folk Dance Movement

In Sweden, Arthur Hazelius created the Nordiskz Museet, or Northland Museum, to house rare folk dances and folk art. In 1893, the Friends of Swedish Folk Dance was formed. This and other organizations have worked to make this phase of Swedish culture known to every generation. The revival movement led to formation of the Danish Folk Dance Society in 1901. In 1911, Cecil Sharp, an English writer and musician, helped found the English Folk Dance Society. Branches of this society have been established throughout the British Commonwealth and America.

A series of events prior to the outbreak of World War II marked the revival of the Folk Dance movement in Europe. In 1928, the International Congress of Popular Arts was held in Prague. The Congress, called together by the Assembly of the League of Nations, was attended by 31 nations. The purpose was to study the geographical distribution of the different artistic forms of folk life and to compile records and devise methods for encouraging and preserving the popular arts still in existence. In 1935, the English Folk Dance Society and the British national Committee on Folk Arts sponsored an International Folk Dance Festival in London. In 1939, a second Congress was held in Stockholm, Sweden. Some 3,000 delegates and officials attended. The program provided opportunity for presentation of papers and discussions as well as for dance demonstrations by the various national groups in attendance.

International Folk Dancing is America's other dance enthusiasm. While millions of Americans Square Dance, thousands of Americans of no particular ethnic heritage spend their prime leisure time dancing a variety of dances from many nationalities and cultural groups. The Folk Dance movement in America is spread like a patchwork quilt from coast to coast. Clubs are the backbone of the movement. Some regional organizations and a few state federations exist. In contrast to the highly organized and standardized American Square Dance movement, the international Folk Dance movement is best described as diverse, autonomous, and fragmented. However unorganized it is at the regional and national level, the movement is bound together by the most universal adhesive known—the desire among participants to share their love of dancing dances from around the world.

The largest concentration of Folk Dance groups is found in major urban areas, such as New York City, Chicago, Detroit, San Francisco, and Los Angeles, where there is a greater mix of ethnic groups. Folk Dance groups are typically sponsored and housed by institutions whose aims include fostering of international understanding. Since learning about other cultures' customs and ways is an outcome of Folk Dance, it is a natural and appropriate activity for such sponsorship. College and university campuses, YMCAs, YWCAs, settlement houses, and churches are, therefore, popular locations for Folk Dance groups.

A major boost to international Folk Dance was felt in 1940 when the New York World's Fair and the San Francisco World's Fair introduced Folk Dance as an attraction for public participation. The enthusiastic response by the general public led to the formation of two major centers for the lay-folk dance movement: the Folk Dance House founded by Michael and Mary Ann Herman in New York City and Chang's International Dancers formed by Soon Chang in San Francisco. These East-West urban strongholds of international dancing have produced thousands of folk dancers who have, in turn, spread the fun and enjoyment of Folk Dance throughout America.

The ever-expanding repertoire of the community Folk Dance club stimulated and broadened the curriculum content found in the public schools and colleges. The movement's growth sparked the production of records for Folk Dancing by folk dancers. A wide variety of records resulted, and music was often recorded in native settings, thus increasing the new materials and the variety of sources available for community and educational programs. The Folk Dancer series by Michael Herman and others such as Kismet, Imperial, and Folkraft freed public schools, particularly, from the need for live musical accompaniment or reliance upon outdated recordings for music for Folk Dance.

America's thirst for performing dances from other countries is attested to by the unprecedented rate at which Americans have been learning dances since World War II. Mary Ann Herman of New York City's Folk Dance House says, "It is often difficult for foreigners to believe in the scope of American interest in folk dance. There may be more traditional folk dancing of other countries being done in the United States today than in the countries of their origin." Fortunately, America has historically been a rich depository of folk traditions by virtue of its cultural mix of immigrants from other countries. Although these traditions and customs were largely limited to the various ethnic groups who danced and performed them only on special occasions, over the years these groups have learned to share their heritage with all other Americans. This has been a rich source of dance material in America for Americans.

Dance Sources

Educators and educational institutions have played a role in research, teaching, and fostering the use of Folk Dance in schools and recreation programs. In the early 1920s, physical educators, recognizing the value of dance in human neuromuscular development, drew from Folk Dance for the content of gymnastic dance routines. Movement from Irish Jigs, Italian Tarantellas, and American Virginia Reel were incorporated into these dance sequences. Paralleling the use of Folk Dance in gymnastics, Folk Dance was also developing as a separate subject in physical education classes and the early playground movement. Elizabeth Burchenal and C. Ward Crampton were two early researchers and collectors of traditional Folk Dances as they were being performed in European countries. By the beginning of the 20th century, Folk Dance was widely used in physical education in secondary schools and colleges.

Elizabeth Burchenal's research and collection of dance materials from original European sources brought a wealth of Folk Dance materials to schools and recreation programs in the early 1900s. As chairman of the Folk Dance committee of the Playground and Recreation Association of America, she was instrumental in introducing Folk Dance to a wide audience as well as training many teachers over several decades. Burchenal became the first president of the American Folk Dance Society, which was formed in 1916.

Mary Wood Hinman, a physical educator of exceptional vision, worked to provide an appropriate and meaningful way for ethnic groups to perform and share their cultural heritage with other Americans. Her work resulted in a series of Folk Dance courses being offered at the New School of Social Research in New York City in 1933. The courses were designed to provide an opportunity for various ethnic groups to teach their native songs and dances to people of all backgrounds. With the same philosophy in mind, Hinman was instrumental in establishing Folk Festival Councils in other American cities.

A third source of Folk Dance materials for the thirsty American folk dancer is the touring, taping teachers. Guided tours to European dance festivals with authoritative leaders give the tour group an opportunity to see the real thing. Dance enthusiasts make full use of new innovations in sound technology for recording authentic music and filming dance as they travel from festival to festival. Participant interest in new dances increases as they tire quickly of old ones. This spurs the traveling researchers to comb the European countryside for more and more dances. The continued demand for new dances has been somewhat answered by more specialization in a single type of dance or a single nationality. These dance groups along with international groups give the added dimension of choice.

Dance Programs

Folk Dance programs and class content vary widely depending on the leader's repertoire and enthusiasm, and the participants' interest. Groups may specialize in the dances of a single nationality, such as Scottish dances. Some groups and classes specialize in dances representative of a geographical area, such as Scandinavia or the Balkans. Where participant interest is more social and recreational, groups tend to offer a wide variety of dances. Since World War II, Americans have been learning new dances at an unprecedented rate. It is not unlikely that in one evening session Folk Dancers will do 30–40 dances just for fun!

International Folk Dance groups, unlike Square Dance groups, typically include Square, Contra, and Round Dances in their programs. Folk Dancers must have a wider range of dance skills; therefore, participation is more selective, influencing club group and class size. Leaders and teachers for clubs and classes are predominantly volunteer enthusiasts. Group finance, including the cost of a guest teacher or nationally known leader, are, even at present, the result of club dues, dance admissions, and special fund-raising efforts. Although there are many outstanding full-time professional teachers, their number pales in comparison to those in the Square Dance movement.

Camps

The *Folk Dance camp* concept became a popular vehicle for dancers and leaders alike to enjoy a total folk experience by learning about other cultures through dance, crafts, songs, games, costumes, and ethnic foods. They even have a chance to celebrate a Swedish Christmas in July! Jane Farwell established the first such camp at Oglebay Institute in West Virginia in the early 1940s. Jane Farwell is easily the "Johnny Appleseed" of Folk Dance camps since she has organized and conducted successful camps from Florida to Maine. The idea spread, and in the late 1940s and early 1950s camps influenced by her idea or led by her enthusiasm were in operation across America.

Today the Folk Dance camp is the prime vacation choice for thousands of folk dancing Americans. Camps attract the top teaching professionals who represent specific ethnic groups. Camp programs include complete syllabi of material taught, adventures in gourmet foods from many nationalities, special classes in folk singing, expert guidance in making costumes, and more often than not all of this *and* college credits! Folk Dance camps have come a long way since Jane Farwell and her campers "washed their faces in the May morning dew midst the fairy rings on a West Virginia hillside."

Performing Groups

International Folk Dance performing groups are predominantly associated with, sponsored by, or came into existence on an American college or university campus. These highly skilled and brilliantly costumed groups give concerts and conduct classes and workshops in the communities in which they perform. Performing groups acquire extensive costume collections, acquire musical instruments unique to the nationalities they represent, and develop musicians for orchestral accompaniment. Members of the group actively participate in the research into the background of the dances and nationalities they represent. Groups travel extensively at home and abroad and are often invited to perform at important national festivals. Groups may perform in 100 or more concerts during the academic year.

Some groups specialize in dances of one ethnic group, and others represent a variety of cultures as well as the dances of the United States. Performance demands have made it necessary for many groups to develop a full-time professional staff to take care of their rehearsal and performance needs. Groups are financially supported by concert and workshop admissions, gifts, grants, and their affiliated college or university. Several of the more outstanding groups have made the step to a full professional dance troupe.

These attractive and polished young college students often tour as ambassadors and official representatives of the United States State Department. Many groups offer aspiring high school dancers a unique opportunity to combine education with travel through full college scholarships. And, not unlike professional athletics, some performing groups are in the process of developing a "farm system" to train future dance performers.

Trends

Trends over the past 40 years reflect a continued enthusiasm for international Folk Dance. The social and recreational aspects of Folk Dancing are still paramount over teaching and learning within the strict framework of authenticity. Dance groups show an avid interest in nonpartner circle and line dances. Balkan and Israeli dances have become widely popular. Groups who love Kolos are tagged as having "kolomania"! Women find the freedom of modern times in the nonpartner dances; no longer must they wait to be asked to dance.

The "generalist"-type teacher has given way to the "specialist." Teachers specialize in line dances or dances of a single nationality. The number of male Folk Dance teachers has had an impact on the role of men in dance in general. Teachers, leaders, and participants are becoming more tolerant of the variations found in a dance. There is a greater tendency to see variations and differences in dances as a result of "natural processes" in the culture from which the dance comes and in its application and use by Folk Dance groups.

College and university Folk Dance performing groups are of near to actual professional caliber. They are extremely popular with audiences and widely admired as representatives of the Folk Dance movement.

Future

Interest in national cultural heritage has continued and accelerated in the 20th century. Efforts to preserve the knowledge and practices of the past have provided a wealth of information and artifacts from which dancers and dance scholars alike can draw for greater appreciation and understanding of dance's role in the cultural life of nations.

Each of the dances included in this chapter contains bits and pieces of the culture from which it comes. The story behind the dance reflects the history, geography, climate, religion, lifestyle, and dance characteristics of the national group from which it is derived. Knowing the background and influence of these components of a dance gives depth and added dimension to teaching and performing. Learning Folk Dance, therefore, carries with it a greater responsibility than merely teaching or performing a physical skill. It is an opportunity to develop appreciation for the customs and traditions of other cultures; to discover that the language of Folk Dancing can be a common bond between people of all nations; and, last, to learn that differences can become exciting adventures in discovering real similarities.

Understanding Folkways Enhances Dance

Eastern and Western Culture

Cultural influences in the form of borrowing and exchanging occur wherever two or more cultures meet along political or geographical boundaries. The Balkans are a historic example of an area that has for centuries been the meeting place for both Eastern and Western culture. Of the many ethnic groups passing in and out, the major cultural influences came from the Slavs, who dominated from about the 6th century A.D. to the Middle Ages; the Romans, both pagan and Christian; and the Ottoman Turks, whose influence lasted into the 19th century.

The Balkans are an ethnic mixture made up of four cultural groups: Greeks, Slavs, Daco-Romans, and Albanians. Linguistically they are represented by seven groups: Romans, Slovenians, Serbo-Croatians, Macedonians, Greeks, Albanians, and Bulgarians.

The long period of domination meant isolation from cultural movements going on in western Europe, and it caused the Balkan people to turn to their native folklore for identity and inspiration. Cultural isolation worked to enrich their cultural heritage and served to make the Balkans an extensive storehouse of folk materials.

Geography and Climate

Worldwide, people have found homes in the desert, steppes, plains, river valleys, and mountains. Each of these settings influence lifestyle in its own unique manner. People who live in mountain terrains tend to be more isolated and less mobile, and they learn to make use of small spaces. It is under these conditions that traditions, folkways, and material cultures are most likely to be found intact and better preserved. The people of the southern Appalachian mountains in the southeastern United States are an example. In contrast, people living in fertile plains, river valleys, or broad plains are more accessible and mobile. These groups, by virtue of their environmental setting, are more exposed to cultural exchange. The dance of mountain people, therefore, should reflect an economical use of space and a uniformity in execution due to lack of cultural borrowing or exchanging. The dance of people living in more accessible settings should reflect a potpourri in style, steps, and lack of uniformity.

Climate is regarded as being a major influence on the quality of dance movement. Although it is a factor, it should not be regarded as an inflexible influence because climatic zones do not adhere to rigid lines of demarcation. Generally, dance movements of people living in a warm climate are fluid, flowing, and slow. They contain few strong, abrupt, or energetic motions. In extremely cold climates, dance movements are perceived to be strong, vigorous, and energetic, with sustained action. They often include acrobatic movements and contrary body actions. In temperate climates, where there is a more gradual change in seasons and temperatures, dance movement is more balanced between vigorous and quiet sustained actions. The climate tends to prune out extraneous movements.

Religion

Dance in the form of pagan rituals was primitive people's means of supplicating the gods. These rituals were performed to communicate with the unseen forces that were perceived to sustain and regulate human survival. With the advent of Christianity, pagan rituals lost their magical content but remained in form and structure to become the earliest known forms of Folk Dance. The Morris, Sword, and Maypole dances are examples.

Historically, dance has been an integral part of Christianity and Christian ritual. The "Hymn of Jesus" described in the apocryphal Acts of John, A.D. 120, was a sacred dance in which the Apostles joined hands and circled slowly around Christ, singing a hymn. The mystical circle symbolized the protection of the Church from the outer world. In the early 12th century, Rabbi Hacin ben Salomo taught Christians to perform a choral dance around the altar in St. Bartholomew at Qauste in the Spanish province of Zaragoza. Ecclesiastical dancing survived in France as late as the 17th century.

The Protestant movement generally frowned on dance, albeit ambivalently. In New England during the Revolutionary years, everybody danced, including the minister, who found his niche in the community via the Ordination Ball. Although the fiddle was said to be the Devil's instrument, dance was credited with developing manners and discipline in the young.

Music

Rhythm is important in Folk Dance music. Rhythm is the musical beat that drives dance movement. It is organized and structured sounds. Rhythm is the musical sound that catches the essential style and quality of movement in a Folk Dance. Authentic music and rhythm are important in keeping the ethnic flavor and spirit of a Folk Dance from being lost.

There are cultural variations in rhythm structure. Western culture is accustomed to 2/4, 3/4, and 6/8 meter with groupings of four, eight, and sixteen bars or measures. In Eastern culture, the Western-type meters are rare, except for 2/4. Irregular rhythms dominate, with 5/16, 7/8, and 11/16 being common. Musical phrases and dance phrases do not always coincide with groupings of three, five, and so forth, bars or measures.

The first musical instrument was the human voice; therefore no culture has been without music or some type of musical instrument. Musical instruments played a major role in the spiritual life and rituals of primitive societies.

The drum—a dried animal skin stretched over a hollow log and beaten to produce sounds—is often believed to be the oldest instrument. Some believe wind instruments—a simple reed blown on to produce a tone—to be first. Still others point to the hunter's bow, which produced a "twanging" sound when the arrow was released. In Africa, the drum was used for dance ritual and communication and was so important that it was referred to as "the pulse of life." The oldest music in America is that of American Indians. Their musical instruments—drums, rattles, bells, and rasps—are nearly as old as human society.

Much of what is known about music in ancient times has been passed along by story and legend. Hard evidence depicting musical instruments, however, has come from surviving pottery, sculpture, tomb paintings, and cave carvings. The Egyptians had great orchestras of flutes and string instruments. Thousands of years ago, the Chinese had royal orchestras of drums, bells, and gongs. In the Old Testament, Jericho was blown down by the sound of seven shofars.

European instruments have counterparts in simple form in Africa and in more elaborate form in Eastern countries. Instruments used for folk music and dance are largely those native to or invented by a particular national or ethnic group. The accordion, for example, was invented in Berlin in the 1820s by Friedrick Buschmann and has been a staple of German folk music and dance. In Sweden, the fiddle is the favorite instrument, although old-time dances are done largely to accordion music. Philippine dance instruments reflect a diverse cultural background. Native rhythm instruments, sticks, bamboo poles, and coconut shells are used along with castanets and Spanish guitars. The study of musical instruments is fascinating, and it is significant in keeping the total background and spirit of folk dancing in perspective.

Costumes

Costumes have an interesting and unique effect on the characteristic dance movements of the dancer. The style and range of movement is freed or restricted by the material and cut of the skirt, coat, or trousers. Headdress and footwear also have an interesting effect on qualities of movement. The effect costumes have on dance movement is an important element in studying the style and background of the dance.

Historically, costumes or clothing has served to protect from the elements, accommodate an occupational use, distinguish or give status, and represent a national or ethnological group. The Folk

Dance costume is worn by national or ethnic groups and by members of international Folk Dance groups all over the United States. Costumes add an exciting and dramatic dimension to Folk Dancing.

Holidays, Festivals, and Special Occasions

Dancing is a social event and, as such, is an integral part of the calendar of events in all cultures. Sundays and holidays are common times when work ceases and families and friends can get together for fun and fellowship, with music and dancing as a special way to express the joy of the occasion. Weddings are times for the traditions and customs of a group to be shared, when all are made merrier by music and dance befitting the occasion.

Friends, neighbors, relatives, and often whole communities gather for cooperative work in the form of barn raisings, corn shuckings, or quilting bees. These occasions feature tables laden with "potluck" food and all the trimmings topped off with music and dancing until the wee hours of the morning.

Religious holidays are times of food, fiesta, and dancing. Celebrations may be in honor of a favorite saint and, as such, include mass, a festive parade, and music and dancing in the streets. In nonreligious groups, tribal or group tradition and custom may call for celebration by sacrificial offering to ancestral spirits and performance of ritual dancing.

Seasons are worldwide times of celebration. Christmas, harvest time, and midsummer are major times to roll out costumes, customs, decorations, food, and dance. Christmas is a time for elegant balls, caroling, and dancing around the Christmas tree. Harvest time, where older traditions still hold, is a community and family time to share work and play together. These are times when special traditions and customs are renewed.

Scandinavia*

Introduction

The native name for the part of Europe we call Scandinavia is *Norden,* literally meaning the North. It encompasses five nations: Denmark, Finland, Iceland, Norway, and Sweden; six cultures: Danish, Faroese, Finnish, Icelandic, Norwegian, and Swed-

---

*This section was written by the late Gordon E. Tracie, founder and director of Skandia Folkdance Society, Seattle, Washington and folklore consultant for the Smithsonian Institution, Washington, D.C.

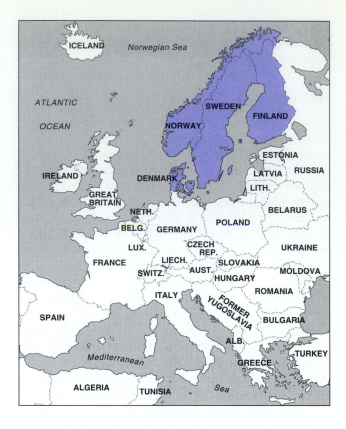

ish; seven flags: Denmark, the Faroe Islands, Finland, Iceland, Norway, Sweden and the Aland Islands; and eight languages: Danish, Dano-Norwegian, Faroese, Finnish, Icelandic, Lappish, Neo-Norwegian, and Swedish. It is therefore not surprising that there is a wide diversity of cultures among the Scandinavians.

Geography, climate, history, lifestyle, and religion all have played a role in the development and acceptance of dance in a given culture. The flat islands of Denmark, the spectacular fjords and mountains of Norway, the rich farmlands and deep woods of Sweden, and the lakes and forests of Finland—each has had an influence on the native music and hence on the traditional dance of the Nordic lands. Of equal if not greater importance is Scandinavia's proximity to other European countries. Germany and the British Isles seem to have been the ultimate source of much material, but Poland and France have also made significant contributions, as has been the case throughout Europe. The cold northern climate has dictated a need for heavy clothes, primarily wool, and for substantial shoes, both of which are reflected in Scandinavian folk costumes.

The pietistic movement of past generations had a devastating effect on dance and dance music in many parts of Scandinavia. Fortunately there were enough "folklore pockets," where musical traditions survived, to be able to pass on a remarkable heritage of true Folk Dances. Today, virtually all dancing in the Northlands is recreational in nature, rather than consciously ceremonial or ritualistic, although remnants of ancient seasonal rites do remain in the Midsummer and Yuletide serpentine dances and in the courting aspects of singing games. In contrast to the Folk Dances in many parts of the world, traditional Scandinavian dancing is almost exclusively coeducational in nature. With but a few exceptions, one always has a partner of the opposite gender with whom to dance. This is true in rings and other formations as well as in couple dances.

Perhaps the single most characteristic feature of Scandinavia's folklore-oriented dances is the predominance of couple rotation. Because this turning is usually relatively fast, factors not present in other types of dancing come into play. The focus is no longer on one or more independent persons, but on a single couple; hence counterbalance and momentum play a vital role. Furthermore, the need for a strong male lead is essential, for it is the man who must "start the wheel turning" and "steer."

It should go without saying that the single most important element in attaining authentic folk spirit in a dance is correct music. Lacking that, a Folk Dance is but a shell without a soul. Proper inspiration and motivation in a given dance can be assured only when the music approximates that with which the dance "grew up." From time immemorial, the dance music of Norway and Sweden has been played on bowed string instruments, usually without the aid of any percussion other than a tapping foot. Predecessors to the violin such as the bowed harp are named in Old Norse literature as far back as the 1300s, and many playing techniques used for instruments predating the violin are still extant in today's Norwegian and Swedish folk fiddling. Open strings characteristically serve as drones, a practice that generates legato rather than a staccato "drive" to the music. In Dalarna, Sweden's folklore district, fiddlers speak of "glued bowing," in which the bow seldom leaves the strings. Norway's Hardanger fiddle and Sweden's keyed fiddle "nyckelharpa" go a step further: Like the viola d'amore, they employ a set of unbowed understrings that vibrate in sympathetic resonance with the bowed strings, thus enhancing the instrument's sonority. All of this contributes to a sustaining legato quality in the music, which is in turn imparted to the dance itself.

The "town orchestra" tradition in Denmark—akin to that in many other parts of Europe—and the predominance of the accordion—an association with Imperial Russia in Finnish tradition—have on the other hand produced a musical style considerably different from that of their Nordic neighbors. Inasmuch as dance naturally reflects music, the variance in dancing style between the Scandinavian countries can be illustrated by a continuum, as follows:

> Legato, loose, "springy" (NORWEGIAN) to
> Legato, more precise, lilting (SWEDISH) to
> Quite precise, smooth (DANISH) to
> Staccato, very precise, "crisp" (FINNISH)

The above differences are readily evident in the various Schottische forms:

Norwegian "Reinlander"—Swedish "Schottis"—Danish "Rheinlaender"—Finnish "Jenkka"

and corresponding Polka forms:

Norwegian "Polka," "Galopp"—Swedish "Polka"—Danish "Polka"—Finnish "Polkka"

The two most important holidays in Scandinavia are Christmas (Danish, Norwegian, Swedish: "Julen"; Finnish: "Joul") and Midsummer (Danish, Norwegian: "Sankt Hans"; "Jonsok"; Swedish: "Midsommar"; Finnish: "Juhannus"). These are occasions to break out one's traditional folk dress if one is a fiddler, dancer, or participant in a procession, and the time to witness and participate in the most Folk Dancing, short of a specific folk music or dance festival.

Denmark

Dance Characteristics

Through all Danish Folk Dance shines a distinctly light-hearted, often whimsical quality that is consistent with the convivial Danish temperament. Not infrequently, an element of satire pervades, for the Dane is blessed with a great sense of humor.

The bulk of Danish Folk Dances bear a close kinship to the dances of the British Isles, with which Denmark has had both cultural and economic ties for centuries. Quadrilles, Longways sets, and dances for two or three couples abound. The melodies often sound a lot like English or Scottish dance turns, and they are obviously cognates. Denmark is the only one of the Nordic lands that has the rollicking Anglo-Celtic 6/8 rhythm, for example, and it has it in abundance. Danish Folk Dance instructions are organized geographically, the material having been meticulously collected from all parts of the land since around the turn of the century. A distinction is made between "folkedanse," Folk Dances, and "gamle danse," old-time dances. The latter (which include the 19th-century Ballroom Dances, Waltz, Polka, and Mazurka) are not accorded the same reverence as the former. But the Folk Dances exist in Denmark today only through the efforts of organized Folk Dance societies, which limit their origin to the century between 1750 and 1850. Like Danish folk costumes, they are no longer a true living tradition.

During the past several years, there has been an effort, which has met with considerable success among young people's groups, to rekindle an interest in old-time dancing and its music, but in a modern setting (i.e., without "folk" costumes). The traditional Folk Dance ensemble of two violins, clarinet, and bass viol, still the norm for the formal Folk Dance movement, has been augmented by accordions, guitars, mandolins, and even bass saxophones. Needless to say, there is precious little cooperation between the advocates of these two approaches and what we in America lump together as Folk Dance.

Norway

Dance Characteristics

A folklorist's delight, Norway is without a doubt the most remarkable of the Scandinavian nations when it comes to the retention of native dance forms. In the remote valleys of this rugged land of fjords and mountains are to be found some of the oldest surviving dances in western Europe. Regional dances, "bygdedansar," such as the *Gangar, Springar, Halling,* and *Pols,* actively learned and danced today, have an unbroken tradition dating back to the 16th century. The formal Folk Dance movement recognizes two other forms: song-dance and figure dances. Song-dance, "songdans," a lyrical dance-song predominant during the Middle Ages, which died out in Norway centuries ago but survived in the Faroe Islands. The form was reintroduced to Norwegian Folk Dancers around 1900 as an adjunct to the promotion of "Nynorsk," the Old Norse-based second language of the land. Figure-dances, "turdansar," consist of Reels, Contras, and Sequence Dances from the 19th century, many of ultimate foreign origin.

Because the Norwegians more than any other Scandinavians have retained the qualities of spontaneity and improvisation in their dancing, the Folk Dances of Norway are the most difficult for foreigners to emulate.

Finland

Dance Characteristics

The folk music and dance of Suomi/Finland reflects two distinct historical influences: the original Finno-Ugric linguistic heritage and the Scandinavian culture of Russia to the east. Finland is bilingual, with just under 10 percent of the population speaking Swedish. Hence there are two distinct Folk Dance movements, the pure Finnish and the Finland-Swedish, each with its own traditions.

The pure Finnish idiom is quite unlike that of the rest of Scandinavia. A different minor mode gives many Finnish tunes a seemingly melancholy quality. Yet the dance is very often brisk in character, which is, of course, reflected in the dancing. The Finns display a great deal of verve and "snap" in their dancing, giving many Folk Dances an element of "fire." Steps are small and danced with a fast, even bounce. Frequently an abrupt change of tempo or rhythm occurs, making for added variety and interest.

Sweden

Dance Characteristics

"The Swedish forest," wrote a 19th-century naturalist, "sings in three-quarter time." A romantic but apt description, because the bulk of Sweden's native melodies are in triple meter, mostly "polska," a rhythmic form older than and unrelated to the Waltz and not to be confused with the relatively modern Polka. Long the national dance of Sweden, the "Polska" has survived from the late 1500s right into the 20th century, its most widely known form being the Hambo. Because the bowed strings of the fiddle have traditionally provided the music for Sweden's native dances, the interpretation is legato, a quality befitting the tranquil nature of the Swedish landscape and people. It has been said that the Swede's distaste for excessive display of emotion likely accounts for the relative conservatism of Swedish Folk Dancing. Nevertheless, Swedish dance style is buoyant with the same lightness as found in Denmark, but with an air of dignity and reserve that mirrors a more serious nature.

The dances promulgated for over a century by the formal Folk Dance societies in Sweden are mainly the products of mid-19th century national romanticism, and thus never actually danced by the "folk." It was not until around 1970, concurrent with a remarkable renaissance of interest in Swedish country fiddling, that true dances of the people became a part of the Folk Dance movement. Thanks to the work of a few devoted researchers, an unbelievable number of old dances, mostly "Polska" types, were rescued from oblivion through interviews with elderly fiddlers and folks who had danced them when young. These "bygdedanser," regional dances, have at last reunited the Folk Dancer with the folk fiddler and the vibrant, unbroken tradition of native Swedish music.

Bitte Mand I Knibe

(Little Man in a Fix) Danish

Bitte Mand I Knibe is a very popular little dance, both in Denmark and all over the United States. *Knibe* means to be in a "spot" or "fix."

Records: EZ 6009; Folk Dancer MH 1054.

Music: Burchenal, E., *Folk Dances of Denmark*, p. 44, and *Folk Dances from Old Homelands*, p. 62, LaSalle, D., *Rhythms and Dances for Elementary Schools*, p. 115.

Formation: Two couples, lady to right of partner. Men hook left elbows and place right arm around partner's waist, ladies place left hand on man's left shoulder.

Steps: Running step, Tyrolian Waltz, Waltz.

■ Directions for the Dance

Meter 3/4 • Directions are same for man and lady, except when specially noted.

Measures

I. Run Around

1 - 8	Beginning left, take small running steps forward, moving counterclockwise. Couples lean away from pivot point.
1 - 8	As **running steps are continued,** men grasp left hands and raise left arms, holding ladies' left hand with their right, and two ladies move under arch and pass each other. Ladies turn counterclockwise to face center, men lower left arms, and ladies grasp each other's right hand on top of men's left-hand grasp. All four continue to take small running steps, moving counterclockwise.

II. Tyrolian Waltz

9 - 12	Men release left hand, ladies right. The two couples turn back to back. Each couple takes couple position, inside hands shoulder height, outside arm relaxed at side. Man beginning left, lady right, take four Tyrolian Waltz steps moving in line of direction. Arms reach forward and draw back with each step. They do not swing forward.
13 - 16	Closed position. Man beginning left, lady right, take four Waltz steps, turning clockwise, progressing in line of direction.
9 - 16	Repeat action of measures 9 - 16.

Note

As the dance repeats, each couple dances with another couple. If a couple cannot find a couple for the first figure, they are **in a fix!** They go to the center and dance the running steps alone, with two hands joined. The next time the man will avoid being the **man in a fix** by hooking arms with another couple quickly for the first figure.

Den Toppede Høne

(The Crested Hen) Danish

Den Toppede Høne means "The Crested Hen," referring to the fact that in Denmark the men wore red stocking caps with a tassel representing a rooster comb. The ladies added to the fun of the dance by trying to pull the man's cap off as he went through the arch. If successful, then the lady became "crested" hen.

Records: Dancecraft DC 162402 LP; Folkraft 1159, 1194; World of Fun LP 4, Side A-6.

Cassette: Dancecraft 162402.

Music: Burchenal, Elizabeth, *Folk Dances of Denmark*, p. 49; LaSalle, Dorothy, *Rhythms and Dances for Elementary Schools*, p. 150. Neilson, N. P., and Van Hagen, W., *Physical Education for Elementary Schools*, p. 300.

Formation: Set of three, two ladies and a man, hands joined to form a circle.

Step: Step-hop.

■ Directions for the Dance

Meter 2/4

Measures

Part I

1 – 8   Beginning left, step-hop around circle clockwise, taking a vigorous stamp on first beat. Dancers lean away from center as they circle.

1 – 8   Jump, bringing feet down sharply on first beat, step-hop around circle counterclockwise.

Part II

9 – 10   Continuing step-hop, ladies release joined hands, place free hand on hip, and right-hand lady dances through arch made by man and left-hand lady.

11 – 12   Man turns under his left arm, following right-hand lady through arch.

13 – 14   Left-hand lady dances through arch made by man and right-hand lady.

15 – 16   Man turns under his right arm, following left-hand lady through arch.

9 – 16   Repeat action of measures 9 – 16.

Mixer

The man may progress forward to the next group at the completion of part II.

Familie Sekstur

Danish

Familie Sekstur mean's "family sixsome" and is pronounced *fa-MEEL-yeh SEKS-toor.* This Danish mixer is similar to American Square Dance figures and steps.

Record: Dancecraft DC 74518.

Music: Farwell, Jane, *Folk Dances for Fun,* p. 20.

Formation: Couples in single circle, lady to right of partner, hands joined, held at shoulder height, elbows V-shaped. Dancers stand close to each other.

Steps: Buzz step, walk.

■ Directions for the Dance

Meter 6/8 • Directions are the same for man and lady, except when specially noted.

Measures

1–8	Introduction. Beginning right, take 16 buzz steps to side (right crosses over left, right knee bending slightly). Circle moves clockwise. Take small light steps, keep circle small with elbows bent, and lean back slightly for better action.

I. In and Out

9–10	Beginning right, take four steps toward center, slowly extending joined hands above head. On fourth step, everyone nods head to greet everyone.
11–12	Beginning right, take four steps backward, to return to original formation, arms gradually lowering to original position (elbows bent, joined hands shoulder height). On fourth step, nod head to partner.
13–16	Repeat action of measures 9–12.

II. Grand Chain

17–24	Face partner and join right hands shoulder high, elbows bent, and continue around circle with grand right and left. Count out loud one to seven for each person met, keeping the seventh person for new partner. This keeps mixers in order. It is especially fun if counted in a Scandinavian language. Danish counting:

one-*en,* pronounced *enn*
two-*to,* pronounced *toe*
three-*tre,* pronounced *tray*
four-*fire,* pronounced *feer*
five-*fein,* pronounced *femm*
six-*sexs,* pronounced *sex*
seven-*syv,* pronounced *syou*

III. Swing

1–8	Swing position, with man's left arm, lady's right, extended straight out at shoulder level. Swing new partner in place, taking 16 buzz steps, ending with lady on man's right. All join hands to form single circle.
	Repeat action of part I–III, measures 9–24, 1–8, until end of record.

❧ Familjevalsen

Familjevalsen means "the family waltz" and is pronounced *fah-MIL-yeh-vahls-en.* Although this dance may be found throughout the Scandinavian countries, the Swedish version is described here as taught by Gordon E. Tracie, Seattle, Washington.

Records: Viking Skandia Album 1; any lively Swedish waltz.

Music: Farwell, Jane, *Folk Dances for Fun.*

Formation: Couples in single circle, lady to right of partner, hands joined, held at shoulder height, elbows V-shaped.

Steps: Waltz balance, Waltz.

■ Directions for the Dance

Meter 3/4 • Directions are for man; lady's part reverse.

Measures

	I. Balance
1	Beginning left, take one Waltz balance turning toward corner.
2	Beginning right, take one Waltz balance turning toward partner.
3–4	Repeat action of measures 1–2.
	II. Waltz
5–8	Take closed position with corner. Arms, man's left, lady's right, are extended straight out, shoulder height. Man places left thumb against the palm of the lady's right hand and closes his hand around the back of her hand. Beginning left, take four Waltz steps turning clockwise, progressing in line of direction. On last Waltz step, form circle, man placing partner on right side. Repeat dance from beginning with new corner.

Style

This should be a very smooth yet lively dance. Be sure to exchange smiles or greetings with corner and partner on the Waltz balance. Remember that the body rises and lowers during a Waltz balance. The Waltz is light, graceful, and fast.

Hambo

The *Hambo* (its full name is *Hambopolska*), often called the national dance of Sweden, is practiced far beyond the borders of its homeland. It is danced in neighboring Scandinavian countries and in Swedish national groups around the world; in the United States it is a top favorite among folk dancers.

The Hambo is the most common living example of the once all-popular Swedish "Polska"—a distinctly Nordic music and dance form dating back to the 16th century. Because the Hambo is a living Folk Dance, yesterday's version is not the same as today's, according to Gordon E. Tracie.* The form most common in the United States is a relatively old style called *nighambo*, referring to the characteristic "dip" on the first beat. It was brought to the United States by Swedish immigrants more than a half-century ago.

Records: Folk Dancer MH 2002, 2003, 2004; Folkraft 1048, 1164; Merit AV 1047 LP; Viking Skandia Album II.

Position: Couple, inside hands joined at shoulder height, outside hands on hip, thumb pointing backwards, fingers forward.

Steps: Step swing or Waltz balance, Polska.

■ Directions for the Dance

Meter 3/4 • Directions are for man; lady's part reverse, except when specially noted.

Measures

I. Introduction

1 Beginning left, take one step swing (dal step) or Waltz balance, turning body slightly away from partner, letting inside hands reach forward.

2 Take one step swing or Waltz balance slightly forward, turning body slightly toward partner, drawing inside hands backward.

3 Take three steps or Waltz step in line of direction.

II. Hambo (Polska) Step

4 Shoulder-waist position.

Man's part: Count 1, beginning right, step (with flat foot and bent knee) forward in line of direction with foot turned outward to start clockwise pivot. Place foot between lady's feet. Count 2, step left slightly forward in line of direction (almost in place) pivoting almost 360° clockwise. Body rises, coming up on ball of left foot. Count 3, touch ball of right foot firmly close behind left heel.

Lady's part: Count 1, beginning left, step almost in place pivoting 180° clockwise, bending left knee slightly. Count 2, right foot describes an arc, skimming floor, and touches toe close behind left heel. Body starts to rise. Count *and*, as body continues to rise, push slightly with left foot and leap into air. Count 3, complete 180° turn while both feet are in air, landing on right foot placed forward in line of direction between man's feet.

5-7 Repeat action of measure 4 three times.

8 Beginning right, take three steps almost in place. Take couple position, facing line of direction.

Hambo (continued)

---

*Gordon E. Tracie, authority on Swedish Folk Dancing, Seattle, WA.

Style

1. The Hambo is a very graceful, smooth-flowing dance. The music should be moderate speed, not fast. At the proper tempo, the dancers appear very relaxed and their movements effortless. Extra turns and twirls are to be discouraged.
2. The upper torso is always upright. The torso is lowered, or settles with the bending of the knee to accompany the primary accent (count 1). It rises on count 2. This body movement is subtle.
3. Both dancers should always be in control of their own body weight. The body is well "grounded" by planting each foot firmly in the step pattern. The touch of the man's right foot (count 3) acts to stabilize the body while pivoting. His weight is actually on both feet momentarily.
4. The lady should not let her right lower leg "fly up," or flick in the air, as it describes the arc (count 2).
5. The man guides the lady while in the air. He does not lift her as she receives her impetus for height from her push (count *and*).
6. Once the basic footwork is learned, perfection and styling of the dance takes several years of regular practice and conscious effort to improve one's style.

Suggestions for Teaching the Hambo (Polska) Step

1. Understand basic rhythm.

Man: 3/4				*Lady: 3/4*			
Step	Pivot	Touch		Step	Touch	Leap	Step
R	L	R		L	R		R
1	2	3		1	2	and	3

2. Men stand single-file, facing a wall; ladies stand single-file, facing an opposite wall.
   a. Analyze basic step (without partner) for each group. Practice basic step in place.
   b. Analyze basic step (with turn) for each group. Emphasize exact placement of each foot in relation to line of direction and a specific wall. Face original wall with each Hambo step.

3. Double-file lines, couples in shoulder-waist position.
   a. Practice step with partner.
   b. Practice individually and then together, alternately.

4. Double circle, couples in shoulder-waist position.
   a. Practice step progressing around room.
   b. Then analyze **Introduction** to Hambo and practice complete dance.

♫ Masquarade

Masquarade is a charming Danish dance consisting of a variety of rhythms and accompanying dance movements.

Records: Folk Dancer MH 1019, Folkraft 1093, 1520.

Formation: Double circle, couples facing counterclockwise.

Steps: Waltz, step-hop, walk.

■ Directions for the Dance

Meter 2/4, 3/4, 4/4 • Directions are for man; lady's part reverse.

Measures

	I.	**Walk**

Music A
1–4 Couples' inside arms are joined, outside arms swinging freely. Dance forward with 16 brisk walking steps.

5–8 Couples turn toward each other to face in reverse direction. Dance clockwise 16 brisk walking steps. Style for Part I should be crisp and brisk rather than slow and ceremonial.

II. Waltz Forward, Waltz Turn

Music B
1–4 Couples face counterclockwise, inside arms joined and elbows bent, outside hands on hips. Beginning man's left, ladies right, take four Waltz steps forward. Style: Dance forward and avoid a back-to-back or face-to-face turning of the body.

5–8 Couples take closed dance position. Beginning man's left, ladies right, dance four Waltz steps, turning clockwise, moving counterclockwise around the circle.

1–8 Repeat measures 1–8 of Music B.

III. Step-Hops

Music C
1–4 Dancers maintain position as in Part II. Beginning man's left, lady's right, move straight forward with four step-hops. Style: Avoid face-to-face, back-to-back turns.

5–8 Dancers take shoulder-waist position. Beginning man's left, lady's right, dance four step-hops, turning clockwise, moving counterclockwise around the circle.

1–8 Repeat measures 1–8 of Music C.

Repeat dance from the beginning.

Norwegian Polka

The *Norwegian Polka* is also known as the *Scandinavian Polka, Seattle Polka,* and *Ballroom Polka.* Gordon E. Tracie* suggests that the Americanized version may come from a simplification of the Norwegian dance *Parisarpolka,* meaning "Parisian Polka." The Norwegian immigrants probably brought the Parisarpolka to America, where it changed somewhat in form but retained the original Scandinavian Polka music.

Records: Viking V-806,** Viking V-812, Folkraft 1411, Folk Dancer MH 2001, 2004, Norse 45; or any good Scandinavian Polka, eight-measure phrase.

Position: Couple.

Steps: Walk, pivot turn.

■ Directions for the Dance

Meter 2/4 • Directions are for man; lady's part reverse.

Measures

Part I

1–2   Beginning left, take three walking steps in line of direction and stamp.

3–4   Beginning right, take three walking steps in reverse line of direction and clap, clap.

Part II

5   Beginning left, walk two steps in line of direction. Face partner on second step and take shoulder-waist position.

6–8   Beginning left, take a six-step pivot turn clockwise, progressing in line of direction. Partners should lean away from each other in turn. Man should end with back to center of room.

Variations

1. Measures 5–6   Walk four steps in line of direction.
    Measures 7–8   Four-step pivot turn clockwise.
2. Measures 1–2   Take two steps in line of direction and a Two-Step in place, facing partner.
    Measures 3–4   Repeat in reverse line of direction.
3. Measures 1–2   Take three-step turn in line of direction. Clap at end of turn.
    Measures 3–4   Repeat in reverse line of direction.

Teaching Suggestions

1. For help teaching pivot turn, see p. 48
2. To simplify dance for the beginner, it is helpful to teach two walking steps in measures 5–8 in couple position, followed by two steps pivoting in shoulder-waist position and repeat. Gradually change the sequence to the regular four- or six-step pivot.

---

*Gordon E. Tracie, director of Skandia Folkdance Society, Seattle, WA.
**Out of print.

Seksmannsril

Norwegian

Seksmannsril means "six persons' Reel," is pronounced *seks-mahns-REEL,* and is classified as a formal Folk Dance. The dance comes from the region of Asker. Mrs. Helfrid Rudd* taught this dance at the University of Washington, 1951.

Record: Viking V 300. Viking Skandia album.

Formation: Three couples in single circle, lady to right of partner; hands joined with arms outstretched, shoulder height.

Steps: Step-hop.

■ Directions for the Dance

Meter 2/4 • Directions are same for both lady and man, except where specially noted.

Measures

	1 – 4	Introduction: no action.

Figure 1

Ring

A	1 – 7	Beginning left, take 14 step-hops to left, circle moving clockwise.
	8	Take three stamps (left, right, left), turning to face counterclockwise.
	1 – 7	Beginning right, take 14 step-hops to right, circle moving counterclockwise.
	8	Take three stamps (right, left, right), clapping hands once on first stamp. Partners face, joining two hands. Arms are outstretched with outside arms slightly higher than inside arms; body leans toward center of circle. Inside hands of all couples almost touch in center of circle.

Two-Hand Hold

B	9 – 15	Man beginning left, lady right, take 14 step-hops, moving in line of direction; man moves forward, lady backward. As couples are leaning slightly toward center of circle, body has banking effect as traveling.
	16	Clapping hands once, take three stamps turning away from partner to face corner; man turns left, lady right, and join two hands with outstretched arms, still leaning toward center.
	17 – 23	Continuing to move in line of direction, repeat action of measures 9 – 15, lady moving forward, man backing up.
	24	Turning back to face partner, (man turns right, lady left) repeat action of measure 16.

Chain

C	25 – 32	Giving right hand to partner, grand right and left around the ring, step-hopping (beginning left). Continue on meeting partner the first time. Second time facing partner, take three stamps and rejoin hands in single circle.

Seksmannsril (continued)

---

*Mrs. Helfrid Rudd, Norwegian Folk Dance authority, Oslo, Norway.

Figure II

Ring

A   1-8   Repeat action of Figure I, A, measures 1-8.

Hand Clapping

B   9-24   Repeat action of Figure I, B, measures 9-24; instead of joining hands, clap hands on each step-hop. Action of arms while clapping is vertical: right hand swinging down, left up for clap, right hand coming up, left down for next clap, and alternating thereafter.

Chain

C   25-32   Repeat action of Figure I, C, measures 25-32.

Notes

1. During Figure I, A, some groups prefer to swing arms in and out while circling.
2. The Reel is a happy dance and must be danced quickly and with abandon. Stamps and claps are very precise. The dancers call "hey" or "ho" as they turn away or toward partners.

🌀 Snurrbocken

Swedish 🌀

Snurrbocken, pronounced *SNOOR-book-en,* means "the whirl and bow." Like the Hambo, it is a form of Swedish Polska. According to Gordon E. Tracie,* the second (bowing) part of the dance is a bit of rustic satire in which the farm folk burlesqued the gentry and their affected mannerisms. Traditionally it was at just this point that the fiddler could have *his* fun with the dancers by setting the timing and tempo of his bow sequence—often with long delays—and it was up to the dancers to follow him!

Records: Folk Dancer MH 1047: Viking V 200.

Music: *Svenska Folkdanser och Sallskapsdancer,* Svendska Ungdomsringen, Stockholm.

Position: Shoulder-waist.

Steps: Polska step, running step.

■ Directions for the Dance

Meter 3/4 • Directions are for man; lady's part reverse.

Measures

I. Polska Turn

1 – 8 Beginning left, take eight Polska steps turning clockwise progressing in line of direction. Analysis of Polska step: Man's part: Count 1, step forward left, pivoting clockwise. Count 2, continue pivoting on left and place ball of right foot near left foot (weight remains on left foot, right foot helps to maintain balance). Count 3, step forward right. Lady's part: Count 1, step on both feet, preparing to pivot clockwise. Count 2, step right, pivoting clockwise. Count 3, step left, pivoting clockwise.

II. Run

9 – 16 Conversation position, with free hand on hips (fingers forward, thumb back). Beginning left, take 24 light, small, running steps forward in line of direction.

III. Bows

17 Place hands on own hips **fingers forward, thumbs back,** and turn slowly toward partner, man with back to center, lady facing the center.

18 Slowly bow low to each other with dignity.

19 Each turn one half-turn, **man counterclockwise, facing center, lady clockwise, facing outward.**

20 Slowly bow while back to back.

21 Each turns one-half more to face each other. Take shoulder-waist position to repeat dance.

Notes

1. This Polska step, sometimes called Delsbopolska, after a district in the province of Halsingland, is related to the Hambo step but begins with the man's **left** and has a pivot, whereas the Hambo-Polska begins with the man's **right** and has a "dip" (first beat) at the beginning of each step.
2. The recording by Folk Dancer begins with a bow instead of a Polska.

---

*Gordon E. Tracie, director of Skandia Folkdance Society, Seattle, WA.

Swedish Varsouvienne

All of the Scandinavian lands have virtually identical Varsouviennes, which are different but related in both music and step pattern to the well-known American Varsouvienne or "Put Your Little Foot."

Records: Folk Dancer MH 1023; Folkraft 1130.

Music: Bergquist, Nils, *Swedish Folk Dances,* p. 12; Herman, Michael, *Folk Dances for All,* p. 32.

Position: Conversation, outside hands on hip, thumb pointing backward, fingers forward.

Steps: Walk, Waltz, Mazurka type.

■ Directions for the Dance

Meter 3/4 • Directions are for man; lady's part reverse.

Measures

I. Walk and Heel

1-2 Beginning left, take three steps, man dancing almost in place; the lady takes a full turn counterclockwise and moves across in front of man to his left side. Man places left arm around lady's waist and lady places right arm on man's left shoulder, outside hands on hip. Place right heel with toe raised (lady's left) slightly forward. Outside hand is always on hip.

3-4 Beginning right, repeat action of measures 1-2, lady turning clockwise, returns to original position. Place left heel with toe raised forward.

5-8 Repeat action of measures 1-4.

II. Mazurka

9-10 Beginning left, step forward with slight accent, draw right to left, hop right, sweeping left across right. Repeat.

11-12 Repeat action of measures 1-2.

13-16 Beginning right, repeat action of measures 9-12.

III. Waltz

17-24 Closed position. Beginning left, take eight Waltz steps, turning clockwise, progressing in line of direction.

Variation

Measures 9-10, as in Sweden, instead of sweeping foot across, kick left foot forward and back fast. This is referred to as "fryksdal-step."

Swedish Waltz

Swedish Waltz has been popular in the United States for at least fifty years. Gordon E. Tracie* in his study of dances in Scandinavia in 1948 discovered that such a Swedish Waltz was not danced in Sweden. However, an elderly couple from the country (Dalarna) recognized it as the nearly forgotten *Norsk Vals* (Norwegian Waltz), which they had danced in their youth. Scandinavian immigrants undoubtedly brought the dance to this country at the turn of the century.

Records: Folkraft N 4510. Any good Swedish Waltz in moderately slow tempo with eight-measure phrases.

Position: Couple, inside hands joined at shoulder height.

Step: Waltz, step-swing, or Waltz balance.

■ Directions for the Dance

Meter 3/4 • Directions are for man; lady's part reverse.

Measures

1   Beginning left, take one step-swing (dal step) or Waltz balance (step touch) almost in place turning body slightly away from partner, inside hands reaching forward as arms are extended forward shoulder height.

2   Beginning right, move slightly forward, taking one step-swing of Waltz balance and turn body slightly toward partner, inside hands drawing backward as arms are extended backward shoulder height.

3–4   Beginning left, take two Waltz steps or six steps in Waltz rhythm in line of direction. More advanced dancers make one solo turn, turning away from partner (man left, lady right) while moving in line of direction. This turn is facilitated by man stepping back in line of direction right, lady left, on second waltz step before continuing turn.

5–8   Closed position or shoulder-waist position. Beginning left, take four Waltz steps, turning clockwise. Lady turns out under man's left arm on last Waltz step to assume couple position.

---

*Gordon E. Tracie, director of Skandia Folkdance Society, Seattle, WA.

❧ To Ting

To Ting means "two things." This refers to the two different rhythms, 3/4 and 2/4.

Records: Folk Dancer MH 1018; Viking Skandia Album I.

Music: Herman, Michael, *Folk Dances for All*, p. 52.

Position: Couple position, outside hands on hips.

Steps: Waltz, walk, pivot turn.

■ Directions for the Dance

Measures

Meter 3/4 • Directions are for man; lady's part reverse.

Part I

1   Moving forward, beginning left, take one Waltz step turning away from partner, swinging inside arms forward, hands at shoulder level.

2   Moving forward, take one Waltz step, turning toward partner, swinging inside arms back.

3-4   Repeat action of measures 1-2.

5-8   Closed position. Beginning left, take four Waltz steps, turning clockwise, progressing in line of direction.

1-8   Repeat action of measures 1-8.

Meter 2/4

Part II

9-12   Conversation position, outside hands on hips. Beginning left, take four walking steps forward.

13-16   Shoulder-waist position. Beginning left, turn clockwise with four steps in a pivot turn.

9-16   Repeat action of measures 9-16.

Variation

9-12   The Danes skip four forward.

13-16   Turn with four step-lifts (svejtril steps) in pivot turn.

Totur or *Two Dance* is a mixer from the district of Vejle in western Denmark. Dancers get new partners at the completion of the "chain" or grand right and left. It is customary to smile at each person you meet in the chain.

Records: Folk Dancer MH 1021; Viking V-401.

Formation: Single circle, couples facing center, lady to right of partner, hands joined, held at shoulder level.

Steps: Walk, Two-Step, Polka.

■ Directions for the Dance

Music 2/4 • Directions are for man; lady's part reverse, except in the introduction.

Measures

Introduction

1 – 8   Beginning left, take 16 walking steps or eight polka steps clockwise.

1 – 8   Repeat action of measures 1 – 8 counterclockwise.

Figure I

9   Single circle. Open position, men facing line of direction, joined hands toward center of circle. Beginning left, take one Two-Step toward center of circle.

10   Continue in same direction with two walking steps.

11 – 12   Beginning right, moving away from center, repeat action of measures 9 – 10 back to place in reverse open position.

13 – 16   Beginning left, take four Polka steps, turning clockwise, progressing in line of direction.

9 – 16   Repeat action of measures 9 – 16.

Figure II

1 – 8   Partners face, grasp right hands and grand right and left around circle with walking or Polka steps.

1 – 8   Continue grand right and left. **Note:** At the end of this figure, dancers may have a new partner for repeat of the dance.

Repeat Figures I and II alternately for remainder of record.

---

*This dance was arranged from the dance used in *The Folk Dancer,* Vol. 5, December 1945, pp. 10 – 11.

British Isles

Introduction

The British Isles were settled by the Celts, who came across from the Continent, as well as by the Milesians, a nomadic Celtic tribe who came to Ireland from northern Italy (Lombardy), and then by invaders from the Basque country (Gallicia). Scotland was settled by the Picts (of uncertain origin) and the Scots, who came from Ireland. Subsequent invading tribes (Romans, Angles, Saxons, Normans, Danes) influenced the culture of the British Isles. The Celts practiced Druid rites, which included dancing, and some of the pagan rites were retained during their conversion to Christianity. A constant exchange of culture existed among the English, the Irish, and the Scottish as the result of natural migration, war, and travel by sailors from one country to another. Hugh Thurston (1964; p. 5) has commented that the figures and the steps of the country dances during the period of 1720–1800 were so similar, with national characteristics lacking, that a particular dance could not be identified as either English, or Scottish, or even American.

England

Dance Characteristics

England's Morris and Sword dances are two ritual dance forms, performed for renewal and continuance of life, that have survived over the centuries.

The third form is the country dance, a term that covers a variety of social dances. According to Douglas Kennedy, "These English country dances came directly from the folk in the form of rounds and squares and longways and contras. Having established themselves as fashionable ballroom forms, they continued through the times of the Stuarts, Commonwealth, the Restoration, Queen Anne and the Hanoverian line right into our own century."[*]

Morris Dance

Morris Dance for centuries has been part of the spring Whitsuntide festival. Whit-Monday was the day for the Morris men to perform, a custom that was little known outside rustic villages in the English countryside until the 19th century. In 1899 Cecil Sharp observed an out-of-season Morris Dance performed by six men dressed in white shirts, adorned with ribbons and padded leg bells, as they pranced and "footed" it in the snow of winter on the outskirts of Oxford. From that experience, Sharp was inspired to delve into the music, dance steps, and history of the Morris. The result was *The Morris Book*, a five-part publication that has been an invaluable source of information concerning this ancient ritual.

The origin of the name Morris is shrouded in the mist of history and speculative at best. The Whitsuntide custom goes back to before the Norman conquest. Whether the dance had a name then is not known. In addition, the Morris has been estimated to have been in existence since the 12th century. Scholars can only theorize about the name; however, the Moorish or Spanish origin of the name has generally been discounted.

In its early form the Morris included character actors such as the Squire, clown, and fool, any one of whom would act as the leader depending on the region and/or Morris tradition from which they came. Other characters taking part in this ancient dance-drama were the Hobby-horse, animal-men, and Maid Marion or "Betsy." During these early times the men dancers played a subsidiary role to the actors. In more recent times, the actors have become secondary to the dancers, who entertain with their spectacular athletic feats.

During its long history the Morris was plagued by ecclesiastical restrictions issued from Rome and Canterbury. In addition, the Puritans waged a vigorous campaign against this traditional rustic pastime. They succeeded in destroying so many of the countryside customs that not even Charles II could restore all the Morris customs and all the Maypoles! This attitude came with the Puritans across the ocean to the colonies where, as occurred in some

---

[*]Kennedy, Douglas. *English Folk Dancing Today and Yesterday.* London: G. Bell and Sons, 1964, p. 112.

southern communities, the word "dance" had to be replaced with the word "game."

The last fifty years has seen a revival of the Morris in America. Contemporary times even finds the Morris danced by women. Today there are three organizations: the Morris Ring for men only, the Women's Morris for women only, and the Open Morris for men and women. At present there are no Federation of Morris teams in the United States or Canada. Communication between groups and about group events is facilitated by the *Morris Newsletter* published in Minneapolis, Minnesota.

Sword Dance

The English Sword Dance is a technically intricate, exciting, and dramatic dance form handed down by example and oral tradition from the remote past. The dance, coupled with the play or dramatic action, has a half-magic and half-religious aura.

The Sword Dance Play consists of two aspects, dancers who blacken their faces or wear masks, and a retinue of characters consisting of (depending on region and tradition) the Hobby-horse, clown, the woman Beson Betty or Dirty Bet, and often a King, Queen, Lord, Lady, and a quack Doctor with his Jack. Although performed at other times of the year the Sword Dance's season traditionally was midwinter on Plough-Monday. It was through the absorbing and diligent work of Cecil Sharp that the details of this fast dying dance tradition and the content and materials of the drama associated with it have been preserved. Sharp's three-part publication of *The Sword Dances of Northern England* remains today the invaluable source for information concerning this ancient custom.

The Sword Dance is distinguished by the type of instrument used. The Yorkshire tradition consisted of a long rigid sword made of wood or iron. The Northumberland and Durham version, which was shorter and more flexible, was called a Rapper. The dance is commonly referred to as the "Long Sword" or the "Rapper" Dance.

The Rapper was fitted with handles at each end and a swivel at the hilt so that the blade could twist and turn within the hand. This turning feature coupled with the shorter blade allowed the dancers to twist and turn as individuals or for the whole group to literally turn inside out. "Stepping," a highly skilled dance movement, was used to change patterns, alternating with the weaving of the swords in a figure. The Rapper style was acrobatic and breathtakingly exciting.

The very nature of the long sword with its more rigid blade eliminated the acrobatic elements found in the Rapper performance. The Long Sword Dance thus was more elaborate and ceremonial in nature yet still dramatic and fascinating. Common to both performances, however, were the "dramatis personae" of the ancient Plough Play, the "Lock," Knott, or Rose, and the "calling on" stage by accompanying actors or characters.

The Long Sword Dance always finished with a "Lock." In some traditions the "Lock" is tied around the neck of one of the accompanying characters, who then dies dramatically. In other traditions the beheaded actor simply gets up, brushes himself off, and leaves, thus signaling the end of the play. In still other traditions the beheading begins the dramatic part of the play. A mock-Doctor appears accompanied by his Jack to undertake a cure of the dead and restore him to life. The symbolism is that of fashioning new life from the ashes of the old, a repeated theme in Sword dance-dramas thought to be associated with the Mummers' plays.

The Rapper Dance tradition seems to be found mostly in the coal mining districts of northern England. Versions of the Rapper dance vary little, which is thought to be a consequence of its existence in closely knit coal mining societies. The design of the sword, its length, and versatility is thought to be a product of the iron workers of antiquity.

Country Dances

English country dances, as early as the 17th century, were contrived dances done by the court and the socially elite at public assemblies. The wealthy landed gentry could afford to hire dancing masters to teach the dances. Indeed, what rustic or peasant would be caught learning, least of all performing, a pas de bourrée!

The country dance formation, then as now, consisted of couples in parallel lines, men in one line, women in the line opposite, partners facing. In the early days, the figure execution was considered democratic in that after one repetition the lead couple moved down the set and back up to place, dancing with one or two couples. The popularity of country dancing hinged on the repetitious nature of the figures and the absence of complicated step combinations, which made the dance easier and thus more enjoyable to all who could afford to learn even at the most rudimentary level.

By the middle of the 17th century the dance form and sequence became simplified into a more repetitive and progressive form, thus accommodating a variety of skill levels and many more dancers. Country dancing was a high point of fashion for the rising middle classes of the time.

English Country Dancing Today

By George A. Fogg

English country dancing is viable and flourishing today, a living tradition. John Playford published *The*

English Dance Master in 1651, the first dance book with music and accompanying dance instructions. Through the years dancing masters have choreographed new dances to fit the social mores of their day. Thus, today on both sides of the Atlantic Ocean dancing masters are presenting new material as well as taking another look at the old masters such as Walsh, Thompson, Kynaston, Bray Neal, and others. In our 20th century mode the dances are performed to a country dance-walk and occasionally employ skipping and slipping steps. The "footwork steps" the dancing masters taught the aristocracy, such as the Pas de Bourrée, Contretemps, Rigadoon, and Balance, have all been replaced with the 20th-century dance-walk. Some of the new country dances are being composed in the American contra-square idiom.

The country dances fell into disuse when the Waltz overran the ballrooms and it became acceptable to hold your partner in your arms in polite company. The Minuet, which was the ultimate elite dance of the assembly rooms and for state occasions, was discarded. No longer did the balls start with Minuets for all those who wished and always in order of class. However, in the villages the traditional country dances continued to use the ballroom position hold and continued to enjoy their country dances. The discarded gentry country dances were discovered by Cecil J. Sharp. He interpreted dance terms that had long gone out of use and took the lead in bringing the English country dances back into vogue. The reconstructed English country dances are very popular with folk dancers today.

Music

Joan Lawson describes the outstanding feature of English Folk Dancing as an "even-tempered quality." "This is due firstly to the specific quality of English folk music" (Lawson 1953; p. 164). Although the melody may move from major to minor keys, it is a smooth (legato) tune that does not build up to climaxes. The dancers reflect this even quality in their posture, which is poised and leans slightly in the direction of movement, and appears even to glide.

For the Morris Dance, a pipe and tabor, a small drum played by one man, are traditional accompaniment. However, today these are replaced by a fiddle or a concertina for all English folk dancing.

Ireland

Dance Characteristic

Despite a common background with the other British Isle countries, Ireland's dance and culture tend to be very different from Scotland's and England's. There are three types of Irish folk dances: Jigs, Reels, and Hornpipes. Jigs and Hornpipes are characterized by clog and tap steps, and Reels by shuffle or gliding steps. The dances follow traditional formations of solos, couples, and groups or sets. The specially trained solo dancers perform step dances based on clog or shuffle steps. The popular dances are Jigs and Reels (simple steps) in round, square, and Longway formations.

The tradition of Feis (a celebration of competitions among the poets, singers, musicians, story tellers, and dancers held after harvest in November) dates back to 1300 B.C. It has been suggested that it was originally a form of Thanksgiving. Different Celtic countries had a similar tradition but referred to it by other names. In the Feis contests, women were allowed to compete. And the minstrel in that period had more status than the warrior. The strong tradition of Feis is credited with keeping Irish folk music and dance alive. Despite difficult times when the Irish came to America, immigrant minstrels perpetuated their heritage, which has become a part of American folk music.

When the famous dancing schools—such as the ones at Limerick, Kerry, and Cork—were established, a polished style evolved and natural expressions were eliminated with emphasis placed on the footwork. Some of the spontaneity of expression was lost. But the dance schools and competitions are to be credited for keeping the Irish dance tradition vibrant.

Style

Characteristics of the Irish people, such as their keen sense of humor, happiness, wit, imagination, and superstition, prevail in their dances and music. The dancer is erect, hands at the sides, and face rather impassive. The range of movement is minimal. The distinguishing characteristic is the intricate and exact footwork. In the most difficult dances, there are about 75 taps per quarter minute. The control of the various sounds produced by the taps of heels and soles on the floor and against each other is of utmost importance in competitive dancing. Although the dances are based on five simple steps, improvisation and elaboration of steps are delightful characteristics of Irish dance.

Music

Originally, the fife and harp were used for dance accompaniment. Today, fiddles, flutes, violins, and accordions are popular. Irish music is very lilting. The secondary rhythm of the tapping feet combines with the melody to create an interesting effect.

Scotland

Dance Characteristics

The unbroken history of Scottish dance has long been preserved as part of Scotland's strong national pride. The practice of regimental troops dancing to relieve tension before battle or to celebrate victories is one aspect of the Scottish heritage. After the 1745 rebellion when the English tried to end the clan system and suppress the Highland culture, the Scottish ways of dress, dance, and music became even stronger when they were forced underground. When the ban was lifted in 1782, Scotland's fierce national pride was stronger than ever. The Highland battalions, moving abroad and eventually around the world, wore their kilts and continued their ceremonies and dance traditions.

Another tradition, the Highland games, continues to stimulate interest through dance, bagpipe, and athletic contests. The Scottish Country Dance Society is to be credited with standardizing steps and techniques, setting up a system of exams and certificates, and publishing many Scottish dances.

Almost all Scots can dance several of their traditional dances. Today, during an evening of social dancing, a *Waltz Country Dance*, a *Petronella*, a *Skip the Willow*, or a *Highland Schottische* are usually included.

Style

The Scots are very enthusiastic about dance and have always entered into it with a great deal of zest.

Highland solo dancing or competitive dancing, such as the *Highland Fling* and *Sword Dance*, are intricate and athletic. The carriage of the body is very erect and the supporting leg is kept straight. The toes are pointed at all times. Arms are used for balance. The hand and arms positions are exact; either the fists are at the hips, the arms curved over the head, with thumb and third finger touching, or one arm is held above the head and the other is held at the hip. The body movement is upward, with hopping or jumping off one or two feet on the first beat. This is referred to as *snap*. The feet beat in the air soundlessly. The body is propelled back upward into the air when the heel touches the floor. Elaborations of steps occur while the body is in the air.

Music

Scottish Highland Dances have been performed traditionally to the music of the bagpipes, which have a nine-note scale. The lilting rises and falls of the tunes influence the dance style. The snap occurs when a sixteenth note is followed by a dotted eighth. Although the first note, the first beat, is light and gives impetus to the next note, which is stressed and louder, the intake of breath when playing the bagpipe has become the snap or sixteenth note. Only the bagpipe can express the peculiar quality and rhythm of Highland Dance music. The violin and piano are now played in many parts of Scotland for Reels and Jigs.

Auretti's Dutch Skipper

English

Presented by George A. Fogg* at the Third Annual English Country Dance workshop at Lost Pines Dance Hall, Bastrop, Texas, fall 1992.

Source: Keller K. & G. Shimer, *The Playford Ball* and Shaw, P., *Holland as Seen in the English Country Dance: 1713–1820.*

Original from: Rutherford's *"Compleat Country Dances,"* Vol. 1, 1756, and Thompson's *"Compleat Collection of Country Dances,"* Vol. 1, 1757.

Record: *Canterbury Country Dance Orchestra* F-72-73.

Music: Barnes, P., *English Country Dance Tunes* and Shaw, P., *Holland as Seen in the English Country Dance: 1713–1820.*

Formation: Duple Minor Longways.

Step: Walking.

■ Directions for the Dance

Meter 6/8

Measures

Part A1

1–4   First couple lead down through second couple and cast up to place.

5–8   First couple two-hand turn.

Part A2

1–4   Second couple lead up through first couple and cast down to place.

5–8   Second couple two-hand turn

Part B1

1–4   First corners (first man and second woman) two-hand turn.

5–8   Second corners (second man and first woman) two-hand turn.

Part B2

1–4   All set twice

5–8   Right and left with hands (3 changes).

Note from *The Playford Ball:* A couplet beneath a picture suggests that Miss Anne Auretti was involved in some sort of scandal.

> The Fair Auretti free from Blame,
> Received of Heaven and of Men,
> The Soul of Balls, and of the dance,
> The gift of Flying in Ballance.

---

*Directions and permission to publish courtesy George A. Fogg, 40 Gray Street, Boston, MA 02116-6210

Bonny Prince Charlie
Crossing the Frew*

Bonny Prince Charlie Crossing the Frew depicts the crossing of Prince Charles at the Frew (1745), the only place to ford the river Forth from the north. The river winds back on itself and the setting and the turnings depict the leaping from stone to stone. The dancers at the bottom of the set watch, as Charles himself did, until all have crossed. The final figure is the flight under fire and farewell to the south as the King's soldiers in King's Park fired only a few shots. Stirling Castle was held, and Prince Charles marched south, then back to Culloden and final defeat.

Record: Dance with Jim Johnson and his Band, FLPS 1853, or any 40-measure Jig in 6/8 time. (Fiesta Record Co., Inc., 1619 Broadway, New York, NY.)

Formation: Longway Reeltime dance. A four-couple set involving three couples. Top of set indicated by first man's left shoulder.

Position: Feet in first position, hands at sides.

Steps: Skip change step, pas de basque, setting.

■ Directions for the Dance

Meter 6/8 • Directions are same for man and lady.

Measures

1–16   Dance begins with honors, men bow, ladies curtsey. First and second couples set (2 measures), join right hands across, and wheel half-way around (2 measures) with two skip change steps.

Second and third couples set (2 measures), join left hands across, and wheel half-way around (2 measures) with two skip change steps.

First and fourth couples set (2 measures), join right hands across, and wheel half-way around (2 measures) with two skip change steps.

First couple dance half-figure-eight up and around fourth couple. First lady will pass in front of partner up and around fourth man to opposite side. First man dances up and around fourth lady to finish at bottom on original side with four skip change steps.

Fourth couple will step up on measures 15 and 16.

17–24   Second, third, and fourth couples advance and retire two skip change steps forward and backward. Join both hands, turn own partner halfway around with two pas de basque steps. Drop hands and fall back to sides on last two pas de basque steps. First couple stand at bottom for these last 8 measures. All dancers are now on original sides.

Bonnie Prince Charlie Crossing the Frew (continued)

---

*This dance was choreographed by Mary McLaren Lindsay of Mesa, AZ. Mrs. Lindsay is a certified teacher of the Royal Scottish Country Dance Society of Edinburgh, Scotland; she was born in Bannockburn and educated in the Stirling area. The dance is used by permission.

| 25–32 | Bottom couple casts up on their own outside of the set to top. (Dance slightly in on first measure toward each other as they cast). Meet each other and dance under bridges (arches) formed by second, third, and fourth couples with eight skip change steps. |

| 33–40 | Second with third, fourth with first, couples dance right and left. **Note:** Dancers retain original number through 1–40 measures. |

Repeat dance from beginning with new first couple.

Scottish Steps and Formations

Wheeling: A four-hand star or mill figure in which dancers turn with either the right or left hand. In this dance, it is used to change lines or turn half around.

Set or Setting: Two pas de basques in place, facing as directed.

Pas de Basque: Push off left foot and leap sideways onto right, weight on ball of foot. Close left foot into third position front and change weight onto ball of left foot. Step back (shift weight) onto right foot, keeping weight on ball of foot as left foot is extended forward in third position. Cues: Leap (count 1), step across (count 2), step in place (count 3). Step, beat, beat.

Skip Change Step: Begin in first position. Skip (hop) on left foot while extending right foot forward, knee straight and toe pointed. Step on right foot, keeping leg straight and firm. Close left to right in third rear position (remain on toes). Step forward onto right foot. Cues: Skip (hop), step, close, step.

Right and Left: Each dancer extends right hand to partner and changes places across the line; each dancer faces up or down the lines, gives left hand to other man or woman dancer, and changes places in line; each dancer gives right hand to partner and changes place across the line; each dancer gives left hand to other man or woman and finishes in original place. Cues: Across the line, up or down the line, across the line, and up or down the line.

Note: The symbols used to represent the man and lady are the reverse of those used by the Royal Scottish Country Dance Society.

Presented by George A. Fogg* at the Third Annual English Country Dance workshop at Lost Pines Dance Hall, Bastrop, Texas, fall 1992.

Source: *Community Dance Manual 1; Country Dances of Today 1* and Sharp, Cecil, *Country Dance Book 1.*

Original: Collected by Cecil J. Sharp.

Record: *Orange and Blue* ED 105.

Music: Any good hornpipe such as *Manchester* or *Rickett's,* also found in *Community Dance Manual 1* and *Country Dances of Today 1.*

Formation: Duple Minor Longways.

Step: Jaunty walking or 1, 2, 3 Hop; a low easy schottische.

■ Directions for the Dance

Meter 4/4

Measures

Part A1

1–8   Right-hand star and left-hand back.

Part A2

1–8   Arching (over and under). (Ones over twos; then twos over ones and repeat.)

Part B

1–8   Couples swing and change places. (In ballroom position, dance one and one-half times around each other to change places.)

---

*Directions and permission to publish courtesy George A. Fogg, 40 Gray Street, Boston, MA 02116-6210.

🌿 Constancy* An Early American Dance in the English Style 🌿

Presented by George A. Fogg at the Third Annual English Country Dance workshop at Lost Pines Dance Hall, Bastrop, Texas, fall 1992. The original from *A Collection of the newest and fashionable Country Dances and Cotillions The Greater Part* by Mr. John Griffith, Dancing Master in Providence. Interpreted by C. C. Hendrickson in *Early American Dance and Music: John Griffith, Dancing Master, 29 Country Dances, 1788.*

Record: *Early American Dance Tunes from John Griffith's Collection, 1788.*

Cassette: THG-2.

Formation: Duple Minor Longways (originally a Triple Minor).

Step: 20th century dance walk or may be danced with the pas de bourrée and balance.

◾ Directions for the Dance

Meter 2/4 • Tune: *The Ton*

Measures

Part A
1–16   First and second couples right hands across (right-hand star) and left hands across back.

First couple leads down the middle; come back and cast down one place.

Part B
1–16   All balance twice (English setting step), and two-hand turn partners.

Right and left with hands (4 changes).

Note: Original text: "No. 11 Constancy: Cross hands—back again lead down the middle—up again and cast off one couple balance all six—turn your partner quite round and right and left to top." The original on file at The Rhode Island Historical Society.

---

*Directions and permission to publish courtesy Charles C. Hendrickson, P.O. Box 776, Sandy Hook, CT 06482.

🍃 Dover Pier*   English 🍃

Source: Keller, K. and G. Shimer, *The Playford Ball*; Simons, A., *Kentish "Hops" 1.*

Original from: Preston's *Twenty Four Country Dances for the Year 1791.*

Record: *Five Country Dances from Printed Collections,* PR-EP 315.

Music: Barnes, P., *English Country Dance Tunes;* Keller, K. and Shimer, G., *The Playford Ball;* Simons, A., *Kentish "Hops" 1.*

Formation: Duple Minor Longways.

Step: Walking.

■ Directions for the Dance

Meter 2/4

Measures

Part A1

1–8 All set twice and right hands across (right-hand star) halfway and fall back.

Part A2

1–8 Repeat A1 with the left hand.

Part B1

1–8 First couple cross over and go below (second couple move up) and first couple two-hand turn one and one-half to end proper.

Part B2

1–8 Right and left with hands (4 changes).

Note from *The Playford Ball:* "The wharfs of Dover are the chief points of departure for the continent, being but twenty-one miles across the English channel to Calais in France."

---

*Directions and permission to publish courtesy George A. Fogg, 40 Gray Street, Boston, MA 02116-6210.

Source: Porter, W. S. and A. and M. Heffer, *The Apted Book of Country Dances.*

Record: *Apted Country Dances,* Lib 1.

Music: Barnes, P., *English Country Dance Tunes;* and Porter, W. S. and A. and M. Heffer, *The Apted Book of Country Dances.*

Formation: Duple Minor Longways.

Step: Walking and slipping.

■ Directions for the Dance

Meter 6/8

Measures

Part A1

1 – 4   First and second couples right hands across (right-hand star) once around.

Part A2

1 – 4   The same couples left hands across, back again.

Part B1

1 – 8   First couple lead down the middle, lead back up, and cast down one place.

Part B2

1 – 8   Hands four (circle) left and back right (slipping).

---

*Directions and permission to publish courtesy George A. Fogg, 40 Gray Street, Boston, MA 02116-6210.

Flowers of Edinburgh*

Scottish Reel

Dances with Jacobite names, like *Flowers of Edinburgh*, may have been composed by the many fiddlers in Scotland. After the 1745 Rebellion, the pipes were banned. The Chiefs had their own fiddlers and the dances usually depict a famous battle, event, or, in many instances, a place name.

Records: Folkraft 1333; Scottish Dance Time Album Volume I, SMT 7028; or any eight-time, 32-measure Reel in 4/4 meter.

Formation: Longway Reeltime dance. A four-couple set involving three couples in each 32-bar repetition. Top of set is indicated by left shoulder of first man.

Steps: Skip change step, pas de basque, poussette.

■ Directions for the Dance

Meter 2/4 • Directions are same for man and lady, except where noted.

Measures

1-6   Dance begins with honors, men bow, ladies curtsey.

First woman turns round by the right, and casts off two places (i.e., dances down behind second and third woman, then crosses over and dances up behind second and third man to her partner's original position, Fig. 1). At the same time, first man follows his partner, crossing over and dancing behind second and third women, then up the middle to his partner's original position, Fig. 2. (Six skip change steps.)

7-8   First couples set to one another. Two pas de basques.

9-14   Repeat bars 1-6, but first man leads as in Fig. 1, and first woman follows, as in Fig. 2. First couples finish in original position. (Six skip change steps.)

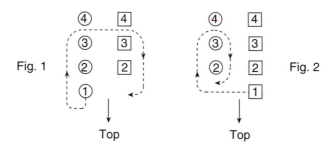

15-16 First couple set to one another. (Two pas de basques.)

17-24 First couple lead down the middle and up again. (Eight skip change steps.)

Flowers of Edinburgh (continued)

*This dance is used by the permission of the Royal Scottish Country Dance Society, 12 Coates Crescent, Edinburgh, Scotland, EH3 7AF. Patron—Her Majesty The Queen; President—The Earl of Mansfield; Secretary—Miss M. M. Gibson. Permission granted April 16, 1986.

25–32   First and second couples poussette. (This is the progression sequence). **Note:** Men begin with left foot.

Repeat, having passed a couple.

Man = □
Lady = ○

Scottish Steps and Formations

Skip Change Step: Begin in first position. Skip (hop), on left foot while extending right foot forward, knee straight and toe pointed. Step on right foot, keeping leg straight and firm. Close left to right in third rear position (remain on toes). Step forward onto right foot. Cues: Skip (hop), step, close, step.

Pas de Basque: Push off left foot and leap sideways onto right, weight on ball of foot. Close left foot into third position front and change weight onto ball of left foot. Step back (shift weight onto right foot, keeping weight on ball of foot as left foot is extended forward in fourth intermediate position, toes down. Cues: Leap (count 1), step across (count 2), step in place (count 3). Step, beat, beat.

Poussette: Both hands joined at shoulder level, elbows at side, hands held firmly. Men begin with left foot. Couples dance eight pas de basque steps. The two couples change places by dancing along the sides of a square, couple 1 down the man's side, couple 2 up on lady's side. Couples dance one step away from center (measure 1); both quarter-turn on corner of square, pull with right hand—men now have backs to top of set. They are on sideline of set (measure 2); both travel up or down the set (measure 3); both quarter-turn, pull with right hand—men have backs to lady's side of set (measure 4); both dance to center of set (measure 5); both turn around to own sides (measure 6); all dancers fall back to sidelines. Dancers have now changed places (measures 7 and 8). **Note:** Pas de basque is used as a traveling step, moving forward and back. Cues: Away from center quarter-turn, up or down quarter-turn, dance into center turn half around, and fall back, fall back.

Set or Setting: Two pas de basques in place as directed.

Note: The symbols used to represent the man and lady are the reverse of those used by the Royal Scottish Country Dance Society.

🌿 Gie Gordons

Records: Express 282; Folkraft 1162.

Cassette: Dancecraft DC 989; Dancecraft DC 162006.

Music: *Folk Dancer,* Volume 7, No. 4, p. 11.

Position: Varsouvienne.

Steps: Walk, Two-step, pas de basque.

■ Directions for the Dance

Meter 2/4 • Directions are same for both man and lady, except when specially noted.

Measures

    I. Walk

1 – 2   Beginning left, walk four steps forward in line of direction. On fourth step, pivot clockwise to face reverse line of direction. Lady is now on man's left.

3 – 4   Continue walking backward four steps in line of direction.

5 – 8   Repeat action of measures 1 – 4 in reverse line of direction.

    II. Two-Step

9 – 12   Man beginning left, takes four Two-Steps in line of direction, as lady, beginning right, turns clockwise under man's right arm four Two-Steps. Or man, beginning left, lady right, pas de basque out and in and man takes four walking steps in line of direction as lady turns twice clockwise under man's right arm.

13 – 16   Closed position. Man beginning left, lady right, takes four Two-Steps turning clockwise, progressing in line of direction. Or takes two Two-Steps turning clockwise, then man walks four steps forward progressing in line of direction as lady twirls under raised right arm. Assume Varsouvienne position.

Note

This dance may be done with inside hands joined instead of Varsouvienne position.

🎵 Greensleeves

Greensleeves is a lively walking dance for four.

Records: Folkraft R6175; Merit AV-1; World of Fun LP 1, B-4.

Cassette: Dancecraft DC 162402.

Formation: Sets of two couples arranged in a double circle, couples facing counterclockwise. Lady to the right of the man, inside hands joined. First couple is 1 and second couple is 2.

Steps: Walking steps.

■ Directions for the Dance

Meter 4/4 • All dancers begin with the left.

Measures

	I.	**Sixteen Walks**
1–8		All walk counterclockwise with 16 crisp walking steps.

	II.	**Stars**
9–12		Couple 1 turns individually a half-turn to the right to form a right-hand star with couple 2. Couples walk briskly eight steps clockwise.
13–16		Couples turn individually a half-turn to the right to form a left-hand star. Couples walk briskly eight steps counterclockwise.

	III.	**Turning the Sleeves**
17–18		Couple 2 forms an arch, with joined inside hands, and walks forward and over couple 1 as couple 1 walks backward and under the arch to couple 1's original position.
19–20		Repeat. Couple 1 forms an arch and walks over couple 2 as couple 2 walks backward and under the arch to original position.
21–24		Repeat measures 17–20 for a second "Turning of the Sleeves."

Repeat dance from the beginning.

Nonesuch

Nonesuch is a dance from John Playford's *The English Dancing Master,* first edition, 1650. Tom Kruskal presented the dance at the 1973 University of Pacific Folk Dance Camp in Stockton, California.

Records: Express FR 3609 B; Westwind International WI 3330, side B, band 1.

Formation: Four couples in a Longway set, numbered 1–4 from top of set; partners facing, man with left shoulder to head of hall. All couples give partners right hands and face up the set to begin the dance.

Steps and Patterns: Walk: Very springy step, almost a run. Slip step: Step left foot to left (count 1), close right to left (count *and*). Two steps per measure. To move right, reverse footwork. A double: Four even running steps in a specified direction, step, step, step, close. Set: Leap right onto right foot (count 1); touch left toe beside right, transferring weight lightly (count *and*); step right in place (count 2); hold (count *and*). Repeat step, beginning left. Turn single: Individual dancer turns clockwise in place with four even steps. Arming: Partners hook right elbows and turn clockwise once (8 counts). Repeat hooking left arms, turning counterclockwise. Movement is "genteel-like," elbow high, forearm parallel with chest. Siding: Partners exchange places with four steps (4 counts), traveling in an arc, passing left shoulders and keeping eye contact with partner; retrace steps, passing right shoulders. **Note:** All step patterns may begin on either foot, except as noted.

■ Directions for the Dance

Meter 2/4

Measures

Chord Introduction: no action.

Figure I. Doubles and Set

Measures	
1–4	All couples forward a double and back a double.
5–8	Repeat action of measures 1–4, Figure I.
9–10	Drop hands and partners face. Beginning right, set right and left.
11–12	Everyone turn single.
13–16	Repeat action of measures 9–12, Figure I.

Figure II. Progression

This figure is danced as though it were a progressive Longway set; couple 1 dances Figure II with couple 2; couple 1 moves down the set and couple 2 begins the Figure II as soon as there is a couple below them. This progression continues until couple 4 reaches the head of set. This couple is the only couple not to dance the couple 1 pattern in the figure. At the end of figure, the couples are in this order: 4, 3, 1, 2.

foot		Progression Down Set					
○ □	4	4	4	1	1	2
○ □	3	3	1	4	2	1
○ □	2	1	3	2	3	3
○ □	1	2	2	3	4	4
head	1st	2nd	3rd	4th	5th	end

Nonesuch (continued)

1-2	First man and lady facing, man beginning right, lady left, take two slight setting steps toward each other.
3	Join two hands, arms outstretched firmly, slightly curved. Take two slip steps down center below couple 2.
4	Release hands. Take two steps, first man turning clockwise, first lady turning counterclockwise, three-quarter turn to face couple 2 and couple 2 turning one quarter to face couple 1. Two men join two hands; two ladies join two hands.
5-8	With four steps (a double), first man pushes second man diagonally forward out of set; second man moves backward and then draws second man backward a double, opening out into a line on last two steps (second man at head of set, first man in second place), inside hands joined. First two ladies dance the same.
9-12	Couples 1 and 2 fall back a double and move forward a double. Two men and two ladies move away from each other and toward each other.
13-16	Partners join two hands, couples 1 and 2, arms slightly curved. Take eight steps, turning clockwise one full turn and falling back into line.
17-80	Repeat action of measures 1-16, Figure II, four more times (total of five times). Remember that, on the third time, the second couple starts dancing while couple 1 dances with couple 4. **Note:** At the **end,** couple 4 will be at head of set. Renumber couples in set: 1, 2, 3, 4

Figure III. Siding, Arming, and Slipping

1-2	Everyone sides halfway with partner.
3-4	Everyone turns single.
5-6	Everyone returns to original position complete siding.
7-8	Everyone turns single.
9-16	At beginning of each measure, each person, in turn (man 1, lady 1, man 2, lady 2, and so forth), leaps into center, landing on both feet, to form a single line, facing partner. Men face down, ladies face up. **Note:** Begin leap so as to land in place on first count (downbeat) of each measure. Leap is subtle, light, and "genteel-like."
17-20	Everyone arms right with partner.
21-24	Everyone arms left with partner, to finish in single lines, partners facing.
25-26	Everyone takes four slip steps to own left.
27-30	Everyone takes eight slip steps to own right, passing partner face to face.
31-32	Everyone takes four slip steps to own left, ending back in line in center of set.
33-40	Each one in turn leaps backward into original place (man 1, lady 1, man 2, lady 2, and so forth). Land in place on downbeat.

Figure IV. Rights and Lefts

Couple 1 faces across set; couples 2, 3, 4 face up the set; couple 1 initiates action. Each couple begins and ends at a different time. Figure is like a grand right and left; set is "oval-like" during action.

1-16	Couple 1 joins right hands and pass; man 1 continues down ladies' line alternating left, right hands; lady 1 does the same, traveling down the men's side, crossing at the foot, coming up the lines. As each person enters the grand right and left, he or she continues in the direction facing until each crosses over at the head or foot of set, alternating hands, until each is back in original position. At end, couple 4 gives right hands to each other and turns halfway to place.

The Northdown Waltz*

Note from *The Playford Ball:* "The North Downs are a long ridge of hills running southwest from Rochester to Dover in Kent."

Source: Keller, K. and G. Shimer, *The Playford Ball;* Simon, A., *Kentish Hops (Third Pickings).*

Original from: Goulding & Cos., *Collection of New & Favorite Country Dances 1820.*

Record: Kentish Hops 2, KH 2.

Music: Barnes, P., *English Country Dance Tunes;* Keller, K. and G. Shimer, *The Playford Ball;* Simon, A., *Kentish Hops (Third Pickings).*

Formation: Duple Minor Longways.

Step: Walking waltz—three steps to the bar.

■ Directions for the Dance

Meter 3/4

Measures

Part A1

1-4   First woman and second man right-hand balance forward and back, then change places.

5-8   First man and second woman do the same.

Part A2

1-8   Repeat A1 back to original places.

Part B1

1-8   First couple leads down the middle and leads back to second couple's place (second couple moves up).

Part C

1-8   Take ballroom position and waltz completely around each other counterclockwise and end progressed.

---

*Directions and permission to publish courtesy George A. Fogg, 40 Gray Street, Boston, MA 02116-6210.

🌀 Oslo Waltz

The *Oslo Waltz* is a lively family-type Waltz mixer. It is of Scottish-English heritage, set to a Norwegian folk song.

Records: Canadian MH 3016; Folk Dancer MH 3016.

Formation: Single circle, couples facing center, lady to the right of partner, all hands joined.

Steps: Waltz, Waltz balance, three-step turn.

■ Directions for the Dance

Meter 3/4 • Directions are for man; lady's part reversed.

Measures

I. Waltz Balance and Lady Turn

1-2   Man begins left; all take one Waltz balance forward. Man begins right; all take one Waltz balance back.

3-4   Man begins left, Waltz balance steps in place as he turns left-hand lady from his left to his right side. Lady makes two clockwise turns in two Waltz steps.

5-16   Repeat measures 1-4 three times.

II. Step-Swing, Three-Step Turn
Singles circle, partners face in butterfly position. Man's new partner is lady on his right.

1-4   Man begins left, steps left to side, swings right across left. Steps right to side, swings left across right. Dropping hands, couples three-step turn individually toward center.

5-8   Man begins right; couples repeat step-swings and three-step turn to place.

III. Draw, Waltz

1-4   Butterfly position: Man begins left; couples take two step-draws toward center. Repeat two step-draws away from center.

5-8   Closed position: Man begins left; couples take four Waltz steps, turning clockwise, progressing counterclockwise around the circle.

Repeat dance from the beginning.

Source: Jackson, R. and G. Fogg, *A Choice Collection of Country Dances.*

Original from: *A Choice Collection of Country Dances with their Proper Tunes, whereof many never before Published, and in an easier Method to be understood than ever yet Printed, Gathered, Composed and Corrected by Many of the Best Masters of this Kingdom.* Dublin Printed & sold by John & William Neal in Christ Church Yard (ca. 1726).

Cassette: Bare Necessities *Take a Dance,* FF90564, will fit. Use the tune "Take a Dance."

Music: Jackson, R. and G. Fogg, *A Choice Collection of Country Dances.*

Formation: Duple Minor Longways.

Step: Walking.

■ Directions for the Dance

Meter 6/8

Measures

Part A1

1 – 4 First couple cross over and go below to second place.

5 – 8 First couple two-hand turn once and a half.

Part A2

1 – 8 Second couple repeat A1.

Part B1

1 – 8 Right- and left-hand star (hands across).

Part B2

1 – 4 Set twice.

5 – 8 Right and left with hands (3 changes).

Original instructions:

1st cu: cross over and turn in 2d cu: place:
2d cu: ye same in their own places:
All 4 right hands across half round, and left hands back again:
All Shuffle, then right and left:

---

*Directions and permission to publish courtesy George A. Fogg, 40 Gray Street, Boston, MA 02116-6210.

Road to the Isles

Road to the Isles is a favorite marching song of the pipe bands. The tune called "Bens of Jura" was composed by Pipe Major MacLellan about 1890 with words by Dr. Kenneth McLeod. The original words are very similar to the song "Border Trail." The dance is relatively new in composition and is similar to the Scottish Polais Glide and the Douglass Schottische.

Records: Folk Dancer MH 3003; Folkraft 1095, 1416; World of Fun LP 3, Side B-5; High/Scope RM-5 Compact Disc.

Cassette: Dancecraft DC 989; High/Scope RM-5.

Music: Rohrbough, Lynn, Cooperative Recreation Service, *Sing it Again, Handy II*, p. 16.

Position: Varsouvienne.

Steps: Schottische.

■ Directions for the Dance

Meter 2/4

Measures

	I. Point, Grapevine
1	Point left toe forward to left.
2–3	Step left behind right (count 1), right to right side (count 2), left in front of right (count 1), and hold (count 2).
4	Point right toe forward to right.
5–6	Step right behind left (count 1), left to left side (count 2), right in front of left (count 1), and hold (count 2).
7–8	Point left toe forward (body leans backward), point left toe back (body leans forward).
	II. Schottische
9–12	Beginning left, take two Schottische steps in line of direction. Without releasing hands, turn clockwise on hop (count 2, measure 12) to face reverse line of direction. Lady is now on man's left.
13–14	Beginning left, take one Schottische step in reverse line of direction. Without releasing hands, turn counterclockwise on hop to face line of direction. Lady is now back in original position on man's right.
15–16	Stamp in place right, left, right.

Style

The Scottish flavor may be added by precise and petite foot movement. Kicking the heel up on the hop of the Schottische step so as to flick the kilt is characteristic.

Siamsa Beirte

Siamsa Beirte is pronounced *SHI-um-suh BEHR-ti* and means "a frolic for two." Siamsa Beirte is a 2/4 Hornpipe time, *not* a Reel. Una and Sian O'Farrell introduced Siamsa Beirte at the Stockton Folk Dance Camp in 1956.

Records: Folkraft 1422, "Bluebell Polka"; Robin Hood 8001; World of Fun LP-5, Side B-4; or any evenly phrased Irish Hornpipe.

Music: "Bluebell Polka," Country Dancer, May 1951, p. 16.

Formation: Double circle, partners facing, man's back to center, right hands joined at shoulder height and left hand hanging relaxed by side.

Steps: Threes, rock, Schottische.

■ Directions for the Dance

Meter 2/4 • Directions are for man; lady's part reverse.

Measures

1–8   Introduction: no action.

"Threes" and Rock

1   Beginning right, hop in place, step to left on left, step right almost behind left, step left (counts *and* 1 *and* 2). Do not dip on second step.

2   Beginning left, repeat action in other direction (counts *and* 1 *and* 2).

3–4   Beginning right, hop in place; bringing left behind right, step on left, hop left; bringing right behind left, step on right, hop right; bringing left behind right, step on left; rock to side on right, rock to side on left (count *and* 1 *and* 2 *and* 1 *and* 2). The rock is side to side with feet close together, the right foot crossed in front of the left. Raise weight onto ball of foot and rock. The lady begins on the left foot but steps one foot behind the other as does the man.

5–8   Beginning with **left hop,** repeat action of measures 1–4 in reverse line of direction.

"Threes" and Change Over

9   Repeat action of measure 1.

10   Beginning with **left hop,** take one Schottische step to change places. Man moves around lady as she turns counterclockwise under joined right hands.

11–12   Repeat action of measures 9–10 and return to original position.

Irish Turn

13–16   Take both hands, crossed so that man's right joins lady's right on top and man's left joins lady's left underneath. Hold at shoulder height, elbows bent. Man pulls right hand toward him and down and under the left, rolling up so that the lady's forearms are resting on him. Beginning with right hop, take four Polka steps, turning clockwise, progressing in the line of direction. Irish Folk Dance teachers refer to this Polka (hop 1–3) as "turning threes." Both pull away slightly, remaining in a true facing position for this turn.

Style

The body is held erect but not stiff, with the head high; the steps are small, lively, and clean cut, with the toes pointing down.

Note

The rhythm hop step step step is taken in even rhythm (*and* 1 *and* 2) even though it is referred to as a Polka.

Three Meet is a dance of greeting from northern England.

Records: Folkraft 1112, 1262.

Music: Gadd, May, *Country Dances of Today, Book 2,* p. 15.

Formation: Sets of three, two ladies and a man, or vice versa, arms linked, facing another set of three. All sets form large circle; alternately one faces line of direction, the other reverse line of direction.

Steps: Running step, buzz step.

■ Directions for the Dance

Meter 4/4

Measures

I. Forward, Back, and Change Sides

1 – 4 Take four steps, moving forward, four steps moving backward. Take eight steps on a diagonal to right, passing opposite set and turning counterclockwise a half-turn to face same set on opposite sides.

5 – 8 In new place, repeat action of measures 1 – 4 to return to original place.

II. Elbow Swing

9 – 10 Taking eight steps, the middle dancer turns right-hand partner with right elbow swing twice around in place.

11 – 12 Middle dancer takes eight walking steps, turning left-hand partner with left elbow swing twice around. On last two steps, the three in set cuddle up (arms reach around each other, middle dancer's arms underneath) to form a basket of three.

III. Basket in Line of Three

13 – 16 In cuddle position, sets progress diagonally to right passing each other, while turning clockwise with a buzz step (right foot crossed in front of left), and meet new set coming in opposite direction.

Repeat dance, each set dancing with new set.

Note

The English Country Dancers are particular about attacking each new phrase of music on time.

Style

The English running step is a light, bouncy, dignified half-walk and half-run step. The body is in a dignified easy posture. The free hand of each outside dancer in the set hangs free to the side. The middle dancer holds the arms of the two partners in closely to his or her sides so that the threes can move easily as a unit. As a dance of greeting, the spirit is as light-hearted as the music. The dancers enjoy visiting around the circle to each new set of three.

---

*Dance arranged from the dance description by May Gadd, *Country Dances of Today, Book 2,* Country Dance Society of America, May 1951.

🎵 The White Cockade*   Scottish Reel 🎵

Dances with Jacobite names, like *The White Cockade,* are believed to have been composed by the many fiddlers in Scotland. After the 1745 rebellion, the pipes were banned. The Chiefs had their own fiddlers and the dances usually depict a famous battle, an event, or a place name.

Records: Scottish Dance Time Album Volume 4; or any eight-time 32-measure Reel in 4/4 meter.

Formation: Longway Reeltime dance. A four-couple set involving three couples in each 32-measure repetition. Top of set is indicated by left shoulder of first man.

Position: Feet in first position, hands by side.

Steps: Skip change step, pas de basque, slip step, setting.

■ Directions for the Dance

Meter 4/4 • Directions are same for man and lady.

Measures

1–8   Dance begins with honors to partner, men bow, ladies curtsey. First, second, and third couples set and cross over with two skip change steps giving right hands, then set and cross back with two skip change sets to original places, again giving right hands.

9–16   First couple leads down the middle and up again to top place in the middle of the dance. (Eight skip change steps.)

17–20 First couple casts off to second place on own side. Second couple steps up on measures 19–20. (Four skip change steps.)

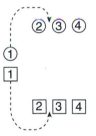

21–24 First and third couples dance four hands round to left. (Eight slip steps.)

25–32 Second and first couples dance rights and lefts with eight skip change steps.

Man = □   ○ ○
Lady = ○   □ □

Repeat, having passed a couple.
(From Preston, *24 New Country Dances for the Year 1797.*)

The White Cockade (continued)

---

*This dance is used by the permission of the Royal Scottish Country Dance Society, 12 Coates Crescent, Edinburgh, Scotland, EH3 7AF. Patron—Her Majesty The Queen; President—The Earl of Mansfield; Secretary—Miss M. M. Gibson. Permission granted April 16, 1986.

Note

Dance is repeated from second position, now involving third and fourth couples. Couple at the top stands and waits. At the end of the second sequence (32 measures), original first couple slips below the fourth couple, who now moves up. A new top couple starts the next 32 measures, or the third sequence. Once at the bottom of the set, the top couple becomes the new first couple.

Scottish Steps and Formations

Set or Setting: Two pas de basques in place facing as directed.

Skip Change Step: Begin in first position. Skip (hop) on left while extending right foot forward, knee straight and toe pointed. Step on right foot, keeping leg straight and firm. Close left to right in third rear position (remain on toes). Step forward onto right foot. Cues: Skip (hop), step, close, step.

Right and Left: Each dancer extends right hand to partner and changes places across the line; each dancer faces up or down the lines, gives left hand to other man or woman dancer, and changes places in line; each dancer gives left hand to other man or woman and finishes in original place. Cues: Across the line, up or down the line, across the line, up and down the line.

Slipping Step: This is used in all circles danced in Reel or Jig time, and in dances where the dancers join both hands to slip down, up or across the dance. The step is started from first position (i.e. heels together, feet turned out at right angles, with heels raised; take a step sideways with left foot (second position), bring right foot to left foot with heels touching (first position). Cue: step, together; step, together. Movements normally done in circles to the left and right.

Note

The symbols used to represent the man and lady are reverse of those used by the Royal Scottish Country Dance Society.

Willow Tree was composed by Hugh Rippon, formerly with the English Folk Dance and Song Society, in 1968. It is based on the Dutch Folk Dance Gort Med Stroop.

Record: Folklore Village FLV 7802 (6/8 and 2/4).

Music: Medley of "Willow Tree," (6/8) "Wabash Cannonball" (2/4), "Golden Slippers" (2/4); Werner, Robert, *The Folklore Village Saturday Night Book,* p. 37.

Formation: Longway set, eight couples. Head and foot couples are active; *do not* cross over.

Note: No call. Could prompt.

Directions for the Dance

Introduction: no action (4 counts).

A1, A2 **Partner change** (32 counts). Head couple, two hands joined, takes eight slides to foot of set (8 counts). Others clap hands. Head man leaves his partner at the foot, joins two hands with foot lady, and they take eight slides to head of set (8 counts). Foot man and lady #1 join two hands and take eight slides to head of set (8 counts). Foot man leaves lady #1 at the head of set and takes his original partner, two hands joined, and takes eight slides to return to original position (8 counts).

B1, B2 **Elbow Reel** (32 counts). Active couples, head and foot couples Reel, hooking right elbows with partner in middle of set, and turn clockwise once and a half, separate. Active men turn counterclockwise next lady in line, with left elbows hooked, once around as active ladies turn next man in line with left elbows hooked once around. Head couples move down, foot couple up the set turning alternately next person in line with left elbow and then partner with right elbow until active couples meet in middle of set (between couples 4 and 5). Each dancer is on original side. Head and foot couples join hands to form a ring of four, raise hands to form four arches.

C 1 **Cast out and Promenade** (16 counts).

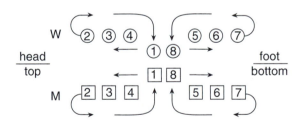

The remaining three head couples (2, 3, 4) face up the set; the remaining three foot couples (5, 6, 7) face down the set. Couples 2 and 7 individually cast out, walk down the outside of the set to the middle of set, move through arch made by head and foot couple; meet partner in center of ring of four, join inside hands. Couple 2 faces up, couple 7 faces down, move through the other arch, returning to head or foot of set. *(See diagram.)* Single-file, couples 3, 4, 5, and 6 move to head or foot of set, cast out, move through arches and promenade up or down set to next position.

C 2 **Swing** (16 counts). All couples swing. Couples 2, 3, and 4 have moved up one position and couples 5, 6, and 7 have moved down one position. Couples 1 and 8 are now in the middle of the set.

Willow Tree (continued)

Notes

1. Repeat dance until all couples have been active once or twice.
2. Forearm grasp may be used for reel.
3. Eight couples work best, but adjustments for six to ten couples are possible. Divide set in half; e.g., three couples and four couples. The Reel can move faster or slower to complete.
4. The first figure must be danced to the proper music. The swing may be shortened or eliminated to accommodate those that are behind.

France

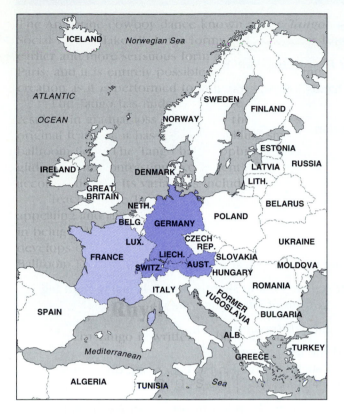

Dance Characteristics

Although originally settled by Celts, France, situated between the sea and the northern plains, with wide river valleys, was easily invaded by one group of settlers and warriors after another. Thus, the ancient dance rituals are quite varied. Although there are characteristics unique to different provinces, French dances tend to have many common features. The dances are simple in form, the behavior of dancers is very polite, and the movement is restrained. Many of the dances are based on one or two steps.

Music

In Brittany, the tunes are sung or played on a biniou (bagpipe) and a bombarde (rustic oboe). For La Farandole, the dancers are preceded by musicians, who play the tambourin (small drumhead with a long body) with the left hand and the galoubet (an oboelike instrument) with the right.

For La Bourrée, the native instruments are the cabrette (a simple form of bagpipe) and the vielle (an oval-shaped mandolin with a very short fingerboard and a resined wheel at the other end that is turned by a handle that strikes the strings as in a hurdy-gurdy). The cabrettaire (player of the bagpipe) often wears a band of small round bells on one ankle and taps the heel on the first beat of each measure to accentuate the rhythm.

🌿 Branle d'Ossau*

This is an open circle dance from Gascogne Pyrénées: Vallée d'Ossau in Béarn. Marilyn Wathen learned this dance from Pierre Corbefin in the summer of 1989.

Cassette: Marc Castanet et Michel Le Meur: *Raccord Duo Swing,* Side B, Band 1.

Formation: Open circle, traveling left (clockwise), hands joined, arms down, men and women alternate positions along the line.

Steps: Rocking step and as analyzed in dance description.

■ Directions for the Dance

Meter 2/4 • Directions are the same for man and lady.

Measures

Introduction: Dancers may begin at the beginning of any musical phrase.

1 Traveling to the left, dancers face center: Step left (count 1), hop slightly on left bringing right leg over in front of left (count 2), step across on right in front of left (count *and*).

2 Backing up slightly in line of direction, step left, right, left (counts 1, 2, *and*).

3 Dancing in place, step on the right slightly behind the left (count 1), hop slightly on right while bringing left leg behind right (count 2), step on left slightly behind right, end facing the center (count *and*).

4 Facing center, step on right in front of left (count 1), step back on left in place (left foot is behind right) (count 2), step on right in place (in front of left) (count *and*). The movement resembles a "rocking step" in place.

Repeat dance from beginning.

---

*Dance description and permission to use Branle d'Ossau courtesy of Marilyn Wathen. Cassette tape available from Marilyn Wathen, 2463 Darla Drive, Santa Rosa, CA 95401.

🎵 La Crouzade*

The bourrée from Auvergne has many names and variants in the Massif Central. This version was learned by Marilyn Wathen in France in the summer of 1986.

Cassette: "La Crouzade," *Le Soleil: Bal Folk en Californie.*

Formation: Two couples, woman on man's right, man's right hand holding woman's left, arms bent. Man has left hand on hip. Couples form a straight line with men side by side in the line, left elbow to left elbow. Women are on the outside (exterior) of the line. Each couple faces ready to travel counterclockwise. Women's right hands down at side.

Steps: Pas de bourrée (traveling forward), man's stamping pattern, man's lateral Pas de bourrée to left, woman's lateral pas de bourrée to left, man's lateral pas de bourrée to right, woman's lateral pas de bourrée to right.

■ Directions for the Dance
Meter 3/8

Measures

Introduction (3 measures)

Part A—Pas de Bourrée

1-6   Two couples side by side in a line as described above under "Formation." Couples dance six pas de bourrée traveling forward counterclockwise, beginning with left.

7-8   Men dance man's stamping pattern while women dance pas de bourrée in place. It is customary for partners to look at each other during these measures.

9-14   Repeat measures 1-6.

15-16   Man turns partner counterclockwise under right arm and places her in front of him. Partners are now face to face in a quadrette. Man may do stamping pattern.

Part B—Va et Vient (Quadrette Formation)

1-4   **Men:** Facing center, dance lateral pas de bourrée to the left, dancing outside the quadrette.

Women: Facing center, dance lateral pas de bourrée to the right, passing each other face to face in center of quadrette.

La Crouzade (continued)

---

*Dance description and permission to use La Crouzade courtesy of Marilyn Wathen. Cassette tape available from Marilyn Wathen, 2463 Darla Drive, Santa Rosa, CA 95401.

5-8   Repeat measures 1–4 with women dancing lateral pas de bourrée to left outside the quadrette and men dancing lateral pas de bourrée to right, passing each other face to face in center of quadrette.

9-16   Repeat measures 1–8. Style: Arms up and slightly forward, elbows slightly bent and palms forward.

Part C—Chaîne Anglaise (Quadrette Formation)

1   Dancers in quadrette formation as in Part B, partners facing each other. Give right hand to partner traveling forward with one pas de bourrée step beginning with left, pass partner's right shoulder.

2   Give left hand to opposite man/woman, traveling forward with one pas de bourrée step beginning with right, pass left shoulders.

3-4   Give right hand to own partner traveling forward with two pas de bourrée steps beginning left, pass partner's right shoulder. Partners look at and acknowledge each other during these measures.

5-6   Give left hand to opposite man/woman, traveling forward with two pas de bourrée steps beginning left, pass left shoulders.

7-8   Give right hand to own partner, women dance two pas de bourrée steps in place, beginning with left. Men dance man's stamping pattern in place. Partners look at each other.

9-10   Continue with Chaîne Anglaise, repeating measures 5–6.

11-12   Repeat measures 3–4.

13-14   Repeat measures 9–10.

15-16   Partners dance two pas de bourrée steps beginning with left while getting into position to begin the dance from beginning (Part A), partners side by side, woman on man's right, man's right hand holding his partner's left hand. **Note:** Throughout the Chaîne Anglaise the women are traveling clockwise and the men are traveling counterclockwise.

        Repeat dance from the beginning.

Steps

Pas de bourrée (traveling forward). Step forward on the left (count 1), step on the right beside left or slightly forward of the left (count 2), step on the left slightly forward (count 3). Step alternates. This step may also be done in place.

Man's stamping pattern (2 measures): Stamp left in place (counts 1–2), hop on left (count 3), stamp right, kicking left forward from knee (count 1), hold (counts 2 and 3).

Man's lateral pas de bourrée to left (4 measures): *Measure 1:* Facing center and traveling left, step on left to left (count 1), close right to left (count 2), step slightly sideward to left on left (count 3). **Note:** Count 1 is a larger step to left than count 3. *Measure 2:* Still facing center and traveling left, cross right in front of left (count 1), step on left (count 2), close right to left or step on right slightly in front of left (count 3). *Measures 3–4:* Man's stamping pattern.

Woman's lateral pas de bourrée to left (4 measures): *Measures 1–2:* Same as man's lateral pas de bourrée to left. *Measure 3:* Repeat measure 1, taking slightly smaller steps and traveling less. *Measure 4:* Step right in place (count 1), step on left beside right (count 2), step right in place (count 3).

Man's lateral pas de bourrée to right (4 measures). *Measure 1:* Facing center and traveling to the right, step on left crossing in front of right (count 1), step on right to right (count 2), step on left beside right or slightly in front of right (count 3). *Measure 2:* Step on right to right (count 1), step on left beside right or slightly in front of right (count 2), step on right slightly to right (count 3). *Measures 3 - 4:* Man's stamping pattern.

Woman's lateral pas de bourrée to right (4 measures). *Measures 1 - 2:* Same as man's lateral pas de bourrée to right. *Measure 3:* Repeat measure 1, taking slightly smaller steps and traveling less. *Measure 4:* Step on right in place (count 1), step on left beside right (count 2), step on right in place (count 3).

Style

Very flat and smooth. Knees slightly bent throughout. Traditionally dancers may begin with either right or left foot. However, for teaching purposes, all steps are described starting with the left foot.

⚘ La Montagnarde* ⚘

La Montagnarde (lah mohn-tahn-YARD) is a bourrée from the Auvergne region of central France. It is done in "cortège" formation, which can accommodate any number of couples. Marilyn Wathen learned the dance in France in 1986, and presented it at the University of Pacific Folk Dance Camp in 1987.

Cassette: "On Y Va," Side A/3 or "Lo Drac," Side A, Band 7.

Formation: Couples, one behind the other in a long column facing "up the set" (cortège). Lady to the left of man, right hands joined behind man's back, and left hands joined behind lady's back. Couples are spaced three to four feet apart and should maintain this distance.

Steps: Pas de bourrée, man's stamping pattern, man's right lateral pas de bourrée, woman's right lateral pas de bourrée, man's left lateral pas de bourrée, woman's left lateral pas de bourrée. Arms: During all right and left pas de bourrée steps both men and women have arms up, slightly forward, elbows bent, palms forward, and hands at or just above head level.

■ Directions for the Dance

Meter 3/8

Measures

Introduction: An improvisation of the bagpipe (cabrette) plus three measures—no action.

I. Avance (Advance)

1-8   Couples in cortège formation move forward "up the set" with pas de bourrée steps. Eight measures is suggested but is not a fixed number when danced in the village or at a bal folk, but at the beginning of an 8-measure phrase and every 8 measures thereafter the "head couple" will begin Figure II.

II. Tour sur Place (Turn in Place)

1-4   Beginning left, the "head couple" turns once and a half clockwise in place with four pas de bourrée steps, and ends facing "down the set."

5-6   Same couple releases hands and separate, bringing arms up. Lady passes in front of man, moves diagonally forward to the right with two pas de bourrée steps, while man moves diagonally forward to left with two pas de bourrée steps. Man ends to left of and just beyond the man of couple 2. Woman ends to right of and just beyond the woman of couple 2.

7-8   Man dances man's stamping pattern. Woman turns once half counterclockwise to end facing "up the set."

III. Croisement (Crossing)

1-4   Couple 1 dances right lateral pas de bourrée in the slot between couple 2 and couple 3, passing face to face.

5-8   Couple 1 dances left lateral pas de bourrée in the slot between couple 3 and couple 4, again passing face to face. In this figure man always faces "down the set" and active woman "up the set." Continue with this figure proceeding down the set until the couples meet at the bottom of the set, where they join hands in position for Figure I. Couples may do a clockwise turn.

Every eight measures the new "head couple" will begin Figure II, then continue "down the set" with Figure III. The cortège continues to dance the pas de bourrée moving "up the set," keeping three to four feet spacing between couples to accommodate those doing Figure III. **Note:** The dance can continue indefinitely!

---

*Dance contributed by Marilyn Wathen and arranged from dance descriptions by Jack Peirce for the Folk Dance Federation of California, Inc. January 1988.

Steps

Pas de bourrée: Step forward on the left (count 1), step on the right beside or slightly forward of the left (count 2), step on the left slightly forward (count 3). The step alternates. It also may be done turning in place or marking time in place.

Man's stamping pattern (2 measures): *Measure 1:* Stamp left in place with weight (count 1), hold (count 2), hop on left (count 3). *Measure 2:* Stamp right kicking left forward from knee (count 1), hold (counts 2 and 3).

Man's right lateral pas de bourrée (4 measures): *Measure 1:* Facing "down the set" and traveling right, step on the left crossing in front of right (count 1), step on right to right (count 2), step on left beside or slightly forward of right (count 3). *Measure 2:* Step on right to right (count 1), step on left beside or slightly forward of right (count 2), step on right slightly to right (count 3). *Measures 3-4:* Man's stamping pattern.

Man's left lateral pas de bourrée (4 measures): *Measure 1:* Facing "down the set" and moving left, step on left to left (count 1), step on right beside left (count 2), step slightly left on left (count 3). *Measure 2:* Step on right crossing in front of left (count 1), step on left to left (count 2), step on right beside or slightly forward of left (count 3). *Measures 3-4:* Man's stamping pattern.

Woman's right lateral pas de bourrée (4 measures): *Measures 1-2:* Facing "up the set" and moving right dance measures 1-2 or man's left lateral pas de bourrée. *Measures 3-4:* Make one full turn clockwise with two pas de bourrée steps, beginning with the right. End facing "up the set."

Woman's left lateral pas de bourrée (4 measures): *Measures 1-2:* Facing "up the set" and moving left dance measures 1-2 or man's left lateral pas de bourrée. *Measures 3-4:* Make one full turn counterclockwise with two pas de bourrée steps, beginning with the left. End facing "up the set."

Style

Arms: During all right and left lateral pas de bourrée steps both man and woman have arms up, slightly forward, elbows somewhat bent, palms forward, and hands at or just above head level.

Generally the styling is very flat and smooth; the knees are slightly bent throughout. The dance may be done an indefinite number of times with any number of couples, but it is less effective with too few couples since the feeling of a long cortège or column of dancers would be lost.

Note

Music on cassette available from Marilyn Wathen, 2463 Darla Drive, Santa Rosa, CA 95401.

🌿 La Tournijaire* 🌿

There are many variants of this dance found in the Massif-Central. This particular variant from Auvergne is an arrangement of figures learned in France from Yvon Guilcher in summer 1984. Three other variants of this dance were observed in the Rouergue. Pronunciation: *lah-toor-nih-JIGH-ruh.*

Cassette: *Bal Folk en Californie* by Le Soleil, Side A/3.

Formation: Couples in a circle, woman on man's left. Hands joined, arms up in a *W* position.

Steps: Pas de bourrée, man's stamping pattern, Waltz.

■ Directions for the Dance

Meter 3/8

Measures

Introduction (3 measures plus 1 count).

I. Ronde

1. Eight measures traveling to left: Facing center and traveling to the left, step on left to left (count 1), close right to left (count 2), step slightly sideward to left on left (count 3). Count 1 is a much bigger step to left than count 3. Styling is smooth, flat, gliding. Knees are slightly bent throughout.

2. Still facing center and traveling to left, cross right in front of left (count 1), step to left, cross right in front of left (count 1), step to left on left (count 2), close right to left (count 3).

3-4. Repeat measures 1-2.

5-8. Repeat measures 1-4, except on measure 8 dance pas de bourrée in place ready to change direction.

1. Eight measures traveling to right: Facing center and traveling right, step on left slightly behind right (count 1), step on right beside left (count 2), step on left beside right (count 3). **Note:** This step travels only slightly to the right. It is used as a transition step to change direction.

2. Step on right to right (count 1), step on left beside right (count 2), step on right slightly to right (count 3).

3. Step on left crossing in front of right (count 1), step on right to right (count 2), step on left beside right (count 3).

4. Repeat measure 2.

5-8. Repeat measures 3-4 two more times. On measure 8 dance pas de bourrée in place or travel only slightly to get ready for refrain, which follows.

Refrain

1-8. **Women:** Form a circle in the center, hands joined and arms up in *W* position. Women repeat Ronde figure traveling eight measures to the left as in Figure I.

Men: Beginning left, dance individual clockwise turns while moving counterclockwise with a small flatfooted waltz step turning smoothly and continuously. End on measure 7 facing center. *Measure 8:* Step right in place (count 1), small step sideward left on left (count 2), close right to left (count 3). Men hold arms up and slightly forward palms forward.

---

*Dance description and permission to use La Tournijaire courtesy of Marilyn Wathen. Cassette available from Marilyn Wathen, 2463 Darla Drive, Santa Rosa, CA 95401.

9-16		**Women:** Reverse direction of Ronde and travel eight pas de bourrée steps to right as in Figure I.
		Men: Facing center, travel to left (clockwise) with basic pas de bourrée step as in Figure I of Ronde. Arms still up and slightly forward.
	II.	**Right and Left Hand Around**
1-8		Facing partner (woman is on man's left), join right hands (arms bent) and dance eight pas de bourrée steps traveling clockwise in a circle with partner beginning with left foot.
9-16		Facing "corner" (the woman on man's right), join left hands and dance eight pas de bourrée traveling counterclockwise in a circle with "corner." Man helps right-hand woman get into formation for the Refrain.
		Refrain
1-16		Repeat measures 1-16 of the Refrain.
	III.	**Panier (Basket Hold)**
1-8		Men form front basket hold by joining hands in front of women. (Women are already in a circle with hands joined from the Refrain. Women lower arms in this figure so men can form basket hold over their arms.) Circle travels to the left eight measures beginning with the left foot.
9-16		On count 1 of measure 9, change to regular hand hold (arms up in *W* position). Circle continues to travel eight measures to the left with basic pas de bourrée (Ronde formation) beginning with the left foot. Circle widens and picks up speed.
		Refrain
1-16		Repeat measures 1-16 of Refrain.
	IV.	**Chaîne**
1-2		Facing partner (woman on man's left), join right hands (arms bent) and begin right and left chain, men traveling diagonally left out of the circle, women traveling diagonally toward center of circle with two basic pas de bourrée steps, beginning with the left.
3-4		Give left hand to next partner, men traveling diagonally toward center of circle and women traveling diagonally right out of circle with two basic pas de bourrée steps beginning left. **Note:** Men travel clockwise, women travel counterclockwise around circle.
5-8		Repeat measures 1-4, traveling around the circle and chaining with partner's number 3 and partner's number 4.
9-10		With partner number 4, do two basic pas de bourrée steps turning one half turn counterclockwise around each other to face in opposite direction (the direction from which you came).
11-16		Repeat measures 1-6: Men now travel counterclockwise, women travel clockwise alternating right hand (measures 11-12) and left hand (measures 13-14), and end facing original partner. Dancers use measures 15-16 to get into closed social dance position with original partner. Man should end with back to center.
	V.	**Valse**
1-16		**Note:** (There is no Refrain after Figure IV Chaîne.) In closed dance position waltz sixteen measures with partner. Man begins left, woman begins right, turning clockwise and traveling counterclockwise around the circle.
		Ending: Musicians play an "ending" motif during which man may turn partner clockwise under their joined hands to finish dance.

Note

Man's stamping pattern may be used in Ronde measures 7-8; in Refrain measures 15-16; or in Panier measures 15-16. Refer to p. 287 for man's stamping pattern.

✿ Mon Père Avait un Petit Bois

Mon Père Avait un Petit Bois is pronounced *mohn pair ah-veh tanh puh-tee bwah* and means "my father had a little woods." This dance is a Branle, a 16th-century court dance. Branle comes from *branler*, to shake, and is also known as "brawls."

This Branle was introduced at Mendocino Folk Lore Camp in 1963, by Madelynne Greene as taught to her in Normandie, France, in 1962 by Madame Jeanne Messager, leader of Ethnic Dance Group in Caen.

Record: "Branle Normand," Folkraft 337-002.

Formation: Single circle, hands joined and held down. No partners.

Steps: Walk, step-hop, branle.

■ Directions for the Dance

Meter 4/4 • Directions are the same for all.

Measures

1–2   Introduction: no action.

1–2   Beginning right, take four walking steps (slow, slow, slow, slow). Circle moves counterclockwise.

3   Facing center of circle, step forward on right (count 1); hop on right, swinging left leg with knee bent backward (count 2); step left (count 3); hop on left, swinging right leg straight forward (count 4). Arms swing backward and body bends forward (counts 1–2), arms swing forward and body leans backward (counts 3–4).

4   Repeat action of measure 3.

5–8   Repeat action of measures 1–4.

9–12   Beginning right, take eight branle steps. Branle step: Step right in place, left foot comes behind and just below right calf, softly touching (count 1), hop on right (count 2). Hands remaining joined, thrust right hand out to right, left elbow bending (count 1), maintaining arm position (count 2). Reverse footwork and arms for branle step, beginning left (counts 3–4).

Lyrics

This dance is frequently done to the singing of the song, unaccompanied.

1. Mon per'avait un petit bois
   d'ou venez-vous bell'promener avec moi
   Il y crossait bien cinq cents noix
   d'ou venez-vous belle D'ou venez-vous donc.
   d'ou venez-vous promener-vous promener la
       belle
   d'ou venez-vous bell'promener avec moi.

1. My father had a little woods
   Where do you come from, pretty (girl),
       stroll with me.
   There grew at least 500 nuts
   Where do you come from pretty girl,
       where do you come from.
   Where do you come strolling from pretty girl
   Where do you come from, pretty girl,
       stroll with me.

2. Il y crossait bien cinq cents noix
   d'ou venez-vous bell'
   Sur les cinq cents j'en mangais trois
   d'ou venez-vous bell'.

2. There grew at least 500 nuts
   Where do you come from pretty girl
   Out of the 500, I ate three
   Where do you come from pretty girl.

3. Sur les cinq cents j'en mangais trois
   d'ou venez-vous bell'
   J'en fus malade au lit des mois
   d'ou venez-vous bell'.

3. Out of the 500, I ate three
   Where do you come from pretty girl
   I was sick in bed for months
   Where do you come from pretty girl.

4. J'en fus malade au lit des mois
   d'ou venez-vous bell'
   Tous mes parents m'y venaient voir
   d'ou venez-vous bell'.

4. I was sick in bed for months
   Where do you come from pretty girl
   All my relatives came to see me
   Where do you come from pretty girl.

5. Tous mes parents m'y venaient voir
   d'ou venez-vous bell'
   mais non et n'y venais pas
   d'ou venez-vous bell'.

5. All my relatives came to see me
   Where do you come from pretty girl
   But no, and don't come
   Where do you come from pretty girl.

🌀 Rondeau de Garein* 🌀

A line dance from Gascogne as learned by Marilyn Wathen in Toulouse in the summer of 1986.

Cassette: "Suite des Rondeaux," *Bal Folk en Californie* by Le Soleil.

Formation: Line leading to the left (clockwise), hands joined right over left, arms bent at the elbows or hands joined down at the side. Alternate position for men and women along the line is preferable.

Step: As analyzed in dance description.

■ Directions for the Dance

Meter 2/4

Measures

Introduction (4 measures)

1   Facing center, lift slightly on right (preparatory left count *ah*), step to left on left (count 1), step on right beside left (count *and*), step slightly to left on left (count 2).

2   Facing center, step on right crossing over in front of left (count 1), step to left on left (count *and*), step on right crossing over in front of left (count 2).

3   Step in place on left (count 1), bounce twice in place on left, kicking right forward slightly from the knee, (knee is bent) and retract right foot slightly (counts 2 *and*).

4   Step back slightly on right (count 1), with slight preparatory lift on right (count *and*), close left to right with left heel next to right toes turned slightly out to the left (count 2).

Repeat dance from beginning.

---

*Dance description and permission to use Rondeau de Garein courtesy of Marilyn Wathen. Cassette tape available from Marilyn Wathen, 2463 Darla Drive, Santa Rosa, CA 95401.

🍃 Scottish*

This variant of the Scottish is from Gascogne in the southwest part of France. Marilyn Wathen learned this dance from Pierre Corbefin in the summer of 1989.

Cassette: Marc Castanet et Michel Le Meur: *Raccord Duo Swing,* Side A, Band 5 or Side B, Band 2.

Formation: Couples in closed ballroom position at random around the room.

Steps: Two-step, buzz turn.

■ Directions for the Dance

Meter 2/4 • Directions are for man, lady's part reversed.

Measures

1   Step sideward left (count 1), close right to left (count *and*), step sideward to left on left (count 2), hold (count *and*).

2   Repeat measure 1 in opposite direction with opposite footwork.

3   Turning to face line of direction (open ballroom position), walk side by side with partner stepping left, right (counts 1, 2).

4   Face partner, repeat measure 1.

5   Repeat measure 2.

6   Repeat measure 1.

7 – 8   Starting with right, make a very flat, smooth, walking-style, "buzz turn" step, turning clockwise in place, ending with left foot free on (count *and*) at end of measure 8.

Repeat dance from beginning.

*Dance description and permission to use Scottish courtesy of Marilyn Wathen. Cassette tape available from Marilyn Wathen, 2463 Darla Drive, Santa Rosa, CA 95401.

Alpine Region—Switzerland, Austria, and Germany

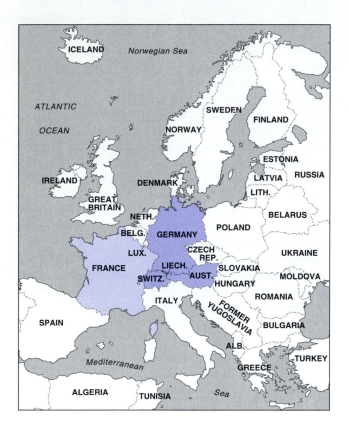

Dance Characteristics

Despite the differences in language, religion, politics, and geography, Switzerland, Austria, and Germany share many similarities in dance, particularly in the Alpine region. The most popular couple dances are the Waltz, Polka, and Schottische. The Ländler is a common dance with many variations. It is basically a courting dance in character: the man leads the lady through many figures in 3/4 or 4/4 time, and eventually the couple ends in closed position, revolving together around the dance floor. In 3/4 time, a flat-footed, even Waltz (smooth) rhythm is maintained, and it is thought to be the forerunner of the Viennese Waltz. The *Schuplatter* is also well known in the Alpine region as a part of the Ländler or as a solo dance for men. Characteristically, the men stamp their feet and slap their knees, thighs, boots, or lederhosen to the rhythm of the music. The dance originated with the woodcutters in their free time, as a possible imitation of a grouselike wild bird during mating season.

The ritual dances are danced on special occasions, particularly at carnival time. Sword Dances and dance-dramas like the English ones are a part of carnival. Dance formations tend to follow the usual European patterns of Longway Sets, Quadrilles, squares, or circles.

Folk Dancing in Switzerland

By Karin Gottier*

The dances of eastern Switzerland are very similar to those of alpine Germany and Austria, while the dances of the western Swiss cantons are related to those of France and in the south, to those of Italy. Most Swiss dances are couple or group dances using the steps of the popular ballroom dances of the 19th century: Mazurka, Waltz, Polka, Schottische, and Gallop. Perhaps because of the austerity of the Calvinist period, few traditional dances survived and many of the contemporary Swiss folk dances are reconstructions based on traditional dance figures that were collected and set either to traditional tunes or to melodies especially composed for these dances. Very few ritual dances have remained and those are usually danced at "driving out winter" ceremonies, carnival, spring and harvest celebrations, and at the time of the ascent and descent of the cattle from the high pastures. There is literary evidence that Switzerland still knew "dances of death" until the middle of the last century. One such source is Gottfried Keller. In his novel *Der grüne Heinrich*** he describes a funeral dance:

> We immediately hurried outside to where, on the corridor and stairs, the crowd began to pair off and form a procession, for without a partner no one was allowed to go up. I took Anna by the hand and fell into line which began to move, led by the musicians. They struck up a lugubrious mourning march, to the rhythm of which we marched three times around the attic, which had been converted into a ballroom, and formed a large circle. Hereupon seven couples stepped into the center and executed a lumbering old dance with seven figures and difficult jumps, kneefalls and intertwinings, accompanied by resounding clapping. After the spectacle had gone on for some time, the host appeared and went through the rows thanking the guests for their sympathy; here and there whispering into the ear of a young man—in such a way that all could hear—that he should not take the mourning too much to heart and to leave him (the host) now alone with his grief. Moreover, the host recommended that the youth should rejoice again in life. Whereupon he walked away and climbed down the stairs with lowered head as if they led directly to

---

*Folk Dancing in Switzerland was written by Karin Gottier, 74 Wilshire Road, Vernon, CT 06066.
**Gottfried Keller, *Der grüne Heinrich*, München: Wilhelm Goldmann Verlag.

Tartarus. The musicians suddenly switched to a gay "Hopser," the older people withdrew and the young swept shouting and stamping across the groaning floor.

In character Swiss dances are more sedate and earthbound than their German counterparts. Among folk dance groups, great emphasis is placed on precision of detail in the placement of hands and arms and in the holds between partners.

The Swiss Folk Dance movement has from its inception been a branch of the Swiss Costume Association (Schweizerische Trachtenvereinigung), which fosters and encourages the practice of all aspects of folk art. One of the pioneers in the field of Swiss folk dance was Luise Witzig. After having come into contact with the German and English folk dance movement, she recognized the importance of folk dance research and its significance to the work of the Costume Association. She began to conduct dance workshops in which she transmitted the results of her research work. This encouraged others to collect and notate existing material in their immediate areas. The Swiss Costume Association then made it its task to systematically collect old tunes and dance figures which were still to be found, especially in the Alpine areas. Because early researchers were able to find only fragments, many Swiss dances are reconstructions or new creations. By 1935 it was possible to publish the first collection of dance notations. Since then, this organization has released records as well as books and pamphlets on the dances of all cantons. It also conducts annual folk dance leader training courses and folk dance workshops, always insisting on high standards of accuracy and precision.

Alongside the folk dance movement of the Swiss Costume Association, there exists the Association of Folk Dance Groups (Arbeitsgemeinschaft Schweizer Volkstanzkreise), which is a collective member in the Swiss Costume Association. This organization was formed in 1956 and consists of independent dance groups who practice all forms of European folk dancing and sponsor specialized workshops in the dances of a given country, conducted by an expert in that particular field. The objectives and practices of the Folk Dance Association are very similar to the recreational folk dance movement in the United States.

D'Hammerschmieds g'selln

(*D'Hammerschmieds g'selln*) is pronounced *duh-HAM-mair-shmeets-guh-sehln* and means "the journeyman blacksmith." This Bavarian dance was originally performed by men only. The intrigue of the clapping pattern has made it a popular dance. It was introduced by Huig Hoffman from Belgium at Stockton, California, and Moorehead, Kentucky.

Records: Folkraft 1458; High/Scope RM 7 and CD.

Cassette: High/Scope RM 7.

Formation: Set of four dancers, two couples, lady on partner's right (a) or four men, partners facing each other (b).

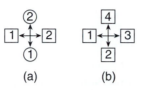

(a)   (b)

Steps: Step-hop, Waltz.

Clap Pattern:

Counts	Two measures = 6 counts
1	Both hands slap own thighs as knees flex slightly.
2	Clap own waist, body turning slightly left.
3	Clap own hands together.
4	Opposites clap right hands.
5	Opposites clap left hands.
6	Opposites clap both hands.

■ Directions for the Dance

Meter 3/4 • Directions are same for both man and lady, except when specially noted.

Measures

Introduction: no action.

Clap Pattern

1–16   If two couples, the men start clap pattern (count 1) and continue through measure 16. The two ladies start clap pattern on count 1 of measure 2 and continue through measure 16. Couple one will be on count 4, clapping opposite dancer's right hand when couple two begins. Or, if four men, man 1 and man 3 start; man 2 and man 4 start on measure 2.

Figure I. Circle

17–24   All four join hands. Beginning left, take eight step-hops, circle moving clockwise.

25–32   Reverse direction, taking eight step-hops, circle moving counterclockwise.

Clap Pattern

1–16   Repeat action of measures 1–16.

D'Hammerschmieds g'selln (continued)

Figure II. Star

17 – 24   Form right-hand star. Beginning left, take eight step-hops, star revolving clockwise.

25 – 32   Form left-hand star. Take eight step-hops, star revolving counterclockwise.

Chorus, Clap Pattern

1 – 16   Repeat action of measures 1 – 16.

Figure III. Large Circle

17 – 24   Circles of four open out to form one large circle. Beginning left, take eight step-hops, circle moving clockwise.

25 – 32   Reverse direction, taking eight step-hops, circle moving counterclockwise.

Variation (Mixer)

1 – 16   Clap pattern.

17 – 24   Figure I or II repeat circle left or right-hand star.

25 – 32   Take corner for new partner. Closed position. Man beginning left, lady right, take eight Waltz steps, turning clockwise, dancing anywhere. Form a new set with a new couple to start clap pattern.

Notes

1. During circle figure, arms should be firm and dancers should lean slightly back, using centrifugal force, which adds zest to the dance.
2. The inner action of partners and couples in the precision of performing the clap pattern adds to the fun-loving spirit of the dance.

Dr Gsatzlig means "exactly" and is from Appenzell in Switzerland. Jane Farwell learned this dance there and introduced it across the United States in 1954. Later, Jane corrected one of the figures slightly, which accounts for two different versions. Although the music is written is 2/4 meter, it has the quality of a Schottische.

Record: Folk Dancer MH 1114.

Music: L. Witzig and A. Stern Pub. Hug and Co., Zurich 12 *Schweitzer Tanze.*

Position: Closed, man's back to center of circle, man's left, lady's right arms extended toward line of direction.

Steps: Side step, Schottische, Two-Step.

■ Directions for the Dance

Meter 2/4 • Directions are for man; lady's part reverse.

Measures

	1–4	Introduction.

I. Dr Gsatzlig (Side Step)

A	1–2	Beginning left, take four side steps forward, moving in line of direction.
	3	Take two side steps in reverse line of direction, swinging joined hands sharply down, elbow bending, upper arm shoulder high.
	4	Take two side steps in line of direction, arms extended toward line of direction. Joined hands always point in the direction traveling.
	5–8	Beginning right, repeat action of measures 1–4, traveling in reverse line of direction.
A	1–8	Repeat action of measures 1–8.

II. Heel and Toe Schottische

B	9	Open position. Beginning left, take one heel and toe.
	10	Take one step-close-step-close in line of direction. Weight remains on left.
	11–12	Swinging joined hands sharply down, elbow bending, upper arm shoulder high, face reverse line of direction. Beginning right, repeat action of measures 9–10, moving in reverse line of direction.
	13–16	Closed or shoulder-waist position (latter preferred). Beginning left, take four slow Two-Steps (Swiss Schottische steps) turning clockwise, progressing in line of direction.
B	9–16	Repeat action of measures 9–16.

III. Dr Gsatzlig (Side Step)

A	1–8	Repeat action of Figure I, measures 1–8.

Dr Gsatzlig (continued)

---

*Dr. Gsatzlig included by permission of Jane Farwell, Folklore Village Farm, Dodgeville, WI.

IV. Schottische

C 17–18 Man faces line of direction, crossed arms held on chest; lady faces man, back to line of direction, hands on hips, knuckles toward body. Beginning left, take two Schottische steps (step close step-hop) (Swiss Polka) in line of direction. Both move diagonally toward center, then away from center, always progressing forward.

19–20 Take four slow step-hops in line of direction, man stamping left on first step, lady turning clockwise twice.

21–24 Repeat action of measures 17–20.

C 17–24 Repeat action of measures 17–24, with right hands joined, free hand on hip. The lady turns clockwise under man's raised arm.

V. Dr Gsatzlig

A 1–8 Repeat action of measures 1–8.

Routine

AABBACCAABBACCA. The record, Folk Dancer MH 1114, allows for this sequence.

Style

The Swiss dance movements are small and precise. Keep the steps simple without much extension of the knee or foot. The side steps are little steps; do not scrape the foot, but lift each foot. Turn head and focus eyes on the direction of travel during the side steps. The abrupt change of direction and focus of a large group is very effective. Keep free hands on hips. Keep step-hops low and subdued. Jane Farwell refers to it as a **leisurely dance.**

Notes

1. It is fun to sing "la-la-la" during the specific tune for Dr Gsatzlig.
2. Add a few shouts "ya'hoo'hoo'hooy" any time.
3. In Switzerland, they call a Polka a Schottische and a Schottische a Polka. Since this book is used primarily by Americans, the terms Schottische and Polka as defined by Americans are used.

Krüz König*

German

"Krüz König" is a German dialect expression for *Kreuz König* which means "king of clubs." "Heinrich Dieckelmann, a German folkdancer and pianist, composed the tune and made a present of it to his friend Ludwig Burkhardt" in 1924. Burkhardt immediately contacted Folk Dance groups in Hamburg and Berlin for ideas. Four couples in a square was very common in northern Germany. There was a desire for dances with more vivacity and more difficult figures. One day the dance was born, with no claim to steps or figures of ancient origin. Krüz König was a new Folk Dance. Ludwig Burkhardt was well known for his leadership in teaching German Folk Dance to young people and teachers, as well as for his early publications of German Folk Dance. He described his dance in *Kneveler, das Tanzbuch mit "Krüz-König,"* Bärenreiter Verlag Kassel, 1927.

Record: "Folk Dancer" MH 1022 or "Tanz" SP 23 030.

Music: Herman, Michael, *Folk Dances for All,* p. 89.

Formation: Set of two couples facing, lady to right of partner, hands joined in a circle of four.

Steps: Running steps, step-hop steps, Mazurka steps, Achtervör steps: step left foot to left, step right foot close behind left, step left foot to left and right across left. **Note:** This is like a grapevine step, but is *not leaped!* It is danced very close to the ground.

Key to symbols: Man facing forward □ Woman facing forward ○

■ Directions for the Dance

Meter 3/8

Measures

1–4	Introduction: no action.

Figure I. Circle of Four

1–4	Beginning left, circle left with one Achtervör step and eight running steps.
5–8	Repeat measures 1–4.

Figure II. Wings

1–8 repeat	Partners take conversation position. Men hook left elbows to form a line of four. Formation turns counterclockwise with 24 running steps. At the end of this figure, men release hold and women take a small step to the right to face center.

①→ ①–② ←②

Figure III. Straight Chain

9–10	With two step-hops men change places by giving left hands. Women dance two step-hops in place. Each man is now facing the opposite woman.

①→ ②–① ←②

Krüz König (continued)

*Krüz König directions translated by Karin Gottier, 74 Wilshire Road, Vernon, CT 06066.

| 11 – 12 | With two step-hops men change places with women by giving right hands. The women are now on the inside of the set. |

| 13 – 14 | With two step-hops women change places by giving left hands to each other while men dance two step-hops in place. Women are now facing their original partners. |

| 15 – 16 | Original partners give right hands and change places with two-step hops. Men are now on the inside of the set. |

| 9 – 14 repeat | Repeat measures 9 – 14 returning to original place. Women are still on the inside. |

| 15 – 16 repeat | With extended right-hand grasp, man pulls partner with momentum and half-turn counterclockwise to his right side to place. At the same time, men release women's right hand and take their left. All join hands to form a circle of four. |

Note: This figure should be executed with well-stretched arms and a large floor pattern.

Figure IV. Circle of Four, Circle of Two with Mazurka

17 – 20	Beginning left, all dance four Mazurka steps clockwise. Release hold with corner.
21 – 22	Take two-hand hold with partner. Continue to turn clockwise with two Mazurka steps.
23 – 24	Without changing hold or direction, couples turn twice clockwise with six running steps.
17 – 22 repeat	Repeat four Mazurka steps in circle of four and two Mazurka steps turning with partner.
23 – 24 repeat	Repeat the 6 running steps turning partner; however, turn only once with three running steps and change to a right-hand hold. Men lead their partners to the center with right arms well extended, so that women stand in the center *right shoulder to right shoulder,* facing in opposite directions. Men take corner woman's left hand in their own left.

Figure V. "King of Clubs"

| 25 – 28 | **Women on inside:** The two men run 12 steps clockwise, turning the two women, who form the center axis, with them. |
| 29 – 32 | **Men on inside:** Left hand is released. With 6 running steps, man leads woman by the right hand outward to his place, taking her place in the center, standing right shoulder to right shoulder with the opposite man. Each woman takes the left hand of corner man into her own. |

They run clockwise with 6 steps, turning the men, who form the axis of the formation, with them.

25 – 28 repeat   **Women on inside:** With 6 running steps women release left-hand hold and lead their partners by the right hand outward, taking men's place in the center. Both men take left hand of corner lady in own left and continue to turn the set clockwise with 6 running steps.

29 – 32 repeat   **Men on inside:** Repeat measures 29 – 32 with women dancing on the outside and men on the inside. During the last measure, men make half a jump-turn clockwise and join hands in a circle of four. Men will have their original partner on their left and the corner lady, who is now their new partner, on their right. The dance is repeated one more time with the new partner.

Styling note: The last figure should be danced with well-stretched arms. Dancers on the outside of the formation need to pull away from center of the set with their left arms. All stand very tall. In circle figures, the momentum is established by pulling away from the center of the set, or from partner. The character of the entire dance is one of restrained energy and controlled strength.

🌀 Man in the Hay

Records: Folk Dancer MH 1051; High/Scope RM 3 LP and compact disc.

Cassette: High/Scope RM 3.

Music: Burchenal, E., *Folk Dances of Germany*, p. 28.

Formation: Set of four couples in Square Dance formation.

Steps: Skip, slide.

■ Directions for the Dance

Meter 6/8 • Directions are same for both lady and man, except when specially noted.

Measures

	1–4	Introduction: All join hands and swing arms forward and back briskly, standing in place. The movement is small and staccato. Keep elbows straight and stand in close formation.

I. Circle

A 1–16   Beginning left, take 16 skips clockwise. Repeat counterclockwise.

Chorus

B 9–10   Head couples take closed position. Man beginning left, lady right, take three slides to center and pause or stamp.

11–12   Man beginning right, lady left, take three slides back to place and pause or stamp.

13–16   Man beginning left, lady right, take six slides across set to opposite side, men passing back to back. Step left, bring right foot to left and hold. Do not turn.

17–20   Repeat action of measures 13–16, returning to home position, ladies passing back to back. Man leads with right foot, lady left.

9–20   Side couples repeat action of measures 9–20, B.

II. Ladies Circle

A 1–8   Four ladies join hands in circle. Beginning left, take 16 skips clockwise. Men clap.

Chorus

B 9–20   Repeat action of measures 9–20, 9–20, B.

9–20

III. Men Circle

A 1–8   Four men join hands in circle. Beginning left, take 16 skips clockwise. Ladies clap.

Chorus

B 9–20   Repeat action of measures 9–20, 9–20, B.

9–20

IV. Basket

A 1–8   Head couples form circle, men's arms around ladies' waists, ladies' arms around men's shoulders. Beginning left, take 16 skips or slides clockwise. A buzz step may be used here with the right foot in front of the left. Keep basket hold firm and lean back.

Chorus

B 9–20   Repeat action of measures 9–20, 9–20, B.

9–20

		V.	**Basket**
A	1 - 8		Side couples repeat action of Figure IV, measures 1-8, A.

Chorus

B	9 - 20	Repeat action of measures 9-20, 9-20, B.
	9 - 20	

		VI.	**Circle**
A	1 - 8		Take 16 skips clockwise and end with a bow to the center of the circle with hands still joined.

Variation

Arrange all the squares so that they are directly behind and beside another square, so that the couples may slide through several squares and return to original position during the chorus.

Measures 13-16, B, man beginning left, lady right, take eight slides across set and on through as many sets as they can go, men passing back to back. Measures 17-20, B, repeat action of measures 13-16, returning home, ladies passing back to back.

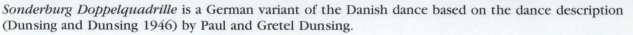

❧ Sonderburg Doppelquadrille   German ❧

Sonderburg Doppelquadrille is a German variant of the Danish dance based on the dance description (Dunsing and Dunsing 1946) by Paul and Gretel Dunsing.

Records: Folkraft 1163; World of Fun LP 4, Side B-1.

Music: Dunsing, Gretel and Paul, *Dance Lightly*, p. 16.

Formation: Two lines facing each other, four couples in each line. Head couples are two couples on each side of line nearest head of set. Foot couples are two couples on each side of line forming remainder of set.

Steps: Walk, Polka.

■ Directions for the Dance

Meter 2/4 • Directions are same for man and lady, except when specially noted.

Measures

I. Two Circles

1–16   Head couples and foot couples join hands and form two separate circles. Beginning left, take 16 walking steps to left, circle moving clockwise; then take 16 walking steps to right, circle moving counterclockwise, ending in original formation (two lines).

II. Heads Down Center

17–24   Head four join inside hands with opposite dancer and take eight walking steps moving down center of set (toward foot) and on eighth step turn individually to face reverse line of direction. Join inside hands and take eight walking steps forward to return to place.

25–32   Foot four repeat action of measures 17–24, moving toward head of set and back to place.

III. Four Circles

17–32   Opposite couples join hands. Take 16 walking steps, moving to left, and take 16 walking steps moving to right, ending in original position.

IV. Chain

33–40   Opposite couples execute grand right and left in small circles, four dancers each. Opposite dancers join right hands, pass, left hand to partner, and so forth, ending in place and bowing to partner.

41–48   Repeat action of measures 33–40.

V. Polka

33–48   Couples take closed position or shoulder-waist position. Man beginning left, lady right, take 16 Polka steps turning clockwise, progressing in line of direction around oval circle formed by two lines, back to place.

Variation

Measures 33–40, opposite couples may execute right and left through across the set, then back to place, instead of grand right and left.

Various forms of this dance were collected in the Alpine regions of Bavaria, Austria and the German settlement areas of Czechoslovakia. The most widely danced variant was collected by Hermann Derschmidt in 1924 in Klaffer, Upper Austria, and published by him and Erna Schützenberger in their five-part collection, *Spinnradl-unser Tanzbuch.*

Record: Tanz EP 58 129, "Osterreichische Tänze"; Tanz EP 58 118, "Volkstänze aus dem Sudetenland," series I; Folkraft 1474.

Formation: One man between two women. He holds their outside hands, while they join their inside hands behind his back. All face line of direction, left shoulder to the center. Arms are loosely stretched.

Steps: "Dreierschritt" (triple-walking step): a smooth, unaccented walk in 3/4 time. One triple-walking step requires three walking steps. Jump, light running steps.

■ Directions for the Dance

Meter 3/4

Measures

1 – 4	Introduction
1 – 8	Beginning left, all move forward with 8 triple-walking steps. These steps are danced close to the ground, smoothly and unaccented. Man looks alternately at the left and right woman.
9	On count 1, man pulls women forward. As their joined hands pass over his head, he bends his knees briefly and immediately stands up again. The joined hands of the women are now in front of him. On counts 2 and 3 the right woman turns once counterclockwise with two steps. She now stands between the man and left woman. (All hands should be held closed together. *Do not* release hold!)
10	As man and left woman form arch by lifting their joined hands, right woman slips under the arch by bending her knees briefly on count one. She continues moving to the right side of man. On counts 2 and 3 the left woman begins to make a clockwise turn.
11	While left woman continues to turn under her own arm to the right on count 1, the man begins to turn left on counts 2 and 3. All are back to the beginning position.
12 – 14	Repeat measures 9 – 11. This time the left woman slips through the arch, which is formed by man and right woman. The right woman turns out counterclockwise and the man clockwise.
15	All move forward with three short, light running steps.
16	All execute a *silent,* soft jump on both feet. Repeat measures 9 – 16.

Note: *At no time do the dancers back up.* The action moves forward over the head of the turning person. The movements of measures 9 – 16 flow into each other. The dancers do not remain in place but continue to move slightly forward in the line of direction. The character of the dance is smooth and flowing. The steps are danced close to the ground with no accent. The jump is soft, elastic, and silent.

Hermann Derschmidt writes in the collection *Spinnradl-unser Tanzbuch* "the man must see that the 'ducking under' does not occur backwards, rather through the pulling of joined hands over head by the other two partners. . . the 'ducking under' must occur exactly on the first count, during the second and third count each partner in turn prepares to duck under." Erna Schützenberger and Hermann Derschmidt, *Spinnradl-unser Tanzbuch,* p. 15, Musikverlag Josef Preissler, Munich, 1974.

---

*Spinnradl zu Dritt directions translated by Karin Gottier, 74 Wilshire Road, Vernon, CT 06066.

Czech and Slovakia

Dance Characteristics

As 1992 dissolved into 1993 so the former country known as Czechoslovakia dissolved its unity and by virtue of a "velvet divorce" peacefully became two separate political units, Czech Republic and Slovakia. Despite the separation many common threads remain. The Czechs are of Slavic origin and speak a common Slavic language. Children's dances and games reflect some of the oldest elements found in Slavic culture and are similar to games and dances found in Poland, Russia, and the general Balkan region.

In the past, the two countries' rich mineral and agricultural resources attracted both Western and Eastern invaders, and migrating tribes and warriors have long used the rivers that flow from east to west.

During the 17th century, Bohemia, Moravia, and Slovakia were a part of the Austro-Hungarian Empire. English Country Dances and Western Court Dances were introduced. About that time, the Italians were invited to the courts. Consequently, the dance tradition of Czech and Slovakia has been influenced by both Western and Eastern culture. In the western regions, the folk songs are in the major key; in the east, in the minor key. In the west, where industrialization is more developed, the folk customs are preserved by societies and through holidays, but in the east, where it is more agriculturally oriented, many of the folk customs, including wearing traditional dress, are very much a part of daily life.

Music

The oldest native instruments are the kobza (like a lyre), the viol, the lucec (hurdy-gurdy), the bagpipe, and the drum. A typical Slovakian folk band also includes a dulcimer and a violin. In southern Bohemia, the bagpipe is played alone or with a violin, and, in eastern Bohemia, the bands are composed of clarinets, violins, double basses, horns, and trumpets.

Doudlebska Polka*

Doudlebska Polka, pronounced *DOH-dleb-ska,* is a simple mixer learned in Czechoslovakia by Jeannette Novak and introduced to American folk dancers through Folk Dance House, New York.

Records: Canadian MH 3016; Festival 114007; Folk Dancer 3016; Folklore Village 45; Folkraft 1413, LP-13.

Formation: Couples in closed position form one large circle or several smaller circles. Directions are for one large circle.

Steps: Polka, walk.

■ Directions for the Dance

Meter 2/4 • The directions are for man, lady's part reverse.

Measures

1–4		Introduction: no action.

I. Polka

1–16   Beginning left, take 16 Polka steps turning clockwise, traveling in line of direction.

II. Walk and Circle

17–32   Open position, lady's free hand on hip. Man stretches left arm out to place hand on left shoulder of man in front as couples take 32 walking steps moving in line of direction. This action moves dancers toward center to form a ring of couples. As ring revolves counterclockwise, everyone sings "tra-la-la," and so forth.

III. Men Clap, Ladies Circle

33–48   Men face center of circle and clap hands throughout figure as follows: clap own hands (count 1), clap own hands (count *and*), clap hands of man on both sides, shoulder high (count 2). Ladies with hands on hips, take one half-turn clockwise to face reverse line of direction and take 16 Polka steps, progressing forward in reverse line of direction around men's circle.

On last measure, each lady steps behind a man, and men turn around and begin dance again with new partner.

Variation

1. Measures 1–16, for beginners a heavy Two-Step and the Varsouvienne position or inside hands joined may be substituted.
2. Measures 33–48, the men may slap a thigh occasionally, duck down, or cross their own hands over when they clap neighbors' hands.
3. Measures 17–32, if group is large, form several small circles.
4. Measures 33–48, if more than one circle is formed, ladies may "cheat" by moving from one circle to another.

Notes

1. Those without partners go to the center (the "lost and found" department) and meet the other one without a partner.
2. If there are extra people, extra men without a partner may join dance during star figure, and extra ladies may join ring as ladies Polka around outside.
3. Encourage group singing during the march, especially loud. It makes the dance fun!

---

*Dance arranged from the dance description by Michael Herman and reproduced by permission of Folk Dance House, New York, NY.

Tancuj

A Czech folk dance pronounced *ton-tsooy*.

Record: Folk Dancer MH 1017.

Formation: Double circle, couples facing, hands joined. Men's backs to center of circle, ladies face center.

Steps: Two-step, runs, hops.

■ Directions for the Dance

Meter: 2/4

Measures

Part I. Step Together Step, Swing

1-2 Moving to men's left, ladies' right. Men step sidewards left, close right to left, step left and swing right across left. Ladies: step sidewards right, close left to right, step right and swing left across right.

3-4 Repeat moving in opposite direction. (Note: Swing joined hands vigorously.)

5-16 Repeat measures 1-4 three times.

Part II. Run

1-8 Partners take a right hip position. Place right hand on partner's left hip, hold own hand on own hip. Run clockwise sixteen steps.

9-16 Change to left hip-to-hip position and run sixteen steps counterclockwise.

Part III. Step Together, Step Swing

1-16 Repeat Part I, Step together, step swing.

Part IV. Heel and Toe

1-8 Partners move away from each other, men to center, ladies away from center. Hop on left, place right heel down, hop on left, place right toe down. Repeat hopping on right. Dance eight "heel-toe" movements away from partner.

Part V. Run

1-16 Repeat Part II, clockwise and counterclockwise run.

Repeat dance from the beginning.

Hungary*

Introduction

By Andor Czompo

Hungarian folk dances can be grouped into five major categories: Herdsmen's dances (Pásztor táncok), Leaping dances (Ugrós táncok), Maidens' round (Leány karikázó), Recruiting dances (Verbunk), and the Csárdás. To establish these categories certain principles of classification were applied, based on the analysis of the spatial, technical, musical-rhythmical, and functional characteristics of the dances. Each of these dance types also represents different historical periods reflecting certain socio-cultural conditions. Although these dances comprise the living dance repertory of the Hungarian peasantry, their existence and popularity vary greatly within Hungary, and show not just functional differences, but varied geographical distributions, too.

The old layer of the Hungarian folk dances includes the Herdsmen's dances, the Leaping dances, and the Maidens' rounds. They date back to the Middle Ages, and show similarities with other European folk dances of the same period. Besides the Maidens' rounds, which are always danced in a closed circle with varied handholds and accompanied by singing, the boundaries of the other older

---

*Introduction written by Andor Czompo, Box 238, Homer, NY 13077.

dances are not always clear. Their formations in particular show great variety from male solo to group and mixed couple variations. The dance tunes that accompany these dances also belong to the old layer of Hungarian dance music as defined by Béla Bartók. Other ancient and common characteristics are the lack of physical contact (or maybe just a handshake hold) between the partners in couple dances, and the unstructured, improvised mode of performance. In the dance repertory of the village folk in the 20th century, these dances reached the last stage of their natural existence. They are performed on rare occasions at weddings, family gatherings, or other festivities.

The recent, newer style of Hungarian folk dances, the Verbunk and the Csárdás, evolved and developed during the 18th and 19th centuries. Assuming a national character, they became the representative Hungarian dances both in Hungary and abroad.

The Verbunk (from the German word *werben:* recruiting) is the result of the 18th-century military recruiting practice, when musical entertainment and jollification were used to attract the attention of the young men and induce them to join the military service. The early Verbunk hardly differed from the male solo Leaping and Swineherd's dances; the technique, formation, and musical accompaniment adjusted later. In western Hungary a semicircle and circle form developed with a regulated structure, and often a dance leader was in charge. In eastern Hungary the dance maintained a solo form with a rich, highly improvised movement repertory of heel clicks, leg swings, and rhythmical boot-slapping. The earlier "Old Style" dance music, notated in 2/4 meter, changed to a more stately 4/4 beat with regular accents. This new style of music became very popular both in folk and national art music, and continued in the popular Csárdás music well into the 20th century. Although it lost its military significance, the Verbunk is still danced on special occasions. During regularly organized dance events, the Verbunk is the first dance of the dance order, followed by a general couple Csárdás.

The Csárdás (from the word *csárda:* roadside inn) is the most recent, the most popular, and the most widely known Hungarian dance. It developed during the 19th century from earlier couple dances by adopting some Western European couple dance components, such as shoulder-waist and waltz positions for closer physical contact, and some turning elements. Improvised and unstructured, the Csárdás is usually danced in two parts. It begins with a Lassú (slow) section, where a Two-Step-like motif is dominant, performed mainly sideways. This is followed by a shorter Friss (fast) part, where turns and vertical movements dominate. The partners occasionally separate, providing an opportunity for the male to dance a solo, utilizing motifs and patterns from the Verbunk.

After the Second World War the traditional lifestyle of the Hungarian peasantry changed drastically. The survival of the folk dances shifted to an institutionalized movement, emphasizing stage performance. During the 1970s and 1980s a new trend emerged, the so-called "Táncház" (dance house) movement. This is mainly an urban phenomenon. Devotees gather in clubs and youth centers to dance traditional folk dances to live music provided by village-style orchestras. The emphasis is on enjoyment, reestablishing the original purpose and function of folk dancing. There are still many well-known village folk ensembles, guarding traditional forms and principles with a conscious effort.

Dance Characteristics

Style

Hungarian dance allows for individual expression and spontaneous improvisation. Very few dances are set. One person is the leader and the others follow. Although the basic step may be simple, the rhythm becomes very complex and the improvisation that occurs with much stamping is a challenge to follow.

The ornamentation that accompanies a basic step may be very involved.

The carriage of the body is important: It is very proper, firm, and erect. The body movement responds to the Hungarian music, which is unique. The element of snap (as in Scottish dancing) is present. The preparatory movement is along or into the ground, which gives the dance abrupt stops and changes in rhythm.

Music

Although Gypsy music is preferred by Hungarian dancers, the Gypsies did not use the native Hungarian instruments. The Gypsy string orchestras consisted of three or more instruments: one or more violins, a bass viol, and a cimbalon.

Some of the native instruments include the following: the tarogato (a wooden wind instrument like a clarinet), the swineherd's horn, the bika (like a bagpipe), the flute (like a whistle), the székler (a plucked string instrument), and the zither. Rhythm from the clicking of spurs was an integral part of many dances. Brass rattles the size of walnuts were fastened on both sides of the leg just below the knee.

Hungarian Motifs*

Technical exercises utilizing basic Hungarian folk dance motifs and their combinations are very useful in increasing the skill level and agility needed to perform Hungarian dances. The exercises may be done in a "follow the leader" style. First try each motif several times in the order listed, making changes at the half point or end of melodies. Later, leaders may arrange their preferred patterns and create new and interesting combinations.

Formation: Circle with a simple side-low hand hold or let individual dancers hold hands on hips and face the center of the room.

Music: Any good medium tempo (quarter note = 140–160 beats per minute) Verbunk, Csárdás, or Kanász-ugrós music in duple meter. Example; Hungaroton LPX 13031-32; Szatmári Verbunk or Dunántúli Ugrós or AC Special #3; Lassú Csárdás.

Motifs

1. **Knee Bends**
   Bend both knees slightly (counts 1–2), straighten both knees (counts 3–4). **Note:** The knee bends can be done in first position (feet together parallel) or second position (feet apart sideways parallel). Repeat the same way.

2. **Knee Bounces**
   Before count 1 bend both knees slightly. Straighten both knees with a slight accent (count 1), bend both knees slightly (count 2). Repeat the same way. **Note:** The preliminary knee bend is necessary only at the beginning. The knee straightenings coincide with the primary accent of the music.

3. **Side Close Step** (Single Csárdás step)
   Step on the right foot to the right side (counts 1–2), close the left foot to the right (no weight) (counts 3–4). Repeat with opposite footwork and direction.

4. **Double Csárdás Step**
   Step on the right to the right side (count 1), step on the left in place (beside right) (count 2), step on the right to the right side (count 3), close the left to the right (no weight) (count 4). Repeat with opposite footwork and direction.

5. **Step Hop**
   Step on the right in place (count 1), hop on the right in place (count 2). Repeat with opposite footwork.

6. **Cifra**
   Leap on to the right side (count 1). step on the left in place (count *and*), step on the right in place (count 2). Repeat with opposite footwork and direction.

   Variation: Cifra (Pas de Basque)
   Leap onto the right foot to the right side (count 1), step on the left in front of the right (count *and*), step on the right behind the left (count 2). Repeat beginning leap to left.

   Variation: Back Cross Cifra
   Leap onto the right foot to the right side (count 1), step on the left behind and across the right (count *and*), step on the right in front of and across the left (count 2). Repeat beginning leap to left.

7. **Leap Hop Kick**
   Leap onto the right in place with a slight knee bend. At the same time lift the left in the back so the left lower leg is close to parallel with the floor (count 1); hop on the right in place. At the same time kick the left to forward-low position (count 2). Repeat beginning to the left.

8. **Run and Click**
   Take two running steps, right and left in place (counts 1–2), close the right to the left with accent (slight heel-click) (count 3), pause (count 4). Repeat the same way.

Hungarian Motifs (continued)

---

*Motifs arranged and permission to use courtesy of Andor Czompo. Music available from A.C. Publications, P.O. Box 238, Homer, NY 13077.

9. **Heel Click**

    Bend both knees slightly. At the same time open both heels (pigeon-toed) (counts 1 – 2), straighten both knees. At the same time close the heels together with a slight accent (counts 3 – 4). **Note:** May be performed with these counts or twice as fast. Repeat the same way.

10. **Cross Jump Heel Click**

    Jump into a "crossed position" (right foot in front of left) (count 1), jump into second position (feet apart and pigeon-toed) (count 2), jump into first position (feet together parallel, knees straight) (count 3), pause (count 4). Repeat the same way.

Csárdás Palócosan*

Csárdás in Paλóc style is from north-central Hungary. This version is arranged by Andor Czompo.

Record: Rounder 5005, side A, band 2, "Play the Bagpipe, Uncle John."

Formation: Independent couples. Partners face and join in a shoulder-shoulder position.

Motifs: Double Csárdás, turning Csárdás, two-step.

■ Directions for the Dance

Motifs

1. **Double Csárdás** (♩♩♩♩)

    Step on the right, to the right side (count 1), step on the left beside the right in place (count 2), step on the right to the right side (count 3), close the left to the right with partial weight (count 4). Repeat beginning left.

2. **Turning Csárdás** (♩♩♩♩)

    Step on the right in place turning 1/4 to the right (count 1), step on the left in place (count 2), step on the right in place turning 1/4 to the right (count 3), close the left to the right with partial weight (count 4).

3. **Two-Step** (♪♪♩)

    Step on the left forward (count 1), step on the right in place (count *and*), step on the left forward (count 2). Repeat beginning right.

■ The Dance

Measures 4/4

Introduction: One note.

1 – 2	Double Csárdás twice starting to the man's right. Woman follows with opposite footwork.
3	Man executes the Turning Csárdás. Woman following the man's lead walks with three steps clockwise about halfway around the man (left, right, left) closing the right to the left with partial weight on the fourth count.
4	Double Csárdás to the man's left.
5 – 8	Repeat measures 1 – 4.
9	Double Csárdás to the man's right.
10 – 12	Two-step three times. During two-step partners release hands and separate. Man makes a small circle to his left; woman with opposite footwork circles to her right. At the end they rejoin in Csárdás position.

Repeat the dance from the beginning four times.

---

*Description and permission to use Cárdás Palócosan courtesy of Andor Czompo. Records and cassettes available from A.C. Publications, P.O. Box 238, Homer, NY 13077.

❧ Kiskanásztác*

Kis means small, short. Kanásztánc is a swineherder's dance. This dance is a short version of a type of dance known as Kanásztánc. Although the majority of these dances are done with an implement (stick, shaft, small ax with a long handle), this version utilizes motifs that can be done without those implements. There are many sources for this dance. This arrangement is by Andor Czompo.

Records: Rounder 5005 "Jew's Harp Music," Side 1, Band 3, or any good moderate tempo Kanásztánc or Ugrós: AC #3, LPX 18007, LPX 18031-32.

Formation: Solo, ie., single dancer, hands on hips.

Motifs: Steps and hop, back cross Cifra, close and step.

■ Directions for the Dance

Motifs

1. **Steps and Hop**   (♩♩♩♩)

   Step on right toward a right forward diagonal into a small knee bend (count 1), step back on the left (count 2), step on the right forward into a small knee bend (count 3), hop on the right, turning about 1/4 to the left, at the same time swing the left lower leg forward (count 4). Repeat beginning left.

2. **Back Cross Cifra**   (♪♪♩)

   Small leap onto the right to the right side (count 1), step on the left behind the right (count *and*), step on the right in front of the left (count 2). Repeat beginning left.

3. **Close and Step**   (♩♩)

   Starting position: Weight is on the left in a small knee bend. The right foot is right-side-low with a slightly bent knee. Close the right to the left with accent (heel click). At the same time straighten both knees (count 1). Small step on the right forward into a small knee bend. At the same time lift the left to the left-side-low position with a slightly bent knee. Repeat beginning right.

Individual dancers have hands or fists on hips. Start the dance at any time with the music.

■ The Dance

Measures 2/4

1–4   Dance the Steps and Hop motif twice.

5–6   Dance the Back Cross Cifra motif twice.

7–8   Dance the Close and Step motif twice.

Repeat this sequence several times until the end of the music.

Note: For those who like to improvise, each motif may be done any number of times or in a different order.

---

*Description and permission to use Kiskanásztác courtesy of Andor Czompo. Records and cassettes available from A.C. Publications P.O. Box 238, Homer, NY 13077.

🌀 Ugrós*

A contemporary recreational folk dance in Hungarian Ugrós style arranged by Andor Czompo.

Record: Rounder 5005, side 2, band 6, "For a Birthday."

Formation: Solo, i.e., a single dancer, hands on hips.

Motifs: Touch and step, back cross Cifra, lift and step with claps, heel click.

■ Directions for the Dance

Motifs

1. **Touch and Step** (♩♩)

   Touch the right heel forward on the floor (leg straight) (count 1), step on the right in place (count 2). Repeat beginning left.

2. **Back Cross Cifra**

   Small leap onto the right to the right side (count 1), step on the left behind the right (count *and*), step on the right in front of the left (count 2). Repeat beginning left in opposite direction.

3. **Lift and Step with Claps** (♩♩)

   Lift the right knee forward and hit the right thigh with the right hand (count 1), step on the right in place. At the same time clap the hands together in the front (count 2). Repeat beginning left foot and hand. **Note:** Man can lift the leg forward with bent and turned out knee and hit the inside of the lower leg (boot top). **Variations on the clap:** Replace the single clap (♪♪) with a double or triple clap. (♪♪♪)

4. **Heel Click** (♩♩♪‖)

   Starting position: Weight on left. The right foot is right-side-low with a slightly bent knee. Close the right to the left with slight accent (knees are straight) (count 1), bend the knees and at the same time turn out (open) both heels (pigeon-toed) (count 2), close the heels together with accent and straighten knees (count 3), pause (count 4).

■ The Dance

Measures (2/4)

Individual dancers face the music or the center of the dance floor. Hands are on hips. During the dance individual dancers can turn and change facing direction at will.

	Introduction; the first full melody.
1–2	Dance the Touch and Step motif #1 twice (right and left).
3–4	Dance the Back Cross Cifra motif #2 twice (right and left).
5–8	Repeat measures 1–4.
9–10	Dance the Lift and Step motif #3 twice (right and left) with single claps.
11	Dance the Lift and Step motif #3 with double or triple claps.
12	Dance the Lift and Step motif #3 with left foot and hand.
13–14	Dance the Back Cross Cifra motif #2 twice (right and left).
15–16	Dance the Heel Click motif #4 one time.
	Repeat the dance from the beginning.

---

*Description and permission to use Ugrós courtesy of Andor Czompo. Records and cassettes available from A.C. Publications, P.O. Box 238, Homer, NY 13077.

Russia

Dance Characteristics

The former Union of Soviet Socialist Republics (USSR), a political unit, was made up of 16 republics and many cultures (Slavs, Turks, Ugrian tribes, Mongolians, and Tartars). Movement of people and intermarriage have existed for a long time. Consequently, a great variety of dance is found in Russia, reflecting these many cultures.

The term *Russian dance* refers to a geographical location in central Russia. These are typical north Slavic dances: fast and slow, musical phrases of six or eight measures, including many prysiadka (knee bend) variations for the men.

Many of the dances favored by American Folk Dancers come from the Ukraine, where the Cossacks lived. Cossack dancing is reflective of the spirit of fearless soldiers and superb horsemen. It is exuberant, exciting, and characterized by fast running, leaping, and pas de basque steps and by the difficult knee bend or prysiadka steps, used by the men. Also characteristic are turning, spinning, stamping, and heel clicking. The Ukrainian dancers are unsurpassed for their vitality, competitive spirit, and endurance.

Georgia is located at the eastern end of the Black Sea. The language of Georgia (belonging to the Turki-Tartar group) relates to that of the Basques. The tall, stately men dance on the tip of their toes, moving at varying tempos but always maintaining an illusion of floating constantly through space.

The Western influence on Russian dance is limited to the Court Dances and the contact with Poland.

Style

The Russian dances are characterized by emotional expressiveness. The movements are fluid in the warm countries and very vigorous in the cold countries. The Russian dances are not always set. On the inspiration and the mood of the dancer, the steps are changed.

Music

The song-dances are sung by choirs with musical accompaniment. There are also ceremonial dances performed today with only vocal accompaniment. When Peter the Great tried to Westernize the musical tastes of his people, the native instruments were banned. The people then sang for the dancers. But, in the courts, imported classical instruments and Western Court Dances became very popular.

Russian music uses the pentatonic scale (five notes in an octave). The stretching or leaping that is followed by a sustained position in dance coincides with the characteristics of the pentatonic scale.

During the latter part of the 17th century and the early part of the 18th century, peasant dances and folk songs became popular with all classes. The Russian minstrels are credited with making the balalaika popular. Eventually, even the aristocrats became interested in learning to play it.

🌀 Alexandrovska

Alexandrovska is a Russian Ballroom Dance, probably named in honor of Czar Alexander.

Records: Folk Dancer MH 1057; Folkraft 1107; Worldtone 10031.

Music: Fox, Grace, *Folk Dancing in High School and Colleges,* p. 10; Beliajus, V. F., *Dance and Be Merry,* Vol. 1, p. 22.

Position: Partners face, two hands joined.

Steps: Waltz, draw step.

■ Directions for the Dance

Meter 3/4 • Directions are for man; lady's part reverse.

Measures

I. Face to Face, Back to Back

1   Beginning left, take one draw step to left.

2   Step left to side (count 1), release man's left hand, lady's right, pivot on left back to back, swinging joined hands and right foot forward (counts 2–3). Join other hands shoulder high. Release right hand.

3   Beginning right, take one draw step in line of direction.

4   Step right to side, touch left to right, weight remaining on right.

5–8   Beginning left, repeat action of measures 1–4 in reverse line of direction. In measure 6, joined hands are swung down and back as partners pivot, bringing them face to face.

9–16   Repeat action of measures 1–8.

II. Lady's Turn

1   Partners face, inside hands joined, outside hands on hip. Beginning left, take one draw step in line of direction (counts 1–3).

2   Man repeats draw step to left as lady turns clockwise once with two steps (right, left) under man's right arm (counts 1–3).

3–4   Repeat action of measures 1–2, part II. On last draw, man touches right to left, lady takes three steps in the turn (right, left, right).

5–8   Man beginning right, lady left, repeat action of measures 1–4, part II, in reverse line of direction.

9–16   Repeat action of measures 1–8.

III. Skating

1   Promenade position. Beginning left, take one Waltz step forward in line of direction.

2   Take one Waltz step, turning toward partner to face reverse line of direction. Movement continues in line of direction.

3–4   Take two Waltz steps backward, moving in line of direction.

5–8   Repeat action of measures 1–4, part III, in reverse line of direction.

9–16   Repeat action of measures 1–8, part III.

IV. Waltz

1–2   Closed position. Beginning left, take one draw step to side, step left to side, touch right to left, weight remaining on left.

3–4	Beginning right, repeat action of measures 1–2, part IV, to right side.
5–8	Take four Waltz steps, turning clockwise, progressing in line of direction.
9–16	Repeat action of measures 1–8, part IV.

⚘ Korobushka

Korobushka, also spelled *Korobotchka,* means "little basket" or "peddlar's pack." According to Michael Herman (1941), this dance was originated on American soil by a group of Russian immigrants, following the close of World War I, to the Russian folk song, "Korobushka."

Records: Canadian MH 1059; EZ 6009; Folk Dancer MH 1059; Folkraft 1170; World of Fun LP 3, Side B-4; Worldtone 1005; High/Scope RM 8 LP and compact disc.

Cassette: High/Scope RM 8.

Music: Beliajus, V. F., *Dance and Be Merry,* Vol. I, p. 20.

Formation: Double circle, partners facing, man's back to center. Two hands joined or man crosses arms on chest, lady places hands on hips.

Steps: Hungarian break step, Schottische, balance, three-step turn.

■ Directions for the Dance

Meter 2/4 • Directions are for man; lady's part reverse.

Measures

I. Schottische Step

1–2	Beginning left, take one Schottische step away from center of circle. Extend right foot on hop.
3–4	Beginning right, take one Schottische step toward center of circle.
5–6	Repeat action of measures 1–2.
7–8	Hungarian break step (cross-apart-together).

II. Three-Step Turn

9–10	Drop hands. Man and lady beginning right, take one three-step turn or one Schottische step, moving away from each other.
11–12	Beginning left, repeat three-step turn or Schottische back to place.
13–14	Join right hands. Man and lady beginning right, balance together, balance back.
15–16	Man and lady beginning right, change places with four walking steps, lady turning counterclockwise under man's arm.
17–24	Repeat action of measures 9–16, returning to original starting position.

Mixer

One may progress to a new partner on the last three-step turn, measures 19–20, by taking turn in place, balancing with a new partner, and changing sides. The man progresses to the lady in front of him at the completion of the three-step turn in place. Before dancers cross over, the man may identify his new partner as the next lady in the line of direction.

🌀 Troika

Troika means "three horses." The dance symbolizes the three horses that traditionally drew sleighs for the Russian noble families.

Records: Canadian MH 1059; EZ 5009; Festival 3617; Folk Dancer MH 1059; Folkraft 1170; World of Fun LP 3, Side B-3; High/Scope RM 2 LP and compact disc.

Cassette: High/Scope RM 2.

Music: Herman, Michael, *Folk Dances for All,* p. 7; Neilson, N. P., and Van Hagen, W., *Physical Education for Elementary Schools,* 1954, p. 373.

Formation: Set of three, man between two ladies, facing line of direction, inside hands joined, outside hands on hip.

Step: Running step.

■ Directions for the Dance

Meter 4/8

Measures

	I.	**Run Forward**
1 – 4		Beginning right, take 16 running steps in line of direction. The first four runs may be done diagonally right, second four, diagonally left, and last eight straight forward.
	II.	**Arch**
5 – 6		Right-hand lady moves under arch made by raised arms of man and left-hand lady with eight running steps. Man runs in place and follows right-hand lady turning under his left arm. Left-hand lady runs in place.
7 – 8		Left-hand lady moves under arch made by raised arms of man and right-hand lady with eight running steps. Man runs in place and follows left-hand lady turning under his right arm. Right-hand lady runs in place.
	III.	**Circle**
9 – 11		Set of three join hands in circle and run 12 steps clockwise.
12		Stamp left, right, left, hold.
13 – 16		Repeat action of measures 9 – 12, moving counterclockwise.

Style

The knees should be lifted high and the body and head held high.

Mixer

The man may move forward to the next group of three as the stamps are taken in the last figure.

Lithuania

Dance Characteristics

Folk Dancing in Lithuania was related to the way of life and reflected the chores and the various aspects of farm life. Although the older dances were slow and restrained, in later years they became livelier. Eventually, the polka arrived on the scene from Poland and became an integral part of Lithuanian Folk Dance. According to Vyts Beliajus, the Polka was "flat footed with more body bounce than foot hop" because the farmers wore wooden shoes and, if their feet came too far off the ground, the shoes would fall off. "The steps were small, rapid and close to the ground. It consisted of three such bouncy steps with a low hop on the fourth, which often terminated with a quick step on the ground" (Beliajus 1959; p. 6).

🌀 Klumpakojis

Klumpakojis means "wooden footed" or "clumsy footed." It is frequently translated erroneously as "wooden shoes." It is a form of the Finger Polka–type Folk Dance found the world over. Notice its similarity to the Swedish Klappdans, the Dutch Hopp Mor Annika, and the Danish Siskind.

Records: Folkraft 1419; Worldtone FDLP 2.

Cassette: Dancecraft 162402.

Formation: Double circle, couples side by side, inside joined, free hands on hips, facing line of direction.

Steps: Walk, stamp, Polka.

■ Directions for the Dance

Meter 2/4 • Directions are for man, lady's part reverse.

Measures

I. Walk

1 – 4	Beginning left, take eight brisk walking steps in line of direction, turning toward partner to face reverse line of direction on last step.
5 – 8	Join inside hands, free hands on hips. Take eight walking steps in reverse line of direction.
1 – 8	Face partner, joining right hands, right elbow bent, left hand on hip. Partners take eight steps, walking around each other clockwise. Join left hands and take eight steps, walking counterclockwise.

II Stamps, Claps

1 – 4	No action (counts 1 *and*, 2 *and*). Then stamp three times. No action (counts 1 *and*, 2 *and*). Clap own hands three times.
5 – 8	Shake right finger, right elbow bent, at partner (counts 1 – 3), hold (count 4). Shake left finger, left elbow bent, at partner (counts 1 – 3), hold (count 4). Clap right hand of partner and turn solo counterclockwise in place once with two steps. Facing partner, stamp feet three times quickly.
1 – 8	Repeat action of measures 1 – 8, Part II.

III. Polka

1 – 8	Varsouvienne position. Beginning left, take 16 Polka steps forward in line of direction. On last two Polka steps, man moves forward to new partner.

Notes

1. Zest is added to the dance if dancers shout "hey hey" or "ya-hoo" spontaneously during the Polka sequence.
2. This dance may be used to introduce either the Two-Step or the Polka step.

Kalvelis

The name means "The young blacksmith." The clapping action imitates the beating of the hammer on the anvil. The dance was introduced to the United States by Vytautas Finadar Beliajus, noted Lithuanian dance teacher.

Record: Folk Dancer MH 1016.

Formation: Couples in a single circle facing center. Lady on man's right.

Steps: Polka, stamping, skips.

■ Directions for the Dance

Meter 2/4

Measures

Music A	**Part I. Circle Polka**
1–8	Circle counterclockwise with seven polka steps. End with three stamps on the eighth measure.
1–8	Repeat circling clockwise.
Music B	**Chorus. Claps and Skips**
9	Clap left hand onto right, right onto left.
10	Repeat left onto right and right onto left.
11–12	Hook right elbows with partner and turn once around with four skips.
13–16	Repeat claps, hook left elbow, and turn once around with four skips.
9–16	Repeat all of Music B.
Music A	**Part II. To Center and Back**
1–4	Ladies dance three polka steps to center, stamp three times.
5–8	Repeat back to place.
1–4	Men dance three polka steps to center, stamp three times.
5–8	Repeat back to place. (**Note:** Men's dance action should be vigorous.)
Music B	Repeat Chorus.
Music A	**Part III. Grand Right and Left**
1–8	Partners face, join right hands. Dance Grand Right and Left for sixteen polka steps to meet new partner. (**Note:** Music A is repeated.)
Music B	Repeat Chorus with new partner.

Variations on Part III: Men stand in place as ladies weave to the right with sixteen polka steps. Repeat Chorus with new partner. Ladies stand in place as men weave around circle with sixteen polka steps, ending, if all goes well, with partner. Repeat Chorus with original partner. Instead of the Grand Right and Left, take ballroom position with partner and dance sixteen polkas around the circle. Repeat Chorus.

Repeat dance from the beginning.

Balkan Countries

Introduction

The Balkan Peninsula includes the former Yugoslavia grouping of Croatia, Bosnia, and Serbia along with Romania, Bulgaria, Greece, and Albania. Originally occupied by Slavic tribes, the area has seen a steady flow of outside influences, including Greeks, Romans, Crusaders, and Turks. Different areas have come under the influence of pagan, Roman Catholic, Greek Orthodox, Bulgarian Orthodox, and Moslem religions. As different countries have emerged from Ottoman Turkish control, boundaries have been established and national unification developed.

The Balkan Peninsula is rich in folk art, music, dance, and tradition. The fact that these countries have remained more agrarian for a longer period of time than other western European countries has made it possible to visit villages in remote areas and find people still wearing their native dress daily and performing traditional dances.

The Folk Dance tradition is a living one. The Sunday hora, a social get-together including dance, is a common custom in small and large communities. Each village has one or several places set aside for a dance: the square, the threshing circle, a barn or a hall for inclement weather, the wide porch of a home, or a level clearing or meadow.

The *Chain Dance* (circle), open or closed, is the common dance among the Balkans but it is referred to by different terms and with different spellings (*Kolo,* Serbia; *Hora,* Romania; *Horo,* Bulgaria; *Oro,* Macedonia; and *Xopos,* Greece [pronounced *hó-rohs*]). The same words are used for the social occasion and the dance. There are many old tunes and songs for the Hora, as well as newly composed ones that still use the complex rhythms that are associated with Balkan music. The rhythm of the songs relates to the length of syllables and goes back to Greek poetry and drama.

Some of the dances originated with the craft guilds; for example, the *Butcher's Dance,* the *Shepherd's Dance,* and the *Tailor's Dance.* Others were named for the place of their origin, and the ritual dances frequently were related to pagan ceremonies that were adapted to another religion. Originally, the chains were for men or ladies alone. The men's movement is more exuberant and dynamic, and the opportunity for the leader to show off is always present. The ladies have traditionally kept their movement more restrained, with feet closer to the floor and eyes downcast.

Such couple dances as the Waltz, Schottische, and Polka did not begin to appear until after 1876, when the Western style began to influence the peasant dances. Today, it is common to include Kolos (Horos) with the Ballroom Dances.

Greece

Dance Characteristics

Dance was a common theme on ancient vases and many frescoes in Byzantine monasteries. The Greek word *chorus* means dance. The chorus in the tragedies sang as well as danced. The continuity of dance tradition among the Greeks persists through their history, through ancient Greece, Byzantium, 400 years of slavery to the Turks, the uprisings, the establishment of Greece as a sovereign kingdom, the European influence, and the social and political reforms following World Wars I and II.

Greek dance has always been an integral part of the people's lives. It is characterized by the display of human emotions, expressing great joy, exuberance, sorrow, aspirations, and hopes. It is a living tradition that may be found at cafés, bars, and religious celebrations, wherever people meet.

Modern Folk Dancing in Greece can be classified in a variety of ways. One is according to rhythm. There are the *Syrtos* or *Kalamatianos,* 7/8 meter; the *Tsamiko,* 3/4 meter; and the *Hasápikos* (sometimes referred to as the Butcher's Dance), 2/4 meter. Some Folk Dances are remnants of ritual drama, such as the survival of the hobby horse during carnival. Sometimes they are classified according to formation: circular, pair, or solo.

Most of the dances follow the circle or the broken circle formation; although men and women used to dance alone, they now dance together without partners. In the broken circle, the leader (traditionally a man, unless it is a ladies' dance) is on the right-hand end, holding two handkerchiefs, one in his right hand, away from the body, to wave and signal variations in step, and the other joining the leader to the next person in the line. The leader improvises steps in time with the music, displaying his ingenuity and skill. As the leader, he encourages the group to become one as they keep the basic step going. In small villages, the leader may use this opportunity to display his personality to the opposite sex. The element of competition among leaders is always present, as one attempts to surpass another. A second dancer can join the leader in improvisation. Occasionally the leader moves to the opposite end and the next person in line becomes the leader.

The body is firm and upright. The women traditionally move in a simple and dignified manner, with footwork close to the ground and eyes downcast. The man is more exuberant in his dance style, leaping, twisting, and turning, but always in time to the basic rhythm. The different regions have definite styles and traditions.

Music

Greek folk music is a monophonic mixture of ancient Greek scales and Byzantine church music. Only the music of the Ionian Islands reflects Western music. Usually the rhythms are 5/4 or 5/8, 7/8, or 9/8 (which are the rhythms of the tragedies). The dance steps are slow and quick, corresponding to the length of syllables of words, rather than to the beat. Musical meter was based on poetic meter.

The dances are performed with the accompaniment of the dancers' singing of folk instruments. The string instruments are the lyra, the violin, the lute, the santouri (dulcimer), the mandolin, and the bouzouki. The wind instruments are the pipiza, the comemusa, the clarinet, the pastoral flutes, the gaida (bagpipe), and the zurna. The percussion instruments include drums, bells, triangles, defi (small tambourines), krotala (wooden spoons), and finger cymbals.

The musicians, not more than four or five, usually stood in the middle of the dancers and responded to the mood of the occasion. Certain instruments and combinations were typical of specific regions.

Former Yugoslavia

Dance Characteristics

In 1945, the Federal Republic of Yugoslavia was established. It was comprised of six republics (Serbia, Croatia, Slovenia, Macedonia, Montenegro, and Bosnia-Hercegovina) and was surrounded by seven nations (Austria, Hungary, Romania, Bulgaria, Greece, Albania, and Italy); it included four nationalities (Serbs, Croatians, Slovenics, and Macedonians), three main languages (Serbo-Croatian, Slovenian, Macedonian), three main religions (Eastern Orthodox, Roman Catholic, and Moslem), and two alphabets (Latin and Cyrillic). The great diversity that this represents speaks dramatically for the present breakup of this section of Europe.

The music, dance, and art of this area have much in common. The Kolo is danced in all parts of the former Yugoslavia, but variations exist because of past influences. In strong Moslem areas, the lady may not be visible; in Croatia, Slovenia, and North Serbia, as the result of Western influence, the men and women may alternate; the silent Kolos have resulted from the Turkish prohibition of native song; and where the Austro-Hungarian Empire dominated the northern section, the influence of the Catholic Church and the church calendar and Western music and dance are seen.

Style

The Kolos combine the Slavic dance traits of liveliness, gaiety, quickness, and gymnastic footwork. The dancers are relaxed from head to foot. The leader frequently carries a handkerchief, waving it to signal step changes or in rhythm to the music. The leader passes it to the next person to relinquish the position.

Serbia emerged as a nation at the end of the 7th century. The clans were fighting each other within; the Greek church and the Roman Catholic Church each were struggling for domination in the Balkans; and the Turks, Russians, and Austrians were pressing from the outside. The Serbian culture is rich with much influence from Turkey. Serbian dances usually move to the right. The steps are quite small, the upper body is "quiet," with most action below the knee. The soft leather, moccasin-type shoe, called *opanci*, allows for the rolling forward and backward action of the foot.

Macedonia is divided into three parts. Of the total population, 40 percent are Macedonian, 50 percent Greek-Macedonian, and 10 percent Bulgarian-Macedonian. Located in the high mountains, the people are separated by streams and rivers; yet they share common traditions. Rich in timber, wheat, and minerals, Macedonia controls the route from central Europe down the valleys to the Aegean Sea. Enemies have always desired Macedonia because of this pathway.

Music

The tone of the music of this region reflects intense feelings from sadness to gaiety. Occasionally a dancer will shout, expressing momentary emotion. The basic instruments are the svrala or frula (shepherd's pipe), the gaida (bagpipe), the gusle (fiddle), and the drum.

Bulgaria

Dance Characteristics

Although the area was originally occupied by Slavic tribes, the Bulgars, a Finno-Ugrian nomadic tribe, became established. Eventually the Slavic princes were driven out, but the ancient Slavic culture persisted, including the language, as the Bulgars settled and intermarried. Bulgarian music and dance reflect the influence of Greece, the Roman Empire, and the Ottoman Empire. Yet, in the mountainous regions, dance and rituals exist that show little influence of the invaders and are almost identical to those of Yugoslavia and southeast Russia.

The social aspect of Bulgarian dance tradition is a part of the Sunday Horos, festivals, and country fairs. The customs (Joukowsky 1965) and dance are closely interrelated. The Chain Dances (Horos) are the most popular. The Bulgarians dance with "devotion and dignity" and in general appear solemn as they move through complex rhythms. The upper body is "quiet," with most of the action in the feet. The skillful dancer is very light on his or her feet, almost "not touching the ground." The footwork is very precise. One word in the name of a dance frequently describes the character of the dance, for example, Tropkano Horo (stamped). There is great variety in steps, and the opportunity for the dancer to improvise and add personality is inherent. Although most Horos move to the right, some move to the left; some move forward and backward with slight movement to the right or left. The tempos vary from slow to fast.

Through the names of Horos, it is suggested that the dance may be of Bulgarian, Romanian, or Turkish origin. Over the years, the Horos have changed to meet the dancing tastes of the people of specific places and times. The Chain Dances used to follow very definite forms (closed, broken, led from one or two ends, straight line dance, crooked, and so on). There are also solo and couple dances, Ruchenitsa being the most common and the liveliest.

Style

Different styles are associated with different regions: In southwest Bulgaria, the dances are small stepped and lively; in the north, they are more free, with humor and gaiety. The Thracian dances are slower and more solemn and yet they are punctuated with stamps; the Drobrudza dances display more emotion, with the dancer's whole body moving at a moderate tempo and knees slightly bent.

Then there are the ritual dances Some relate to nature, emphasizing the belief in the magic that certain dances are said to hold; others relate to religious holidays, marriage, and so forth. In Bulgaria, carnival dances and customs occur the week preceding Lent as well as at other feast days in the year.

It is only recently that modern Ballroom Dancing has reached the villages.

Music

Singing, mostly by women, while dancing the Horo is very common. The words express a wide range of moods. In some areas, diaphonal songs are common, two or three singing and then two or thee others responding. Sometimes the folk instruments in various combinations are used as accompaniment. The instruments include three kinds, wind instruments like the gaida (bagpipe), various pipes, and the common whistle; string instruments like the gudulka, the gusla (a mandolin type), and the lute; and percussion instruments, including various sizes of drums and tympans. In place of folk instruments, orchestras of clarinets, violins, and drums are becoming popular, as is the use of military bands in small villages.

The most common meter is 2/4. But Bulgarian rhythms of unequal beats (5/16, 7/16, 9/16, and 11/16 meter) are characteristic of their music.

Romania

Dance Characteristics

The Roman Empire extended its influence in the northeast as far as Romania, and, despite a history of many ethnic influences (Slavic, Turkish, Germanic), the language, based on Latin, has remained a unique feature of this Balkan country. Romanian dance and music reflect these many cultural influences, especially the Slavic. The pageant of Cuci,* a pantomine-dancing pageant with masks celebrating the arrival of spring at Shrovetide, can be found in southern Romania, Bulgaria, and Yugoslavia. Tradition links Cuci to the Day of Fools, which originated in the Roman Empire.

*See "Pageant of Cuci at Shrovetide in Romania," in *Viltis*, March 1970, p. 4.

The Vlachs, descendents of the Romanized colonials who are shepherds in the Carpathian mountains, have interesting dances similar to the Hungarians, Basques, and Gypsies. The dancers perform their complicated leaps, turns, deep-knee bends, and intricate footwork to the music of a drummer and a flute or a bagpipe.

The Sunday Hora, a living tradition in the villages of people gathering together to socialize and dance at the square, keeps their Folk Dances alive. And, as in other Balkan countries, the native dances are mixed with modern Ballroom Dancing (Foxtrot, Tango, Twist, and so on).

The Circle Dances, also called Hora, are the most common. The dance usually begins with a slow rhythm and gradually accelerates in tempo.

Music

The Romanians have a tradition of singing (mouth music) while dancing, as well as playing the common Slavic folk instruments and the accordion. The influence of the Gypsies must also be noted, as there are many in Romania, and frequently the musicians are Gypsies who interpret the Romanian music with their special flair and moods. The rhythms are frequently syncopated, in 2/4 meter.

Alunelul, pronounced *ah-loo-NAY-loo,* means "little hazelnut."

Records: Canadian MH 1120; Folk Dancer MH 1120; Folkraft 1549; High/Scope RM 5, LP and compact disc; National 4573; Worldtone 10005.

Cassette: High/Scope RM 5.

Formation: Single circle, all facing center, hands on shoulders of person on either side, arms straight. Small circles of eight to ten dancers are best.

Steps: Step, stamp.

■ Directions for the Dance

Meter 2/4

Measures

B	1–4	Introduction: no action.

I. Five Steps

A	1–2	Beginning right, take five steps sideward; step right to right side, step left behind right, step right to right side, step left behind right, step right to right side. Circle moves counterclockwise. Stamp left heel twice, close to right.
	3–4	Beginning left, repeat the action of A, measures 1–2. Circle moves clockwise.
	1–4	Repeat the action of A, measures 1–4.

II. Three Steps

B	5	Beginning right, take three steps sideward; step right to right side, step left behind right, step right to right side. Circle moves counterclockwise. Stamp left heel once.
	6	Beginning left, repeat the action of B, measure 5. Circle moves clockwise.
	7–8	Repeat action of B, measures 5–6.

III. One Step

	5–6	In place, step right, stamp left heel close to right once; step left, stamp right heel close to left once; step right, stamp left heel close to right **twice.**
	7–8	Beginning left, repeat action of part III, measures 5–6, reversing foot pattern.

Notes

1. Dancers need to be light on their feet; use small, precise steps; and support weight of their own arms. Do not let arms sag, and hold heads erect.
2. The tempo of the music of some recordings accelerates at the end. The dancers enjoy the competitiveness of testing their agility of footwork with the musicians. A leader can adjust the speed of control if using a variable record player.

Čukaričko Kolo

The *Čukaričko Kolo* is a Serbian dance from former Yugoslavia.

Record: Folk Dancer MH 1002.

Formation: Nonpartner broken circle or line dance. Joined hands held down by dancers' sides.

Steps: Grapevine (sevens), twos, threes

■ Directions for the Dance

Meter 2/4 • Directions are the same for all dancers.

Measures

Music A	**I.**	**Grapevine (Sevens), Pas de Basque**
1–4		Step left to side, step right across in front of left. Catch weight on right heel. This is a quick "left-right" movement. Keep feet close to the floor. Dance seven quick "left-right" grapevine-like steps to the left. Weight ends on left. Beginning right, dance two pas de basques to the right and left as follows:

Moving right: Leap to side on right (count 1), leap right across left (count 2), leap right in place (count 3).

Moving left: Leap to side on left (count 1, leap right across left (count 2), leap left in place (count 3). Counts are quick, "1-2-3 and 1-2-3." Keep leaps low to floor.

5–8		Repeat moving right with left foot crossing over the right in the grapevine or sevens. Repeat two pas de basques left, right, left, and right, left, right.
9–16		Repeat all of Part I.
Music B	**II.**	**Kolo Steps**
17–24		Dance eight Kolo steps moving to the left and to the right as follows:

Moving left: Hop on right (count 1), leap onto left (count 2), step right behind left (count *and*), step on left in place (count 3), hop on left (count 4).

Moving right: Hop on left (count 1), leap onto right (count 2), step left behind right (count *and*), step on right in place (count 3), hop on right (count 4). Cue as follows: "hop, ball-change, step, hop" or "one, two-and, three, four."

Hasápikos

Greek

Hasápikos means "butcher's dance." Whereas the Americans call this dance Hasápikos, the Greeks refer to it as *Serviko* and reserve the word *Hasápikos* for the slow Hasápiko. This dance, known by different names, is common throughout the Balkans, the character of the variations differing.

Records: Festival 3513; Folk Dancer MH 4052; Folkraft 1021 "The Paro," Folkraft LP 3 and 8; High/Scope RM 4, LP and compact disc; Worldtone 10025.

Cassette: High/Scope RM 4.

Formation: Broken circle, arms extended, resting on adjacent dancer's shoulder (right in back of adjacent dancer's left), *T* position.

Steps: Walk, slide, step swing.

■ Directions for the Dance

Meter 2/4

Measures

	I.	**Basic Step**
1		Line always progresses to right. Beginning right, step to right, step left behind right.
2–3		Take two step swings, stepping right, then left, in place.

Variation

1	Cross in front and step-hop swing: Beginning right, step right, step left, crossing in front of right.
2–3	Take two step-hop swings in place.

	II.	**Turn**
1		Release arms, raise overhead, and, beginning right, take two walking steps, making one complete turn clockwise. Resume *T* position.
2–3		Repeat action of basic step, measures 2–3.

	III.	**Progressive Turn**
1		Leader makes one turn while others in line dance basic step.
2–3		Repeat action of basic step, measures 2–3.
1–3		Leader and second dancer make one turn and then two step swings, while others dance basic step. Each time the next dancer joins the dancers turning until the whole line is turning on measure 1. Or the leader may call "oli" ("all turn") after two or three dancers are turning with the leader.

	IV.	**Slide**
1 – 3		Beginning right, take six slides (two per measure) in line of direction. Toward end of musical phrase, take smaller steps to change pace back to basic step.
	V.	**Slide-Step Swing**
1		Beginning right, take two slides, moving in line of direction.
2 – 3		Take two step swings in place.
	VI.	**Leap Pas de Basque**
1		Beginning right, leap to right, leap left behind right.
2 – 3		Take two pas de basque steps in place.
	VII.	**Twisting Step**
1		Moving to right, feet together, weight on heels, pivot toes to right side (count 1) weight on toes, pivot heels to right (count 2). Knees slightly bent, body twists with each pivot.
		Repeat action as long as desired.
	VIII.	**Skip Pas de Basque**
1		Face slightly right. Beginning right, take two skipping steps in line of direction.
2 – 3		Face center. Hop left slightly and take two pas de basque steps in place.

Notes

1. The Greeks in the cafés cross in front and the Folk Dancers cross behind.
2. The leader indicates the order of figures.
3. The leader holds a kerchief in his or her right hand, arm raised, elbow bent, hand about the level of head, and signals change by twirling the kerchief.

Style

The dancer's movement responds to the music. The step swing is more of a step lift, the knee bending slightly and straightening (body rises slightly) on the step. If the leader is a man, he shows his virtuosity by performing fancy acrobatic steps in time with the music, still leading the line. They are not as vigorous as Tsaimiko.

Hora Pe Gheata is pronounced *HOAR-ah pay GYAH-tsah* and means "the dance on the ice." It is a Ballroom-type dance known in many of the villages of Muntenia, which is in the south-central part of Romania.

Sunni Bloland, Romanian dance specialist from the University of California, learned this dance from Teodor Vasilescu.

Records: High/Scope RM 4, LP and compact disc; Nevofoon LP 5005; Noroc NA-1074.

Cassette: High/Scope RM 4.

Formation: Broken circle, hands joined, held at shoulder height, *W* position.

Step: Walk.

■ Directions for the Dance

Meter 2/4

Measures

1–2	**Introduction****: no action.
1–2	Face slightly right, right shoulder leading. Beginning right, take four steps, moving in line of direction.
3	Face center as stepping right to side, bending right knee slightly, swaying to right, letting left leg come off floor slightly.
4	Transfer weight to left foot, swaying sideways left, right leg coming off floor slightly.
5	Step forward right, bending right knee slightly, upper torso rising to roll up in a forward direction (skating gesture) as left foot comes off floor slightly.
6–7	Moving backward, beginning left, take five small steps; alternately step left, twisting right heel and hip slightly to left, step right, twisting left heel and hip slightly to right.
8	Stamp right in place (weight remains on left).
9	Floor pattern zigs and zags as circle continues to move in line of direction, measures 9–16. The change of direction occurs on the **step lift.** Face slightly right, beginning right, take two steps forward.
10	Take one more step forward (right) and turn counterclockwise to face left on right foot. The turn is actually **step lift,** body rising as bent right knee straightens.
11	Take two steps backward (left, right).
12	Step backward left, turning clockwise to face right (step lift).
13–16	Repeat action of measures 9–12.

Style

The dancers move quietly and elegantly, as if skating on ice, reflecting the step pattern and the music.

---

*Hora Pe Gheata included by permission of Sunni Bloland.
**Noroc NA 1074: no introduction; Nevofoon 15005: four beats.

Lesnoto, or *Lesno,* is a common dance type in the regions of Macedonia and former Yugoslavia. Prior to World War II, the Macedonians traditionally danced it in separate lines; one for men and one for women. Currently, men and women dance together, particularly in the city, and when only the basic steps are performed.

Records: Fez 70a; Folk Dancer MH 3037; Folkraft 1552; Folkraft LP-25, Side A, Band 5.

Formation: Broken circle, hands joined, held at shoulder height, *W* position.

Steps: Walk, step swing.

◼ Directions for the Dance

Meter 7/8 • Directions are same for man and lady.

Measures

I. Basic Pattern

1   Face slightly right. Line travels right. Beginning right, step right (slow), lifting left knee across right (quick); step left diagonally to right (crossing in front of right foot) (quick).

2   Facing center, step right sideward to right, bending knee slightly, body rises as leg straightens (slow); men lift left knee in front so that thigh is parallel to ground (quick, quick); women lift left foot just off the ground and touch toe lightly in front of right foot.

3   Step left sideward to left, bending knee slightly, and body rises as leg straightens (slow); men lift right knee in front so that thigh is parallel to ground (quick, quick); women lift right foot just off the ground and touch toe lightly in front of left foot.

Variations

II. Turn

1   Release hand hold. Turning once clockwise, step right to side, pivoting to face out of circle (slow) step left, pivoting to face the center of the circle (quick, quick). Line continues to travel right. Men crouch slightly while turning. Rejoin hands.

2-3   Repeat action of measures 2-3 of the basic pattern.

III. Squat (Men Only)

1   Repeat action of measure 1 of the basic pattern.

2   Facing center, men squat with weight on balls of both feet, almost sitting on heels; knees face forward (slow), body rises, weight on right, lifting left knee as in basic pattern, measure 2 (quick, quick).

3   Squat with weight on balls of both feet (slow), body rises, weight on left, lifting right knee as in basic pattern, measure 3 (quick, quick).

IV. Combination

1-3   Variations II and III may be combined with both men and women turning on measure 1; and on measures 2-3, men dance squats and ladies dance the basic pattern.

V. Step Hop

     If the tempo is fast, add a step-hop on measures 2-3 with the knee lift.

Lesnoto (continued)

Notes

1. No introduction. Start dancing at the beginning of a phrase.
2. The variations may be introduced in any order at the discretion of the leader.

Style

When men and women dance in same line and join hands shoulder level, with right elbow bent downward and right palm facing upward, holding next dancer's left hand, left arm is held diagonally out to left side, with left palm facing downward and held by next dancer's right hand. Men (only) form separate line, using a shoulder hold; women use hold described above. Leader on right end holds handkerchief in right hand above head for signaling changes. The step is very simple; the subtlety of body movement reflects the Macedonian interpretation of the music and mood. The following suggestions will enable dancers to "catch the flavor" of the dance:

1. Hold the hands in the *W* position, slightly in front.
2. The footwork in Macedonia is light, close to the ground; not really bouncy or on "tippy toe."
3. In measures 2–3, during step lift of knee, there is a subtle double bounce following the step. The knee flexes slightly twice after the step. Cue: Slow quick quick, slow quick quick. Step flex flex, step flex flex.
4. Leader signals the variations by waving a handkerchief in a circle above head, anticipating a variation. To signal the turn, the right hand moves in front of the chest on the step left, swing right. This cues the line that a Two-Step turn follows.

Misirlou

Greek-American

The origin of *Misirlou* is most interesting inasmuch as it originated at Duquesne University, Pittsburgh, Pennsylvania (Holden and Vouras 1965). In 1945, Professor Brunhilde Dorsch, hoping to find a Greek dance for a program, contacted a Greek-American student, Mercine Nesotas, who taught several Greek dances to their dance group. The group enjoyed the dance *Syrtos Haniotikos* the most; Miss Nesotas called it the Kritikos. Because the appropriate music was not available, someone suggested that the steps be adapted to a slower piece of music, Misirlou. This dance was taught by Monty Mayo of Pittsburgh, Pennsylvania, at Oglebay Folk Dance Camp, Wheeling, West Virginia, in 1948. It is danced all over the world now, and by Greeks too!

Record: Folkraft 1060; High/Scope RM 8 LP and compact disc.

Cassettes: Dancecraft 162006; High/Scope RM 8.

Music: "Misirlou," by M. Roubanis, Colonial Music Publishing Company, 168 West 23rd Street, New York, NY.

Formation: One large broken circle, hands joined, lead dancers at right end of line.

Steps: Two-Step, grapevine.

■ Directions for the Dance

Meter 4/4

Measures

1 Beginning right, step in place (count 1). Hold (count 2). Pointing left toe in front of right, describe an arc to left toward right heel (counts 3–4). Circle moves counterclockwise.

2 Step left behind right (count 1). Step right to side (count 2). Step left across in front of right (count 3), and pivot counterclockwise a half-turn on left to face reverse line of direction (count 4).

3 Beginning right and moving clockwise, take one Two-Step.

4 Step back on left (count 1). Step right to side, body facing center (count 2). Step left across in front of right (count 3). Hold (count 4).

Note

The dancer at the right end of the broken circle leads the line in serpentine fashion, coiling it counterclockwise, then reversing and uncoiling it clockwise, while executing the dance pattern.

Variation

Measure 4: Beginning left, take one Two-Step backward, moving counterclockwise, and on last step pivot right on ball of left foot to face center.

Pljeskavac Kolo*

Pljeskavac kolo, pronounced *PLYE-skah-vahts KO-lo,* means "clapping Kolo." It is a Serbian Folk Dance and a quick, easy, and charming introduction to the Kolo.

Records: Canadian MH 1009; Carousel Cr-701 (45 EP); Folk Dancer MH 1009; Folkraft 1548.

Cassette: Dancecraft DC 387.

Formation: Broken circle, joined hands held down.

Steps: Walk, stamp.

■ Directions for the Dance

Meter 2/4

Measures

I.	**Walk, Step in Place**
1	Beginning right, take two walking steps (slow, slow) diagonally forward. Circle moves counterclockwise.
2	Face center. Beginning right, take three steps (quick, quick, quick) in place.
3	Beginning left, take two walking steps backward (slow, slow). Circle continues to move counterclockwise.
4	Beginning left, take three steps (quick, quick, quick) in place.
1–4	Repeat action of measures 1–4.
II.	**Stamps and Claps**
5–6	Face center. Beginning right, take two walking steps (slow, slow) toward center. Stamp three times right, left, right (quick, quick, quick).
7–8	Beginning left, take two walking steps (slow, slow) backward, away from center. Clap hands three times (quick, quick, quick).
5–8	Beginning right, repeat action of measures 5–8.

Notes

1. Each walking step is done with a bounce and tremble of the entire body.
2. The leader may use a skip step instead of a walking step. Dancers follow the leader and use skip step too.
3. Spontaneous Kolo shouts (Veselo . . . hoopat svp—hup, hup, hup, tss, tss, tss, . . . or ceceya) add to the interest of this dance.

---

*Dance arranged from the dance description by Michael Herman and reproduced here by permission of Folk Dance House, New York, NY.

🎵 Rumunjsko Kolo

Serbian-American 🎵

Records: Folk Dancer MH 1010; Folkraft 1402; Festival 4811.

Formation: Broken circle, joined hands held down.

Steps: Schottische, rock, stamp, step-hop.

■ Directions for the Dance

Meter 4/4

Measures

Introduction. Dancers stand in place and feel the basic rhythm for the first four measures and start with part II or they may begin on the first beat with part I.

I. Step-Hop, Schottische

1 – 4 Face line of direction. Beginning right, take two step-hops and one Schottische step, turning on hop to face reverse line of direction. Moving backward in line of direction and beginning left, take two step-hops and one Schottische step, turning on hop to face center. On each hop, free foot swings forward. Circle moves counterclockwise.

II. Rock Stamp

5 Face center. Beginning right, cross right over left (count 1), rock back onto left (count 2), rock forward onto right (count 3), hop right and swing left forward into position to repeat (count 4).

6 Beginning left, cross left over right (count 1), rock back onto right (count 2), rock forward onto left (count 3), hop left and swing right forward into position to repeat (count 4).

7 – 8 Beginning right, cross right over left (count 1), rock back onto left (count 2), rock forward onto right (count 3), hop right and place left beside right (weight remains on right) (count 4). Stamp left three times (counts 1 – 3), hold (count 4).

9 – 12 Beginning left, repeat action of measures 5 – 8. Finish with stamp on right.

Style

The dancers are close together, standing straight, hands joined below waist level. The basic body movement comes from below the hips, knees relaxed. The footwork is close to the floor. The body does not sway on the rock, but the rock comes from the knees. Leader at right end leads line in a serpentine fashion, coiling and uncoiling while traveling.

Sarajevka Kolo*

Sarajevka Kolo is pronounced *SAH-rah-yev-kah KO-lo.* The dance was introduced in this country by Michael Herman.

Records: Folk Dancer MH 1002; Folkraft 1496.

Formation: Broken circle, joined hands held down. Dancer at each end of circle places free arm behind back, fist clenched.

Steps: Step-hop, grapevine, pas de basque, walk, step-touch.

■ Directions for the Dance

Meter 2/4

Measures

		I. **Fast Music**
A	1-2	Face slightly right. Beginning right, take two step-hops, line moving right.
	3	Facing center, step right to right side, step left behind right (grapevine).
	4-6	Beginning right take three small pas de basque steps (right, left, right).
	7	Face slightly left. Beginning left, take two walking steps to left.
	8	Step-hop left, turning on hop to face slightly right. The hop is a lift, ball of foot does not quite leave the floor.

Repeat action of part I, measures 1–8 three times.

Meter 4/4

		II. **Slow Music**
B	1	Beginning right, take two slow walking steps, line moving right.
	2	Facing center, step right to right side, step left behind right, step right, touch left near right.
	3	In place, step left, touching right near left; step right, touching left near right.
	4	Beginning left, take three walking steps, line moving left. Pivot on left (count 4) to face right.
	1-4	Repeat action of part II, measures 1–4.

Notes

1. Since there is no introductory music, dancers may wait through the fast music and begin dancing with part II, slow music.
2. The sequence of the music is AABBAAAABBAAAA, and so forth.

---

*Sarajevka Kolo included by permission of Michael Herman, director of Folk Dance House, New York.

Savila Se Bela Loza*

Savila Se Bela Loza is pronounced *SAH-vee-lah say BAY-lah LOH-zah,* and means "a (grape) vine entwined in itself." The dance comes from Sumadija, Serbia. Dick Crum and Dennis Boxell introduced this dance in this country.

Records: Carousel CR-701 (45 EP); Festival 109; Folkraft 1496; High/Scope RM 6, LP and compact disc.

Cassette: High/Scope RM 6.

Formation: Broken circle, joined hands held down.

Steps: Run, Schottische.

■ Directions for the Dance

Meter 2/4

Measures

Part 1

1–9   Face slightly right. Beginning right, take 18 small running steps. Line moves right (counterclockwise).

10   Step-hop right in place, to change direction.

11–20   Face slightly left. Beginning left, repeat action of measures 1–10. Line moves left (clockwise).

Part II

21–22   Beginning right, take one Schottische step, moving right. Or, facing center, step right, step left behind right, step-hop right.

23–24   Beginning left, take one Schottische step, moving left. Or, facing center, step left, step right behind left, step-hop left.

25–32   Repeat action of measures 21–24 two times.

Variations

1. Measures 21–22: Face center, step right slightly forward, step left in place, step right beside left; hop right.
   Measures 23–24: Beginning left, repeat footwork.
   Measures 25–32: Beginning right, repeat action of measures 21–24 of variation 1.
2. Part II, a hop, step, step, step-hop may be substituted for the Schottische step, traveling right and left or facing center and moving in place.

Notes

1. No introduction. Music for part I usually serves as an introduction, and dancers begin with part II.
2. During part I, measures 1–10, the leader on the right end may lead line anywhere, winding or coiling the line in a **counterclockwise** direction, even through an arch made by two of the dancers in the line. Measures 11–20, the dancer on the left end may lead line anywhere in a **clockwise** direction. The dancer

Savila Se Bela Loza (continued)

---

*Savila Se Bela Loza included by permission of Richard George Crum.

on the left end never initiates the coiling; he coils only if the leader has coiled on measures 1 – 10. Neither the leader nor the end dancer should ever lead the line so that dancers will have their backs to one another.

Lyrics

Singing these words while dancing adds a natural zest.

Verse I

A. Savila se bela loza vinova
   Uz tarabu vinova (repeat two times)
     (Repeat A)

A pretty grapevine entwined itself
Along a fence, a grape (vine)

B. Todor Todi podvalio
   Triput curu poljubio
     (Repeat B twice)

Todor tricked Toda
Kissed the girl three times

Verse II

A. To ne beše bela loza vinova
   Uz tarabu vinova (repeat two times)
     (Repeat A)

It was not a pretty grapevine
Along a fence a grape (vine)

B. Todor Todi podvalio
   Triput curu poljubio
     (Repeat B twice)

Todor tricked Toda
Kissed the girl three times

Verse III

A. Vec to beše dvoje mili i dragi
   Dvoje mili i dragi (repeat two times)
     (Repeat A)

It was, rather, two lovers,
Two lovers

B. Todor Todi podvalio
   Triput curu poljubio
     (Repeat B twice)

Todor tricked Toda
Kissed the girl three times

Šetnja*

Serbian

Šetnja is pronounced *SHAYT-nyah* and is from Šumadija, Serbia. This dance is frequently done at Serbian festive occasions. A young man pays a Gypsy musician to play and he gathers his friends to join his line as they dance around the area. Dick Crum introduced this dance to this country in 1955.

Records: Festival 4816; Folk Dancer MH 3029; Folkraft 1490.

Formation: Broken circle, left forearm held at waist level; right hand hooks and rests on left forearm of neighbor during slow music; joined hands held down during fast music. Leader at right end of broken circle.

Steps: Walk, step-hop.

■ Directions for the Dance

Meter 2/4

Measures

I. Walk, Slow Music

1   Face right. Beginning right, take two walking steps (slow, slow) in line of direction.

2   Take three more walking steps (quick, quick, quick) moving in line of direction and face center (quick).

3   Moving away from center, step left behind right (slow), step right behind left (slow).

4   Step backward left (quick), step right next to left (quick), and step left across in front of right (slow).

5–8   Repeat action of measures 1–4 for slow music.

II. Step-Hop, Fast Music
Joined hands, held down.

1   Face right. Beginning right, take two step-hops in line of direction.

2   Moving in line of direction, take two steps (quick, quick); step-hop right, turning to face center on hop.

3   Moving away from center, step-hop left behind right, step-hop right behind left.

4   Step backward left (quick), step right next to left (quick), and step-hop left across in front of right.

     Repeat action of part II, measures 1–4 until end of music.

Notes

1. No introduction. Start action with the beginning of a phrase.
2. During part I, the manner is quite casual, with flexing knees. Part II is more exuberant as the dancer runs, taking the step-hops and Two-Steps.

Lyrics

These words may be sung while dancing.
I. Dodji, Mile, u naš kraj, pa da vidiš, šta je raj. (repeat)
   Hej, haj, u naš kraj, pa da vidiš šta je raj. (repeat)
II. Prodje, Mile propeva, i volove protera. (repeat)
   Hej, haj, propeva, i volove protera. (repeat)

---

*Šetnja included by permission of Richard George Crum.

Syrtós

Syrtós is the most traditional Folk Dance in Greece. Basic footwork is always the same but varies in styling. The music may be 2/4, 4/4, or 7/8 meter. *Kalamatianos,* a Syrtós from Kalamata, is 7/8 rhythm. Whatever the meter, it is counted slow, quick, quick. Syrtós means "to pull or lead," which is characteristic of the dance movement.

Record: Most Greek albums include a good Syrtós.

Formation: Broken circle, hands joined, shoulder high, elbows bent, *W* position. Dancer at either end of broken circle may place free hand on hip, fingers pointing backward, or arm extended, snapping fingers.

■ Directions for the Dance

Meter 2/4

Measures

1   Face center. Beginning right, step to right (slow), step left behind right (quick), step right to right (quick).

2   Step left crossing in front of right (slow), step right to right (quick), and step left crossing in front of right (quick).

3   Step right, facing slightly left (slow), touch ball of left slightly forward toward center (slow).

4   Step left backward (slow), touch ball of right slightly behind left (slow).

Repeat pattern throughout the dance.

Style

The leader may be a man or a woman. A kerchief is usually held between the first and second dancers in line. This allows the leader greater freedom to execute variations. The second dancer gives the needed support to the leader to perform acrobatic moves. The dancers continue the basic step.

Variations for Leader

1. Measure 4: Leader makes one solo turn counterclockwise, spins on left, touches right.
2. Measures 1 – 2: Leader steps right (slow), makes two solo turns clockwise (quick, quick, slow, quick), and steps left (quick).
3. Measures 1 – 2: Leader makes three solo turns clockwise (slow, quick, quick, slow, quick, quick) and joins the group on measure 3, step point.

Tropanka

This "lively" stamping dance is ideal for beginning an evening of fun with folk dancing for novice groups.

Record: MH 1020.

Formation: Single circle, nonpartner dance. Joined hands, shoulder height, *W* position.

Steps: Walking, step-hop, stamp.

■ Directions for the Dance

Meter 2/4

Measures

Walk and Stamp (Music A)

1–2   Beginning right, move with five quick walking steps (shuffle-like) counterclockwise, stamp left foot twice and pause.

3–4   Repeat beginning left, moving clockwise, stamp right foot twice.

5–8   Repeat measures 1–4 (Music A).

Step Hop and Stamp (Music B)

1–2   Face center, step hop on right, swing left slightly across right. Step hop on left, swing right slightly across left. Step on right in place and stamp left foot twice and pause.

3–4   Repeat measures 1–2 beginning left and end stamping right twice and pause.

5–8   Repeat measures 1–4 (Music B).

To Center and Back (Music C)

1–2   Beginning right, step hop twice toward center, step on right and stamp left twice.

3–4   Repeat measures 1–2. Moving backward, begin left.

5–8   Repeat measures 1–4 (Music C). **Note:** During the move to center, joined hands are raised as dancers move in and lowered as they move out.

Israel

Dance Characteristics

Since Biblical times Jewish dance* has been spiritual in nature and very much a part of the religious experience. As the Jews wandered about the world, they assimilated the culture of each new home into their own tradition. Dance has always been a part of the Jewish child's education and family life. During the Middle Ages, the popular "tanzhaus" (dancing hall) was established in the ghettos of France, Poland, and Germany, and Jewish dance leaders developed.

About 1736 Israel Baal Shem Tov, a young mystic who came from the Carpathian Mountains, inspired a new Jewish religious movement known as Chassidism (also spelled Hassidism). The movement flourished in the ghettos of Poland and eastern Europe. Baal Shem encouraged dance movement and singing with prayer to realize the nearness of God. A new ritual of dancing and humming in worship took place. Improvisation of dance "arose as a conscious attempt to create human joyousness out of misery."**

With a long tradition of dance, the Jews immigrated to the new state of Israel (formed in 1948), bringing with them many diverse cultures and traditions. The Israeli Folk Dances danced today are dances they have brought from other cultures, like east European ones. But a large number of the currently popular Folk Dances have been created by

such folk choreographers as Gurit Kadman, Sara Levi, Yoav Ashriel, Rivka Sturman, Dvora Lapson, and Dani Dassa. Using German interpretive dance techniques and old and newly composed tunes, they have blended dance movements from the Yemenites, the Arabs, the Druzi, the Kurds, and the Hassidim (the largest impact being played by the Yemenites).

The Yemenites, Jews originally from the southwest corner of Arabia, started immigrating to Palestine about 1910, and, in 1949 they were transported by airplane to the new state of Israel. Although the Yemenites had many things in common with the Arabs, their religion was different, and they could read and write. The Yemenites were a link with the Biblical Hebrews. They had maintained old religious and cultural patterns, songs in the language of the Bible, and dances of Oriental rhythm. Their dances were slow and gentle, gradually accelerating as danced to drumming, hand clapping, and singing. Their basic dance forms inspired a new trend in Israeli dances and the Yemenite step in many variations became a basic step. A group of well-known dances (*Dodi Li* and *Ma Na'avu*) came from the Song of Songs.

The dance of the Bukhara Jews† emphasizes hand movements. Their melodies are mostly in 3/4 and 6/8 meter and sound like a Iändler; therefore people frequently mistake them for Bavarian dances.

The newly created Folk Dances involve a variety of themes: Biblical (*Shibbolet Bassedeh*—a harvest festival), the great need for water (*Mayim Mayim*); experiences that have occurred in modern times (*Sisu Yerusalyim*—choreographed after the Six-Day War, celebrates the joy of being in Jerusalem again), and discotheque dance (*Shir Hashalom*), referred to as "The Madison Avenue Dance" by Israelis. The movement in the dance rarely pantomimes its theme.

Line, circle, and couple dance formations are used. It is interesting to note that the Jewish Square Dance differs from European Quadrilles in that the ladies of the side couples stand on the left side of their partners so that two ladies or two men are at each corner. The lady was not to touch a "strange man."

Characteristically the total body is involved in movement, frequently with a fluid, undulating movement; the knees and ankles are flexible; hand movements may be reaching upward, clapping hands symbolic of clapping cymbals in ecstasy, or reaching behind their back in a mood of restraint.

The music, also a blend of many cultures, may be tunes from other lands or newly composed ones. The music on Israeli recordings could be identified as German, illustrating the many cultures that Israeli dance represents. The melodies have a strong rhythmic pulse.

---

*See "The Story of Jewish Dance," in *Viltis*, October–November 1968.
**Berk, Fred. *Ha-Rikud, The Jewish Dance.* American-Zionist Youth Foundation, Union of American Hebrew Congregations, U.S.A. 1972, 1975.

---

†See "Jews from Bukhara," by Vyts Beliajus in *Viltis*, May 1962.

Cherkessiya

Tscherkessia or *Cherkessiya* is a dance for men from Circassia. They were followers of the Mohammedan faith, who sought religious freedom in the czarist days of Russia. They left southeastern Russia and migrated to Palestine and Syria. The Circassians were noted for their horsemanship. The rhythmic movement of the dance portrays either horses or riders.

Records: Folkraft R 4140; Dancecraft DC 74627; High/Scope RM 2, LP and compact disc; Merit AV LP; Worldtone 10040 (vocal), 10043 (instrumental).

Cassettes: Dancecraft DC 162303; High/Scope RM 2.

Music: Beliajus, V. F., *Dance and Be Merry,* Vol. I, p. 12; Chochem, Corinne, and Roth, Muriel, *Palestine Dances,* p. 31; Lapson, Dvora, *Dances of the Jewish People,* p. 34.

Formation: Groups of four or five dancers in a line, arms linked about one another's waist, or any number of dancers in a single circle.

■ Directions for the Dance

Meter 2/4

Measures

Part I

A 1–2 Keeping the left foot in place, step right across left, step left in place, step back right, step left in place. As cross step is taken, body leans forward, left knee bends to give flexibility to movement. As backward steps are taken, body should lean back as far as possible.

   3–8 Repeat action of measures 1–2 three times.

Part II

B 9 Line or circle moves to the right. Beginning right, step to the side, step left behind right.

   10–16 Repeat action of measure 9 seven times.

Variations for Part II

1. Sixteen scissor kicks (cut steps) in front.
2. Sixteen scissor kicks (cut steps) in back.
3. Combination of scissor kicks in front and back.
4. Eight slow skips to the right (one per measure).
5. Keep feet together, move both toes, then both heels to the right.
6. Semicrouch position, execute a shuffle step, moving to the right.

Note

The action described in part II may be used each time or a different action selected from the variations may be used for each repeat of the B music. The dance should be started in a slow tempo. Each repetition becomes faster until a climax of great excitement is reached. If done in a line, each group moves independently, allowing the action of part II to carry it anywhere on the floor.

🎵 Harmonica*

Harmonica means "accordion." The dance movements are symbolic of the action of an accordion. The dance was choreographed by Rivka Sturman.

Records: Folk Dancer MH 1091; Folkraft 1108; Worldtone 10030.

Music: Lapson, Dvora, *Dances of the Jewish People,* p. 13.

Formation: Single circle, hands joined and held down.

Steps: Grapevine, run, hop.

■ Directions for the Dance

Meter 4/4

Measures

I. Grapevine

1   Moving counterclockwise, cross left in front of right (count 1), step right to side (count 2), cross left behind right (count 3), leap right to side with slight accent (count 4).

2   Continue moving counterclockwise and step-hop left (counts 1–2), step-hop right (counts 3–4).

3–8   Repeat action of measures 1 and 2 three times.

II. Cross Step, Hop

9   Beginning left, cross left over right (count 1), step right in place (count 2), step left in place (count 3), and hop slightly on left (count 4), turning body to left side on hop.

10   Beginning right, cross right over left (count 1), step in place (count 2), step right in place (count 3), and hop slightly on right (count 4), turning body to right side on hop.

11   Beginning left, repeat action of measure 9.

12   Moving clockwise, step-hop right (counts 1–2), step-hop left (counts 3–4).

13–15   Beginning right, repeat action of measures 9–11.

16   Moving counterclockwise, step-hop left (counts 1–2), step-hop right (counts 3–4).

III. Friendship Circle, Swaying

17   Place hands on upper arms of adjacent dancers. Dancers sway to left (counts 1–2), sway to right (counts 3–4). Action of feet may be step left, touch right to left; then step right, touch left to right.

18   Beginning left, moving clockwise, take four running steps.

19–24   Repeat action of measures 17–18 three times.

---

*Dance arranged from the dance description by Dvora Lapson, *Dances of the Jewish People,* 1954 (p. 13).

Hava Nagila*

Hava Nagila means "come let us be joyful." This couple dance is done to an old hora melody, "Hava Nagila."

Records: Folkraft 1110, 1116; High/Scope RM 4, LP and compact disc; Worldtone 10001.

Cassette: High/Scope RM 4.

Music: Lapson, Dvora, *Dances of the Jewish People,* 1954, p. 18.

Formation: Double circle, partners facing, man's back to center, two hands joined. Partners stand close together, elbows bent, and hands close in.

Steps: Walk, leap, hop, jump, running step.

■ Directions for the Dance

Meter 4/4 • Directions are for both lady and man, except when specially noted.

Measures

I. Pull Away and Circle

A 1   Beginning right, take four steps backward, knees bend slowly taking body into crouch position by fourth step. Back remains fairly straight.

2   Beginning right, take four steps forward, moving immediately into left reverse open position (count 1). Stand straight with left elbow bent and close to body, right arm is straight across in front of partner. Turn clockwise in reverse open position (counts 2–4).

3–4   Repeat action of measures 1–2.

1–4   Repeat action of measures 1–4. On fourth measure, partners face line of direction and take back cross position.

II. Leap and Turn, Balance and Run

B 1–2   Beginning right, leap forward, body bending forward (count 1), step left beside right (count 2), step right back, body straightens (count 3), step left beside right (count 4). Repeat.

3   Drop left hands. Beginning right, take four steps, lady making three-quarters turn to face man who turns one-quarter clockwise to face her. Partners join left hands under right.

4   Beginning right, take four steps, lady in place, man turning a full turn clockwise under their joined upraised hands. Now in original starting position, with joined hands crossed.

5–6   Man beginning left, lady right, take four balances to side. (Man—left, right, left, right; lady—right, left right, left.)

7–8   Hook right elbows and extend left arm diagonally upward and outward. Take eight running steps around each other, turning clockwise once around to face original starting position. Drop hands and move apart about three feet.

III. Clap, Hop, and Turn

C 1   Bend over to right and clap hands to one's own right side about knee level (counts 1–2). Repeat bending to left (counts 3–4). Sing "Uru Uru Achim."

Hava Nagila (continued)

---

*Dance arranged from the dance description by Dvora Lapson, *Dances of the Jewish People,* 1954 (p. 19).

2	Bend forward and clap in front (count 1), gradually raise hands to outstretched arm position, in three upward lifts (counts 2–4). Head follows hand positions. Sing "Uru Uru Achim."
3	Hands on hips. Jump in place (count 1). Take three hops on right, extending left foot forward (counts 2–4).
4	Repeat action of measure 3, hopping on left foot and extending right.
5–6	Repeat action of measures 3–4.
7	Repeat action of measure 3, letting left foot trail behind while turning clockwise around in place once on three hops.
8	Repeat action of measure 4, letting right foot trail behind while turning counterclockwise around in place once on three hops.

Lyrics

A. Hava Nagila	Let's be joyful
Hava Nagila	Let's be joyful
Hava Nagila Venismecha	Let's be joyful
Repeat A	
B. Hava Neranena	Let's sing
Hava Neranena	Let's sing
Hava Neranena Venismecha	Let's sing and be joyful
Repeat B	
C. Uru Uru Achim	Wake up, Wake up, brothers
D. Uru Achim Belev Sameach	Wake up, brothers, with a happy heart
Repeat D three times	
E. Uru Achim	Wake up, brothers
Uru Achim Belev Sameach	Wake up, brothers, with a happy heart

🎵 Hineh Ma Tov

The words *Hineh Ma Tov* are taken from the Bible. Their meaning—"How good it is to dwell together as brethren"—admonishes people to live in the world as brothers, friends, and good neighbors.

Record: Folk Dancer MH 1091; Folkraft 1434, LP-2; Worldtone 10018.

Formation: Nonpartner circle or line dance. Lines may be composed of four to eight dancers moving freely in any direction.

Steps: Walk, twinkle, yemenite.

■ Directions for the Dance

Meter 2/4

Measures

Part I

1–2 Beginning right, move counterclockwise four walking steps. Flex knees during "slow walk," hold hands down and straight.

3–4 Beginning right, continue counterclockwise, run lightly eight steps. Run in a "quick, prancing style."

Repeat measures 1–4.

Part II

5–6 Face center, raise joined hands to shoulder level. Leap softly onto right and bring joined hands down (counts 1–2). Twinkle: Step back on left (count 3), step right to left (count 4), step forward on left (counts 1–2). Stamp right softly beside left (counts 3–4). Weight remains on left. Hands remain down during twinkle.

7–8 Yemenite: Step right to side (count 1), shift weight back to left (count 2), step right across left (count 3). Repeat to left: Step left to left side (count 1), shift weight to right (count 2), step left across right (count 3), stamp right softly. Weight remains on left.

Repeat dance from the beginning.

Words

Hineh ma tov, uma naim (hee-nay-ma-tov, ooma nayim). She-vet a chim gam ya chad (sheh-vet-akim-gahm-ya-khad).

⚓ Hora

The Jewish people, dispersed over the earth for many years, have kept their religion alive, but many of the folk traditions have become broken or lost. When the people returned to Israel, they brought dances from their former homelands.

The Sephardic Jews, who left Spain during the Inquisition, settled in the Balkan area. They danced the Balkan *Hora,* adopting it and incorporating it into their festivities.

The word *hora,* a Croatian-Serbian word, means "tempo" or "movement." Although the earlier Hora dances were probably a part of primitive agricultural rites (the leaps and high jumps in the dance suggest and were supposed to induce high growth of corn); the Hora became more subdued and restrained as the people danced it indoors in small spaces. As danced in Israel today, it has absorbed the flavor of the people living there and is once again danced out of doors.

Records: Folk Dancer MH 1052, 1053; Folkraft 1110, 1118, 1431, 1476, LP-12.

Cassette: Dancecraft DC 162303.

Music: Chochem, Corinne, and Roth, Muriel, *Palestine Dances,* p. 15; Beliajus, V. F., *Dance and Be Merry,* Vol. I, P. 37.

Formation: Single circle, hands on shoulders of person on either side, arms straight.

■ Directions for the Dance

Meter 4/4

Measures

1–3   Moving counterclockwise, step right to side, place left behind right, and step right. Kick left in front of right while hopping on right. Step left to side, kick right across left while hopping on left.

This same pattern is repeated throughout the dance.

Note

Begin the Hora slowly in order to establish the rhythm, keep the tempo slow and the music soft, and then gradually accelerate the rhythm and increase the volume. If the group is large, it is interesting to have several concentric circles, some circles beginning with the right foot, moving clockwise, and others beginning with the left foot, moving counterclockwise.

Style

If the movement of the dance begins mildly, with a tiny hop, it can build gradually to a larger hop as the tempo increases.

If dancers extend arms and lean back, keeping head up, the momentum is easier. Dancers should hold up their own arms, not press down on shoulders of the person to each side.

🎵 Ma Na'avu

Ma Na'avu is a lovely nonpartner circle or line dance. The lyrics are from the Bible, Isaiah 52–57. The music was composed by Joseph Spivak, and the dance was choreographed by Rajah Spivak.

Records: High/Scope RM6, LP and compact disc: Tikva 45-102; Worldtone 10020.

Cassette: High/Scope RM 6.

Formation: Single open circle or single line, hands joined and held down.

Steps: Touch, twinkle, rocking, yemenite.

■ Directions for the Dance

Meter 2/4

Measures

Introduction (4 measures).

1–2   Touch: Beginning right, touch right forward (count 1), touch right to side right (count 2). Twinkle: Step back onto right (count 3), step left next to right (count *and*), step forward onto right (count 4). Rock: Rock weight back onto left (count 1 *and*), rock weight forward onto right (count 2 *and*), rock weight back onto left (count 3), step right forward in place (count *and*), close left to right (count 4). Lift body upward as if taking a deep breath. Weight ends on right for repeat beginning left.

3–4   Repeat action of measures 1–2 beginning left.

5   Yemenite: Step right to side right (count 1), step left next to right (count *and*), step right forward and across left (count 2), turn to face counterclockwise by pivoting slightly on the right (count *and*). Move counterclockwise three steps left, right, left (counts 3 and 4). Bring joined hands to shoulder level during the three steps. End facing forward.

6–8   Repeat action of measure 5 three times.

Repeat dance from the beginning.

Mayim*

Mayim is a Jewish folk tune. Translated, Mayim means "water." The dance movements express the joy of finding water in arid land and emulate the motion of waves as they break on the shore. The dance originated in a kibbutz on the shores of Galilee.

Records: Folkraft 1108, 1475 LP-12; High/Scope RM 5, LP and compact disc; Tikva LP 106; World of Fun LP 6, Side B-3; Worldtone 10040.

Cassette: High/Scope RM 5.

Music: Lapson, Dvora, *Dances of the Jewish People,* p. 8.

Formation: Single circle, hands joined and held down.

Steps: Grapevine (tscherkessia), running step.

■ Directions for the Dance

Meter 4/4

Measures

1–2   Introduction: no action.

I.   Grapevine (Tscherkessia)

1–4   Moving clockwise, cross right in front of left (count 1), step left to side (count 2), cross right behind left (count 3), step left to side with a light springy step, accenting step (count 4). Repeat three times.

II.   To Center and Back

5   Beginning right, move to center with four running steps. Leap slightly, bending the knee on first step. Lift joined hands gradually above heads as dancers move to center. Sing "Mayim, Mayim, Mayim, Mayim" while moving to center.

6   Beginning right, repeat action of measure 5, moving away from center. Lower joined hands gradually down to sides.

7–8   Repeat action of measures 5–6.

III.   Run, Toe Touch, Clap

1   Beginning right, move clockwise with three running steps (counts 1–3), turn to face center, weight remains on right (count 4).

2   Hop on right and touch left across front to right side (count 1); hop on right, touch left to side (count 3); hop on right, touch left in front to right side (count 3); hop on right, touch left to side (count 4).

3   Repeat action of measure 2, part III.

4   Hop on left, touch right in front to left side and clap hands directly in front at arm's length (count 1); hop on left, touch right to side and swing arms out to sides shoulder high (count 2); hop on left, touch right in front to left side and clap hands directly in front at arm's length (count 3); hop on left, touch right to side and swing arms out to sides shoulder high (count 4).

5   Repeat action of measure 4, part III.

Lyrics

I.   1–4   V-Shav-tem Mayim Bi-Sa-Son, Mi-ma-Yi-Wey Ha-Y'Shu-ah

     3–4   V-Shav-tem Mayim Bi-Sa-Son, Mi-ma-Yi-Wey Ha-Y'Shu-ah

---

*Dance arranged from the dance description by Dvora Lapson, *Dances of the Jewish People,* 1954, p. 8.

II. 5 – 6   Ma-Yim Ma-Yim Ma-Yim, Ma-Yim, V-Ma-Yim Bi-Sa-Son

    7 – 8   Ma-Yim Ma-Yim Ma-Yim, Ma-Yim, V-Ma-Yim Bi-Sa-Son

III. 1   Hey! Hey! Hey! Hey!

     2   Mayim Mayim Mayim Mayim

     3   Mayim Mayim Bi-Sa-Son

     4   Mayim Mayim Mayim Mayim

     5   Mayim Mayim Bi-Sa-Son

✤ Ve' David ✤

The full title of *Ve' David* is *Ve' David Y'Fey Enayim,* meaning "And David of the Beautiful Eyes." It is a couple mixer choreographed by Rivkah Sturman.

Records: Festival FS-201; Folk Dancer MH 1155; Folkraft 1432; High/Scope RM 3, LP and compact disc; Worldtone 10043.

Cassette: High/Scope RM 3.

Formation: Double circle, couples facing counterclockwise. Lady to the right of partner, inside hands joined.

Steps: Walking steps.

■ Directions for the Dance

Meter 2/4

Measures

Part I (Music A)
Introduction (6 measures)

1 – 2   Beginning right, walk forward four steps. Couples turn to face center, join hands in a single circle on fourth step. Walk away from center four steps.

3 – 4   Beginning right, walk four steps to center and four steps away from center.

Part II (Music B)
1 – 2   Men clap hands, ladies walk four steps to center, and four steps back to place.

3 – 4   Men clap hands and walk four steps to the center, turn to the right and walk four steps away from the center to new partner. New partner is the lady to the right of original partner.

5 – 6   Hungarian-turn position: Partner stand right side to right side, right hands on partner's left hip, left hands curved overhead. Turn clockwise eight "buzz-steps."

Repeat dance from the beginning.

Italy

Dance Characteristics

The Italian dance is not only an expression of the native Mediterranean people, but also reflects the influence of the invaders from Asia, northern Europe, and Africa. The dances are simple in form and pattern. The dances may be classified in the following groups: Processional and Religious Dances, Sword Dances, Chain Dances in closed or open circles, and Couple Dances. The *Tarantella,* which originated in the southern part of Italy, is one of the best-known dances.

Style

The dancers are free and easy. The body is held loosely, often swaying from side to side with arms held high in the air and the head erect. In the mountainous areas of Italy and in the Sword Dances, the steps are precise. Pantomime and flirtation are parts of the dance, especially in courting dances. The dances sometimes are accompanied by castanets or tambourines used by the dancers themselves.

🎵 Il Codiglione

Il Codiglione means "the cotillon" and is pronounced *eel koh-deel-YOH-neh.* Vyts Beliajus first saw this dance performed at Chicago's Hull House about 1928 by an Italian group of dancers, and he introduced it at Idyllwild in 1954.

Record: Folkraft 1426.

Formation: Double circle of couples, Varsouvienne position, facing line of direction.

Steps: Walk, pas de basque.

◼ Directions for the Dance

Meter 6/8

Measures

1–4	Introduction: no action.

I. Walk

1–16	Beginning left, take 32 walking steps forward in line of direction.
17–24	All join hands to form a single circle and take 16 walking steps to right. Circle moves counterclockwise.
25–32	Take 16 walking steps to left. Circle moves clockwise.

II. Two Circles

1–8	Ladies form circle and take 16 walking steps to left, circle moving clockwise. Men form circle around ladies and take 16 walking steps to right, circle moving counterclockwise.
9–16	Each circle moves in the opposite direction, ladies counterclockwise, men clockwise.

III. Basket

1–8	Men join hands and raise over and in front of ladies to form basket as ladies join hands. Lady remains to right of partner. Take 16 walking steps to right. Circle moves counterclockwise.
9–16	Ladies' hands remain joined. Men raise joined hands over ladies' heads, release hands, and reach under ladies' arms to rejoin hands in front of ladies and form basket again. Take sixteen walking steps to left. Circle moves clockwise.

IV. Walk

1–16	Repeat action of measures 1–16, part I.
17–24	Men turn and walk clockwise single-file in reverse line of direction while ladies continue to walk counterclockwise in line of direction.
25–32	Reverse. All turn half around and men walk counterclockwise while ladies walk clockwise. Ladies turn on the last measure to Varsouvienne position, facing line of direction.

V. Walk, Pas de Basque, Do-sa-do

1–3	Varsouvienne position. Take six walking steps forward in line of direction.
4	Release hands. Partners turn to face and back away from each other two steps. End facing partner, man's back to center.

Il Codiglione (continued)

5–8	Snap fingers with arms outstretched above head and beginning right, take four pas de basque steps in place.
9–12	Lower arms to side and partners do-sa-do, passing right shoulders first, taking eight steps.
13–16	Partners do-sa-do, passing left shoulders first, taking eight steps and progress to new partner on left by moving diagonally left on last four steps.
1–16	Repeat action of measures 1–16.

VI. Ending

1–2	With feet slightly apart, take weight on right foot and clap hands (counts 1–3); pause (counts 4–6), step left and clap hands (counts 1–3); pause (counts 4–6).
3–4	Repeat action of measures 1–2.
5–8	Hook right elbow with partner and turn clockwise seven steps, then stop. Turn back on partner and clap hands overhead on last beat.

Note

Directions above are given for the Folkraft record.

Style

There should be smooth transitions when changing directions. The walking steps are on the ball of the foot; a flat walk is heavy and ugly. The hands are joined shoulder high, elbows down, without an extended arm. The body is carried high. The success of this dance depends on the style of execution. The body is **high** and **light.**

Sicilian Tarantella

The *Sicilian Tarantella* is a flirtatious dance for four based on a number of typical Sicilian steps. Real tambourines add an exciting flavor to the dance. Snapping fingers and sharp hand claps may be substituted for shaking and hitting of tambourines.

Records: Folkraft 1173; High/Scope RM 6, LP and compact disc; Worldtone 10033.

Cassettes: Dancecraft DC 162105; High/Scope RM 6.

Music: Herman, Michael, *Folk Dances for All*, p. 45.

Formation: Sets of two, partners facing. Men are side by side and ladies are side by side. Couple 1 is nearest the music. Couple 1 may be designated the "head couple," couple 2 the "foot couple."

Steps: Step-hop, running steps.

■ Directions for the Dance

Meter 6/8 • Directions are same for man and lady.

Measures

	I.	**Step Clap, Hop Swing**
1		All dancers step left, clap hands (count 1). Hop on left, swing right across (count 2). Striking tambourine or claps should be made in front of dancer, not overhead.
2		Repeat measure 1, beginning right, and swing left across.
3 – 4		Beginning left, four rounds in place. Men snap fingers, ladies shake tambourines or snap fingers.
5 – 8		Repeat measures 1 – 4.
1 – 8		Repeat Part I.
	II.	**Runs Forward and Back**
9 – 10		Beginning left, four runs forward toward partner. Dancers begin bending low. Men snap fingers, ladies shake tambourines or snap fingers.
11 – 12		Beginning left, four runs backward away from partner. Dancers slowly straighten up and raise arms upward. Men snap fingers, ladies shake tambourines or snap fingers.
13 – 16		Repeat measures 9 – 12.
9 – 16		Repeat Part II.
	III.	**Run and Turn**
17 – 20		Man 1 (head) and lady diagonally opposite (foot) run toward each other, hook right arms, turn once around and return to place.
21 – 24		Man 2 (foot) and lady 1 (head) repeat action of measures 17 – 20.
17 – 24		Repeat measures 17 – 24, turning with left arms.
	IV.	**Do-Si-Do**
1 – 4		Man 1 (head) and lady diagonally opposite (foot) run toward each other; pass right shoulders, back to back; pass left shoulders, and dance backward to place. Do not fold arms across chest. Snap fingers as dancers pass each other.
5 – 8		Man 2 (foot) and lady 1 (head) repeat action of measures 1 – 4.
1 – 8		Repeat action, except pass left shoulders when moving forward and right shoulders when running backward to place.

Sicilian Tarantella (continued)

9–12	Dancers face a quarter-turn to the right; hands on hips, left shoulders to center of circle, move counterclockwise with eight skipping steps.
13–16	Repeat measures 9–12, right shoulders to center of circle.

VI. Stars

17–20	Dancers form a left-hand star and move counterclockwise with eight skipping steps.
21–24	Repeat measures 17–20, forming a right-hand star and moving clockwise.

Note

This arrangement is based on a piano score of 24 measures. Recordings may only have eight measures of Music A and eight measures of Music B. The dance may be done with only four parts to best fit the recording.

Mexico

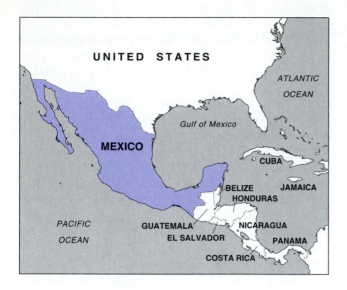

The Dance in Mexico*

By Nelda G. Drury

If you were to visit Mexico you would probably find a civil or religious celebration or parade in which dances are featured. Dance is an integral part of Mexican life. The costumes worn by the dancers add a high note of color to the occasion. Let's take a look at the history of the dance in Mexico. Three phases become immediately apparent: pre-Hispanic, the period of conquest, and the dances of modern Mexico.

Pre-Hispanic

The first inhabitants of Mexico were the Nahuas, Toltecas, Zapotecas, Mixtecos, Totonacos, and Mayas. Each group made dance a part of their existence. They taught their children to dance even before they attended school, for they believed it an essential part of growing into adulthood. Unfortunately, little is known about these ancient dances. Our knowledge of them is derived from ancient codices that have been discovered and from the writings of some of the priests who entered Mexico with Hernando Cortez.

These sources indicate the importance of dance to native Mexicans. They performed dances in their religious celebrations that often lasted several days. The dances were performed in concentric circles with the eldest of the group in the center directing the change of steps. Participants of higher

*The Dance in Mexico was written by Nelda G. Drury, Associate Professor, Emeritus, San Antonio College, San Antonio, TX.

rank were bestowed a place in the inner circle closer to the center. These dances had many similarities to those of ancient Egypt. Dances were performed before going off to war or as tribute to the god of rain or other gods as the occasion required. They were also performed in adoration of the sun or the moon. Some of the gods were bloodthirsty so human sacrifices were part of the rituals.

The Deer Dance is one of the few pre-Hispanic dances that has survived in its pure form over the centuries. It is a dance of the Yaquis from the states of Sonora and Sinaloa. It enacts the killing of a deer and is considered a classic of this era.

Dance accompaniment was predominantly by percussion instruments and woodwinds, such as flutes usually made of bamboo canes. These instruments were elaborately decorated and very colorful. A few instruments that have survived the ravages of time may be seen in the Museum of Anthropology and History in Mexico City.

Period of Conquest

In the second phase of the dance in Mexico a new lifestyle evolved with the arrival of the Spanish. This period is characterized by astounding changes. The people were confronted with new customs, new ideologies, a new religion, new beliefs, and even a new language! Along with the Spanish conquistadors came evangelists bringing Christianity to the New World. When the new religious leaders realized the importance of dance in the life of the Indians and found that it could not be suppressed, they adapted the dances to Christian rituals. If the native Indians held a festival to honor one of their idols or gods, the priests would substitute a Christian saint in its stead. The Spanish introduced new dance rhythms as well as new string instruments.

The blending of the two cultures produced the *danza Mestiza*, which rapidly spread to all the states of the republic. These dances were warlike reenactments of the conquest. One of the most famous dances of this type is *La Danza de la Pluma* (dance of the plumes). In the dance, from the state of Oaxaca, the performer dons a splendid headdress that is covered with feathers, beads, and mirrors in beautiful designs and breathtaking colors. The dance simulates the struggles between the Indians and the Spaniards. The choreography is simple, but the steps are quite difficult. The dance is performed by men only and is very popular even today.

Most of the dances of this era are of the same type. Examples are *Mores y Cristrianos* (Moors vs. Christians) and the *Danza do los Diablitos* (devils). There are also dances of pre-Hispanic origin that have had their music and costumes embellished by the European influence. Examples of these are *La Danza de los Quetzales* (Quetzales is a bird) from the state of Puebla and *La Danza de los Voladores* from Papantla, Veracruz. The latter is sometimes called the dance of the "Flying Indians."

Dances that depict the work ethic are demonstrated by such dances as *Los Sonarjeros*, a planting dance, and *La Tortuga del Arenal*, which reenacts the gathering of turtle eggs, an important part of the diet of the Juchitecas. Most of these dances were performed at fiestas and in the courtyard of the church, a custom that still exists. Every region has its own *danzas mestizas*, which correspond to its own way of life. Each embodies a reminder of what used to be and an acceptance of the new.

Dances of Modern Mexico

The third phase of the dance of Mexico evolved from the intermarriage of the Spanish with native Mexicans. As time went by, the children of this union, called *Mestizos*, began to acquire more and more of the Spanish customs and slowly discarded that which was purely indigenous. During the colonial period other nationalities also added their influence. The French who came with Maximilian brought the ballroom dances that were popular in the courts of Europe (*Bailes de Salon*) such as the polka, waltz, schottische, mazurka, and varsouvienne. The Germans favored the northern part of Mexico and left their stamp on the music and dance of that region. Dance, however, took a new direction. Each region developed its own *zapateado* (footwork) and with it, its own jarabe.

El Jarabe Tapatio is considered the national dance of Mexico. From the state of Jalisco, it is the most popular of all the Jarabes. It is a dance of courtship and tells about the Charro (young cowboy) who has taken a fancy to a beautiful "China" (young señorita) and decides to visit her and declare his passion. She shares the same feelings but does not want to seem overanxious. So she shyly repulses his advances. Dejected over the rejection, he goes off to a cantina where he imbibes a little too much tequila and proceeds to get a little tipsy. On coming to his senses, he decides to try once more to show his serious intentions. He throws his most prized possession, his sombrero, at her feet and allows her to dance in the brim. Upon observing the manifestation of his true love for her, as a gesture of acceptance, she picks up the hat and places it on her head, after which they dance a *Diana*, a dance of triumph.

The word *jarabe* actually means a syrup or sweet mixture of different herbs and sugars. In music it is a medley of different tunes and in dance it consists of steps characteristic of a particular region. These are truly Mexican dances, Indian in origin and influenced by the Spanish, giving them the true flavor of Mexico. The most popular, recognizable, and best known of the Jarabes are Jarabe Tapatio, Jarabe de la Botella (Jalisco), Jarabe Michoacano, Jarabe Tlaxcalteco, and Jarabe Mixteco. Yucatan has produced the Jaranas; the Huapango is from Huastica; and the polkas are from the northern part of the country.

Music is also unique to each region. Jalisco, in the central part of Mexico, has mariachis or groups of strolling, singing musicians using the violin, different sized guitars, and more recently the trumpet. The typical musicians of Veracruz use the harp and violins and sing in a high pitch. The music of the north includes the guitar and accordion, often a button accordion, and in the south the marimba and the jaranas. Music has had deep influence on dance and vice versa.

An added attraction is the colorful costumes worn in each of the different regions of Mexico. From the predominantly white costumes from the warm climates of Veracruz and Yucatan, to Jalisco's colorful and beribboned costumes, to the heavy woolen skirts of Michoacan, to the fringed leather garments of the vaquero (cowboy) of northern Mexico, there are more than six hundred regional costumes. Dance in Mexico is the spontaneous manifestation of the feelings, the passions, and the pleasures of its people.

Corrido

Corrido was introduced to the California Folk Dance Federation by Avis Landis, a former member of the research committee of the California Folk Dance Federation. The Corrido is actually a folk ballad. Several steps are commonly done spontaneously to this type of music, namely, soldado, grapevine, and step close.

Records: Folkraft 1458; High/Scope RM 5, LP and compact disc.

Cassette: High/Scope RM 5.

Music: California Folk Dance Federation Reference II, Vol. IV (p. 1).

Position: Closed, man's back to center of circle.

Steps: Step-close, grapevine, shuffle.

■ Directions for the Dance

Meter 4/4 • Directions are for man; lady's part reverse.

Measures

Part I

Step-Close

A   1–5   Beginning right, take ten step-close steps in reverse line of direction. Small steps; Merengué and Rhumba action in displacement of weight.

Grapevine

B   1–7   Beginning right, take seven grapevine steps (crossing in front first) in line of direction.

     8   Step right across in front of left, stamp left, stamp right in place, and hold. Weight remains on left foot.

Step-Close and Soldado

C   9–10   Beginning right, take four step-close steps in reverse line of direction.

     11   Left reverse position. Beginning right, take four shuffle steps (soldado), couples moving **diagonally** to center of circle to man's left. (Man moves backward, lady forward.) Body action like Samba. During the soldado, the couple travels diagonally in and out, like "cutting pie."

     12   Take four shuffle steps (soldado) moving diagonally away from center of circle to man's left.

   13–17   Repeat action of measures 11–12 two and a half times, progressing forward in line of direction while moving diagonally in and out of circle.

     18   Moving away from center of circle, step forward on right, stamp left, stamp right, and hold and move into closed position.

Corrido (continued)

Grapevine

B   1–18   Repeat action of measures 1–8, B, part I.

Part II

Step-Close

A   1–5   Repeat action of measures 1–5, A, part I.

Cross-Step With One Turn

B   1   Partners face, man's hands clasped behind back, lady's skirt held out to side. Beginning right, moving in line of direction, step right across in front of left (accent), left coming off floor in back (count 1), step left in place (count 2), step right in place (count 3), cross left in front of right, right coming off floor in back (count 4).

       2   Starting a full turn, step right behind left (count 1), step left in place, pivoting counterclockwise to face away from partner (count 2), step right to side, pivoting counterclockwise to face partner (count 3), step left, facing partner (count 4).

       3–6   Repeat action of measures 1–2, B, part II, twice.

       7   Repeat action of measure 1, B, part II.

       8   Step right across in front of left, stamp left, stamp right in place, and hold.

Step-Close and Soldado

C   9–18   Repeat action of measures 9–18, C, Part I.

Grapevine with Two Turns

B   1–7   Partners face, right hands joined at shoulder height, man's left placed behind back, lady's left holds skirt. Beginning right, moving in line of direction, man takes seven grapevine steps. Lady takes one grapevine step (measure 1), and four steps turning clockwise twice under man's left arm (measure 2). Lady repeats this action twice, and takes one grapevine step on measure 7.

       8   Step right across in front of left stamp left, stamp right in place, and hold.

Part III

Step-Close

A   1–5   Repeat action of measures 1–5, A, part I.

Grapevine

B   1–8   Repeat action of measures 1–8, B, part I.

Step-Close and Soldado

C   9–18   Repeat action of measures 9–18, C, part I.

Grapevine

B   1–7   Inside hands joined, held at shoulder height and man's left hand placed behind back, lady's left holds skirt. Beginning right, take seven grapevine steps in line of direction. Dancers turn toward and away from each other as lady alternately holds skirt out to side and then folds it across the front of her body with the action of the grapevine steps.

       8   Step right across in front of left, stamp left, stamp right in place and hold.

El Jarabe Tapatio*

El Jarabe Tapatio is often referred to as the Mexican Hat Dance. It is considered to be the national dance of Mexico. The more proficient dancer will add steps and flourishes; others will simplify the dance.

Records: Folkraft R 4127; Imperial 1002; Peerless 1918; Victor 23-5901.

Formation: Any number of couples scattered informally around the dance area. Partners face each other or the front with inside hands joined, man's right holding lady's left.

Jarabe step: The basic step is like a very small two-step with accent on the first count. Example: step forward on right foot (count 1), step on left foot close to right instep (count 2), step forward on right foot. Repeat starting with left foot. This counts as two Jarabe steps, six counts, one measure. There are many styles of *Jarabe* step execution, such as: count 1 being done with just the heel, or the second count being done with the heel, rather than the whole foot. The steps should be very small since the music is very fast.

Steps: Jarabe step, heel toe, stamp, run, buzz step, chug.

■ Directions for the Dance

Meter: 6/8 • Directions are the same for both lady and man.

Roll of music   **Introduction:** Length of roll of music varies. The lady turns to her left under partner's joined hand and both move away from each other about three short steps. Man's hands are held low behind his back, lady holds skirt out to side. Body should lean forward slightly.

Measures

Part I

8 measures   **A.** Beginning right, move toward partner using fourteen basic Jarabe steps. Stamp right foot and hold. At this point couple should be in center of stage, right shoulder to right shoulder with partner.

8 measures   Continue in same direction to partner's place with twelve Jarabe steps, turning to right on 13th and 14th steps, and stamp on right. Now facing partner.

Cue words: Heel step, toe step.

8 measures   **B.** Step on right heel slightly in front of left foot, small step forward on left foot, step on right toe slightly back (but not behind) left foot, very small step forward on left foot. Use same floor pattern as **A** to partner (center) and stamp. Seven heel step, toe steps to the center and stamp. Continue across and turn to face partner and stamp.

8 measures   Pass right shoulders and continue to own original place, seven more heel-toe steps, turn to right to face partner, and stamp.

8 measures   **C.** Using fourteen Jarabe steps, go all the way to partner's place, turn and stamp right.

Meter 3/4

Part II

4 measures   Take three running steps toward partner (right, left, right), then cross left over right to do a full turn to right (in center, close to partner). Continue to opposite side, with three runs and cross left over right to a half-turn right to face partner. The running should be done lightly, like scissor kicks, straight legs lifting the free foot high from the hip. Pass by right shoulder.

El Jarabe Tepatio (continued)

---

*Directions by Nelda Drury, Associate Professor, Emeritus, San Antonio College, San Antonio, TX.

4 measures	**Turns:** Beginning right, take three buzz steps, turning right, stamp left. Turning left, repeat stepping left, stamp right.
4 measures	Repeat turns to right and to left. The stamp should be done facing toward partner.
12 measures	Repeat first twelve measures, runs and turns.

Part III Borrachito (Drunken) Step

This is like a waltz step. Fall forward onto right foot (count 1), step on left close to (and behind) right ankle (count 2), step on right foot (count 3). Repeat, starting with left foot. Dip right shoulder slightly forward when falling onto right foot. Dip left shoulder when falling onto left foot.

6 measures	Beginning right, take six borrachito steps, traveling to opposite side. Do not stop at center.
2 measures	Cross right foot over left and dance six little rocking steps while turning to the right (clockwise) in place. End facing partner.
8 measures	Repeat all, crossing back to original side.
Meter 2/4	

Part IV Hojas de Te

Hojas de te are the rhythmic words for practicing this step. This step is similar to Part I B; just add a chug to it. Step on right heel, step left. Step on right toe, step left, chug.

8 measures	Beginning right, take seven of these steps to center and stamp. Right shoulder to right shoulder with partner. Continue to other side, step left, turning right, stamp right. Each should be in own original place, facing partner.

Part V

6 measures	Run lightly forward, right, left, right, and cross left over right do full turn (pivot) to right (clockwise) ending with right shoulder toward home. Beginning right, take four push steps back to place. Push step is similar to buzz step, without turning, but traveling in straight line. The number of push steps varies according to proficiency.
6 measures	Repeat runs toward center; right, left, right, and cross left over right, do full turn, remain in center. Man throws hat on the floor at lady's feet during these push steps. Take six push steps, facing partner, leading with left shoulder, traveling around hat clockwise.

Part VI

8 measures	Left shoulder leading, stepping on left foot, dancers move around the hat with sixteen push steps.
8 measures	The man and lady travel around the hat in opposite directions: man clockwise, lady counterclockwise. End up at own side.

Lady leaps lightly into brim of the hat, cross right over left and dance six rocking steps (weight onto right, lifting left heel, pointing left toe down, then transfers weight onto left, lifting right heel). During these rocking steps, maneuver to end up on lady's original side. Use last two measures to get out (step, jump, leap, whatever) of the hat, onto "her" side. Today the lady seldom leaps into the hat, because they want to save the hat.

Man's step like a polka. (Lunge or fall forward on right, lifting left heel high in back, step on ball of left, step on right. Repeat starting with left.

3 measures	**Interlude:** Lady sinks down, picks up hat with both hands, places hat on her head. Man swings right leg over her head, crosses right over left, pivots to left. Man extends his right hand to her left hand to help lady up, and she rises. They stand side-by-side facing front, inside hands joined.

Meter 2/8

Part VII

8 measures Take four light running steps forward, four backing up to place. Repeat four forward, four back.

8 measures Hop on left, at same time place right heel out to right (count 1), hop on left, at same time cross right in front of left and touch right toe to floor (count *and*), hop on left, at same time place right heel to right (count 2), bounce lightly on both feet (count *and*). Repeat starting left. Repeat all.

8 measures Take four running steps forward, four backward. Skip in place. Raise joined inside hands, lady turns left under that arch. Man kneels on left knee, lady places left foot on man's right knee. Lady holds her skirt out to the side with right hand, man extends left arm out, and both lean away from each other and hold pose!

🌀 Jesucita En Chihuahua* 🌀

Jesucita En Chihuahua is a vigorous and exciting polka from northern Mexico. This is a choreographed sequence, arranged by Señora Alura Flores de Angles.

Records: Folkraft 1513; Peerless 3248; Polka 1489 (Pepe Villa); Victor 70-7609.

Formation: Couples in varsouvienne position facing the line of direction.

Steps: Two-step, walk, heel toe, slide, step-close, stamp.

■ Directions for the Dance

Meter 4/4 • Directions are the same for both lady and man.

Measures

Part I

8 measures   Beginning right, take sixteen two-steps in line-of-direction. Use last two measures, without releasing hands, to do a half-turn to right and face reverse line of direction. Lady remains on outside. Turn as in Road to the Isles (p. 274), measure 12.

Part II

8 measures   Beginning right, take sixteen two-steps in reverse line of direction. Use last two measures to do a half-turn to left to face original line of direction. Lady remains on outside.

Part III

8 measures   Take four walking steps forward (right, left, right, left) (4 counts). Release left hand. Take four more small walks forward while lady turns right under held hands (4 counts). Rejoin left hands and repeat this combination three more times. Four times in all.

Part IV

8 measures   Repeat Part I. Take sixteen two-steps forward. Do not turn around, do not reverse.

Part V

8 measures   Lower joined right hands to lady's waist. Both stamp forward with the right, close left foot up to right foot. Step back with right, draw left foot back toward right foot. Take eight of these steps, maneuvering to turn clockwise.

8 measures   Repeat same footwork, but turn counterclockwise.

Part VI
Cue words: Heel, toe, heel, toe, slide, slide, slide, bounce.

8 measures   Hop on left foot and at same time touch right heel to right side. Hop on left foot and at same time cross right in front of left and tap right toe to the left of left foot. Repeat heel toe. Take two slides to the right, step right to side (like a gallop) and bounce on both feet. Beginning left, repeat to the left. Repeat all.

Part VII

8 measures   Repeat Part V, forward, close, back, close, for eight measures, turning clockwise.

Part VIII

8 measures   Repeat Part I, sixteen two-steps in line of direction.

Part IX

8 measures   Repeat Part III, walk and lady turns.

Part X

8 measures   Face partner, take closed position, man's back to center. Man beginning left, lady right, step to man's left side, close with right. This step is similar to the Merengue. Take sixteen step-close steps in line of direction. End with a stamp.

---

*Directions by Nelda Drury, Associate Professor, Emeritus, San Antonio College, San Antonio, TX.

🐚 La Adelita*

La Adelita is a charming couple dance from northern Mexico.

Record: Peerless 4-3248.

Position: Partners side-by-side facing front. Lady is to the right of the man. Man's thumbs in belt, lady holds her skirt out to sides.

Steps: Stamp, slide, heel toe.

■ Directions for the Dance

Meter 2/4 • Directions are the same for both lady and man.

Measures

	Part I
16 measures	Stamp right foot. Beginning right, take two slides to the right, step side right. Repeat starting with left foot. Eight times in all.
	Part II
16 measures	Partners face each other. Hop on left and at same time tap right heel at side, toe out, hop on left and at same time tap right toe across left foot. Hop left, step right to side, close left to right, step right to side. Repeat to left. Four times in all. End facing front.
	Part III **Cue words: Heel, toe, stamp, hold.**
16 measures	Hop on left, at same time place right heel in front. Hop on left, at same time place right toe in back. Stamp right foot and hold. Repeat all. Do three consecutive "heel-toe" steps turning to right. End with stamp on right, facing front. Repeat pattern, starting with left. End facing front.
	Part IV **Cue words: Heel, toe, run, run, run.**
16 measures	Hop on left and place right heel in front. Hop on left and place right toe in back (as in Part III). Take three running steps forward (right, left, right). Repeat heel, toe with left foot. Run three steps backward to place (left, right, left). Four times in all.
	Part V Taconazo (Northern Zapateado)
16 measures	Face front. In place, leap onto right foot. Step on left heel in place. Step on right foot in place. Tap (or strike) left heel in place without taking weight. Repeat starting with left foot. Alternate right, left. The man takes sixteen Taconazo steps in place; the lady takes eight in place and then travels forward with eight more. On the last step, the lady travels forward and turns to face partner.
	Part VI Square or Diamond
16 measures	Partners facing, they describe a square around each other, using "heel, toe, run, run, run" steps as in Part IV (four sequences to make one square). On the third run, turn one-quarter to own left, ready for new direction. To begin turn slightly to own right, hop left, right heel, hop left, right toe, run, run, run traveling right diagonally forward, (slight turn to own left on last run); hop right, left heel, hop right, left toe, travel diagonally forward to partner's place (turn one-quarter to own left on last run); hop left, right heel, hop left, right toe, run, run, run traveling diagonally forward (turn one-quarter turn to own left on last run); hop right, left heel, hop right, left, toe, and end up at home position. Repeat sequence. Two sequences in all.

Repeat dance from Part II.

---

*Directions by Nelda Drury, Associate Professor, Emeritus, San Antonio College, San Antonio, TX.

🌿 La Bruja* 🌀

La Bruja or "The Witch" is a stately dance from the Mexican state of Veracruz.

Records: RCA Camden CAM-108; Express E-S 1 (45 RPM); Folkraft 1515.

Formation: A group dance for women or women and men. These directions, however, are for individuals scattered, facing front. Each carries a glass three-quarters full of water in the right hand. The Jarochas, women from Veracruz, wear very full white skirts, which adds much to the dance.

Steps: Waltz, two-step, step swing.

■ Directions for the Dance

Meter 3/4

Measures

Part I

16 Beginning on right, take eight very small waltz steps forward. Take four small waltz steps in a small circle to the left. Use measures 13–16 to place and balance glass on own head. A heavy glass is easier to balance.

Part II

16 Step to side right with right foot, close left foot to right foot, step to right with right, and swing left foot across right. Repeat to left starting with left. Take eight of these step-close-step-swings, alternating to the right and left, each time turning gradually to the right, making a complete revolution.

Part III

16 Step right, swing left to right, step left, swing right to left, step right, close left to right, step right, swing left to right.

Beginning left, repeat to left. Repeat all. Four times in all.

Part IV

16 **Cue words: Step, brush, brush.** Beginning left, take a small step forward, brush ball of right foot forward, brush ball of right foot back. Repeat starting with right. Sixteen step, brush, brush, alternating feet. This step should move—just take longer steps.

Part V

16 Walk forward with four small stamps (right, left, right, left), brush, ball of right foot forward, brush it back. Repeat same footwork eight times in all.

Part VI

16 Step on right foot, tap left heel in place by right foot. Slowly turn in place to right with 24 of these (three per measure for eight measures). Repeat, turning to left.

Repeat action of Parts II, III, IV, and V.

Ending

Stamp right foot, point left foot forward. Remove glass from head. Bow.

---

*Directions by Nelda Drury, Associate Professor, Emeritus, San Antonio College, San Antonio, TX.

La Cucaracha*

The song that accompanies the dance was popularized during the Mexican Revolution. There are many versions of La Cucaracha. An original version and an adapted version for recreational groups are presented.

Records: DL P5; DC 162105 LP; EZ 5009; FD LP5; Folkraft 1458; R 4134; Merit AV Album 5.

Cassette: DC 162105 C.

Formation: Couples scattered informally around the dance area. Partners face each other, man's left shoulder, lady's right shoulder toward the front. Man places thumbs in belt, lady holds skirt out to the side.

Steps: Walk, stamp.

■ Directions for the Dance

Meter 3/4 • Footwork is the same for man and woman, both beginning right.

Measures

Part I

1	Step on right foot diagonally across left, step back on left in place, step back right in place.
2	Step on left foot diagonally across right, step back on right in place and hold (count 3).
3–4	Spin to left with four steps (left, right, left, right). Hold (counts 2, 3).
5–8	Repeat measures 1–4, beginning with left foot, toward the right. Face front.
9–16	Repeat measures 1–8 facing front.

Part II

17–18	Beginning right, walk forward diagonally left three steps (right, left, right). Stamp left twice (no weight).
19–20	Walk back to place (left, right, left). Stamp right foot twice (no weight).
21–24	Repeat measures 17–20 diagonally right. Face partner for measures 25–32.
25–32	Repeat measures 17–24 to partner's right shoulder and back to place, then to partner's left shoulder and back to place.

Variation (La Cucaracha, adapted)

Formation: Couples in a circle, facing center, both beginning right.

Part I

1–8	Action of measures 1–8 is original version, facing center of circle.
9–16	Repeat measures 1–8 facing partner.

Part II

17–24	Action of measures 17–24 is original version to partner's right shoulder and back, then to left shoulder and back.
25–26	Weave the ring **three places:** Walk three steps to partner's right shoulder (right, left, right), stamp, stamp.
27–28	Continue forward to next person's left shoulder with three walks and two stamps.
29–32	Continue forward to next person's right shoulder with three walks and two stamps. This is a new partner.
31–32	Join both hands, walk four steps, turning 3/4 around and face center, lady to right of man, drop hands.

---

*Directions by Nelda Drury, Associate Professor, Emeritus, San Antonio College, San Antonio, TX.

🌿 La Raspa

Frequently, *La Raspa* is called *Mexican Hat Dance* by the public. The true Mexican Hat Dance, *Jarabe Tapatio,* is an entirely different dance.

Records: Coast 7018; EZ-716; Folkraft 1457; High/Scope RM 3, LP and compact disc; Merit AV LP; World of Fun LP 6, Side B-5; Worldtone 10042.

Cassettes: Dancecraft DC 887; Dancecraft DC 162303.

Music: Sedillo, Mela, *Mexican and New Mexican Folk Dances,* p. 36.

Position: Partners face, man holds clasped hands behind back, lady holds skirt, or two hands joined.

Steps: Bleking step, running step.

◼ Directions for the Dance

Meter 2/4

Measures

Part I

A 1-4 Beginning right, take one bleking step.

5-8 Turn slightly counterclockwise away from partner (right shoulder to right shoulder) and, beginning left, take one bleking step.

9-12 Repeat action of measures 1-4, facing opposite direction (left shoulder to left shoulder).

13-16 Repeat action of measures 1-4, facing partner.

Part II

B 1-4 Hook right elbows, left hands held high. Take eight running steps, clapping on eighth step.

5-8 Reverse direction, hook left elbows. Take eight running steps, clapping on eighth step.

9-16 Repeat action of measures 1-8, B.

Variation

Measures 1-8: Take 16 running steps, right elbows hooked. Measures 9-16: Reverse and take 16 running steps.

Icebreaker

No partners, all stand in single circle. Turn slightly left and right for action of measures 1-16, A; run in line of direction and reverse line of direction for action of measures 1-16, B. Halfway through record, everyone may take a partner.

🌿 Las Chiapanecas* 🌾

Las Chiapanecas is a woman's dance from the state of Chiapas.

Records: EZ 716; Folkraft 1483; LS E 20.

Formation: There are many options. As a couple dance, both on same foot, moving in the same direction, or opposite feet, moving in opposite direction. As a solo dance, dancers scattered, or group dance with a lot of choreography.

■ Directions for the Dance

Meter 3/4

Measures

Part I

1	Beginning left, step left in place (count 1), hop on left (count 2), step on right diagonally forward left, across left (count 3).
2	Step on left in place (count 1), hop on left (count 2), step backward on right (count 3).
3–6	Repeat measures 1 and 2 two more times.
7–8	Do four stamps, left, right, left, right (no weight on last stamp).
9–16	Repeat measures 1–8 to the right, starting with right.
17–32	Repeat measures 1–16.

Part II

1–3	Beginning right, turn to right with three-step turn or take three waltz steps.
4	Lean slightly to right and clap hands twice about shoulder high.
5–8	Repeat measures 1–4 to the left, beginning left.
9–16	Repeat measures 1–8.

Part III A

1	Beginning right, step to right (count 1), tap left heel close to right (count 2), step on left close to right (count 3).
2–3	Repeat measure 1 two more times. Three times in all.
4	Two stamps, right, left (no weight on left).
5–8	Repeat measures 1–4 to left, starting with left.
9–14	Repeat measure 1 six times.
15–16	Do a pivot turn to right (step on right, cross left over right and turn).

Part III B

17	Beginning left, step to left on left (count 1), hop left and at same time lift right foot (keep it close to left ankle) (count 2), step on right close to left (count 3).
18–32	Repeat pattern of Part III A to the left, substituting the "lift" instead of tapping heel.

Variation

Part I and/or Part III: Individuals may waltz around, turning instead of suggested pattern.

---

*Directions by Nelda Drury, Associate Professor, Emeritus, San Antonio College, San Antonio, TX.

🌀 Santa Rita*

Santa Rita is a couple dance from northern Mexico.

Records: CBS - E.P.C. 393; Folkraft 1513.

Formation: Couples in semi-open position, facing line of direction, in a circle.

Steps: Two-step, slide, polka.

■ Directions for the Dance

Meter 2/4 • Directions are for man; lady's part reverse.

Measures

	Part I
1–4	Beginning left, take four two-steps forward. In Mexico this is called a polka. There is no hop, but rather a scuff forward on the foot that starts the two-step.
5–6	Closed position, man's back to center of circle. Cross left over right, cross right over left. Stamp left foot three times, weight ends on left.
7–8	Step right to right side, close left to right, step right (like a two-step to side). Stamp left twice (no weight).
9–16	Repeat measures 1–8.
	Part II
17	Closed position, man's back to center of circle. Moving to the left side, step left, close right, step left.
18	Cross right over left, cross left over right.
19–20	Repeat measures 17–18 in reverse line of direction, beginning right.
21–32	Repeat measures 17–20 three more times.
	Part III Polka
33–48	Closed position. Take sixteen polka steps (traditional real polka, not a two-step). Turn clockwise while progressing in line of direction.
	Part IV Wrap Up
49–50	Join two hands, man's back to center of circle. Beginning right, balance forward (right shoulder near right shoulder), balance away (backward).
51–52	Both hands remain joined, man lowers right hand, lady's left, as lady turns to her left (counterclockwise), taking two small two-steps, under her right hand, his left. Lower joined hands. Partners are side by side, lady to **right** of man.
53–54	In wrap position, balance forward, balance backward, using two small two-steps.
55–56	Unwind her back to place.
57–58	Balance forward (left shoulder to left shoulder), balance backward.
59–60	Wrap up lady to man's **left side.** Man's left, lady's right hand stays down. The lady turns to her right (clockwise) taking two small two-steps, under her left hand, man's right. Lower joined hands.
61–64	In wrap up position, facing line of direction, balance forward, balance backward, balance forward, balance backward. Do not unwrap.

---

*Directions by Nelda Drury, Associate Professor, Emeritus, San Antonio College, San Antonio, TX.

Part V

65–68 In wrap up position, take four small two-steps in place (right, left, right, left).

69–72 Take seven push steps sidewards right (counts 1–7). Bounce on both feet on count 8.

73–80 Repeat measures 65–72 to the left, starting with left foot.

Interlude

81–82 Dancers are facing line of direction, lady on left side of man. Release man's right hand. Beginning left, lady takes a three-step turn to her left.

83–84 Release inside hands and both turn. Man does a four-step-turn to his left (left, right, left, right) in place. Lady does one and a half turn to right, with four steps (right, left, right, left). She ends up in front of man. Closed position, man facing line of direction.

Part VI Apache Step

May be done cheek-to-cheek, bend forward at the waist, "tush" protruding in back.

85–86 **Man's step:** rock forward onto left foot and push joined hands (man's left) forward (count 1). Step back onto right foot (back at home position) (count 2). Step far back with left foot, pull joined hands back, toward man's left hip (count 1). Step on right foot, it never left home (count 2).

87–88 Repeat measures 85–86.

89–92 Man walks forward eight steps: step forward left, at same time right heel turns up and out, right toe remains on floor.

93–100 Repeat 85–92 starting with right. Bring joined hands to man's left hip.

85–88 **Lady's step** is the opposite. Beginning right, lady rocks back and forward, back and forward.

89–92 Then she walks backward eight steps. If possible, do "broken ankle" step. Step back on right, at same time turn left ankle to left so that left edge of foot is on the floor, do not put weight on turned ankle.

93–100 Repeat starting left.

Part VII

Closed position, man facing line of direction.

Cue words: Heel, toe, slide, close, step; cross, cross, close, bounce.

101 Hop on right and tap left heel to left side. Hop on right and cross left foot over right ankle, left toe taps floor.

102 Step left to side, close right to left, step side left, toward center.

103–104 Cross right over left, cross left over right. Close right foot to left foot. Bounce on both feet.

105–108 Repeat measures 101–104 to right, starting with right.

109–116 Repeat measures 101–108.

Part VIII

117–132 Repeat Part I, measures 1–16.

Part IX

133–148 Repeat Part II, measures 17–32.

Part X

149–161 Repeat Part I, measures 1–16.

CHAPTER 8

Social Dance

Introduction

Social Dance in America is a form of silent language in that it tends to reflect, in music and movement, the mood of people. An in-depth analysis of dance in relation to socioeconomic change would no doubt show the changing status of human anxieties and pressures, crises and competitions, and joys and depressions, as well as changes in manners and dress.

Nearly every dance on the ballroom floor today was ushered in with wild hysteria and daring, but throughout history those dances that were once shocking have, with time and refinement, evolved into an acceptable mode of expression.

Social Dance had its start with the Court Dances when, during the Renaissance period, all the courts of Europe were trying to outdo each other with the most elaborate ball. Dance masters were hired to dignify many of the peasant dances and teach them to the aristocracy. Even the great masters, Beethoven, Brahms, Strauss, and others, wrote special music for these great court occasions. Exquisite dress and polished manners were essential

for any lady and gentleman of the court. These same elements were part of the military balls and elaborate cotillions of early social dancing in America, and they still appear on a limited scale in the college proms and formal dances of organized clubs today, although the earlier dances—Polka, Two-Step, Waltz, and Minuet—have been replaced by a long line of changing forms in the 20th century and continue into the 21st century.

Parallel with the development of Ballroom Dance in early America was the spread of dance in the tavern and honky-tonk during the trail-blazing period. The night clubs of the 20th century display all levels and types of Social Dance, and all levels of society are represented by dancers in those night clubs.

Ballroom dance is not limited to nightclubs. Nonalcoholic events, receptions, celebrations, and family occasions feature social dancing too.

Phases of Social Dance

Since the 1900s seven periods have marked the progress of Social Dance, and each was stimulated or motivated by a new style of music.

The Foxtrot Period

The *Foxtrot* had its beginning in the early 1900s as a fast, trotting step to a new jazz beat called "ragtime," and it was destined to undergo numerous transitions as it developed. Novelty dances like the *Bunny Hug* and the *Grizzly Bear* rocked the population in an early dance revolution around the time of World War I.

The Charleston Period

Ushered in by Dixieland jazz was a huge dance fad accompanying the short haircut, the shorter skirt, and the whole flapper style of the Roaring Twenties—the *Charleston*. Although strenuous and tricky to do, it reappears frequently due to its blend of syncopated beat and action, which has tremendous natural attraction for all ages.

The Swing Era

The *Swing* was spearheaded by the big-band music of 1930–1950, bringing in thousands of tunes that have become classics. During this period, the Foxtrot changed to a beautiful, smooth dance with a multitude of variations. The Waltz took on a new sophistication, and the Lindy, often referred to as the Jitterbug and later as the Swing, found its way deep into the hearts of a dancing public. The *Big Apple,* the *Shag,* and the *Lambeth Walk* were the big fads of the college crowd in 1937, while the new Latin American dances were setting off still another trend in Social Dance. Everybody was humming a tune. It was a time when song and dance became the milestones for marking important events in people's lives. Dance studios sprang up everywhere, and large public ballrooms held thousands who were captivated by these toe-tapping, swinging, and swaying melodies. The '80s and '90s have brought Swing dancing back, but to many different rhythm styles—big band, rock and roll, rhythm and blues, Country Western, Salsa, and Cajun.

The Latin Dance Craze

Although the *Tango* was a fad in the 1920s, it has been restyled several times and remains a favorite, even though other *Latin dances* have overshadowed it at times. In the 1930s, the Cuban *Rumba* started a whole new trend toward Latin American dance, stimulated by electric Latin melodies. It was followed by the *Samba* from Brazil, and these two became a sort of slow-fast partnership. During World War II, the *Mambo* stirred up the dancing population but was soon replaced by the *Cha Cha Cha,* the *Calypso,* the *Merengue,* and a few others that had only brief periods of popularity. Finally, in 1960 came the *Bossa Nova,* a slower and easier form of the Samba. All during the period of rock that followed, one had to belong to a dance club to have the opportunity to dance the Latin dances to any extent. Now with the big-band music back again, the Latins may see a revival, particularly the Rumba, the Cha Cha Cha, the Bossa Nova, and the Tango, which remained firmly established in the repertory of standard Ballroom Dances.

Rock and Roll

The military draft of World War II reduced the big bands to small combos of from three to five instrumentalists and a vocalist. The tiny dance floors of the smaller night clubs were crowded, and the mood was rhythm and blues. Later, the younger set began a new style of dance at the coffeehouses and discotheques. The disc jockey and recorded music reigned at these establishments. Rock and roll was a more syncopated version of the lindy but with a greater freedom of the torso, a dropping action in the knees, and numerous swing-out patterns. This hysterical fad led, in the 1960s, into a new feeling about dance, which was to spread throughout the world. Whereas the body in Social Dance had generally been used in a single movement with most action in arms and legs and with emphasis on morals and manners, the active beat of rock music

began to demand a freer and more energetic response. Dance from the black culture brought an explosive movement from the pelvic area and the center of the body. Television was the vehicle for disseminating a wide variety of rock variations, starting at first with the low-down, gutsy delivery of Elvis Presley carrying through to the Beatles, the Rolling Stones, and the Beach Boys. With Rock and Roll dancing the dress code disappeared. A series of dances came and went, starting with the Twist, the Slop, the Mashed Potato, the Swim, the Monkey, the Pony, the Bug, the Frug, the Hitchhiker, the Watusi, the Hully Gully, and the Jerk.

Between 1965 and 1975, young people in the U.S. rebelled against the Vietnam War, the establishment, and the traditional values. Small singing-moving groups performed with a booming beat, discordant effects, and strobe lights. The trend manifested itself through swinging hair, hippie clothing, and a new wave of social mores. The "free" dance, unencumbered by pattern or partner, reflected an age of anxiety, confusion, and affluence. The popularity of Rock and Roll is still strong today.

Country Western

Songs from the cowboys after the Civil War lingered. Country western music grew from this beginning and was reinforced with music and folk songs from Appalachia and the southwest. By the 1930s this music became widespread through the use of radio and became known as country or country western. Country Western dance has developed with the country western music.

Approaching the 21st Century

With the return of the big bands and partner dancing, popular taste has come full circle. Not too many people can name the step, but they like the rhythms and are comfortable propelling their partner around the dance floor. The 1980s was a period of eclectic dance.

"Touch Dancing," a newly coined term, refers to holding one's partner again and includes Hustle, Disco, Swing, and Social Dances from Waltz to Cha Cha Cha.

The changes in dance styles are intricately connected to the changes in music that people want to hear. The desire for more variety is shown by the greater number of people back on the dance floor. *Disco* brought back in vogue partners dancing together and it lowered the decibels. Country singer Willie Nelson and rock singer Joe Jackson produced albums that featured the sound of swing.

Live music is also back in style, with a wider range of sounds and rhythms. Bands are comfortable playing a variety of styles—foxtrot, swing, shuffle, Latin music, rock, rhythm and blues, salsa, reggae, ska, and soul. *Salsa* music entered the dance scene in the mid-1960s when Cubans settled in Miami and southern Florida. Their Latin music became a blend of Afro–Cuban jazz, the big band sound, and disco rhythms. *Salsa* is the Spanish word for *sauce* and, as the Spanish sauces are spicy, the name seems appropriate. The Afro–Cuban rhythms influence soul music and Jamaican rhythms the reggae music. Shuffle, 4/4 swing, is the bridge between swing and rock and roll, or music of the 1940s and music of the 1950s and 1960s. Once again people are dancing a smooth SSQQ,* the old magic step, or a QQSS, the shuffle beat.

Swing dance is back, danced to country western, big band sound, rhythm and blues, rock, and Cajun. Salsa music and the Broadway dance revue El Tango Argentino have rekindled interest in *Latin dances.* Country western has an array of dances based on ballroom and folk forms. Line dances have also become popular: they offer the opportunity for everyone to dance without a partner.

Break dancing, an acrobatic form coming from the South Bronx, is also a product of the 1980s. The dance soon took off across the country. The Rock Steady Crew Breakers had a brief spot in the movie *Flashdance.* Break dancing was a part of the Hip Hop culture—real folk art—that also included graffiti art, rapping, and scratching. The Hip Hop culture was a positive force in staving off boredom and channeling hostilities for black and Hispanic teenagers in the Bronx. It was warmly received because of its antidrug and antiviolence approach.

Hip Hop has its roots in rap, a black music form. It also embraces soul, funk, and jazz, dance hall reggae and other forms of primarily black music. Hip Hop is a combination of rap music, break dancing, and graffiti art. The rhythm is 4/4, essentially a rhythm-driven dance music in which the beat and drum are essential. The music is electronic-funk with its machine-gun-style chanting called Rap. The motion (dance) is faster than the beat.

Meanwhile, *International Style* from England has become firmly entrenched in the dance studio and competitive world since 1960 and deserves mention here because of its patterns and precise style, almost as an art form. Those who have reached the advanced stage of dance look to International Style for greater stimulation and challenge. Although beautiful, it is demanding in terms of form

and has not caught on with the dancing public, who have not had the sustained interest, the time, nor the discipline to develop it thoroughly. Interest in **competitive Ballroom Dancing** is also growing. Viennese Waltz, Waltz, Quickstep, Tango, Bolero, Foxtrot, Cha Cha Cha, Rumba, Samba, and Paso Doble are some of the categories. Country Western Dance also sponsors competitions in 4- and 6-count swing.

Vintage Dance

There is considerable interest in reconstructing the ballroom dances of the 19th and early 20th centuries. Related areas of costuming, makeup, lighting, and sound are involved. Dance skills are expanded through the staging of quadrilles, contras, waltzes, polkas, rags, and tangos.

Dances through the ages have cast their spell. They are a part of the common culture. They are the American heritage to be borrowed, shared, and recreated. Each generation will continue to find its own way of relating dance to life itself.

Phenomenon of Social Dancing

Strangely enough, in spite of the term *Social Dance,* it may be and usually is a way of actually being asocial. It is the form of dance where one does not have to mix with others. One can go out for an evening of dancing, perform every dance with the same partner, and remain completely disassociated and private from the others in the crowd.

Unlike what happens in Square, Contra, or Folk Dance, there is no obligation to be part of the total group. The atmosphere is completely unstructured. One can sit and listen to the music or dance. The movement of any one couple is the interpretation of the man who is leading. His only concern for other dancers is that he tries to make his way around the floor without bumping anyone else. It is fascinating how hundreds of couples can maneuver in and out and around the dance floor with almost no contact with others, either physically or mentally. Subconsciously, there is a pattern of general consideration for others that exists to keep the atmosphere serene and pleasant. A considerable amount of attention at times is given the musical ensemble, particularly if they have exceptional performers.

On the other hand, Social Dances are the prime social events of nearly all civic and fraternal organizations several times a year. Sociability is far more apparent both on and off the dance floor. Many communities, both urban and rural, have dance clubs that meet on a regular basis and repre-

---

*SSQQ—see footnote on p. 379.

sent people with a mutual concern for each other and an interest in having fun together.

In any case, Social Dance fulfills a need for recreation and is high on the list of leisure-time pursuits. Most individuals will be involved in Social Dance sometime in their lives. It is a social phenomenon unparalleled in any other form of dance.

Teaching of Social Dance

The ever-present need of our youth to keep up with their contemporaries makes it imperative that they know how to dance. The Rock Dance period was very bewildering to the dance teachers and the recreation leaders who were trying to sort out what to teach and how to teach it. In many schools and recreation departments, the teaching of Social Dance came to an abrupt halt. In some settings, teachers learned from their students, worked out the analysis of the movements, and with the help of skilled students, taught the Discotheque Dances. It is significant that, even during a time when dance was most individual and to do "one's own thing" was the fashion, many young people did not take part because they did not know what to do and could not readily copy what they saw.

Now, with a new era of music and dance ahead, it is a time for dance to be revived for all, youth and adult. It is the leader-teacher's responsibility to provide the opportunity for every boy and girl to learn to dance.

Chapter 2 gives pertinent, detailed information about facilities and equipment for dance, organization and program planning, and effective teaching procedures.

Dance Class

The makeup of a class often affects whether interest is sustained. Traditionally, teenagers separate themselves into two common interest groups. Younger teenagers do not particularly enjoy being with the older group for recreational activities. Adults need this same consideration for class instruction. Older adults need to move slowly and tend to prefer only a few patterns, in contrast to younger adults, who desire to keep up with the innovations. Although all dance, more or less, to the same bands, the ways of handling a class for instruction will differ greatly depending on the ages of the students.

Some guidance in the selection of materials comes from a look at past preferences, but all should be consulted about their preferences.

1. Junior teenagers will request dances to rock but need the Foxtrot and Swing. The Cha Cha Cha and Samba are popular with them because those dances are active and have an open positioning. Line Dances assist rhythm training and allow everyone to dance solo.
2. Senior teenagers will dance to rock since they grew up with it, but they are now requesting instruction in the closed dance position. Foxtrot and Waltz appeal strongly, and the Tango is a favorite. Swing is a must. The Rumba requires slow sophistication and is fun if students are not drilled on the style too much.
3. Young to middle-aged adults need to be divided into two groups—the absolute beginners and the dancers. One group will want just enough to get by on, while the other is hungry for everything from the Tango to Viennese Waltz.
4. The older adult will prefer to review the slower dances, particularly the Foxtrot, Waltz, moderate-tempo Swing, and Rumba.

Detailed suggestions for teachers and recreation leaders in the orientation to the dance class, procedures and management of a class, planning guides and grading, are to be found in Chapter 2.

Additional Dance Material

Chapter 3, Dance Fundamentals
 Schottische, Two-Step, Polka
Chapter 4, American Heritage Dance
 Line Dances, Plain and Novelty Mixers, Heel Toe Polka, Novelty Dances

Sample Series of Lessons

1. Junior teenagers—ten lessons. Change partners often.
   a. Foxtrot basic plus three variations—three lessons.
      Swing basic plus three variations—three lessons.
      Overall review, grading day, final party—four lessons (grading is unnecessary except at school).
   b. Swing basic plus two variations—two lessons.
      Cha Cha Cha basic plus two variations—two lessons.
      Review and grading—one lesson.
      Samba basic plus two variations—two lessons.
      Review, grading, and final party—three lessons.
   c. Charleston (optional).
2. Senior teenagers—ten lessons. Change partners often, but have times of free choice.
   a. Foxtrot review plus three variations—two lessons.

Tango basic plus two variations—two lessons.
Review and grading—one lesson.
Swing review plus two variations—two lessons.
Waltz basic plus two variations—two lessons.
After-school dance.

   b. Rock dances—every day for ten minutes.
Swing, new variations—two lessons.
Waltz basic plus three variations—two lessons.
Foxtrot, new variations—one lesson.
Overall review—one lesson.
Grading—two lessons.
Cha Cha Cha and Samba review—one lesson.
Final party—one lesson.

   c. Charleston and Polka (optional).

3. Adults—perhaps one 2-hour lesson a week for 15 weeks. It is best to teach one dance through the basics plus two or three variations before going on to another dance. When into the second dance, keep reviewing and dancing material previously taught. Avoid, for the beginner, teaching a dab of each dance and jumping from one dance to another. It is very confusing. Adults usually sign up for lessons by couples; therefore, for initial instruction of new styles, it is best not to have husbands and wives together until free practice time.

4. Senior adults—perhaps a series of ten lessons of 1 hour each in which they learn one or two new steps each time and do lots of dancing just for review and enjoyment. They will also enjoy the Polka and the Schottische, as well as Mixer Dances. Often there is an uneven number of men and women. The best way to handle that situation is to have the leader bring extra men to help out.

Analysis of Variables in a Lesson

Certain aspects of teaching Social Dance are variable, depending on the circumstances of class size, available space, and length of the teaching unit and also on the particular step, variation, or style being taught at any given time. It seems wise to think through these variables and their relationship to the learning process.

1. **Formation of the Class:** * Beginning steps usually are more quickly and easily understood if the class is in line formation, all facing the same direction, so that dancers can hear and see the demonstration of the action from the same angle that they will perform it. Partners should be side by side or opposite each other so they can quickly get together when needed. The teacher's

---

* □ = Man; ○ = Lady; △ = Teacher.

position is in front of the line, facing the group when talking, but turning his or her back to the class to demonstrate (a). Both teacher and class may be turned on a diagonal so that each can see by looking sideways toward the other (b). When the class is fortunate enough to have two teachers, a favorite formation is to have men standing in a line opposite their partners with the two teachers in between (c).

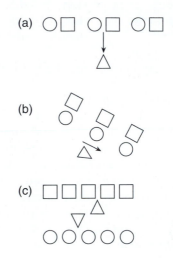

Immediately after the class has learned the step in line formation, it is wise to scatter the group about the floor, moving counterclockwise in the normal traffic pattern for Social Dance. Intermediate and advanced material is sometimes best taught from the traffic pattern and also with partners in a designated position.

2. **The Walkthrough:** The teacher should be able to talk while demonstrating the action of a new step. Then alone, in slow motion, in unison, with a starting cue, the class will try the action with the teacher several times through. The speed may be gradually increased until it is the same as the music to be played. Then the step may be tried with the music, or it first may be done with a partner and then to the music. When a partner is added, aspects of leading one's partner nearly always have to be brought in. During the walkthrough, group corrections and style corrections are made. Opportunity for questions gives the class freedom and ease. The walkthrough should never approach a "drill" in duration. It is merely a stage of progression when a student can learn one thing at a time, gradually getting a whole step, with a partner, all fitted together logically. Then a free practice time with music is in order, at which time the teacher is free also to wander about, giving individual help where needed.

3. **The Cue:** The whole principle of unison practice developing rhythmic awareness is contingent on the accuracy of a system of cueing when in a group class. A signal, such as "ready and," will

serve to get everyone started at the same time. Various other types of cues help keep time and help the student remember the duration or the foot pattern, but most important is the fact that cues should be given rhythmically. This helps the learner get the feeling of the timing.

For example: 4/4   *1 - 2*   *3*   *4*

	1-2	3	4
a rhythm cue:	slow	quick	quick
a step cue:	step	side	close
a direction cue:	turn	side	close
a style cue:	down	up	up
an advance cue or warning cue:	get ready for the break		

Good teachers frequently change from one type of cue to another in search of the right combination to help a student. The cue should be only a "help," not a "crutch." Overcueing means that the teacher cues after there is no longer a need for it or cues where the students should be on their own to listen and respond to the music. Any cueing when the music is playing should be done over the microphone and should be short.

4. **The Demonstration:** Learning takes place faster when students see what they are trying to do. It must not take the place of the walkthrough and unison practice, but it is a definite advantage in terms of getting the style or flow of an action. Demonstration also means that less talking and more practicing take place. It is helpful to demonstrate at the following times.

   a. At the beginning—a total picture of the pattern, with partner and music, occasionally is a good motivational device.
   b. To start a new step—demonstrate the man's part, then the lady's, and then the leads as students take partners to do it.
   c. Demonstrate for emphasis on style, lead, partner relationships, and timing.
   d. Occasionally demonstrate incorrect form followed by correct form.
   e. When students ask to see it again for clarification. Overuse of demonstration causes copying instead of thinking, and standing instead of dancing.

5. **Unison versus Free Practice:** Each must have its own time. The walkthrough of something new should be done in unison; that is, with everyone starting together and responding to cue. This way students and teacher alike become keenly aware of the group motion and can see or feel whether they have it or not. Teachers can spot problems easily and proceed to repeat, slow up, or demonstrate to correct errors as they develop. However, the whole concept of Social Dance is violated if a class is kept constantly in the control of the teacher-leader as he or she

calls out what to do. As quickly as unison practice shows that the majority of the group has caught on to the new action, students should be free to practice on their own with the music, to move freely about the dance floor, and to use the step, variations, or learned package in their own way. Free practice is healthy and transposes the class into a more nearly real social situation. Students must learn to cope with this situation rather than always being teacher directed.

6. **Space Awareness:** The traffic pattern is always counterclockwise around the dance floor. This is also the *line of direction* or the *line of dance.* Dancing the wrong way, against the natural flow of traffic, is like driving the wrong way on a one-way street. It is in obvious poor taste and causes problems for all dancers. The man should avoid moving down the center line. There is no marking to divide the two sides of the floor, but generally when the man finds himself in that vicinity he should plan his next dance pattern to maneuver himself away from the center or to turn so that he will be traveling with the traffic on the other side of the floor. One of the hardest lessons for the man, who guides the dance, to learn is that the patterns he uses must be maneuvered into the open spaces on the floor and around other moving couples without bumping them or using more than his share of the total space. A simple example of this is that the man may use open position freely as long as it carries him along with the traffic rather than across traffic. This does not preclude his dancing from side to side or in place, even backward or into a corté, so long as he is aware of others around him and there is space for him to perform the desired pattern without interfering with the progress of others. Even beginning dancers should practice this concept in order to develop a space awareness at an early stage.

7. **Rhythm Awareness:** A sense of being with the music is vital for the man who sets the beat and for the woman who must follow her partner. Excellent suggestions are given on pp. 53 – 54 for the teacher who must cope with the problems of helping students who have trouble learning the beat of the music. It is important to differentiate the melody and the rhythm. The percussion instruments carry the rhythm. Musical phrasing is important, especially for the Tango. Special emphasis here is needed to encourage students to listen to the music. Students in Social Dance, more than any other, need to understand the relationship of slow beats and quick beats in any given pattern. The teacher must understand this relationship and cue the correct timing of slow and quick beats as he or she teaches each step. Through encouragement

and practice in listening for those patterns in the music, students gradually become aware of the changing relationship of beats as dance patterns are combined. Greater pleasure as well as challenge develops for both man and woman when they are aware of combining steps that vary in rhythm as well as floor pattern and style.

8. **The Learning Package:** Here is a way of talking about tying all objectives for the day, or several days, into a complete set. Such a package is involved with any step that is taught, the understanding of its proper rhythmic pattern, and the use of the step in maneuvering with a partner about the dance floor. This method suggests that any given dance step all by itself is useless. It must be understood in relation to its rhythmic structure, and there must be some transition from the step itself to its related basic and its use with a partner on the dance floor in the moving traffic of other dancers.

Even with beginning dancers on their first basic step in closed position, it is possible to show how that one basic step can be maneuvered forward or backward, right or left, or danced on the spot in place. Now the man is prepared to cope with moving in space without bumping other dancers, holding up the traffic, or dancing his partner into the wall. Soon learning packages will involve tying together basic steps and several variations all in the same rhythm pattern. Eventually, tying together combinations of several rhythm patterns and their respective variations brings the whole complex picture into perspective. Thinking about dance in terms of packages or units that fit together gives purpose to learning and direction to teaching, and also progression toward a meaningful goal for both student and teacher.

The materials under each type of dance in this chapter have been organized with a basic step, followed by its variations, in an effort to try to help teachers put together effective learning packages.

9. **Creativity versus Practice Combo:** Use of learning packages helps the student know how to tie the variations to the respective basic steps. From then on, it is a matter of remembering what variations one knows to be able to keep the dance interesting. Practice routines may help to show the man what variations combine excitingly. It is not necessary to have an even number of measures. Short practice routines of four to eight measures are handy and easy for the learner to repeat over and over for practice. The creative students will be anxious to try to put dance variations together and will be eagerly asking questions. It is important that the dancer learn to think in terms of phrasing and coordinated sequences of movement.

Preparation of the Lesson

The Teacher's Preparation of a Basic Step

1. *Selection of the dance:* Foxtrot and the basic step are to be taught—magic step, p. 424.
2. *Understanding of the basic rhythm:* 4/4 time, p. 421—to be used with all of its parts.

Basic magic step rhythm

uneven rhythm (SSQQ)

a. It is an uneven rhythm pattern in 4/4 time with a pattern of slow, slow, quick, quick.
b. It takes a measure and a half and repeats from the middle of the measure.
c. The accent of the music is on the first and third beats of each measure.
d. The style, p. 422, is for the man—a heel walk, left, right, plus a side close, left, right, with small steps.

Pattern diagram

start

For the lady—a long leg reach to the toe and backward two steps and with the man side, close right, left.

3. *Practice:* The teacher should practice the step to the music so that an accurate demonstration can be made. One teacher will need to know both the man's and the lady's parts and be able to demonstrate with one of the students from time to time. Two teachers working together, a man and a lady, can best show the partner positions and the leads, of course, but one well-prepared teacher can lead a good student after a class walkthrough on all the parts—usually without out-of-class practice.
4. *Analysis:* The teacher should analyze the positions, leads, style, and teaching cues for both the man's and the lady's parts, p. 381.

---

*S = slow; Q = quick.

5. *Structuring of the materials into a learning package:* Analysis and practice of ways to maneuver the magic step in the traffic pattern (forward or backward, right or left, or danced in place) should be part of the teacher's preparation.

Sample Organization of the Lesson Plan*

1. *Learning objectives:* Dance the basic magic step of Foxtrot. Understand the rhythm pattern SSQQ. Recognize the music and move to the beat. Demonstrate correct closed dance position, lead or follow a partner, and maneuver in a variety of ways in traffic.

2. *Selection of music:* Select five to seven records in moderate Foxtrot tempo with a good basic beat. Detailed assistance in selection of Social Dance records is on p. 494.

3. *Information about the dance:* Describe country and origin, give interesting facts or pictures, make notes of what to write on the chalkboard (i.e., name and rhythm pattern).

4. *Step-by-step progression:* Approximate time (50 minutes total).
   Warm-up dancing: 6 minutes
   Review from previous lesson: 6–8 minutes
   Presentation of new material: 20 minutes
     Formation of the class
     Walkthroughs, magic step, forward or backward, right or left, in place, turning
     Demonstrations
     Style
     Leads
     Cues
     Unison practice and free practice
     Partner changes
   Free practice time: 16 minutes
   Individual help

5. *Evaluation and reminders for next lesson.*

Sample Progression of a Learning Package

1. Dance the basic step the class has already learned to the music. Give reminders on style or lead.

2. Exchange partners and take line formation.

3. Pick out any position not previously learned that is involved in the variation and:
   a. Demonstrate the position.
   b. Walk through without involving the rhythm pattern.

---

*For detailed information on lesson and unit plans see pp. 24–26.

c. Teach how to lead into it and out of it from closed position.

4. Teach the new variation:
   a. Demonstrate it with or without partner, depending on nature of the step and cue.
   b. Walk through with rhythm pattern, making use of new position learned above.
   c. Add partners if not used in above.
   d. Allow free practice briefly.

5. Teach how to lead into the new variation from the basic step in closed position:
   a. Demonstrate when and how to lead.
   b. Practice it in unison.

6. Teach how to get out of the new variation back to basic in closed position:
   a. Demonstrate when and how to lead.
   b. Practice it in unison.

7. Put it all together, and practice in unison the basic step, the variation, and the basic step.

8. Try it with the music and have free practice moving in the traffic pattern.

9. Change partners. Make corrections and practice with at least one more record.

10. Give individual help while they are dancing: Be available for questions or encouragement.
    a. Students who need help, particularly those who are too shy to ask questions before the whole group, can be assisted during free practice time, when the teacher is circulating about and is available for questions.
    b. Instructing both man and lady to say to their partner "Let's go ask the teacher what we are doing wrong" frees students from criticizing each other and brings them to seek help, not just to continue the struggle.
    c. By dancing briefly with a person who is having difficulty, it is often easy to find what the problem is and make the correction without embarrassing the student in front of a partner; that is, it may be that the man does not have an effective lead or it may be that the lady is leading or leaning heavily on her partner.
    d. Additional ideas may be given to those who learn quickly and are ready to try out a bit more style or a variation that is not given to the class as a whole.
    e. Words of encouragement go a long way to build up confidence. "That's right," "good," "you look good today," "that's better"—all help students gain assurance.
    f. A teacher can help the group be more at ease if he or she encourages partners to learn together, talk things over, encourage and compliment each other, laugh at their mistakes, and have fun rather than being sensitive, overly serious, and embarrassed.

g. Sometimes a few minutes of assistance after class will help an individual student and may make the difference between a student wanting to or hating to come to class the next time.

Style of Social Dance

American Ballroom Dancing has borrowed steps and dances from many, many countries. Few of these are now done in the authentic style of any country. In most cases, it was the rhythmic quality that was fascinating, and not its meaning. Therefore, only a semblance of the original style remains in the Latin American dances done on our dance floors.

Particular consideration needs to be given to the importance of the individual as a person and the development of one's own style. Since all individuals are different, it is folly to try to get them all to perform exactly alike. The individual who likes to dance will work for the right feeling and take a pride in the way it looks. The dance will gradually reflect an easy confidence and become part of the individual's personality. This is a priceless possession, because it is one's own style. One of the greatest satisfactions in teaching is to watch this style develop.

At the beginning, few students realize the importance of good basic posture and footwork to the beauty and style of any dance. An easy, upright, balanced posture and motion of the feet in line with the body will make the dancer look good regardless of how limited the knowledge of steps. A detailed discussion of correct posture for dance may be found on p. 54. Beyond this, style means the specific way of moving in any one dance as influenced by rhythmic qualities of the music, cultural characteristics of a country, or the current style of the movement. It is true that styles of dances change from time to time with the rising popularity of a new star, a new band sound, or a new promotional venture by the popular dance studios.

Footwork in Social Dance

Footwork is a term used to discuss the manner of using the feet in the performance of dance steps. With the exception of body posture, it has the most significant bearing on form and style. Far too often the placement of the feet and the action of the legs give a distorted appearance to the dance. The beauty, continuity, and balance of a figure may be lost entirely due to any comic and, at the same time, tragic caricature unintentionally given to the motion.

Some general principles are involved in the application of good footwork to good dance style.

1. The weight should be carried on the ball of the foot for easy balance, alert transfer of weight from step to step, and change of direction.
2. The feet should be pointing straight ahead. When moving from one step to another, they should reach straight forward or backward in the direction of the desired action and in line with or parallel to the partner's feet.
3. Any action will start with feet together. When moving, feet should pass as closely as possible. With a few exceptions, the feet should always come together before reaching in a new direction. This is known as a follow-through with the feet, and it is used in the Foxtrot, Waltz, and Tango.
4. The feet are never dragged along the floor from one step to another, but are picked up and placed noiselessly in the new position. Occasionally, as in the Tango, the foot glides smoothly into place with the two reaching and without a scraping sound on the floor.
5. The legs should reach forward or backward from the hip. The action is initiated by stabilizing the trunk and swinging the leg freely.
6. The faster the rhythm, the shorter the step. The slower the rhythm, the more reaching the step.
7. Changes of direction are more readily in balance and under control if initiated when the feet are close together rather than when they are apart.
8. For the specific actions of reaching with one foot forward or backward, as in a corté or a hesitation step, the arch of the foot should be extended and the toe pointed.
9. Turning and pivoting figures are most effectively executed from a small base of support with the action of the man's and the lady's feet dovetailing nicely. This is possible when the action of the foot is a smooth turn on the ball of the foot with the body weight up, not pressing into the floor.
10. In accordance with the characteristic cultural style of a dance, the footwork will involve specific and stylized placement of the feet. This styling is described with each dance.

One-Step/Dance Walk

All smooth dances used to have a gliding motion with the ball of the foot. However, change in style now dictates a *dance walk* that is much like a regular walk when moving forward. It is a step forward on the heel of the foot, transferring the weight to the ball of the foot. This action is used by both man and lady when they are moving forward.

The backward step is a long reach to the toe, transferring the weight to the ball of the foot.

In closed dance position, the man is reaching forward and the lady backward, simultaneously. There is a tendency for the man to step sideways so as not to step on the lady's foot, but he should step forward directly in line with her foot. The lady consequently must reach backward into her step not only to avoid being stepped on but to give him room for his step. Master dance teachers have been quoted as saying, "If the lady gets her toe stepped on, it is her own fault." This reemphasizes the point that the dance walk is a long reaching step and both man and lady must learn to reach out confidently. It is this reach that makes the style smooth and beautiful and provides contrast to other smaller steps. Taking all small steps gives the style a cramped, insecure feeling. The following points describe the mechanics of the forward dance walk.

1. The body sways forward from the ankles. The weight is on the ball of the foot.
2. The trunk is stabilized firmly. The leg swings forward from the hip joint. The reach results in a long step rather than a short, choppy step. An exaggerated knee bend will cause bobbing up and down.
3. The foot swings forward and the heel is placed on the floor first, followed by a transfer of weight to the ball of the foot. The feet never drag along the floor.
4. The legs are kept close together, with the feet passing closely together. The toes are facing straight ahead.
5. Man and lady dance on the same forward line. One should avoid letting one's feet straddle the partner's feet.

The backward dance walk is not an easy movement, because one feels unstable moving backward. It should be practiced particularly by the lady since she will be moving backward a large part of the time.

1. The body weight is over the ball of the foot. One should take care not to lean forward or backward. The lady is pressing against the man's hand at her back.
2. The trunk is stabilized firmly. The leg swings backward from the hip joint with a long, smooth reach. Avoid unnecessary knee bend of the standing leg.
3. The foot is placed backward on the toe with weight transferring to the ball of the foot. The weight remains on the ball of the foot, the heel coming down only momentarily during the next step.
4. The legs and feet pass as closely as possible and in a straight line. One should avoid toeing out, heeling out, and swinging backward outside of the straight line.

Dance Positions

As early as the first time dance requires a grasp with a partner, students should be instructed in the correct position. Teachers of dance should give more attention to demonstrating and teaching the necessity for accurate dance positioning, as it is so often the determining factor of good balance, comfort, confidence in leading, security in following, and, therefore, a successful performance. There are five positions generally used in Social Dance—the **closed position;** the **open** or **conversation position;** the **left parallel position** or **right parallel position;** the **flirtation position** or **swing-out position;** and the **side-by-side position.** The basic closed position will be discussed here in detail. The others are adaptations of it and are fully described in the Glossary.

Closed Position

Each factor in the analysis of the closed position is significant. It is not a mere formality. Those who are learning dance will tend to form better dance habits if they understand specifically how the position aids the dance rather than being left to manage as best they can.

1. **Partners should stand facing each other squarely with shoulders parallel.** When standing almost toe to toe, partners can maintain a comfortable distance and have freedom in leading and following. The body posture is in good alignment.
2. **The feet should be together and pointing straight ahead.** The weight is over the ball of the foot.
3. **The man's right arm** is placed around the lady so that his arm **gives her security and support. The right hand is placed in the center of the lady's back, just below the shoulder blades.** The fingers should be closed and the hand almost flat so that the man can lead with the fingers or the heel of the hand. The man's arm is away from his body with the elbow pointing slightly out to the right side. A majority of leads are initiated by the man's shoulders, right arm, and hand.
4. **The lady's left arm rests gently but definitely in contact with the man's upper arm** and the hand should lie along the back of the man's shoulder as is comfortable. The lady's ability to follow is often determined by her response to the action of the man's arm.
5. **The lady should arch her back against the man's right hand and move with it.** All pressure leads for change of step will come from the man's right hand and she will feel them instantly.

6. **The lady's free hand is raised sideways and the man holds the lady's right hand in his left hand approximately between them at a level just above the lady's shoulder.** The man may let her fingers rest on his upturned palm, or he may grasp lightly with his thumb against her fingers and close his fingers around the back of her hand. He should not push with his hand.
7. **Both man and lady should look at each other or over the partner's right shoulder.**
8. **Resistance is essential.** A limp body or a limp hand is the surest indication of insecurity; a poor lead elicits a slow response. Dancers need to understand the difference between tension, which does not allow for easy moving along with one's partner, and relaxation, which cannot respond readily to change. An in-between state of body alertness—called resistance—is most desirable.

Some **common errors** in the use of closed position are the following:

1. Partner standing at an angle in a half-open position. This causes diagonal motion of the footwork and is uncomfortable.
2. Partner too far away.
3. Lack of support in the man's right arm.
4. Lack of contact of the lady's left arm.
5. Primary use of man's left hand to lead by a pushing or pumping action.
6. Lack of resistance by either man or lady.
7. Man's right hand too high on lady's back, pulling her off balance.
8. Lady's weight back on heels.
9. Man leaning forward from the waist off balance.
10. Man pulling back with his left shoulder and hand, causing an awkward angle of motion.
11. Lady leaning heavily on partner's arm.

Techniques of Leading and Following

Dancing is like conversation. A person's interest is held through the use of natural, interesting speech. In dancing, a partner's interest must be held through the use of varied, interesting steps. The man sets the rhythm, decides what steps are to be used, and controls the direction and progression around the floor. The lady is completely dependent on her partner. Through the use of a gentle but definite lead, the man can make dancing a mutually pleasant experience rather than a tugging on the part of one and a hoping and groping on the part of the other.

Leading

Good leading results from seven basic understandings:

1. An alert posture that moves as a complete unit.
2. Body weight is slightly ahead of the leg and foot.
3. A basic position that gives security and support.
4. Knowledge of the cues used to lead specific positions or directions.
5. Knowledge of the basic steps and a few simple variations.
6. Proper application of pressure timed to indicate in advance the new steps.
7. Consciousness of musical tempos and styles.

The use of the body, arms, and hands is the chief technique of leading. If the whole body is part of the dance, there is a perfectly natural lead felt through the shoulders and chest if the couple is in correct dance position. In other words, if the man's body turns the way he wants to go, his body along with arms and hand supporting the lady will carry her along. In addition, firmness of his hand at her back is a guiding force for all changes indicated by a pressure lead. Last, there is an increased tension of the upper body that indicates certain distinctive motions such as a hold, sudden change, pivot, or dipping action.

In summary, the three principal leads are **body and arm action** in desired directions, **hand pressure** indicating change and direction, and **sudden body tension** indicating certain distinctive actions. It is important that the lady understand these three so that she will recognize the leads and be able to respond to them.

The leads should serve as a continual barometer of action, giving gentle but confident warning of the changes of step or direction.

General Rules for Leading

1. Hold partner confidently, not tensely.
2. Listen to the music to get the beat before starting.
3. Step out on the accented beat.
4. Start each new step with a left-foot lead.
5. Give the lead for the new step or direction just before stepping out into it.
6. Start with easy steps. Before going into variations be sure that your partner is following.

Specific Directions for Leading

1. **To lead the first step,** the man should precede the step off with the left foot by an upbeat, forward motion of the body.

2. **To lead a forward moving pattern,** the man should give a forward motion in the body, including the right arm, which will direct the lady firmly in the desired direction.

3. **To lead a backward moving pattern,** the man should use pressure of the right hand. This will draw the lady forward in the desired direction.

4. **To lead a sideward moving pattern in closed position,** the man should use pressure of the right hand to the left or right to indicate the desired direction.

5. **To lead a box step,** the man should use a forward body action followed by right-hand pressure and right-elbow pull to the right to take the lady into the forward sequence of the box. Forward pressure of the right hand followed by pressure to the left side takes her into the back sequence of the box.

6. **To lead a box turn,** with slight pressure of the right hand, the man should use the right arm and shoulder to guide or bank her into the turn. The shoulders press forward during the forward step and draw backward during the backward step.

7. **To lead into an open position,** or conversation position, the man should use pressure with the heel of the hand to turn the lady into open position. The right elbow lowers to the side. The man must simultaneously turn his own body, not just the lady, so that they end facing the same direction. The left arm relaxes slightly and the left hand sometimes gives the lead for steps in open position.

8. **To lead from open to closed position,** the man should use pressure of the right hand and raise the right arm up to standard position to move the lady into closed position. She should not have to be pushed, but should swing easily into closed position as she feels the arm lifting. She should come clear around to face the man squarely.

9. **To lead into right parallel position** (left reverse open position), the man should not use pressure of his right hand, but rather should raise his right arm, rotating her counterclockwise one-eighth of a turn while he rotates counterclockwise one-eighth of a turn. This places the man and the lady off to the side of each other, facing opposite directions. The lady is to the right of him but slightly in front of him. The man should avoid turning too far so as to be side by side as this results in poor style and awkward and uncomfortable motion. The man's left hand may assist the lead by pulling toward his left shoulder.

10. **To lead from right parallel position to left parallel position** (right reverse open position), the man should pull with his right hand, lowering the right arm, and push slightly with his left hand causing a rotation clockwise about a quarter turn until the lady is to the left of him but slightly in front of him. They are not side by side.

11. **To lead a hesitation step,** the man should use pressure of the right hand on the first step and sudden body tension to control a hold of position as long as desired.

12. **To lead all turns,** the man dips his shoulder in the direction of the turn, and his upper torso turns before his leg and foot turn.

13. **To lead into a pivot turn,** clockwise, the man should hold the lady slightly closer, but with sudden body tension. Resistance is exerted outward by both man and lady leaning away from each other in order to take advantage of the centrifugal force of the circular motion. The right foot steps between partner's feet, forward on the line of direction, while the left foot reaches across the line of direction and turns on the ball of the foot about three-quarters of the way around.

14. **To lead into a corté** (dip) the man should use firm pressure of the right hand with sudden increased body tension going into the preparation step. Then the man should draw his partner forward toward him as he steps back into the dip. The left foot taking the dip backward should carry the weight, and careful balance of the weight should remain over that foot. Pressure is released as they recover to the other foot.

15. **Finger pressure leads and arm control** are important. Many times the man's only contact with his partner is with one hand or changing from hand to hand. A soft, gentle hand hold and a limp arm make it impossible to lead the variations of Swing, Cha Cha Cha, or Rumba. It is necessary that the lady exert slight resistance to the man's grasp so that pressure in any direction is reacted to instantly. Both man and lady should maintain elbow control by holding the arm firmly in front of the body with elbows down and always slightly bent. The arm is seldom allowed to extend in the elbow as this destroys the spring action needed to move out and in and under without jerking. The fingers often need to slip around the partner's without actually losing contact, in order to maintain comfortable action of the wrist and arm.

16. **To change the rhythm pattern,** the man exerts extra pressure with the right hand and pushes a little harder from the chest.

17. **Visual lead.** When partners are apart, as in the shine position of Cha Cha Cha, the lady watches her partner closely.

Following

The lady's responsibility in dancing is to follow her partner and adapt to any rhythm or style he dances. She should maintain an easy resistance (not rigidity or tension) throughout the body that gives the man an alert, movable partner whom he can lead. If the lady is too relaxed or too light, leading becomes very difficult, for there is no resistance. In other words, it takes cooperation for two people to dance well, the same as it takes two people for a satisfactory handshake. The lady should always maintain contact with her partner's upper right arm and shoulder and give resistance against his hand at her back, moving with it as it guides her. If the man is a poor leader, then the lady must pay close attention to his body movement, particularly his chest and shoulder movement, in order to follow. Following, when in an apart position, requires a firm, controlled arm that responds to a lead by simultaneous action of the body. A limp arm with no resultant body response makes leading difficult in Swing, Rumba, and Cha Cha Cha. In the challenge position, the lady's only lead is visual. She must be alert and follow her partner's action by watching him. The good dancer will aim to dance with beauty of form. The lady can make a poor dancer look good or a good dancer look excellent. She can also cramp his style if she takes too small a step, has poor control of balance, dances with her feet apart, dances at an awkward angle, or leans forward.

General Rules for Following

1. Keep the man's rhythm.
2. Be alert to partner's leads.
3. Support one's own weight. Arch the back and move with the partner's hand.
4. Step straight backward with reaching motion so as to give the partner room to step straight ahead.
5. Pass the feet close together.
6. Know the basic steps and basic leads.
7. Try not to anticipate partner's action, just move with it.
8. Give careful thought to proper body alignment and good posture.

🦋 Swing (Jitterbug)

Swing is an umbrella term for a wide variety of dance, such as West Coast Swing, East Coast Swing, Jive, Jitterbug, Shag, and Lindy Hop. With the advent of Dixieland jazz during the Roaring Twenties, a variety of dances appeared, including the *Lindbergh Hop*. Lindbergh had just completed his successful trans-Atlantic trip, a "hop" over to France. Later the dance was just called the *Lindy*. Cab Calloway is credited to referring to the Lindy hoppers as "jitterbuggers." It went through a fad period of being extremely eccentric with its wild acrobatics inspired by the rising popularity of boogie woogie. The Big Apple, the Shag, and the Lindy were all products of that period. They changed after World War II to a more syncopated rhythm called Rock and Roll with the double Lindy pattern and to the Swing with the smooth, sophisticated triple rhythm, which came in a short time later. All during the Rock period, both Double and Triple Lindy could be seen on American Bandstand. A softer sound called boogie, but no relation to boogie woogie, has greater synthesization of electronic equipment.

Swing is danced to a wide variety of music and reflects the dance style of the particular music— Big Band music of the '50s, Rock and Roll, Rhythm and Blues, Salsa, Reggae, Country Western, and Cajun—all written in 4/4 or cut time. Swing includes the rhythm of Single Lindy, Double Lindy, Triple Lindy, 4-Count Swing (page 403). Some refer to these as Jitterbug. The term "Swing" is also applied to Country Western Two-Step; "Jitterbug" to Cajun step-close, step-close. The common denominator is a myriad of figures as the couple covers a *circular space* in one area. There is wide variation in the footwork and figures.

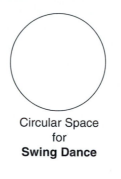

Circular Space
for
Swing Dance

East Coast Swing and **Triple Lindy** are synonymous. **West Coast Swing** is a more difficult and sophisticated dance. West Coast Swing is referred to as a *slot dance* because the couple moves back and forth in a *narrow* space, always the same space. The dance evolved in the '50s on the West Coast in the small clubs where dance space was limited.

Anchor Step

Anchor Step

Narrow Space
for
West Coast Swing Dance

We will continue to use the term *Swing* for Single, Double, and Triple Lindy.

■ Swing Rhythm

Swing is written in 4/4 or cut time. It is extremely adaptable to fast or slow rhythm or to 4/4 time from foxtrot to hard rock in quality. The Shag was actually the first dance to be called Jitterbug, and its slow slow quick quick rhythm set the pattern for all of the others. The Single Lindy has the same rhythm. It is done occasionally by older adults because of the slower pace it sets, but was not really in use much in the 1980s. It is shown here to demonstrate the transition into the more active Swing patterns.

Single Lindy

The Double Lindy is very adaptable to slow or fast music and is the rhythm that is coming back as the new Jitterbug. Accent is on the offbeat.

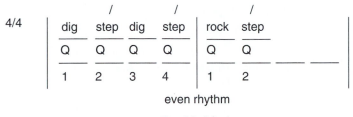

Double Lindy

The Triple Lindy is more often danced to the slow, mellow, sophisticated tempos.

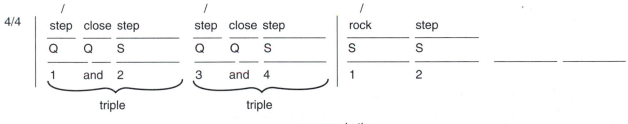

Triple Lindy—East Coast Swing

■ Swing Style

Exciting styles and positions are in use for Swing. It is a matter of taste for the individual dancers whether they use a dig step, a step-hop, or a kick step. However, the basic rhythm must be maintained by both man and lady in order to coordinate the pattern together, unlike Discotheque, in which the step or rhythm pattern of each partner is unstructured. The man is able to lead the dance because of the magnificent body alertness of both partners. A firm body and a calculated resistance in the arm and fingers enable quick response in any direction. The space between partners is controlled by a spring tension in the elbow, which never extends fully but allows the pull away and the spring back smoothly and with control. The lady uses her arm as a pivot center. The elbow is down and the hand is up for the underarm turns, and she turns around her arm but does not let it fly in the air. There should never be the appearance of arms flying loose or entangled. The fingers slip easily around one another without losing contact. Even the free arm is bent and remains close to the body.

Swing steps tend to cover a circular space in one area of the floor. The footwork is at all times small and close together, with rolling and turning on the ball of the foot. The turning action for beginner steps

Swing (continued)

is always on the first step (count 2) of the pattern when the lady is on her right foot and the man is on his left. The rhythm pattern is generally the same over and over but the changes of position and direction and the constant subtle smooth roll to offbeat rhythm generates a fabulous excitement for both dancer and observer.

■ West Coast Swing Rhythm

West Coast Swing Rhythm is 6 or 8 beats. It is a slower rhythm than East Coast Swing.

All Uneven Rhythm

4/4 | step | step | step | step | anchor step step step | | |
|------|------|------|------|------|
| S | S | S | S | Q Q S |
| 1 | 2 | 3 | 4 | 1 & 2 |
| 1 | 2 | 3 | 4 | 5 & 6 |

triple

uneven rhythm—6 count

4/4 | step | step | step step step | anchor step step step step |
S	S	Q Q S	Q Q S
1	2	3 & 4	1 & 2
1	2	3 & 4	5 & 6

double | triple | triple

uneven rhythm—6 count

4/4 | step | step | step step step | step | step | anchor step step step step |
S	S	Q Q S	S	S	Q Q S
1	2	3 & 4	1	2	3 & 4
1	2	3 & 4	5	6	7 & 8

double | triple | double | triple

uneven rhythm—8 count

■ West Coast Swing Style

The lady's step is different than the man's; partners do not mirror each other. The step is like the Cuban walk (page 458). Little kicks and toe touches on the beat give flair for a sophisticated look. The anchor steps (quick, quick, slow) occur at the end of the slot. The couples move in a narrow space.

Directions are for the man; the lady's part is reversed, except when noted.

■ The Double Lindy

(Beginners—Two hands joined; experienced—Semiopen position)

Steps	4/4 Counts	Rhythm Cue
Touch L to instep of R	1	quick
Step L in place	2	quick
Touch R to instep of L	3	quick
Step R in place	4	quick
Step L backward, a little behind R heel	1	quick
Step R forward	2	quick

Step Cue: Dig step, dig step, rock step.

Style: The body takes a *slight* motion, tipping forward from the waist and dipping the outside shoulder (man's L, lady's R) on the first dig step like an upbeat. Take care not to exaggerate this motion. It is very subtle. The dig is a touching of the toe lightly to the instep of the other foot. It should not be a tap step that makes noise on the floor. The feet are close together for this beat. The weight is carried on the ball of the foot and the steps are small throughout the step. The amount of knee bend depends on individual preference as to style; however, the action should be smooth and rolling rather than bouncy.

Note: Beginners must learn this pattern alone until they can move accurately with the rhythm. Then dancers take two hands joined, man's hands palm up. The elbow is down, forearm is firm, and fingers exert resistance against partner's. On the rock step there is a spring tension in the arms that allows an "apart-together" action that is smooth and has arm control.

Lead: The man holds both of their hands close together and dips slightly with his left shoulder on the first dig step. The lady pushes slightly against his hands on the first dig step so as to receive his lead. This technique teaches the lady to give the necessary resistance for all future leads.

Note: The above progression provides instant success with Swing. The variations listed are arranged in the order recommended. In describing the variations, the analysis will refer to action on the first dig, the first step, the second dig, the second step, the rock step or the first dig step, second dig step, or the entire pattern, rather than by counts as in other dances.

■ Double Lindy Variations

Collegiate	Swing Out Break	Wrap
Break to Semiopen Position	Continuous Underarm Turns	Double Brush Off
Semiopen Basic	Brush Off	Dish Rag
Basic Turn	Tuck Spin	Overhead Swing

■ COLLEGIATE

(Two hands joined, man's hands palm up)

Steps	Step Cue
Man brings both hands close together and dips the left shoulder	first dig
Man steps L forward close to the L of the lady, pivots clockwise at close range on the L foot	first step

Fundamental Swing Steps (continued)

Lady steps R diagonally forward across to the R of the man at close range
    and pivots clockwise on the R foot ....first step
Both take dig and step in place...second dig step
Both rock out and in using arm control ....rock step

Step Cue: Dig turn, dig in place, rock step.

Style: Resistance in the arms and fingers hold the couple in a tight, close-facing position on the pivot turn. Each needs to step in close to partner on the pivot foot (man's L, lady's R). The steps are small.

Lead: The man can help the lady pivot by the pull of his hands and body. He dips the left shoulder on the first dig to give her the cue for this turn. When used in combination with other variations, the man will take or release hands on the rock steps. (a) An optional lead is to reach sideways with each hand shoulder high on the first step and bring the hands back together on the second step. This creates a butterfly turn effect. (b) A second optional and more advanced lead is the man may pivot to right parallel position on the first dig and to left parallel on the first step. It is a quick change of position like a cock turn and is led by a push and pull action in the hands. The second dig step and rock step are the same as before.

■ BREAK TO SEMIOPEN POSITION

(Two hands joined)

Steps   *Step Cue*

Dig in place, the man preparing to pull the lady toward him..first dig
Man and lady step toward each other, the man pulling the L hand downward and
    placing R arm around her waist...first step
Both take dig step, pivoting to semiopen position ....second dig
Both step backward a short step in semiopen position ....second step
Rock step in same position...rock step

Step Cue: Pull down, come together, rock step.

Style: The steps are small.

Lead: The man pulls down on her hand so that, as they come into semiopen position, the man's left hand holding the lady's right hand ends up in the correct position for basic.

■ SEMIOPEN BASIC

(Semiopen position)

Steps   *Step Cue*

Dig in place, L to instep of R...first dig
Step forward a short step L ....first step
Dig R to instep of L ....second dig
Step backward a short step R ....second step
Rock step..rock step

Step Cue: Dig step, dig step, rock step.

Style: Dancers remain in semiopen position throughout. All steps are small. The hand grasp is low with a straight elbow and held in close to the body. The man's fingers reach around the little-finger side of the lady's hand.

■ BASIC TURN

(Semiopen position)

The basic turn is used in semiopen position as previously described. When repeated over and over, it should be done turning the couple around in place clockwise. The man makes the step turn by taking the first step with his left foot on a clockwise curve toward the lady and pivoting about a quarter-turn on the ball of the left foot. He finishes the remainder of the pattern from that new direction. Repeat as desired. As the dancers become skillful at this turn they will find they can turn a half-turn or more each time by pivoting a greater degree on the stepping beat.

Step Cue: Dig turn, dig-step, rock step.

Style: The lady will have no trouble adjusting to this turning action. She will roll on the ball of her foot.

Lead: A dip of the man's left shoulder and a slight pull of his right arm around her waist take her along easily into the turn.

■ SWING OUT BREAK

(Semiopen position)

The man takes the entire pattern in place once as he turns the lady out under his left arm to face him.

Steps	*Step Cue*
Man moves his L hand from the low position to a position in close at waist level	first dig
Man raises his L hand above her head and turns her under to face him. Lady on R foot pivots clockwise halfway around to face him	first step
Both take a dig step in place facing partner	second dig step
Both rock away and together using elbow control	rock step

Step Cue: Dig turn, dig step, rock step.

Style: Lady keeps the R elbow level with shoulder and forearm at right angles, and turns around her own arm, not under it. His arm is high enough so that she does not have to duck to get under. The lady's pivot step is short so that they do not get too far apart. They must have room to take the rock step with elbow control.

Lead: The man leads the starting motion by bending his left elbow to bring his hand in to waist level on the first dig. This cues the lady. She is waiting with her right foot in dig position and with the lead she can step with him into the first step. His arm must be raised high enough on the first step to clear her head as she turns under.

Note: The face-to-face position is called swing out position—dancers will have one hand joined (man's L, lady's R). The man should bring her back to position by using the break to semiopen position.

■ CONTINUOUS UNDERARM TURNS

(Swing out position)

The man and lady exchange places as he turns her counterclockwise across to his position and steps around her to her position.

Steps	*Step Cue*
Man increases pressure on lady's hand	first dig
Both man and lady take a short step forward. Man turns clockwise on his L foot while turning lady under counterclockwise on her R foot	first step
Take dig and step in place	second dig step
Rock step out and in, controlling with firm arm	rock step

Step Cue: Dig turn, dig step, rock step.

Style: Both turn halfway around on the first step but stay in close so that there is room for the remainder of the basic step. They have exactly exchanged places after one complete pattern.

Lead: The man turns his hand knuckles up, fingers down, so that the lady's fingers can slip around his fingers as she turns. Then he brings his hand down palm up.

Note: This underarm turn can be repeated over and over. It will serve as a connecting step to any other variation. The man may lead back to semiopen basic or reach for the lady's other hand for any of the two hands joined variations that follow.

Fundamental Swing Steps (continued)

■ BRUSH OFF

(Also called flirtation pass) (Swing out position)

This step begins with the lady in swing out position after one underarm turn, leaving the man's hand in palm-up position. It is basically a man's left turn.

Steps	*Step Cue*
Take dig in place	first dig
Man steps forward toward L side of the lady, shifting her R hand into his R hand, while he turns counterclockwise one-quarter on his L foot until his back is to the lady. Lady steps diagonally forward, pivoting on her R foot clockwise as in the collegiate and moving around behind the man	first step
Take dig in place, continuing to turn	second dig
Man brings both of his hands behind his back. He steps on the right foot, turning counterclockwise one-quarter more to face the lady, and changes her R hand into his L hand. The lady steps on the L foot, turning clockwise to face the man	second step
Rock step out and in, using arm control	rock step

Step Cue: Man turns and turns rock step.

Style: While doing this pattern, the couple have exchanged places, each turning a half-turn. The lady can control the space factor because she can stay in close to him as she goes around him.

Lead: The transfer of hands should be done smoothly and without losing contact.

Note: It is especially fun to follow the brush off with an underarm turn. The man should be prepared to lead into it immediately after the rock step.

■ TUCK SPIN

(Swing out position)

Steps	*Step Cue*
Man moves both of lady's hands to his R (lady turns slightly to her L), pulls lady toward himself in a sharp action	first dig
Man steps in place, releasing her hands; he pushes her in the opposite direction with a quick flip, spinning her clockwise once around on her R foot	first step
Lady catches her balance with the digging foot, man resumes joined-hand position	second dig
They step in place together	second step
Rock step out and in	rock step

Step Cue: Tuck spin, dig step, rock step.

Style: The lady must spin smoothly a full-turn around in place on right foot without losing her balance.

Lead: There must be firm arm and finger control in order for the lady to respond to this with the proper timing. Lady offers arm resistance. Man catches her left hand in his left, then changes to swing out position.

Note: The man may also spin at the same time. His turn will go counterclockwise on the left foot.

■ WRAP

(Two hands joined)

Steps	*Step Cue*
Take dig, man lifts his L arm and prepares to turn the lady counterclockwise	first dig
Step forward a short step, and, without releasing hands, the man will move his raised L hand across in front of her and up over her head as she is turning counterclockwise one-quarter on her R foot	first step

Dig in place still turning ....second dig

Step backward, as the lady finishes in a position close to him on his R side.
   His R arm is around her waist and her arms are crossed in front as they finish
   in the wrap position (his R joins her L) ....second step

Rock step back and forward together ....rock step

Style: A smooth roll is important.

Note: To unwrap, the man initiates a reverse roll, turning the lady clockwise back to starting position and assisting with a gentle right-arm push. Another variation on the unwrap is for the man to release with his left hand and pull with the right hand, rolling the lady out to his right. Again this should be taken on the two dig steps and they finish off with the rock in face-to-face position.

■ DOUBLE BRUSH OFF

(Swing out position)

The couple must know how to do a single brush-off step. The double brush-off step is twice through the rhythm pattern. Starting position is swing out position (man's L, lady's R hand joined).

First time through the rhythm pattern (dig step, dig step, rock step):

Steps   *Step Cue*

Man starts first brush-off step, turning L one-half, lady steps forward slightly ....first dig step

He reaches out palm up with his L hand to take her L hand, they are side
   by side, the lady on the L; the lady's step is in place.......................................second dig step

The man releases her R hand behind his back and reaches around in front
   under their L hands to take her R hand ....rock step

Second time through the rhythm pattern (dig step, dig step, rock step):

Steps   *Step Cue*

Man raises L hand, pulling the lady under with the R and turning her
   counterclockwise as both hands go up over her head ....first dig step

He releases the L hand, as he begins to turn his second brush off, turning
   counterclockwise as his R arm comes down behind his back ....second dig step

He changes her R hand into his L as he finishes his turn to face the lady ....rock step

Style: This must have the look of a complete flowing action. The lady must stay in close to the man. Both man and lady must keep the dig step, dig step, rock step pattern going in their feet. Steps are small.

Lead: The most important lead is when the man reaches out palm up to take her left hand. The second lead is when he pulls with the right hand and both hands go over her head.

■ DISH RAG

(Two hands joined)

The couple rolls to the man's left, lady's right, turning back to back and rolling on around face to face. They must keep the footwork of the Double Lindy going. It is one complete pattern.

■ OVERHEAD SWING

(Two hands joined)

The couple steps forward right side to right side. Each swings the right arm over partner's head, behind the neck and slides the right hand down the right arm of partner to a right-hand grasp. The dancers must keep the basic footwork going. It is one complete pattern.

Fundamental Swing Steps (continued)

The Triple Lindy—East Coast Swing

The Triple Lindy is lovely and so pleasant to do to a nice swingy foxtrot. It should be smooth and relaxing.

■ TRIPLE RHYTHM

(Semiopen position) (Three little steps to each slow beat; these are similar to a fast Two-Step.)

Steps	4/4 Counts	Rhythm Cue
Step L forward		
Close R to L, take weight R .... } 1 *and* 2		quick quick slow
Step L forward		
Step R backward		
Close L to R, take weight L .... } 3 *and* 4		quick quick slow
Step R backward		

Rock Step

Step L backward, a little behind R heel	1	slow
Step R in place	2	slow

Step Cue: Shuffle step, shuffle step, rock step.

Style: The triple rhythm should be small shuffling steps, keeping the feet close to the floor. Weight is on the ball of the foot. Basic style is that of Double Lindy.

Lead: The man cues the lady for the triple steps by increasing the tension in his right hand as he starts the shuffle step forward. Other leads are the same as for the Double Lindy.

Note: Any of the variations for Double Lindy can be done in triple rhythm, and dancers frequently change from one rhythm to another during one piece of music.

■ TRIPLE LINDY SWIVEL STEP

(Semiopen position and traveling in line of direction, forward; rhythm pattern changes)

Steps	4/4 Counts	Rhythm Cue
Man's Part (lady's part is the reverse)		
Step L forward		
Close R to L .... } 1 *and* 2		quick quick slow
Step L forward		
Step R forward		
Close L to R .... } 3 *and* 4		quick quick slow
Step R forward		
Pivot on R foot to face partner, and bring L foot alongside of it, shifting weight to L foot	1	slow
Pivot on L foot to face open position, bring R foot alongside of it, shifting weight to R foot	2	slow
Repeat pivot on R foot	3	slow
Repeat pivot on L foot	4	slow
Step L forward		
Close R to L .... } 1 *and* 2		quick quick slow
Step L forward		
Step R backward		
Close L to R .... } 3 *and* 4		quick quick slow
Step R backward		
(turning lady out clockwise in an underarm turn)		
Rock step (in swing out position)	1, 2	slow slow

Step Cue: Triple step, triple step
  swivel 2 3 4
  triple step, triple step, rock step.

Style: The swivel steps are tiny, crisp, and neatly turning, just a quarter turn on each pivot. The body turns with the foot closed, open, closed, open.

Lead: The man must lead the swivel step by turning the lady from open to closed, and so forth.

Note: The couple progresses along the line of direction as the pivot turn is being done in four quick steps.

Swing Combos

The Swing routines are combinations for practice, which are listed from simple to complex. They may be used for either Shag, Single Lindy, Double Lindy, or Triple Lindy. (Two hands joined or semiopen position, unless otherwise indicated.)

1. *Basic Swing Out and Close*
   1 basic
   single underarm break
   break to original position
2. *Basic—Swing Out—Underarm Turn Close*
   1 basic
   single underarm break
   break to original position
3. *Swing Out and Collegiate*
   2 basics
   single underarm break
   3 collegiate steps
   underarm turn
   original position

4. *Swing Out and Brush Off*
   2 basics
   single underarm break
   brush off
   underarm turn
   original position
5. *Collegiate—Brush Off*
   2 basic
   single underarm break
   underarm turn
   3 collegiate steps
   underarm turn
   brush off
   underarm turn
   original position

6. *Collegiate—Tuck—Spin*
   2 collegiate steps
   tuck spin
   underarm turn
7. *Collegiate—Wrap*
   2 collegiate steps
   wrap
   unwrap
8. *Wrap—Unwrap Spin*
   2 collegiate steps
   wrap
   unwrap
   tuck spin
   underarm turn

⚘ West Coast Swing

Refer to West Coast Swing definition, diagram, West Coast Rhythm, and West Coast Swing Style pages 386 and 388.

■ SUGAR PUSH

(Basic step) (Two hands joined)

Steps	Counts	Step Cue
Man's Part		
Step back L	1	Step
Step R to L	2	Together
Touch L	3	Touch
Step forward L	4	Step
Step R behind L (hook) in place and release man's R, lady's L hand (swing out position)	5	Hook
Step L in place, pushing off	*and*	Step
Step R in place	6	Step
Lady's Part		
Step forward R	1	Step
Step forward L	2	Step
Touch R to L instep	3	Touch
Turning R towards partner, step back R (continue to travel in slot)	4	Step
Step L behind R (hook) and release lady's L, man's R hand	5	Hook
Step R in place	*and*	Step
Step L in place	6	Step

Step Cue: The cue "walk" may be used for counts 1, 2, 4.

Style: The footwork and hips are like the Cuban walk (refer to page 458). Dig, pressing the foot into the floor while moving forward.

Lead: The arms need to be firm (give weight) as the lady moves forward, the man pulling toward him. On count 3 the lady leans a little more forward, body rising to receive the *push*. On count 4 the man *pushes* as the lady moves backward. Both dancers must offer resistance. The man initiates the *pull* and *push*.

Note: The steps on counts 5 and 6 are the "anchor steps." The lady may choose to do a "coaster step" for counts 5 and 6. Coaster step is step back L, close R to L, step forward L.

Variation: Triple step. Counts 3, 4 become "3 and 4" (QQS). Instead of Touch Step, man steps LRL, lady steps RLR.

■ UNDERARM TURN

(Swing out position)

Lady passes the man's R side, turns under her arm to face opposite direction.

Steps	Counts	Step Cue
Man's Part		
Moving to L side, step L	1	Step
Step forward R	2	Step

Moving toward slot, step L, pivoting clockwise	3	.... Side
Step R, still turning	*and*	.... Step
Raising L arm, step L into the slot. Now facing opposite direction	4	.... Step
Step R behind L	5	.... Hook
Step L	*and*	.... Step
Step R in place	6	.... Step

Lady's Part

Step forward R	1	.... Step
Step forward L	2	.... Step
Take 3 running steps (R, L, R) to the end of slot, turning counterclockwise under R arm, on count 4	3 *and* 4	.... Run, run, turn
Step L behind R	5	.... Hook
Step R	*and*	.... Step
Step L in place	6	.... Step

Lead: Man pulls the lady forward, left hand down, raises arm for turn on count 4.

Note: Alternate one Sugar Push sequence with one Underarm Turn.
Lady may use "coaster step" for counts 5 and 6.

■ LEFT SIDE PASS

(Swing out position)

Lady passes man's left side.

Steps	*Counts*	*Step Cue*

Man's Part

Moving to R side, step L across R	1	.... Step
Pivoting counterclockwise on L, step R near L (now facing slot)	2	.... Step
Following lady, take 3 steps (L, R, L)	3 *and* 4	.... Step, step, step
Facing opposite direction, step R behind L	5	.... Hook
Step L	*and*	.... Step
Step R in place	6	.... Step

Lady's Part

Step forward R	1	.... Step
Step forward L	2	.... Step
Passing partner (man's left side), traveling in the slot, take 3 short running steps (R, L, R) pivoting counterclockwise on last run	3 *and* 4	.... Run, run, turn
Facing opposite direction, step L behind R	5	.... Hook
Step R	*and*	.... Step
Step L	6	.... Step

Note: The Left Side Pass is usually preceded by one Sugar Push.

Style: Lady holds L arm, elbow bent, to chest as she passes partner and turns.

Lead: On count 4 man drops L shoulder, pulls his L hand down as lady passes.

West Coast Swing (continued)

■ WHIP

(Swing out position)

Starting in Swing out position, couple moves into closed position, makes one complete turn clockwise as a couple at the center of the slot, separates into Swing out position, and ends in original position.

Steps	Counts	Step Cue
Man's Part		
Step back L	1	Step
Moving to L side, step R across L and move into closed position	2	Cross
Step L forward, pivoting clockwise as a couple	3	Turn
Continuing to turn, step R in place	*and*	And
Step L across slot (L and R feet straddle slot)	4	Step
Step R behind L (hook), continuing to turn as a couple	5	Hook
Releasing man's R, lady's L hand and separating, step L forward into slot. Now facing original direction	6	Step
Step R behind L, step L, step R in place	7 *and* 8	Hook, step, step
Lady's Part		
Step forward R toward partner	1	Step
Moving into closed position step L pivoting clockwise to face partner	2	Pivot
Step back R	3	Back
Close L to R	*and*	Together
Step R forward between the man's two feet	4	Step
Continuing to turn clockwise as a couple, step L	5	Step
Release lady's L, man's R hand and step back R	6	Step
Step L behind R, step R, step L in place	7 *and* 8	Hook, step, step

Note: Lady's Part, counts 3 and 4, is a *coaster step.* It may be cued as "coaster step" (3 and 4) (QQS).

❧ Country Western

Country Western Dance has been around for a long time; it is definitely a grass-roots dance. As country western music has increased in popularity so has Country Western Dance. Country western music, a twangy honky-tonk sound as played by Bob Wills and his Texas Playboys in the late 1930s, was just the beginning. The music is influenced by spirituals, Dixieland jazz, and the big band sound. The fiddle, steel guitar, and deep bass give country western music its character. The fiddle was part of the band. Wherever country western music is played, people dance. The dances are based on old Folk Dances, Square Dances, and Social Dances, topped off with a new look, called Country Western. Swing, One-Step, Two-Step, Schottische, Waltz, and Line Dances are all part of the repertory.

■ Country Western Style

The dance is very smooth, gliding and elegant. The upper body is quiet, with a straight back and very little hip movement; the knees are slightly bent, and are used as a spring to lower the center of gravity; the feet stay close to the floor. There is no pumping of the hands, no bounce, no waddle. In closed position, the dancers are apart. A relaxed, friendly, easy-going attitude is ever present.

The country western look starts with cowboy boots for both men and women. The men frequently wear Levis, and are proud of their large silver belt buckles. Many dance with their cowboy hats on. One writer commented that real cowboys now wear caps that say "Coors," "Mac," or "Bull Durham." Nonetheless, it is the Stetson type one sees on the dance floor. The women also enjoy wearing Levis or a western skirt, cowboy shirt or blouse, and scarves.

When the man has one or two hands free, he inserts his thumb into his belt, near the buckle, fingers pointing down casually. The lady may put her thumb in her belt too, or, if both hands are free as in a line dance, behind her back. She overlaps them, palms facing out, which is typical of Mexican-style dance.

Line Dance Style

The steps are precise, and they have a "calculated look." The feet are close to the floor, and the steps, if traveling, glide. Dancers keep their weight on the balls of their feet, bending their knees slightly for balance. They keep their upper torso quiet, with arms and shoulders relaxed. There is no arm movement. Refer to the previous description for the position of hands. High kicks are discouraged.

■ Country Western Music

Country Line dances may be danced to any popular country tune. The exceptions, Achy Breaky and Cotton-Eyed Joe, are danced to the tune by the same name. When a particular tune fits well to the step routine, a match is made. Then the routine takes the name of the tune, for example, Elvira. Obviously the Waltz, Schottische, One-Step, Swing, and Two-Step need the correct meter.

■ Dance-Hall Etiquette

At country western dances, several types of dancing may take place simultaneously. The perimeter of the dance floor is for round dances; the slower ones dance in the inside lane. Fast and slow dancers move counterclockwise around the floor. The Swing Dancers and Line Dancers split the center area, with line dancers closer to the band.

The gentleman takes the lady's hand, arm, or offers his arm to escort her onto or off the dance floor and to return her to her seat. The gentleman always leads; the lady follows graciously.

Country Western (continued)

■ Names of Steps Not Standardized

Frequently there are several names for the same dance. Real confusion exists on the names for basic steps, like a Shuffle, a Two-Step, and a Two-Step Waltz. This mix-up is reminiscent of the early American Bandstand days when they announced "Now we will do the Mexican Hat Dance," and proceeded to play and dance La Raspa. Could the strut of John Travolta in *Saturday Night Fever* have started the misnomers? Technically a Shuffle is a One-Step, a Two-Step is a step close step, and a Waltz is a step side close. They dance the Polka without a hop. "Hang loose" with the terminology till the dust settles!

■ Country Western Dances

Texas Two-Step   Electric Slide
Texas Two-Step Swing   Four Corners
Country Western Swing   Freeze
Ten-Step Shuffle   Slappin' Leather
Achy Breaky   Tush Push
Cowboy Boogie

Refer to Chapter 3, Dance Fundamentals—Two-Step and Waltz; and Chapter 4, American Heritage Dance—Cotton-Eyed Joe (Line Dance) and Jessie Polka (same as Cowboy Polka and Eight-Step Shuffle).

🎵 Texas Two-Step

The *Texas Two-Step* is also known as the *Texas Shuffle*. The dance is done in a smooth, flowing style. The rhythm—slow, slow, quick, quick—is referred to as *shuffle beat*. It is like the Foxtrot magic rhythm. The name is confusing because the real Two-Step, also done in Texas, is quick, quick, slow, or step-together-step.

■ Texas Two-Step Rhythm

The music is written in 4/4 time. The step pattern takes a measure and a half of music. It is an uneven rhythm pattern—slow, slow, quick, quick.

■ Texas Two-Step Style

The dance has smooth, controlled steps; there is no pumping of arms or bouncing. The closed dance position has several variations. The body has good posture alignment, with a straight back and knees slightly bent. Quite a bit of space should be left between partners in variations of the closed dance position. Man's left palm faces up and lady's right palm faces down, resting lightly in man's left; man's right arm may be straight, right hand folding over lady's left shoulder. The position of the lady's left arm varies. The lady may fold her left hand over his right elbow; her elbow is down, her arm is limp, which gives a "careless look." Her left arm may be extended to rest on top of man's right arm. Or she may hook her thumb into one of the man's belt loops on his right side. They face each other squarely, shoulders parallel.

The dancers glide around the floor in a counterclockwise direction and cover a lot of territory. Although there are many variations, most dancers relax and move forward, with an occasional turn, or the man dances backward, but always they move in the line of direction.

Records: MH 35.

Cassette: MH C35.

Music: Suggested tunes: "If It Was Easy" or "Everything a Waltz."

Position: Closed.

Directions are for the man; the lady's part is reversed.

Steps	4/4 Counts	Rhythm Cue
Step L forward	1-2	slow
Step R forward	3-4	slow
Step L forward	1	quick
Step R forward	2	quick

Style: The forward steps should be long, smooth, gliding steps, straight ahead. The lady, moving backward, takes a long step, reaching from hip to toe. If the music is slow, for balance on the slow steps, dancers may step forward L, touch R to L (for balance), step forward R, touch L to R.

Lead: A body and right-arm lead forward.

Variations: The variations usually start on the QQ.

1. Turn left to face the reverse line of direction, QQ.
2. Man travels backward in line of direction until ready to face the line of direction, then turn left on the QQ.
3. The man raises his left arm and the lady twirls clockwise under his arm, once or twice, on the QQ.
4. On the SS beats, step left to the side, step right to the side, travel forward QQ.
5. Open position, moving toward the center on the SS beats, step left, cross right in front of left. Closed position, travel left, right forward on the QQ.

Texas Two-Step Swing

Position: Two hands joined.

Directions are for the man; the lady's part is reversed.

Steps	4/4 Counts	Step Cue
Step L in place	1	step
Touch R to L	2	touch
Step R in place	3	step
Touch L to R	4	touch
Step L backward, a little behind R heel	1	rock
Step R forward	2	step

Figures: Swing out position. The variations occur on the first 4 counts.

1. Lady turns clockwise under her R arm, in place.
2. Man turns clockwise under his L arm in place.
3. Man and lady exchange places as he turns her counterclockwise across to his position and steps around her to her position.
4. Two hands joined. Man raises L arm, lady steps R toward partner, turning counterclockwise under his arm, steps L as she is side by side on his R. Lower man's L, lady's R arms.
   Now in Cuddle position (Wrap). Rock, step. In this position, dancers may go forward, travel clockwise or counterclockwise in place dancing the Texas Two-Step. To unwrap, the man initiates a reverse roll, turning the lady clockwise back to starting position. Refer to page 392.

Country Swing

Country Swing Rhythm

The music is the primary difference between *Country Swing, Disco Swing,* and *Swing.* The syncopated rhythm of rock and roll permeates the country western music for Swing.

Country Swing is danced to faster, 2/4 or 4/4 time, western music. There is 4-count, 6-count, and 8-count swing. The 4-count swing has a smooth, even rhythm, and is especially comfortable for learning all the figures. The 6-count swing (Double Lindy) also has an even rhythm. The 8-count swing (Triple Lindy) has uneven rhythm. For analysis and dance directions of Double and Triple Lindy refer to pp. 386–395.

4-Count Swing

4/4	step	step	rock	step
	Q	Q	Q	Q
	1	2	3	4

Meter: 4/4

Record: MH 37.

Cassette: MH C37.

Music: Even rhythm. Four-count swing, "Jose Cuervo," "Wild Turkey," "Hey Bartender," and "The South's Gonna Do It." Six-count swing, "Bebop," "Step That Step," "Lay Down Sally."

Position: Two hands joined.

Steps	4/4 Counts	Step Cue
Step L in place	1	step
Step R in place	2	step
Step L backward, a little behind right heel	3	rock
Step R forward	4	step

Style: Dancers step on every beat, no rush. The weight is carried on the ball of the foot. On the rock step, the arms are extended and dancers give a small snap as they come back together. In the basic step, the dancers may pivot as a couple.

Figures: Refer to Double Lindy, pp. 389–393, Triple Lindy, p. 394.

Terminology

Double Lindy	Country Western
Collegiate	Basic 6-Count Swing
Swing Out Break	Outside Turn
Continuous Underarm turns	Inside Turns
Brush Off	Brush Off
Tuck Spin	Free Spin
Wrap	Wrap, Basket, Cradle, Curl, Cuddle, Sweetheart
Double Brush Off	Double Brush Off, Double Brush
Dish Rag	Barrel Roll, Egg Beater
Overhead Swing	Slide
Triple Lindy Swivel Steps	Double Two-Step

Teaching Suggestion: Teach the figures first. Then add the basic step pattern.

Ten-Step Shuffle is also known as *Ten-Step Polka*. A similar dance, 8 beats, is the Jessie Polka (see Chapter 4). Country western dancers call the Jessie Polka the *Eight-Step Shuffle* or *Cowboy Polka*.

Meter: 2/4 fast or 4/4 slow. Directions are presented in beats.

Record: Grenn 25371.

Music: Fiddle music; suggested tunes: "Uncle Pen," "Cajun Moon," "New Cut Road," "On the Road Again," "East Bound and Down."

Position: Couples in Varsouvienne position; lady's right-hand fingertips touch man's right for ease of turn; man's left hand reaches over (fingers down) lady's left, holding just above waist.

■ Directions for the Dance

Beats

Starting position: feet together, weight on right.

1–8	**Part I** Beginning left, take four Two-Steps forward in line of direction (quick, quick, slow—four times).
	Part II
9–10	Beginning left—right knee bent—touch left heel forward, left foot turned to a 45° angle, and return. Shift weight to left.
11	Touch right toe backward.
12	Brush (scuff) right heel as returning (no weight).
13	Touch right heel forward, right foot turned to a 45° angle.
14	Sweep right, heel leading, across in front of left.
15–16	Touch right heel forward, right foot turned to a 45° angle, and return, taking weight.
17	Touch left heel forward, left foot turned to a 45° angle.
18	Sweep left, heel leading, across in front of right.

Style: Review Line Dance style, p. 399.

Variations for Part I

During Part I, partners may improvise with a wide variety of maneuvers. The number of Two-Steps may be increased by an even number. Part II is referred to as "think steps" because the leader decides what variation to do.

1. Lady turns under man's left arm once or twice while moving forward.
2. Man lifts right hand over lady's head, lady taking four Two-Steps turns toward the man, and moves to his left side to face line of direction in promenade position. Repeat Part II; then man raises his right arm over his head like a lariat and lady taking four Two-Steps travels behind the man. She starts to turn counterclockwise 360° (third Two-Step); her right shoulder comes to his right shoulder; man lifts his left arm up and extends his right arm down at his side, shoulder to shoulder; she pivots to face forward in original position (fourth Two-Step).
3. *The Train.* Taking four Two-Steps, lady moves in front of man, two hands still joined and resting on her shoulders. Repeat Part II in this position. Lady Two-Steps back to place.
4. Take two Two-Steps forward; on the next two Two-Steps, the man raises his right arm over her head, and the lady travels in front of man to face him. Arms are crossed, extended and firm, with right hand on top. Repeat Part II. Pivoting counterclockwise, take four Two-Steps. Repeat Part II. Man lifts right arm over his head as she travels around behind him, turning 360° as in **2** to face original position.

5. *Wheel Around.* In Varsouvienne position, take four Two-Steps; the couple turns counterclockwise, the man dancing almost in place as the lady travels forward. Or turn clockwise, the lady dancing almost in place, as the man travels forward.

Style

1. Keep knees slightly bent.
2. Keep it smooth.

Achy Breaky

Achy Breaky is a Country Western Line Dance to the song "Achy Breaky Heart." Don Von Tress wrote the song, calling it "Don't Tell My Heart." Unable to remember the title, the audience would request Billy Ray Cyrus to sing that "Achy Breaky" song. Mercury is credited with capitalizing on the country dance craze and packaging a videotape with the *Achy Breaky* line dance when it released a single. The song and dance caught on fast. "Achy Breaky Heart" became a hit and Billy Ray Cyrus won a 1993 American Music Award.

Meter: 4/4. Directions are presented in beats.

Music: "Achy Breaky Heart."

Formation: Scattered, all facing music.

■ Directions for the Dance

Beats

Starting position: feet together, weight on both feet.

1–4	Grapevine. Beginning right, step sidewards right, cross left behind right, step sidewards right, stomp left in place.
5–8	Bump hip left, right, and twice left. (Single, single, double.)
9–12	Star. Point right toe back, side, front, step right in place.
13–16	Step left, right in place, lift left knee up (hitch), step left in place.
17–20	Moving backward, step right, left, right, stomp left.
21–24	Bump hip left, right, twice left.
25–26	Step right, scuff left forward.
27–28	Step left, pivoting left one-quarter turn, scuff right forward.
29–32	Grapevine. Step sideward right, cross left behind right, step right sideward, step left. Now right foot is free to begin grapevine from the beginning. There are two consecutive grapevines in a row (first step and last step of the dance), *both to the right.*

Variation

25–26	Step right, pivoting almost one-quarter turn right, scuff left forward.
27–28	Pivot will be almost a half-turn to face new direction.

⚜ Cowboy Boogie

Cowboy Boogie, also called *Country Boogie,* is a Country Western Line Dance with no partners.

Meter: 4/4 medium to fast. Directions are presented in beats.

Music: "Friends in Low Places," or popular 4/4 Country Western tune.

Formation: Scattered, all facing music.

■ Directions for the Dance

Beats

Starting position: feet together, weight on both feet.

1–4	Grapevine. Beginning right, step sideward, cross left behind right, step sideward right, scuff left heel forward and clap.
5–8	Repeat grapevine beginning left.
9–10	Step right in place, scuff left heel.
11–12	Step left in place, scuff right heel.
13–16	Moving backwards, step right, left, right, and lift left knee up (hitch).
17–18	Rock forward left, touch right in back.
19–20	Rock backward right, touch left in front.
21–24	Rock forward left, rock back right, rock forward left, pivoting on left foot, one-quarter turn left and swing right knee up (hitch).

Electric Slide

Electric Slide is a Country Western Line Dance with no partners.

Meter: 4/4, medium to fast. Directions are presented in beats.

Music: Any popular 4/4 Country Western tune.

Formation: Scattered, all facing music.

■ Directions for the Dance

Beats

Starting position: feet together, weight on both feet.

1 – 4	Beginning right, step sideward right, close left to right, step sideward right, close left to right, step touch.
5 – 8	Repeat same action to left.
9 – 12	Moving backward, step right, close left to right, step right and touch left heel to right foot.
13 – 14	Rock forward left, touch right (dig) in place. May swing right arm in arc, bending over, and touch floor in front of left foot on the "dig."
15 – 16	Rock backward right, touch left (dig) in place.
17 – 18	Step left (count one), pivoting on left one-quarter turn left and brush right foot forward (count two).

Variations

1 – 4	Take three fast slides to right, letting left foot drag, step right, touch left. Repeat to left.
1 – 4	Or grapevine right (right, left, right), touch left heel. Repeat left.

Style: Bend knees on grapevine.

■ ELECTRIC SLIDE TO FUNK MUSIC

Music: Any popular Funk tune.

Style: Bring knees up high. Bend elbows and work arms like a hammer alternately. On the rock, twist shoulders and torso forward and back. Add hops, at every opportunity. Whole body makes exaggerated moves to the music.

🎵 Four Corners

Four Corners is a Country Western Line Dance with no partners.

Meter: 4/4 medium to fast. Directions presented in beats.

Record: MH 35.

Cassette: MH C35.

Music: Suggested tunes: "Tulsa Line," "Swingin'," "Elvira."

Formation: Free formation, all facing music.

■ Directions for the Dance

Beats

Starting position: feet together, weight on both feet.

1-2	Swivel heels to left and return.
3-4	Swivel heels to right and return.
5	Touch right heel forward, foot turned out to 45° angle.
6	Sweep right heel in front of left.
7-8	Touch left heel forward, foot turned out to 45° angle, and return. Weight on right.
9	Touch left heel forward, foot turned out to 45° angle.
10	Sweep left heel in front of right.
11	Touch left heel forward, foot turned out to 45° angle.
12	Touch left toe backward.
13-14	Step left forward, chugging with right knee raised.
15	Step backward right.
16-19	Repeat action of beats 12-15.
20	Touch left toe backward.
21-22	Turning foot slightly left, step left forward, chugging while turning a quarter-turn left with right knee raised.
23-26	Grapevine: step right, crossing in front of left; step left sideward; step right behind left; touch left toe to left side.
27	Return left to right, stepping on left.
28-29	Touch right toe to right side and return right to left. Weight on both feet.

Style: Review Line Dance style, p. 399.

🌿 Freeze

Freeze is a Country Western Line Dance with no partners.

Meter: 4/4, medium fast. Directions presented in beats.

Record: MH 37.

Cassette: MH C37.

Music: Suggested tunes: "Tulsa Line," "Swingin'," "Elvira."

Formation: Free formation, all facing music.

■ Directions for the Dance

Beats

Starting position: feet together, weight on right.

1 – 4	Grapevine: beginning left, step left sideward; step right behind left; step sidewards left; lift right knee turned out, crossing right heel in front of left, then kick right foot out.
5 – 8	Grapevine: beginning right, repeat action of measures 1 – 4 to the right.
9 – 12	Traveling backward, step back left, right, left; lift right knee turned out, crossing right heel in front of left, then kick right foot out.
14 – 15	Freeze! Weight remains forward till beat 16. Or rock backward on left; lifting right foot, rock forward on right.
16	Turning one-quarter turn right, pivot on right foot with left knee bent, foot off the floor.

Style: Review Line Dance style, p. 399.

❧ Slappin' Leather ❧

Slappin' Leather is a Country Western Line Dance with no partners.

Meter: 4/4, medium to fast. Directions presented in beats.

Music: Suggested tunes: "Elvira," "Tulsa Times," "Swingin'," "Baby's Got Her Blue Jeans On."

Formation: Free formation, all facing music.

■ Directions for the Dance

Beats

Starting position: feet together, weight on both feet.

1–4	Swivel, weight on balls of feet; spread heels apart, heels together; spread heels apart, heels together.
5–8	Touch right heel forward, step right in place. Touch left heel forward, step left in place.
9–12	Repeat action of beats 5–8.
13–14	Tap right heel in front twice, foot turned out.
15–16	Tap right toe in back twice.
17–20	Star. Touch right toe forward, to right side, behind left, and to right side.
21	Slap leather! Weight remains on left. Swing right foot behind left and slap right boot with left hand.
22	While turning a quarter-turn left (pivot on left foot), swing right foot to right side and slap right boot with right hand.
23–26	Grapevine: beginning right, step right; step left behind right; step sideward right; chug (scoot) right, lifting left knee up (hitch), and clap hands.
27–30	Beginning left, repeat action of beats 23–26 to the left.
31–34	Traveling backward, step right, left, right; chug (scoot) right, lifting left knee up (hitch), and clap hands.
35–36	Stomp forward left; stomp right next to left. Weight on both feet.

Style: Review Line Dance style, p. 399.

Tush Push

Tush Push is a Country Western Line Dance with no partners.

Meter: 4/4, medium to fast. Directions presented in beats.

Music: Any popular 4/4 Country Western tune.

Formation: Scattered, all facing music.

■ Directions for the Dance

Beats

Starting position: feet together, weight on both feet.

1–4	Beginning right, lift heel and tap (press) heel four times.
5–8	Beginning left, lift heel and tap (press) heel four times.
9–12	Swivel, heels together, right, left, right, clap.
13–16	Swivel, heels together, left, right, left, clap.
17–20	Bump hips right, left, right, clap.
21–24	Bump hips left, right, left, clap.
25–28	In a circular counterclockwise motion, bump hips first to right, circling twice.
29–32	Cha Cha Cha. Beginning right, step forward, close left to right, step forward right (counts one and two), step forward left, right.
33–36	Moving backward, step left, close right to left, step left (counts one and two), step right, left.
37–44	Repeat cha cha cha step forward and backward.
45–48	Step right in place, step left pivoting one-quarter turn, stomp right (weight remains on left foot), clap.

Variation

Cha Cha Cha. On the third and fourth cha chas, pivot a half turn.

37–40	Step right forward, close left to right, step forward right, step left forward, pivoting one-half turn counterclockwise, step right in place. Now facing opposite direction.
41–44	Moving forward, step left, close right to left, step left, step right forward, pivoting one-half turn clockwise to face original direction, step left in place.

Disco Dance

Disco stands to the seventies as Rock stood to the sixties. *Disco* comes from the word *discotheque*, which in France is a place where records and disques are stored. In the United States, a discotheque is a place where records are played and one can listen or dance to rock music. Disco Dance has become a descriptive term that encompasses a wide variety of dance steps to many musical rhythms. Originally the partners did not touch and the patterns were simple, characterized by (1) stationary base, (2) response to a steady beat—predominantly 4/4 time, (3) action in the upper torso (this is styling of hands and movement of body above the hips), and (4) not following the lead of a partner.

What began as fury and inspiration became fashion. How to keep the momentum going became a major concern as record sales declined and disco attendance dropped. Two events occurred that increased the desire of the whole nation for dance. Studio 54 in New York City proved that a discotheque could work on a grand scale. People wanted an opportunity to exhibit themselves. Gone were the glitter balls; they were replaced by video screens with computer graphics. The disc jockey continued to be in the driver's seat. The dance floor was more spacious. The music and the atmosphere for overstimulation was shared with a profusion of lights, sound, rhythm, and spectacles that could be interpreted as the formula for "pleasure and high times."

The other event was the movie *Saturday Night Fever.* John Travolta strutted and presented a virile young man's need to be assertive, seeking a stage on which to perform.

"Touch dancing" was the new phrase for holding one's partner. The Hustle is credited with bringing people together again on the dance floor. One of the common tunes for dancing was "Feelings"—the dance included body contact, dancing in one spot, responding to the music, and a 4/4 rhythm.

Clubs reopened and new ones arrived to meet the new disco interest. With the Hustle, partners touching once again, the dance studios were back in business. Many of the old forms, like the Lindy and the Latin Dances, as well as the closed dance position or variations, reappeared. Disco in the '90s refers to dance. The music is rock or a blend of soul, reggae, and disco—an irresistible mix of sounds. The music may be live or recorded.

Disco Swing

Disco Swing follows the syncopated rhythm of rock and roll. Many are dancing 4-count swing (even rhythm, Single Lindy) or 6-count swing (uneven rhythm, the Double Lindy). The dance is smoother and glides more like Country Western than Jitterbug. The turns are the same as Swing, but perhaps with different names. The approach to Disco Swing is more casual as the dancers explore one move after another; the feet pause or ignore the step pattern while turns or twirls are in progress; when the maneuvers are completed, the dancers pick up the beat and resume the step pattern. In the discos, with today's social climate and the advent of assertive feminism, it is acceptable for the lady to lead the moves.

Whoever knows the leads, leads. The leads may be pressure from the hands, or eye or verbal contact. Refer to Country Western for analysis of 4-count Swing (p. 403); Swing for 6-count Swing (Double Lindy)(p. 389). Follow the directions for the many turns of the Double Lindy.

🌀 The Hustle

The Hustle is written in 4/4 time. The accent is on the first beat of each measure. Traditionally the Hustle is danced to 6 counts of music (one and a half measures). The tap (touch) step is characteristic of all Hustles.

4/4	/					/	
	tap	step	tap	step		step	step
	Q	Q	S	Q	Q	S	S	S
	1	2	3	4		5	6

🌀 California Hustle

There are many Hustles, some for no partners, others for couples. The *California Hustle* is also called the *Los Angeles Hustle* and, in New York, *Bus Stop*.

Meter: 4/4. Directions presented in beats.

Records: High/Scope RM9; DC 74528.

Cassette: High/Scope RM9.

Music: Betty White Records, How to Hustle D115.

Formation: Free formation, all facing music. No partners.

■ Directions for the Dance

Beats

Starting position: feet together, weight on left.

Back and Forward Steps

1–3   Beginning right, take three steps backward.

4   Tap left foot to right foot or point left toe backward. Weight remains on right.

5–7   Beginning left, take three steps forward.

8   Tap right foot to the left foot or point left toe forward. Weight remains on left.

9–12   Repeat steps 1–4.

Grapevine to Side

1   Step left to left side.

2   Step right, crossing in front of left.

3   Step left to left side.

4   Tap right toe to left foot. Weight remains on left.

5   Step right to right side.

6   Step left, crossing in front of right.

7   Step right to right side.

8   Tap left toe to right foot. Weight remains on right.

9–10   Step left to left side; tap right to left—no weight.

11–12   Step right to right side; tap left to right—no weight.

Take a quarter-turn to left to face a new direction and repeat dance.

✿ Hustle with Partner

Directions are for the man; the lady's part is reversed, except when noted.

■ BASIC STEP

(Closed Position)

Steps	4/4 Counts	Rhythm Cue
Tap L to side	1	quick
Close L to R, take weight on L	2	quick
Tap R to side	3	quick
Close R to L, take weight on R	4	quick
Step L in place	5	quick
Step R in place	6	quick

Step Cue: tap step, tap step, step, step.

Style: Knees are soft; action should be smooth and rolling rather than bouncy.

■ TURN

(Clockwise)(Closed position)

Steps	4/4 Counts	Step Cue
Tap L to side	1	tap
Close L to R, take weight on L	2	step
Tap R to side	3	tap
Step forward right between partner's feet	4	step
Step L forward, turning right (clockwise) pivoting on ball of foot	5	turn
Step R in place, completing turn	6	turn

■ LINDY

(Closed position)

Steps	4/4 Counts	Step Cue
Moving into open position step L behind R	1	cross
Step R in place	and	step
Moving into closed position, step L to side	2	step
Moving into reverse open position, step R behind L	3	cross
Step L in place	and	step
Moving into closed position, step R to side	4	step
Step L in place	5	step
Step R in place	6	step

■ HUSTLE SWING TURNS

The turns are the same as swing, sometimes with different names. The tap (touch) steps precede the turns, which are made on counts 5, 6. Refer to Double Lindy Variations.

Salsa

Salsa music entered the dance scene in the mid-1960s when the Cubans settled in Miami and southern Florida. Their Latin music became a blend of Afro-Cuban jazz. *Salsa* is the Spanish word for *sauce* and, as the Spanish sauces are spicy, the name seems appropriate.

The Salsa is written in 4/4 cut time. The rhythm is quick, quick, slow. It is counted 1 and 2 of the cut-time beat. The music is fast and lighthearted.

Salsa Style

Salsa Steps

The style is very similar to the rumba: bent knees, *small flat footsteps* (weight over the heel), hip action of the Cuban walk as it rolls, and upper body held firmly poised, never sagging, rib cage moving subtly side to side, following the action of the feet.

Directions are for the man, lady's part reversed, except as noted.

■ BASIC STEP

(Closed position)

Steps	C Counts	Rhythm Cue
Step L forward	1	quick
Step R backward	*and*	quick
Step L beside R	2	slow
Step R backward	1	quick
Step L forward	*and*	quick
Step R beside L	2	slow

Use basic step to turn L or R in place.

■ SIDE STEP

(Closed position)

Steps	C Counts	Rhythm Cue
Step sideways L	1	quick
Close R to L	*and*	quick
Step sideways L	2	slow
Reverse to R	*1 and 2*	quick, quick, slow

Salsa (continued)

■ CROSS STEP

(Two hands joined)

Cross L over R (with exaggeration)	1	quick
Step back R	*and*	quick
Step L close to R	2	slow

Repeat crossing R.

■ THROW OUT

(Closed position)

2 Basic Steps (LRL, RLR).
Man releases his right hand, gives lady a slight push, and takes 2 more Basic Steps in place.
Lady moves away from partner (R, L, R) and comes back (L, R, L) to closed position.

♫ Charleston

The Roaring Twenties saw the advent of Dixieland jazz and the *Charleston*. Definitely a fad dance, the Charleston comes and goes, only to reappear again. The dance, with its fancy footwork and carefree abandon, is a challenge to young and old.

Black dock workers of Charleston, South Carolina, are credited with performing the dance steps eventually referred to as the Charleston. In 1923, the Ziegfeld Follies popularized the step in a show called "Running Wild." Teachers toned the kicking steps down and interspersed them with the Two-Step and Foxtrot, and the United States had a new popular dance. The *Varsity Drag* was one of many dances that incorporated the basic Charleston step. The dance permitted individuals to express their ability with many Charleston variations, independent of their partner.

■ Charleston Rhythm

The Charleston rhythm is written in 4/4 time. The bouncy quality of the music occurs in the shift of accent, becoming highly syncopated rhythm.

```
          /    /   /   /   /
4/4   Q |  Q  Q  Q  Q  Q  Q  Q  Q |
      — | —  —  —  —  —  —  —  — |
      — | —  —  —  —  —  —  —  — |
      & | 1  &  2  &  3  &  4  & |
```

The rhythm is an even beat pattern of quicks counted "*and* 1, *and* 2, *and* 3, *and* 4." The knee bends on the *and* before the step. It is the *and* that gives the Charleston its characteristic bounce. Rhythmically, the beats are:

The accent shifts from the first beat to the eighth note tied to the third beat, which gives punch to the rhythm. The rhythm is jerky, staccato as well as syncopated.

■ Charleston Style

The twisting of the feet and the bending of the knees before each step, then the straightening of the leg, are basic. The arms move in opposition to the feet: For example, step left, point right and swing both arms across to the left; step right, point left and swing arms across right. The Charleston may be danced as a solo; in a line with a group; or with a partner, side by side, on the same foot, or facing each other, hands joined or closed position.

Charleston with Partner

Partners may be side by side, on the same foot or facing each other, hands joined or closed position. The lead is visual. The man starts with his L, lady R. Any step changes start with man's L. Man and lady stop together.

Charleston (continued)

■ Teaching Suggestions

1. Practice rhythm first. Feet slightly apart and parallel, bend knees *(and)*, straighten legs (count 1). Repeat the action of "*and* 1, *and* 2, *and* 3, *and* 4." Then add the music.
2. Practice pivot on balls of feet. Heels out *(and)*, heels in (count 1). Repeat.
3. *Charleston Twist.* Combine **1** and **2.** Bend knees and heels out *(and)*, straighten legs and heels in (count 1). Repeat.
4. Add arm movement, swinging arms in opposition to feet. Swinging arms helps to maintain balance.
5. If balance and timing are difficult, try sitting on the edge of a chair to establish the rhythm; then stand behind the chair, holding onto the back for support.
6. Teach all figures in place. Then move forward and backward. Practice without music, slowly. If record player has a variable speed, introduce music as soon as possible. Gradually increase tempo until the correct tempo is reached.

Fundamental Charleston Steps

Record: "The Golden Age of the Charleston," EMI Records LTD., GX 2507; or any good recording of the 1920s.

Formation: Free formation, all facing music.

■ POINT STEP

(Feet together, weight on R)

Steps	4/4 Counts	Direction Cue
Bend R knee	and	and
Step forward L	1	step forward
Bend L knee	and	and
Point R toe forward, straighten knees	2	point forward
Bend L knee	and	and
Step back R	3	step back
Bend R knee	and	and
Point L toe back, straighten knees	4	point forward

Arms: Swing arms in opposition to legs. R toe forward, L arm swings forward, R arm swings back; L toe forward, R arm swings forward, L arm swings back.

■ SINGLE KICK STEP

(Feet together, weight on R)

Steps	4/4 Counts	Direction Cue
Bend R knee	and	and
Step forward L	1	step forward
Bend L knee	and	and
Kick R leg forward, straighten knees	2	kick forward
Bend L knee	and	and
Step back R	3	step back
Bend R knee	and	and
Kick L leg back	4	kick back
Straighten knees	and	and

Arms: Swing arms in opposition to the kick. Kick R leg forward, L arm swings forward, R arm swings back; kick L leg forward, R arm swings forward, L arm swings back.

■ Variations

1. *Double Kick.* Step forward left; kick right forward, then backward; step right in place. Repeat kicking left forward, then backward; step left.
2. *Single Diagonal Kick.* Step sideward left, kick diagonally forward across left leg, step sideward right, kick diagonally forward across right leg.

Fundamental Charleston Steps (continued)

■ THE CHARLESTON TWIST

(Weight on the balls of both feet, heels touching, toes pointing out)

1. The twist comes from pivoting on balls of feet, heels turned out, then pivoting on balls of feet, heels turned in. Heels are slightly off the floor to allow the pivot action.

Steps	4/4 Counts	Direction Cue
Bend knees, pivot in on balls of feet	*and*	heels out
Pivot out, straighten knees	1	heels in
Repeat over and over.		

2. Twist and snap (heels touching, toes pointing out, weight on R).

Steps	4/4 Counts	Direction Cue
Bend R knee, pivot in on ball of foot, lifting L leg up, knee turned in	*and*	heel out
Pivot out on ball of R foot; straighten knees; place L foot by heel of R, toe pointed out; L takes weight	1	heel in
Bend L knee; pivot in on ball of foot, lifting L leg up, knee turned in	*and*	heel out
Pivot out on ball of L foot, straighten knees, place R foot by heel of L, toe pointed out; R takes weight	2	heel in

■ JUMP

Steps	4/4 Counts	Direction Cue
Bend both knees together	*and*	bend
Jump forward diagonally L, both arms swing L, shoulder height	1	jump
Bend both knees	*and*	bend
Jump back, both arms swing down	2	jump
Repeat jump and arms forward and back	*and* 1 *and* 2	
Bend both knees together	*and*	
Jump forward diagonally R, both arms swing R, shoulder height	1	jump
Bend both knees together	*and*	
Jump back, both arms swing down	2	jump
Repeat jump and arms forward and back	*and* 1 *and* 2	jump jump
Alternately jump L R L R, arms swing L R L R	*and* 1 *and* 2	jump

■ SWIVEL

Weight on heel, pivot toes R (count *and*); weight on toes, pivot heels R (count 1). Continue to move R, heel, toe, heel, toe. Arms swing L and down, repeating with heel, toe. Travel on counts *and* 1 *and* 2. Reverse movement to travel L.

■ SUZY Q

Pivoting on L heel and R toe simultaneously (count *and*), then pivoting on L toe and R heel simultaneously (count 1). Continue alternating, traveling R. Hands in front of chest, elbows out as heels are apart; drop elbows as toes are apart; alternate elbows out and dropped with foot movement. Reverse footwork to travel L.

The *Foxtrot,* as a present-day form, is of relatively recent origin. The only truly American form of Ballroom Dance, it has had many steps and variations through the years. The Foxtrot gets its name from a musical comedy star, Henry Fox, of the years 1913–1914 (Hostetler 1952), who danced a fast but simple trotting step to ragtime music in one of the Ziegfeld shows of that time. As an additional publicity stunt, the theater management requested that a star nightclub performer, Oscar Duryea, introduce the step to the public but found that it had to be modified somewhat, because a continuous trotting step could not be maintained for long periods without exhausting effort. Duryea simplified the step so that it became four walking steps alternating with eight quick running steps. This was the first Foxtrot.

Since that time, under the influence of Vernon and Irene Castle and a series of professional dancers, the Foxtrot has been through a gradual refining process and has developed into a beautifully smooth dance. It claims considerable popularity today.

Music from ragtime through the blues on down to modern jazz and swing has had its effect on the Foxtrot. The original Foxtrot was danced to a lively 2/4 rhythm. Its two parent forms were the One-Step, 2/4 - - - - quick quick quick quick rhythm; the other was the Two-Step, 2/4 | - - – | - - – | quick quick slow or step-close-step. Both of these forms are danced today but have given way to a slower, smoother 4/4 time and a more streamlined style. The Foxtrot is danced in three tempos (slow, medium, and fast) and can be adapted to almost any tempo played in the music.

The basic Foxtrot steps can be used together in any combination or sequence. A dancer who knows the basic steps and understands the fundamentals of rhythm can make up his or her own combinations easily and gradually develop the possibilities for variation in position, direction, and tempo.

■ Foxtrot Rhythm

The modern Foxtrot in 4/4 time, or cut time, has four quarter beats or their equivalent to each measure. Each beat is given the same amount of time, but there is an accent on the first and third beats of the measure. When a step is taken on each beat (1-2-3-4), these are called *quick beats.* When steps are taken only on the two accented beats (1 and 3), they are twice as long and are called *slow beats.*

4/4	— — — —	
	Q Q Q Q	One-step
	1 2 3 4	

4/4	—— ——	
	S S	Dance walk
	1–2 3–4	

4/4	— — ——	
	Q Q S	Two-step
	1 2 3–4	

4/4	—— � — —	
	/ /	
	S Q Q	Westchester
	1–2 3 4	

Foxtrot (continued)

A use of these quick and slow beats and a combination of them into rhythm patterns form the basis for all of the modern Foxtrot steps. There are two patterns used predominantly: the magic step and the Westchester box step.

Magic Step

The magic step pattern represents broken rhythm as it takes a measure and half of music and may be repeated from the middle of the measure. It is an uneven rhythm pattern, slow slow quick quick.

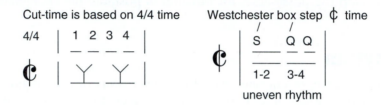

Westchester Box Step

The Westchester box step is a one-measure pattern, but it takes two measures to complete the box. The rhythm is uneven, slow quick quick. The rhythm may also be played in cut time, but it is still slow quick quick. Beats 1 and 2 are put together to make 1 beat. Beats 3 and 4 are put together to make 1 beat. The time signature for cut time is ¢ . It is played faster and feels very much like 2/4 time.

■ Foxtrot Style

Foxtrot style truly reflects its American origin. It is the least affected of any of the Ballroom Dances. Completely without stylized or eccentric arm, foot, head, or torso movement, the Foxtrot is a beautifully smooth dance. The body is held easily erect and follows the foot pattern in a relaxed way with little up and down or sideward movement. The good dancer glides normally along the floor and blends the various steps together without bobbing or jerking. This effect is accomplished by long, reaching steps with only as much knee bend as is needed to transfer the weight smoothly from step to step. It gives the Foxtrot a streamlined motion and a simple beauty of form that can be enjoyed without strain or fatigue, dance after dance. As one becomes more and more skillful at putting together steps for the Foxtrot, there will be increasing joy derived from the tremendous variety of quick and slow combinations.

❧ Fundamental Foxtrot Steps

Directions are for man, facing line of direction; lady's part is reversed, except when noted.

■ Introductory Steps

■ ONE-STEP

(Closed position)

Steps	4/4 Counts	Rhythm Cue
Step L forward	1	quick
Step R forward	2	quick
Step L forward	3	quick
Step R forward	4	quick

Style: It is like a regular walk, heel first.

Steps	4/4 Counts	Rhythm Cue
Step L backward	1	quick
Step R backward	2	quick
Step L backward	3	quick
Step R backward	4	quick

Style: Reach straight back with toe of foot.

Note: Refer to detailed analysis of One-Step, p. 381.

■ TURN

Counterclockwise (L) step on each beat (L, R, L, R) in place.

Variation: Alternate 4 quick and 4 slow. Try different combination of rhythms, moving forward, backward, turning, and sideward.

■ DANCE WALK

(Forward or backward*) (Closed position)

Steps	4/4 Counts	Rhythm Cue
Step L forward	1–2	slow
Step R forward	3–4	slow
Step L forward	1–2	slow
Step R forward	3–4	slow

Style: It is like a regular walk, heel first, but should be a long, smooth, reaching motion.

Steps	4/4 Counts	Rhythm Cue
Step L backward	1–2	slow
Step R backward	3–4	slow
Step L backward	1–2	slow
Step R backward	3–4	slow

Style: It is a long, smooth, reaching motion to the toe of the foot, straight back.

Note: Refer to detailed analysis of Dance Walk, p. 381.

Fundamental Foxtrot Steps (continued)

---

*Check lead indication, p. 383.

■ SIDE CLOSE

(Chasse; a sideward-moving step) (Closed position)

Steps	4/4 Counts	Rhythm Cue
Step L sideward	1	quick
Step R to L, take weight on R	2	quick

Style: Steps should be short, smooth, sideward motion, on the ball of the foot.

Note: Repetition of this step will continue action to man's left.

■ Magic Step Series

Magic Step (Basic step)	Right and Left Parallel	Pivot Turn
Open Magic Step	The Conversation Pivot	
Magic Left Turn	The Corté	

The magic step series was created by Arthur Murray (1954). It is called by this name because it can be varied in a surprising number of ways. The pattern is uneven rhythm and requires a measure and a half for one basic step. This is called broken rhythm.

■ MAGIC STEP

(Basic Step) (Closed position)

Steps	4/4 Counts	Rhythm Cue
Step L forward	1 - 2	slow
Step R forward	3 - 4	slow
Step L sideward, a short step	1	quick
Close R to L, take weight on R	2	quick

Step Cue:

forward forward   side close   Floor pattern ———┐

long steps   short steps

start

Style: The forward steps should be long, smooth, walking steps, straight ahead. The lady, moving backward, takes a long step reaching from hip to toe.

Lead: A body and right arm lead forward.

Variations on the Magic Step Pattern: The following three techniques are used for maneuvering in a closed dance position.

1. Forward or backward—the man may maneuver forward or backward if he is aware of the traffic around him. The lead to move backward is a pressure lead at the lady's back during the quick quick beats and then a step into the backward direction on the next slow beat. Generally the man will not have room to move backward more than one or two consecutive patterns.

2. Right or left—the man may maneuver to the right or to the left to go around another couple. He will change direction on the quick quick beats by use of a pressure lead with his right hand and turn his body at the same time one-eighth of a turn to the right so as to travel diagonally outward or one-eighth turn to the left so as to travel diagonally inward beginning with the next slow beat. The right turn is particularly

handy in leading a partner out of a crowded situation away from the center of the floor. Closed position is retained throughout.

3. Dance in place—used on a crowded dance floor. Closed dance position:

Steps	4/4 Counts	Rhythm Cue
Step sideward L, slide R to L, no weight change	1-2	.... slow
Step sideward R, slide L to R, no weight change	3-4	.... slow
Step sideward L	1	.... quick
Close R to L, take weight R	2	.... quick

Step Cue: Step slide, step slide, quick quick.

Style: The steps are very small.

Lead: Increase pressure with the right hand to keep the lady from stepping back. Indicate sideward action.

Note: The man may maneuver this in-place pattern into a turn counterclockwise by the use of the right hand and elbow.

■ OPEN MAGIC STEP

(Closed position)

Steps	4/4 Counts	Rhythm Cue
Step L forward	1-2	.... slow
Step R forward	3-4	.... slow
Step L forward a short step, turning to open dance position	1	.... quick
Close R to L, take weight R	2	.... quick
Step L forward in open position	3-4	.... slow
Step R forward	1-2	.... slow
Step L forward a short step	3	.... quick
Close R to L, take weight R	4	.... quick
Step L forward	1-2	.... slow
Step R forward	3-4	.... slow
Step L forward a short step, turning to closed position	1	.... quick
Close R to L, take weight R	2	.... quick

Step Cue: Slow slow quick quick.

Style: It is a heel lead on the slow beats in open position for both the man and lady.

Lead: See lead indications 7 and 8, p. 384. The man may wish to return to closed position on the quick beats following the first two slows in open position.

Note: It is possible to maneuver when going into open position so that the couple opens facing the line of direction and afterward closes with the man still facing the line of direction, starting from closed position as follows:

Steps	4/4 Counts	Rhythm Cue
Step L forward	1-2	.... slow
Step R forward	3-4	.... slow
Step L, R moving around the lady on the L side while turning her halfway around to open position	1-2	.... quick,quick
Step L forward in open position moving in line of direction	3-4	.... slow
Step R forward	1-2	.... slow
Step L, R in place, bringing the lady around to face the closed dance position	3-4	.... quick quick

Fundamental Foxtrot Steps (continued)

Step Cue: Slow slow come around/slow slow in place.

Style: The lady must be sure to swing around, facing the man, into a correct closed dance position while taking two quick beats.

Lead: The man must start bringing his right elbow up to indicate to the lady that he is going into closed position on the first quick beat.

Note: Any number of open magic steps may be done consecutively when traveling in the line of direction without fear of interfering with the dancing of other couples.

■ MAGIC LEFT TURN

(Closed position)

Steps	4/4 Counts	Rhythm Cue
Step L forward a short step	1 – 2	slow
Step R backward, toe in and turn counterclockwise one-quarter	3 – 4	slow
Step in place L, toeing out L, and turning one-quarter counterclockwise	1	quick
Step R to L, take weight R, and finish the one-half turn.	2	quick

Repeat to make a full turn.

Step Cue: Rock   rock   step   close.
               S   S   Q   Q

Style: The slow steps forward and backward are like short rocking steps, but the body is straight, not leaning.

Lead: The man must strongly increase pressure at the lady's back on the first step so that she will not swing her left foot backward. Then he uses his firm right arm to turn the lady with him counterclockwise. As the lady reacts to these two leads, she will step in between the man's feet and pivot on her left foot as he guides her around.

Note: The pattern may be reduced to a quarter-turn at a time, or it may be increased to make a full turn at a time. This variation provides a means of turning in place or of turning to maneuver into position for another variation or for recovering the original line of direction. Because of this, it is often used to tie together all types of Foxtrot variations.

■ RIGHT AND LEFT PARALLEL MAGIC STEP

(Closed position)

This is a delightful variation involving right and left parallel position.

Steps	4/4 Counts	Rhythm Cue
Step L forward	1 – 2	slow
Step R forward	3 – 4	slow
Step L sideward a short step, turning to R parallel position	1	quick
Close R to L, take weight on R	2	quick
Step forward L, diagonally in R parallel position	3 – 4	slow

Step forward R	1-2	.... slow
Step in place L, turning in place one-quarter clockwise into L parallel position	3	.... quick
Close R to L, take weight on R	4	.... quick
Step forward L in L parallel position	1-2	.... slow
Step forward R	3-4	.... slow
Step in place L, turning to R parallel	1	.... quick
Close R to L, take weight on R	2	.... quick
Step L forward in R parallel position	3-4	.... slow
Step R forward	1-2	.... slow
Step L in place, turning to closed position	3	.... quick
Close R to L, take weight on R	4	.... quick

Step Cue: Slow slow quick quick.

Style: The lady in parallel position must reach back parallel to the man's forward reach.

Lead: See lead indications 9 and 10, p. 384.

Note: The couple should move forward in a zigzag pattern, down the floor, changing from one parallel position to the other. The man must be careful to take the quick beats in place as he is changing position in order to make a smooth transition. A more advanced use of this variation is to make a half-turn clockwise in place on the quick beats as the man changes from right parallel position to left parallel position so that the man would then travel backward in the line of direction and the lady forward. A half-turn counterclockwise in place would then turn the couple back to right parallel position. Innumerable combinations of this variation will develop as dancers experiment with changes of direction.

■ THE CONVERSATION PIVOT

(Open position)

Steps	*4/4 Counts*	*Rhythm Cue*
Step L forward	1-2	.... slow
Step R forward	3-4	.... slow
Step L around the lady clockwise going into closed position	1-2	.... slow
Step R between lady's feet and pivot on the R foot, turning clockwise	3-4	.... slow
Step L forward a short step, taking open position again	1	.... quick
Close R to L, taking weight R	2	.... quick

Note: Two extra slow beats have been added for this variation, S S S S Q Q.

Step Cue: Step step pivot pivot quick quick.

Style: Couples must hold the body firmly and press outward to move with the centrifugal force of the motion on the pivot turn. The lady will step forward in between the man's feet on the third slow beat and then around him with her left foot on the fourth slow beat, followed by a quick quick to balance oneself in place.

Lead: See lead indication 10, p. 384. The pivot turn is only the third and fourth slow beats. Then the man will lead into open position and take the quick beats.

Note: Following this variation it is usually wise to dance one more magic step in open position before leading into the basic closed position. Note details on pivot turn, p. 431.

Fundamental Foxtrot Steps (continued)

■ THE CORTÉ

(A fascinating dip step in magic step rhythm) (Closed position)

Steps	4/4 Counts	Rhythm Cue
Step L forward	1–2	slow
Step R forward	3–4	slow
Step L sideward a short step	1	quick
Close R to L, take weight on R	2	quick
Dip L backward	3–4	slow
Transfer weight forward onto R foot	1–2	slow
Step L sideward, a short step	3	quick
Close R to L, take weight R	4	quick

Step Cue: Slow slow   quick quick   dip   recover quick quick.
            (preparation (corté) (weight forward)
            beats)

Style: *Man*—The weight is transferred onto the left foot as the man steps backward into the dip. The left knee is bent, the back is straight, the right toe extends forward. *Lady*—Her weight is transferred onto the right foot as she steps forward into the dip. The right knee is bent and directly over her foot. The back is arched, keeping her straight up and down. The left leg is extended strongly from the hip through the knee of the pointed toe. Her head should be turned left to glance at the extended foot. For additional style details, see Tango, p. 441.

Lead: See lead indication 13, p. 384. The man must take care not to step too long backward or to dip too low as it is difficult for both man and lady to recover in good style.

Note: The exciting part about the corté is that it may be used as a variation in the dance or it may be used as a finishing step at the end of the music. It is perfectly acceptable to end a beat or two in advance and hold the position to the end of the music. It is also acceptable to corté after the music has finished. There is no pressure to get the corté on the last note of the music.

■ Box Step Series—Westchester

Westchester Box Step   Cross Step   Grapevine Step
Box Turn   Twinkle Step

The Westchester box is based on slow quick quick rhythm in 4/4 or cut time. It is a one-measure pattern—but it takes two measures to complete the box—with uneven rhythm, but it is done in a smooth style. It is a combination of dance walk and side close.

■ WESTCHESTER BOX STEP

(Closed position)

Steps	4/4 Counts	Rhythm Cue
Step L forward	1–2	slow
Pass R alongside of L, no weight change; step R sideward	3	quick
Close L to R, take weight on L	4	quick
Step R backward	1–2	slow
Pass L alongside of R, no weight change; step L sideward	3	quick
Close R to L, take weight on R	4	quick

Step Cue: (a) Forward   side   close.
           S   Q   Q

       (b) Backward   side   close
            long steps   short   steps.

Floor pattern

Style: The forward step is a heel step. Both forward and backward steps should be long reaching steps. Dancers must not lose a beat by pausing as they slide alongside the standing foot.

Lead: Refer to lead indications for the box step, p. 384.

Note: The man must understand the concept of the forward side close as being the forward sequence of the box and the backward side close as being the back sequence of the box. It is important because this terminology will be used in future patterns and leads.

■ BOX TURN

(Left) (Closed position)

Steps	4/4 Counts	Rhythm Cue
Step L forward, toe out; turn one-quarter to L	1–2	slow
Step R sideward	3	quick
Close L to R, take weight on L	4	quick
Step R backward, toe in; turn one-quarter to L	1–2	slow
Step L sideward	3	quick
Close R to L, take weight on R	4	quick
Step L forward, toe out; turn one-quarter to L	1–2	slow
Step R sideward	3	quick
Close L to R, take weight on L	4	quick
Step R backward, toe in; turn one-quarter to L	1–2	slow
Step L sideward	3	quick
Close R to L, take weight on R	4	quick

Step Cue: Turn side close, turn side close.

Style: The lady is taking the reverse of this pattern except that, when the lady steps forward with her left foot, instead of toeing out as described for the man, she steps forward between man's feet. This style for the lady greatly facilitates the turn.

Lead: Refer to lead indications, p. 384. A cue for the lead might be bank side close, draw side close.

Note: The man may use this turn to maneuver himself into any direction he may wish to use next.

■ CROSS STEP

(Closed position)

This is a simple but pretty step turning to open dance position momentarily on the forward sequence.

Steps	4/4 Counts	Rhythm Cue
Step L forward	1–2	slow
Step R sideward, turning to open position	3	quick

Fundamental Foxtrot Steps (continued)

Close L to R, take weight on L	4	quick
Step R forward in open position	1-2	slow
Step L forward, turning on L foot to face partner in closed position	3	quick
Close R to L, take weight R	4	quick

Step Cue: Forward side close, cross side close.

Style: The man and lady do not open up to a side to side position but open just enough to step forward on the inside foot, which feels like a crossing step. It should be accented by a long reaching step on the heel but not a dipping knee or body action.

Lead: Same as the lead to turn to open position and then back to closed position. See lead indications 7 and 8, p. 384.

Note: It is possible to go into this step when the man is facing out so that the cross step may travel into the line of direction.

●

■ TWINKLE STEP

(Closed position)

This is a slow quick quick rhythm using right and left parallel positions, led from the forward sequence of the box pattern.

Steps	*4/4 Counts*	*Rhythm Cue*
Step L forward	1-2	slow
Step R sideward	3	quick
Close L to R, take weight on L	4	quick
Step R diagonally forward in R parallel position	1-2	slow
Step L sideward, turning from R parallel to L parallel position	3	quick
Close R to L, take weight on R	4	quick
Step L diagonally forward in L parallel position	1-2	slow
Step sideward R, turning from L parallel to R parallel position	3	quick
Close L to R, take weight on L	4	quick
Step R diagonally forward in R parallel position	1-2	slow
Step L sideward turning to closed position	3	quick
Close R to L, take weight on R	4	quick

Step Cue: Slow quick quick.

Style: The quick steps are small. Changing from one parallel position to the other is done in a very smooth rolling manner. The lady needs lots of practice alone to learn the back side close pattern because it is on the diagonal backward parallel to the man.

Lead: Refer to lead indications 9 and 10, p. 384.

Note: Progress is a zigzag pattern down the floor. The parallel part of the steps may be repeated as many times as desired before going back to closed position.

■ GRAPEVINE STEP

(Closed position)

It is a beautiful pattern in slow quick quick time with four quick steps added to make the grapevine design, using parallel position.

Steps	4/4 Counts	Rhythm Cue
Step L forward	1 - 2	slow
Step R sideward, turning into R parallel position	3	quick
Close L to R, take weight on L	4	quick
Step R diagonally forward in R parallel position	1	quick
Step L sideward, turning to L parallel position	2	quick
Step R diagonally backward in L parallel position	3	quick
Step L sideward, turning to R parallel position	4	quick
Step R forward in R parallel position	1 - 2	slow
Step L sideward turning to closed position	3	quick
Close R to L, take weight on R	4	quick

Step Cue:

slow quick quick | quick quick quick quick | slow quick quick

forward sequence of box | grapevine pattern | transition back to closed position

Style: Practice on the grapevine step alone will help dancers get this pattern smoothly and beautifully. Cue man: forward side back side (R, L, R, L) on the grapevine step. Cue lady: back side forward side (L, R, L, R) on the grapevine step.

Lead: Refer to lead indications 9 and 10, p. 384. The lead is from the forward sequence of the box.

Note: The man should maneuver so that he is facing out before he starts this step in order that the grapevine step may travel in the line of direction. He may maneuver into this by use of a three-quarter turn or a hesitation step.

■ The Pivot Turn

The continuous pivot turn is a series of steps turning clockwise as many beats as desired. The man should be careful that he has room to turn, as the pivot turn progresses forward in the line of direction if done properly, and he should not turn so many steps as to make his partner dizzy. The principle involved in the footwork is the dovetailing of the feet, which means that the right foot always steps between partner's feet and the left foot always steps around the outside of partner's feet. The pivot turn described here has two slow beats as a preparation followed by four quick beats turning and comes out of it into the box step.

■ THE PIVOT TURN

(Closed position)

Steps	4/4 Counts	Rhythm Cue
Step L forward	1 - 2	slow
Step R forward, starting to turn the body clockwise increasing the body tension	3 - 4	slow
Step L, toeing in across the line of direction and rolling clockwise three-quarters of the way around on the ball of the L foot	1	quick
Step R, between partner's feet forward in the line of direction, completing one turn	2	quick
Step L, toeing in and reaching forward but across the line of direction, turning clockwise three-quarters as before	3	quick
Step R, between partner's feet forward in the line of direction, completing the second turn	4	quick
Step L forward in the line of direction, not turning but controlling momentum	1 - 2	slow
Step R sideward	3	quick

Fundamental Foxtrot Steps (continued)

Close L to R, take weight on L	4	....	quick
Step R backward	1 – 2	....	slow
Step L sideward	3	....	quick
Close R to L, taking weight R	4	....	quick

Step Cue: Step ready
              S   S

             turn turn turn turn
             Q Q Q Q

             forward side close
             S   Q   Q

             back side close
             S   Q   Q

The Lady: On the second slow beat, the lady receives the lead as the man increases body tension. She does the same. Then, on the first quick beat, she has been turned far enough to place her right foot forward in between his feet on the line of direction, left foot across the line of direction, right foot between, left across, and into the box step.

Style: They both must lean away, pressing outward like "the water trying to stay in the bucket." The concept of stepping each time in relation to the line of direction is what makes it possible to progress while turning as a true pivot turn should do.

Lead: See lead indications 12 and 13, p. 384.

Foxtrot Combos

The Foxtrot routines are listed here merely as examples to show how the various steps can be used in combination for practice routines. They are listed from simple to complex. (Closed position, unless otherwise indicated.)

1. *Dance Walk*
   4 dance walk forward
   4 dance walk backward
   4 dance walk forward
   4 dance walk, travel left in a circle
2. *Dance Walk*
   4 dance walk forward
   2 open magic step
   conversation pivot

3. *Magic Step*
   2 magic steps
   2 open magic steps
   conversation pivot
4. *Magic Step—Box*
   2 magic steps
   1 box step
   2 magic steps (open)

5. *Magic Step/Corté*
   1 magic step (open or closed)
   corté (recover)
   1 side close
   1 box turn
   corté (recover)
6. *Advanced Combo*
   1 magic step
   1 single twinkle to open
   1 single twinkle to left parallel
   1 single twinkle to open
   1 single twinkle to close

Although a majority of the middle European countries lay some claim to the origin of the Waltz, the world looked to Germany and Austria, where the great Waltz was made traditional by the beautiful music of Johann Strauss and his sons. It has a pulsating, swinging rhythm, which has been enjoyed by dancers everywhere, even by those who dance it only in its simplest pattern, the Waltz Turn. Its immediate popularity and its temporary obscurity are not unlike other fine inheritances of the past, which come and go with the ebb and flow of popular accord. Early use of the Waltz in America was at the elegant social balls and cotillions. Its outstanding contribution to present-day dancing is the Waltz position. Even in its early stages, it was quite some time before this position was socially acceptable. Now the closed position is universally the basic position for Ballroom Dancing.

The Waltz music is played in three different tempos—slow, medium, and fast. The slow or medium Waltz is preferred by most people. However, the fast Waltz is a favorite of those who know the Viennese style. The slower American style is danced for the most part on a box pattern, but the use of other variations has added a new interest.

■ Waltz Rhythm

The Waltz is played in 3/4 time. It is three beats per measure of music, with an accent on the first beat. The three beats of Waltz time are very even, each beat receiving the same amount of time. The three movements of the Waltz step pattern blend perfectly with the musical tempo or beat of each measure. The tempo may be slow, medium, or fast.

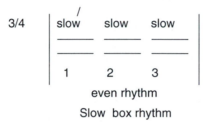

Slow box rhythm

Canter rhythm in Waltz time is a means of holding the first and second beats together so the resultant pattern is an uneven rhythm, or slow quick slow quick. It is counted 1, 3, 1, 3.

Canter rhythm

The Viennese Waltz is an even three-beat rhythm, played very fast. It is a turning pattern. There is only one step on the first beat of the measure and a pivot of the body on that foot for the two remaining counts of the measure.

Viennese rhythm

Waltz (continued)

■ Waltz Style

The Waltz is a smooth dance with a gliding quality that weaves an **even pattern** of swinging and turning movement. The first accented beat of the music is also accented in the motion. The first step of the Waltz pattern is the reaching step forward, backward, sideward, or turning. Because it is the first beat that gives the dance its new impetus, its new direction, or a change of step, there evolves a pulsating feeling, which can be seen rather markedly and is the chief characteristic of the beauty of the Waltz. This should not be interpreted as a rocking or bobbing motion of the body. On count 1, the man steps *flat* on the sole of the foot; on counts 2–3, the body rises stepping on the ball of the foot. The rising action is sometimes described as a *lift*. The "fall and rise" action of the body is seen in every step. The footwork is most effective when the foot taking the second beat glides past the standing foot as it moves into the sideward step. The feet should never be heard to scrape the floor, but should seem to float in a silent pattern. In closed position, it is important for the lady to be directly in front of the man, their shoulders parallel.

Directions are for the man, facing line of direction; lady's part is reversed, except as noted.

■ BOX STEP

(Closed position)

Steps	3/4 Counts	Style Cue
Step L forward	1	flat
Step R sideward, passing close to the L foot	2	lift
Close L to R, take weight L	3	lift
Step R backward	1	flat
Step L sideward, passing close to the R foot	2	lift
Close R to L, take weight R	3	lift

Step Cue: Forward side close/back side close.

Style: The forward step is **on the heel.** Follow through on the second beat, moving the free foot closely past the standing foot, but do not lose a beat by stopping. Body rises on counts 2, 3 as stepping on ball of foot. The floor pattern is a long narrow rectangle rather than a square box.

Floor pattern

Lead: Refer to lead indication 5, p. 384.

Note: The man must understand the concept of the forward side close as being the forward sequence of the box and the backward side close as being the back sequence of the box. This terminology will be used in future patterns.

■ BOX TURN

(Left)—(Closed position)

Steps	3/4 Counts	Style Cue
Step L forward, toe out, turning one-quarter L	1	flat
Step R sideward, gliding past the L foot	2	lift
Close L to R, taking weight L	3	lift
Step R backward, toe in, turning one-quarter L	1	flat
Step L sideward, gliding past the R foot	2	lift
Close R to L, taking weight R	3	lift
Step L forward, toe out, turning one-quarter L	1	flat
Step R sideward, gliding past the L foot	2	lift
Close L to R, taking weight on L	3	lift
Step R backward, toe in, turning one-quarter L	1	flat
Step L sideward, gliding past the R foot	2	lift
Close R to L, taking weight R	3	lift

Step Cue: Turn side close, turn side close.

Lady: The lady is taking the reverse pattern, except that, when the lady steps forward with the left foot, instead of toeing out as described for the man, she steps forward between the man's feet, her left foot next to the instep of the man's left foot. This style greatly facilitates the turn.

Fundamental Waltz Steps (continued)

Man: A common error is that the man tries to step around his partner. The lady must be directly in front of her partner.

Style: Accent the first step by reaching with a longer step. However, man must be careful not to overreach his partner. There is no unnecessary knee bending or bobbing up and down.

Lead: See lead indication 6, p. 384.

Note: For the right turn, start with the right foot. Follow the same pattern with opposite footwork.

Teaching Strategy for Changing Leads—Turn Right, Turn Left

It is important to learn to turn counterclockwise and clockwise. The foot must be free to *lead* in the direction of the turn: left lead for left turn; right lead for right turn. There are several ways to change the lead. With the left, step balance or a hesitation step, then start the box with the right foot (right side close, left side close). Another is to take two Waltz steps forward, take the third Waltz step backward; right foot is now free to turn right. To return to the left lead, either step (R) balance or take two Waltz steps forward and the third one backward; then the left foot leads again. Once the student can turn left and right, the teacher should present a definite routine that drills this change. When students learn this concept for the Waltz, they will be able to transfer the principle to other rhythms.

■ Waltz Step Variations

Hesitation Step   Weaving Step   Streamline Step
Cross Step   Twinkle Step   Viennese Waltz

■ HESITATION STEP

(Closed position)

Steps	3/4 Counts	Style Cue
Step L forward	1	flat
Bring R foot up to the instep of L and hold, no weight change	2, 3	lift
Step R backward	1	flat
Bring L foot up to the instep of R foot, no weight change	2, 3	lift

Step Cue: Step close hold.

Style: Smooth.

Lead: Refer to lead indication 11, p. 384.

Note: As in the Foxtrot, a beautiful combination is to dance two hesitation steps, then the first half of the box turn, two hesitation steps and then the second half of the turn. The hesitation step repeated may also be done turning either counterclockwise or clockwise and may be useful in maneuvering for the next step.

■ CROSS STEP

(Closed position)

Steps	3/4 Counts	Style Cue
Step L forward	1	flat
Step R sideward, turning to open position	2	lift

Close L to R, taking weight L	3	lift
Step R forward, in open position	1	flat
Step L forward, turning on L foot to face partner in closed position	2	lift
Close R to L, taking weight R	3	lift

Step Cue: Forward side close, cross side close.

Style: The position is opened to semiopen position, just enough to step forward on the inside foot, which feels like a crossing step. It should be accented by a long, smooth, reaching step on the heel, not a dipping or bobbing action.

Lead: Same as for open position and back to closed position. Refer to 7 and 8, p. 384.

Note: When man is facing out in closed position, he can go into this step and the cross pattern will travel in line of direction.

■ WEAVING STEP

Same as above but crossing from side to side. (Closed position)

Steps	3/4 Counts	Style Cue
Step L forward	1	flat
Step R sideward, turning to open position	2	lift
Close L to R, taking weight L	3	lift
Step R forward in open position	1	flat
Step L forward, turning to side by side position facing the reverse line of direction	2	lift
Close R to L, taking weight R	3	lift
Step L forward, in side by side position	1	flat
Step R forward, turning to open position	2	lift
Close L to R, taking weight L	3	lift
Step R forward in open position	1	flat
Step L forward, turning to closed position	2	lift
Close R to L, taking weight R	3	lift

Step Cue: Forward side open/cross side reverse/cross side reverse/cross side close.

Style: Reach into crossing step on the heel. It is a long reaching step on the accented beat.

Lead: Turn lady to semiopen position for first cross step and then drop right arm and lead through with the left hand to side by side position, facing the reverse line of direction. Next time, as they reverse direction, the man puts his arm around her in open position and follows standard procedure for returning to closed position.

Note: The weave pattern may be repeated back and forth, crossing as many times as desired, but should go back to closed position as described above.

■ TWINKLE STEP

(Closed position)

It is led from the back sequence of the box step.

Steps	3/4 Counts	Style Cue
Step L forward	1	flat
Step R sideward turning into R parallel position	2	lift
Close L to R, taking weight L	3	lift
Step R, diagonally forward in R parallel position	1	flat
Step L sideward, turning from R parallel to L parallel position	2	lift
Close R to L, taking weight R	3	lift
Step L diagonally forward in L parallel position	1	flat

Fundamental Waltz Steps (continued)

Step R sideward, turning from L parallel position to R parallel position	2	.... lift
Close L to R, taking weight on L	3	.... lift
Step R diagonally forward in R parallel position	1	.... flat
Step L sideward turning to closed position	2	.... lift
Close R to L, taking weight on R	3	.... lift

Step Cue: Step turn close.

Floor pattern

start

Step Cue: The second beat has a short step and a smooth roll from one position to another. The lady reaches parallel to the man's step, except that she is stepping diagonally backward, which takes a lot of practice for the lady to do it well.

Lead: Refer to lead indications 9 and 10, p. 384.

Note: Progress is in a zigzag pattern down the floor in the line of direction and may repeat over and over as desired.

Suggestions for Variations

Any student or teacher who has followed these directions this far should be prepared to make use of the advance twinkle, corté, and pivot turn described under the Foxtrot by transposing a slow, quick, quick in 4/4 time into slow, slow, slow in 3/4 time.

■ STREAMLINE STEP

(Closed position)

An advanced step seen in the International Style and competition. Dancers travel in the line of direction and need a lot of space to move. Step on every beat, each step forward. The feet are never together, always moving forward! Step flat on the first beat; body rises on counts 2–3. The floor pattern, although forward, zigs and zags. In addition to moving forward, the dancers may rock or grapevine.

Rock: Forward, backward, forward; backward, forward, backward.

Grapevine: Semiopen position, travel in line of direction.

■ VIENNESE WALTZ

The **rhythm** is three even, quick beats now instead of slow. The Viennese Waltz music is fast and it is hard to keep one's balance on the pivot step when it is slowed down, so that students get discouraged learning the step. An experiment of a half-Viennese has proved successful in getting students to learn the pivot step by doing it first on the right foot and then taking a regular Waltz step on the left sequence.

3/4	step	side	cross	step	pivot	
	1	2	3	1	2	3
	quick	quick	quick	right	pivot	

Half-Viennese step

Half-Viennese Step:

1. Both man and lady need to practice this pattern alone, traveling down line of direction.

Steps	3/4 Counts	Rhythm Cue
Step L forward, turning one-quarter counterclockwise .	1	.... quick
Step R sideward, turning one-quarter counterclockwise	2	.... quick
Slide the L foot, heel first, in across R to the R of the R foot. Transfer weight to L foot. Both toes are facing the reverse line of direction, feet are crossed	3	.... quick
Step R backward and pivot one-half counterclockwise on the R foot	1	.... quick
Bring the L foot up to the instep of the R foot and with the L toe help balance on the R foot	2, 3	.... quick quick

2. Closed position, the man facing the line of direction.

Steps	3/4 Counts	Rhythm Cue
Starting L, the man takes the step side cross while ..... the lady, starting R, takes the back pivot .... }	1, 2, 3	.... all quick
Starting R, the man takes the back pivot while .... the lady, starting L, takes step side across .... }	1, 2, 3	.... all quick

Style: The couple remains in closed position throughout. The steps are small as the lady is turning on a small pivot base while the man takes step side cross. Since the man turns one-quarter on his forward step, his second step is in line of direction, a small step and cross on third beat. Then he steps back a short step and pivots while lady takes the step side cross. The dancers always progress in the line of direction. Use two Waltz steps for one complete turn. The body resistance is firm for both man and lady. They must lean away, pressing outward but keeping the center of gravity over the pivoting feet. The shoulders tilt slightly in one direction and then the other; tilt left as the left foot leads, right as the right foot leads. Do not resist the momentum of body weight, but rather give into the momentum.

Lead: Firm body and arms in correct position. The momentum comes from the rapid transfer of the body forward in the line of direction every time on count 1.

Cue: 1, 2, 3, 1, 2, 3.

Viennese Step:

3. The true Viennese with a step pivot repeated over and over is in closed dance position. Man starting L forward, lady R backward.

Steps	3/4 Counts	Rhythm Cue
Step L forward, pivoting on the ball of the foot one-half counterclockwise; the right foot coming up to the instep of the L and with the R toe, helps to balance on the L foot	1, 2, 3	.... all quick
Step R backward, pivoting on the ball of the foot one-half counterclockwise; the L foot coming to the instep of the R helps to balance on the R foot	1, 2, 3	.... all quick

Step Cue: Step pivot, step pivot.

Style: There is a lift of the body going into the pivot, which lifts the body weight, momentarily allowing the feet to pivot with less weight. Take care not to throw the weight off balance.

Lead: Same as before.

Variations: The hesitation step as given under the box pattern is very helpful in giving a rest from the constant turning. Also, by using an uneven number of hesitation steps, the right foot is free and the whole Viennese turn may be changed to a clockwise turn starting with the right foot and applying the pattern with opposite footwork.

🎵 Waltz Combos

These Waltz routines are combinations for practice, listed from simple to complex. (Closed position, unless otherwise indicated.)

1. *Balance and Box*
   2 balance steps
   (forward, backward)
   4 box steps
2. *Waltz Box*
   1 box step
   2 forward Waltz steps
   1 box turn
3. *Cross Box and Turn*
   2 cross steps
   1 box turn

4. *Hesitation and Box Turn*
   2 hesitation steps
   (forward, backward)
   1 box turn
5. *Cross Step and Weaving*
   2 cross steps
   1 weaving step
6. *Advanced Combo*
   1 box turn
   4 twinkle steps
   2 hesitation steps
   2 pursuit Waltz steps
   1 corté
   1 forward Waltz step

7. *Advanced Combo*
   6 streamline steps (18 beats)
   2 twinkle steps
   4 streamline steps
   2 hesitation steps

❧ Tango

The Argentine cowboy dance known as the *Tango* has won itself an accepted place in our modern-day Social Dance. Like all dance forms, the Tango has been through much evolution and adaptation from its earlier and more sensuous form as a gaucho dance. The American version of the Tango comes to us via Paris, and it is entirely possible that the Argentine cowboy would have a difficult time recognizing this creation as it is performed today.

The Tango has undergone more changes than any of the other Ballroom Dances. Each change has resulted in gradual loss of many of the Tango's Latin characteristics. However, in losing some of its original features, it has gained a thrilling smoothness, and it is one of the most beautiful dances on the ballroom floor. The Tango has a sophistication and suave style that cannot be matched. Its slow, accented glide and the contrasting excitement of the Tango close are enhanced by unusually beautiful musical accompaniment. Its variations include the corté, the fans, the flares, and the rock steps.

Teaching the Tango is one of the greater thrills in teaching Ballroom Dance. The Tango style is appealing and the feeling of the unique figures is exciting. A dancer has a sense of real accomplishment in being able to dance the Tango. Students take a great pride in learning it. Experience with the Tango develops confidence and poise in the dancer, which often carry over into the Foxtrot and the other Ballroom Dances in general.

■ Tango Rhythm

The modern Tango is written in both 2/4 and 4/4 time. Here it will be presented 2/4 time.

The Tango rhythm is a deliberate accented beat that is easily distinguished. Few dancers have trouble following the Tango rhythm. There is a calculated contrast between the slow promenade beats of the first measure and the staccato of the Tango break in the second measure.

■ Tango Style

The Tango is characterized by a deliberate glide, not sliding the foot on the floor, but a long reach from the hip with a catlike smoothness and placement of the ball of the foot on the floor. The knees remain straight. The break, which is quick quick slow, is a sudden contrast ending in the subtle draw of the feet together. It is this combination of slow gliding beats and the sharp break that makes the Tango distinctive. Restraint is achieved by the use of continuous flow of movements and a controlled, stylized break presenting disciplined and sophisticated style, instead of a comic caricature. The dancer should strive to effect the idea of floating. Care should be taken to avoid the look of stiffness. Since the long reaching glide is used, the feet should pass each other close together. The draw in the Tango close is executed slowly, taking the full length of the slow beat to bring the feet together and then sweep quickly into the beginning of the basic rhythm again. The lady should synchronize the action of her drawing step with that of the man. The body and head are carried high and the lady's left hand, instead of being on the man's shoulder as in other dances, reaches around the man at his right shoulder-blade level. The fingers of the hand are straight and the arm is in a straight line from the elbow to the tip of the fingers.

Once in a while, deliberately move the shoulders forward in opposition to the feet. For example, stepping left, the right shoulder moves forward. The fan steps, most glamorous of all tango patterns, turn, whip, or swirl in a most exciting, subtle way. The fan style is described in detail with the variations used.

Fundamental Tango Steps

Directions are for the man, facing the line of direction; the lady's part is reversed, except as noted.

■ BASIC TANGO STEP

(Closed position)

A combination of the promenade or walking step and the break.

Steps	2/4 Counts	Rhythm Cue
Step L forward	1	slow
Step R forward	2	slow
Step L in place	1	quick
Step R sideward abruptly	*and*	quick
Draw L to R, weight remains on R	2	slow

Step Cue: Slow slow Tango close.

S   S   Q   Q   S

Floor pattern

start

Style: The slow beats are long, smooth, gliding steps. The feet pass each other closely. The break quick quick slow is in place or slightly forward.

Lead: Man must draw to the right with right hand and elbow to guide the lady in the break step.

Note: This step repeats each time from the man's left foot, because there is no change of weight on the draw. This pattern will tend to carry the couple outward toward the wall. It immediately becomes necessary to know how to vary the step in order to counteract this action. Open position, right parallel position, or quarter-turn all may be used for this purpose.

■ Tango Step Variations

Open Position Basic Tango	Half-Turn Clockwise	Right Parallel Basic Tango
The Box Step	Quarter-Turn	The Corté
Cross Step and Quarter-Turn	Open Fan	Half-Turn Counterclockwise

■ OPEN POSITION BASIC TANGO

(Closed position)

Steps	2/4 Counts	Rhythm Cue
Step L into open position, turning abruptly	1	slow
Step R forward, in open position	2	slow
Step L forward, a short step, pivoting on L foot abruptly to face partner in closed position	1	quick
Step R sideward, in closed position	*and*	quick
Draw L to R, no change of weight	2	slow

Step Cue: Open step close side draw.

Style: The abrupt turning to open position on the first slow step and the turn back to closed position are sharp and only a firmness in the body can accomplish this.

Lead: Refer to leads 7 and 8, p. 384. The lead is sudden and on the first slow beat.

■ RIGHT PARALLEL BASIC TANGO

(Closed position)

Steps	2/4 Counts	Rhythm Cue
Step L diagonally into R parallel position turning abruptly	1	slow
Step L forward	2	slow
Step L a short step forward, turning abruptly to closed dance position	1	quick
Step R sideward	*and*	quick
Draw L to R, no change of weight	2	slow

Step Cue: Parallel step close side draw.

Style: Right parallel travels diagonally forward; lady's foot reaches parallel to man's left foot. The second slow is an exaggerated reaching step forward.

Lead: Refer to lead 9, p. 384. A lift of right arm is given on the first slow beat.

■ QUARTER-TURN

(Closed position)

Steps	2/4 Counts	Rhythm Cue
Step L forward	1	slow
Step R forward	2	slow
Step L, turning one-quarter counterclockwise	1	quick
Step R sideward	*and*	quick
Draw L to R, no change of weight	2	slow

■ CROSS STEP AND QUARTER-TURN

(Closed position)

Steps	2/4 Counts	Rhythm Cue
Step L sideward	1	slow
Step R across in front of L, take weight R	2	slow
Step L sideward, turn toe out, turn one-quarter counterclockwise	1	quick
Step R sideward	*and*	quick
Draw L to R, no change of weight	2	slow

Fundamental Tango Steps (continued)

Step Cue: Side cross turn side close.

Style: All of this pattern is taken in closed position. The turn actually begins by a pivot on the crossing foot at the end of the second slow beat.

Lead: As above for quarter-turn.

■ HALF-TURN COUNTERCLOCKWISE

(Closed position)

Steps	2/4 Counts	Rhythm Cue
Step L into open position, turning abruptly	1	slow
Step R forward, a short step, pivoting one-quarter counterclockwise on the R foot; bring up R arm and turn the lady around the man a three-quarter turn to closed position	2	slow
Step L bringing L foot next to R foot	1	quick
Step R sideward	and	quick
Draw L to R, no weight change	2	slow

Step Cue: Step pivot break side draw.

Style: The lady pivots counterclockwise on her left foot (second slow beat) around the man a three-quarter turn into closed position. The lady's step on this beat was a longer step than the man's, giving her freedom to pivot. She must bring her first quick step with R foot alongside of left foot.

Lead: Man must bring up his right arm and elbow firmly, almost lifting her so that she can pivot easily on her left foot on the second slow beat.

■ HALF-TURN CLOCKWISE

(Closed position)

Steps	2/4 Counts	Rhythm Cue
Step L into open position, turning abruptly	1	slow
Step R forward, a long step, pivoting one-half clockwise on the R foot around the lady into closed position	2	slow
Step L sideward, a short step apart from where R foot is at the end of the pivot	1	quick
Step R sideward	and	quick
Draw L to R, no weight change	2	slow

Step Cue: Step pivot break side draw.

Style: The man smoothly pivots on his right foot clockwise about halfway around the lady. The lady turns clockwise in place on her left foot. This step is very easy for the lady.

Lead: Refer to lead indications 7 and 8, p. 384, for open and closed position. The main lead is increased resistance in hand, arm, and body as the man pivots halfway around the lady.

■ THE BOX STEP

The rhythm of the Tango box step is like that described in the Foxtrot—slow quick quick—forward side close, back side close. The Tango gliding action will be used on the first slow beat. The box step variations for Foxtrot may also be used here, including the box turn and the grapevine step.

■ THE CORTÉ

The corté is a dip, most often taken backward on the man's left or right foot. It is a type of break step used to finish off almost any Tango variation and is used as an ending to the dance. The skilled dancer will learn to use the corté in relationship to the music of the tango so that the feeling of the corté will correspond to the climax or the phrase of the musical accompaniment.

The left corté will be described here. A right corté may be taken by starting on the right foot and reversing the pattern. There is nearly always a preliminary step used as preparation for going into the corté. It is described here as a part of the rhythm of the corté.

■ PREPARATION STEP

Steps	2/4 Counts	Rhythm Cue
Step forward L, a short step	1	quick
Shift weight back onto R	*and*	quick

CORTÉ

Steps	2/4 Counts	Rhythm Cue
Step L backward, take weight, and bend L knee slightly	2	slow
Recover forward, take weight R	1	slow
Step L in place beside R	2	quick
Step R in place beside L	*and*	quick

Step Cue: Rock and dip recover quick quick.
Q   Q   S   S   Q   Q

Style: As the *man* steps backward into the corté, the weight is all taken on the standing foot with a bent knee. The man should turn his bent knee slightly outward so that the lady's knee will not bump his as they go into the dip. His left shoulder and arm move forward (the left leg and left shoulder are in opposition). His back should remain straight. He should avoid leaning either backward or forward. His right foot should be extended (arched) so that the toe is only touching the floor.

The *lady* should step forward on the right, arch her back, and place all of her weight over the forward right foot. The right knee is bent. The left leg is extended behind and should be a straight line from hip to toe. A bent line makes the whole figure sag. The left arch of the foot should be extended so that the toe is pointed and remains in contact with the floor. If the lady steps forward too far or does not bend the forward knee, she will be forced to bend at the waist, which destroys the form of the figure. She may look back over her left shoulder.

The execution of the dip should be as smooth as any slow backward step. The man should avoid leaping or falling back into the dip.

Lead: The left shoulder leads forward as the man goes into the preparation step on the first beat. There is an increase of tension of the man's right arm and hand also on the first beat plus general resistance throughout the upper body. The man will draw the lady with his right arm when stepping into the dip and release on the recovery step. The lead is essential for the corté as the pattern cannot be executed correctly unless both man and lady are completely on balance and ready for it.

Note: The recovery step is followed by two quick steps left right, which finish count 2 and complete the measure of music. These may be omitted when they follow a variation that takes up those extra counts.

Learn the footwork first, then work on the style.

Fundamental Tango Steps (continued)

■ FAN STEP

The fan is a term used to describe a manner of executing a leg motion, in which the free leg swings in a whiplike movement around a small pivoting base. This should not be a large sweeping movement in a wide arc but rather a small subtle action initiated in the hip and executed with the legs close together. The balance is carefully poised over the pivoting foot at all times. When the man and lady take the fan motion, the action is taken parallel to partner; that is, the right leg, which is free, swings forward. When it reaches its full extension, just barely off the floor, the right hip turns the leg over, knee down, while pivoting on the standing foot to face the opposite direction. The right leg then swings through forward and the weight is taken on the right foot. This action usually is done in slow rhythm. Accompanying the hip action there is also a lift and turn on the ball of the standing foot. This lift permits the free leg to swing through gracefully extended and close in a beautiful floating style.

■ OPEN FAN

(Open position)

Steps	2/4 Counts	Rhythm Cue
Step L forward	1	slow
Step R forward	2	slow
Step L in place, releasing R arm around lady, and turn halfway around to the right to a side-by-side position with lady on man's L	1	quick
Step R sideward, a short step	and	quick
Draw L to R, no weight change (the man's L hand is holding the lady's R)	2	slow
Step forward L	1	quick
Swing the R leg forward, pivoting on L foot while fanning the R, coming halfway around to open position	and	quick
Step forward R in open position	2	slow
Step L forward, pivoting toward the lady into closed position	1	quick
Step R sideward	and	quick
Draw L to R, no weight change	2	slow

Step Cue: Slow slow open side draw/fan through break side draw.

Style: When the man releases his arm around her, the lady turns halfway around to the left. On the fan, the lady steps right, swings left leg forward, hip turns over, knee faces down. Foot is kept close to the floor and sweeps through pivoting clockwise to open position, and weight is transferred forward onto left foot. She then goes into break step with partner.

Lead: The man drops his right arm and pulls away from the lady to side-by-side position. Then, with his left hand, he pulls in as he fans through to open position and from there lifts his right arm into closed position for Tango close.

Note: This is an easy beginner step in fan style and gives them the thrill of the Tango.

Tango Combos

The Tango routines are combinations for practice, listed from simple to complex. (Closed position, unless otherwise indicated.)

1. *Basic*
   2 basic steps
   1 basic step (open position)
2. *Basic, Cross Step*
   2 basic steps
   4 cross steps and quarter-turn
3. *Box, Basic, Cross Step*
   2 box steps
   1 basic step
   1 cross step and quarter-turn

4. *Basic, Cross, Corté*
   2 basics
   1 cross step, quarter-turn
   1 corté
5. *Advanced Combo*
   2 box steps
   1 basic
   1 cross step
   open fan

6. *Advanced Combo*
   2 basics
   open fan
   half-turn clockwise
   corté
   1 basic

✤ Cha Cha Cha

A Cuban innovation of the old basic Latin form (danson), the *Cha Cha Cha* is said to be a combination of the Mambo and American Swing. A close look shows its rhythm to be that of a Triple Mambo, its style that of the Rumba, and its open swingy variations that of the Triple Lindy. It does not have as heavy a quality or as large a foot pattern as the Mambo; nor has it the smooth sophistication or the conservative figures of the Rumba. It reflects a light, breezy mood, a carefree gaiety, and a trend, in the challenge steps, for dancers to ad-lib variations to their heart's content. Consequently one sees variations in almost every known position.

■ Cha Cha Cha Rhythm

In 4/4 time, the catchy rhythm and delightful music of the Cha Cha Cha have brought dancers and musicians alike a new treat in the undeniably Latin flavor. The rhythm has been a controversy. Originally it was done on the offbeat of the measure, and then there was a widespread acceptance of the onbeat rhythm, which is the easier way, but again the trend is to go back to the offbeat rhythm. Analysis in this edition will be done with the offbeat rhythm.

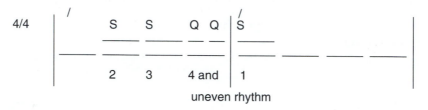

The rhythm is an uneven beat pattern of slow slow quick quick slow and will be counted 2 3 4 *and* 1, with the 4 *and* 1 being the familiar Cha Cha Cha triple. Rhythmically the beats are as follows:

Note that the last beat of the triple is a quarter note, not an eighth note as is sometimes misinterpreted.

■ Cha Cha Cha Style

The Cha Cha Cha is seen danced in a variety of positions as it moves in and out of the variations. However, the three basic positions are closed position, face-to-face position, and challenge position (which is completely apart from but facing partner). Beginners like the facing position with two hands joined. The lady holds her arms up with the elbows just in front of her body. The hands are up, fingers pointing inward. The man reaches over the top of the lady's forefingers and grasps her fingers with his fingers and thumb. The lady exerts a little resistance against his fingers. Both man and lady hold the forearms firm so that the man can push, pull, or turn her, and she responds, not with arm motion or shoulder rotation, but with body motion forward, back, or turning. The arm and hand, when free, are **held up parallel to the floor in bent-arm position** and they turn with the body as it moves.

The Cha Cha Cha, with its light bouncy quality, is delightfully Latin as it carries with it some of the subtleness of the Rumba movement. The forward foot should be placed nearly flat on the floor. The knee is bent over the stepping foot. The back step (instead of a flat step that tends to give the appearance of a sag) is a toe step, holding the body firmly so as to avoid the sag. The Cha Cha Cha triple is taken with very small steps in place or traveling but is kept close to the floor. The upper body is held comfortably upright and the head focuses on one's partner in a typical gracious Latin manner. The eye contact brings the dance to life.

🎶 Fundamental Cha Cha Cha Steps 🎶

Directions are for man, facing line of direction; lady's part is reverse, except as noted.

■ BACK BASIC STEP

(Challenge or Two hands joined)

Steps	4/4 Counts	Rhythm Cue
Step L sideways (preliminary step)	1	slow
Step R backward	2	slow
Step L forward in place	3	slow
Step R in place next to L	4	quick (cha)
Step L in place	and	quick (cha)
Step R in place	1	slow (cha)

Note: There is a side step on the accented first beat to begin the dance only and it is not used again.

■ FORWARD BASIC STEP

Steps	4/4 Counts	Rhythm Cue
Step L forward	2	slow
Step R back in place	3	slow
Step L in place next to R	4	quick (cha)
Step R in place	and	quick (cha)
Step L in place	1	slow (cha)

Step Cue: Back forward Cha Cha Cha/forward back Cha Cha Cha.

Style: The back basic has the toe step, the forward basic has the flat style (see Cha Cha Cha style). Dancers have a tendency to pound the feet on the floor for the Cha Cha Cha. It should be neither a pounding nor scuffing sound.

Lead: The man leads by pulling with his right hand going into the back basic or pushing with the left hand going into the forward basic. If arm and elbow are firm, finger resistance aids in getting the message across. The body should respond by moving backward or forward.

Position: The basic Cha Cha Cha may be done in closed, facing, or challenge position.

Note: This is the basic step of Cha Cha Cha. The forward half is also called the "forward break"; the back half is the "back break." They may be used with either foot leading when called for in a particular variation. Sometimes the Cha Cha Cha part of the step is used to travel rather than being in place.

■ Cha Cha Cha Step Variations

Open Break	Cross Over Turn	Jody Break	Kick Swivel
Cross Over	Chase Half-Turn	Reverse Jody	Kick Freeze
	Full Turn	Shadow	

■ OPEN BREAK

(Two hands joined or Closed position)

The purpose of the break is to change position from face to face to side by side. The couple may open to either right or left. The right break is described next.

Fundamental Cha Cha Cha Steps (continued)

■ RIGHT BREAK

Steps	4/4 Counts	Rhythm Cue
Step R backward, releasing R hand hold with lady ..	2	slow
Step L forward in place	3	slow
Step R in place, turning one-quarter clockwise to face R in a side-by-side position	4	quick
Step L in place	*and*	quick
Step R in place	1	slow

Step Cue: Break open turn Cha Cha Cha.

Style: The released hand and arm remain up in place and turn with the body.

Lead: The man releases right hand for right turn, left hand for left turn, and guides through to the side-by-side position with the other joined hand. As the man does this, the lady should exert slight resistance against his arm with her arm or wrist to facilitate following forthcoming leads in side-by-side position.

Note: The left break will start forward with the left foot and turn one-quarter left.

■ CROSS OVER

(Side-by-side position, having taken the open break to the right)

Man's left is holding lady's right hand. Start with the inside foot (man's left, lady's right).

Steps	4/4 Counts	Rhythm Cue
Step L forward	2	slow
Step R back in place	3	slow
Step L in place, turning to face lady, and release her R hand	4	quick
Step R in place, still turning on around, take lady's L hand	*and*	quick
Step L in place, finishing a half-turn to face opposite direction in side-by-side position	1	slow

Repeat, starting with the inside foot (man's right, lady's left) and turning back to starting position.

Step Cue: Forward turn Cha Cha Cha.

Style: On the forward step, the inside foot should step straight ahead. The body is upright and the head is looking over the inside shoulder at partner. The free hand is up. Avoid bouncing, leaning forward, turning back on partner, or looking at the floor.

Lead: The man's inside hand guides forward into the forward step and pulls back to start the turn. If the arms of both man and lady remain up when turning, the arms are ready to receive the lead when changing from one hand to the other.

Note: If the open break was taken to the left side, then the cross over step will begin with the inside foot (man's right, lady's left). The cross over step may be repeated from side to side any number of times.

■ RETURN TO BASIC

(Side-by-side position, facing right starting with the inside foot)

Steps	4/4 Counts	Rhythm Cue
Step L forward	2	slow
Step R backward in place, turning to face partner ...	3	slow
Step L, R, L in place taking both of the lady's hands	4 and 1	quick quick slow
With R foot now free, go into a back basic		

■ RETURN TO BASIC

(Side-by-side position, facing left starting with the inside foot)

Steps	4/4 Counts	Rhythm Cue
Step R forward	2	slow
Step L backward in place, turning to face partner	3	slow
Step R, L, R, in place taking both of the lady's hands	4 and 1	quick quick slow
With the L foot now free, go into a forward basic		

Lead: If the man uses pressure against the lady's fingers of the hand he holds just before he takes both hands, she will recognize the intent to go back to basic and will facilitate the transition.

■ CROSS OVER TURN

(Side by side, facing left, starting with the inside foot [man's right, lady's left])

Steps	4/4 Counts	Rhythm Cue
Step R forward, turning counterclockwise away from the lady about halfway around	2	slow
Step L in place, continuing to turn counterclockwise, completing the turn around to face the lady	3	slow
Bring feet together and hold	4 and 1	quick quick slow
Free the L foot and step into a forward basic on count 2		

Step Cue: Out around *hold* Cha Cha Cha/forward step Cha Cha Cha.

Style: A smooth spin on the ball of the foot is taken on counts 2 and 3 and then a sudden hold during the Cha Cha Cha part gives this variation a bit of special pizazz. It is necessary to count the timing carefully so as to step forward into basic again on count 2. The lady is turning clockwise.

Lead: The man, knowing he is going into the cross over turn, will not grasp the lady's hand as he comes through from the other side but will place the heel of his hand against the back of her hand and push out slightly into the turn. He must then direct her into a back basic as he steps into his forward basic.

Note: Of course, the turn may be taken from either side. The man may use this variation as a lead into challenge position, in which case he will not rejoin hands with partner but will remain apart, facing partner.

Fundamental Cha Cha Cha Steps (continued)

■ CHASE HALF-TURN

(Challenge position or Two hands joined)

It is a turning figure in which the man is always one turn ahead of the lady. He will start the turn while she takes a back basic. On her next forward basic she starts the turn. After the desired number of turns he will finish with a forward basic while she completes her last turn to face him. The forward break is used with alternating feet for all turns.

Steps	4/4 Counts	Rhythm Cue
Man's Part		
Step L forward, turning clockwise on both feet		
halfway around with back to lady	2	slow
Take weight on R foot	3	slow
Step L, R, L in place	4 *and* 1	quick quick slow
Step R forward, turning counterclockwise a		
half-turn, on both feet, to face lady's back	2	slow
Take weight on L foot	3	slow
Step R, L, R in place	4 *and* 1	quick quick slow
Lady's Part		
Step R backward	2	slow
Step L forward in place	3	slow
Step R, L, R in place	4 *and* 1	quick quick slow
Step L forward, turning clockwise on both feet		
halfway around with back to man	2	slow
Take weight on R foot	3	slow
Step L, R, L in place	4 *and* 1	quick quick slow

Step Cue: Turn about Cha Cha Cha.

Style: The turn about is called a swivel turn and is done with both feet in an apart position. The step is forward, the swivel turns toward the back foot, with the weight on the balls of the feet. There is a cocky manner as man and lady look over the shoulder at partner.

Lead: The man drops both hands when stepping forward left foot, and the rest is a visual lead for the lady. She keeps turning if he does. When the man wishes to go back to basic, he will take a forward basic while she does her last turn and then rejoin hands and go into a back basic on the right foot.

Note: The half-turn may be done again and again. A familiar styling is to tap partner's shoulder when facing partner's back.

■ FULL TURN

(Challenge position)

Step L forward, pivoting clockwise a half-turn. Step right in place, again pivoting clockwise a half-turn. Take Cha Cha Cha in place, facing partner.

Lead: The lead is a visual one, having let go of hands to start the turn and taking the hands to finish it.

Style: The manner is a bit cocky as each looks over the shoulder at partner. The pivoting steps are small and on the ball of the foot for good balance and smoothness.

Note: The man will make a complete turn while she does a back basic, and then she follows with a complete turn while he does a back basic.

■ JODY BREAK

(Two hands joined)

Steps	4/4 Counts	Rhythm Cue

Step L backward, and at the same time changing hands from a two-hand grasp to a right-hand grasp .... 2 .... slow

Step R forward, and at the same time pull with the R hand to guide the lady into a counterclockwise turn .... 3 .... slow

Take Cha Cha Cha (L, R, L) in place, guiding the lady into Varsouvienne position (see p. 51) beside the man .... 4 *and* 1 .... quick quick slow

Step R backward in Varsouvienne position .... 2 .... slow

Step L forward in place and, at the same time, release the left hand and guide the lady with the R hand to turn clockwise .... 3 .... slow

Take Cha Cha Cha (R, L, R) in place, guiding the lady back out to original position, facing man completing half-turn clockwise .... 4 *and* 1 .... quick quick slow

Note: This may be repeated over and over without changing the right-hand grasp. When the man desires to go back to regular basic, he will change to two-hand grasp and forward basic when the lady returns to facing position.

Lady's Part: Starting right foot into regular back break.

Step R backward, allowing man to change from two-hand grasp to a R-hand grasp .... 2 .... slow

Step L forward, toeing out and pivoting on L counterclockwise, being guided by man's lead toward Varsouvienne position .... 3 .... slow

Take Cha Cha Cha (R, L, R), finishing the turn into Varsouvienne position beside the man .... 4 *and* 1 .... quick quick slow

Step L backward in Varsouvienne position .... 2 .... slow

Step R forward, toeing out and pivoting on the R clockwise, being guided by the man's lead towards the original facing position .... 3 .... slow

Take Cha Cha Cha (L, R, L) in place finishing the turn to face partner .... 4 *and* 1 .... quick quick slow

Step Cue: Back forward Cha Cha Cha.

Style: Both man and lady should keep steps small and not get too far apart. Large steps and big movement spoil the beauty of this lovely figure and make it awkward to maneuver.

Lead: Arm tension control makes it possible for the man's lead to guide the lady smoothly in and out of Varsouvienne position.

■ VARIATIONS FROM JODY POSITION

(Also called Varsouvienne position)

1. **Reverse Jody:** While in Varsouvienne position, both break back on the inside foot, and while stepping forward turn one-half clockwise in place to reverse Varsouvienne, with the lady on the left of the man, and take Cha Cha Cha in place. Repeat, starting with the inside foot, and turn counterclockwise to end up in original position. This may be repeated any number of times. Steps are very small. Both partners are using back break continuously.
2. **Shadow:** While in Varsouvienne position, both break on the inside foot, then releasing the Varsouvienne grasp, step forward, the man guiding the lady across in front of him. Take the Cha Cha Cha, finishing the cross over, and catch inside hands. Lady is to left of man. Repeat, starting with the inside foot and crossing the lady in front of the man to a hand-grasp position on his right. This may be repeated any number of times. Return to Varsouvienne position with the lady on the right when ready to go back to a facing position and back to a regular basic.

Fundamental Cha Cha Cha Steps (continued)

Style: In the shadow, couples do not get farther apart than a bent-elbow control. The footwork in the apart position changes on count 2 to a back-cross style; that is, the inside foot crosses behind the standing foot. The action of the changing sides with partner is done on the Cha Cha Cha beats like a running motion.

Step Cue: Cross step Cha Cha Cha.

Lead: The man leads with his fingers, pulling her on count 4.

Note: The man may lead the lady across in front of him or in back of him.

■ KICK SWIVEL

(Two hands joined)

Steps	4/4 Counts	Rhythm Cue
Step L sideward	2	slow
Kick R across in front of L	3	slow
Put both feet together and swivel both toes to the R and then both heels to the R	4 *and* 1	slow slow
Repeat stepping R sideward	2	slow
Kick L across in front of R	3	slow
Put both feet together and swivel both toes to the L and then both heels to the L	4 *and* 1	slow slow

Return to basic from either side by using the free foot, if left to lead a forward basic, if right to lead a back basic.

Step Cue: Step kick swivel swivel.

Style: Dancers should take small steps. Keep the kick low and take the swivel steps with the feet and knees close together. One may bend the knees slightly. The man and lady kick in the same direction.

Lead: The man pulls both of the lady's hands in the direction of the step kick, and then he puts the hands close together and gives a push-pull action for the swivel. Part of the lead the lady picks up visually.

Note: The two swivel steps take the place of the three cha cha cha steps and are even rhythm, being the equivalent of counts 4, 1.

■ KICK FREEZE

(Facing position or Closed position)

Steps	4/4 Counts	Rhythm Cue
Step L sideward	2	slow
Kick R across in front of L	3	slow
Touch R foot sideward to the R in a stride position (no weight change); count 4—hold count 1	4, 1	slow slow
Step R, L, R, moving to the R without changing position	2 *and* 3	quick quick slow
Repeat on the same foot	4, 1, 2, 3, 4, *and* 1	

Step Cue: The posture on the freeze straightens to be extra firm and holds with the leg extended sideward. Arms extend sideward to butterfly position. The body may turn slightly to the right during the Cha Cha Cha but should end up facing partner.

Lead: The man pulls both of the lady's hands in the direction of the kick and then suddenly increases tension as arms and legs swing to freeze position. They hold the position 1 beat. Then he releases pressure and leads sideward for the quick slow beats.

Note: The freeze is on counts 4, 1. These are two extra counts added to the regular pattern. It is best to take the kick freeze twice in order to make it fit rhythmically with the music. Return to basic by leading into a back basic with the right foot.

Cha Cha Cha Combos

The Cha Cha Cha routines are combinations for practice, listed from simple to complex. (Partners facing, unless otherwise indicated.)

1. *Open Break and Cross Over*
   2 forward and back basics with
     open break
   4 cross overs
2. *Cross Over With Turn*
   2 basics with open break
   3 cross overs and turn
   repeat
3. *Cross Over and Freeze*
   2 basics with open break
   2 cross overs
   2 freeze
   1 cross over and turn

4. *Basic and Chase*
   2 basics
   4 half turns
   2 full turns
5. *Basic and Jody*
   2 basics
   4 jody breaks

6. *Jody Variations*
   2 basics
   jody break
   2 double jody
   2 shadow
7. *Basic and Kick Freeze*
   2 basics (closed position)
   2 kick freeze

🌀 Rumba

The Latin American dances are to American dancing what garlic is to the good cook. Used sparingly, they can add a tangy interest to our dancing. The *Rumba* is a Cuban dance (along with the Mambo, Bolero, and Cha Cha Cha) but it has enjoyed greater popularity than any of the others, probably because of its slower, more relaxed, smoother style. The music is usually identified by the tantalizing rhythms of the percussion instruments known as the maracas, which carry the continuous quick beat, and the sticks or bongo drum, which beat out the accented rhythm of the dance.

■ Rumba Rhythm

The Rumba is written in 4/4 time and is played both fast and slow. Many Americans prefer the slower Bolero-type tempo, but actually in the Latin American countries the rumba is danced considerably faster. The rhythm is tricky as it is a 1 2 3, 1 2 3, 1 2 count in 4/4 time.

It was taught in the United States for many years as a quick quick slow rhythm, but it has gradually shifted over to a slow quick quick beat with the accent on the first and third beats of the measure. This is the rhythm that will be used in this text.

Rumba music has a subtle, beautiful melody with a rolling quality that requires the subtle rolling Rumba movement. It is seldom mistaken for the Cha Cha Cha or mambo music because of its smoothness and continuity.

■ Rumba Style

Naturally, in the transition, the Rumba lost a lot of its original character. The style has been greatly exaggerated and distorted at times. Some people dance it like the Foxtrot, without attempting to get any of the Cuban flavor. It is hoped that dancers will feel sufficiently challenged to put in a little extra time in order to get the feeling of the subtle, continuous, rolling motion. Three characteristics make it different from other dances:

1. The action is in the feet and the knees.
2. There is a delayed shift of weight.
3. The upper body is upright and quiet, with a focus on one's partner.

The step itself is comparatively short and flat-footed, with the knee leading. The weight tends to be maintained over the heel of the foot more than in any other dance. The Cuban Rumba movement is a springlike action, resulting from placing the left foot on the floor first, without taking weight but with a bent knee. This is followed by pressing the weight into the floor and straightening the left knee. Accompanying this press into the floor there is a smooth roll of the weight being shifted to that left foot. The right knee begins to bend and leads the right foot, then free of weight, into its new position. The roll is completed as the weight is transferred gradually to the newly placed right foot. Then the entire action is repeated by pressing the weight into the right foot and straightening the right knee rolling smoothly. As the left foot is freed of weight, the knee leads, shifting the left foot to its new position with the weight coming over it, completing the roll.

The knees should be bent directly over the foot, and the feet should be placed with the toes pointing straight ahead. A pigeon-toed effect should be avoided. As the feet pass each other, the steps are small and close together, with the toes pointed straight ahead in the line of direction. The movement of the hips is merely the subtle result of the specific action of the feet and the knees. There should be no intentional swinging of the hip from side to side. There needs to be a stabilization of the upper trunk at the waist in order to keep it easily upright and the shoulders straight.

The head is held with the focus constantly on one's partner. The arm and hand, when free from partner, are held in a bent-elbow position, waist level, palm down. The man does not hold his partner close. There is seldom any body contact.

The Rumba, with its open and encircling patterns, is generally danced within a small space and reflects a dignified, although flirtatious, quality.

Teaching Suggestions for Rumba Style

First, practice the motion described above, moving forward in a slow, slow rhythm, working to achieve the feeling of the roll. Practice in front of a mirror is usually helpful. Second, practice the same motion forward in a slow quick quick rhythm (Cuban walk). Third, practice the motion as in the box step. Finally, practice with partner in closed dance position.

✿ Fundamental Rumba Steps

Directions are for the man, facing line of direction; lady's part is reversed, except as noted.

■ Basic Rumba Steps

■ CUBAN WALK

Steps	4/4 Counts	Rhythm Cue
Place L forward, roll weight slowly onto L	1–2	.... slow
Place R forward, roll weight quickly onto R	3	.... quick
Place L forward, roll weight quickly onto L	4	.... quick

Step Cue: Place—roll roll roll.

1 - 2   3   4

Style: The roll is the springlike action of pressing into the floor. The knee of the free foot bends and leads the foot into its new position, followed by the transfer of weight to that foot.

Note: The Cuban walk step is used for all moving variations when not in closed position. It may move forward, backward, or in a circle.

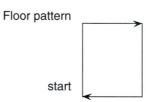

■ BOX STEP

(Closed position)

Steps	4/4 Counts	Rhythm Cue
Place L forward, roll weight slowly onto L	1–2	.... slow
Place R sideward, roll weight quickly onto R	3	.... quick
Place L close to R, roll weight quickly to L	4	.... quick
Place R backward, roll weight slowly onto R	1–2	.... slow
Place L sideward, roll weight quickly onto L	3	.... quick
Place R close to L, roll weight quickly onto R	4	.... quick

Step Cue: Forward side close/back side close.

Floor pattern

start

Style: The knee leads each step. The feet are placed flat on the floor, in a small box pattern.

Lead: Refer to lead indication 5, p. 384.

Note: Students need to understand that this forward, side, close constitutes the forward sequence or forward basic and that back, side, close constitutes the back sequence or back basic. These will be referred to in the variations.

■ Rumba Step Variations

Box Turn	Circular Turn	Bolero Break	Varsouvienne Break
Flirtation Break	Parallel Turn	Walk Around	
Side by Side		Parallel Turn	
		Circular Turn	

■ BOX TURN

(Closed position)

The Rumba box step is the same foot pattern as the Westchester box step in the Foxtrot. The box turn will follow the same pattern as the Foxtrot box turn, p. 429. The style is different and one needs to shorten the step and add the Cuban movement.

■ FLIRTATION BREAK

(Closed position)

Starting from closed position, dancers will change to flirtation position (see number 17, p. 51) and travel with the Cuban walk either forward or backward.

Steps	4/4 Counts	Rhythm Cue
Step L forward	1-2	slow
Step R sideward	3	quick
Close L to R, roll weight L	4	quick
Step R backward, a larger step changing to flirtation position, removing his right arm from around the lady	1-2	slow
Step L sideward	3	quick
Close R to L, roll weight to R	4	quick
Step L forward	1-2	slow
Step R forward	3	quick
Step L forward	4	quick
Step R forward	1-2	slow
Step L forward	3	quick
Step R forward	4	quick

Step Cue: Slow quick quick.

Style: In flirtation position, the dances use the Cuban walk step, all forward or all back. The man steps back a little larger step when he is changing to flirtation position. Finger pressure and arm control are essential as they are the only way the man has to lead. The free arm is held up, elbow bent, parallel to the floor.

Lead: Refer to lead indication 12, p. 384. The man's left-hand position changes to palm up, finger grasp in flirtation position. Man may lead with fingers to push the lady backward, or to pull to bring her forward. Pressure should come on the quick beats, so that change of direction actually occurs on the next slow.

Note: The man may lead as many steps in either direction as desired. To return to closed position and basic Rumba box step, the man will be moving the lady forward in flirtation position. During a back sequence on the right foot, the man will go into closed position as follows:

Steps	4/4 Counts	Rhythm Cue
Step R backward, pulling the lady into closed position	1-2	slow
Step L sideward, changing L-hand position	3	quick
Close R to L, roll to R	4	quick
Step L forward into the forward sequence		

■ SIDE BY SIDE

(Flirtation position)

Starting from flirtation position with the couple traveling either forward or backward in flirtation position, the man turns one-quarter to the right (lady to the left), to side-by-side position, lady on the man's left.

Fundamental Rumba Steps (continued)

Lead: On the quick quick beats, his left hand guides her into side-by-side position. She must then press with her arm against the man's arm or wrist to follow the leads in this position. The man may direct them forward or backward in this position, changing on the quick beats.

■ CIRCULAR TURN

(Side-by-side position)

Starting from side-by-side position, the couple is traveling forward. The man on the quick beats will change his direction so as to move backward, pulling with his lead hand toward himself to direct the lady to continue forward. This will result in a turn clockwise, side by side. They should focus on each other over the shoulder.

a. Side-by-side position   b. Circular turn (man moves backward)

Note: The man may return to basic box when he is on a back sequence with the right foot by facing the lady, taking close position, guiding into the quick quick beats sideward left, and starting the forward sequence on the left foot.

■ PARALLEL TURN

(Starting from circular turn)

When traveling in circular turn, the man backward, the lady forward, the man on the quick beats will turn suddenly one-half counterclockwise into right parallel position and, turning clockwise, both man and lady will be moving forward, around each other. Return to basic box as noted above.

a. Circular turn:
man moving backward,
lady forward

b. Parallel turn:
both man and lady move forward

■ BOLERO BREAK

(Closed position)

Starting in closed dance position, the dancers execute the forward sequence of the box step. Then, as the man starts the back sequence, he turns the lady clockwise under his left arm. The man continues to take the box step in place while the lady travels in a circular pattern clockwise until she faces him again at arm's distance. He has maintained hand contact (his left, her right) during this time and he finally guides her forward toward him back into closed dance position.

Step Cue: Slow quick quick.

Style: The lady will use the Cuban walk when moving around clockwise and keep the man's rhythm until back in closed position. She should keep the body upright, outside arm up and focus on her partner.

a.   b.

Lead: The man gives the lead by lifting his left hand high enough so that the lady does not have to duck her head to get under his arm. He also guides her under with his right hand. His left hand guides her around clockwise and finally draws her toward him to closed position.

Note: Any number of basic sequences (slow quick quick) may be taken, and, if the partners both keep the pattern going, they can move right back into the box step when they come together in closed position.

Variations of Bolero Break

1. *Walk Around.* As the lady comes around from Bolero break, instead of going into closed position, the man with his left hand will lead the lady toward his right side and past his right shoulder, bringing her around behind him and toward his left side. He then turns one-half left to face her, and they move into closed dance position.

Step Cue: Slow quick quick.

Style: The lady will use Cuban walk and keep her circle in close to the man. The man will keep the box step going until she passes his right side, and then he will go into the Cuban walk on a forward sequence and come around to his left to meet her. Both focus on each other. From closed position:

a. Bolero break   b. Walk around

Lead: The man should raise his left arm high enough so that he does not have to duck his head as she goes around. He will move under his own left arm and turn left to meet the lady.

Note: When the man and lady meet, they should go back into closed position and box step on whichever foot is free.

2. *Parallel Turn.* As the lady comes around in her wide arc at arm's distance, the man will move in toward her, coming into right parallel position, and they will turn clockwise as far as desired. The man may then lead lady to closed position or twirl the lady clockwise once around in place to finish in closed position. The lead for the twirl should come as the man steps into the forward basic sequence with the left foot so that the lady may turn on one basic step starting with her right foot. They finish together in the back part of the box step in closed position.

Step Cue: Slow quick quick.

Style: They use the Cuban walk. Focus on each other.

a. Bolero break   b. Man moves forward to parallel position   c. Parallel turn

3. *Circular Turn.* Immediately after the man turns the lady under his left arm to start the Bolero break, he brings his left arm down to a pressure position against her right elbow and turns one-quarter right to be in a side-by-side position. Then the man moves backward, the lady forward, turning in place clockwise. To get out of this turn, the man turns to face the lady and steps back with his right foot into the back basic sequence, taking closed dance position.

Step Cue: Slow quick quick.

Style: They must be in a tight side-by-side position. They will use the Cuban walk. Focus should be on the partner, outside arm up.

Lead: Firmness in the arm is necessary by man and response to this firm pressure is needed by the lady.

■ VARSOUVIENNE BREAK

(Closed position)

This is a delightful series of turns with the couple rolling from one to the other all the while keeping the basic Cuban walk rhythm, slow quick quick, going in the feet. There are four changes of position that should be practiced before the rhythm is added.

1. *Turn into the Varsouvienne Position:* The man releases the lady's right hand and reaches across in front of his right shoulder to take her left hand, pulling it across in front of him,

Fundamental Rumba Steps (continued)

causing the lady to turn clockwise a half-turn until she is by his right side, facing in the same direction. The man now holds the lady's left hand in his left and has his right around her waist to take her right hand at her right side. They circle clockwise one complete turn. To do this effectively, the man moves forward, the lady backward to turn in place.

2. *Turn into Reverse Varsouvienne Position:* The man releases the lady's right hand and turns to his own right, bringing their joined left hands across in front of lady as she turns left until she is by his left side and slightly behind him, facing in the same direction. She reaches around behind him with her right hand to take his right hand at his right side. They continue to circle clockwise another complete turn, the man now moving backward, the lady forward.

3. *Return to Varsouvienne Position:* The man releases the lady's right hand and, turning to his left, brings their joined left hands across in front of him, turning the lady halfway around clockwise until she is to the right of the man. His right arm is around her waist, holding her right hand. They continue turning clockwise, the man again moving forward, the lady backward, one full time around.

4. *Turn Back to Closed Position:* The man releases the lady's left hand and by pulling with his right toward him he turns the lady clockwise halfway around into closed dance position. He changes her right hand into his left and the man leads into the basic box step, usually on the back sequence with his right foot.

Step Cue: Slow quick quick or change quick quick.

Style: Although this is described in four parts, the transitions into each part should be smooth so as to make the entire maneuver blend into one figure rather than four disconnected parts. There is no set number of Cuban walk steps to be taken for each part. The couple should turn continuously clockwise throughout the figure. Dancers should be careful to maintain good Rumba style throughout.

🌀 Rumba Combos 🌀

The Rumba routines are combinations for practice, listed from simple to complex. (Closed position, unless otherwise indicated.)

1. *Cuban Walk and Box*
   4 Cuban walks
   2 box steps
2. *Box and Bolero Break*
   2 box steps
   Bolero break
3. *Box and Flirtation Step*
   2 box steps
   flirtation break forward and back

4. *Bolero Break and Walk Around*
   2 box steps
   Bolero break and walk around
5. *Bolero Break and Parallel Turn*
   2 box steps
   Bolero break
   parallel turn

6. *Flirtation Break and Reverse Turn*
   2 box steps
   flirtation break
   side by side
   parallel turn

🎵 Samba

The *Samba,* from Brazil, is the most active of the Latin American dances. It was introduced to the United States about 1929. It is interesting to discover how similar it is to some of the native dance rhythms of Africa. The Samba is sensitive and smooth. The music is fiery, yet lyrical; and the dance is characterized by tiny, light footwork, and the rise and fall of the body (always turning and at the same time swaying back and forth at a most deceiving pendular angle).

■ Samba Rhythm

Samba is written in 4/4 cut time and may be either slow or fast, although it is generally preferred at the faster tempo. The rhythm is slow quick slow, an uneven rhythm pattern. It has a double accent, one on each of the two major beats, and these downbeats are represented by the down movements of the dance. It will be counted as 1 *ah* 2 of the cut-time beat.

The execution of the up down weight change is the secret to the smooth, springing rhythm. There is a change of weight from one foot to the other on each of the three beats, down up down, but a preliminary uplift of the body on the upbeat of the music sets the rhythmical swing in motion. The music is fast and lighthearted.

■ Samba Style

In contrast to the Rumba, which has a lower body movement, the Samba has a total body action. The easy springing motion comes from the ball of the foot, the flexible ankle, and the easy relaxed knees. The upper body is held firmly poised, never sagging, and it seems to sway forward and back about an axis that centers in the pelvic area. The arm, when not in contact with partner, is held out from the body, a little above waist level, bent at the elbow, parallel to the floor, palm down. The first accented step, count 1, is the largest of the three steps, the other two being like a quick-change weight step. It has been called a "step-ball-change" in the language of tap dancing. It is important to get the correct rhythm and foot pattern before working on the body sway. However, having that mastered, the body sways backward as the feet take the forward basic and forward as the feet take the back basic. Always the pattern is small and on the ball of the foot.

Fundamental Samba Steps

Directions are for man; lady's part reversed, except as noted.

■ BASIC STEP

(Forward and back; Closed position)

Steps	4/4 Counts	Rhythm Cue
Step L forward	1	slow
Step R forward next to L	ah	quick
Step L in place	2	slow
Step R backward	1	slow
Step L backward beside R	ah	quick
Step R in place	2	slow

Step Cue: Forward change weight/back change weight.

Style: The steps are small. Feet are close together on the change step. The rise and fall of the body begins on the upbeat with the rise of the body. This is the preparatory motion for each step. With the first step, the down motion is executed on the first slow beat, followed by an up motion on the quick beat and down again on the slow beat. The body is controlled. It does not bend at the waist.

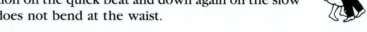

Lead: With the increased pressure of his right hand, the man sways backward slightly when stepping forward with his left foot and sways forward when stepping backward with his right foot. The lady sways forward when the man sways backward, backward when he sways forward, so that the appearance is a rocking action parallel to each other.

■ Samba Step Variations

Basic Turn   Slow Side Close   Copa Step
Forward Progressive Step   Sideward Basic

■ BASIC TURN

(Closed position, counterclockwise)

Steps	4/4 Counts	Rhythm Cue
Step L forward, turning one-quarter counterclockwise	1	slow
Step R forward beside L	ah	quick
Step L beside R	2	slow
Step R backward, toe in, and turn one-quarter counterclockwise	1	slow
Step L backward beside R	ah	quick
Step R beside L	2	slow

Step Cue: Turn step step.

Style: Keep the down up down motion going. Sway backward and then forward.

Lead: Bank right arm in direction of turn, and pull into the back step.

Note: It is important to turn on a small base, turning on the ball of the foot, not trying to step sideward around partner.

■ FORWARD PROGRESSIVE STEP

(Closed position)

Steps	¢ Counts	Rhythm Cue
Step L forward	1	slow
Step R beside L	*ah*	quick
Step L beside R	2	slow
Step R backward, changing from closed position to two hands joined with partner	1	slow
Step L beside R	*ah*	quick
Step R beside L, drop L hand	2	slow

Into Forward Progressive Step (Side-by-side position)

Steps	Counts	Rhythm Cue
Step L forward and diagonally outward to the L (lady R)	1	slow
Step R beside L	*ah*	quick
Step L beside R	2	slow
Step R forward and diagonally inward toward partner (lady L)	1	slow
Step L beside R	*ah*	quick
Step R beside L	2	slow

Back to Closed Position

Steps	Counts	Rhythm Cue
Step L, turning diagonally outward	1	slow
Step R beside L	*ah*	quick
Step L beside R	2	slow
Step R, turning diagonally inward, and take closed position	1	slow
Step L beside R	*ah*	quick
Step R beside L	2	slow
Into basic, step forward on the left foot		

Step Cue: Forward step step change step step/out step step in step step/out step step close step step/forward step step back step step.

Style: The couple turns only diagonally away from each other and back, not back to back. When they come in, the outside hand, which is up turning with the body, touches partner's hand, palm to palm. Arm when free stays up.

Lead: The man's right hand controls the motion and the diagonal position by reaching forward and back with the hand as he turns.

Note: The diagonal step should reach in the line of direction each time, so that the couple will progress down the floor. The progressive step may be repeated over and over as desired.

Fundamental Samba Steps (continued)

■ SLOW SIDE CLOSE

(Closed position)

A resting step.

Steps	¢ Counts	Rhythm Cue
Step L sideward	1	slow
Close R to L, take weight R	2	slow

Repeat three times moving left. The last time, do not take weight right but be ready to go back the other direction. Take four side-close steps to the right.

Step Cue: Side close side close.

Style: The sway of the Samba is discontinued as is the down up down motion. The rhythm is an even-beat step close.

Lead: Following a basic Samba step forward and back, the man has his left foot free. Stopping the sway and motion by control of his body and right arm, he steps left sideward into the pattern. Check lead indication 4, p. 384.

Note: Many beginners find the Samba basic step very tiring, so this step may be used to permit the dancers a resting variation.

■ SIDEWARD BASIC

(Closed position)

Steps	¢ Counts	Rhythm Cue
Step L sideward	1	slow
Step R behind L heel	ah	quick
Step L in place	2	slow
Step R sideward	1	slow
Step L behind R heel	ah	quick
Step R in place	2	slow

Step Cue: Side back step/side back step.

Floor pattern

Style: Both man and lady may rock the body and turn the head in the direction away from the leading foot. The steps are small. A long step is awkward.

Lead: The man directs the sideward step with his right arm, but the body leans in the opposite direction.

Note: For variation, the man may (1) turn the lady one-quarter counterclockwise as he steps to the left side, so that she turns her back on the direction they are traveling. As he repeats the step to the right, he turns her a half-turn clockwise. (2) They may both turn from reverse open position to open position.

■ **COPA STEP**

(Open position)

Steps	¢ Counts	Rhythm Cue
Step L forward	1	.... slow
Step R back in place on ball of foot, leaving the L foot forward	*ab*	.... quick
Drag L foot back half the distance, taking weight on L	2	.... slow
Step R forward	1	.... slow
Step L back in place on ball of foot, leaving R foot forward	*ab*	.... quick
Drag R foot back half the distance, taking weight R .	2	.... slow

Step Cue: Down up drag.

Style: The left step forward is flat with the knee bending, and the body leans backward slightly. The right step backward on the ball of the foot is accompanied by a raise of the body, which stays up during the drag of the left foot backward.

Lead: The man leads into the open position on the back right sequence of the basic step and then starts the copa with the left foot in open position. The man leads the copa action by a back lean and down up up action in the body.

Note: Dragging the foot only halfway back allows the copa step, when repeated over and over, to progress forward in open position. If the man opens in reverse open position, the copa will begin on the inside foot.

🌀 Samba Combos

The Samba routines are combinations for practice, listed from simple to complex. (Closed position, unless otherwise indicated.)

1. *Basic Slow Side Close*
   8 basic (forward and backward)
   8 side close (4 left, 4 right)

2. *Basic Step and Turn*
   4 basic steps
   4 turning left
   8 side close (4 left, 4 right)

3. *Basic: Forward and Sideward*
   8 basic (forward and backward)
   4 sideward steps

4. *Basic Turn—Copa*
   4 basic turn
   4 slow side close
   4 copa steps

5. *Advanced Combo*
   4 basic
   4 sideward basic
   8 forward progressive
   8 copa steps (open)

6. *Advanced Combo*
   4 basic
   8 copa steps
   8 basic turn
   4 slow side close

🌿 Merengue

This clever little dance from the Caribbean could very well be a favorite with the young adult set if they really had a chance to explore it. The music is a peppy, pert, marchlike rhythm, and the dance patterns are the most simple of all the Latin dances. There are two styles: the original "limp step" from the Dominican Republic and the more even, smooth Haitian style. The Haitian style will be described here.

■ Merengue Rhythm

In 4/4 time, there is a very pronounced beat of the music, which has an exciting uneven beat in the rhythm pattern, but the dance follows the basic beats of the measure and is in even rhythm.

■ Merengue Style

Perhaps merengue style could be described as a combination of the rumba movement and a majorette swagger step. The feet are placed flat, but the *weight is on the ball of the foot for easy balance*. It is a controlled hip movement resulting from the bent-knee action with each step as in the rumba, but it has the almost sassy quality and breezy manner of the majorette. A slight rock sideways with the shoulders to accompany the foot pattern is optional. It is not meant to be an exaggerated body movement, but the lively music and the character of the step give this dance a delightful touch of humor.

With a simple step, the footwork must be disciplined or it may look sloppy. The feet face squarely forward and close tightly together. The step is small.

Fundamental Merengue Steps

Directions are for the man; lady's part is reversed, except as noted.

■ BASIC SIDE STEP

(Closed position)

Steps	4/4 Counts	Rhythm Cue
Step L sideward	1	quick
Close R to L, take weight on R	2	quick
Step L sideward	3	quick
Close R to L, take weight on R	4	quick

Step Cue: Side close.

Style: Steps are small, head high, focus on partner. Rock body left, right with the step.

Lead: See lead indication 4, p. 384.

Note: Could travel sideways any number of side steps. Should travel in line of direction.

■ BOX STEP

(Closed position)

Steps	4/4 Counts	Rhythm Cue
Step L forward	1	quick
Close R to L, take weight on R	2	quick
Step L backward	3	quick
Close R to L, take weight on R	4	quick

Step Cue: Forward together back together.

Style: The same foot leads each time. The shoulders lead the rock from side to side.

Lead: See lead indication 5, p. 384. Note that the left foot is the lead foot each time.

■ BOX TURN

(Closed position)

Steps	4/4 Counts	Rhythm Cue
Step L, toeing out to a L one-quarter turn counterclockwise	1	quick
Close R to L, take weight on R	2	quick
Step L backward	3	quick
Close R to L, take weight on R	4	quick

Step Cue: Turn close back close.

Style: A shoulder rock on the turn makes it very easy to lead.

Lead: See lead indication 6, p. 384.

Note: Repeat three times to make a full turn.

Fundamental Merengue Steps (continued)

■ CROSS STEP

(Closed position)

Steps	4/4 Counts	Rhythm Cue
Step L sideward, turning to open position	1	.... quick
Step R forward, in open position	2	.... quick
Step L sideward, turning to closed position	3	.... quick
Close R to L, take weight on R	4	.... quick

Step Cue: Open step side close.

Style: Each step must be precisely taken in the closed or open position. If the footwork is not square with each position, the merengue loses all of its distinctive character.

Lead: Check lead indications 7 and 8, p. 384. The lead is given rather suddenly.

Variation: The flick is like the cross step, except that there is a *leap* onto the left foot in open position, bending the right knee and flipping the right foot quickly up in back, and then right foot steps forward and side close as above. The man raises his right elbow as he turns to open position into the leap.

■ SWIVEL

(Open and closed traveling in line of direction)

Steps	4/4 Counts	Rhythm Cue
Leap L forward in open position flick R foot	1	.... quick
Step R forward in open position	2	.... quick
Pivot on R foot to face partner, bringing L foot alongside of R, shift weight to L	3	.... quick
Pivot on L foot to open position, bringing R foot alongside of L, shift weight to R	4	.... quick
Repeat pivot on R	1	.... quick
Repeat pivot on L	2	.... quick
Step L, turning to closed position	3	.... quick
Close R to L, taking weight R	4	.... quick

Step Cue: Leap step, swivel, swivel, swivel, swivel, side close.

Style: Steps are tiny and neat, turning exactly a quarter-turn each time. The body turns with the foot.

Lead: The man is quickly turning the lady from open to closed position. Check lead indications 7 and 8, p. 384.

■ LADDER

(Closed position)

Steps	4/4 Counts	Rhythm Cue
Step L sideward	1	quick
Close R to L, take weight on R	2	quick
Step L forward	3	quick
Close R to L, take weight on R	4	quick

Step Cue: Side close forward close.

Style: Footwork small and neat. Face partner squarely.

Lead: Moving squarely into position helps lead the body. Since there are a lot of direction changes in the merengue, the lady must be extremely alert to the action of his right arm and shoulder.

■ SIDE CLOSE AND BACK BREAK

(Closed position)

Steps	4/4 Counts	Rhythm Cue
Step L sideward	1	quick
Close R to L, take weight on R	2	quick
Step L sideward	3	quick
Close R to L, take weight on R	4	quick
Step L sideward	1	quick
Step R, in place, turning to open position	2	quick
Step L backward, in open position	3	quick
Step R, in place, turning to closed position	4	quick

Step Cue: Side close side close side open back step.

Style: There is a rather sudden swing to open position on count 2 of the second measure and then immediately back to closed position on count 4.

Lead: Man uses his left hand to push lady out quickly to open position.

■ MERENGUE COMBOS

1. 4 basic steps
   4 box steps
   4 basic steps
   4 box turns

2. 4 basic steps
   4 cross steps
   8 box steps

3. 4 basic steps
   4 box turns
   4 swivels

4. 4 basic steps
   4 ladder
   4 box turns
   4 side close and back break

Appendixes

Model for Test Construction

The Model for Test Construction is presented as a guideline for students in teacher training classes and for teachers. These questions are also helpful to students in understanding how test questions are phrased, thereby enabling students to comprehend the extent of details they need to know. A variety of questions are presented so that student teachers may comprehend different ways of testing student knowledge as well as of presenting clear and concise directions for test construction. Some types are more difficult and more complicated than others; some are specifically for teacher training classes. Once the objectives and content for a dance unit are established, the type of questions are selected and composed of material following the models. This model *is not* a sample test because the coverage is incomplete.

I. Dances or steps will be demonstrated. As soon as you recognize the dance or step, write the title in the correct space.

1. _Polka Step_   3. _Grapevine_
2. _Korobushka_   4. _Black Hawk Waltz_

II. Music will be played. Circle the step that would be used.

5. Waltz, Schottische, Polka, (Two-Step,) Mazurka
6. (Waltz,) Schottische, Polka, Two-Step, Mazurka
7. Waltz, (Schottische,) Polka, Two-Step, Mazurka
8. Waltz, Schottische, Polka, Two-Step, (Mazurka)

III. Complete the Chart.

Name of Dance	Give the Nationality	Give information indicated for each dance
9. Texas Star	_American_	Formation _Square_
10. Man in the Hay	_German_	Number of Dancers _8_
11. Spinnradl Zu Dritt	_Austrian_	Basic Step _Waltz_
12. Hora Pe Gheata	_Romanian_	Name of Locomotor Step _Waltz_
13. Il Codiglione	_Italian_	Position of Couple _Varsouvienne_
14. Broken Sixpence	_American_	Type of Dance _Contra_

IV. Write the letter of the technique or term from Column II next to its description in Column I. Letters may be used more than once.

Column I

_G_ 15. Couple with back to music.

_A_ 16. Man turns lady on his left with his left hand.

_E_ 17. Lady on man's left.

_I_ 18. Pass back to back with a person.

_J_ 19. Move in couples around the set.

_D_ 20. Let go hands.

Column II

A. Allemande left
B. Allemande right
C. Balance
D. Break
E. Corner lady
F. Couple 1
G. Couple 3
H. Do Paso
I. Do-sa-do
J. Promenade

V. Write the letter of the Fundamental Step from Column II next to the Dance in Column I in which it is used.

Column I
Dances

_C_ 21. Texas Star

_A_ 22. Varsouvienne

_E_ 23. Masquarade

Column II
Fundamental Steps

A. Mazurka type
B. Polka
C. Shuffle
D. Slide
E. Waltz

VI. Write the letter of the Dance Step from Column II that is analyzed in Column I.

Column I
Step Patterns

_D_ 24. Hop, step, close, step

_C_ 25. Leap, step, step

_A_ 26. Step (crossing behind), step side, step (crossing in front)

_B_ 27. Step left, draw right to left, hop right, sweeping left

Column II
Dance Steps

A. Grapevine
B. Mazurka
C. Pas de basque
D. Polka

VII. Multiple Choice: Write the letter that indicates the proper word or phrase.

_B_ 28. The Waltz step consists of (A. two; B. three; C. four; D. five) counts or steps.

_A_ 29. The Polka is like a Two-Step with a hop that (A. precedes the Two-Step; B. comes after the first step; C. is used after step together; D. follows the Two-Step).

a. _B_ b. _G_ 30. A single Schottische step consists of (A. four; B. three; C. one; D. six) steps and a hop executed to (E. two; F. three; G. four; H. six) counts of music.

_B_ 31. One box Waltz is composed of (A. one; B. two; C. three; D. four) Waltz step or steps.

VIII. Circle the letter that precedes the best answer for each question or statement.

32. In dancing, the weight of the body is

A. equally distributed on the heels and toes.
B. centered over a wide base.
C. carried mainly over the balls of the feet.
D. transferred from heel to toe on each step.

33. What musical factor helps the dancer to recognize when to change from one dance step or unit to another?

A. Measure
B. Phrase
C. Underlying beat
D. Accent

34. Krüz König means
   A. The King from König
   B. Beloved Knight
   C. King's Cross
   D. King of Clubs ✓

35. Which of the following are executed to a three-beat rhythm?
   A. Waltz and Mazurka ✓
   B. Two-Step and Waltz
   C. Polka and Two-Step
   D. Schottische and Waltz

36. When executing a backward dip,
   A. the trunk remains erect, the back knee bends, and the free leg extends forward. ✓
   B. the trunk leans slightly backward, the back knee turns slightly out, and the forward toe points straight ahead.
   C. the trunk leans slightly forward, the back leg remains straight, and the forward knee bends.
   D. the trunk remains erect and both knees bend slightly.

37. A Polka step is described as which of the following?
   A. Step-close-step-hop
   B. Side-close-side-hop
   C. Hop-step-close-step ✓
   D. Side-close-side-close-hop
   E. All of the above.
   F. None of the above.

38. In closed position, most leading cues are given with the man's ——————— arm and hand.
   A. Right ✓
   B. Left
   C. Either
   D. Both
   E. None of the above.

IX. Short Answers.

_____4_____ 39. How many people are involved in a right and left through?

_____8_____ 40. How many people are involved in a grand right and left in a square?

a. __2__ 41. What are the numbers of the side couples?
b. __4__

_____1_____ 42. What is the number of the couple that has their backs to the music?

Figure 8 43. What *floor pattern* does the man make when he dances "All around your left-hand lady, see-saw your pretty little taw"?

Let go
hands 44. What does the term *break* in Square Dancing mean?

X. Short Answers.
   45. Give the *count* for the following Social Dance steps.

   A. Samba
      1 and 2, 1 and 2

   B. Tango
      1, 2, 1 and 2

   C. Triple Lindy
      1 and 2, 3 and 4

   D. Charleston
      and 1, and 2, and 3, and 4

46. Fill in the *name* of the Folk Dance that includes the following:

Cotton-Eyed Joe _____ A. Buzz Step   *Black Hawk Waltz* _____ D. Waltz balance

Virginia Reel _____ B. Slide   *Gie Gordons* _____ E. Pas de basque

Corrido _____ C. Grapevine   *Korobushka* _____ F. Three-step turn

47. Give the *rhythm cue* for the following Social Dance steps.

A. Magic step

slow slow quick quick

B. Twinkle step

slow quick quick

C. Rumba

slow quick quick

D. Cha Cha Cha

slow slow quick quick slow

XI. In the space provided, indicate by letter the starting formation for each dance.

FORMATIONS:

Key to Figures:
○→ Women facing in direction of arrow.
□→ Men facing in direction of arrow.

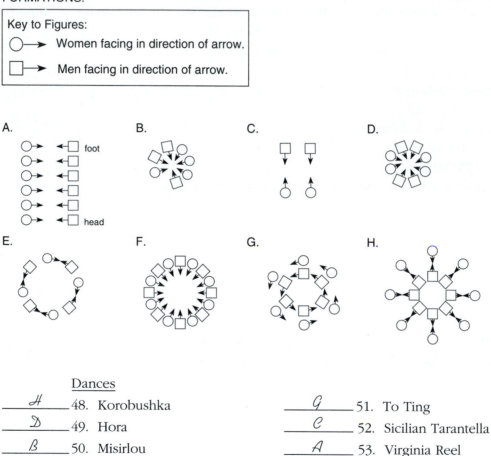

A.   B.   C.   D.

E.   F.   G.   H.

Dances

_H_ 48. Korobushka   _G_ 51. To Ting

_D_ 49. Hora   _C_ 52. Sicilian Tarantella

_B_ 50. Misirlou   _A_ 53. Virginia Reel

XII. The steps of each dance are listed. Write the letter of the progression of each dance in terms of *change* in step.

Dances

Road to Isles

54. _D_

55. _B_

56. _A_

57. _C_

Steps

A. Schottische
B. Point forward and back
C. Stamp
D. Grapevine

58. ____C____ A. Pivot
59. ____B____ B. Walk
60. ____D____ C. Side step, stamp
61. ____A____ D. Two-step

XIII. Complete the chart. See example.
    Column I: Indicate by letter from column VI the position that describes the starting position for each dance.
    Column II: Write *left* or *right* after each dance indicating with which foot the man starts the dance.
    Column III: Write *left* or *right* after each dance indicating with which foot the woman starts the dance.
    Column IV: Indicate by letter from column VII the description of the first sequence of the dance.
    Column V: Indicate by letter from column VIII the last sequence of the dance.

	I	II	III	IV	V
	Starting Position	What foot does the man start with?	What foot does the lady start with?	Name the 1st dance step of sequence.	Name the last dance step.
EXAMPLE: Gie Gordons	G	left	left	M	R
62. To Ting	G	left	right	L	P
63. Korobushka	D	left	right	I	O
64. Corrido	B	right	left	H	2
65. Misirlou	E	right	right	J	N

VI	VII	VIII
Dance Position	Description of First Movement	Description of Last Movement
A. Arms around waist of neighbors	H. Draw or side step	N. Grapevine
B. Closed position	I. Schottische	O. Partners cross over
C. Conversation position	J. Soft stamp	P. Pivot
D. Facing partner	K. Step swing	Q. Stamp
E. Hands joined with neighbor	L. Waltz balance	R. Two-step
F. Inside hand joined	M. Walk	S. Waltz
G. Varsouvienne		

SUGGESTED QUESTIONS FOR STUDENTS IN TEACHER TRAINING CLASSES

1. Give a method for including "extras" (dancers) in a square dance.

   Extras stand behind a dancer. When the call is "Swing your partner," extra person steps into swing. The new extra moves to another set. Avoid more than one extra per set.

2. List the eight Level IA: Beginning Basics a Square Dance class needs to know in order to maneuver in the set.

   Shuffle, Honors, Do-sa-do, Promenade, Twirl, Single-file Promenade, Waist Swing, Allemande left.

3. Give a short practice call for any *one* of the above basics.

   Honor your partner, Corners all, Swing your partner, and Promenade the hall.

4. Mixers enhance the social atmosphere of a class, party, or evening of dancing. List two mixers and give the basic step involved.

Mixer	Basic Step
Korobushka	*Schottische step*
Oh Johnny	*Shuffle/walk*

5. Analyze the following basic dance steps.

   Schottische   *step, step, step hop*

   Mazurka   *step left, bring right up to left with a cut-step displacing left, hop right while bending left knee so that left foot approaches the right ankle.*

   Waltz   *step forward left, step to the side with the right, close left to right, take weight on left.*

6. Describe the process you would use in teaching a Polka turn.

   Practice individually "hop step close step," alternating left, right, in the line of direction. Then turn clockwise a half-turn on each hop. Individual faces out, then toward the center alternately.

7. Define a *measure* in music.

   A group of beats made by a regular accent.

8. Explain the foot positions for the man in executing a Two-Step turn with a partner.

Man's back to center of circle. Man steps side left, close right to left, step side left, pivot half-turn, body turning clockwise; step side right, close left to right, step forward right, pivot half-turn, body turning clockwise. (Often students forget they need to step forward when the right foot is free.)

9. Give the rhythm for the following Social Dance steps.

A. Magic step

slow, slow, quick, quick

B. Westchester box step

slow, quick, quick,

slow, quick, quick

C. Basic Tango step

slow, slow,

quick, quick, slow

D. Cha Cha Cha

slow, slow, slow

quick, quick, slow

10. A grand right and left in European dancing is referred to as *chain* or *grand chain*. Why do they call *ladies chain* in Contra and Square Dancing a "chain"?

In a ladies chain, two ladies give right hands to each other, left hand to opposite man, alternating right and left hands, same as in chain or grand chain.

11. List five common errors in the use of the closed position.

A. *Partner too far away*

B. *Lack of resistance by either man or lady*

C. *Lady leaning heavily on partner's arm*

D. *Lack of support in the man's right arm*

E. *Lack of contact of lady's left arm*

12. What contribution did each of the following make to the American Folk Dance scene?

A. Ralph Page *Credited with stimulating growth of Contra Dance.*

B. Lloyd Shaw *Credited with reviving interest in Western Square Dance.*

C. Elizabeth Burchenal *One of the earliest Americans to publish Folk Dances and teach folk dancing in physcial education classes.*

D. John Playford *English author of first dance books that were used in America.*

E. Vyts Beliajus *Editor/founder of Viltis, a Folk Dance magazine.*

13. After each of the following words, write whether they are the same or different in Contra dancing and Square Dance.

A. Formation _different_

B. Balance _different_

C. Ladies chain _same_

D. Circle four _same_

14. Give the names of the following dance positions:

A. Lady is slightly to the right of the man and in front of him. Man holds lady's right hand in his right and her left hand in his left.

Varsouvienne

B. Man and lady face. Man places hands on lady's waist, lady places hands on man's shoulders.

Shoulder-waist

15. Name four different types of American Folk Dance and give an example of each.

	Type	Example
A.	_Square_	_Texas Star_
B.	_Contra_	_Rory O'More_
C.	_Play Party Games_	_Alabama Gal_
D.	_Round_	_Black Hawk Waltz_

16. Correctable True/False: If the statement is entirely correct, circle the _T._ If the statement is totally or partially incorrect, circle the _F,_ and _correct the statement to make it true._

A. A three-step turn to the right is started with the ~~left~~ _right_ foot.   T (F)

B. In a grand right and left, the ladies progress around the circle clockwise.   (T) F

C. The fundamental step in the Norwegian Polka is the ~~Polka step.~~ _walk or pivot turn_   T (F)

D. During each promenade in the Texas Star, the man is with ~~his original partner.~~ _the lady one position right of his original position_   T (F)

E. To Ting means "two things" because there are ~~a balance type step and waltz step.~~ _two rhythms, 3/4 and 2/4, or a walk and waltz step_   T (F)

F. When clogging, the upper body should move very little.   (T) F

G. When clogging, the weight should stay over ~~the ball of the foot.~~ _center of foot or entire foot_   T (F)

H. Generally, either both legs are straight or both are bent when performing clogging steps and step combinations.   (T) F

I. The following step combination takes ~~4 measures:~~ _2 measures_ Double-toe Step Brush Slide Touch Slide Toe Heel.   T (F)

17. Complete the Chart. For each basic step, check under one of three columns: Downbeat, Upbeat, Either.

Basic Step	Downbeat of music ("beat")	Upbeat of music ("and")	Either beat of music
A. Brush		X	
B. Double-toe		X	
C. Drag		X	
D. Heel	X		
E. Rock		X	
F. Slide	X		
G. Step	X		
H. Toe		X	
I. Touch		X	

18. Write a behavioral objective for the Alexandrovska.
The student needs to identify the behavior, conditions, and criteria.

Periodicals

The following periodicals are of two types. The first type is an association or federation publication dealing with news and current dance events aimed at a particular geographic area. The second type is a more traditional publication that specializes in one dance form and gives in-depth coverage of the social and cultural background of that particular dance form.

Allons Danser. Rand Speyrer, ed., Acadian Music and Dance Co., P. O. Box 15908, New Orleans, LA 70175-5908; (504) 899-0615. Dedicated to preserving Cajun music and culture.

American Squaredancer Magazine. Jon Sanborn, ed., 661 Middlefield Road, Salinas, CA 93906; (408) 443-0761; Fax (408) 443-6402. Covers Square and Round Dances.

Bridges. Lithuanian American News Journal, 2715 E. Allegheny Ave., Philadelphia, PA 19134-5914.

Country Dance and Song Society News. Country Dance and Song Society, 17 New South Street, Northampton, MA 01060; (413) 584-9913.

The Dance Gypsy. 57 Sleepy Hollow Road, Essex Junction, VT 05452; (802) 899-2378. Publishes monthly calendar and sponsors dance events in northern New England.

Ethnomusicology. Society of Ethnomusicology, Morrison Hall 005, Indiana University, Bloomington, IN 47405; (812) 855-6672; Fax (812) 855-6673. Good folklore and music dealing with dance.

Folk Dance Scene. Published monthly by the Folk Dance Federation of California So., Inc., 22210 Miston Dr., Woodland Hills, CA 91364.

Footnotes. Square and Folk Dance Federation of Washington, Box 26, Puyallup, WA 98371.

Gotta Dance Magazine. P.O. Box 265, Southeastern, PA 19399-0265; (215) 695-0430. Ballroom, Country Western, Folk, Polka, Swing—New York City to northern Virginia.

Laografia. A newsletter of the International Greek Folklore Society, 6 Golden Star, Irvine, CA 92714; (714) 559-8579.

Let's Dance. Folk Dance Federation of California, Inc., P.O. Box 1282, Alameda, CA 94501.

Northwest Folkdancer. c/o Linda Caspermeyer, 1023 NE 61st St., Seattle, WA 98115-6601.

Round Dancer Magazine. Brian E. Bassett, publishing ed., RR 1 Box 843, Petersburg, PA 16669-9304; (814) 667-2530. An integral part of Round Dance legacy.

Slovakia. A Slovak Heritage newsletter of the Slovak Heritage and Folklore Society of North America, 151 Colebrook Dr., Rochester, NY 14617-2215; (716) 342-9383.

Swing Your Partner Where? Box 1750, Seattle, WA 98111; (206) 624-9699.

Viltis. V. F. Beliajus, ed., 1337 Marion St., Denver, CO 80218; (303) 839-1589.

Organizations and Resources

Caller Lab. International Association of Square Dance Callers, 829 3rd Ave., S.E., Rochester, MN 55904; (507) 288-5121; Fax (507) 288-5827. Standardization of dance programs, accreditation of callers, liability insurance, guidelines for buildings, and Foundation for preservation and promotion of Square Dancing.

Contralab. c/o Glen Nickerson, 606 Woodland Way, Kent, WA 98031. International Association of Contra Callers.

Country Dance and Song Society. 17 New South Street, Northampton, MA 01060; (413) 584-9913. Promotes the preservation of American Country Dance. English Country Dance also included. Publishes **Country Dance and Song Society News** six times a year and **Country Dance and Song** annually, books, and **Group and Membership Directory**; produces records; sells records, cassettes, videos, books; sponsors dance camps.

Country Dance and Song Society Library and Archives. This collection is located with the Ralph Page Collection, Dimond Library, University of New Hampshire, Durham, NH 03824.

Ethnic Folkarts Center (EFAC). 325 Spring St., Room 314, New York, NY 10013; (212) 691-9510. Aims to visually record world leaders who have contributed to the folk music and folk dance scene.

Flying Cloud Academy of Vintage Dance. Richard Powers, director, 3623 Herschel Ave., Cincinnati, OH 45208; (513) 321-4878.

Folk Alliance. Division of North American Folk Music and Dance Alliance, P.O. Box 5010, Chapel Hill, NC 27514; (919) 542-3997. Sponsors annual conferences and coordinates those involved with performing arts. Music is primary focus, dance is included.

Folk Arts Center of New England. 1950 Massachusetts Avenue, Cambridge, MA 02140. Promotes traditional dance, music, and related arts of many cultures. Quarterly newsletter; Folk Dancing 'Round Boston bi-monthly calendar; Folk-Fone (recording) in Boston area (617) 491-6084.

Folk Dance Federation of California, Inc. P.O. Box 1282, Alameda, CA 94501. Encourages the study and advancement of Folk Dancing and related arts. Publishes **Let's Dance** and books, sponsors festivals, institutes teaching training and research in dances, music, and costumes.

Folkmoot. Box 523, Waynesville, NC 28786; (704) 452-2997.

Historical Dance Foundation, Inc. 31 Union Square West, Suite 15D, New York, NY 10003.

Library of Congress. 10 1st St. S.E., Washington, D.C. 20540. Information (202) 707-2905. Largest collection of dance books in USA.

1. American Folklife Center (202) 707-2905. Goal is to preserve and present programs relating to folklife and cultural heritage in United States. Publishes newsletter, quarterly.
2. Archive of Folk Culture (202) 707-5510, founded by the Lomaxes in 1928. Archives include dance material in tape recordings, documentaries. Available for research.
3. Research. Write National Reference Service, Library of Congress, Washington, D.C. 20540-5570. Will respond to questions *only* relating to material held by the Library of Congress. *Will not* respond to questions that local libraries can answer.

The Lloyd Shaw Foundation. Preserves and promotes American Square and Round dance. Membership: c/o Ruth Ann Knapp, 2124 Passolt, Saginaw, MI 48603.

Archives: c/o Dr. Wm. Litchman, 1620 Los Alamos SW, Albuquerque, NM 87104.
The Lloyd Shaw Foundation publishes *The American Dance Circle*. Quarterly. Box 224, Baldwin City, KS 66006.
Sales: P.O. Box 11, Macks Creek, MO 65786. Sponsors camps, workshops, publishes books, and produces records.

National Clogging and Hoedown Council (NCHC). 507 Angie Way, Lilburn, GA 30247.

National Dance Association. Division of AAHPERD, 1900 Association Drive, Reston, VA 22091-1502; (703) 476-3436; Fax (703) 476-9527.

National Folk Organization of U.S.A. (NFO). c/o L. DeWayne Young, 359 S. Cleveland Ave., Blackfoot, ID 83221; (208) 785-2427. Networking with national groups, performing and recreational, is primary focus through exchange of information and resources for folk arts and cultural heritage. Publishes quarterly. Coordinates with international folk organizations.

The National Folk Organization of United States of America. c/o Ms. Lola Walker, 72 North First E., Rexburg, Idaho 83440.

National Square Dance Directory. P.O. Box 880, Brandon, MS 39043; (601) 825-6831 or (800) 542-4010. Directory includes 10,000 Square, Round, Clogging and Contra dance clubs in U.S., Canada, and around the world.

New England Folk Festival Association (NEFFA). 1950 Massachusetts Avenue, Cambridge, MA 02140; (617) 491-6083. Sponsors annual New England Folk Festival.

New England Square Dance Caller. New England Caller Association, Box 8069, Lowell, MA 01853; (508) 452-3222, (800) 33DoCdo. New England Square Dance information.

New York Public Library for Performing Arts Dance Collection. Located at the Lincoln Performing Arts Center, 111 Amsterdam Avenue, New York, NY 10023. (212) 870-1657. Holdings include 40,000 books plus films, videotapes, oral history tapes. The *Complete Catalogue of Dance Collections* of the New York Public Library is available.

1. Published directory in reference section of large libraries.
2. CD ROM—copy of disc at large libraries.

Orff-Schulwerk Association. P.O. Box 391089, Cleveland, OH 44139-8089; (216) 543-5366. National association that promotes the Orff-Schulwerk approach to understanding rhythm.

People's Folk Dance Directory. P.O. Box 8575, Austin, TX 78713.

Ralph Page Collection. Special Collections Room, Dimond Library, University of New Hampshire, Durham, NH 03824. Ralph Page's personal collection of dance and music books is available for research.

Smithsonian Institution. 1000 Jefferson Drive S.W., Washington, D.C. 20560; (202) 357-2139.

1. Office of Folklife and Cultural Studies sponsors the annual Festival of American Folklife on the National Mall every summer.
2. Film Archives. Anthropological films from around the world, dance included.

Society of Folk Dance Historians. 2100 Rio Grande St., Austin, TX 78705-5513. Publishes *Folk Dance Phone Book,* sponsors dance opportunities, and preserves history and practice of international folk dancing.

United States Amateur Ballroom Dancers Association (USABDA). 1427 Gibsonwood Road, Baltimore, MD 21228; (800) 447-9047.

Record, Cassette, Video Sources: Distributors and Producers

Record, Cassette, Video Sources

The sources listed are of two types: producers who make recordings and distributors who supply retailers. Ordering from a nearby distributor is not only convenient and time-saving but, more important, it alerts the distributor to the dance records and supplies most commonly used in that area. Producers can supply catalogs of their products and suggest sources from which they may be obtained.

United States

■ ARIZONA

Mail Order Master Record Service. P.O. Box 37676, Phoenix, AZ 85069; (602) 993-9932. Distributor of Folk and Square dance records.

■ CALIFORNIA

Blue Ribbon Square, Round Dance, and Clogging, *DJ Square Dance Records,* and *Hi Hat Square Dance Records.* Producer: Ernie Kinney Enterprises, 3925 N. Tollhouse Rd., Fresno, CA 93726; (209) 227-2764.

Ed Kremers' Folk Showplace. 155 Turk St., San Francisco, CA 94102; (415) 775-3444. Dance records, books, and supplies for schools and recreation. Imports foreign records. Public address systems and cassettes of "unavailable" music.

Festival Records. 2773 West Pico Blvd., Los Angeles, CA 90006; (213) 737-3500. Foreign and Folk Dance records, cassettes, videos, books, and folklore imports.

Gold Star Video Productions. P.O. Box 417802, Sacramento, CA 95841; (916) 331-2550, outside CA (800) 87HINGE. Square, Round, and Ballroom Dance including Jive, West Coast Swing, Paso Doble, Quickstep, etc. videos.

Hilton Audio Products, Inc. 1033-E Shavy Circle, Concord, CA 94518; (415) 682-8390; Fax (415) 682-8497.

Square Dancetime. Jack Murtha Enterprises, P.O. Box 3055, Yuba City, CA 95992-3055; (916) 673-1120. Square Dancetime records and teaching material. Some Round dances included.

Sundance. 10331 Lindley #145, Northridge, CA 91326; (818) 363-4454. Distributor of Square and Round Dance records.

Wagon Wheel Records and Books. Paul James, 17191 Corbina Lane #203, Huntington Beach, CA 92649; (714) 846-8169. Excellent source for Folk, Square, Clogging, Ballroom dance records, cassettes, and teaching material.

Wagon Wheel Records and Books. Bob Ruff, 8459 Edmaru Ave., Whittier, CA 90605; (310) 693-5976. Producer of Wagon Wheel records, cassettes, and video.

Windsor Record Co. 312 Monterey Pass Road, Monterey Park, CA 91754; (818) 282-5181. Producer of Windsor Records.

■ COLORADO

Norsk, Ltd. Jofrid Sodal, 800 Linden Ave., Boulder, CO 80302; (303) 442-6452. Carries Scandinavian folk music, primarily Norwegian and Swedish. LP, CD, cassette.

Square Dance Record Roundup. 957 Sheridan Blvd., Denver, CO 80214; (303) 238-4810. Dealer of Square, Folk, Line, Round, and Clogging records.

■ CONNECTICUT

The Hendrickson Group. P.O. Box 766, Sandy Hook, CT 06482; (203) 426-9266. Country Dance books, music, and cassettes.

■ ILLINOIS

Human Kinetics Publishers. P.O. Box 5076, Champaign, IL 61825-5076; (800) 747-4457; Fax (217) 351-1549. Social Dance cassettes.

International Folk Rhythms, Ltd. P.O. Box 1402, Northbrook, IL 60065; (708) 564-2880. Folk Dance records, cassettes, ethnic and educational music and books, electronic equipment, imported clothing, and specialties.

■ KENTUCKY

Folk Circle Association Incorporated, Russel Action Folk Recreation Center, P.O. Box 488, Berea, KY 40403; (606) 986-8033 or (606) 986-9344 ext. 5141. Records and cassettes.

Ox dances from Appalachia, song dance music to poetry to folk tales, as well as locally made crafts.

■ MASSACHUSETTS

Country Dance and Song Society. 17 New South Street, Northampton, MA 01060; (413) 584-9913. Large selection of English and American traditional dance, music, and song records, cassettes, books, videos.

Folk Arts Center of New England. 1950 Massachusetts Avenue, Cambridge, MA 02140; (617) 491-6083. Distributors of Folk Dance records, CDs, cassettes, videos, sheet music, and books.

Hands Four Book and Record Service. P.O. Box 641, Bedford, MA 01730. Stocks Contra Dance items.

■ MICHIGAN

High/Scope. 600 N River Street, Ypsilanti, MI 48198-2898; (313) 485-2000; Fax (313) 485-0704. Produces High/Scope books, records, CDs, cassettes, videos.

■ MISSOURI

4-Bar-B Records, Inc. Box 7-11, Macks Creek, MO 65786; (314) 363-5432; Fax (314) 363-5820. Produces Cardinal and Quadrille records. Supplies Square Dance records and cassettes.

Lloyd Shaw Foundation, Inc. (Sales Division). P.O. Box 11, Macks Creek, MO 65786; (314) 363-5868.

■ NEW JERSEY

Folkraft Records and Tapes. P.O. Box 404, Florham Park, NJ 07932; (201) 377-1885. Produces Folkraft products.

Hoctor Products for Education. P.O. Box 38, Waldwick, NJ 07463-0038; (201) 652-7767; Fax (201) 652-2599. Produces and retails records, cassettes, videos.

Kimbo Educational. P.O. Box 477, Long Branch, NJ 07740; (908) 229-4949; Fax (908) 870-3340. Producers of a wide variety of dance and musical play activities, videos, cassettes, and records for school and recreational use.

Princeton Book Company. 12 West Delaware Avenue, Pennington, NJ 08534; (609) 737-8177; (800) 326-7149. Dance books and videos.

■ NEW HAMPSHIRE

Supreme Audio, Inc. P.O. Box 50, Marlborough, NH 03455-0050; (800) 445-7398. Fax (603) 876-4001. Distributor of Square, Round, Folk, and Ballroom dance records, cassettes, videos, and audio equipment.

■ NEW YORK

Andy's Front Hall. Folk, Traditional, Acoustic music store. P.O. Box 307, Voorheesville, NY 12186; (518) 765-4193, (800) 759-1775; Fax (518) 765-4344. Books, records, cassettes for American Country Dance, including Contra, New England and West Virginia Squares, English Country Dance. Many folk instruments.

Educational Frontiers. 132 West 21st St., New York, NY 10011; (212) 675-8567. Distributes software, filmstrips, videos, records, and cassettes.

Michael Herman's Folk Dance House. P.O. Box 2305, North Babylon, Long Island, NY 11703; (516) 661-3866. Distributes a wide assortment of records for Folk, Square, Contra, and Round dance.

Roper Records. 45-15 21st St., Long Island City, NY 11101; (718) 786-2401. Produces a wide variety of Social Dance records—45s, LP, and cassettes.

Worldtone Music, Inc. 230 Seventh Avenue, New York, NY 10011; (212) 691-1934; Fax (212) 691-2554. Distributes Folk, Square, Ballroom, Jazz, Contra, Clogging, and floor exercise records. Producer of Worldtone Folk Music.

■ NORTH CAROLINA

Folk Dance Videos International. P.O. Box 470907, Charlotte, NC 28247.

■ OHIO

Grenn, Inc. 2775 Yellow Creek Road, Akron, OH 44313; (216) 836-5591. Producer of Grenn records for recreational dancing—Square, Round, Line, and Clogging.

Palomino Square and Round Dance Service. 1050 Toulon Dr., Marion, OH 43302; (800) 328-3800. Distributor of Square, Round, Folk and Ballroom dance records.

■ OKLAHOMA

Melody House Publishing Co. 819 N.W. 92nd St., Oklahoma City, OK 73114; (405) 840-3383; Fax (405) 840-3384. World of Fun records and cassettes. Collection includes American Play Party Games, American Square Dances, many International Dances.

■ TEXAS

Kalox-Belco-Longhorn Records. Produced by Kalox Record Distributing Co., 2832 Live Oak Drive, Mesquite, TX 75150; (214) 270-0616.

Merrbach Record Service. 323 W. 14th Street, Houston, TX 77008; (713) 862-7077. Distributors of Square and Round Dance records.

Reeves Record, Inc./Eddie's & Bobbie's Records. 1835 South Buckner, P.O. Box 17668, Dallas, TX 75217-0668; (214) 398-7508. Square, Round, and Clogging records and books.

Rocket Records. 5238 Appleblossom Lane, Friendswood, TX 77546; (713) 482-0374. Contemporary Square Dance music.

■ VERMONT

Alcazar Records. P.O. Box 429, South Main St., Waterbury, VT 05676-0429; (802) 244-8657, (800) 541-9904; Fax (802) 244-6128. Excellent source for Bluegrass, Folk, Country Western, Cajun and Zydeco, R&B, Blues, Jazz, Rock, traditional dance and British recordings. LP, CD, cassette.

■ WASHINGTON

Avalon Dance Shop, Inc. Waltraud Stanzl, 1021 Stewart St., Seattle, WA 98101; (206) 628-6195. Ballroom records and cassettes, including foreign records desirable for competition.

Viking Record Sales. 1221 NE 140th, Seattle, WA 98125; (206) 363-0975. Excellent source of Scandinavian records.

Other Countries

■ CANADA

Can-Ed. Media Ltd. 43 Moccasin Trail, Don Mills, Ontario, Canada M3C 1Y5; (416) 445-3900. Publishers of Dancecraft records and books. Folk and Square Dance records and cassettes.

■ SWITZERLAND

Swiss Records. Francis Feybli, Postfach 2, CH 8332 Russikon, Switzerland.

Instructional Aids: Records/Cassettes and Videos

Records/Cassettes

■ AMERICAN COUNTRY DANCE

Suggested American Country Dance Records/Cassettes:

American Country Dances (1775–95), eight tunes. Cassette. George A. Fogg, 40 Gray Street, Boston, MA 02116-6210.

Dances from Appalachia, Series I, II, III. Berea College, Box 287, Berea, KY 40404.

■ CLOGGING

Any musical selection with a 2/4 time signature may be used for clogging. Square Dance music without calls (hoedown music) is a good choice when the tempo is appropriate for the skill level of the dancers. Many musical selections can be made more appropriate if the instructor uses a variable-speed record player. The following are examples of records with music of a moderate tempo.

Suggested Clogging Records/Cassettes:

Chinese Breakdown/Rockabout, Sets In Order 2123. *Phase Craze/Pavalon Stomp,* Sets in Order 2114.

Clog Dancers' Choice, Old Time Fiddle Tunes for Clogging Practice. Bob Dalsemer. Cassette.

Dixie on My Mind, Rhythm Records RR 157. *I'm Just a Redneck in a Rock and Roll Bar,* Rhythm Records RR 118. *Trucking Fever,* Rhythm Records RR 151.

Dueling Banjos/Pitter Patter, Wagon Wheel WW 125. *Rain/Timber,* Wagon Wheel WW 134.

Gladys Stomp/Clogging Down Yonder, Red Boot Records RB 301.

Louisiana Saturday Night, Chaparral Records C-311.

Melody Hoedown, Lamon Records LR 10076.

Minstrel Man, Jay-Bar-Kay Records JBK 6018.

Ragtime Annie/Sasafrass, Blue Star BS 1612.

■ CONTRA

Suggested Contra Records/Cassettes:

Contra Dance Music from Western Massachusetts, Fourgone Conclusions. Record FHR 029L.

Eight American Contras and Squares as called by the dean of New England callers. Cassette. George A. Fogg, 40 Gray Street, Boston, MA 02116-6210.

Farewell to the Hollow, New England Tradition. Cassette CSWM 9860 C.

Fluke Hits, The Fish Family Dance Band. Reels and jigs, couple dances from Scandinavia, a few Cajun tunes. Cassette MAR 9012C.

Hold the Mustard, Hold the Mustard. Contra music for dancing and listening. Record HTM IL.

Kitchen Junket, Yankee Ingenuity. Traditional New England Square Dances, suitable for Contra. Cassette ALC 200A/BC. Side 1—music only, Side 2—Tony Parkes's calls.

Live from Contrafornia, The Glasnotes. Spirited collection of Bay Area favorites. Cassette AVO 103C.

Mistwold, Canterbury Country Orchestra. Traditional dance tunes. Record F&W 5L.

New England Chestnuts, Vol. 1 & 2, Randy and Rodney Miller. Tunes for New England Contras. Cassette ALC 203/4C.

Southerners Plus Two Play Ralph Page, The English Folk Dance and Song Society, RP 500.

■ FOLK DANCE

Single records are recommended as a primary music source for instruction. Multiband, long-playing records arranged in a series are useful and economical. Records or cassettes packaged in series form offer a variety of basic steps, nationalities, and formations. They are usually graded easy to difficult; thus they are adaptable to all ability levels. These would also be suitable for One-Night Stands. Single records or audio cassettes make it less expensive to upgrade dance selections, thus keeping dance materials current.

Suggested Folk Dance Records/Cassettes:

Easy Folk Dance Lessons for Children, Dancecraft Cassette Series. A series of six cassettes supervised by Jack Geddes, lecture at MacMaster University School of Physical Education (Canada). The series contains graded dances from a number of nationalities based on locomotor skills. Dance directions accompany each cassette. Series numbers are DC 387, 487, 587, 687, 787, 887.

Folk Dances from 'Round the World, Merit Audio Visual. A seven-album series containing twelve or more dances each from the United States and abroad. Each album presents steps for dancers of increasing ability. Well-illustrated manuals of dance instructions accompany each album. It is especially useful to beginning folk dance teachers. (Formerly the RCA Victor Series supervised by Michael and Mary Ann Herman.)

■ ONE-NIGHT STANDS

Suggested One-Night Stands Records/ Cassettes:

Lloyd Shaw—Elementary Kit.

Melody House (World of Fun).

When the Work's All Done. A Square Dance Party for Beginners and Old Hands. Bob Dalsemer. TC 125C (with), TC 126 (without).

■ SOCIAL DANCE

Music for Social Dance or Ballroom Dance is subject to the particular "sound" in vogue in each generation. "Standards" are records that are recognized by musicians and public alike as favorites and do, indeed, survive several generations. In addition to local distributors, the four most extensive sources are: Grenn, Hoctor, Roper, and Windsor. Refer to Appendix D for distributors.

Suggested Social Dance Records/Cassettes:

Betty White Records. *Foxtrot* D101; *Waltz* D102; *Cha Cha Cha* D103; *Rumba* D104; *Mambo* D105; *Tango* D106; *Charleston* D107; *Lindy* D109; *Merengue and Samba* D110.

Windsor Ballroom Dance Records, 45s, LPs.

Die Tanzplatte Des Jahnes, Günter Mois. TELDEC Record Service (Germany), Warner Communications Co.

Swing Mit Mir—Tanz Mit Mir, Hugo Strasser. EMI Electrola.

Tanzgala '92, Abros Seelos. Cassette, CDs. KOCH 322665.

■ SQUARE DANCE

Records without calls should be chosen for musical key, beat, and overall good phrasing. Callers and teachers who specialize in patter calls will find a wealth of instrumentals or Hoedowns available. Instructors should listen to and select their own background music.

Records with calls are excellent supplementary instructional aids. Videos add a visual as well as an auditory dimension during the beginning learning stages.

Suggested Square Dance Records/Cassettes:

Smoke on the Water. Square Dance Classics, Bob Dalsemer. TC 123C (with), TC 124C (without).

Square Dance Party for the New Dancer, No. 1. Bob Ruff, Wagon Wheel Cassette or LP 1001. Includes eight singing calls, 1 Contra, and 1 Hoedown. Callerlab movements 1–22.

Square Dance Party for the New Dancer, No. 2. Bob Ruff, Wagon Wheel Cassette or LP 1002. Includes eight singing calls, 1 Contra, 1 Hoedown. Callerlab movements 1–34.

Suggested Hoedown Records:

Banjo Plucking/The Other Side. Wagon Wheel 126.

Billy John/Freddies Fancy. Wagon Wheel 121.

Dueling Banjo/Pitter Patter. Wagon Wheel 125.

Get Down Number One/Long Journey. Windsor 4167.

Golden Reel/Chordex. Windsor 4166.

Rock Island Ride/Mt. Mist. Windsor 4185.

Sherbrooks. Grenn 12204.

Sugarfoot Rag. Grenn 12201.

Yellow Creek. Grenn 12209.

Videos

Allons Danser! Randy Speyrer, P.O. Box 15908, New Orleans, LA 70175-5908; (504) 899-0615. "Cajun Dancing" step by step instruction. Waltz, Two-Step, One-Step, Cajun Jitterbug.

Best Film and Video Corp., Great Neck, NY 11021. "Fred Astaire Dancing: Ballroom (Fox Trot, Waltz), Latin (Cha Cha, Salsa)."

Brentwood House Video. 5740 Corsa Ave., Suite 102, Westlake Village, CA 91362. "Line Dancing," "New Line Dancing," "Fun and Funky Freestyle Dancing," "Line Dancing Vol. 2," Christy Lane.

Coffey Video Productions. 3300 Gilbert Lane, Knoxville, TN 37920; (800) 423-1417. "Texas Two Step."

Country Dance and Song Society. 17 New South Street, Northampton, MA 01060; (413) 584-9913. "Clogging and Buck Dancing," "Dances of the World: Appalachia." Clogging groups with history and commentary. "Talking Feet" Solo Southern Dance, Buck Flatfoot and Tap by Mike Seeger and Ruth Pershing.

Duke Publishing Co. Jerry Duke, 14 Ardenwood Way, San Francisco, CA 94132; (415) 338-1850. "Appalachian Clog Dance Steps."

Ethnic Folkarts Center (EFAC). 325 Spring St., Room 314, New York, NY 10013; (212) 691-9510. "Pericles in America" video of Greek dance and Pericles Halkias, Greek clarinet player; "Salute to Immigrant Cultures" film, three days of folk dance in Manhattan.

Flower Films and Video. 10341 San Pablo Avenue, El Cerrito, CA 94530; (415) 525-0942. "Talking Feet" Solo Southern dance: buck, flatfoot, and tap by Mike Seeger and Ruth Pershing.

Folk/Ethnic Dance Videos Catalogue. Published by International Dance Discovery, 1025 South Minor Road, Bloomington, IN 47401.

High/Scope Videos. 600 N. River Street, Ypsilanti, MI 48198-2898; (313) 485-2000; Fax (313) 485-0704. "Folkdances" 1, 2, 3, 4.

Hoctor Products for Education. P.O. Box 38, Waldwick, NJ 07463; (201) 652-7767; Fax (201) 652-2599. "Hip Hop," "Charleston."

National Association of Country Dances. P.O. Box 9841, Colorado Springs, CO 80932. "28 Country Swing Moves and Combinations."

New England Caller, Inc. P.O. Box 8069, Lowell, MA 01853. "Line Dancing for Seniors, Vol. I," Grant F. Longley.

PPI Parade Video. 88 St. Francis St., Newark, NJ 07105. "Texas Dance Styles" by Valerie Moss and Scott Schmitz; "Texas Two-Step," "Down and Dirty" (Jerk, Twist, Stroll, Monkey, Hustle, etc.).

Princeton Book Co. 12 West Delaware Avenue, Pennington, NJ 08534. "Arthur Murray Dance Magic Series." Waltz, Tango, Swing, Samba, Merengue, Night Club, Rumba, Salsa, Cha Cha, Dancin' Dirty, Fox Trot, Mambo.

Quality Video Inc. 7399 Bush Lake Road, Minneapolis, MN 55439. "Country Line Dancing for Kids," "Country Line Dancing," "More Country Line Dancing," Diane Horner.

R & R Video International Dancing in America Series. 3649 Whittier Blvd., Los Angeles, CA 90023. "West Coast Swing," Skippy Blair.

Rushing Productions. 5149 Blanco Rd., #214, San Antonio, TX 78216. "Kicker Dancin' Texas Style." How to do the top ten Country and Western Dances like a Texas cowboy, 1982.

Sarver, Mary J. 1224 SW Normandy Terrace, Seattle, WA 98166. "Pattern Ballroom Dances for Seniors," 27 dances, 1992.

Schild, Myrna Martin. SIU Box 1126, Edwardsville, IL 62026. "Smooth Dances" (Fox Trot, Waltz, Tango). "Rhythm Dances" (Polka and Regional Dances, Samba, Merengue, Swing, Mambo, Cha Cha, and Rumba).

Supreme Audio, Inc. P.O. Box 50, Marlborough, NH 03455-0050; (800) 445-7398; Fax (603) 876-4001. Large collection of Square, Clogging, Country Western, Texas, East Coast Swing, and West Coast Swing videos.

Video Vacation. 306 West Ave., Lockport, NY 14094. "Line Dancing Video for Seniors," "Clogging Appalachian Free-Style Techniques."

Wagon Wheel Records and Books. Bob Ruff, 8459 Edmaru Ave., Whittier, CA 90605; (310) 693-5976. "The Fundamentals of Square Dancing," Parts I & II.

Worldtone Music, Inc. 230 Seventh Avenue, New York, NY 10011; (212) 691-1934; Fax (212) 691-2554. "High Scope Dances," Phyllis Weikart; "Favorite Folk Dances of Kids and Teachers," Sanna Longden; "Easy American Dances #105" and "Easy Israeli Dances," Yehuda Emanuel of Israel.

Bibliography

General

Armstrong, Alan. *Maori Games and Hakas.* Wellington, New Zealand; St. Paul, Auckland, New Zealand and Sidney, Australia: A. H. & A. W. Reed, 1971.

Ashton, Dudley. "Contributions of Dance to Physical Education," *Journal of Health, Physical Education and Recreation,* vol. 27, no. 4, April 1956, p. 19.

Bandem, I. Made and Fredrik Eugene deBoer. *Kaja and Kelod Balinese Dance in Transition.* Oxford, New York, Melbourne, Kuala Lumpur: Oxford University Press, 1981.

Basso, Keith H. *The Gift of Changing Woman.* Anthropological Papers, No. 76. Smithsonian Institute, Bureau of American Ethnology. U.S. Government Printing Office, Washington, D.C., 1966.

Bauer, Marion, and Ethel R. Peyser. *Music Through the Ages: An Introduction to Music History.* 3rd ed. Revised by Elizabeth E. Rogers, ed. New York: G. P. Putnam's Sons, 1967.

Blum, John M., et al. *The National Experience: A History of the United States.* New York: Harcourt Brace Jovanovich, 1973.

Botkin, B. A. "The Play-Party in Oklahoma," in *Follow the Drinkin' Gou'd.* J. Frank Dobie, ed. Publications of the Texas Folk-Lore Society, no. VII. Austin, TX: Texas Folk-Lore Society, 1928.

Boulton, Laura. *Musical Instruments of World Cultures.* Revised Edition 1975. Arizona State University, Tempe, AR 85287.

Bowers, Faubion. *Theatre in the East, A Survey of Asian Dance and Drama.* New York: Thomas Nelson & Sons, 1956.

_____. *The Dance in India.* New York: Columbia University Press, 1953.

Campbell, I. C. *A History of the Pacific Islands.* Berkeley, California: University of California Press, 1989.

Campbell, Joseph. "The Ancient Hawaiian Hulas," *Dance Observer,* vol. 13, no. 3, 1946, pp. 32–33.

Chapline, Claudia. "Dance and Religion," *Journal of Health, Physical Education and Recreation,* vol. 28, no. 8, November 1957, p. 39.

Cole, Arthur C. *The Puritan and Fair Terpsichore.* Brooklyn, NY: Dance Horizons, 1942. (This article is reprinted from *The Mississippi Valley Historical Review,* vol. XXIX, no. 1, June 1942.)

Costa, Mazeppa King. "Dance in the Society and Hawaiian Islands Presented by Early Writers 1767–1842." Master of Arts thesis, University of Hawaii, HI, 1951.

Craddock, John R. "The Cowboy Dance," in *Coffee in the Gourd.* J. Frank Dobie, ed. Publications of the Texas Folk-Lore Society, no. II. Austin, TX: Texas Folk-Lore Society, 1925. (Reprint edition, 1935.)

Czarnowski, Lucille. "Folk Dance in Education," *Focus on Dance I.* Gertrude Lippincott, ed. Washington, D.C.: American Association for Health, Physical Education and Recreation, 1960, pp. 6–7.

Damon, S. Foster. *The History of Square Dancing.* Barre, MA: Barre Gazette, 1957.

Daniel, Ana. *Bali Behind the Mask.* New York: Alfred A. Knopf, 1981.

Dansley, Harry and Kenneth and Jean Bigwood. *The New Zealand Maori in Color.* Wellington, New Zealand, St. Paul, Auckland, New Zealand and Sidney, Australia: A. H. & A. W. Reed, 1963.

deZoete, Beryl and Walter Spies. *Dance and Drama in Bali.* London: Faber and Faber Ltd., 1988.

Dickinson, Mildred. "Dance in Psychotherapy," *Country Dance and Song,* vol. 1, 1968, pp. 28–32.

Ericson, Jane Harris (ed.). *Focus on Dance VI.* Washington, D.C.: American Association for

Health, Physical Education and Recreation, 1972.

Gadd, May. "A Survey: Folk Dance in the Western World," *Dance and Song Society,* no. 2, 1969.

Goodwin, Grenville. *The Social Organization of the Western Apache.* Chicago: University of Chicago Press, 1942.

Grove, Lilly, F. R. G. S. *Dancing: A Handbook of the Terpsichorean Arts in Diverse Places and Times, Savage and Civilized.* London: Longmans, Green, and Company, 1895. (Detroit: Reissued by Singing Tree Press, Book Tower, 1969.)

H'Doubler, Margaret F. *Dance: A Creative Art Experience.* New York: F. S. Crofts and Co., 1940.

Hill, Kathleen. *Dance for Physically Disabled Persons. A Manual for Teaching Ballroom, Square and Folk Dances to Users of Wheelchairs and Crutches.* Washington, D.C.: American Alliance for Health, Physical Education and Recreation, 1976.

Howard, Alan. *Polynesian Readings on a Cultural Area.* Bernice P. Bishop Museum, Honolulu: Chandler Publishing Co., 1971.

Howard, Alan and Robert Borofsky. *Developments in Polynesian Ethnology.* Honolulu, HI: University of Hawaii Press, 1989.

Jobes, Gertrude (ed.). *Dictionary of Folklore, Mythology, and Legends.* New York: Scarecrow Press, 1962.

Kaepplu, Adrienne L. "Folklore as Expressed in the Dance in Tonga," *Journal of American Folklore,* 80(316): 160–168, 1967.

_____ . "Tonga Dance: A Study in Cultural Change," *Ethnomusicology* 14(2): 266–277, 1970.

Kealūnohomoku, Joann Wheeler. "Dance History Research: Perspectives from Related Disciplines." Warrenton, Virginia: Proceedings of the Second Annual Conference on Research in Dance of the Committee on Dance Research, July 4–6, 1969.

_____ . "A Court Dance Disagrees with Emerson's Classic Book on the Hula," *Ethnomusicology* 8(2): 161–164, 1964.

_____ . "Hopi and Polynesian Dance—A Cross Cultural Comparison," *Ethnomusicology* 11:343–58, 1967.

Kennedy, Douglas. *English Folk Dancing Today and Yesterday.* London: G. Bell and Sons, 1964.

Kraus, Richard. *History of the Dance in Art and Education.* Englewood Cliffs, NJ: Prentice-Hall, 1969.

Kurath, Gertrude P. "Basic Techniques of Amerindian Dance," *Dance Notation Record,* vol. VIII, no. 4, 1957, pp. 2–8.

_____ . "Mexican Moriscas: A Problem in Dance Acculturation," *Journal of American Folklore,* vol. 62, no. 244, April–June 1949, pp. 87–106.

Lawler, Lillian B. *The Dance in Ancient Greece.* Middletown, CT: Wesleyan University Press, 1964.

Lawson, Joan. *European Folk Dance: Its National and Musical Characteristics.* New York: Pitman Publishing Co. 1953.

Martin, John. *Introduction to Dance.* Brooklyn, NY: Dance Horizons, 1965.

Mason, Kathleen Griddle (ed.). *Focus on Dance VII.* Washington, D.C.: American Association for Health, Physical Education and Recreation, 1974.

Meerloo, Joost A. M. *The Dance: From Ritual to Rock and Roll—Ballet to Ballroom.* New York: Chilton Co., 1960.

Nevell, Richard. *A Time to Dance: American Country Dancing from Hornpipes to Hot Hash.* New York: St. Martin's Press, 1977.

Pollenz, Phillippa. "Change in Form and Function of Hawaii Hulas," *American Anthropologist,* 52: 225–234, 1950.

_____ . "The Puzzle of Hula," *American Anthropologist,* 50: 647–656, 1948.

Poort, W. A. *The Dance in the Pacific.* Katwijk, Netherlands: Van Der Lee Press, 1975.

Richardson, Philip J. S. *The Social Dances of the Nineteenth Century in England.* London: Herbert Jenkins, 1960.

Rust, Frances. *Dance in Society.* London: Routledge and Kegan Paul, 1969.

Sachs, Curt. *World History of the Dance.* New York: W. W. Norton and Co., 1937.

Sauthoff, Hermine. "Folk Dance: An Expression of Culture," *Journal of Health, Physical Education and Recreation,* vol. 10, no. 7, September 1939, p. 390.

Shapiro, Harry. *The Peopling of the Pacific Rim.* The Thomas Burke Memorial Lecture, 1964.

Stearns, Marshall Winslow, and Jean Stearns. *Jazz Dance.* New York: Macmillan Pub. Co., 1968.

Terry, Walter. *The Dance in America.* New York: Harper and Row, 1956.

Van Zile, Judy. *Dance in Africa, Asia, and the Pacific.* New York: MSS Information Corporation, 1976.

Vuillier, Gaston. *A History of Dance.* London: William Heineman, 1898.

Wallace, Carol McD., et al. *Dance: A Very Social History.* New York: The Metropolitan Museum of Art, 1986.

Wang, Kefen. *The History of Chinese Dance.* Translated into English by Ke Ruibo. Beijing, China: Foreign Languages Press, 1985.

Waterman, Richard A.   "Role of Dance in Human Society," *Focus on Dance II*. Bettie Jean Wooten, ed. Washington, D.C.: American Association for Health, Physical Education and Recreation, 1962, p. 47.

Wood, Melusine.   *Some Historical Dances, Twelfth to Nineteenth Century: Their Manner of Performance and Their Place in the Social Life of the Time*. London: The Imperial Society of Teachers of Dancing Publisher to the Society, 1952.

Youmans, John Green.   "History of Recreational and Social Dance in the United States," University of Southern California, Ph.D. dissertation (Microcard), 1966.

American Heritage Dance

Boyd, Neva. L., and Tressie M. Dunlavy.   *Old Square Dances of America*. Chicago: H. T. Fitzsimmons Co., 1932.

Brewster, Mela Sedillo.   *Mexican and New Mexican Folk Dances*. Albuquerque: University of New Mexico Press, 1938.

Burchenal, Elizabeth.   *American Country Dances*. New York: G. Schirmer, 1918.

Casey, Betty.   *Dance Across Texas*. Austin, TX: University of Texas Press, 1985.

Chase, Gilbert.   *America's Music*. New York: McGraw-Hill Book Co., 1966.

Czarnowski, Lucille.   *Dances of Early California Days*. Palo Alto, CA: Pacific Books, 1950.

Damon, S. Foster.   *A History of Square Dancing*. Barre, MA: Barre Gazette, 1957.

Demille, Agnes.   *The Book of the Dance*. New York: Golden Press, 1963.

Duggan, Anne Schley, Jeanette-Schlottmann, and Abbie Rutledge.   *Folk Dances of the United States and Mexico*. The Folk Dance Library, vol. 5. New York: Ronald Press, 1948.

Duke, Jerry.   *Dance of the Cajuns*. San Francisco, CA: Duke Publishing Co., 1987.

_____ .   *Clog Dance in the Appalachians*. San Francisco, CA 94 121-0368: Duke Publishing Co., 1984.

Engel, Carl.   *Music from the Days of George Washington*. Washington, D.C.: United States George Washington Bicentennial Commission, 1931.

Ericson, Jane Harris (ed.).   *Focus on Dance VI*. Washington, D.C.: American Association for Health, Physical Education and Recreation, 1972.

Evanchuk, Robin.   "Cajun—Sight, Sound and Movement," *Ethnic and Recreational Dance: Focus on Dance VI*. Dance Division of American Association for Health, Physical Education, and Recreation, Washington, D.C., 1972, pp. 43-46.

Ferrero, Edward.   *The Art of Dancing*. New York: Dick Fitzgerald, 1859.

Ford, Henry, and Mrs. Henry Ford.   *Good Morning*. 4th ed. Dearborn, MI: Dearborn Publishing Co., 1943.

Greene, Hank.   *Square and Folk Dancing*. New York: Harper and Row Pub., 1984.

Hamilton, Frank.   *Round Dance Manual*. Los Angeles, CA: Sets in Order, American Square Dance Society, 1975.

Hartsfield, Joyce.   *Solo Dancing II*. New York: Joyce Hartsfield.

_____ .   *Solo Dancing*. New York: Worldtone Music Inc., 1980.

Hipps, R. Harold, and Wallace E. Chappell.   *World of Fun*. Nashville, TN: Board of Education of the United Methodist Church, 1970.

Holt, Ardern.   *How to Dance the Revived Ancient Dances*. London: Horace Cox, 1907.

Howard, John Tasker.   *Our American Music: A Comprehensive History from 1620 to the Present*. New York: Thomas Y. Crowell Co., 1965.

Keller, Kate Van Winkle.   *If the Company Can Do It!: Techniques in Eighteenth-Century American Social Dance*. Sandy Hook, CT: The Hendrickson Group, 1990.

Keller, Kate Van Winkle, and Ralph Sweet.   *A Choice Selection of American Country Dances of the Revolutionary Era, 1775-1795*. New York: Country Dance and Song Society of America, 1975.

Kraus, Richard.   *History of the Dance in Art and Education*. Englewood Cliffs, NJ: Prentice-Hall, 1969.

Longley, Grant F.   *Line Dance Manual, Vol. I*. Lowell, MA: New England Caller, Inc., 1987.

_____ .   *Solo (Line) Dance Manual, Vol. II*. Lowell, MA: New England Caller, Inc, 1979, 1985.

_____ .   *Solo (Line) Dance Manual, Vol. III*. Lowell, MA: New England Caller, Inc., 1990.

McDowell, William.   *Tennessee Play Party*. Delaware, OH: Cooperative Recreation Service, 1960.

McIntosh, David Seneff.   *Singing Games and Dances*. New York: Association Press, 1957.

Mayo, Margot,   *The American Square Dance*. New York: Sentinel Books, 1948.

Melamed, Lanie.   *All Join Hands: Connecting People Through Folk Dance*. Montreal: Lanie Melamed, 1977.

Meyers, Rick.   *Traditional American Dance Book*. Published 1983. Available from: Rick Meyers, 1827 S.E. 76th, Portland, OR 97215.

Millar, Jolen Fitzhugh. *Country Dances of Colonial America.* Williamsburg, VA: Thirteen Colonies Press, 1990.

Morrison, James. *Twenty-Four Early American Country Dances, Cotillions and Reels.* New York: Country Dance and Song Society, 1976.

Nevell, Richard. *A Time to Dance: American Country Dancing from Hornpipes to Hot Hash.* New York: St. Martin's Press, 1977.

Ray, Ollie M. *A Fun Encyclopedia of Solo and Line Dances: The Steps That Came and Stayed.* Whitewater, WI: Siddall and Ray Research Foundation, Publications for Dance, 1987.

Rohrbough, Lynn. *Handy Play Party Book.* Delaware, Ohio: Cooperative Recreation Service, 1940.

_____. *Play Party Games of Pioneer Times.* Delaware, Ohio: Cooperative Recreation Service, 1939.

_____. *Quadrilles, Thirty American Square Dances.* Delaware, Ohio: Cooperative Recreation Service, 1941.

Ryan, Grace L. *Dances of Our Pioneers.* New York: A. S. Barnes Co., 1939.

Sharp, Cecil J., and Maud Karpeles. *The Country Dance Book.* London: Novello and Co., 1918. (Reissued, 1946.)

Shaw, Lloyd. *Cowboy Dances.* Caldwell, ID: Caxton Printers, 1939.

_____. *The Round Dance Book.* Caldwell, ID: Caxton Printers, 1948.

Spizzy, Mable Seeds, and Hazel Gertrude Kinscella. *La Fiesta: A Unit of Early California Songs and Dance.* Lincoln, NE: The University Publishing Co., 1939.

Strobell, Adah Parker. *Bicentennial Games 'n' Fun.* Washington, D.C.: Acropolis Books, 1975.

Thomas, Jean, and Joseph A. Leeder. *The Singin' Gatherin'.* New York: Silver Burdett Co., 1939.

Thompson, Sydney. *Old Time Dancing.* London: John Dilworth, 1950.

Tolman, Beth, and Ralph Page. *The Country Dance Book.* Weston, VT: Countryman Press, 1937.

Wakefield, Eleanor Ely. *Folk Dancing in America.* New York: J. Lowell Pratt and Co., 1966.

Werner, Robert. *The Folklore Village Saturday Night.* Dodgeville, WI: Folklore Village Farm, Inc., 1981.

Clogging

"American Clogging Abbreviations," *American Clogging,* vol. 2, no. 5, October 1984, pp. 22–31.

Austin, Debra E., and Diana L. Callahan. *Modern Clogging.* n.p.: The Tennessee Moonshine Cloggers, 1977.

Austin, Debra, and Diana Hatfield. *Modern Clogging II.* n.p.: The Tennessee Moonshine Cloggers, 1981.

Bernstein, Ira. *Appalachian Clogging and Flatfooting Steps.* Malverne, NY: Ten Toe Percussion, 1992.

Bonner, Frank X. *Clogging and the Southern Appalachian Square Dance.* Acworth, GA: Bonner Publishing Company, 1983.

Doss, Jane. "A Prospective on Dance in the South," *GAHPERD Journal,* vol. 23, no. 2, Spring 1989, pp. 10–11.

Duke, Jerry. *Clog Dance in the Appalachians.* San Francisco: Duke Publishing Co., 1984.

Hillas, Marjorie, and Marian Knighton. *Athletic Dances and Simple Clogs.* New York: A. S. Barnes and Company, 1926.

Linnington, Darryl. "An Old English Dance," *Flop-Eared Mule,* October/November 1990, p. 7.

March, Stephen, and David Holt. "Chase That Rabbit," *Southern Exposure Long Journey Home,* vol. 5, nos. 2–3, Summer & Fall 1977, pp. 44–47.

Meyers, Rick. *Traditional American Dance Book.* Portland, OR: Rick Meyers, 1983.

Nieberlein, Judy. "Step Dancing, Clogging's First Cousin," *Flop-Eared Mule,* March/April 1986, p. 4.

Popwell, Sheila. *Almost Everything You Always Wanted to Know About Teaching Clogging Except How You Ever Let Yourself Get Talked Into Doing This in the First Place!* Huron, OH: Burdick Enterprises, 1980.

Rhodes, Sally. *Fontana Fall Jubilee Clogging.* n.p.: Fontana Village Resort, 1979.

Schild, Myra Martin. *Square Dancing Everyone.* Winston-Salem NC: Hunter Textbooks Inc., 1987.

Seeger, Mike. *Talking Feet.* Berkeley, CA: North Atlantic Books, 1992.

Smith, Steve. "The History of Clog Dancing," *Rock-Step Gazette,* vol. 2, no. 2, August/September 1983, p. 8.
"The Clog Shoe," *American Clogging,* vol. 2, no. 11, April 1985, p. 15.
"The Great Ones," *Clogging,* July/August/September 1984, p. 8.
"The History of Clog Shoes," *American Clogging,* vol. 2, no. 12, May 1985, pp. 16–17.
"Traditional Terminology," *Flop-Eared Mule,* January/February 1987, pp. 29–35.

Woodall, Chip. "The Revival of Folk Dance," *Flop-Eared Mule,* July/August 1986, pp. 10–11.

Contra Dance

Armstrong, Don. *Contra.* Lakewood, CO: The Lloyd Shaw Foundation, 1960.

_____ . *The Caller-Teacher Manual for Contras.* Los Angeles: American Square Dance Society, 1973.

Briggs, Dudley T. *Thirty Contras from New England.* Burlington, MA: Dudley T. Briggs, 1953.

Brundage, Al, and Reuben Merchant. *Contras Are Fun.* 1952.

Burchenal, Elizabeth. *American Country Dances.* New York: G. Schirmer, 1918.

Community Dance Manual. Numbers 4 (1954) and 5 (1957). New York: Country Dance Society, Inc.

Fix, Penn. *Contra Dancing in the Northwest.* Spokane, WA: Penn Fix, 1991.

Ford, Henry, and Mrs. Henry Ford. *Good Morning.* 4th ed. Dearborn, MI: Dearborn Publishing Co., 1943.

Gadd, May. *Country Dances of Today.* Vol. 2. New York: Country Dance Society of America, 1951.

Gaudreau, Herbie. *Modern Contra Dancing.* Sandusky, OH: American Square Dance Magazine, 1971.

Henrickson, Charles Cyril. *A Colonial Dancing Experience: Country Dancing for Elementary School Children.* Sandy Hook, CT: The Hendrickson Group, 1989.

Hinds, Tom. *Dance All Night* and *Dance All Night 2.* Arlington, VA: Tom Hinds, 1991.

Hubert, Gene. *Dizzy Dances Volumes I and II.* Bethseda, MD: Gene Hubert, 1986.

_____ . *More Dizzy Dances: Volume III.* Bethseda, MD: Gene Hubert, 1990.

Jennings, Larry. *Zesty Contras.* Cambridge, MA: The New England Folk Festival Association, 1983.

Kaynor, David A. *Calling Contra Dances for Beginners by Beginners.* Montague Center, MA: David A. Kaynor, 1991.

Keller, Kate Van Winkle and Ralph Sweet. *A Choice Selection of American Country Dances of the Revolutionary Era.* New York: Country Dance and Song Society, 1975.

Knox, Roger, ed. *Contras as Ralph Page Called Them.* Ithaca, NY: Roger Knox, 1990.

Nevell, Richard. *A Time to Dance. American Country Dancing from Hornpipes to Hot Hash.* New York: St. Martin's Press, 1977.

Page, Ralph. *An Elegant Collection of Contras and Squares.* Denver, CO: The Lloyd Shaw Foundation, Inc., 1984.

_____ . *Heritage Dances of Early America.* Colorado Springs, CO: Lloyd Shaw Foundation, 1976.

_____ . *The Ralph Page Book of Contras.* London: English Folk Dance and Song Society, 1969.

Parkes, Tony. *Contra Dance Calling, A Basic Text.* Bedford, MA: Hands Four Books, 1992.

_____ . *Shadrack's Delight.* Bedford, MA: Hands Four Books, 1988.

Sannella, Ted. *Balance and Swing.* New York: Country Dance Society, Inc., 1982.

_____ . *Swing the Next.* Northampton, MA: Country Dance and Song Society, in preparation.

Shacklette, Stew. *Contra Calling Made Easy.* Bradenburg, KY: Kentucky Dance Institute, 1980.

Twork, Eva O'Neal. *Henry Ford and Benjamin B. Lovett: The Dancing Billionaire and the Dancing Master.* Detroit, MI: Harlo Press, 1982.

International Folk Dance

Alford, Violet. *The Traditional Dance.* London: Methuen and Co., 1935.

_____ . *Dances of France. Vol. III: The Pyrenees.* New York: Crown Publishers, 1963.

Banbra, Audrey, and Muriel Webster. *Teaching Folk Dancing.* New York: Theatre Arts Books, 1972.

Beliajus, V. F. *Dance and Be Merry.* Vols. I and II. Evanston, IL: Summy-Birchard Co., 1940.

Bergquist, Nils W. *Swedish Folk Dances.* Cranbury, NJ: Thomas Yoseloff, 1928.

Berk, Fred. *Ha-Rikud, The Jewish Dance.* American Zionist Youth Foundation, Union of American Hebrew Congregations, United States of America, 1972, 1975.

Brehthnach, Breandan. *Folk Music and Dances of Ireland.* Dublin, Ireland: Mercier Press, 1986.

Bryans, Helen L., and John Madsen. *Scandinavian Dances.* Toronto: Irwin Clarke and Co., 1942.

Burchenal, Elizabeth. *Folk Dances from Old Homelands,* 1922; *Folk Dances and Singing Games,* 1922; *National Dances of Ireland,* 1929; *Folk Dances of Germany,* 1938; *Folk Dances of Denmark,* 1940. New York: G. Schirmer, Inc.

Butenhof, Ed. *Dance Parties for Beginners.* Mack Creek, MO: Lloyd Shaw Foundation, 1990.

Casey, Betty. *International Folk Dancing U.S.A.* Garden City, NY: Doubleday & Co., Inc., 1981.

Chapru, Doleta. *A Festival of the English May.* Dodgeville, WI: Folklore Village Farm, Inc., 1977.

Chochem, Corinne, and Muriel Roth. *Palestine Dances.* New York: Behrman's Jewish Book House, 1941.

Covarrubias, Luis. *Regional Dances of Mexico.* Mexico, D.F.: Eugenio Fischgrund, n.d.

Cwieka, R. *The Great Polish Walking Dance, Volume I; The Polish Running Dance, Volume II; The Polish Figure Dance Book, Volume III: The Krakowiak Dance Workbook, Volume IV; The Kujawiak Dance Workbook, Volume V; The Oberek Dance Workbook, Volume VI; The Zakopane Mountain Dance Workbook, Volume VII.* Copyright © 1983. Order from R. Cwieka, 1375 Clinton Avenue, Irvington, NJ 97111.

———. "Spanish Mexican Dance: California and the Southwest," *Focus on Dance VI.* Jane Harris Erickson, ed. Washington, D.C.: American Association of Health, Physical Education and Recreation, 1972, p. 23.

Damon, S. Foster. *The History of Square Dancing.* Barre, MA: Barre Gazette, 1957.

Duggan, Anne Schley, Jeanette Schlottmann, and Abbie Rutledge. *The Teaching of Folk Dance, Volume I; Folk Dances of Scandinavia, Volume II; Folk Dances of European Countries, Volume III; Folk Dances of the British Isles, Volume IV; Folk Dances of the United States and Mexico, Volume V.* The Folk Dance Library. New York: Ronald Press, 1948.

Dunsing, Gretel and Paul Dunsing. *A Collection of the Descriptions of Folk Dances,* 1972; Second Collection, 1976; Third Collection, 1977.

———. *German Folk Dances.* Vol. 1, Leipzig: Verlag Friedrich Hofmeister, 1936.

———. *Dance Lightly.* Delaware, OH: Cooperative Recreation Service, 1946.

Eisenberg, Helen, and Larry Eisenberg. *The World of Fun Series of Recreation Recording.* Nashville, TN: Board of Education of the United Methodist Church, 1970.

Ellfeldt, Lois. *Folk Dance.* Brown Physical Education Activity Series. Dubuque, IA: William C. Brown and Co., 1967.

English Country Dances of Today. Delaware, OH: Cooperative Recreation Service, 1948.

The English Folk Dance and Song Society. *Community Dance Manual, Books 1–7.* Princeton, NJ: Princeton Book Co., 1986.

Farwell, Jane. *Folk Dances for Fun.* Delaware, OH: Cooperative Recreation Service, n.d.

———. *The Folklore Village Saturday Night Book.* Dodgeville, WI: Folklore Village Farm, Inc., 1981.

Flett, J. P., and T. M. Flett. *Traditional Dancing in Scotland.* Boston, MA: Routledge and Kegan Paul, 1986.

Folk Dance Federation of California, Inc. *Folk Dances from Near and Far. International Series,* A1, 2, 3 Beginners; B1, 2 Intermediate; C1, 2 Advanced; D1, 2 Nonpartner. Alameda, CA: Folk Dance Federation of California, Inc.

Folklore Village Farm. *Folk Dances and Music.* Booklets Vol. 1, 1975; Vol. 2, 1976. Dodgeville, WI: Folklore Village Farm, Inc.

Fox, Grace I., and Kathleen G. Merrill. *Folk Dances in High School and College.* New York: Ronald Press, 1957.

Gault, Ned and Marian. *Half a 100 and 1 More Easy Folk Dances.* 17632 Via Sereno, Monte Sereno, CA, 1983.

———. *100 and 1 Early Folk Dances.* 17632 Via Sereno, Monte Sereno, CA, 1980.

Gilbert, Cecile. *International Folk Dance at a Glance.* Minneapolis: Burgess Publishing Co., 1974.

Haire, Frances H. *The Costume Book.* New York: A. S. Barnes and Co., 1937.

Hall, J. Tillman. *Dance! A Complete Guide to Social, Folk and Square Dancing,* Belmont, CA: Wadsworth Publishing Co., 1963.

———. *Folk Dance.* Goodyear Physical Education Series. Pacific Palisades, CA: Goodyear Publishing Co., 1969.

Harris, Jane A. *File O'Fun.* Minneapolis: Burgess Publishing Co., 1970.

Herman, Michael. *The Folk Dancer,* vol. 1. April 1941. Folk Dance House, P.O. Box 2305, North Babylon, NY 11703.

———. *Folk Dances for All.* New York: Barnes and Noble, 1947.

Hinman, Mary Wood. *Group Dances, Gymnastics and Folk Dancers.* Vol. IV. New York: A. S. Barnes and Co., 1930.

Hipps, R. Harold, and Wallace E. Chappell. *World of Fun.* Nashville, TN: Board of Education of the United Methodist Church, 1970.

Holden, Rickey, and Mary Vouras. *Greek Folk Dance.* Newark, NJ: Folkraft Press, 1965.

Hunt, Beatrice A., and Harry Robert Wilson. *Sing and Dance.* Chicago: Hall and McCreary Co., 1945.

Isbary, Hanni. "A Long Life Serving Folkdancers," *Viltis,* vol. 34, no 3, October 1975, p. 18.

Jaffe, Nigel Allenby. *Folk Dance of Europe.* Lambert's Halt, Kirby, Malham, Skipton, North Yorkshire BD23 4BT, England: Folk Dance Enterprises, 1990.

Jankovic, Ljubica, and Danica Jankovic. *Dances of Yugoslavia.* New York: Crown Publishers, 1952.

Jensen, Mary Bee, and Clayne R. *Folk Dancing.* Provo, UT: Brigham Young University Press, 1973.

Joukowsky, Anatol M. *The Teaching of Ethnic Dance.* New York: J. Lowell Pratt and Co., 1965.

Katzarova-Kukudova, Raina, and Djener, Kiril. *Bulgarian Folk Dances.* Sophia, Bulgaria: The Science and Art State Publishing House, 1958.

Keller, Kate Van Winkle and Genevieve Shimer. *The Playford Ball, 103 Early English Country Dances.* North Hampton, MA: The Country Dance and Song Society, 1990.

Kennedy, Douglas, ed. *Community Dances Manual, Books 1 – 7.* London: English Folk Dance and Song Society, 1991.

_____. *English Folk Dancing Today and Yesterday.* London: G. Bell and Sons, Ltd., 1964.

Khumer, Gertrude with Eliot Khumer. *The Golden Gate Book of Original Solo/Line Dances.* Vol. I. 1324 Bay View Place, Berkeley, CA.

Kraus, Richard G. *Folk Dancing: A Guide for Schools, Colleges, and Recreation Groups.* New York: Macmillan Pub. Co., 1962.

Lapson, Dvora. *Dances of the Jewish People.* New York: The Jewish Education Committee of New York, 1954.

LaSalle, Dorothy. *Rhythms and Dances for Elementary Schools,* New York: Ronald Press, 1951.

Lawson, Joan. *European Folk Dance: Its National and Musical Characteristics.* New York: Pitman Publishing Co., 1953.

Leeming, Joseph. *The Costume Book for Parties and Plays.* Philadelphia: J. B. Lippincott Co., 1938.

Lidster, Miriam D., and Dorothy H. Tamburini. *Folk Dance Progressions.* Belmont, CA: Wadsworth Publishing Co., 1965.

Lloyd, A. L. *Dances of Argentina.* London: Max Parrish and Co., n.d.

Lobley, Robert and Priscilla. *Your Book of English Country Dancing.* London: Faber and Faber, Ltd., 1980.

Lucero-White, Aurora. *Folk Dances of Colonials of New Mexico.* Santa Fe, New Mexico: Examiner Publishing Company, Inc., 1946.

Martin, Phil. *Across the Fields. Traditional Norwegian-American Music from Wisconsin.* Dodgeville, WI: Folklore Village Farm, Inc., 1982.

Milligan, Jean C. *Won't You Join the Dance.* Available from: The Royal Scottish Country Dance Society, 12 Coates Crescent, Edinburgh, Scotland, EH3 7AF.

Mooney, Gertrude X. *Mexican Folk Dances for American Schools.* Coral Gables, FL: University of Miami Press, 1957.

Mynatt, Constance V., and Bernard D. Kaiman. *Folk Dancing for Students and Teachers.* Dubuque, IA: William C. Brown and Co., 1968.

O'Keefe, J. G. *A Handbook of Irish Dances.* Dublin: M. H. Gill and Sons, 1944.

People's Folk Dance Directory. P. O. Box 8575, Austin, TX 78712.

Petrides, Ted P. *Greek Dances.* Athens, Greece: Lyeabettus Press, 1975.

Petrides, Theodore, and Elfleida Petrides. *Folk Dances of the Greeks.* New York: Exposition Press, 1961.

Pinon, Roger, and Henri Jamar. *Dances of Belgium.* London: Max Parrish and Co., 1953.

Pittman, Anne, Marlys Swenson, and Olcutt Sanders. "Cotton-Eyed Joe," *Foot 'n' Fiddle,* September 1947, pp. 9 – 12.

Playford, John. *The English Dancing Master: Or, Plaine and Easie Rules for the Dancing Country Dances, With the Tune to Each Dance.* Reprinted Princeton, NJ: Princeton Book Co., 1986.

Rath, Emil. *The Folk Dance in Education.* Minneapolis: Burgess Publishing Co., 1939.

Rohrbough, Lynn. *Treasures from Abroad.* Delaware, OH: Cooperative Recreation Service, 1938.

Ross, F. Russel, and King, Virginia. *Multicultural Dance,* Box 18227, Cleveland Heights, OH: Russel & King, 1984.

Sedillo, Mela Brewster. *Mexican and New Mexican Folk Dances.* Albuquerque: University of New Mexico Press, 1948.

Shambaugh, Mary Effie. *Folk Festivals for Schools and Playgrounds.* New York: A. S. Barnes and Co., 1932.

Sharp, Cecil J., and Maud Karpeles. *The Country Dance Book.* London: Novello and Co., 1918. (Reissued, 1946.)

Sharp, Cecil J. and A. P. Oppé. *The Dance, An Historical Survey of Dancing in Europe.* London: Halton and Truscott Smith, Ltd.: New York: Murton, Balch and Company, 1924. (Republished EP Publishing Ltd., 1972.)

Spicer, Dorothy Gladys. *The Book of Festivals.* New York: The Woman's Press, 1937.

Spiesman, Mildred C. *Folk Dancing.* Philadelphia: W. B. Saunders Co., 1970.

Spizzy, Mable Seeds, and Hazel Gertrude Kinscella. *La Fiesta: A Unit of Early California Songs and Dance.* Lincoln, NE: University Publishing Company, 1939.

Thurston, Hugh. "History of Scottish Dancing," *Viltis,* March 1964, p. 5.

Turner, Margery J. *Dance Handbook.* Englewood Cliffs, NJ: Prentice-Hall, 1959.

Van Clef, Frank C. *24 Country Dances from the Playford Editions.* Princeton, NJ: Princeton Book Co., 1986.

Viski, Karoly. *Hungarian Dances.* London: Simpkin Marshall, 1937.

Wakefield, Eleanor Ely. *Folk Dancing in America*. New York: J. Lowell Pratt and Co., 1966.

Weikart, Phyllis S. *Teaching Movement and Dance*. Ypsilanti, MI: High/Scope Press, 1982.

_____. *Teaching Intermediate Folk Dance*. Ypsilanti, MI: High/Scope Press, 1982.

Werner, Bob. *Scandinavian Folk Dances and Tunes. A compilation*. Dodgeville, WI: Folklore Village Farm, 1981.

Witzig, Louise. *Dances of Switzerland*. New York: Chanticleer Press, 1949.

Zielinski, Stefan J. *Dances of Poland*. Chicago: W. H. Sajewski Music and Publishing Co., 1953.

Tune Books

Brody, David. *The Fiddler's Fakebook*. Oak Publications, 1983.

Cahn, David. *A Dozen Waltzes*. Seattle, WA: 1992.

Cole, M. M. *One Thousand Fiddle Tunes*. 1940, 1991.

Edelman, Larry. *Timepieces: Vintage Originals*. Baltimore, MD: Larry Edelman, 1989.

Geisler, Richard. *The Bulgarian Collection, The International Collection, The Yugoslav Collection*. The Village and Early Music Society, 15181 Ballantree Lane, Grass Valley, CA 95949.

McQuillen, Bob. *Bob's Note Books: Jigs, Reels, and Other Tunes*. Volumes 1–8. Petersborough, NH: Bob McQuillen, 1982–1992.

Miller, Randy and Jack Perron. *The New England Fiddler's Repertoire*. East Alstead, NH: Fiddlecase Books, 1983, 1986.

Sweet, Ralph. *The Fifer's Delight*. Hazardville, CT: Ralph Sweet, 1964, 1981.

Williams, Vivian, ed. *Brand New Old Line Fiddle Tunes, Vol. 1, 2, 3*. Seattle, WA: Voyager Recordings & Publication, 1992.

Square Dance

Burdick, Stan. *Show and Sell the Square Dance Story*. Huron, OH: American Square Dance Magazine, 1982.

Burleson, Bill. *Square Dance Encyclopedia*. 2565 Fox Avenue, Minerva, OH 44657.

Cassey, Betty. *The Complete Book of Square Dancing and Round Dancing*. Doubleday & Co., Inc., Garden City, NY, 1976.

Clossin, Jimmy, and Carl Hertzog. *West Texas Square Dances*. El Paso, TX: Carl Hertzog Printing, 1949.

Dalsemer, Bob. *New England Quadrilles and How to Call Them*. Baltimore, MD: Bob Dalsemer, 1985.

_____. *Smoke on the Water, Square Dance Classics*. Baltimore, MD: Traditional Caller Productions, 1989.

_____. *West Virginia Square Dances*. New York: Country Dance and Song Society of America, 1982.

_____. *When the Work's All Done: A Square Dance Party for Beginners and Old Hands*. Baltimore, MD: Traditional Caller Productions.

Damon, S. Foster. *The History of Square Dancing*. Barre, MA: Barre Gazette, 1957.

Durlacher, Ed. *Honor Your Partner*. New York: Devin-Adair Co., 1949.

Edelman, Larry. *Square Dance Caller's Workshop, Fourth Edition*. Baltimore, MD: D & R Productions, 1991.

Everett, Bert. *Fifty Canadian Square Dances*. Toronto: Can-Ed Media, 1983.

Ford, Henry, and Mrs. Henry Ford. 3rd ed. 1941. 4th ed. 1943. Dearborn, MI: Dearborn Publishing Co.

Gadd, May. *Country Dances of Today*. Vol. 2. New York: Country Dance Society of America, 1951.

Gilmore, Ed. "The Science of Calling," *Square Dancing*. Vol. XXII, No. 3, 1970, Ch. I, pp. 19–22; Vol. XXII, No. 4, 1970, Ch. II, pp. 27–30; Vol. XXII, No. 5, 1970, Ch. III, pp. 21–25.

Greene, Hank. *Square and Folk Dancing. A Complete Guide for Students, Teachers and Callers*. New York: Harper & Row, 1984.

Gunzenhauser, Margot. *Square Dancing at School*. Virum, Denmark: Square Dance Partners, 1991.

Helsel, Lee. "Leadership," *Square Dancing*. Vol. XXII, No. 11, 1970, pp. 31–33.

Holden, Rickey. *The Square Dance Caller*. Newark, NJ: American Squares, 1951.

Howard, Carole. *Just One More Dance: A Collection of Old Western Square Dance Calls*. Chelsea, MI: Book Crafters, 1989.

The Illustrated Basic and Mainstream Movements of Square Dancing. Handbook Series. Official Publication of Sets In Order American Square Dance Society, 426 North Robertson Blvd., Los Angeles, CA 90048.

The Illustrated Plus Movements of Square Dancing. Handbook Series. Official Publication of Sets in Order American Square Dance Society, 426 North Robertson Blvd., Los Angeles, CA 90048.

Jensen, Clayne R., and Mary B. Jensen. *Square Dancing*. Provo, UT: Brigham Young University Press, 1973.

King, Jay. *How to Teach Modern Square Dancing.* Lexington, MA: 1972.

Kraus, Richard G. *A Pocket Guide of Folk and Square Dances and Singing Games for Elementary School.* Englewood Cliffs, NJ: Prentice Hall Inc., 1966.

_____ . *Square Dances of Today and How to Call Them.* New York: Ronald Press, 1950.

Linnell, Rod and Louise Winston. *Square Dances from a Yankee Caller's Clipboard.* Norwell, MA: The New England Square Dance Caller, 1974.

Lyman, Frank Jr. *One Hundred and One Singing Calls.* Woodbury, NJ: American Squares, 1951.

Nevell, Richard. *A Time to Dance. American Country Dancing from Hornpipes to Hot Hash.* New York: St. Martin's Press, 1977.

Owens, Lee, and Viola Ruth. *Advanced Square Dance Figures of the West and Southwest.* Palo Alto, CA: Pacific Books, 1950.

Page, Ralph. "A History of Square Dancing," *Square Dancing.* Vol. XXVI, No. 1–5. 1974.

Pete, Piute. *Piute Pete's Down Home Square Dance Book.* NY: Grosset & Dunlap, 1977.

Ryan, Grace L. *Dances of Our Pioneers.* New York: Ronald Press, 1939.

Schild, Myrna M. *Square Dancing Everyone.* Winston-Salem, NC: Hunter Textbooks, Inc., 1987.

Shaw, Dorothy. "The Story of Square Dancing: A Family Tree," *Sets in Order,* vol. XIII, no. 11, 1961, pp. 33–48.

Shaw, Lloyd, *Cowboy Dances.* Caldwell, ID: Caxton Printers, 1939.

Stultz, Sandra J. *Contemporary Square Dance.* Minneapolis: Burgess Publishing Co., 1974.

Social Dance

Aldrich, Elizabeth. *From the Ballroom to Hell, Grace and Folly in Nineteenth-Century Dance.* Evanston, IL: Northwestern University Press, 1991.

Blake, Dick. *Discotheque Dance.* Cleveland: The World Publishing Co., 1965.

Buckman, Peter. *Let's Dance: Social, Ballroom and Folk Dancing,* New York and London: Paddington Press Ltd., 1978.

Casey, Betty. *Dance Across Texas.* Austin, TX: University of Texas Press, 1985.

Clark, Sharon Leigh. "What Do You Dance, America?" *Focus on Dance VI.* Jane Harris Ericson, ed. Washington, D.C.: American Association for Health, Physical Education and Recreation, 1972, pp. 51–55.

Dannett, Sylvia, and Frank Rachel. *Down Memory Lane.* New York: Greenberg Publishers, 1954.

Dow, Allen with Mike Michaelson. *The Official Guide to Ballroom Dancing.* Northbrook, IL: Domus, 1980.

_____ . *The Official Guide to Latin Dancing.* Northbrook, IL: Domus, 1980.

Duke, Jerry. *Social and Ballroom Dance Lab Manual.* San Francisco, CA: Duke Publishing Co., 1988.

Elfman, Bradley. *Breakdancing.* New York: Avon Books, 1984.

Ellis, Havelock. *The Dance of Life.* New York: Grosset and Dunlap, 1923.

Fischer-Munstermann, Uta. *Jazz Dance and Jazz Gymnastics Including Disco Dancing.* New York: Sterling Publishing Co., Inc., 1978.

Franks, A. H. *Social Dance: A Short History.* London: Routledge and Kegan Paul, 1963.

Fresh, Mr., and the Supreme Rockers. *Breakdancing.* New York: Avon Books, 1984.

Goldman, Albert. *Disco.* New York: Hawthorn Books, Inc., 1978.

Hager, Steven. *Hip Hop: The Illustrated History of Break Dancing, Rap, Music, and Graffiti.* New York: St. Martin's Press, 1984.

Heaton, Alma, and Israel Heaton. *Ballroom Dance Rhythms.* Dubuque, IA: William C. Brown Co., 1961.

Heaton, Alma. *Disco with Donny and Marie, Step by Step Guide to Disco Dancing.* CA and MT: Osmond Publishing Co., 1979.

_____ . *Techniques of Teaching Ballroom Dance.* Promo, UT: Brigham Young University Press, 1965.

_____ . *Techniques of Teaching Ballroom Rhythms.* Dubuque, IA: Kendall/Hunt Publishing Co., 1971.

_____ . *Fun Dance Rhythms.* Provo, UT: Brigham Young University Press, 1976.

Hostetler, L. A. *Walk Your Way to Better Dancing.* Rev. ed. New York: A. S. Barnes and Co., 1952.

Javna, John. *How to Jitterbug.* New York: St. Martin's Press, 1984.

Kilbride, Ann, and Angelo Algoso. *The Complete Book on Disco and Ballroom Dancing.* Los Alamitos, CA: Hwong Publishing Co., 1979.

Kraus, Richard G., and Lola Sadlo. *Beginning Social Dance.* Belmont, CA: Wadsworth Publishing Co., 1964.

Kraus, Richard. "Dance in the Age of Aquarius," *Focus on Dance VI.* Jane Harris Ericson, ed. Washington, D.C.: American Association for Health, Physical Education and Recreation, 1972, pp. 56–58.

Laird, Walter. *Technique of Latin Dancing: International Dance.* London: Book Service, 1972.

Livingston, Peter. *The Complete Book of Country Swing and Western Dance and a Bit About Cowboys.* Garden City, NY: Doubleday & Co., Inc., 1981.

Lustgarten, Karen. *The Complete Guide to Disco Dancing.* New York: Warner Books, Inc., 1978.

——. *The Complete Guide to Touch Dancing.* New York: Warner Books, Inc., 1979.

Marlow, Curtis, *Break Dancing.* Cresskill, NJ: Sharon Publications, Inc., 1984.

McDonagh, Don. *Dance Fever.* New York: Quarto Marketing Ltd., 1979.

McGuigan, Cathleen, Mark D. Uehling, Jennifer Smith, Sherry Keene-Osborn, Barbara Burgower, and Nadene Joseph. "Breaking Out: America Goes Dancing," *Newsweek,* July 2 1984, pp. 46–52.

Monte, John. *The Fred Astaire Dance Book.* New York: Simon and Schuster, 1978.

Moore, Alex. *Ballroom Dancing.* London: Sir Isaac Pitman and Sons, 1974.

Morton, Virgil L. *The Teaching of Popular Dance.* Columbus, OH: Charles E. Merrill Publishing Co., 1968.

Murray, Arthur. *How to Become a Good Dancer.* Rev. ed. New York: Simon and Schuster, 1959.

National Association of Country Dancers. *Country and Western Dance Manual.* P. O. Box 9841, Colorado Springs, CO 80932.

Pillich, William F. *Social Dance.* Brown Physical Education Activity Series. Dubuque, IA: William C. Brown and Co., 1967.

Romain, Elizabeth, and Flick Colby. *Let's Go Dancing.* London: Octopus Books Ltd., 1979.

Rushing, Shirley and Patrick McMillan. *Kicker Dancin' Texas Style.* Winston-Salem, NC: Hunter Textbooks, 1988.

Schild, Myrna Martin. *Social Dance.* Dubuque, IA: Wm. C. Brown, 1985.

Sherratt, Brian, and Nalani M. Leong. *Disco Chic: All the Style, Steps, and Places to Go.* New York: Harmony Books, Crown Publishers, Inc., 1979.

Silvester, Victor. *Modern Ballroom Dancing: The Maestro's Manual.* London: Book Service, 1971.

Spencer, Frank, and Peggy Frank. *Come Dancing.* London: Book Service, 1970.

Stearns, Marshall and Jean. *Jazz Dance, the Story of American Vernacular Dance.* New York: Schirmer Books, Macmillan Publishing Co., Inc., 1968, 1979.

Stephenson, Richard M. and Joseph Iaccarino. *The Complete Book of Ballroom Dancing.* New York: Doubleday, 1980.

Veloz and Yolanda. *Tango and Rumba.* New York: Harper and Brothers, 1938.

Villacorta, Aurora S. *Step by Step to Ballroom Dancing.* Danville, IL: Interstate Printers and Publishers, 1974.

——. *Charleston, Anyone?* Danville, Il: Interstate Printers & Publishers, Inc., 1978.

Villari, Jack, and Kathleen Sims Villari. *Disco Dance Steps.* Secaucus, NJ: Chartwell Books, Inc., 1978.

Williams, Jill. "Keeping Fit to a Fiddle (Western)," *Saturday Evening Post,* October 1981, pp. 74–77.

White, Betty. *Teen Age Dance Book.* New York: David McKay Co., 1952.

——. *Teen Age Dance Etiquette.* New York: David McKay Co., 1956.

——. *Latin American Dance Book.* New York: David McKay Co., 1958.

——. *Ballroom Dancebook for Teachers.* New York: David McKay Co., 1962.

Wright, Dexter, and Anita Wright. *How to Dance.* New York: Doubleday and Co., 1952.

Wright, Judy Patterson. *Social Dance: Steps to Success.* Champaign, IL: Leisure Press, 1992.

Glossary

Above Contra Dance term. Refers to the next couple or the couples up the set from the actives.

Accent The stress that is placed on a beat that makes it stronger or louder than the others. The primary accent is on the first beat of the measure. Sometimes there is more than one accent per measure. Some dance steps have the accent on the off-beat, which makes the rhythm syncopated.

Active Couple Relating to Square Dance and Quadrilles, refers to lead couple. Relating to Contra Dance, refers to every other couple (1, 3, 5, and so forth) or every third couple (1, 4, 7, and so forth). Same as first couple, head couple, or top couple.

Alamo Style A Square Dance term. A variation of grand right and left. All eight dancers do an allemande left, hold on to the corner, but shift to a hands-up position and take partner by the right, making a complete circle with the men facing in and the ladies facing out. Dancers balance forward and back. They release the left hand halfway around so that the men now face out and the ladies face in. They join hands as before and repeat balance. Dancers release with the right hand and turn with the left hand halfway around. They join hands as before and repeat balance and right-hand turn. They repeat balance and left-hand turn and meet partner.

All Around Your Left-Hand Lady A Square Dance term. Corners move one time around each other in a loop pattern, the man starting behind the corner, continuing on around her and moving back to place. The lady starts in front of the man and continues on around him and back to place. As they move, both partners always remain facing the center of the square. This completes half of the loop. See-saw your partner is a similar action around partner that completes the other half of the loop.

All Eight A Square Dance term. Refers to all eight members in set.

Allemande Left A Square Dance term. Corners take a left-forearm grasp and turn each other once around and go back home. Left elbow is bent, and dancers pull away from each other to take advantage of the centrifugal force.

Allemande Right A Square Dance term. Man and lady designated to take a right-forearm grasp and turn each other once around. Right elbow is bent, and dancers pull away slightly as in allemande left.

Allemande Thar A Square Dance term. A star formation involving all four couples in the set. Dancers go allemande left, return to partner, give a right hand, pull by, and take the next with a left-forearm grasp. The man then turns this lady about a half-turn counterclockwise until he can put his right hand into the box star position with all the other men. The men travel backward in the star; the ladies travel forward. To "shoot the star," the men release the box star position, turn the ladies on their left halfway around so that the ladies are facing clockwise and the men are facing counterclockwise. They release arm position, move forward to the next person, give a right hand, pull by, and take the next with a left-forearm grasp. The men turn as before into another box star, backing up. They shoot the star once more, pulling around to meet original partner.

All Jump Up and Never Come Down A Square Dance term. All jump into the air; usually followed by partner swing.

Along the Line A Square Dance term. This refers to the persons in the same line. If the call is ladies chain along the line, each side of the line turns to face the other couple in the line and chains the ladies.

Anchor Step West Coast Swing term. Step right behind left (hook) (count 1), step left in place (count *and*), step right in place (count 2). Usually danced at the end of the slot.

Arch in the Middle A Square Dance term. The two persons in the center of a line take hands and make an arch for others to duck under. After the arch is made, the couple, if facing out, turns a California twirl to face the center of the set. Also called make an arch.

Arm Around   *See* Cast Off.

Around One or Two   A Square Dance term used following split the ring, pass thru, or cross trail thru. Couples separate; one goes right, the other left around the outside of the set, just passing one person. They come into a line or into the middle of the set. Sometimes the call is "come around two," meaning the person going on the outside passes two persons before coming in.

Back Cross Position   Man and lady stand side by side, the lady on the right. Arms are crossed behind them so that the lady's left arm is behind him and her left hand holds his left hand at his left side; his right arm is behind her and his right hand holds her right hand at her right side.

Back to Back   *See* Face to Face.

Back Track   A Square Dance term referring to a double turn back from a grand right and left. *See also* Single-File Turn Back; Turn Back.

Balance

1. *Contra.* The following is suggested.
   a. Step swing: step left (count 1) and swing right across in front of left (count 2). Repeat beginning right.
   b. Refer to Folk Dance balance in 2/4 time.
2. *Folk Dance.* The balance may be done forward, backward, or sideward.
   a. *3/4 Time.* Step left (count 1); touch right to left, rising on balls of both feet (count 2); and lower heels in place (count 3). Repeat same movement, beginning right.
   b. *2/4 Time.*
      1) Step left (count 1); touch right to left, rising on balls of both feet (count *and*); lower heels (count 2); and hold (count *and*). Repeat, beginning right.
      2) Or step left (count 1) and touch right to left (count 2). Repeat same movement, beginning right. Omit the pronounced lift of the heel in this analysis. However, there should be a slight lift of the body as the movement is executed.
   c. *English Country Dance.* 3/4 Time. Balance forward. Step forward onto right, bring left close to right, step back on left (3 counts). Balance back. Step backward onto left, bring right close to left, step forward onto left. **Note:** Change of weight allows moving forward into a traveling figure (3 counts).
3. *Square Dance.* Partners face, inside hands joined; or man may hold lady's left hand in his right.
   a. Each takes two steps backward, dipping back on second step; then two steps forward to original position.

   b. Or man rocks back on left, taking weight on left, pointing right front (counts 1 – 2); then steps forward right to original position (counts 1 – 2). Lady's part reverse.
4. *Social Dance.* Same as the Folk Dance balance described above.

Balance in Line   A Contra Dance term. Four in line, hands joined at shoulder height, elbows bent. Beginning right, balance to the right, then left. Look at the person with whom you are balancing.

Banjo Position   *See* Right Parallel Position.

Basketweave Grasp   A Square or Folk Dance term. Usually involves four or more people. Each puts the right hand into the center, and they all face left, one behind the other, and put the right hand on the wrist of the person in front of them.

Becket Formation   Contra Dance formation, but couples stand side by side with partner. Each couple faces an opposite couple. Couples 1, 3, and 5 start as active on the ladies' line; couples 2, 4, and 6 start as inactive on the man's line.

Below   Contra Dance term. Usually refers to the next couple or the couples down the set from the actives.

Bend the Line   A Square Dance term. From any line of even numbers (four usually), the line breaks in the middle, the ends move forward, and the centers back up, so that one half of the line now faces the other half.

Bleking Step   2/4 time. A quick change of the feet, moving in place, in an uneven rhythm. Hop right (count *ah*); touch left heel forward (counts 1 – 2); leap onto left, bringing it back into place (count *ah*); touch right heel forward (counts 1 – 2); leap onto right in place (count *ah*); touch left heel forward (count 1); leap onto left in place (count *ah*); touch right heel forward (count 2); leap onto right in place (count *ah*); touch left heel forward (counts 1 – 2). The *ah* count comes on the pickup beat, and the heel touch on the accented beat of the music.

Bossa Nova   A Social Dance from Brazil.

Bow   A Square and Folk Dance term. In Square Dance, it is the term that has replaced "honor." It is a slight turn to face partner while shifting the weight to the outside foot and pointing the inside foot toward partner. One may dip slightly as the weight shifts and one nods to partner.

Bow and Swing   A Square Dance term. Bow, then step forward into swing position and swing once around. *See* Bow; Swing, item 3.

Box Star Position   Also referred to as Pack Saddle Star and Basketweave Grasp. Each person places right (left) hand on wrist of the person in front to form a star.

Box the Flea   A Square Dance term. Similar to box the gnat, except that both man and lady use the left hand instead of the right. The lady is turned clockwise under the man's right arm; the man walks around her counterclockwise. They end up facing each other, as they started, but they have exchanged places. Also called swat the flea.

Box the Gnat   A Square Dance term. A man and lady face each other, take right hands, and exchange places, the lady turning counterclockwise under the man's right arm while he walks around her clockwise. They end up facing each other, but they have exchanged places.

Break   Drop clasped hands.

Break and Form a Line   A Square Dance term. This occurs when two couples are in a circle. The lead man drops his left hand and pulls the others into a line square with the visited position. If first couple leads out to second couple, the man circles about two-thirds of the way to the left and breaks to form a line in the second position.

Break and Swing   Drop clasped hands and partners swing with a waist swing.

Break and Trail Along that Line   A Square Dance term. Drop hands, turn and face in opposite direction, move in single file to home position; the lady leads, the man follows.

Broken Circle   A single circle of dancers in which all hands are joined except two.

Brush   A Clogging term. The Brush is a toe movement (*see* Toe Movement) occurring on the upbeat (count *and*). The leg performing the movement swings forward as the ball of the foot brushes the floor. No weight change occurs in the Brush. Brushes also may cross in front of the body or swing out to the side. Less frequently they are performed brushing backward. Both legs are straight on the Brush; on the following downbeat (accent), both knees bend slightly while performing the next movement.

Butterfly Position   Couple faces, arms extended shoulder high and out to the sides, hands joined. In this position, couple may dance forward and backward or to the right or left, and in the line of direction and reverse line of direction.

Buzz Step   A turning step used in Folk, Square, and Social Dance. Done alone or with a partner, turning clockwise or counterclockwise in swing or shoulder-waist position. Buzz step may be used to travel sideways. The rhythm is uneven (long, short).

1. *Clockwise turn.* Step right (turn toe right), pivoting clockwise on ball of foot (long); push with ball of left foot placed slightly to side of right (short). Repeat as required. Reverse footwork for counterclockwise turn. **Note:** The weight remains on the right or pivot foot; the impetus for turn is given by left foot.

2. *Sideways.* Step left sideways (long); push with right foot as it moves to the left, displacing left foot (short). **Note:** The turning action of the pivot foot is omitted.

Buzz-Step Swing   A Contra and Square Dance term. Use swing position for Contra and Square Dance. Folk Dance position as directed. Step right on long count into swing position; the left foot takes the short count in a pushing off motion to propel the turn. Couples generate centrifugal force by pulling away of upper torso. **Note:** Contra swings are usually eight measures; Square Dance swings usually two turns and open up to face center of set.

California Twirl   A Square Dance term. Used by couples to change or reverse direction without changing relation of couple position. Lady's left in man's right, man walks around lady clockwise as lady executes a left-face turn, moving under raised right arm of man. If partners began movement side by side, facing center of set, they now are side by side, facing away from center of set. A repeat of the movement puts dancers in original position. Also referred to as frontier twirl.

Canter Rhythm   An uneven pattern in 3/4 time, resulting from a long beat (counts 1–2) followed by a short beat (count 3). A step is taken on count 1 and held over on count 2. Another step is taken on count 3. The three-step turn in canter rhythm is step left (count 1); pivot on left a half-turn counterclockwise (count 2); step right (count 3), pivoting almost a half-turn counterclockwise; step left (count 1), completing the turn; and hold (counts 2–3). Close right to left (count 3), but keep weight on left. It may be done clockwise by starting with the right foot.

Cast   Refers to English Country Dance. Partners turn away from each other and move outside the set to a new position; other dancers move up or down as indicated.

Cast Down   A Contra Dance term. Dancer faces up the set, turns outward, and travels down the outside of the set.

Cast Down   An English Country Dance term. Cast down means first or active couple face up, separate, and move down outside one place.

Cast Off   A Contra Dance term. Refers to one of the following ways to progress in the set:

1. *Walk Around.* Active couple separates, walks around the inactive and finishes below inactive, facing partner. Inactives do not turn.

2. *Arm Around.* Active couple separates and the inactive faces up the set; the active and nearest inactive put their nearest arm around each other's waist. May be same sex. The inactive person acts as a pivot or backs up, turning as the active moves forward, the two turning side by side. The active ends one position below, both facing partner.

3. *Unassisted, Two Dancers.* Like the arm around, the two dancers stand side by side, shoulders close together, but they do not touch. They turn as a unit, active ends one position below, with both facing partner.

4. *Hand Cast Off.* Coming up in a line of four, joined hands shoulder height, elbows down, active couple separates, active and inactive turn forward. The inactive acting as a pivot, the two turn; active ends one position below, with both facing their partners. Or active couple separates and joins hands with inactive, as in an allemande and the two turn.

5. *Two Couple.* Active couple leads up the set, followed by inactive. Active couple separates and travels in a small circle to one position below inactive. The inactive couple separates and turns almost in place, backing into the line above the active couple.

6. *Separately.* Sometimes one person casts off, as in a star figure, and the other person casts off in the next figure.

CCW   Symbols referring to *counterclockwise*. *See* Counterclockwise.

Center   The space in the middle of the square (set) or circle formed by dancers.

Centrifugal Force   The force exerted outward from the center that is created by dancers rotating as in a buzz step swing or pivot turn.

Cha Cha Cha   A Social Dance from Cuba.

Chain   For Contra and Square Dance, *see* Ladies Chain. For Folk Dance, *see* Grand Right and Left.

Challenge Position   A term used in Social Dance to refer to position of man facing lady, at approximately arm distance. Hands are not joined.

Charleston Step   A step in 4/4 meter, accent on count *and*. Put weight on right bent knee, left foot in the air. Flip left foot up behind (count *and*); step forward left (count 1); bend left knee and flip right foot up behind (count *and*). Point right toe forward; straighten knees (count 2); bend left knee and flip right foot up behind (count *and*). Step back on right (count 3); bend right knee and flip left foot up behind (count *and*); point left toe behind and straighten knees (count 4).

Chassé   A series of sliding steps; one foot displaces the leading one, moving forward, backward, or sideward. In Square Dance, called sashay.

Chug Step   Move forward or backward on one or two feet or sideward on one foot. Moving backward on left foot, with weight on left foot and right foot slightly off the floor and knee flexed, the left foot pulls (drags) backward as the left knee straightens (count *and* 1). Body bends forward slightly with action.

Circle   Four, six, eight, or more dancers join hands in a circle and move left or right as directions of the call or dance indicate. In a Contra or Square Dance call, if the direction is not indicated, circle left.

Circle to a Line—Line of Four   Couples 1 and 3 lead to the right, join hands and circle three-quarters around, lead men (men 1 and 3) drop left hands with left-hand lady to form lines of four dancers. Couples 1 and 3 will be on the end of the line opposite their home position. Lines will be facing across the set from the side couples (couples 2 and 4) position. Also done with side couples 2 and 4, leading out to couples 1 and 3. Lines will be formed, facing from the head couple position.

Circle Wide   Dancers join hands and circle left. In a Square Dance call, it may also mean that dancers enlarge circle as they circle left.

Circulate   A Square Dance term. From two ocean-wave lines, dancers on the outside (or the inside) of the line circulate by moving forward to the next outside (or inside) position in a circle. Refer to diagram, p. 159.

Clockwise   Refers to the movement of dancers around a circle in the same direction as the hands of a clock move or to a turning action of one dancer or couple as they progress around the floor. In directional terms, clockwise is to the left (e.g., "circle to the left").

Close   Free foot is moved to supporting foot. Weight ends on free foot. Begin weight on left, move right (free foot) to left, and take weight on right.

Closed Position   Partners stand facing each other, shoulders parallel and toes pointed directly forward. Man's right arm is around the lady and the hand is placed on the small of her back. Lady's left hand and arm rest on man's upper arm and shoulder.

Man's left arm is raised sideward to the left, and he holds her right hand in his palm. For detailed description, refer to p. 382.

Coaster Step   West Coast Swing term. Step back left (count 1), close right to left (count *and*), step forward left (count 2).

Contra Corners Turn (16 counts)   Contra corners are diagonally across the set for each person. The *first contra corner* is diagonally right and the *second contra corner* is diagonally left. For the call "turn contra corners," active partners crossing set take right hands, turn halfway, take left hand of *first contra corner,* turn all the way around, take right hand of partner, turn three-quarters around in middle of set, take left hand of *second contra corner,* turn all the way around and return to center of set and await next call. The actives use their right and left hands alternately; the corners **always** use their left hands. Each turn is 4 counts.

Contra Dance Formation   Parallel lines, men in one line or on one side and ladies in other line or on opposite side. Head or top of set to man's left, lady's right. Foot or bottom of set to man's right or lady's left when couples face partner. In Longway or Contra sets, dancers may face partners across lines; all dancers may face top or head of set; or couples 1, 3, and 5 may change sides or lines to put odd-numbered couples facing each other on opposite sides of set.

Contra Set   *See* Longway Set.

Conversation Position   As described for open position, but with the forward hand released and arm (man's left, lady's right) hanging at the side.

Corner   The lady on the man's left. Also called left-hand lady. The lady's corner is the man on her right.

Corners   An English Country Dance term. In duple minor formations the *first corners* are the first man and second lady. *Second corners* are the first lady and second man.

Corner Swing   Square Dance term. A waist swing or buzz-step swing with left-hand lady.

Corté   Social and Round dance term. *See Dip.*

Counterclockwise   Refers to the movement of dancers around a circle in opposite direction from the movement of the hands on a clock or to a turning action of one dancer or couple as they progress around the floor. In directional terms, counterclockwise is to the right (e.g., "circle to the right").

Couple   A man and a lady. Lady stands at man's right.

Couple Position   Partners stand side by side, lady on man's right, inside hands joined, both facing in same direction. Also referred to as strolling, side-by-side, or open position, or inside hands joined.

Courtesy Turn   A Square Dance term. A couple is standing side by side, with the lady on the right of the man. They turn counterclockwise. The man takes the lady's left hand in his left. He puts his right arm around her waist and guides her forward as he moves backward. It is a spot turn in place.

Cross   An English Country Dance term. Actives go directly across the set to the other side, passing right shoulders or as directed.

Cross Over   A Contra Dance term. Two facing dancers exchange places, passing right shoulders.

Cross-Over Position   Social Dance term for Cha Cha Cha. The couple is side by side, with inside hands joined. *See* Couple Position.

Cross Trail Thru   A Square Dance term. Active couples meet, pass right shoulder to right shoulder; lady then crosses in front of partner to her left, man crosses behind lady to his right. Wait for caller's direction.

Curtsey   The term used occasionally to refer to the action of honors in which the lady nods her head to partner, at the same time shifting her weight to the outside foot as she turns to face partner. Usually accompanied by a smile. *See also* Bow.

Cut-Step   Step left (count 1); bring right quickly up to left and step right displacing left (count 2). Used in Mazurka.

Cut Time   A rhythm that comes from 4/4 time. Refer to diagram on p. 36.

CW   Symbols referring to clock*wise. See* Clockwise.

Dal Step   A Swedish step in 3/4 time. Step left (count 1), swing right across in front of left (count 2), raise left heel from floor as weight rolls to ball of left foot, and complete swing of right across left (count 3). Repeat movement, beginning right.

Dance Walk   A Social Dance term that describes the basic walking step. May move forward, backward, or sideward in Foxtrot, Waltz, or Tango.

Dig Step   Place slight weight on the ball of one foot; usually followed by stepping on the foot.

Dip (Corté)   Step back on foot indicated, taking full weight and bending the knee. The other leg remains extended at the knee and ankle, forming a straight line from the hip. The toe remains in contact with the floor.

Disco Dance A descriptive term that encompasses a wide variety of dance steps to many rhythms of recorded music. (*See* Disco Dance, p. 412).

Discotheque A French word meaning "a place where records (disques) are stored." In common usage, it describes a place for contemporary dancing to records as opposed to live music.

Dish Rag Whirl A Square Dance term. Man and lady who are facing join both hands and turn under their joined hands, starting under man's left arm and lady's right. As they turn, their hands come up over their heads. They make one complete rotation and end up facing the side couples.

Dive Thru A Square Dance term. Active couple will duck under an arch made by the couple they are facing. If the arching couple then faces the outside of the square, they turn a California twirl to reverse direction and end facing in.

Dixie Chain A Square Dance term. Two couples meet in single-file and move past each other as in a grand right and left. The first two to meet use right hands; the second two to meet use left hands. Remain in single-file; wait for caller's directions.

Docey Doe A Square Dance term. *See* Do-Si-Do, Shaw Style.

Do Paso A Square Dance term. Starting position is a circle of two or more couples. Partners face, take a left forearm grasp, and turn each other counterclockwise until facing corner. They turn corner with right-forearm grasp until facing partner and take partner with the left hand. Man turns lady with a courtesy turn.

Do-Sa-Do A Square Dance term. The man and lady face, pass each other right shoulder to right shoulder, move around each other back to back, and return to original position. In Contra Dance, this is the correct action for the call "do-si-do."

Do-Si-Do
1. *Contra Dances.* The call "do-si-do" in Contra Dances is the same as defined by "do-sa-do."
2. *Shaw Style* (for two couples in a circle). A square Dance term. Form a circle of four and release hands; ladies pass left shoulders, turn left, and give left hand to partner. As the ladies move around behind partner, the men do **a** or **b.**
   a. Always facing partner and moving forward and backward to minimize the amount of space that the lady must travel, man releases partner's hand and gives right to opposite lady, who moves around behind him once.

   b. Partners pass back to back; man releases partner's hand, gives right to opposite lady, and turns once around until the partners again pass back to back. Then man takes partner's left hand and turns lady with a courtesy turn.
3. *Texas-Southwest Style* (for two or more couples in a circle). A Square Dance term. Partners face, join left hands, and turn once around to face corner; corners join right hands. Turn once around to face partner. Dancers describe a figure-eight pattern as they execute the figure. The Texas-Southwest style do-si-do is generally repeated until the caller calls "one more change and promenade." The last time the man turns his partner, the man puts his right arm around the lady's waist and turns her counterclockwise into place to promenade.

Double Pass Thru Starting position. Couple 1 stands with backs to couple 4; couple 3 stands with backs to couple 2. All couples move forward, passing right shoulders with two dancers (men pass two men; ladies pass two ladies), to end facing away from center of set. Couples 1 and 3 can get into starting position by circling couple 4 in center until backs are to designated couples. Danced also with couples 2 and 4 circling into positions with couples 1 and 3.

Double Progression A Contra Dance term. Each couple moves two positions within one dance sequence. *See* Progression.

Double-Toe A Clogging term. The Double-Toe is a toe movement (*see* Toe Movement) occurring on the upbeat (count *and*). The foot performing the movement makes two clicking sounds with the ball of that foot. A small brushing movement of the ball of the foot forward and a small brushing movement backward occur during the "and-ah" count. No weight change occurs in the Double-Toe. The knee of the supporting leg is straight; the knee of the leg performing the movement straightens on the small brushing movement forward and relaxes on the small brushing action backward. On the following downbeat (accent), both knees bend slightly while performing the next movement.

Double Turn Back from Grand Right and Left A Square Dance term. Dancers meet partner on grand right and left, take forearm grasp, turn halfway around to face reverse direction. Go grand right and left in reverse direction to meet partner for the second time, then turn halfway around to face original direction. Go grand right and left in original direction to meet partner for the third time. A promenade usually follows. Also called back track.

Down Contra Dance term. Refers to the foot of the set and away from the music.

Drag A Clogging term. The Drag is a toe movement (*see* Toe Movement) occurring on the upbeat (count *and*). A weight-bearing movement that may be performed on both feet simultaneously or on one foot. Similar to a chug step, the Drag is a movement that scoots *backward* a few inches as the weight is shifted to the balls of the feet. Heels skim the floor during the movement. Both knees are straight (not stiff) on the Drag; on the following downbeat (accent), both knees bend slightly while performing the next movement.

Draw Step In 2/4 time, step sideward on left (count 1) and draw right to left, transferring weight to right (count 2). To draw, the foot is dragged along the floor. In 3/4 time, step sideward on left (counts 1 – 2) and draw right to left (count 3).

Drop the Gate A Square Dance term. Called to form one circle of eight from two circles of four. Men of active couples release hands with corner lady in circle of four and join hands with original corner ladies to form a circle of eight.

Duple Minor A Contra set is divided into minor sets, two couples each.

Eight Chain Thru A Square Dance term. For starting position, first and third couples take the opposite person and face the side couples. Four couples are lined up across the floor. Two are on the outside facing in, while two are on the inside facing out. The action is like a grand right and left across the set and back, using a right and left thru when facing out. Refer to p. 157.

Elbow Swing Hook right elbows (or left) with person indicated and turn once around.

Ends Turn In A Square Dance term. Starting position is two lines of four, facing out. The two persons in the center of the line form an arch; the two persons on the ends of the line drop hands, walk forward, and go together under the arch, moving into the center of the square. The arching couple does a California twirl.

Escort Position Couple faces line of direction, lady to man's right. The lady slips her left arm through the man's right arm, which is bent at the elbow so that her left hand may rest on his right forearm. Free arm hangs to side.

Even Rhythm When the beats in the rhythm pattern are all the same value, the rhythm is said to be even.

Face to Face, Back to Back A pattern of movement used by a couple moving in the line of direction or reverse line of direction. Partners face, inside hands joined. The basic steps most generally used to effect this movement are the Two-Step, Polka, or Waltz. For example, in the Two-Step, the man would begin left, the lady right. They would take the first Two-Step in the line of direction, turning toward each other. Inside joined hands are swung back and arms are extended. They would take the second Two-Step in the line of direction, turning away from each other. Inside joined hands are swung forward, and arms are extended. Repeat pattern.

Facing Position *See* Two Hands Joined Position.

Fan A term used to describe a manner of executing a leg motion, in which the free leg swings in a whip-like movement around a small pivoting base. Should be a small, subtle action initiated in the hip.

File A type of formation. Dancers stand one behind the other, all facing the same direction.

First Four Refers to the first and third couples in the set. Also called the head couples, first two couples, or heads.

First Position One of five basic positions of the feet used in classical ballet. The heels remain touching as the feet are rotated 180° to form one line.

First Two Couples Refers to the first and third couples in the set. Also called head couples, first four, or heads.

Flare An exaggerated lift of the foot from the floor accompanying a knee bend. It is often used in the Tango.

Flirtation Position Partners are facing; man's left hand and lady's right hand are joined. The arms are bent and are firm so as to indicate or receive a lead.

Foot Four In Longway sets, refers to the last two couples.

Foot of Set In Contra and Longway sets, the end of the set farthest from the caller and musicians.

Forearm Turn A Square Dance term. Partners grasp each other by the forearm just below the elbow with either right or left hand, as directions indicate. They press the palm of the hand against the person's forearm, pulling back slightly and keeping the elbow bent as the two people turn each other around. Avoid grasping with the fingers and thumb. This grasp is used in Square Dance for all arm turns, particularly for allemande left, back track, do paso, do-si-do, and allemande thar.

Form a Ring Join hands and circle left.

Forward and Back Move forward four steps and back four steps into place.

Four Gents Star   A Square Dance term. All four gents go into the center, take a box star position with their right hand (or left hand), and turn the star as far as designated by the caller.

Four Sides   A Square Dance term referring to all four couples in the set.

Four-Step Turn   One complete turn is made in four steps. The turn may be made to the left (counterclockwise) or to the right (clockwise). To right, step right to side (count 1); pivot clockwise on right and step left to face opposite direction (count 2); pivot clockwise on left and step right to side to face original direction (count 3); and step left across right in line of direction (count 4).

Foxtrot   An American Social Dance.

Frontier Whirl   *See* California Twirl.

Full Turn 'Round   A Square Dance term meaning one full turn around from where the turn was started.

Gallop   A basic form of locomotion in uneven rhythm, moving forward diagonally with a step close step close pattern (slow quick slow quick).

Gents Turn Back   A Square Dance term. When couples are promenading in a circle, this call indicates that the man will drop promenade position, turn to his left, take four steps around to the next lady behind him, and take promenade position with her. It is a good means of changing partners quickly.

Grand Right and Left   A Square and Folk Dance term. Partners take right hands, move past partner, take next with the left hand, move past, take next with the right hand, move past, and so on until partners meet. In European Folk Dance, the term *chain* indicates the same movement.

Grand Square   A Square Dance term. This is a no-patter, geometric figure that keeps all dancers in the set active at the same time. First and third couples have one action, while second and fourth couples have a different action. Refer to detailed instructions, p. 152.

Grapevine   Step left to side (count 1), step right behind left (count 2), step left to side (count 3), and step right in front of left (count 4). Bend knees, let hips turn naturally, and keep weight on balls of feet.

Grapevine Schottische   Beginning right, step right to side, step left behind right, step right to side, and hop right.

Gypsy (8 counts)   Two dancers face each other and continuing to face each other with eye contact, move clockwise around each other once. "Left gypsy" travels counterclockwise.

Half Promenade   Opposite couples take promenade position, pass each other to the right

in the middle of the set (men pass left shoulders), and turn as a couple in the opposite position.

Half Right and Left   A Contra Dance term. Same as right and left thru. Couples cross over with a courtesy turn but *do not* return.

Half Sashay   *See* Sashay Halfway Around; Roll Away With a Half Sashay.

Half Square Thru   A Square Dance term. *See* Square Thru.

Halfway Around   Move in one direction, left or right, halfway around the circle (180°). In a circle of four couples, move left or right until on the opposite side of circle from original position.

Hand Cast Off   *See* Cast Off.

Head Couple   Refers to first and third couples in a set of four couples. In Contra and Longway sets, head couple is the first couple (man's left shoulder is to top or head of the set).

Head Four   Refers to first and third couples in a square.

Head of Set   In Longway (Contra) sets, the end of the set closest to the caller and musicians.

Heads   Refers to first and third couples in the set. Also called head four.

Heel   A Clogging term. The Heel step is a weight-bearing heel movement (*see* Heel Movement) occurring on the downbeat (accent). Weight is shifted from the ball of the foot to the heel as it snaps to the floor.

Heel and Toe Polka   Moving to the left, hop right (count *and*), place left heel close to right instep (count 1), hop right (count *and*), place left toe close to right instep (count 2), and take one Polka step to the left (counts *and* 1 *and* 2). Repeat beginning hop on left, moving to the right.

Heel and Toe Scottische   Moving to the left, place left heel close to right instep (counts 1–2), place left toe close to right instep (counts 3–4), and take one Schottische step to the left (counts 1–4). Repeat, beginning right.

Heel Movement   A Clogging term. The heel movements in clogging (step, slide, heel) take place on the downbeat (accent) of the music. Both legs are slightly bent. Heel movements are accented as the weight is transferred to the entire sole of the foot.

Hesitation   A Social Dance step that cues step hold, step hold.

Hey for Four   An English dance figure, also used in Contra Dance. Four dancers in a line, center two facing, weave without touching hands, moving in a figure-eight pattern with an additional loop at end. For detailed analysis, refer to p. 193.

Hitch   A Country Western Dance term. Swing right (left) knee almost waist height as one step hops on the other foot, slight chug back. Step hop is subtle.

Home Position   Original position of each dancer or couple in the set.

Honey   Partner.

Honors   Man bows to lady, lady curtseys to man. "Honors right" means bow to partner; "honors left" means bow to corner. *See also* Bow.

Hop   A basic form of locomotion in even rhythm. It is a transfer of weight by a springing action from one foot to the same foot. Refer to diagram on p. 39.

Hub Flies Out, Rim Flies In   A Square Dance term called from star promenade position. The man, starting in the center, breaks the star and, with arm around partner, wheels counterclockwise around one full turn and a half more to put the lady into the center to form the star (rim flies in).

Hungarian Break Step   (cross apart together). Hop left, touching right toe in front of left (count 1); hop left in place, touching right toe to right side (count 2); draw right foot to left, clicking heels together (count 3). Hold (count 4).

Hungarian Turn   Partners face in opposite directions with right side to right side. Right hands on partner's right hip, left arm curved overhead. Turn using a push step, buzz step, or hop-step-step. Lean weight away from partner during turn. Reverse position for counterclockwise turn.

Improper   A Contra Dance term. Refers to Contra Dances in which the active couples cross over (partners exchange places).

Inactive Couple   In Contra Dance, refers to 2, 4, or 6 couples in duple minor dances; 2, 3, 5, 6, 8, or 9 in triple minor dances.

Indian Style   A Square Dance term. *See* Promenade Single-File.

Inside Hands Joined Position   Partners stand side by side, lady on man's right, inside hands joined, both facing same direction. Also referred to as side-by-side, open, or strolling position.

Inside Out. Outside In   A Square Dance term. When two couples are facing, the couple designated by the call ducks under an arch made by the other couple. Immediately after they get under the arch, they stand up, make an arch, and back up, letting the other couple duck and move backward under that arch to starting position.

Jitterbug   An American Social Dance done to jazz or swing music. *See* Lindy.

Jody Position   *See* Varsouvienne Position.

Jump   A basic form of locomotion in which one or both feet leave the floor, knees bending; both return to the floor together, landing toe-heel with an easy knee action to catch body weight. Spring off the floor on the upbeat of the music and land on the beat.

Kolo Step   Moving right: hop on left foot, leap onto right foot, step on left foot behind right, step on right in place, and hop on right foot. Moving left: hop on right foot, leap onto left foot, step on right foot behind left, step on left in place, and hop on left foot.

Ladies Chain

1. *Two Ladies Chain.* A Contra and Square Dance term. Ladies meet in center, clasp right hands, pass right shoulders, and give left hand to opposite man. Man puts his right arm around lady's waist and turns her with a courtesy turn. Ladies return to partner in the same manner.

2. *Four Ladies Chain.* A Square Dance term. All four ladies place right hands in the center, forming a star as they catch hands, and move to the left around circle to opposite man. He turns lady with a courtesy turn. Ladies return to partner in the same manner.

3. *Three-Quarters Chain.* A Square Dance term. Ladies chain three-quarters of the way around the ring instead of half of the way. Finish with a courtesy turn.

Ladies Line   A Contra Dance term. When a Contra set is formed, the ladies are to the left of the caller. Even though they may cross over, this term refers to the original line.

Lady by Your Side   A Square Dance term. Left-hand lady, corner, or lady on man's left.

Lady Go Gee. Gent to Haw   A Square Dance term. Lady goes to right, man goes to left.

Lead Couple   In Square Dancing, refers to the couple indicated to *move* (lead out) and progress through a figure. If two couples are requested to lead out, there are two lead couples. Also called active couple.

Leap   A basic method of locomotion involving a transfer of weight from one foot to the other foot. Push off with a spring and land on the ball of the other foot, letting the heel come down; bend the knee to absorb the shock.

Left-Face Turn   Dancer turns individually one full turn to the left, or counterclockwise.

Left Parallel Position   *See* Parallel Position.

Left Square Thru   A Square Dance term. Same as square thru (full), except begin with left-hand grasp instead of right.

Lindy An American Social Dance done to jazz or swing music in 4/4 or cut time. There are three Lindy rhythms—single, double, and triple.

Line A type of formation. Dancers stand side by side, all facing in the same direction.

Line of Direction Refers to the direction of movement of dancers around the circle *counterclockwise.*

LOD Symbol for *line of direction.*

Long Lines, Join Hands Along the line, join hands with neighbor.

Longway Set Couples stand in a double line (file or parallel lines), men in one line and ladies in opposite line. Partners face in a double line or partners face head of set in a double-file. This is also known as Contra formation.

Magic Step A Social Dance term. A basic step of the American Foxtrot.

Major A Contra Dance term. The whole Contra set is referred to as the major set. The major set is divided into minor sets.

Make an Arch A Square Dance term. Any two dancers facing the same direction make an arch by raising their joined inside hands. The next call will be for someone to duck under, so arching couples need to separate slightly and make room for that, so that people do not bump each other. Also, if short people are making the arch, they may release hands in the arch in order to allow more room for the ducking couple to go under.

Mazurka Step left (slight stamp), bring right up to left with a cut step displacing left, and hop right while bending knee so that left foot approaches right ankle.

Measure One measure encloses a group of beats made by the regular occurrence of the heavy accent. It represents the underlying beat enclosed between two adjacent bars on a musical staff.

Men's Line A Contra Dance term. When a Contra set is formed, the men are to the right of the caller. Even through they may cross over, this term refers to the original side.

Meter Refers to time in music or group of beats to form the underling rhythms within a measure.

Minor or Minor Set A Contra set is divided into smaller sets that dance together. Two couples dancing together is called duple minor; three couples dancing is called triple minor.

Minuet Position Man extends right arm forward about waist high or to accommodate lady, bending elbow slightly and with palm down and fingers straight. Lady places her left hand, palm down, lightly upon his, keeping her forearm gracefully extended to side, palm down and fingers softly straight. Arms are horizontal; partners are side by side.

Motifs A short step pattern, for example, two-step. Several patterns (motifs) may be combined. Refer to Hungarian dances.

Neighbor A Contra Dance term. Same as the opposite person (different sex) or corner. It is not your partner.

Neutral Couple Relating to Contra Dance. A couple waiting out at either end of the set is called the "neutral couple."

Note Values A term used to refer to the relative value of the musical notes or beats that make up the rhythmic pattern.

Ocean Wave A Square Dance term. A line of dancers—usually four, facing in alternate directions—join hands and balance (e.g., step or rock, forward and back). Count 1–2 for forward movement, counts 3–4 for backward movement.

Open Position Partners stand side by side, lady on man's right, facing in the same direction. Man's right arm is around lady's waist. Lady's left hand rests on man's right shoulder. Man holds lady's right hand in his left. Arms extend easily forward.

Open the Gate A Square Dance call when four dancers are side by side in a line in the center of the ring. "Open the gate" will indicate that the two persons on the right of the line will step forward two steps and the two on the left will step back two steps, opening a space in the line. Usually the inactive couples will chain their ladies through the gate. The call "close the gate" will indicate that the active dancers will step back in line and wait for the next call.

Opposite The person standing in opposite position across the set.

Parallel Position Refers to right or left parallel position. Right parallel is a variation of closed position, in which both man and lady are turned one-eighth turn counterclockwise to a position facing diagonal. The lady is slightly in front of but to the right of the man. Also referred to as banjo position. In left parallel position, man and lady are turned clockwise to face diagonally on the other side. Lady is in front of and to the left of the man.

Partner Lady to immediate *right* of man and man to immediate *left* of lady. Also called taw and honey.

Pas de Basque

1. *3/4 Time.* Leap to side on left foot (count 1), step right in front of left (count 2), and step left in place (count 3).
2. *2/4 Time.* Leap to side on left (count 1), step right in front of left (count *and*), step left in place (count 2), and hold (count *and*).

Pas de Bourrée   Step forward on left (count 1), step on right beside left or slightly forward of left (count 2), step on the left slightly forward (count 3). Step alternates. This step can be done in place.

Pass Thru   A Square Dance term. Two couples face. They move toward each other, each passing his opposite by the right shoulder, and then wait for the next call.

Phrase   A musical term that represents a short division of time comprising a complete thought or statement. In dance, it is a series of movements considered as a unit in a dance pattern. It is a group of measures, generally four or eight, but sometimes 16 to 32.

Pigeon-Wing Handhold   Man and lady face each other and place their forearms, held vertically, close together. The palms are held together, open and upright, and elbows are almost touching.

Pirouette   A turn clockwise or counterclockwise. To go clockwise, step right foot across left and turn, pivoting on the balls of both feet halfway around until feet are uncrossed.

Pivot   Turn clockwise or counterclockwise on balls of one or both feet.

Pivot Turn   Closed or shoulder-waist position. Step left, pivoting clockwise (count 1), continuing in same direction step right (count 2); step left (count 3), and step right (count 4). Make one complete turn progressing in line of direction. May also be done counterclockwise. Refer to pp. 48 and 431.

Pivot Turn Dip   Step left, turn clockwise (count 1); step back on right, continuing turn (count 2); step left, facing forward (count 3); dip back on right foot, still facing forward (count 4).

Polka   Hop right, step left forward, close right to left, and step forward left. Repeat, beginning hop left.

Posture   The position of the body. An easy, upright standing position is a tremendous advantage in helping one to move efficiently in dance.

Pressure Lead   A lead in which extra pressure is exerted by the fingers, arm, or body in order to lead the lady into a particular position or step.

Progression   A Contra Dance term. Refers to the movement of each couple to new positions during the dance. Active couples move down the set, inactive move up the set. A new minor set forms for each time through the dance. For most Contras, each couple progresses only one position.

Promenade   Couples move counterclockwise around the set or large circle in promenade position. *See* Promenade Position. In Square Dance, the man may give his partner a finishing whirl, bow, and/or swing before resuming ready position facing the center of the set. *See also* Twirl.

Promenade But Don't Slow Down   A Square Dance term. Couples continue promenading until caller gives the next call. They do not stop in home position.

Promenade Eight   A Square Dance term. All four couples promenade once around the set and return to home position.

Promenade Inside Ring   A Square Dance term. Promenade counterclockwise around the inside of the square.

Promenade Outside Ring   A Square Dance term. Promenade counterclockwise around outside of square.

Promenade Position   Partners stand side by side, facing line of direction. The lady stands to the right of the man. The man holds the lady's right hand in his right and her left in his left. The man's right arm is crossed above the lady's left arm. In some sections of the country, it is customary for the man to cross his right arm underneath the lady's left arm. The promenade position is also referred to as the skater's position.

Promenade Single-File   A Square Dance term. Promenade one behind the other in single-file, lady in front, man behind. The line may move clockwise or counterclockwise or down the middle of the set. May also be referred to as Indian style.

Proper   A Contra Dance term. Refers to Contra Dances in which the men and ladies remain on the original sides to start the dance.

Push Step   Moving to the left, beginning left, step (chug) to the side (count 1); bring right toe close to left instep; and push right foot away from body (count *and*). Repeat pattern. The push step is similar to a buzz step, except that the action is taken to the side instead of in a turning or circling movement.

Q   Symbol for Quick. Used for Rhythm Cue. For example, QQSS, Quick Quick Slow Slow.

Quadrille Formation   *See* Square.

Quick   A rhythm cue. For example, 4/4 time, 4 quarter beats to each measure; each beat is given the same amount of time, an accent on the first beats of the measure. When a step is taken on each beat (1-2-3-4), these are called *quick* beats. When steps are taken only on 1 and 3, they are twice as long and are called *slow* beats.

Red Hot A Square Dance term. Executed during a promenade by all four couples. Man releases lady's right and walks partner to center with left forearm grasp. Man moves forward to meet right-hand lady, with right forearm turns once around to meet partner, turns partner with left once and a half counterclockwise, faces corner, turns corner with the right once clockwise, moves back to partner with a left, and turns once around counterclockwise. Wait for caller's directions.

Reel A figure used in Longway dances. Head couple meets in middle of set and hooks right elbows, turns once and half around. Man faces ladies' line, lady faces men's line. Couple separates and head man hooks left elbows with second lady in line; head lady hooks left elbows with second man in line and turns once around. Head couple returns to middle of set. They hook right elbows, turn once, and return to respective lines to swing third dancer. Repeat the "reeling action" until head couple reaches the foot of the set.

Re-Sashay After having done a half sashay (*see* Half Sashay) dancers retrace steps to original position. Often the call "go all the way around" is given following a re-sashay. To "go all the way around" dancers, beginning in original positions, encircle each other once and go back to position. Men generally move in front of partner first. Dancers usually face center of set while traveling on any variation of a sashay.

Reverse Line of Direction Refers to the direction of movement of dancers around the circle *clockwise*. Dancers move in the opposite direction from the line of direction.

Reverse Open Position From an open Social Dance position, facing line of direction, partners turn in toward each other to face reverse line of direction but do not change arm or hand positions.

Reverse Varsouvienne Position Couples are standing almost side by side, with the lady on the left side of the man. She is slightly behind him. The man reaches across in front of the lady to hold her left hand in his left. Her right arm is around his shoulders and her right hand grasps his right hand at shoulder level. For Social Dance, the right arm is sometimes extended behind partner at waist level and grasps his hand at the waist. Still a different concept of reverse Varsouvienne position is merely to turn half about from Varsouvienne position. Now lady is on man's left side but slightly in front of him, and his left arm is around her shoulders. Her right arm is across in front of him.

Rhythm Pattern The rhythm pattern in dance is the grouping of beats for the pattern of a dance step. The rhythm pattern must correspond to the underlying beat of the music.

Right and Left Eight *See* Grand Right and Left.

Right and Left Four *See* Right and Left Thru.

Right and Left Thru A Contra and Square Dance term. Two couples are facing each other. Both man and lady, using the right hand, pass by the opposite person on the right side and then immediately give the left hand to their own partner. The man, putting his right arm around his lady, turns her halfway around (courtesy turn) to face the same couple. The two couples have exchanged places.

Right-Face Turn Dancer turns individually one full turn to the right, or clockwise.

Right Hands Across Men or ladies join right hands in center and turn clockwise. Usually followed by the call "back with the left," which means break with the right, join left hands in the center, and turn counterclockwise.

Right-Hand Lady A Square Dance term. The lady in the couple on the right, not partner.

Right Parallel Position *See* Parallel Position.

Ringing Circle formed by two or more dancers joining hands, usually moving left, unless otherwise indicated.

Rip and Snort A Square Dance term. Four couples join hands in a circle. The designated couple, without releasing hands, leads down the center under an arch made by the opposite couple, pulling the whole circle with them. Once under the arch, the lead couple drop each other's hands. The lady pulls her line around to the right, and the man pulls his line around to the left until both man and lady are back to starting position. The arching couples turn under their own joined hands without letting go and face the center of the circle once more.

RLOD Symbol for *reverse line of direction*. *See* Reverse Line of Direction.

Rock A Clogging term. The Rock is a toe movement (see Toe Movement) occurring on the upbeat (count *and*). A weight-bearing movement in which the weight is taken on the ball of the foot. Both knees are straight (not stiff) on the Rock; on the following downbeat (accent) of the music, both knees bend slightly while performing the next movement.

Rock A dance term used when the dancer steps forward (or backward) a short step and then backward (or forward) a short step. With the body weight shifting forward and backward over the foot, this creates a rocking motion. The term is used in Social Dance and in American Round Dance and Folk Dance.

Rock-and-Roll When the second and fourth beats are accented in country-western and folk blues music, it is referred to as rock-and-roll music. Contemporary fad dances are done to rock-and-roll music. Rock-and-roll is a rhythm; but the term *Rock Dance* is used.

Roll Away with a Half Sashay A Square Dance term. Partners are side by side, facing the same direction, lady on the man's right. The lady rolls across in front of the man to his left side. As she rolls, she makes one complete turn counterclockwise. The man guides the lady across with his right hand and simultaneously steps to his right so that they end up having exchanged places.

Roll Back A Square Dance term. From a star promenade position with the lady on the outside, the lady is released. She rolls out and around once to meet the man who is behind her. If the star is turning counterclockwise, she will roll back clockwise. If the star is turning clockwise, she will roll back counterclockwise.

Roll Promenade A Square Dance term. A man and lady meet with the left hand. The man rotates to face the same way as the lady with her on his right in promenade position. They wheel around until they face standard promenade direction.

Rumba A Latin-American Dance from Cuba in 4/4 time.

Run A basic form of locomotion in fast, even rhythm. It is similar to a walk, except that the weight is carried forward over the ball of the foot with a spring-like action.

Running Step A light, bouncy, dignified half-walk, half-run as in English dances. *See* Run.

Russian Polka The customary Polka hop is omitted. Step left (count 1), close right to left (count *and*), step left (count 2), and hold (count *and*). Repeat, beginning right.

S Symbol for slow. Used for Rhythm Cue. For example, SSQQ, slow, slow, quick, quick.

Samba A Latin-American Dance from Brazil in 4/4 or cut time.

Sashay Dancers move once around each other. Man moves sideways to the right and behind the lady and the lady moves sideways to the left and in front of the man. Dancers face center of circle throughout the sashay.

Sashay Halfway Around *See* Roll Away with a Half Sashay.

Schottische Step left (count 1), step right (count 2), step left (count 3), and hop left (count 4). Repeat, beginning right.

Scissor Kick Kick the left leg (stiff-legged) forward (count 1) and exchange by kicking the right leg forward and left back to place (count *and*). Continue action.

Scoot A Country Western Dance term. *See* Chug Step.

Scuff A Country Western Dance term. A brush of the heel forward.

Second Corners An English Country dance term. Refer to Corners.

See Saw A Square Dance term. Man moves to his right around behind and then in front of partner and back to home position.

Semiopen Position A Social Dance position halfway between open and closed position.

Separate A Square Dance term meaning to turn one's back on the partner and do what the next call says. Couples frequently separate to go around the outside ring (man goes left, lady right) until they meet each other. Wait for next call.

Separate Go Around One Couple 1 moves into center, man goes left between couple 4 and around lady 4 and back to place; lady 1 goes right between couple 2 and around man 2 and back to place. Also done with two couples facing. Example: couple 1 leads out to couple 2, couple 1 moves between couple 2 man moving around lady and back to place as lady one moves around man two and back to place.

Set An English Country Dance term. Setting steps are done either in place, advancing toward or retiring from another dancer. A single set is to the right and the left. Dancer springs lightly on right, usually to side, steps onto left, then back onto right with a quick change of weight. Repeat to the left. (Slow, quick, quick, slow, quick, quick.)

Set Refers to a group formation. In Square Dancing, it refers to the arrangement of four couples in a square formation. The term *set* is used interchangeably to refer to Square, Contra, and Longway formations. The term *set* is also used to describe a group of three dance (i.e., "set of three").

Shoulder-Waist Position Partners stand facing each other, shoulders parallel and toes pointed directly forward. The man extends his arms in a "barrel shape" around the lady, both hands are placed below the lady's shoulder blades. Lady's raised arms rest gently on man's arms; her hands folding over his shoulder, point slightly toward each other. The lady supports the weight of her arms and give a firm pressure with her hands. Both lean slightly away from each other against the firm hand support of the other.

Shuffle An easy, light one-step, keeping feet lightly in contact with the floor as they move. Principal step used in Square and Contra dancing.

Sicilian Circle A double circle with *couples facing,* lady to man's right. Couples may be numbered 1, 2, 3, and so forth. All *even*-numbered couples face line of direction, while all *odd*-numbered couples face reverse line of direction.

Side Refers to second and fourth couples.

Side-by-Side Position *See* Inside Hands Joined Position.

Sidecar Position *See* Left Parallel Position; Parallel Position.

Side Couples Refers to second and fourth couples in a set of four couples.

Side Four Refers to second and fourth couples.

Side Step Step to the left with the left foot (count 1). Close right to left, take weight on right (count 2).

Side Two Couples Refers to second and fourth couples in the set. Also called side four.

Single-File Promenade *See* Promenade Single-File.

Single-File Turn Back A Square Dance term. From a single-file promenade, traveling counterclockwise, either man or lady may be designated by the caller to step out of the circle, about-face to the right, and go the other way, making another circle on the outside, traveling clockwise.

Skater's Position *See* Promenade Position.

Skip A basic form of locomotion in uneven rhythm. The pattern is a step and a hop on the same foot in slow quick slow quick rhythm.

Slide A basic form of locomotion in uneven rhythm. The movement is sideward. It is a step close step close pattern (slow quick slow quick).

Slide A Clogging term. The Slide is a heel movement (*see* Heel Movement) occurring on the downbeat (accent). A weight-bearing movement that may be performed on both feet simultaneously or on one foot. Feet scoot *forward* a few inches as weight is shifted from balls of feet to heels. Heels skim along the floor. Both knees are slightly bent on the Slide; on the following upbeat (count *and*), both knees straighten while performing the next movement.

Slip the Clutch A Square Dance term. Starting from the allemande thar star position, man will release partner on his left arm, move forward one place to the corner for an allemande left, and follow the call.

Slipping Step An English Country Dance term. Spring sideways to the right (or left) (count 1), bring trailing foot up taking weight (count *and*), spring again to right (or left).

Slow A rhythm cue. *See* Quick.

Split the Ring A Square Dance term. From square formation, the lead-off couple joins hands and goes between the couple they are facing, splitting them apart. After going through, they wait, facing out, for the next call.

Square The formation for Square Dancing. A square is composed of four couples, each standing on the imaginary sides of a square, facing the center. Each couple stands with their backs to one side of the room. Also called a set.

Square Sets A Square Dance term. At home: Man has his lady on the right and they are standing side by side, inside hands joined. Away from home: After a swing or promenade, man is on the left, lady is on the right, inside hands joined. The couple faces the center of the set.

Square Thru (full) A Square Dance term. The square thru is executed when two couples are facing. Couples move forward, take opposite's right hand, pull by; do quarter-turn to face partner, join left hands, pull by; do quarter-turn to face original opposite again, join right hands, pull by; make quarter-turn to face partner, join left hands, pull by; and wait for caller's directions.

Square Thru (half) A Square Dance term. The half square thru is executed when two couples are facing. Couples move forward, take opposite right hand, pull by; do quarter-turn to face partner, join left hands, pull by; do quarter-turn to face partner, join left hands, pull by; and wait for caller's directions. This is one half of a full square thru.

Square Thru (three-quarters) A Square Dance term. The three-quarters square thru is executed when two couples are facing. Couples move forward, take opposite's right hand, pull by; do quarter-turn to face partner, join left hands, pull by; do quarter-turn to face original opposite again, join right hands, pull by; and wait for caller's directions. This is three-quarters of a full square thru.

Stamp   Place the ball of one foot firmly on the floor, accenting the placement. The weight is not usually transferred to the foot taking the stamp; however, in some instances, it does take the weight.

Star Promenade   A Square Dance term. Either man or lady may be on the inside of the set, forming a star (box star position). The free arm is around partner, who travels in the same direction. If right hand forms the star, it will travel clockwise with left arm around partner. If left hand forms the star, it will travel counterclockwise with right hand around partner.

Star Thru   A Square Dance term. When two couples are facing, each person works with the opposite. The man takes the lady's left hand in his right hand and turns her quarter-turn counterclockwise as he walks around her one-quarter of the way clockwise. They end up side by side. This lady is now his new partner and is on his right.

Step   A Clogging term. The Step is a weight-bearing flat-footed heel movement (*see* Heel Movement) occurring on the downbeat (accent). Both knees are slightly bent on Step; on the following upbeat (count *and*) both knees straighten.

Step Close   Step sideward left (count 1), and close right to left, take weight on right (count 2). The right foot does not draw along the floor, but moves freely into place beside left.

Step-Hop   Step on the left foot (count 1) and hop on the same foot (count *and*). Even rhythm.

Step Swing   Step left (count 1) and swing right across in front of left (count 2). Repeat movement, beginning right.

Stride Position   A Social Dance term. Legs straight, feet apart.

Strut   Walk forward, upper torso high and leading, left knee slightly bent, toe pointed, preparing to step. Step on *ball of foot first* and then lower heel gently.

Suzy Q   Moving sideward, toes are together, heels apart, "pigeon toes." Weight on both feet, shift weight to left heel, right toe simultaneously, pivoting to "pigeon toe" position; shift weight to left toe, right heel, pivoting to toes out, "roach toe." Alternating toe heel, heel toe, move sideward.

Sweep   Cue word for Varsouvienne and Country Western Line Dances as left heel swings across in front of right instep. Same as wing.

Swing
1. *Right or Left-Hand Swing*. The lady and man clasp right (or left) hands and swing around clockwise. Forearm grasp may be used.

2. *Two-Hand Swing*. The lady and man face each other, join both hands, and one-step or shuffle once around clockwise. The elbows are held in close to the body.
3. *Waist Swing*. Couples take swing position (right parallel position) and turn clockwise with a shuffle, Two-Step, or buzz step. In Square Dance, make two turns. In Contra, turn for eight measures. Couples should lean back slightly for a swing.

Swing Out Position   See Flirtation Position.

Swing Position   The man and lady step into right parallel position, the lady and man are almost right side to right side. The man's right arm is around the lady's waist, and his right hand is firm at her waist so that she may lead back against it. The lady places her left hand on his right shoulder. His left hand holds her right hand. The couple look at each other and lean back as they shuffle around in a clockwise direction.

Swing the Right-Hand Lady   A Square Dance term. The ladies all stay in home position. The men pass in front of partner on the inside and move to the right to swing right-hand lady twice around and square the set in that position.

Swing Thru   A Square Dance term. From an ocean-wave position, the two on each end of the line turn each other with right arm halfway around. Then the two in the center of the line turn each other with left arm halfway around. All balance forward and back and follow the next call.

Swing Your Opposite   A Square Dance term. The ladies stay in home position. The men move straight across the inside of the set to the opposite lady, but the man must allow the man in the couple to his left to cross in front of him. He swings the opposite lady twice around and opens up to square the set from that new position. Another call to swing the opposite will take him back to his own original partner, but the caller may choose to get him back to his partner in another way.

Swivel   Toes and heels move sideward, either weight on toes, pivoting heels, or weight on heels, pivoting toes. Also called Suzy Q. Or, pivoting on one toe and one heel simultaneously, then pivoting on the other toe and heel, alternating toe heel, heel toe, moving sideward; or, in place by shifting weight, feet are "pigeon toes," then heels together, toes pointed out "roach toe."

Swivel Turn   In one spot, a complete turn on the ball of one foot, either direction. Free foot may be lifted, bending knee, or close to other heel.

Syncopation   A temporary displacement of the natural accent in music. For instance, shifting the accent from the naturally strong first and third beat to the weak second and fourth beat.

Tango   A Latin American Dance from Argentina.

Tempo   Rate of speed at which the music is played, or the speed of the dance.

Those Who Can   A Square Dance term meaning that those who are in the right position should do what the next call says. Those who are not in the right position should just stand and wait.

Three-Quarter Chain   *See* Ladies Chain.

Three-Step Turn   One complete turn made in three steps. The turn may be made to the left (counterclockwise) or to the right (clockwise). To turn right (clockwise), step right to side (count 1), pivot clockwise on right, and step left to face opposite direction (count 2); pivot clockwise on left and step right to side to face original direction (count 1). Hold the last count of 2/4 or 4/4 music. For 3/4 time, *see* Canter Rhythm.

Throw in the Clutch   A Square Dance term. Executed from an allemande thar or wrong way thar movement. On the call "throw in the clutch," dancers in the center retain hold on the star but release hand with outside dancers. The star changes direction and moves forward while the dancers on the outside (once released) continue in same direction (e.g., forward). Dancers then follow the next call.

Time Signature   A symbol indicating duration of time. Example: In 2/4 time, the upper number indicates number of beats per measure, while the lower number indicates the note value that receives one beat.

Tip   A Square Dance term. One completed Square Dance call (sequence).

Toe   A Clogging term. The Toe step in clogging is a weight-bearing toe movement (*see* Toe Movement) occurring on the upbeat (count *and*). Weight is placed on the ball of the foot, followed by a Heel step.

Toe Movement   A Clogging term. The toe movements in clogging (rock, drag, toe, double-toe, brush) occur on the upbeat (count *and*) of the music. Both legs are straight (but not stiff).

Touch   A Clogging term. The Touch is a variation of the Toe step. The Touch step involves no change of weight. The ball of the foot touches the floor on the upbeat (count *and*) and lifts on the downbeat (accent).

Triple Allemande   A Square Dance term. Men turn corner ladies with a left allemande and send them to the center. Ladies form a right-hand star and move star clockwise, while men walk counterclockwise around star. Men again turn corners with left allemande one full turn, move to center, and form a right-hand star. Star moves clockwise, as ladies walk counterclockwise, around star. Men again, third time, turn corners (original always) with left allemande one full turn and move into a grand right and left or wait for caller's directions.

Triple Minor   A Contra set is divided into minor sets, three couples each.

Triple Set   A set of three couples.

Turn   Dancers may move around individually clockwise or counterclockwise or with a partner. With a partner, dancers join right, left, or both hands as directed and move around clockwise (or counterclockwise).

Turn as a Couple   A Contra Dance term. Hands may or may not be joined. Partners, side by side, turn as a unit counterclockwise, the lady moving forward, the man pivoting almost in place.

Turn Back   A Square Dance term.
1. Sometimes used as "gents turn back and swing the girl behind you."
2. May be used as a single-file turn back.
3. *See* Back Track.

Turn Contra Corners   *See* Contra Corners Turn.

Turn Single   An English Country Dance term. One dancer turns clockwise (or counterclockwise) individually, taking four walking steps.

Turn Thru   A Square Dance term. Two dancers are facing each other. They take a right forearm grasp and turn each other around clockwise 180°, so as to end up facing the direction they had their backs to when they started.

Twinkle Step   A variation based on box rhythms for both Foxtrot and Waltz.

Twirl   In Square Dance, the twirl may be used to get into and out of a promenade. To get into a promenade, partners face and join right hands. The man lifts his right hand, twirling the lady clockwise one time around under his right arm. As she comes around, he takes her left hand underneath the right and they are ready to promenade. To get out of a promenade at home position, the man, as he nears his home position when promenading, releases with the left hand and raises the right hand, twirling the lady clockwise under one-half turn into her home position. Then they both face the center of the set. In some areas of the country, this twirl out is followed by a swing. To go from a swing into a promenade, the man, as he completes the swing, will not open out to face center but will come around to face the line of direction. He raises his left hand and twirls the lady clockwise under his left hand once around. As she comes around, he puts her right hand in his right and reaches underneath for her left hand. This needs practice so that the lady can be moving in the line of direction while twirling under because the total movement should be continuous.

Two Hand Swing   *See* Swing.

Two-Hand Turn   *See* Swing, Two-Hand Swing.

Two Hands Joined Position   Partners stand facing each other, shoulders parallel, and toes pointed directly forward. Two hands are joined, man's palms up, his thumbs on top of her hands. The elbows are bent and held close to the body.

Two-Step   Step left (count 1), close right to left (count 2), step left (count 3), and hold (count 4).

Tyrolian Waltz   A series of Waltz steps taken in the line of direction. Beginning left, step diagonally forward left on first Waltz step, step diagonally forward to the right on the second Waltz step. Repeat pattern. Partners tend to face away and toward each other, with alternate steps, as they *glide* forward.

Unassisted, Two Dancers   *See* Cast Off.

Uneven Rhythm   When the beats in the rhythm pattern are not all the same value but are a combination of slow and quick beats, the rhythm is said to be uneven.

U Turn Back   A single dancer, either man or lady, or both, turn around in place 180°, ending facing in opposite direction.

Varsouvienne Position   Couple faces in line of direction, lady in front and slightly to the right of man. Man holds lady's left hand in his left at shoulder level. Man's right arm extends back of lady's shoulders and holds lady's raised right hand in his right. In Social Dance, this is sometimes called jody position.

Walk   A basic form of locomotion in even rhythm. Steps are from one foot to the other, the weight being transferred from heel to toe.

Walk Around   *See* Cast Off.

Waltz   Step forward left (count 1), step sideward right (count 2), close left to right, and take weight left (count 3).

Waltz Balance   *See* Balance, 3/4 time.

Weave the Ring   A Square Dance term. Same as grand right and left, except that dancers *do not* touch hands in passing each other.

Wheel and Deal   A Square Dance term. From a line of four, facing out, the right-hand couple in line pivots counterclockwise halfway around the person nearest the center. The left-hand couple moves forward two steps and then pivots clockwise halfway around the person nearest the center and comes in behind the right-hand couple. Both end up facing the center, one behind the other.

Wheel Around   A Square Dance term that is also used in Contra. From the promenade position, couples wheel around as a unit to face in opposite direction. Men back up, ladies move forward around men. Dancers retain the promenade position handhold.

Whirl   Term used for waist swing in Square Dance. Also refers to several rather rapid individual right- or left-face turns.

Whirlaway With a Half Sashay   *See* Roll Away With a Half Sashay.

Wrap Position   The lady is at the right of the man. His right arm is around her waist and his hand holds her left hand. His left hand is holding her right hand in front.

Yemenite Step   In 4/4 meter. Begin left, with flexed knees, and step to left (count 1); step right behind left (count 2); step left in front of right (count 3); and hold (count 4).

Index Contents

Classified Index of American Heritage Dances

Name of Dance	Page	Type	Formation	Basic Steps	Mixer	Degree of Difficulty	Exhibition
Alabama Gal	93	Play Party Game	Longway set	Shuffle, slide		Easy	
All-American Promenade	121	Mixer	Circle, couples	Walk	■	Easy	
Alley Cat (Popcorn)	116	Novelty Dance	Nonpartner	Touch, kick, jump		Easy	
Amos Moses	114	Novelty Dance	Nonpartner	Grapevine, stamp		Easy	
Big Circle Square Dance	78	Running set	Circle, couples	Shuffle		Easy	
Black Hawk Waltz	107	Round Dance	Couples	Waltz		Moderate	
Blue Pacific Waltz	108	Round Dance	Couples	Waltz, three-step turn		Moderate	■
Boston Two-Step	103	Round Dance	Couples	Two-Step, step swing		Easy	
Cajun Jitterbug	114	Round Dance	Couple	Step-close		Moderate	
Cajun One-step	113	Round Dance	Couple	One-step		Easy	
Cajun Two-step	113	Round Dance	Couple	Two-step		Easy	
Cajun Waltz	113	Round Dance	Couple	Waltz		Easy	
Clogging 101	88	Clog Dance	Nonpartner	Double-toe, rock, brush, drag		Easy	
Cotton-Eyed Joe	105	Round Dance	Couples	Polka or Two-Step		Moderate	■
Cotton-Eyed Joe	106	Line Dance	Nonpartner or Varsouvienne	Two-Step, kick		Easy	
Digging Dutchman, The	122	Mixer	Circle, couples	Walk, balance, swing	■	Easy	
Double Toe Tapping	91	Clog Dance	Nonpartner	Double-toe, rock, drag, brush, slide		Easy	
Fancy Step Out	89	Clog Dance	Nonpartner	Double-toe, rock, brush, slide		Easy	
Garden Waltz	109	Round Dance	Set of three	Waltz, Two-Step, or Polka		Easy	
Glowworm	102	Round Dance	Couples	Walk, Two-Step, grapevine		Easy	
Glowworm Mixer	123	Mixer	Circle, couples	Walk	■	Easy	
Grand March	63	March	Couples	Walk		Easy	

Dance	Page	Type	Formation	Steps	Difficulty		
Grand Square Quadrille	70	Quadrille	Square	Shuffle	Easy		
Heel and Toe Polka	104	Round Dance	Couples	Polka, heel and toe Polka	Moderate		
Hokey Pokey	95	Play Party Game	Circle, nonpartner	Walk	Easy		
Jessie Polka (Cowboy Polka, Eight-Step Shuffle)	115	Round Dance	Two or more	Polka or Two-Step	Moderate		
Jiffy Mixer	125	Mixer	Circle, couple	Walk, step-close-step, chug	Easy		
Kentucky Running Set	76	Running set	Square	Run	Easy		■
Levi Jackson Rag	124	Mixer	Five couples	Walk, swing	Moderate		
Loomis Lancers	65	Lancer	Square	Dance walk	Moderate		■
Lovely Lane Chain	75	Progressive Dance	Four couples	Shuffle	Moderate	■	
Mexican Mixer	126	Mixer	Circle, couples	Walk, balance	Easy	■	
Mixers, Plain and Novelty	119	Mixers	Circle, couples	Walk	Easy	■	
Ninepin Reel	73	Square Dance	Square	Shuffle, buzz step	Easy	■	
Nobody's Business	94	Play Party Game	Circle, couples	Walk	Easy	■	
Oh Johnny	128	Mixer	Circle, couples	Shuffle	Easy	■	
Patty-Cake Polka	127	Mixer	Circle, couples	Heel toe, slide, walk	Easy		
Paul Jones Your Lady	72	Mixer	Circle, couples	Walk, Two-Step	Easy		
Ping-Pong Schottische	97	Round Dance	Couples	Grapevine, Two-Step	Easy		
Popcorn	116	Novelty Dance	Nonpartner	Touch, kick, jump	Easy		
Portland Fancy	74	Progressive Dance	Four Couples	Shuffle	Moderate		
Red River Valley	129	Mixer	Two sets of three	Shuffle	Easy	■	
Salty Dog Rag	101	Round Dance	Couples	Grapevine, Schottische	Easy		

Name of Dance	Page	Type	Formation	Basic Steps	Mixer	Degree of Difficulty	Exhibition
Schottische	96	Round Dance	Couples	Schottische		Easy	
Southern Special	90	Clog Dance	Nonpartner	Double-toe, rock, drag, slide		Moderate	■
Steppin' Out	118	Novelty Dance	Nonpartner	Step brush, grapevine, walk		Moderate	■
Ten Pretty Girls	100	Line Dance	Two or more	Grapevine, walk		Easy	
Tennessee Wig-Walk	130	Mixer	Circle, couples	Walk	■	Easy	
Teton Mountain Stomp	131	Mixer	Circle, couples	Walk, Two-Step	■	Easy	
Texas Schottische	98	Round Dance	Couples	Grapevine, Two-Step		Moderate	■
Texas Schottische for Three	98	Mixer	Circle, threes	Heel toe, walk, Two-Step	■	Easy	
Tricky Footwork	92	Clog Dance	Nonpartner	Double-toe, rock, drag, slide, brush		Moderate	■
Twelfth Street Rag	117	Novelty Dance	Nonpartner	Charleston, grapevine		Easy	
Varsouvienne	111	Round Dance	Couples	Mazurka		Easy	■
Virginia Reel	69	Contra Dance	Longway set	Shuffle		Easy	
Waltz of the Bells	110	Round Dance	Couples	Waltz		Easy	

Classified Index of Square Dances*

532

Dance	Page	Type	Description	Level
Shindig in the Barn	180	Singing	Begin. 3 and four ladies chain, right and left thru	Begin. 3
Sides Break to a Line	165	Patter	Begin. 3 and double pass thru, wheel and deal	Interm. 5
Sides Divide	171	Patter	Begin. 2	Begin. 2
Smoke on the Water	179	Singing	Begin. 1 pass thru, star	Begin. 3
Split the Ring, Around Just One	160	Patter	Pass thru, split the ring	Begin. 2
Split the Ring Variation 1	161	Patter	Pass thru, split the ring, right and left thru, ladies chain	Begin. 2
Split the Ring Variation 2	162	Patter	Begin. 2 and cross trail	Begin. 3
Star Thru, California Twirl	163	Patter	Begin. 3 and half-square thru, star thru	Interm. 4
Star Thur and Square Thru Combo	163	Patter	Begin. 3 and square thru, star thru	Interm. 4
Take Me Home Country Roads	182	Singing	Promenade, do-sa-do, allemande left	Begin. 1A, 1B
Tea Cup Chain	171	Patter	Four ladies chain	Begin. 2
Texas Star	160	Patter	Texas star basics	Begin. 2
There's Your Corner	162	Patter	Roll away to half-sashay, cross trail, box the gnat	Begin. 3
Tie Me Kangaroo Down	178	Singing	Begin. 2 and four ladies chain	Begin. 3
Truly Fair	176	Singing	Begin. 3 and star thru, wheel around	Interm. 4
Turn Thru Combo	166	Patter	Interm. 4 and turn thru	Interm. 5
Woman in Love	177	Singing	Begin. 2 and do paso, allemande thar	Begin. 3

*Key to Classified Index:

Beginner 1 consists of preliminary basics 1–8; *Beginner 2* consists of Beginner 1 plus basics 9–20; *Beginner 3* consists of Beginner 2 plus basics 21–33; *Intermediate 4* consists of Beginner 3 plus basics 34–44; *Intermediate 5* consists of basics 1–50 in any combination. For teaching and calling materials beyond the 50 basic levels, refer to Handbook Series "Plus Movements of Square Dance" and the "Advanced" or "Challenge" levels published by The Sets in Order American Square Dance Society, 462 North Robertson Boulevard, Los Angeles, CA, 90048.

Classified Index of Contra Dances

Classified Index of International Folk Dances

Name of Dance	Page	Nationality	Formation	Basic Steps	Mixer	Degree of Difficulty	Exhibition
Alexandrovska	316	Russian	Couples	Waltz		Moderate	
Alunelul	326	Romanian	Circle, non partner	Step, stamp		Moderate	
Auretti's Dutch Skipper	258	English	Longways duple minor	Walk		Easy	
Bitte Man I Knibe	239	Danish	Two couples	Run, Waltz		Moderate	
Bonny Prince Charlie Crossing the Frew	259	Scottish	Longway	Skip change, pas de basque		Moderate	
Branle D'Ossau	282	French	Circle nonpartner	Rock		Moderate	
Butterfly Hornpipe	261	English	Longways duple minor	Walk		Easy	
Cherkessiya	343	Israeli	Line dance nonpartner	Grapevine		Easy	
Constancy	262	American/English	Longways duple minor	Walk		Easy	
Corrido	359	Mexican	Couples	Grapevine		Moderate	■
Csárdás Palócosan	312	Hungarian	Couples	Double and turning Csárdás		Difficult	
Čukaričko Kolo	327	Serbian	Broken circle nonpartner	Kolo		Moderate	
Den Toppede Høne	240	Danish	Set of three	Step-hop	■	Easy	
D'Hammerschmieds g'selln	295	German	Two couples	Step-hop, Waltz	■	Easy	
Doudlebska Polka	307	Czech	Couples	Polka	■	Moderate	
Dover Pier	263	English	Longways duple minor	Walk		Easy	
Dr Gsatzlig	297	Swiss	Couples	Schottische, slow Two-Step		Moderate	
El Jarabe Tapatio	361	Mexican	Couples	Jarabe step, push step, Borrachito step		Difficult	■
Familie Sekstur	241	Danish	Couples in circle	Walk, buzz step	■	Easy	
Familjevalsen	242	Swedish	Couples	Waltz, Waltz balance		Easy	
First of April, The	264	English	Longways duple minor	Walk		Easy	

Dance	Page	Nationality	Formation	Steps	Difficulty	
Flowers of Edinburgh	265	Scottish	Longway	Skip change, pas de basque	Moderate	
Gie Gordons	267	Scottish	Couples	Two-Step, walk	Moderate	
Greensleeves	268	English	Two-couple sets	Walk	Easy	
Hambo	243	Swedish	Couple	Polska, Waltz balance	Difficult	
Harmonica	344	Israeli	Circle, nonpartner	Grapevine, run	Moderate	■
Hasápikos	328	Greek	Broken circle, nonpartner	Walk, step swing	Easy	
Hava Nagila	345	Israeli	Couples	Walk	Easy	
Hineh Ma Tov	347	Israeli	Broken circle	Leap, yemenite	Easy	
Hora	348	Israeli	Circle, nonpartner	Step behind, step swing	Easy	
Hora Pe Gheata	320	Romanian	Circle, nonpartner	Walk	Easy	
Hungarian Motifs	311	Hungarian	Nonpartner	10 motifs	Difficult	
Il Codiglione	353	Italian	Couples in circle	Walk, pas de basque	Easy	■
Jesucita En Chihuahua	364	Mexican	Couples	Two-step, heel toe, slide	Moderate	
Kalvelis	321	Lithuanian	Couple in a circle	Polka	Moderate	
Kiskanásztác	313	Hungarian	Singles	Step-hop, Cifra, close step	Difficult	
Klumpakojis	300	Lithuanian	Couples	Polka	Easy	
Korobushka	317	Russian	Couples in circle	Schottische	Easy	■
Krüz König	299	German	Sets of threes	Achtervor step, run step-hop, mazurka	Moderate	■
La Adelita	365	Mexican	Couples	Stamp, slide, heel toe, run	Moderate	
La Bruja	366	Mexican	Nonpartner	Waltz, two step, step swing	Difficult	■
La Crouzade	283	French	Two couples line of four	Pas de bourrée, stamping pattern, right and left	Difficult	
La Cucaracha	367	Mexican	Couples	Walk, stamp	Easy	
La Montagnarde	286	French	Couples in a column	Pas de bourrée, stamping pattern, right and left	Difficult	

Name of Dance	Page	Nationality	Formation	Basic Steps	Mixer	Degree of Difficulty	Exhibition
La Raspa	369	Mexican	Couples	Bleking, run		Easy	
La Tournijaire	288	French	Couples in a circle	Pas de bourrée stamping pattern, waltz		Moderate	
Las Chiapanecas	370	Mexican	Nonpartner	Waltz, stamp		Easy	
Lesnoto	331	Macedonian	Broken circle, nonpartner	Walk, step swing		Easy	
Ma Na'avu	349	Israeli	Broken circle	Yemenite		Easy	
Man in the Hay	302	German	Four couples	Slide, skip		Easy	
Masquarade	245	Danish	Circle couples	Walk, waltz		Moderate	
Mayim	350	Israeli	Circle, nonpartner	Grapevine		Easy	
Misirlou	333	Greek-American	Broken circle, nonpartner	Grapevine, two-step		Moderate	
Mon Père Avait un Petit Bois	290	French	Circle, nonpartner	Walk, step-hop, branle		Easy	
Nonesuch	269	English	Four couples	Walk, run		Easy	■
Northdown Waltz, The	271	English	Longways duple minor	Walk		Easy	
Norwegian Polka (Scandinavian Polka)	246	Norwegian	Couples	Walk, pivot turn		Moderate	
Oslo Waltz	272	Scotch-English	Couple circle	Waltz	■	Moderate	
Pljeskavac Kolo	334	Serbian-Croatian	Broken circle, nonpartner	Walk, stamp		Easy	
Ragg, The	273	English	Longways duple minor	Walk		Easy	
Road to the Isles	274	Scottish	Couples	Schottische		Easy	
Rondeau de Garein	291	French	Line nonpartner	Grapevine		Moderate	
Rumunjsko Kolo	335	Serbian-American	Broken circle, nonpartner	Scottische		Easy	
Santa Rita	371	Mexican	Couples	Two-step, slide, stamp, polka		Difficult	■

Dance	No.	Origin	Formation	Steps	Difficulty
Sarajevka Kolo	336	Bosnian	Broken circle, nonpartner	Grapevine, pas de basque	Easy
Savila Se Bela Loza	337	Serbian	Broken circle, nonpartner	Run, schottische	Easy
Scottish	292	French	Couples	Two-step, buzz turn	Easy
Seksmannsril	247	Norwegian	Couples	Step-hop	Easy
Šetnja	339	Serbian	Broken circle, nonpartner	Walk, step-hop	Easy
Siamsa Beirte	275	Irish	Couples	Threes	Moderate
Sicilian Tarantella	355	Italian	Two-couple sets	Run, skip	Moderate
Snurrbocken	249	Swedish	Couples	Polka, run	Advanced
Sonderburg					
Doppelquadrille	304	German	Four couples	Polka, walk	Moderate
Spinnradl zu Dritt	305	Austrian	Threes	Waltz, stamp, jump	Moderate
Swedish Varsouvienne	250	Swedish	Couples	Mazurka, Waltz	Moderate
Swedish Waltz	251	Swedish	Couples	Waltz	Moderate
Syrtós	340	Greek	Broken circle, nonpartner	Grapevine	Easy
Tancuj	308	Czech	Couples in double circle	Step close, heel and toe	Easy
Three Meet	276	English	Set of three	Run	Easy
To Ting	252	Danish	Couples	Walk, Waltz	Moderate
Totur	253	Danish	Couples, single circle	Walk, Two-Step, Polka	Moderate
Tropanka	341	Bulgarian	Circle nonpartner	Shuffle, step, hop, stamps	Easy
Troika	318	Russian	Set of three	Run	Easy
Ugrós	314	Hungarian	Singles	Touch step, back cross Cifra, lift step	Difficult
Ve'David	351	Israeli	Circle couples	Walk	Easy
White Cockade, The	277	Scottish	Reel	Skip change, pas de basque	Moderate
Willow Tree	279	English	Longway	Walk	Easy

Classified Index of Social Dances

Name of Dance	Page	Partner	Nonpartner	Exhibition
Merengue continued				
Ladder	471			
Side close and back break	471			
Swivel	470			
Rumba				
Bolero break, variations	456			
Box step	460			
Box turn	458			
Circular turn	459	■		■
Cuban walk	460			
Flirtation break	458			
Parallel turn	459			
Side by side	460			
Varsouvienne Break	459			
	461			
Salsa				
Basic step	415	■		
Side step	415			
Cross step	416			
Throw out	416			
Samba				
Basic step	463	■		
Basic turn	464			
Copa step	464			
Forward progressive step	467			
Sideward basic	465			
Slow side close	466			
	466			
Swing				
Double Lindy	386	■		■
Basic turn	389	■		■
Break	390			
Brush off	390			
Continuous underarm turns	392			
Collegiate	391			
Dish rag	389			
	393			

Name of Dance	Page	Partner	Nonpartner	Exhibition
Double brush off	393			
Overhead swing	393			
Semiopen basic	390	■		■
Swing out break	391			
Tuck spin	392	■		■
Wrap	392			
Triple Lindy—East Coast Swing	394			
Triple Lindy swivel step	394			
West Coast Swing	396			
Sugar push	396			
Underarm turn	396			
Left side pass	397			
Whip	397			
Tango	441			
Basic step	442	■		■
Box step	445			
Corté	445			
Cross step and quarter turn	443			
Fan step	446			
Half-turn clockwise	444			
Half-turn counterclockwise	444			
Open fan	446			
Open position basic Tango	442			
Right parallel basic Tango	443			
Quarter-turn	443			
Waltz	433			
Box step	435	■		■
Box turn	435			
Cross step	436			
Hesitation step	436			
Streamline step	438			
Twinkle step	437			
Viennese Waltz	438	■		■
Weaving step	437	■		■

Index of Mixer and Nonpartner Dances

Subject Index